Library of Congress Control Number 2016903850

ISBN: 978-0-9911048-6-4

ISBN-10 0-9911048-6-2

Samskrta Bhāratī संस्कृत भारती

--Indus Script Dictionary, Epigraphia Mlecchita Vikalpa, 'Meluhha cipher'

Sarasvati Research Center, Herndon, VA

Samskrta Bhāratī संस्कृत भारती

--Indus Script Dictionary, Epigraphia Mlecchita Vikalpa, 'Meluhha cipher'

Samskrta Bhāratī संस्कृत भारती is a tribute to Bharatam Janam who have contributed significantly to the evolution of an industrial revolution demonstrated by the metallurgical excellence of artisans, lapidaries and metalcaster people.

Bhāratī (vāk) is the language, *lingua franca* (common language, vehicular language) of Bharatam Janam, an expression used in Rigveda by Rishi Visvamitra signifying metalcaster people.

This Bhāratī (vāk) is derived from Samskrtam which is par excellence reconstruction of the *lingua franca* of Bharatam Janam. This reconstruction of Samskrta Bhāratī संस्कृत भारती is a cultural reality, unparalleled in the annals of civilization and is documented in over one million manuscripts constituting a monumental body of literary resources of nighantus, धातुपाठ dhātupātha . The *catalogus catalogorum* includes complementary works of unsurpassed brilliance of Panini, Hemacandra, Bharata, Yaska, Patanjali, Bhartrhari, Tolkappiyan, Kautilya, Pingala, Nagarjuna and thousands of savants who have devoted their life-times to the study and veneration of Bhāratī (vāk) as *brahman*, a divine dispensation of paramātman, as vāgdevi derived from [√vac].

The recognition of [√vac] *vāk* as central to the enquiries in knowledge systems leads to the personification of this expression as a Divinity, resulting in the Rigveda Sukta venerating राष्ट्री rASTrI, the feminine form of राष्ट्रं बाहुबलाश्रितम् Ms.9.255, 'dependent on'. She is (वाग्देवता, वाग्देवी), she is saṅgamanī vasūnām 'the path for moving/transporting wealth'.

The *samskrti* of Bharatam finds expression in this metaphor of राष्ट्री

Bhāratī (vāk) is राष्ट्री because, every phenomenon in the universe is explained by *s'abdabrahman*. A civilization which was wonderstruck by the phenomena of mere earth and stone *–dagoba* or *dhAtugarbha* -- getting transformed into metal of utility value through the messenger (*purohitam)* of fire and intervention by the artificers, results in *chandas*, a musical, prosodic inquiry into the cosmic dance, the ताण्डव नृत्यम् as a metaphor for that चषाल, that octagonal brick embellished with सुदर्शन चक्र signifying the transformation processes from Being to Becoming. The multi-layered metaphors of rudra-s'iva and sudars'ana fuse into paramAtman and the inquiry becomes a quest to unite the Atman with the paramAtman. This is the *Samskriti*, exemplified in langue expression as Samskrtam, the *weltanschuaang* elaborated in ancient texts, starting with Indus Script Corpora and iconographic metaphors in *utsava bera* उत्सवबेर. This is Bharata Nidhi, the treasure of Bharatam Janam. Archaeometallurgical enquiries have resulted in an understanding of the transformation processes involved in hardening soft metals – the processes of pyrolysis and carburization. चषाल, that octagonal brick is a metaphor which explains this process of infusing carbon through smoke from *godhUma*, wheat chaff into soft metal (e.g. *mRdu* 'wrought iron') to produce ductile, but hard metal for sharp instruments such as blades, swords, sickles, axes, pots and pans, and other metallic objects of utility and exchange value.

धातु--गर्भ [p= 513,3] *m.* (with Buddh.) is a receptacle for ashes or relics, a Dagaba or Dagoba (Sinhalese corruption of पालि Dhatu-gabbha) MWB._Xxxv (Monier-Williams). The stupa is a dhatu-gabbha and hence, venerated by the worshippers.

धातु--पाठ [p= 514,1] *m.* " recital of grammatical roots " N. of an ancient list of roots ascribed to पाणिनि. dhātuḥ धातुः -पाठः a list of roots arranged according to Pāṇini's grammatical system (the most important of these lists called धातुपाठ being supposed to be the work of Pāṇini himself, as supplementary to his Sūtras).

Decipherment of Indus Script (mlecchita vikalpa) is धातुपाठ, with rebus reading of the word dhAtu (element, ore, mineral) using Indus Script cipher of rebus mleccha, early Prakrtam, identifying early speech forms of meaningful words or sememes signified by hieroglyphs.

Suh veneration of dagoba, dhAtugarbha is evidenced by the Sit Samshi bronze, morning libations to Sun divinity, as Meluhha metalwork with Indus writing hieroglyphs transmitted along the Tin Road of Antiquity. The morning libations occur in front of a dagoba, a ziggurat. The shape is comparable to the shape of yupa found in Kalibangan fire-altar or yajna kunda.

Maquette d'un lieu de culte, dite le Sit-shamshi ou "(cérémonie du) lever du soleil" XIIe siècle avant J.-C. Suse, Tell de l'Acropole Bronze Fouilles J. de Morgan 1904 - 1905 Département des Antiquités orientales Sb 2743 Plateau de bronze représentant un haut lieu comparable à ceux qu'utilisaient les Cananéens. A côté des prêtres accoupis sont dressés des stèles, des bassins et un bosquet sacré.
http://louvre.suzie.fr/pages/sb2743.html I suggest that this bronze model signifies through Indus Script hieroglyphs the सन्ध्यावन्दनम् sandhyAvandanam to Sun divinity by Bharatam Janam, metalaster people

Pointing to this photograph of an object, Gian Pietro Basello quizzes: "Do you know this object? I hope so. It is perhaps the most stimulating object found in the entire Ancient Near East, even if handbooks on Mesopotamian art do not talk much about it. It is a three-dimensional bronze model whose base measures about 60X40 cm, excavated in the 1904-1905 campaign by the French mission at Susa. The scene is focused on two squatted human figures: one stretches its hands out, the other seems to be pouring water over them from a jug. Around them, there are possibly some kinds of altars, a large vessel, two basins, a stela and three trunks of trees. This act, perhaps a cultic scene which took place in the second half of the 12th century BCE, was fixed for eternity by will of Silhak-Insusinak (1140-1120 BCE), king of Ansan and Susa, according to the short inscription in a corner of the base." http://bharatkalyan97.blogspot.in/2015/01/sit-shamshi-bronze-morning-libations-to.html

The expression is derived from भारती N. of a deity (in RV._often invoked among the आप्री deities and esp. together with इला and सरस्वती accord. to Nir._viii , 13 a daughter of आदित्य ; later identified with सरस्वती , the divinity of speech) RV._&c; speech , voice , word , eloquence , literary composition , dramatic art or recitation MBh.Ka1v._&c; the Samskrta speech of an actor L. Classifying language as divine, the Rigveda presents an extraordinary sukta rendered as a soliloquy by Vagdevi, the divinity of speech. भारती-इतिहासः, -कथा the story of the Bhāratas (महाभारत). -मण्डलम्, -वर्षम् India (Apte. Samskrtam) .

The objective of this work is to correct the distortions caused by a false hypothesis which emerged as a 'linguistic doctrine' that the explanation for the formation and evolution of Samskrta Bhāratī संस्कृत भारती can be explained by 'Aryan invasion'. There are alternative explanations possible to explain the formation and evolution of Samskrta Bhāratī संस्कृत भारती as a kaleidoscope of vāk or parole. In Bhartiya tradition vāk is divine, sacred and venerated in the worship of Sarasvati on two days every year: 1. on vasanta pancami day and 2. on ayudhapuja day during Navaratri (Dusserah). This pan-bharatiya cultural reality celebrated in kumbhamela every 12 years as the sangamam (confluence) of Rivers Ganga, Yamuna and Sarasvati, provides a framework for further studies in the cultural history of Bharatam Janam, complementing the stellar work done in understanding the reality of Vedic River Sarasvati which had protected and nurtured Sarasvati's children, the Bharatam Janam.

Another historical distortion relates to the linguistic evaluation of 'classical Sanskrit' as 'regulated by the grammarians but may be conveniently used more widely as equivalent to Old Indo-Aryan'. (Burrow, Thomas., 1955, *Sanskrit Language*, London, Faber & Faber, p.2) This arbitrary invention of linguistic categories of Pre-classical or Vedic language or Old Indo-Aryan, Middle Indo-Aryan (Prakrtam) and Modern Indian languages has led to lopsided studies missing the reality of Indian *sprachbund*. Burrow's work assumed that there was linguistic history in this land only for 3000 years, wrongly classifying Prakrtam as a post-Indo-European language phenomenon, governed by the false premise of 'aryan invasion' as a 'linguistic doctrine'.This work demonstrates that Prakrtam lexis is a repository which documents the formation and evolution of all languages of Bharatam Janam. An example of such a demonstration is provided by Jules Bloch's *Formation of Marathi language*. The evidence of over 7000 inscriptions of Indus Script as metalwork catalogs provides a firm foundation for a Prakrtam metalwork lexis (vocabulary) which was part of the *lingua franca* of the civilization for millennia.

I suggest that the term Indo-Aryan in language categories should be replaced by the term 'Prakrtam' which is defined as the *lingua franca* or parole, to identify cognate lexis with *dhātupātha* derived from Vedic prosody, chandas and to signify a composite Samskrti of Bharatam Janam.

The significance of Prakrtam metalwork lexis as documentary evidence of an industrial revolution of the bronze age (with brilliant inventions of alloys, metal casting techniques including lost-wax *cire perdue*) is best exemplified by a painting which adorns the Institute of Steel Authority of India, Ranchi. The painting shows Purushottama presenting a steel sword to Alexander on the banks of Jhelum (Vitasta, one of tht pencanada which constituted the glacial drainage system of Vedic River Sarasvati). The *wootz* or *urukku* or *ukku* steel also called the Damascus sword is an indicator of the journeys of artisans among Bharatam Janam who had travelled the Maritime Tin Route from Hanoi (Vietnam) to Haifa (Israel). These journeys of seafaring merchants and artisans may provide an alternative to the linguistic doctrine that ther were contact areas which stretched along the Tin road which preced the Silk Road by two millennia. These contacts explain the reason why the Samskrtam word mRdu 'soft iron' finds expression as meḍ 'iron, copper'; med 'copper' (Munda. Slavic. Ho. Santali) mẽṛhẽt, meD 'iron' (Mu.Ho.Santali). Another example of the spread of metallurgical products is the word poLa 'magnetite' which finds cognate in polad 'steel' (Russian). It has been demonstrated that the pyrolysis or carburization of wrought iron (by infusing carbon into molten metal, resulting in hardening of metals/alloys) was achieved by the processes of caSAla as explained in Rigveda, Taittiriya Samhita and Satapatha Brahmana and celebrated in the sculptural splendor of caSAla, snout of a boar in Varaha temple of Khajuraho, Eran and other sites.

The ancient texts note that an octagonal yupa is a signifier of a Soma yaga. Such an octagonal yupa as a brick has been discovered in a yajna kunda (fire altar) at Binjor on the banks of Vedic River Sarasvati close to Anupgarh where the river forks into two channels, one flowing southwards to Jaisalmer and another westwards to Ganweriwala, Bahawalpur Province, Chilistan.

Binjor. Yajna kunda with octagonal brick.

Binjor seal. Documents metalwork. The 'fish' hieroglyph-multiplex signifies aya 'fish' rebus: *aya* 'iron' *ayas* 'metal' PLUS *khambhaṛā* m. 'fin' rebus: *Ta. kampaṭṭam* coinage, coin. *Ma. kammaṭṭam,* kammiṭṭam coinage, mint. *Ka. kammaṭa* id.; *kammaṭi* a coiner(DEDR 1236). The circumscript of fourt short strokes: gaNDa 'four' rebus: kanda 'fire atar'. koD 'flag' rebus: koDa 'workshop' baTa 'quail' rebus: bhaTa 'furnace'. The one-horned young bull PLUS standard device denote engraver, joinery work. sangaDa 'lathe' rebus: sangAtha 'vajra, adamantine metal glue'. dulo 'hole' rebus: dul 'cast metal' pota 'hole' rebus: potR, potti purifier'; पोतदार [pōtadāra] *m* (P) An officer under the native governments. His business was to assay all money paid into the treasury. He was also the village-silversmith (Marathi).

King Purushottama (Porus) presents Indian ukku (wootz) steel sword to Alexander in the battle on River Hydaspes (Jhelum, Vitasta) Painting in SAIL, Ranchi. khaNDa 'sword' Rebus: kanda 'fire-altar'; khanda 'implements'.

Focus on the 'frog' and 'heron' hieroglyphs on a Dong Son bronze drums.

Includes also cire perdue crafted tympanum to signify kanka 'heron' rebus: kanga 'brazier'. The depiction of frogs on the Dong Son drums is significant. I suggest that it is a hieroglyph signifying metal ingot: *Kur. mūxā* frog. *Malt. múqe* id.*mūkaka-* id. (Samskrtam) (DEDR 5023) Rebus: *mū̃h* 'ingot'. Muha. The quantity of iron produced at one time in a native smelting furnace. (Santali) Hieroglyph: maraka 'peacock' (Santali. Mu.) Rebus: मारक loha 'a kind of calcining metal' (Samskritam) Kariba 'trunk of elephant' ibha 'elephant' rebus: karba 'iron' ib 'iron'.

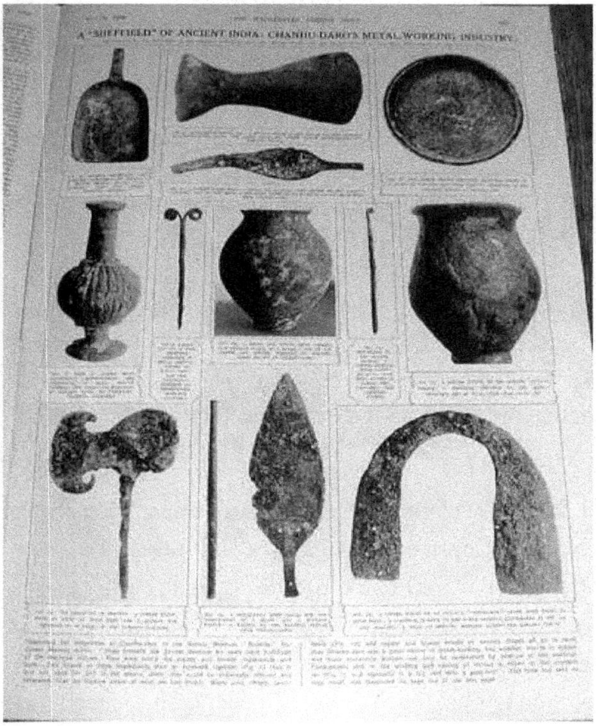

A "SHEFFIELD" OF ANCIENT INDIA: CHANHU-DARO'S METAL-WORKING INDUSTRY.

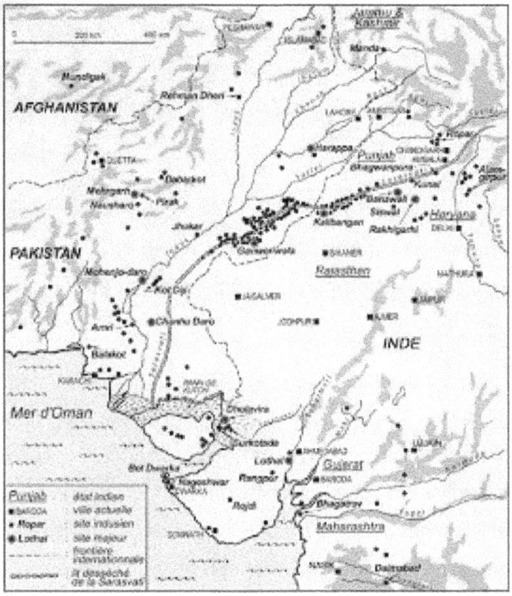

I

llustrated London News 1936 - November 21st

Chanhudaro. Sheffield of Ancient Near East. Metalware catalog in London News Illustrated, November 21, 1936.A 'Sheffield of Ancient India: Chanhu-Daro's metal working industry 10 X photos of copper knives, spears, razors, axes and dishes. The words used in the *lingua franca*of such tin-processing families constitute the words invented to denote the Bronze Age products and artifacts such as tin or zinc or the array of metalware discovered in the Sheffied of the Ancient East, Chanhu-daro as reported in the London News Illustrated by Ernest Mackay.

Depiction of torana, or gateway, of stupa, a fragment of a Jaina stupa railing, Kankali Tila, near Mathura (Government Museum, Lucknow). *dām* 'rope, string, garland' rebus: *dhāu* 'ore'. The artisans producing alloys are *dhā̆vaḍ* m. 'a caste of iron smelters', *dhāvḍī* 'composed of or relating to iron')(CDIAL 6773)..

Sanchi Stupa. Northern Gateway Toraṇa, 'row of hieroglyphs on the top architrave.

This is a proclamation of mintwork, engraver work, metalwork by sippi 'artificers'. *sippi* 'snail' 'date palm spathe' rebus: *sippi* 'artisan, sculptor' aya 'fish' rebus: *aya* 'iron' *ayas* 'metal' PLUS *khambhaṛā* m. 'fin' rebus: *Ta. kampaṭṭam* coinage, coin. *Ma. kammaṭṭam,* kammiṭṭam coinage, mint. *Ka. kammaṭa* id.; *kammaṭi* a coiner.(DEDR 1236). *tAmarasa* 'lotus' (Prakrtam) rebus: *tAmra* 'copper'.*kariba* 'trunk of elephant' *ibha* 'elephant' rebus: *karba* 'iron' (Kannada) *ib* 'iron' (Santali) *eraka* 'nave of wheel' rebus: *eraka* 'moltencast copper'; *arka* 'copper, gold' *agasAle* 'goldsmith' (Kannada)

This work is a preface to this effort, based on two landmark developments: 1. decipherment of Indus Script Corpora as metalwork catalogues; and 2. compilation of comparative dictionary of all 25+ ancient Bharatiya languages reinforcing Indian *sprachbund* (language union) of the Bronze Age and earlier eras. We now have a continuous linguistic history recorded in over 7000 Indus Script Corpora inscriptions. The idiom of these inscriptions spread over the entire Ancient Near East and Ancient Far East, exemplified by the seal of Bogazhkoy and by the Hinduised States of the Far East (pace George Coedes). This spread has resulted in the formation and evolution in various languages now spoken in Bharatam, in Austro-Asiatic zone and in Indo-European zone extending westwards from Tocharian in Central Asia. The earliest available document to unravel this spread is the Rgveda from which the Vagdevi Sukta and Ganapati SUkta will be cited and explained. The language of the Rgveda is the source from which all language developments in the contact zones of Bharatam Janam have arisen. Pre-history of Chandas (Prosody, the language of Rgveda) is for linguists an extraordinary challenge which can be met by further studies of (1) comparison of Prakrtam lexis with the dhātupātha derived from Rgveda; (2) comparison of Prakrtam and Austro-Asiatic, Iranian, Tocharian and other Indo-European languages. It is a moot question if 'the original language' or even the 'urheimat' can ever be reconstructed even in general outlines with the available documents. Exemplary efforts have resulted in the comparison of Vedic Samskrtam with Avesta attesting to the latter as a derivative from Rgveda. Scores of Nighantus which document lexis of flora and fauna can be compared with the words in vogue in contact areas of the Vedic civilization as a general framework for History of Medicine. It is notable that about 70% of British Pharmacoepia of the nineteenth century (1865), was founded on ancient Bharatiya herbals identified in the Nighantus.

Bogazkoy seal impression with 'twisted rope' hieroglyph

*skambha2 ' shoulder -- blade, wing, plumage '. [Cf. **skapa* -- s.v. *khavaka --]S. *khambhu, °bho* m. ' plumage ', *khambhuṛi* f. ' wing '; L. *khabbh* m., mult. *khambh* m. ' shoulder -- blade, wing, feather ', khet. *khamb* ' wing ', mult. *khambhaṛā* m. ' fin '; P. *khambh*m. ' wing, feather '; G. *khā̃m* f., *khabhɔ* m. ' shoulder '.(CDIAL 13640) khambh 'wing' rebus: *Ta.* kampaṭṭam coinage, coin. *Ma.* kammaṭṭam, kammiṭṭam coinage, mint. *Ka.* kammaṭa id.; kammaṭi a coiner. (DEDR 1236) *eruvai* 'kite' *dula* 'pair' *eraka* 'wing' Rebus: *eruvai dul* 'copper cast metal' *eraka* 'moltencast' PLUS *dhāu* 'strand of rope' Rebus: *dhāv* 'red ore' (ferrite) ti-*dhāu* 'three strands' Rebus: *ti-dhāv* 'three ferrite ores: magnetite, hematite, laterite'.

The seal thus describes a mint with a smelter for three ferrite ores and copper.

The findspot of this seal is Bogazkoy where a treaty was also found attesting to the presence of Samskrtam speakers. Bogazkoy texts also include horsemanship manual (written by a Mitanni called Kikkuli, c. 1400 BCE) which contained Samskrtam words to describe the technical details of training horses (aika (one), tera (tri, three), panza (panca, five), satta (sapta, seven), na (nava, nine), vartana (round). A treaty between Mitanni and Hittites (Shattiwaza and Suppiluliuma), c. 1380 BCE mentions Vedic divinities Mitra, Varuna, Indra and Nasatya (Asvins).

Samskrta Bhāratī संस्कृत भारती is the language which unified Prakrtam (vernacular) of Bharatiya *sprachbund* (language union), which had many phonetic variants in an extensive area from Assam to Gujarat, from Kashmir to Sri Lanka. This is treasure, nidhi, heritage of Bharatam. The variations in pronunciation were identified as mleccha (mis-pronunciations or ungrammatical forms) and were sought to be corrected through a touchstone, the medium of studies in Samskrtam grammar. The word mleccha has a cognate in meluhha used in cuneiform Akkadian texts and on a cylinder seal showing an Akkadian translator in front of a Meluhha merchant carrying a goat (as a phonetic/semantic determinant: mlekh 'goat' rebus: milakkhu, mleccha-mukha, meluhha 'copper') and his female companion carrying a kamandalu (cf. ranku 'liquid measure' rebus: ranku 'tin')..

Samskrtam is a structured reconstitution of the semantics, syntax, morphology and phonetics of Prakrtam. This reconstruction is documented in ancient texts such as Yaska's Niruktam, Bhartrhari's Vakyapadiya, Panini's Ashtadhyayi, Tolkappiyam, Patanjali's Mahabhashya, Bharata's Natya Sastra, various Nighantus, Hemacandra's Desinamamala, and scores of other literary evidences. These basic texts have provided the resources for scholarly studies defining Bharatam as a Linguistic Area (Indian *sprachbund* or language union). Ancient scripts were called Brahmi, Kharoshthi attesting the divine dispensation of Vakdevi and speech forms from the lips of artisans (khar 'smith' osti 'lip') This discovery of the language of a civilization provides a foundation for further civilization studies including a re-assessment of general semantics, the formation and evolution of all Bharatiya language forms and cultural contacts with neighbouring cultural regions of Eurasia for nearly 8 millennia. The word *Samskriti* relatable to Samskrtam is the *weltanschauung* defining both the material resources and adhyatmika foundations for the mores of people of a vibrant region of the globe with a civilizational foundation which dates back to more than 8 millennia.

Samskrta Bharati absorbs the features of Chandas and provides a framework for the invention of two writing systems: Brahmi and Kharoshti (ca. 5th cent. BCE). Both writing systems are syllabic and follow the Vedic sound system as may be seen from the diagram presented by Frits Staal (Source: *Lecture given by Frits Staal, during the Inaugural Session of the International Conference on"Sanskrit in Asia" to celebrate the Golden Jubilee of Her Royal Highness Princess Mahachakri Sirindhorn at Silpakorn University,Bangkok, June 23, 2005. Subsequently published in Sanskrit Studies Central Journal. Journal of the Sanskrit Studies Centre, Silpakorn University, 2 (2006) 193-200.*

Note that the invention of a syllabic writing system was necessary because Indus Script was essentially adopted in metalwork and to document technical specifications of work in mints, smithies, forges and in lapidary crafts and was NOT designed to provide for syllabic hieroglyphs for phonemes. This is the principal reason why Indus Script hieroglyphs continue to be used in mints and hence, on early punch-marked and cast coins.

A long excerpt from the lecture of Frits Staal are apposite to demonstrate that Samskrtam (as was chandas) was premised on a perfect understanding of the science of production of sounds in spoken forms of language:

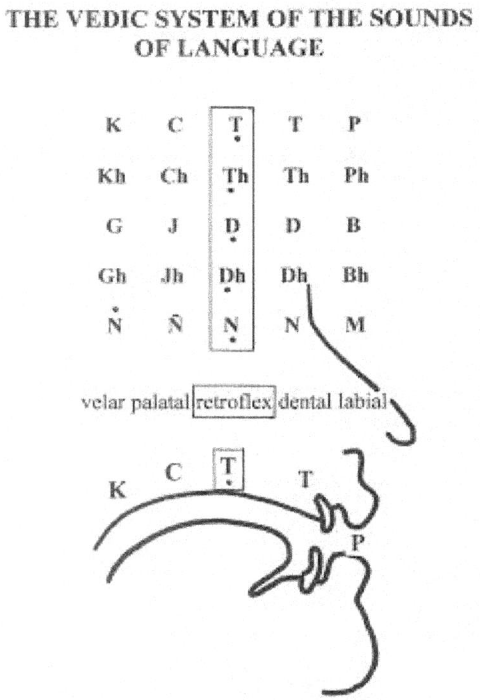

*[quote]*Toward the end of the Vedic period and at the western extremity of Vedic India, in Kośala or Videha, – not far in time and place from the Buddha's birth – reciters of the Veda made a major discovery (Figure 1). They found that the consonants of a language are produced by constricting the vocal tract at a particular point along its stationary portion -- the palate or upper lip. If we move from the larynx or throat to the lips, we pronounce *ka, ca, ṭa, ta, pa.* Each of these syllables may be unvoiced or voiced, provided with more or less breath, which may be made to pass through the nasal cavity as well. Thus we produce, in the case of *ka*, the sequence *ka, kha, ga, gha, ṅa*; and similarly for the other four consonantal stops. The two directions are combined in the two-dimensional square or varga that is depicted here. In order to complete the picture, a few other syllables have to be added along with semi-vowels and vowels…

… The Sanskrit inscriptions from Cambodia contain words that are not found in Sanskrit dictionaries. One of them is *lekhin* which refers to a scribe or secretary. We also find*abhyantaralekhin*, "personal secretary" or, as Kamaleswar Bhattacharya translates it, "secrétaire intime." The Sanskrit root is *likh*, "scratch" or "write," and in Indic Sanskrit we come across derivatives such as *lekha-* "document," *lekhaka-* "writer," *lekhana* "writing," etc.; but not *lekhin*. In Old-Javanese, similar derivatives are at least apparent. Thus we have*lekita* which means "written evidence" and is used in a court

of law. It also refers to "by-laws of the village." It may come from Sanskrit *lekhita* "written" or "caused to be written," but may be connected with Javanese *lukita* which means "thought expressed in words" or "literary composition" and may in turn be related to another term that is certainly native: *lukis* "drawn with a pen." All this evidence suggests that the introduction of Sanskrit had something to do with writing…
… The sound pattern of Sanskrit was adopted and adapted in a large part of Asia - including Central Asia, Korea, Japan and, momentarily, in a grammar of Arabic composed in Iran. I refer to *adoption* and *adaptation* because, in most cases, the Indic system was not imitated slavishly but adapted creatively to new languages and language structures…
… the script of Kharoshthi, probably the earliest Indic script, which was used in northwest India and spread to Central Asia from about the fourth century BCE to the third century CE. The order of syllables starts with *a ra pa ca na la da ba èa ṣa* . . . That order is unexplained and the script is called *Arapacana* after the first five syllables. It possesses clearly Indic features: each syllable ends in a short *–a* and diacritic signs are added when that short *–a* is replaced by another vowel. The order of vowels, however, is not Indic but Aramaic: *a e i o u* and not *a i u e o*. That order is also adopted by diacritics attached to consonants from top to bottom when changing a into *e, i, o* and *u*. The other early Indic script is Brahmi. It is the paradigm of the Vedic system. It influenced, directly or indirectly, via Pallava or other medieval Indian scripts, all the scripts of South and Southeast Asia that include (again in *alphabetic* order) Balinese, Bengali, Burmese, Devanagari, Grantha, Gujrati, Gupta, Gurmukhi, Kannada, Khmer, Lao, Malayalam, Nepali, Oriya, Pallava, Sinhala, Tamil, Telugu and Thai. The evidence for these influences is constituted by the scripts themselves. Textual evidence for how the transmission occurred is less common. The same applies to the evidence for Indian numerals. But there is circumstantial evidence, in both cases. It is probable, for example, that one of the Indian brahmans who transmitted the Vedic paradigm to Cambodia, was the South Indian who belonged, according to a seventh century Cambodian inscription, to the Yajurvedic school of *Taittirîya*. The reason is that among the Prâtiśâkhya compositions that explain the Vedic system, only the *Taittirîya Prâtiśâkhya* depicts the Vedic square (*varga*) of *Figure 1* in full…

… The numbers of South, Southeast and Central Asian scripts that adopted the Indic order is large. An attractive estimate occurs in the tenth chapter of the *Lalitavistara*, called*Lipiśâlâsaṃdarśanaparivarta*, "the revolution of displays of the mansions of writing." It lists 64 different scripts that were mastered by the Bodhisattva. The title of the chapter is reminiscent of the Buddha's own *dharmacakrapravartana*. It emphasizes instructively that the carriers of the sound pattern of Sanskrit to other Asian regions were not only Indian Brahmans but also, and in increasing numbers, Buddhist monks. It is explained at least in part by the geographical facts with which I started: the discovery of the sound pattern of language by Vedic reciters occurred close in place and time to the areas where early Buddhism flourished. It was a feature of civilization that Buddhists carried across Asia…

… I derive five conclusions from our brief discussion. The first is that the sound pattern of Sanskrit was adopted and adapted by many writing systems of Asia. The exporters were Indian brahmans and Buddhist monks. The second is that the pattern that underlies the system was not always understood. The third is that those Asian writing systems are applications of a theory of language, just as airplanes are applications of the laws of aerodynamics. The fourth, closely connected, is that a writing system is only as good as the theory upon which it is based. (Since the accuracy of theories is measured in degrees, absence of any theory points to probability zero.) My fifth and final conclusion is hypothetical in character. If the sound pattern of Sanskrit had also reached the Near East and Europe, there would not be so many clumsy alphabets around and the modern world would have the benefit of rational and practical Indic syllabaries in addition to rational and practical Indic numerals*[unquote]*

Evolution of four Brahmi syllables from Indus Script hieroglyphs *ḍha- dha-, ka-, ma-*

There are indications that some orthographic features from Indus Script were adopted into Brahmi and Kharoshthi writing systems which are both syllabic scripts.

Orthography of four consonants ***ḍha- dha-, ka-, ma-*** signified by Brahmi syllables are traceable to the tradition of Indus Script Corpora which is a *catalogus catalogorum* of metalwork.

Evolution of Brahmi script syllable ka- possibly from Indus Script hieroglyph kaṇḍa, 'arrow' rebus: 'implements/sword'

Brahmi syllabic orthography

Image source for Brahmi: vocalized consonant http://www.ancientscripts.com/brahmi.html

See also:http://www.payer.de/exegese/exeg03.htm#5.2.2.

On the Rakhigarhi seal, a fine distinction is made between two orthographic options for signifying an arrow

with fine pronunciation variants, to distinguish between an arrowhead and an arrow: kaNDa, kANDa. The word kANDa is used by Panini in an expression ayaskANDa to denote a quantity of iron, excellent iron (Pāṇ.gaṇ) i.e., metal (iron/copper alloy). This expression ayas+ kāṇḍa अयस्--काण्ड is signified by hieroglyphs: aya 'fish' PLUS kāṇḍa, 'arrow' as shown on Kalibangan Seal 032. An allograph for this hieroglyph 'arrowhead' is gaNDa 'four' (short strokes) as seen on Mohenjo-daro seal M1118.

Rebus: ayaskāṇḍa 'a quantity of iron, excellent iron' (Pāṇ.gaṇ) aya = iron (G.); ayah, ayas = metal (Skt.)

Thus, the arrowhead is signified by the hieroglyph which distinguishes the arrowhead as a triangle attached to a reedpost or handle of tool/weapon.

As distinct from this orthographic representation of 'arrowhead' with a triangle PLUS attached linear stroke, an arrow is signified by an angle ^ (Caret; Circumflex accent; Up arrow) with a linear stroke ligatured, as in the Rakhigarhi seal. To reinforce the distinction between 'arrow' and 'arrowhead' in Indus Script orthography, a notch is added atop the tip of the circumflex accent. Both the hieroglyph-components are attested in Indian sprachbund with a variant pronunciation: khANDA. खांडा [kāṇḍā] m A jag, notch, or indentation (as upon the edge of a tool or weapon) (Marathi)

It is thus clear that the morpheme kANDa denotes an arrowhead, while the ^ circumflex accent hieroglyph is intended to signify rebus: kāṇḍā 'edge of tool or weapon' or a sharp edged implement, like a sword. In Indian sprachbund, the word which denotes a sword is *khaṁḍa* -- m. 'sword'(Prakritam).

In the hieroglyph-multiplex of Rakhigarhi seal inscription, the left and right parentheses are used as circumscript to provide phonetic determination of the gloss: *khaṁḍa* -- m. 'sword' (Prakritam), while the ligaturing element of 'notch' is intended to signify खांडा [kāṇḍā] 'A jag, notch, or indentation (as upon the edge of a tool or weapon)' Rebus: kaNDa 'implements' (Santali).

Hieroglyph-multiplexon Rakhigarhi seal

Thus, the hieroglyph-multiplex is read rebus as kaNDa 'implements' PLUS *khaṁḍa* 'sword'. The supercargo is thus catalogued on the seal as: 1. arrowheads; 2. metal implements and ingots; 3. swords.

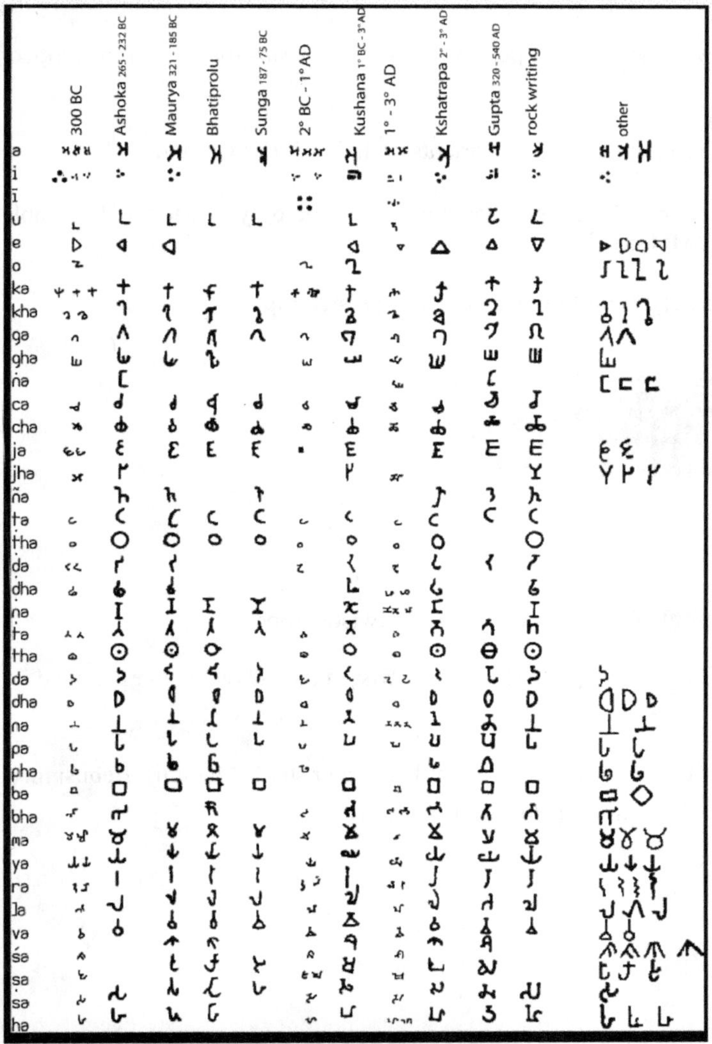

The hieroglyph 'rhinoceros is: kANDA rebus: kaNDa 'implements/weapons'.

The entire inscription or metalwork catalogue message on Rakhigarhi seal can be deciphered:

kaNDa 'implements/weapons' (Rhinoceros) PLUS खाण्डा [kāṇḍā] 'weapons' PLUS *mūhā* 'cast ingots'(Left and Right parentheses as split rhombus or ellipse).

Thus, the supercargo consignment documented by this metalwork catalogue on Rakhigarhi seal is: metal (alloy) swords, metal (alloy) implements, metal cast ingots.

A review of the evolution of Brahmi syllable ka seems relatable to the Indus Script hieroglyph, which signified rebus the gloss: kaṇḍa, 'arrow' as explained in the decipherment of the Rakhigarh seal.

The Brahmi script symbol is almost analogous to the hieroglyph used on Indus Script, thus the orthography of *ka-* syllable was possibly identified as *ka-* for *kaṇḍa*, 'arrow'

Evolution of Brahmi script syllable ma- possibly from meḍ 'iron, copper, metal' in the context of smelting, metalwork tradition of Ancient Near East. Proving svastika signifies zinc metal

Evolution of Brahmi syllable for *ma-* and presents comparable deciphered hieroglyphs from Indus Script Corpora to affirm the continuum of the writing tradition of *Bhāratam Janam*, 'metalcaster folk'.

Image source for Brahmi: vocalized consonant
http://www.ancientscripts.com/brahmi.html See also:
http://www.payer.de/exegese/exeg03.htm#5.2.2.

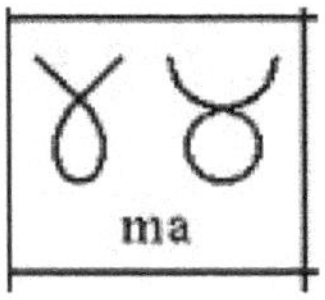

Brahmi syllable ma- is a 'knot' hieroglyph, a continuum fom Indus Script Corpora wherein the 'knot' hieroglyph signified *meḍ* 'iron, copper, metal'.

The orthography of *ma-* syllable was possibly identified as *ma-* for *meḍ*, 'iron, copper, metal'.

The 'knot' hieroglyph has many variants on Indus Script Corpora.

Mohenjo-daro. m1457 Copper plate with 'twist' hieroglyph. Mohejodaro, tablet in bas relief (M-478)

The first hieroglyph-multiplex on the left (twisted rope):

m478a tablet

The hieroglyph may be a variant of a twisted rope.

dhāu 'rope' rebus: dhāu 'metal' PLUS मेढा [mēḍhā] 'a curl or snarl; twist in thread' rebus: mẽṛhẽt, meḍ 'iron'. Thus, metallic ore.

Hieroglyph: मेढा [mēḍhā] A twist or tangle arising in thread or cord, a curl or snarl (Marathi). Rebus: meḍ 'iron, copper' (Munda. Slavic) mẽṛhẽt, meD 'iron' (Mu.Ho.Santali)

med' 'copper' (Slovak)

h131 4271Text

Decipherment from l. to r.:'ant' hieroglyph

Hieroglyph: చీమ [cīma] *chīma*. [Tel.] n. An ant. కొండచీమ. the forest ant. రెక్కలచీమ a winged ant. పారేచీమను వింటాడు he can hear an ant crawl, i.e., he is all alive.చీమదూరని అడవి a forest impervious even to an ant. చలిచీమ a black ant; పై పారేపక్షి కిందపారే చీమ (proverb) The bird above, the ant below, i.e., I had no chance with him. చీమంత of the size of an ant. **చీమపులి** *chīma-puli*. n. The ant lion, an ant-eater.

Rebus: †**cīmara** -- ‘ copper ’ in *cīmara* -- *kāra* -- ‘ coppersmith ’ in Saṁghāṭa -- **sūtra** Gilgit MS. 37 folio 85 verso, 3 (= *zaṅs* -- *mkhan* in Tibetan Pekin text Vol. 28 Japanese facsimile 285 a 3 which in Mahāvyutpatti 3790 renders *śaulbika* -- BHS ii 533. But the Chinese version (Taishō issaikyō ed. text no. 423 p. 971 col. 3, line 2) has *t'ie* ‘ iron ’: H. W. Bailey 21.2.65). [The Kaf. and Dard. word for ‘ iron ’ appears also in Bur. *čhomār*, *čhumər*. Turk. *timur* (NTS ii 250) may come from the same unknown source. Semant. cf. lōhá --]Ash. *ċímä*, *ċimə* ‘ iron ’ (*ċiməkára* ‘ blacksmith ’), Kt. *čimé;*, Wg. *čümā´r*, Pr. *zíme*, Dm. *čimár*(*r*), Paš.lauṛ. *čimā´r*, Shum. *čímar*, Woṭ. Gaw. *ċimár*, Kal. *čīmbar*, Kho. *čúmur*, Bshk. *čimer*, Tor. *čimu*, Mai. *sẽwar*, Phal. *čímar*, Sh.gil. *čimĕr* (adj. *čĭmārī*), gur. *čimăr* m., jij. *čimer*, K. *ċamuru* m. (adj.*ċamaruwu*).(CDIAL 14496) చీముంత [cīmunta] *chīmunta*.. [Tel.] n. A metal vessel. చెంబు.

'bow and arrow' hieroglyph-multiplex.

kāmaṭhum = **a bow**; *kāmaḍ, kāmaḍum* = a chip of bamboo (Gujarati) rebus: *kammaṭa* 'mint' (Kannada) ***Ta.*** **kampaṭṭam** coinage, coin. ***Ma.*** **kammaṭṭam, kammiṭṭam** coinage, **mint**. ***Ka.*** **kammaṭa** id.; **kammaṭi** a coiner.(DEDR 1236) kaNDa 'arrow' rebus: kANDa 'pots and pans, implements'

'twist' hieroglyph PLUS (ligature) 'linear stroke' hieroglyph. meD 'twist, curl' rebus: meD 'iron, copper,metal' PLUS koD 'one' rebus: koD 'workshop' dhAv 'strand' rebus: dhAv 'ore, element, dhAtu'

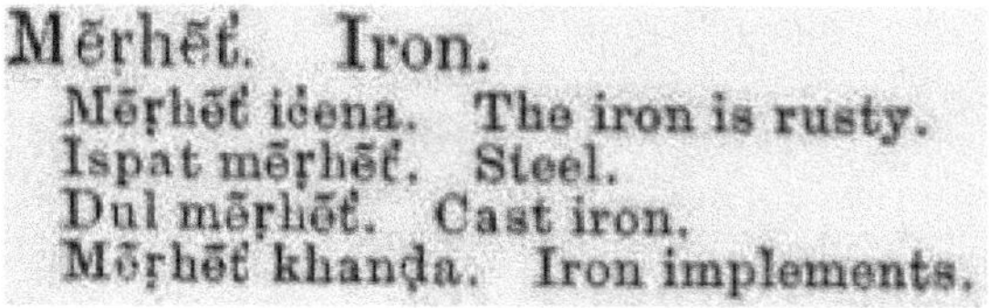

Mērhēt. Iron.
Mērhēt icena. The iron is rusty.
Ispat mērhēt. Steel.
Dul mērhēt. Cast iron.
Mērhēt khanda. Iron implements.

Obj. No. 1049

Together, the inscription on h131 reads: meD koD 'metals ores workshop or smelter/smithy' PLUS meD kANDa 'metal (iron) implements' PLUS *cīmara* 'copper' *kammaṭa* 'mint'.

The Shahdad standard has the 'twisted strand' hieroglyph together with tree, zebu, lion, woman. kuTi 'tree' rebus: kuThi 'smelter' poLa 'zebu' rebus: poLa 'magnetite' arye 'lion' rebus: Ara 'brass' meD 'twist' rebus: meD 'iron, copper, metal'. kola 'woman' rebus: kolhe 'smelter' kol 'working in iron'.

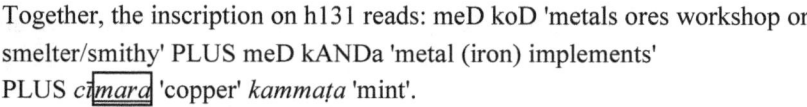

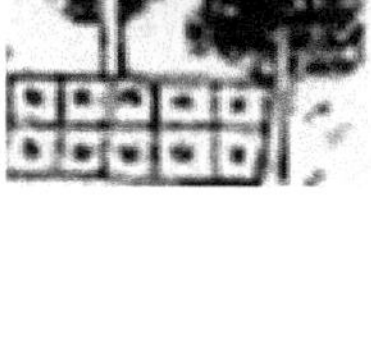

kuṭi 'tree'. Rebus: kuṭhi 'smelter' (Santali). The two trees are shown ligatured to a rectangle with ten square divisions and a dot in each square. The dot may denote an ingot in a furnace mould.

Glyph of rectangle with divisions: *baṭai* = to divide, share (Santali) [Note the glyphs of nine rectangles divided.] Rebus: *bhaṭa* = an oven, kiln, furnace (Santali)

meṛhao = v.a.m. entwine itself; wind round, wrap round roll up (Santali); maṛhnā cover, encase (Hindi) (Santali.lex.Bodding) Rebus: *meḍ* 'iron' (Mu.Ho.) mẽṛh t iron; ispat m. = steel; dul m. = cast iron (Mu.) meṛed-bica = iron stone ore, in contrast to bali-bica, iron sand ore (Munda) *mẽṛhẽt* 'iron'; *mẽṛhẽt icena* 'the iron is rusty'; *ispat mẽṛhẽt* 'steel', *dul mẽṛhẽt* 'cast iron';*mẽṛhẽt khaṇḍa* 'iron implements' (Santali) *meḍ.* (Ho.)(Santali.lex.Bodding) *meṛed, mṛed, mṛd*iron; enga meṛed soft iron; *sanḍi meṛed* hard iron; *ispāt meṛed* steel; *dul meṛed* cast iron; *i meṛed* rusty iron, also the iron of which weights are cast; *bica meṛed* iron extracted from stone ore; *bali meṛed* iron extracted from sand ore (Mu.lex.)

Evolution of Brahmi script syllables ḍha-, dha- from Indus Script. Ur cylinder seal, Harappa tablet with 5 svastika deciphered.

The archaeo-metallurgical enquiry starts with the decipherment of an Ur cylinder seal of 3rd millennium BCE as a metalwork catalogue of a mint.

The objective of this monograph is to demonstrate the association of hieroglyphs of Indus Script Corpora with smelting of ores in ancient mints, by ancient smiths of Sarasvati-Sindhu Civilization who spoke Prakritam (aka Meluhha/Mleccha as spoken *parole*, as distinct from the prosody and precise pronunciations of Chandas of Vedic diction).

The Meluhha lexis related to metalwork is a frame of reference for the evolution of Brahmi script syllables.

This monograph traces the Brahmi script syllables *ḍha-, dha-* from Indus Script hieroglyphs: *dhāv* 'string, dotted circle' rebus: *dhāu*'ore'

h182A, h182B

The drummer hieroglyph is associated with svastika glyph on this tablet (har609) and also on h182A tablet of Harappa with an identical text.

dhollu 'drummer' (Western Pahari) Rebus: *dul* 'cast metal'. The 'drummer' hieroglyph thus announces a cast metal. The technical specifications of the cast metal are further described by other hieroglyphs on side B and on the text of inscription (the text is repeated on both sides of Harappa tablet 182).

kola 'tiger' Rebus: kol 'alloy of five metals, pancaloha' (Tamil). ḍhol 'drum' (Gujarati.Marathi)(CDIAL 5608) Rebus: large stone; dul 'to cast in a mould'. Kanac 'corner' Rebus: kancu 'bronze'. dula 'pair' Rebus: dul 'cast metal'. *kanka* 'Rim of jar' (Santali); *karṇaka* rim of jar'(Skt.) Rebus:*karṇaka* 'scribe' (Telugu); *gaṇaka* id. (Skt.) (Santali) Thus, the tablets denote blacksmith's alloy cast metal accounting including the use of alloying mineral zinc -- *satthiya* 'svastika' glyph.

sattu (Tamil), satta, sattva (Kannada) jasth जसथ् ।रपु m. (sg. dat. jastas ज्तस), zinc, spelter; pewter; zasath ़ ज़स्ऺथ् ़or zasuth ज़सुथ ़। रप m. (sg. dat. zastas ु ज़्तस),़ zinc, spelter, pewter (cf. Hindī jast). jastuvu; । रपूभवः adj. (f. jastüvü), made of zinc or pewter.(Kashmiri).
The hieroglyph: svastika repeated five times.
Five svastika are thus read: taṭṭal sattva Rebus: zinc (for) brass (or pewter). ***ṭhaṭṭha**1 'brass'. [Onom. from noise of hammering brass?]N. *ṭhaṭṭar* ' an alloy of copper and bell metal '. ***ṭhaṭṭhakāra** ' brass worker '. 1.Pk. *ṭhaṭṭhāra* -- m., K. *ṭhö̃ṭhur* m., S. *ṭhā̃ṭhāro* m., P. *ṭhaṭhiār*, °*rā* m.2. P. ludh. *ṭhaṭherā* m., Ku. *ṭhaṭhero* m., N. *ṭhaṭero*, Bi. *ṭhaṭherā*, Mth. *ṭhaṭheri*, H.*ṭhaṭherā* m.(CDIAL 5491, 5493).
Rebus: ṭhaṭṭar 'an alloy of copper and bell metal' (Nepalese)

The drummer hieroglyph is associated with svastika glyph on this tablet (har609) and also on h182A tablet of Harappa with an identical text.

dhollu 'drummer' (Western Pahari) Rebus: *dul* 'cast metal'. The 'drummer' hieroglyph thus announces a cast metal. The technical specifications of the cast metal are further described by other hieroglyphs on side B and on the text of inscription (the text is repeated on both sides of Harappa tablet 182).

kola 'tiger' Rebus: kol 'alloy of five metals, pancaloha' (Tamil). ḍhol 'drum' (Gujarati.Marathi)(CDIAL 5608) Rebus: large stone; dul 'to cast in a mould'. Kanac 'corner' Rebus: kancu 'bronze'. dula 'pair' Rebus: dul 'cast metal'. *kanka* 'Rim of jar' (Santali); *karṇaka* rim of jar'(Skt.) Rebus:*karṇaka* 'scribe' (Telugu); *gaṇaka* id. (Skt.) (Santali) Thus, the tablets denote blacksmith's alloy cast metal accounting including the use of alloying mineral zinc -- *satthiya* 'svastika' glyph.

Evolution of Brahmi script syllables *ḍha-, dha-* traced from Indus Script hieroglyph dotted circle, *dām* 'rope (single strand or string?)', *dā̃u* 'tying', *ḍāv* m. 'dice-throw' rebus: *dhāu* 'ore'

The following monographs have presented evidence and arguments that Indus Script hieroglyph dotted circle, signified *dā̃u* 'tying', *ḍāv* m. 'dice-throw' read rebus: *dhāu* 'ore' in the context of glosses: *dhā̆vaḍ* m. 'a caste of iron -smelters',

dhāvḍī 'composed of or relating to iron'.

The fillet worn on the forehead and on the right-shoulder signifies one strand; while the trefoil on the shawl signifies three strands. A hieroglyph for two strands is also signified.

 Single strand (one dotted-circle)

Two strands (pair of dotted-circles)

Three strands (three dotted-circles as a trefoil)

These orthographic variants provide semantic elucidations for a single: *dhātu, dhāū, dhāv* 'red stone mineral' or two minerals: dul PLUS dhātu, dhāū, dhāv 'cast minerals' or *tri- dhātu, -dhāū, -dhāv* 'three minerals' to create metal alloys'. The artisans producing alloys are *dhā̆vaḍ* m. 'a caste of iron -- smelters', *dhāvḍī* 'composed of or relating to iron')(CDIAL 6773)..

dām 'rope, string' rebus: *dhāu* 'ore' rebus: मेढा [*mēḍhā*] A twist or tangle arising in thread or cord, a curl or snarl (Marathi). Rebus: *meḍ* 'iron, copper' (Munda. Slavic) *mẽṛhẽt, meḍ* 'iron' (Munda).

Semantics of single strand of rope and three strands of rope are: 1. Sindhi *dhāī* f. ' wisp of fibres added from time to time to a rope that is being twisted ', Lahnda *dhāī̃* id.; 2. *tridhā́tu* -- ' threefold ' (RigVeda)

Evolution *ḍha-, dha-* in Brahmi script syllables are evocative of 'string' and 'circle, dotted circle' as may be seen from the following orthographic evidence of epigraphs dated from ca. 300 BCE:

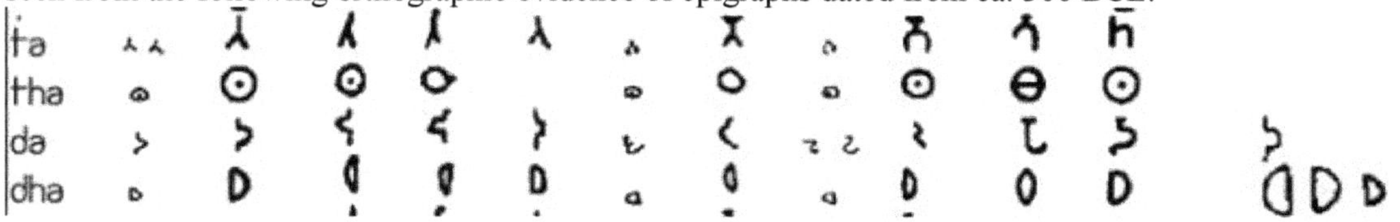

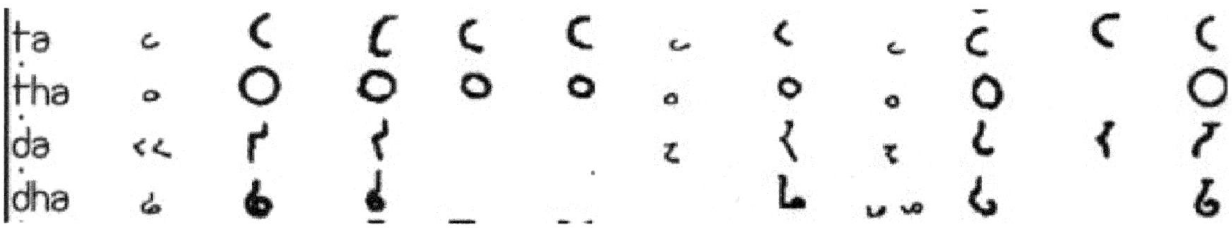

It may be seen from the table of evoution of Brahmi script orthography that

1. a circle signified the Brahmi syllable '*ṭh*a-' and a dotted circle signified the syllable '*tha-*';

2. a string with a twist signified the syllable '*da-*', a string ending in a circled twist signified the syllable '*ḍha-*' and a stepped string signified the syllable '*ḍa-*'.

Importance given to the study of spoken forms of language may be seen from two Ajmer epigraphs and one Dhar epigraph on stone with tables of two Samskrtam plays. Also at Dhar, the pillars of Bhojashala which is an ancient grammar school, ca. 1150, provide charts engraved in stone as sarpabandha, of 1. the Samskrtam alphabet and 2. Verbal terminations from the Katantra.

Varṇanāga-kṛipāṇikā 'dagger of Samskrtam grammar rules'

Selected epigraphical inscriptions of 12th century from Bharat detail ancient methods of teaching Samskrtam language and the grammar rules of the language to school-children. The methods documented in epigraphs include details of forms and use of ancient Samskrtam syllabaries and verbal roots, called *dhātuḥ*.

Varṇanāga-kṛipāṇikā is a metaphor mentioned in an ancient Dhar inscription of 12th century. The phrase refers to 'Samskrtam language (syllables, pronunciation and morphology) rules depicted pictured in a metaphor of 'dagger of Samskrtam grammar rules'.

"On the right side of where the *Māhēśvara-sūtras* end, we find the beginning of the *bandha* known as *Varṇanāga-kṛipāṇikā,* which is, as the expression indicates, a scimitar or a dagger formed by (the combination) of the letters and a snake. The head of the snake is represented by the broad barbed blade of the dagger, and its coiled body, after forming a sort of hilt of the dagger, curls up, making a serpentine loop representing a tail. In the head of the dagger are engraved the fourteen vowels from a to au, and below in its body, the letters *ha, ya, va, ra* and *la*. The portion below is divided into 25 squares, arranged obliquely, and in each of them is to be seen an *akshara* from *ka* to ma, known as *sparśas*, in their classes, five in each line. The portion still below is shaped as a triangle ; and in its right arm, which has four square compartments, are engraved the aksharas *śa, sha, sa* and *ha*, one in each square, from top to bottom. The base is also divided in four columns, each of which shows the *jihvāmūlīya*, the *upadhmānīya*, the *anusvāra* and the *visarga*, respectively from left to the right; and in the left-hand side of the triangle are engraved the aksharas *ru, yu* and *u*, in columns two to four. The syllable which was engraved in the first of these columns has altogether disappeared."

The *Māhēśvara-sūtras are also part of the Dhar inscription. In Hindu tradition, these are also called* ***Shiva Sutras*** (IAST: śivasūtrāṇi; Devanāgarī: शिवसूत्राणि) or *Māheshvara Sutras* (Devanāgarī: माहेश्वर सूत्राणि) are fourteen verses that organize the phonemes of the Samskrtam language as referred to in the Aṣṭādhyāyī of Pāṇini.

IAST	**Devanāgarī**
1. a i u ṇ 2. ṛ ḷ k 3. e o ṅ 4. ai au c 5. ha ya va ra ṭ 6. la ṇ 7. ña ma ṅa ṇa na m 8. jha bha ñ 9. gha ḍha dha ṣ 10. ja ba ga ḍa da ś 11. kha pha cha ṭha tha ca ṭa ta v 12. ka pa y 13. śa ṣa sa r 14. ha l	१. अ इ उ ण्। २. ऋ ऌ क्। ३. ए ओ ङ्। ४. ऐ औ च्। ५. ह य व र ट्। ६. ल ण्। ७. ञ म ङ ण न म्। ८. झ भ ञ्। ९. घ ढ ध ष्। १०. ज ब ग ड द श्। ११. ख फ छ ठ थ च ट त व्। १२. क प य्। १३. श ष स र्। १४. ह ल्।

Dhar (Mahākāleśvara Temple) sarpabandha inscription. Fro

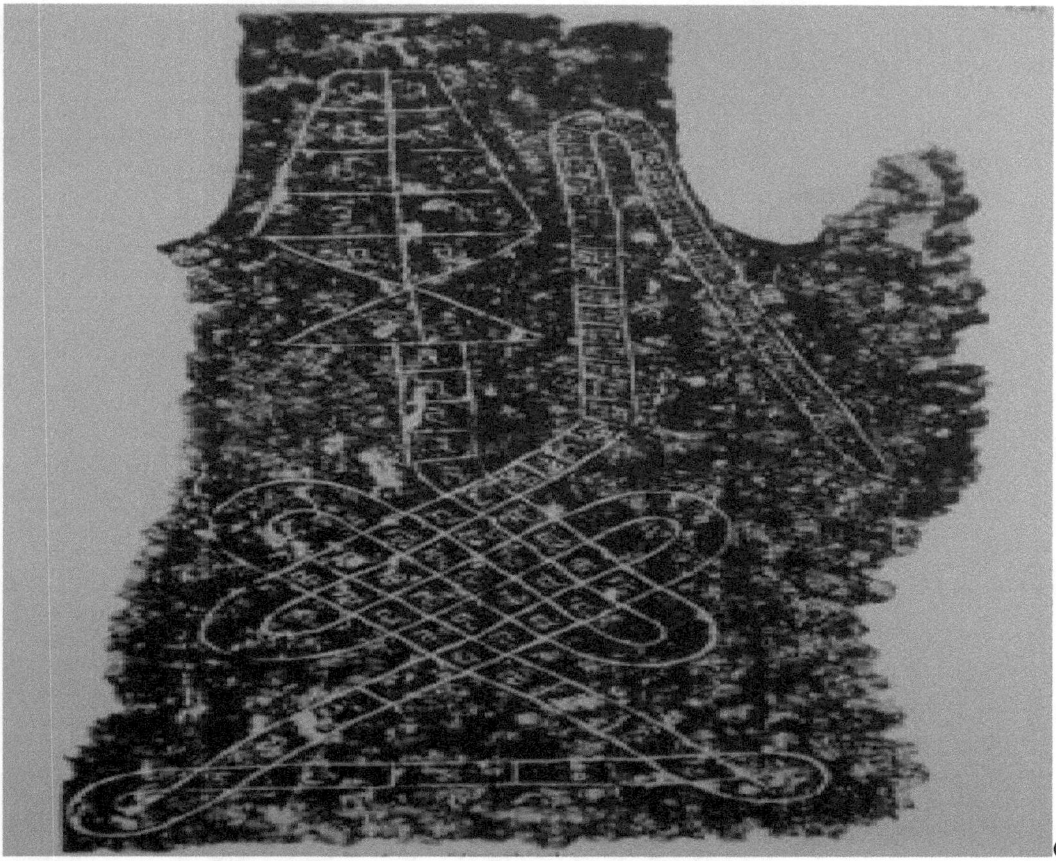

C
m CII 7.2, pl. XXVII II: Vol. VII, Plate VII DHAR SARPA-BANDH

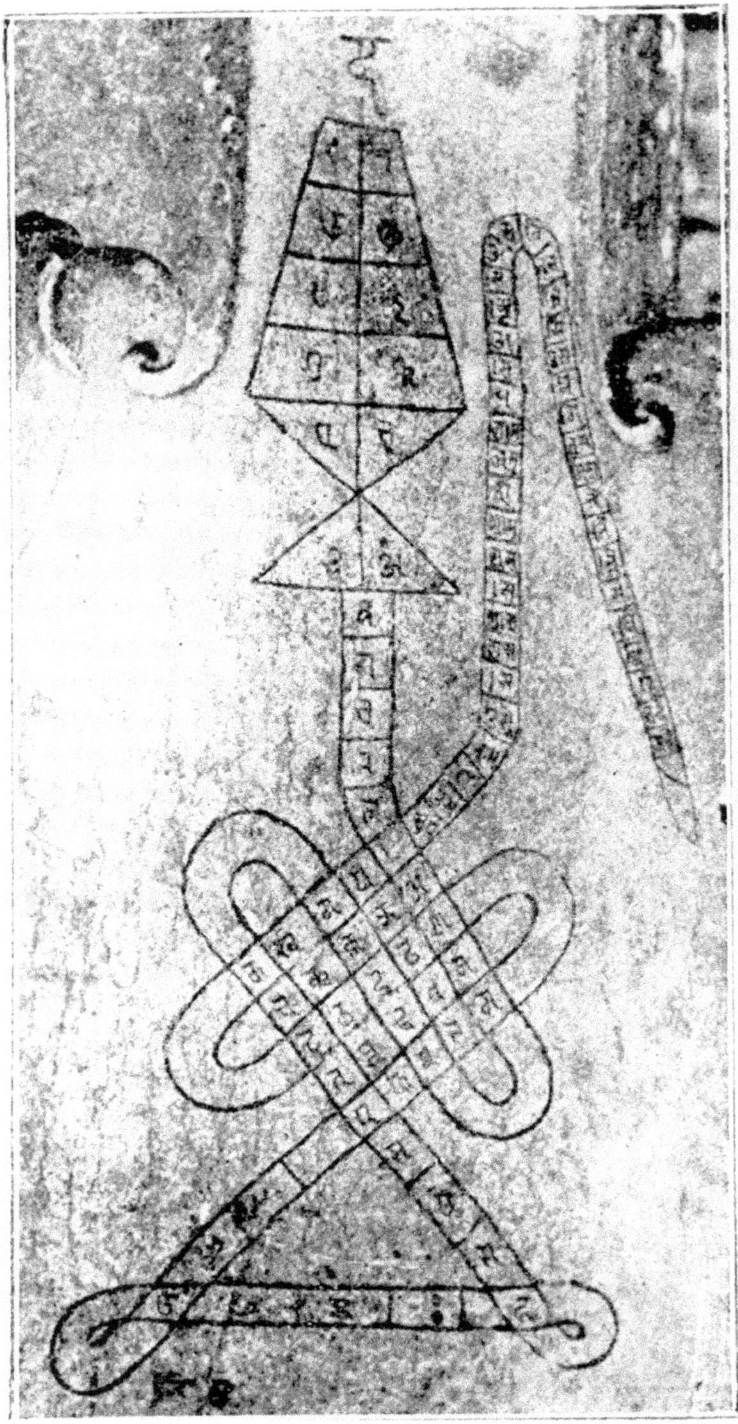

Samskrtam grammar inscriptions, Bhojashala, Dhar

Background

An article in Jan. 2012 issue of Journal of the Royal Asiatic Society, attempted to show that the Sarasvati statue in British Museum is NOT that of Sarasvati but that of Ambika. (Michael Willis, 2012, Dhar Bhoja and Sarasvati: from Indology to Political mythology and back, *JRAS*, Series 3, 22,1, pp. 129-153), While Michael Willis has failed in his attempt (as detailed in the note Annex A in the embedded document), there has been a greater failure in not reporting on a crucial piece of evidence establishing that the two Sarasvati statues now in the British Museum were IN FACT, taken from the Sarasvati Temple at Dhar in Madhya Pradesh. These statues now in the British Museum belong to the temple in Dhar and SHOULD BE RETURNED FORTHWITH by British Government and British Museum Authorities.

This evidence relates to two inscriptions of Samskrtam grammar in the Samskrtam school set up there by King Bhoja in the temple. This note discusses the provenance and details of these two inscriptions.

Importance of the finds

1. *Bomb. Gaz.* Vol. I, p. 180, states that the mosque was an old Samskrtam School founded by Bhoja himself.
2. The contents of these Dhar *sarpabandha* (serpentine chart) inscriptions have been read and are demonstrated to relate to teaching Samskrtam grammar to students in a class room in Bhoja *śālā*, i.e. Bhoja's Samskrtam school.
3. These two Samskrtam grammar inscription charts on stone were found on the pillars which support the dome of what is today Kamal Mosque.
4. The pillars on which the inscriptions were found relate to the temple for Sarasvati.
5. The Sarasvati statue in British Museum contains an inscription on its base and refers to her as *Ambā*, NOT *Ambikā*. Ambā is another name for Sarasvati as noted in a Annex A citing Rigveda: ***ambi****tame, devitame, naditame Sarasvati.* The second statue of Sarasvati in British Museum is that of *Vāgdevi* (Divinity of Language. A reference to this statue also occurs on the inscription at the bast of the first Sarasvati statue where Vararuchi refers(in the inscription) to the fact that he had a statue of Vāgdevi made and now he is getting the statue of *Ambā*..
6. The occurrence of the Samskrtam grammar inscriptions CONCLUSIVELY demonstrates evidence for the Hindu tradition of Sarasvati as divinity of education, learning, knowledge.
7. Temple for Sarasvati was part of the temple for Īśvara (i.e.śiva). An iron pillar (now broken into 3 pieces) comparable to the Delhi iron pillar lies in front of the temple complex of Dhar, attesting to the possibility that this pillar was a *dvhajastambham* (sacred pillar) of the temple.

I suggest that Samskrtam experts should try to transcribe Inscription B also and make both the Samskrtam grammar charts an essential part of all schools teaching Samskrtam.

I also suggest that a booklet be made of these inscriptions to constitute a guide for students and teachers of Samskrtam grammar in all institutions devoted to the study of Samskrtam.

Excerpt from *Corpus Inscriptionum Indicarum*, 1991, Harihar Vitthal Trivedi, ed., Vol. VII, Part 2 Inscriptions of the Paramaras, Chandellas, Kachchapaghatas and two minor Dynasties, Director General, Archaeological Survey of India, New Delhi (pp.86 - 88):
[quote]

No. 26; Plates XXVII-XXIX (Inscription A + duplicate and Inscription B) The Dhar inscriptions. These inscriptions, which are two in number and called here as A and B, were first brought to light by Ernest Barnes in his article on Dhar and Mandu, published in the Journal of the Bombay Branch of the Royal Asiatic Society, Vol. XXI, 1900-02, pp. 330 ff., with a photolithograph between pp. 350 and 351, in which he also incorporated a note on them by KK Lele, Superintendent of Archaeology in the former State of Dhar. Lele also prepared two official notes on the records (One of these was written in May, 1902, for presentation to Lord Curzon on the occasion of his visit to Dhar; and the other, in 1929. I am indebted to

Shri AW Wakankar of Dhar, for lending me the only copies of these notes with him, for utilising them in this article); and a description of the inscriptions appeared also in his work entitled Dhar and Mandu, on pp. 29-30, along with that on the preceding one, as already stated. Subsequently the inscriptions were noticed briefly in the *Annual Reports of the Western Circle of the Survey,* for 1904-05, p. 8 (No. 2081) and again for 1912-13, pp. 21 and 55 (No. 2601); and finally, they were edited by KN Sastri, without facsimiles, in the*Epigraphia Indica*, Vol. XXXI, p. 29 f., along with the one that precedes and the other that follows.The inscriptions are edited here from my personal examination of the originals and from an excellent impression of one of them (B) which I owe to the Chief Epigraphist of the Archaeological Survey of India.

These inscriptions are on two separate pillars near the tomb of Kamal Maula mosque in the monument known as Bhoja-shala, in the south-west part of Dhar, the principal town of a district of the same name in Madhya Pradesh. The pillars are of grey lime stone and are among those that support the dome of the prayer hall, one on each side of the raised pulpit, Each of the inscriptions is complete in itself, though they are allied inasmuch as they deal with the same subject of Nagari alphabet and grammatical terminology. The letters are beautifully engraved and well preserved except that they have suffered from partial decay and peeling off in some places, as the material of grey lime stone on which they were cut was not quite suitable for incisions. (I am thankful to Shri Deshpande, technical assistant in the Arch. Surv. Of India at Mandu, for the information that the stones of the pillars are similar to those found in quarries in the adjoining region, for example, at Tarapur, etc.) Here we may also point out that quite a large number of some other inscriptions which were incised on the floor or pavement of the same structure, appear to have been deliberately chiseled off so as to leave a letter here and there, in some later time, were all on durable black stone, whereas the inconspicuous position of the pillars appears to have saved them from the fate which the other inscriptions have undergone due to vandalism. (Now nothing can be made out of these inscriptions except that they were in Samskrtam and Prakrit).

A. The first of these inscriptions, which is on the proper right side of the pulpit and faces the east, measures about 70 cms. in height and 30.5 cms. in breadth. The letters of the alphabet are about 1 cm. in size, while those of the terminations in the tail are slightly smaller. The inscription is written in the Nagari alphabet of about the 11-12th century. The language is Samskrtam.

It is an alphabetical chart and its contents are identical with those of its counterpart in the Mahakala temple inscription, as seen above. As the alphabet plays the chief part in this inscription, it has rightly been called alphabetical.

B. This inscription, which is on the proper left side of the raised platform and faces the south, is bigger in size, being 91.55 cms. high and 45 cms. in breadth. The language is Samskrtam; and the palaeographical and orthographical peculiarities are the same as stated above. The inscription commences with two verses in the *Anushtubh* metre, with the symbol for *svasti* in the beginning. They are written in four lines, in a space 17 cms. broad and by 5 cms. high. They are identical with verses 86-87 of the Ujjain inscription and are not marked. Below the verses and leaving a vacant space measuring 13 cms. in height, we find a chart (*bandha*) made up by the intertwining of two serpents, probably male and female, as Lele has rightly remarked, exhibiting on their body the personal terminations of ten *lakāras (tinvibhaktis)* together with 16 *dhātu-pratyayas.* The chart may be divided in three parts, viz., the top, the middle and the bottom portions. In the top section the letters are very indistinct except for the initial *atha*, and they have been conjecturally restored by Sastri as *atha tin-vibhakti-bandhah*; but as already remarked by Sircar while publishing Sastri's article, the letters appear as *atha… dhātuh.* (See *Ep. Ind.,* Vol. XXXI, p. 29, n. The letters are rather indistinct; but I read *atha dhātuh* between the heads of the serpents and the word *pratyaya* straight down the base.)

The middle section of the chart is shaped as a square standing vertically on one of the angles of the top section. It is divided into 180 compartments, each of which is a parallelogram cut by 'drawing nine parallel lines one way and seventeen the other way across.' The space between each pair of parallel lines, as remarked by sastri, 'is alternately closed by means of projecting loops at either end along the four sides of the square turning the sets of parallel lines into two running spirals end to end.' The five loops and the five intervening open spaces between them, in the upper left arm of the square, contain the initial letters of the terms denoting the different senses in which the ten *lakāras*, i.e., the tenses and moods of Samskrtam verbs, are used. These letters are, in serial order, *va, sa, vi, hy, a, pa, sva (śva), ā, bha* and *kri*, respectively standing for *vartamāna, sambhāvanā, vidhi, hyastana-atīta, atīta-sāmānya, parokṣa, śvastana-bhaviṣyati, āśīr, bhaviṣyat and kriyātipatti* or *kriyākrama,* indicating, respectively, the ten *lakāras* from *laṭ* to *lṛin,* excepting the Vedic *lōṭ* and taking *vidhi-lin* and *āśīrlin* separately. Thus there are altogether 18 X 10 = 180 verbal terminations, of which, 90 of each set

(known as *parasmai-* and *ātmanepada*) are given in the chart.

(In his note Lele red the letter *hya* as *pa* and the preceding letter as *sa*, and took them as for *pancamī and saptamī,* remarking that they are so called because they are the 5th and 7th in the usual enumeration of the tenses. But to me the consonant of this letter appears as *p* and the sign of the *mātrā* is clear, though mutilated.)

They are all duly numbered on the right hand side and arranged in slanting columns from the left to the right, given in the spaces left between the 'zigzag cross-turnings' of the serpents. The two sets of terminations (*parasmai-* and *ātmane-*), the three persons (*prathama, madhyama and uttama*) and the three numbers (singular, dual and plural) are marked on the left-hand side, in order, by the initial letters representing them; and the names of the tenses and moods are marked at the top of each column by the initial letter of each. They may be arranged as under:

Intials	Full name	Panini's name	English name
Va	*vartamāna*	*laṭ*	Present
sa	*sambhāvanā*	*lin*	Potential
vi	*vidhi*	*lōṭ*	Imperative
hya	*hyastanī*	*lan*	Imperfect
a	*adyatanī*	*lun*	Aorist
pa	*parokṣā*	*liṭ*	Perfect
śva	*śvastanī*	*luṭ*	First Future
ā	*āśīh*	*āśīrlin*	Benedictive
bha	*bhaviṣyantī*	*lṛiṭ*	Second Future
kri	*Kriyātipatti* or *kriyākrama*	*lṛin*	Conditional

The last section of the table is triangular, with its apex above. In its looped corner and also in the hollow circles along its arms, are engraved the several derivative bases showing causality, desire, intensity, etc. The portion of the stone in the right corner side, which appears to have contained at least three circles with a letter in each, is entirely lost; but, to judge from what remains, the total number of these circles appears to have been 19, as also stated inside the triangle in its middle. (Sastri read this number as 16, but I am tempted to take the unit figure as 9 because of the curve at the top which is broader than the one below). These terminations are only of grammatical interet and therefore need not be dealt with here in detail. (For details of these, see Sastri's article referred to above. He also remarked that the terminations are in agreement with the Chāndra system of grammar whereas, according to Lele, it is in agreement with that of Kātantra.)

Both these inscriptions are of educational interest, also showing the high interest of the public in teaching and learning grammar. In this respect, what KK Lele writes in his note referred to above is highly appealing, and it is given here in his own words. He says: 'they must have been designed by some ingenious teacher and permanently engraved on the pillars as charts in modern schools...They confirm the tradition that the mosque (on the pillars of which they are engraved) was merely a transformation of the Samskrtam School formed by Raja Bhoja and maintained by his successors. The old foundation too tells the same tale. It is, therefore, beyond doubt that the mosque was not only built out of the materials of, but stands on the site of the old Schools.' (Note: In this connection, see *Bomb. Gaz*. Vol. I, p. 180, where it is stated that the mosque was an old Samskrtam School founded by Bhoja himself. Attention is also invited to the inscription on the pedestal of the Sarasvati image, edited above (No. 14).

[unquote]

INSCRIPTIONS OF THE PARAMARAS OF MALWA

Nos. 25-27 ; PLATES XXVII-XXX

THREE SERPENTINE STONE INSCRIPTIONS FROM MĀLWĀ (All undated)

25. THE MAHĀKĀLA TEMPLE (UJJAIN) INSCRIPTION (PLATE XXVII)

...THIS inscription was briefly noticed by K. K. Lele, Superintendent of Archaeology in the former Dhār State, in his work entitled *Dhar* and *Mandu*, pp. 29-30, and subsequently its contents were noticed by D.R. Bhandarkar in the*Reports of the Western Circle of the Survey,* for 1904-05, p. 8, and again for 1912-13, pp. 21 and 55 (Nos. 2601 and 2599). It was finally edited by K.N. Sastri in the Epigraphia Indica, Vol. XXXI, pp. 25 ff., with a photolithograph between pp. 28-29. The record is edited here from the original stone and an estampage which I owe to the Chief Epigraphist.

...The inscription is incised on a black basalt, now set in a small I in the compound of the Mahākāla temple at **Ujjain**, the principal city of a district of the same name in Madhya Pradesh. It consists of 28 closely written lines, measuring 35 cms. broad by 44 cms. high. The length of the first three lines is a little less than the usual length of the other lines so as to accommodate two or three letters less on either of their sides ; and line 17 is only about half in length of the others. Lines 18 to 28, which are engraved only on the left side, again vary in length, the first of these is 20 cms. long ; the next three about 23 cms. long each (except that the first of these is also continued on the right side) ; and the last seven lines show the length of each of them to be 12.5 cms. The lower right side of the slab contains an alphabetical-cum-grammatical chart, with its top being almost parallel to 1. 18 and showing a total height of about 55 cms. The average height of letters in 11. 1-17 is 1 cm., and below, it varies slightly, being more or less, as allowed by the space for engraving them. The inscription is tolerably well preserved, except some of the syllables which are damaged or have disappeared on account of flaking, as also on the lower left side of the stone.

...The inscription is written in the **Nāgarī** alphabet of the 11-12th century A.C. They are beautifully engraved. With reference to its **palaeography**, we note that in 11. 1-17 the syllable ṅ is devoid of its dot, as in *liṅga,* 1. 1, and *-saṅga,*1.8 ; that *dh* has a horn on its forelimb, for example in *–dhyāna*, 1.2, though we have exceptions as in *dhātrā,* 1. 16 ; and the slightly different forms or r are to be seen in –
rapi and *charaṇa-,* in 11. 16 and 17, respectively. It is interesting to note that in the alphabetical chart engraved below, ṅ exhibits the same form, the lingual ḍ is formed so as to resemble *r* ; *dh* has begun developing a horn, and finally, the letter *b* has a separate sign of its own, resembling a parallelogram, the height of which exceeds its breadth, with the side on the right drawn below.

...The **language** is Samskrtam. The inscription begins with a *praśasti* eulogising Śiva in six stanzas, each of which is complete in itself. The **purpose** of it, as can only be guessed, appears to record the restoration of the temple of Mahākāla where it is found, and along with it, also to give the type of the alphabet and some grammatical terminations, the details of which we shall presently see. The record is grammatically correct. With reference to **orthography**, we note the same peculiarities as to be found in contemporary inscriptions, for example, the use of the dental for the palatal sibilant, as in *pasyanti,* 1. 5 ; the occasional reduplication of a consonant following *r*, as in *–archchita* and *–arppita*, both in 1.2, but not in *hartā*, 1.7 ; the general use of the *pṛishṭha-mātrā*, which, in a few cases is marked above the letter, as in the three *anushṭubh* verses below ; and finally, the use of the sign for v to denote b, which too is given as a separate letter in the chart below. The word dhyāna in 1. 2 is spelt with the lingual ṇ, and yasmin in 1. 11 ends wrongly in an anusvāra.

...The six stanzas of the *praśasti* are marked from 79 to 84 ; and this naturally raises a question as to the existence of another fragment containing stanzas No. 1 to 78. It is likely, as suggested by Sastri, that the earlier portion of the *praśasti* which contains stanzas 1 to 78 may have been engraved on a stone slab built in a niche in the upper story of the Mahākāla temple. The resemblance in style and the subject matter, along with the kind of stone, tends to support the suggestion of Sastri, though we cannot be absolutely certain about it. This is why Dr.D. C. Sircar, while publishing Sastri's article, remarked that it is likely that the two fragments form the beginning and end of two different inscriptions.[1]

...Here we may give a general idea of the record in the upper story and consider its relation with the one number review. The inscription on the upper story of the temple is about 43 cms. broad by 55 cms. high ; and the surface of the stone being highly worn out, it cannot be completely read. But what one can make out from the fragmentary reading of it is that it contains 19 stanzas, of which the first sixteen are devoted to the eulogy of Śiva and the description of the Arbuda mountain. This account is followed, as we find in a number of the Paramāra inscriptions, by an allusion to the sacrificial offering of the sage Vasishṭha and the creation of a warrior from his fire-pit. The portion that follows is lost ; it appears to have contained the genealogy of the Paramāra rulers bringing it down to Udayāditya, whose name appears in the present inscription. Viewing this all, it appears possible, though not certain, that the present inscription was in continuation of the one on the upper story, and some time subsequently the two fragments were separated. This consideration alone appears to justify the fact that the verses in the present inscription are numbered from 79 onwards.

...Of the three stanzas in the *Anushṭubh* metre which are incised in 11. 23-28 and below the alphabet on the left hand side, the first dedicates the *Varṇa-nāgakṛipāṇikā, i.e., the alphabetical snake-scimitar, to Udayāditya ;* and the second stanza states that this sword of kings Udayāditya and Naravarman, the worshippers of Śiva, was ready equally for the protection of the (four) *Varṇas* (classes of society) and of the *Varṇas* (alphabet), (by encouraging learning), with a pun on the word *Varṇa*. The third and the last of these stanzas purports to state that this serpentine sword of king Udayāditya, intended for the protection of letters (learning) and social classes has been set up as a badge for the poets and kings (rulers). It also says that the string of (poetic) gems was composed by "the friend of the talented poets'' *(sukavibandhunā)*, which, as Sastri rightly pointed out, presumably refers to king Naravarman himself, who appears to have composed the *praśasti.* [2] Thus the drift of all these three verses taken together goes to show, as already indicated by Sastri, that the *praśasti* was incised by Naravarman himself, during his reign, to commemorate the restoration of a temple of Śiva (the Mahākāla temple itself where the stone was found), [3] and also that he associated his father's name with his own as an expression of honour and filial love. The case appears analogous to that of the Nagpur Museum stone inscription which is Naravarman's own composition and which contains as many as twenty-one verses to eulogise his brother Lakshmadēva for whom he had deep devotion [4] .

...Immediately following the *praśasti* and in 11. 18-19 are engraved the *akshara* of the Nāgarī alphabet, class-wise, each group being followed by a numerical indication showing the number of aksharas in it. Thus the number 14 in 1. 18 indicates the vowels from a to au, then the number 2 the *anusvāra* and *visarga*, and following it, again the number 2 is engraved consonants from ka to ha, indicating their total number 51, at the end. The sub-total is also indicated just after each of the groups. Line 20 of the inscription gives the long vowels *ā, ī, ū, ṛī, and lṛī,* and following these, we find (in 11. 20-22) the well-known *Māhēśvara-sūtras*. The total number of letters in them, which is 47, is given at the end, and the sub-total of each group is also mentioned along with it. This alphabetical arrangement is followed by the three stanzas (11. 23-28), as already discussed above.

...On the right side of where the *Māhēśvara-sūtras* end, we find the beginning of the *bandha* known as *Varṇanāga-kṛipāṇikā,* which is, as the expression indicates, a scimitar or a dagger formed by (the combination) of the letters and a snake. The head of the snake is represented by the broad barbed blade of the dagger, and its coiled body, after forming a sort of hilt of the dagger, curls up, making a serpentine loop representing a tail. In the head of the dagger are engraved the fourteen vowels from a to au, and below in its body, the letters *ha, ya, va, ra* and *la*. The portion below is divided into 25 squares, arranged obliquely, and in each of them is to be seen an *akshara* from *ka* to ma, known as *sparśas*, in their classes, five in each line. The portion still below is shaped as a triangle ; and in its right arm, which has four square compartments, are engraved the aksharas *śa, sha, sa* and *ha*, one in each square, from top to bottom. The base is also divided in four columns, each of which shows the *jihvāmūlīya*, the*upadhmānīya*, the *anusvāra* and the *visarga*, respectively from left to the right ; and in the left-hand side of the triangle are engraved the aksharas *ru, yu* and *u*, in columns two to four. The syllable which was engraved in the first of these columns has altogether disappeared. The object of engraving these three aksharas is not known to me. [1] In the end we find the number 15 which gives the total.

...In the loop representing the tail of the snake are engraved the *sup* and *tiṅ* terminations as they are technically known. It is divided into 39 compartments, 21 of which are occupied by the noun terminations of the seven classes (three for each of the numbers, *i.e.*, singular, dual and plural), and the remaining 18 are the verbal inflexions of the two (*parasmai and ātmanē-*) padas. 9 for each of them, respectively, for the three numbers known as the *prathama* (third), madhyama (second) and the *uttama* (first) person.

[1] See *Ep. Ind., Vol. XXXI,* p. 25, n. 3. In my personal examination on the spot I was convinced that Sastri is correct in his remarks.

[2] Agreeing with Sastri and also with Lele who expressed the same opinion while noticing the alphabeticalcum-grammatical chart found at Dhār (the next one), I hesitate to agree with Dr. Sircar who suggests that the verses were composed by the talented poet Bandhu (*su-kavi-bandhunā*) who was probably

a protégé of Naravarman, for Sircar himself has also felt the difficulty that the poet Bandhu would not indulge in calling himself "a talented poet''. See Ep. Ind., Vol. XXXI, p. 26, n. In our view as expressed here. Sircar's justification of calling Naravarman a king (mahībhuj) by taking him a governor of a district of his father's kingdom, does not arise.

[3] The time of the actual construction of the temple of this jyōtirliṅga being unknown. this view is expressed here.

[4] See No. 33, vv. 34-54.

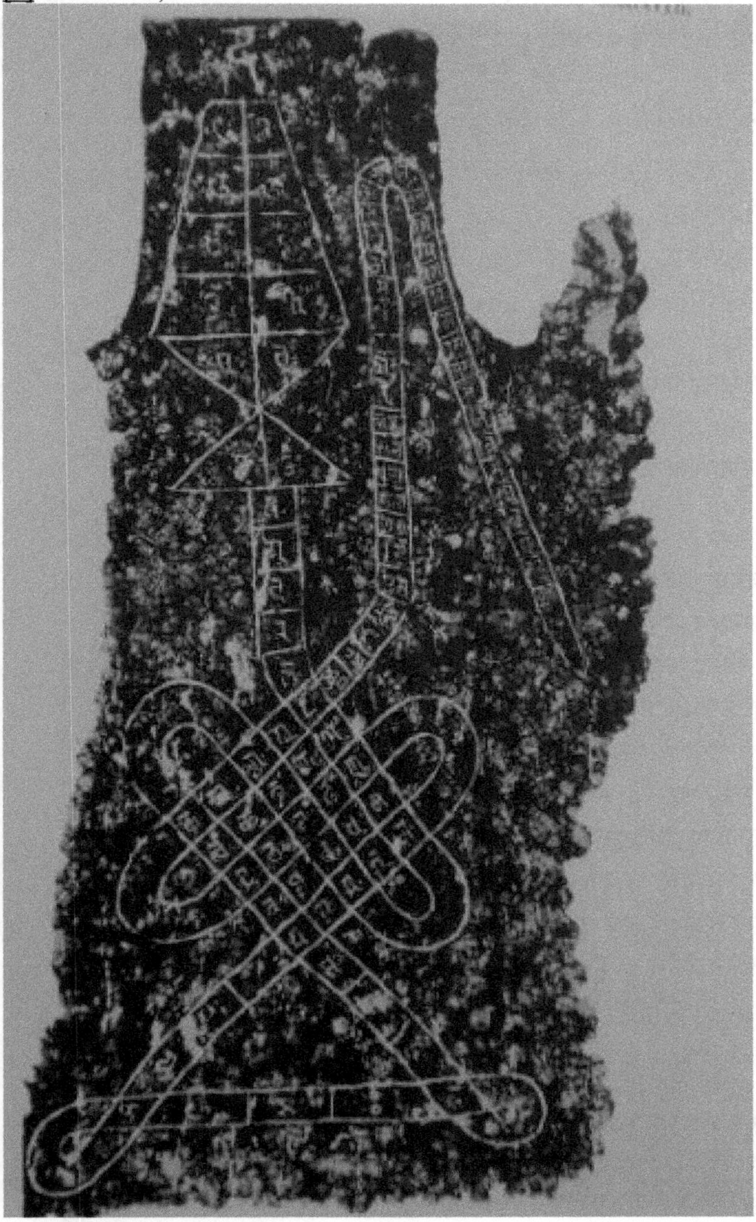

DHAR SARPA-BANDH INSCRIPTION : A (DUPLICATE AND UNDATED)

13 म्व(म्ब)रानुस्वारं कलयन्नकाररुचिराकारः कृपार्द्रः प्रभुः । विष्णोर्विश्वतनोरवन्तिनग-

14 रीहृत्पुण्डरिके वसन्नोंकाराक्षरमूर्त्तिरस्यतु[1] महाकालोन्तकालं सताम् ॥-३॥ भुज्य-

15 न्ते भुवनानि सप्त वसुधा साम्भोनिधिर्द्दीयते कल्पान्तेपि न नश्यते न कुपितान्मृत्यो-

16 रपि त्रस्यते । ध्यायद्भिर्यदपास्तकर्म्मनिगडैर्धात्रापि न प्राथ्र्यते तद्वः स्वान्तमलंकरो[2]-

17 तु चरणाम्भोजद्वयं सा(शा)म्भवम् ॥-४॥

18 श्प श्पा इ ई उ ऊ ऋ ॠ लृ लॄ ए ऐ श्पो श्पो १४० : २ - - २

19 क ख ग घ ङ २ च छ ज झ ञ २ ट ठ ड ढ ण २ त थ द ध न २ प फ ब भ म २ य[3] र ल व ४ [श][4] ष स ह २१]

20 श्पा ई ऊ ॠ लॄ [।*] श्पाइउण(ण्) [ऋ]लृक(क्) १० ए श्पौ ङ(ङ्) ऐश्पौच(च्) हयवरट् लण(ण्) ञ-

21 मङ[ण*] झभञ(ञ्) घढध[ष्] जबगडदश(श्) २०।३४ खफछठथचटतव(व्)

22 कपय(य्) शषसर(र्) १३ हल(ल्) ३३।४७॥

23 उदयादित्यदेवस्य वर्ण्णनागकृपाणिका ।

24 कवीनां च नृपाणां च वेषो वक्षसी रोपितः ॥[-२॥*][5]

25 ए[के]यमुदयादित्यनरवर्म्ममहीभुजोः[5] ।

26 [महे]शस्वामि[नोर्व्वर्ण्णस्थित्यै सिद्धासिपुत्रिका] ॥[-६॥*]

27 [उदया][6]दित्यनामाङ्कवर्ण्णनागकृपाणिका ।

28 [पद्यमुक्ता]मणिश्रेणी सृष्टा सुकविबं(बं)धुना ॥[-७॥*]

1 - -[3]हा (हे?)न्द्रसद्दक्षशक्तिरशनारम्यं[4] वियद्वेदिकं ज्योतिर्लिङ्ग-

2 मनादि सिद्धनिवि (बि) डध्यानप्रसूनार्च्चितम्। नासाग्रार्प्पितचक्षुषः[5]

3 कतिपये पश्यन्ति यद्योगिनस्तद्भूयादणिमादिदिव्यफल-

4 दं रूपं सतां शाम्भवम्[6] ॥७६॥ नित्यं व्यापकमेकम् [ज्ज्व] लचलं ज्योतिः स्फुरद्रत्नव-

5 द्योगोन्मीलितामीलितेक्षणपुटाः पस्य(श्य)न्ति पातंजलाः। सांद्रैव्यो (र्व्यो) मकदम्व (म्ब)नीप[7]-

6 कुसुमैरभ्यर्च्चितं चिन्तितं तद्भूयादपुनर्ह (र्भ) वाय परमं रूपं सतां शाम्भवम् ॥-०॥ [नाम्भः][8]

7 क्लेदयति प्रकम्पयति न व्र(ब्र)ह्माण्डहर्त्ता मरुन्नाग्निः प्लुष्यति नावृणोति [च नभः]

8 क्षोणी न चाक्रामति। योगाभ्यासवसा (शा)द्विमुक्तविषयासङ्गान्यदन्तर्व्विनिल्लीना-

9 न्त[:*]करणां (णं)हृदि स्फुरतु तज्ज्योतिः सतां शाम्भवम् ॥-१॥ वैराग्यातिशयाद्वितीय[10]-

10 सतताभ्यासप्रसूतिर्गुरुवृ त्तीनां मनसो निरोध उदितो योगः स योगीश्व-

11 रैः। यस्मिं(स्मिन्) संश्न(स्न)पितेर्च्चिते परिचिते ध्याते नते संस्तुते स्पृष्टे दृष्ट उपार्ज्जितेस्तु

12 पुरजित्स व्र(ब्र)ह्ममूयाय वः। ॥-२॥ क्रीडाकुण्डलितोरगेश्वरतनूका[रा*]धिरूढो-

Two views: Varṇanāga-kṛipāṇikā (Serpentine dagger)tine Dagger) of King Udayāditya (Mahākāleśvara Temple, Ujjain, early twelfth century)--Archaeological Survey of India. (The grammatical chart found in Bhojaśālā in Dhārā is also found in a ruined temple outside the city.) Naravarman, Paramāra king restored the temple. A sarpabandha is engraved on a stone slab of the temple. It is a table used by students to learn

Samskrtam. The verse refers to the preservation of language sounds which matches with the preservation of *varṇasthiti* (language sounds).

Alphabets are in the snake's body, nominal and verbal endings are in the tail; to the left of the snake's head, verses note: *CII* 7.2: 83 ff., vv 85–86:

उदयादित्यदेवस्य वर्णनागकृपाणिका कवीनाम् च नृपाणां च वेषवक्षसि रोपितः एकेयं उदयादित्यनरवर्ममहीभुजोः महेशस्वामिनोर् वर्णस्थित्यै सिद्धासिपुत्रिका (पत्रिका?)

Translation: This is the serpentine dagger of King Udayāditya and is a badge to be worn on the chest of poets and kings. This unique magical sword belonging to the worshippers of Śiva, the kings Udayāditya and Naravarman, for var*n*asthiti, the preservation of language sounds. Hence the inscription.

Langue and Parole: *bhāsā* and *vakka*

Early words used to signify langue and parole (categories of language identified later by Saussure) were: Prakrtam: *bhāsā* -- f. 'language ' and vakka 'speech'

bhāṣā f. ' speech ' Mn.Pa. Pk. *bhāsā* -- f. ' speech, language '; Wg. *bāṣ* ' word '; Dm. *bâṣa* ' language ', Sh. *baṣ* f. (→ Ḍ. *bāṣ* f.), Ku.gng. *bhāś*, N. B. Mth. *bhās*; OG. *bhāsa* f. ' song '; Ko. *bhās* ' language '; Si. *baha* ' word, saying ', Md. *bas*, *baha.* <-> Deriv.: H. *dubhāsiyā* m. ' interpreter '.*bhāṣpa -- ' vapour ' see bāṣpá -- .BHĀS ' shine ': bhāsá -- , bhā´sati, bhāsura -- , bhāsyatē, bhāsvará -- ; avabhāsa -- , udbhāsayati, prabhāsatē, prabhāsayati.Addenda: bhāṣā -- : WPah.poet. J. *bhāś* f. ' language, speech '.(CDIAL 9479)

[√vac] 'speech': uktá ' spoken ' RV. [√vac]Pa. *utta* -- , *vutta* -- ' spoken ', °*aka* -- n. ' a saying ' (*v* -- from *vattuṁ*, *vakkhati*, &c. and *vadati*); Pk. *utta* -- , *vutta* -- , Aś. gir. *vutaṁ*, dh. *vute*, KharI. *uta* ' was said '; S.*utaṇu* ' to say, tell ' prob. < *vutta* -- ; OSi. pp. *vataka* (*utu* ' spoken, described ' prob. ← Pa.); -- M. *utāṇṇẽ* ' to describe, declare ' X *ukhāṇā* m. ' saying, riddle ' (CDIAL 1626) vākya n. ' speech, words ' MBh. [√vac]Pa. *vākya* -- n. ' speech ', Pk. *vakka* -- n.; K. *wākh*, dat. °*kas* m. ' speech, voice ', adj. at end of cmpds. -- *wôku*; S. *vāko* m. ' outcry '; P. *vāk*, *bāk* m. ' word, speech '; Ku.*bākā*, *ākā* -- *bākā* ' abusive language '; Or. OAw. *bāka* ' word, speech '; H. *bāk* m. ' word, proverb '.kuvākya -- , suvākya -- .Addenda: vākya -- : †nirvākya -- .†vā´c -- f. ' speech ' RV. [√vac](CDIAL 11468) vāc

वाच् *f.* [वच्-क्विप् दीर्घोऽसंप्रसारणं च Uṇ.2.67] 1 A word, sound, an expression (opp. अर्थ); वागर्थाविव संपृक्तौ वागर्थप्रतिपत्तये R.1.1. -2 Words, talk, language, speech; वाचि पुण्यापुण्यहेतवः Māl.4; लौकिकानां हि साधूनामर्थं वागनुवर्तते । ऋषीणां पुनराद्यानां वाचमर्थोऽनुधावति U.1.1; विनिश्चितार्थामिति वाचमाददे Ki.1.3 'spoke these words', 'spoke as fol- lows'; R.1.49; Śi.2.13,23; Ku.2.3. -3 A voice, sound; अशरीरिणी वागुदचरत् U.2; मनुष्यवाचा R.2.33. -देवता, -देवी (वाग्देवता, वाग्देवी) Sarasvatī, the goddess of speech; वाग्देवतायाः सांमुख्यमाधत्ते S. D.1.

Bharata's *Nāṭya Śāstra* (c. 200 BCE), a treatise on performing arts, theatre, dance and music provides a documentation of provincial or des'I or vernacular forms of speech which may be variant pronunciation of sememes (root words of dhātupātha). This work in 6000 karikas or verse stanzas incorporates 36 chapters three of which relate to messaging systems: Rules of Prosody and Rules on the use of languages, Modes of address and intonation. This work had united Bharatam Janam, the way Prakrtam (spoken version of Samskrta Bharati) had united Bharatam Janam in a Bharatiya *sprachbund* (language union).

Dhātupātha was the earliest attempt to clearly identify sememes (root morphemes, the smallest linguistic units of meaning) from among multifarious forms of pronounced words in speech forms of Prakrtam.

Similarly, Indus Script was the earliest attempt to signify sememes through orthographic signifiers as hieroglyph components in a writing system for parole, speech form of language.

Thus, for example, a sememe, kuTi is signified by a water-carrier hieroglyph; a sememe baTa is signified by a rimless pot hieroglyph.

वाक्य--पदीय is the title of a celebrated work on the science of grammar by भर्तृहरि (divided into ब्रह्म-काण्ड or आगम-समुच्चय ,वाक्य-काण्ड , पद-काण्ड or प्रकीर्णक). Bhartṛhari (c. 5th century CE) *Vākyapadīya in Bharatiya grammatical tradition explains the theories on the word and on the sentence and elaborates on* sphoṭa, 'spurt, bursting, opening' as a framework to explain how the mind orders linguistic units into meaningful utterances.

वाक्य, in grammar, signifies speech, saying, assertion, statement, command, words (मम वाक्यात्, in my words, in my name). According to Panini, it is a sentence, a period. It also signifies a declaration in law.

पदम् padam means 'a foot-step, foot- print, foot-mark'. The adverbial form is पद्य padya which means 'consisting of padas or lines'. Thus padya is part of a word, it belongs to a word. Padam also signifies in grammar of language 'a complete or inflected word'. In the context of semantics of Vedic texts, it is a process of 'detachment of the Vedic words from one another, separation of a Vedic text into its several constituent words; वेदैः साङ्गपदक्रमोपनिषदैर्गायन्ति यं सामगाः Bhāg.12.13.1'.

Vākyapadīya of Bhartṛhari thus means a mode of expression to create the mental construct of meaning. The title of the work by Bhartrhari signifies the explanation of methods by which meaning is recognized in human speech when uttered and heard, so that such spoken forms get identified as 'meaningful' parts of a language. One such method is explained by Ferdinand de Saussure whose ideas have contributed to the development of linguistics and semiotics, 'the study of meaning-making'.

Just as Bhartṛhari's *Vākyapadīya is an ordering of utterances into linguistic units to yield meaning, t*he method of decipherment of Indus Script as a writing system is a method in semiotics, a study of meaning-making together with a study of orthography deployed to signify linguistic units. Framed on the hypothesis that Indus Script is a linguistic sign system, the decipherment is a process of identifying fine distinctions between langue (French, meaning language) and parole (meaning speaking). In Indian tradition, the expression mlecchita vikalpa is an expression which signifies a linguistic sign system, as an alternative method of representation of speech (spoken form of language). "Langue involves the principles of language, without which no meaningful utterance, 'parole' would be possible. Parole refers to the concrete instances of the use of langue. This is the individual, personal phenomenon of language as a series of speech acts made by a linguistic subject." (de Saussure, F., 1972, *Course in general linguistics*, (R. Harris, Trans.), Chicago, Open Court Publishing Company, pp. 9-10, 15.)

Prakrtam lexicons provide concrete instances of the use of langue and thus constitute a lexis (vocabulary) for parole. Study of this parole yields the structure of Prakrtam langue. Since many variants in pronunciations of words (speech expressions) were noted by early grammarians, attempts were made to evaluate the structure of a lingua franca (trade language or vehicular language) by reconstructing the common features of native languages or dialects in grammatical terms of morphology, phonetics, syntax and semantics.

A monumental evidence of such efforts is the work documented by Pāṇini in अष्टाध्यायी Ashtadhyayi, a work par excellence in grammatical studies of all times. Pāṇini (ca. 4th century BCE, 'descendant of Pāṇi'; Pāṇi, 'a place of sale, shop, market') was a grammarian of Samskrtam from the early mahajanapada era of ancient Bharatam. Pāṇini is also the author of several other works such as धातु-पाठ, गण-पाथ, लिङ्गानुशासन and शिक्षा. Thus, a substantial documentation is available to unravel, with evidence, the nature of Prakrtam (parole) and Samskrtam (langue) of the linguistic area of Bharatam during periods Before Common Era.

Orthographic methods of Indus Script to signify linguistic units

Orthographic forms of natural objects are mirrored to create a writing system. This mirroring is comparable to the *cire perdue* or lost-wax method of metal casting. An image is first made in bees-wax and a mirror image is attained by a coating of fine clay from a river-bed which imprints the iconographic units to create a metal casting as a mirror image of the wax sculptural casting.

Examples of orthographic forms used in Indus Script are presented to demonstrate how encryption of Indus Script is organized.

Sign 12 of Indus Script. In Prakrtam kuTi is a word which signifies a water-carrier. This word is evidenced in a Telugu lexicon. A mirror- or inflected-pronunciation of this word is kuThi which signifies a smelter. This word is evidenced in a Santali lexicon. The evidences provided from languages of Bharatam is premised on the fact that Bharatam was a linguistic area (*sprachbund*) with demonstrated patterns of mutual acquisitions of language features from among the dialects or speech forms in the lingua franca which included earlier forms of Telugu or Santali which are derived from Prakrtam. Comparative language lexicons and linguistic studies have demonstrated the existence of Bharatiya *sprachbund* traceable to Prakrtam.

The pictorial of a kneeling 'worshipper' is echoed in the script signs, ligatured with the 'pot' sign:

The orthographic form 46 has a head-gear (like a scarf). dhaṭa2, *dhaṭī* -- f. ' old cloth, loincloth ' [Drav., Kan. *daṭṭi* ' waistband ' etc., DED 2465]Ku. *dhaṛo* ' piece of cloth ', N. *dharo*, B. *dhaṛā*; Or. *dhaṛā* ' rag, loincloth ', *dhaṛi* ' rag '; Mth. *dhariā* ' child's narrow loincloth '.*dhaṭavastra -- .Addenda: *dhaṭa -- 2. 2. †*dhaṭṭa -- : WPah.ktg. *dhàṭṭu* m. ' woman's headgear, kerchief ', kc. *dhaṭu* m. (also *dhaṭhu* m. ' scarf ', J. *dhāṭ(h)u* m. Him.I 105). (CDIAL 6707) Rebus: dhatu 'element, mineral (ore)'.

The homonymous word denoting element, ore: dhā´tu n. ' substance ' RV., m. ' element ' MBh., ' metal, mineral, ore (esp. of a red colour) ' Mn., ' ashes of the dead ', ' *strand of rope ' (cf.*tridhā´tu* -- ' threefold ' RV., *ayugdhātu* -- ' having an uneven number of strands ' KātyŚr.). [√dhā]Pa. *dhātu* -- m. ' element, ashes of the dead, relic '; KharI. *dhatu* ' relic '; Pk. *dhāu* -- m. ' metal, red chalk '; N. *dhāu* ' ore (esp. of copper) '; Or. *ḍhāu* ' red chalk, red ochre ' (whence *ḍhāuā* ' reddish '; M. *dhāū, dhāv* m.f. ' a partic. soft red stone ' (whence *dhā̆vaḍ* m. ' a caste of iron -- smelters ', *dhāvḍī* ' composed of or relating to iron '); -- Si. *dā* ' relic '; -- S. *dhāī* f. ' wisp of fibres added from time to time to a rope that is being twisted ', L. *dhāī˜* f. (CDIAL 6773)

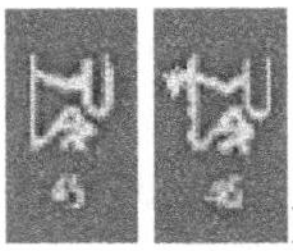I suggest that these orthographic forms signify: బత్తుడు*battuḍu*. n. A worshipper. భక్తుడు. The caste title of all the five castes of artificers as వడ్లబత్తుడు a carpenter. కడుపుబత్తుడు one who makes a god of his belly. L. xvi. 230. వడ్లత or వడ్లది *vaḍlata*. n. A woman of the carpenter caste. వడ్లబత్తుడు *vaḍrangi*. [Tel.] n. A carpenter. వడ్రంగము, వడ్లపని, వడ్రము orవడ్లంగితనము *vaḍrangamu*. n. The trade of a carpenter. పాంచాలుడు *pānchāluḍu*. n. A member of any one of the five castes of artificers, viz., the carpenters, weavers, barbers, washermen, painters. వడ్లవాడు, సాలెవాడు, మంగలవాడు, చాకలవాడు, ముచ్చివాడు, ఈ అయిదు జాతులందు దేనిలోనైనను చేరినవాడు.

A worshipper is signified by cognates in Bharatiya *sprachbund*: 9366 bhaṭṭa2 m. ' mixed caste of bards ' lex. [Cf. *bhaṭa* -- m. ' mixed caste ' lex., *bhaḍa* -- m. Cat., *bhaṇḍa* -- m. BrahmavP.Pk. *bhaṭṭa* -- m. ' bard '; K. *bāṭh*, dat. °*ṭhas* m. ' bard, panegyrist ', S. *bhaṭu* m., P. *bhaṭṭ* m., Ku. N. A. B. *bhāṭ*, Or. *bhāṭa*, Bhoj. Aw.lakh. H. G. M. *bhāṭ* m., Si. *bäṭṭayā*; -- S. *bhaṭiṇī* f. ' woman of this caste ', P. *bhaṭṭaṇ*, °*ṇī* f., N. *bhaṭini*, H. *bhāṭan* f.; -- N. *bhaṭyāunu* ' to lead a chorus '.
bhaṭṭāra -- see bhártṛ -- . bhaṭṭa -- 2: WPah.kṭg. (kc.) *bhā`ṭ* m. ' poet and singer ', kṭg. *bhā`ṭṭəṇ*, kc. *bhāṭiṇ* f. ' his wife '; Garh. *bhāṭ* ' bard '.(CDIAL 9366).

To designate the specific work performed by this 'worshipper', a rimless pot is ligatured to the outstretched hand of the person seated in a worshipful posture.

This pot is signified by the word: baTa (cf. Prakrtam *vaṭṭa 'cup';* Oriya. *baṭā* ' metal pot for betel '.): *varta2 ' circular object ' or more prob. ' something made of metal ', cf. *vartaka* -- 2 n. ' bell -- metal, brass ' lex. and vartalōha -- . [√vṛt?]Pk. *vaṭṭa* -- m.n., °*aya* -- m. ' cup '; Ash. *waṭā´k* ' cup, plate '; K. *waṭukh*, dat. °*ṭakas* m. ' cup, bowl '; S. *vaṭo* m. ' metal drinking cup '; N. *bāṭā*, ' round copper or brass vessel '; A. *bāṭi* ' cup '; B. *bāṭā* ' box for betel '; Or. *baṭā* ' metal pot for betel ', *bāṭi* ' cup, saucer '; Mth. *baṭṭā* ' large metal cup ', *bāṭī* ' small do. ', H. *baṭrī* f.; G. M. *vāṭī*f. ' vessel '.(CDIAL 11347).

Thus, the word బత్తుడు*battuḍu* signified by the worshipper orthography is reinforced by a phonetic determinant baTa 'pot, cup'.

A homonymous word (with an inflected pronunciation) is bhaTa which signifies 'a furnace' (Prakrtam *bhaṭṭha* -- m.n. 'gridiron'; Punjabi. *bhaṭṭh* m., °*ṭhī* f. ' furnace ',*bhaṭṭhā* m. 'kiln' : bhrā́ṣṭra n. ' frying pan, gridiron ' MaitrS. [√bhrajj]Pk. *bhaṭṭha* -- m.n. ' gridiron '; K. *büṭhü* f. ' level surface by kitchen fireplace on which vessels are put when taken off fire '; S. *baṭhu* m. ' large pot in which grain is parched, large cooking fire ', *baṭhī* f. ' distilling furnace '; L. *bhaṭṭh* m. ' grain -- parcher's oven ', *bhaṭṭhī* f. ' kiln, distillery ', awāṇ. *bhaṭh*; P. *bhaṭṭh* m., °*ṭhī* f. ' furnace ',*bhaṭṭhā* m. ' kiln '; N. *bhāṭi* ' oven or vessel in which clothes are steamed for washing '; A. *bhaṭā* ' brick -- or lime -- kiln '; B. *bhāṭi* ' kiln '; Or. *bhāṭi* ' brick -- kiln, distilling pot '; Mth. *bhaṭhī*, *bhaṭṭī* ' brick -- kiln, furnace, still '; Aw.lakh. *bhāṭhā* ' kiln '; H. *bhaṭṭhā* m. ' kiln ', *bhaṭ* f. ' kiln, oven, fireplace '; M. *bhaṭṭā* m. ' pot of fire ',*bhaṭṭī* f. ' forge '. -- X bhástrā -- q.v.bhrāṣṭra -- ; *bhraṣṭrapūra -- , *bhraṣṭrāgāra -- .bhrā́ṣṭra -- : S.kcch. *bhaṭṭhī keṇī* ' distil (spirits) '.(CDIAL 9656)

धातु element , primitive matter (= महा-भूत L.) MBh. Hariv. &c (usually reckoned as 5 , viz. ख or आकाश , अनिल , तेजस् , जल , भू ; to which is added ब्रह्म Ya1jn5. iii , 145 ; or विज्ञान Buddh.) primary element of the earth i.e. metal , mineral , are (esp. a mineral of a red colour) Mn. MBh. &c element of words i.e.grammatical or verbal root or stem Nir. Pra1t. MBh. &c (with the southern

Buddhists धातु means either the 6 elements [see above] Dharmas. xxv ; or the 18 elementary spheres [धातु-लोक] ib. lviii ; or the ashes of the body , relics L. [cf. -गर्भ]).

The search for the primary elements धातु leads to the formation and evolution of two strands of knowledge systems: 1. Metallurgy; 2. Grammar of language. This two-stranded enquiry (veda) leads to the expressions in early Bharatiya thought of धातु--गर्भ and धातु--पाठ , respectively. धातु -कुशल *a.* skilful in working in metals, metallurgist. -क्रिया metallurgy, mineralogy; - प्रसक्त *a.* devoted to alchemy; -माक्षिकम् 1 sulphuret of iron. -2 a mineral substance.

cīmara 'black**ant**' Rebus: cīmara '**copper**'. cīmara kāra -- ' **coppersmith** ' See: Indus Script signs 54 to 57 which signify ants and flies (bees).

माक्षिक [p= 805,2] *mfn.* (fr. मक्षिका) coming from or belonging to a bee Ma1rkP. Rebus: *n.* a kind of honey-like mineral substance or pyrites MBh. This signifier is found in Indus Script signs 54 to 57.

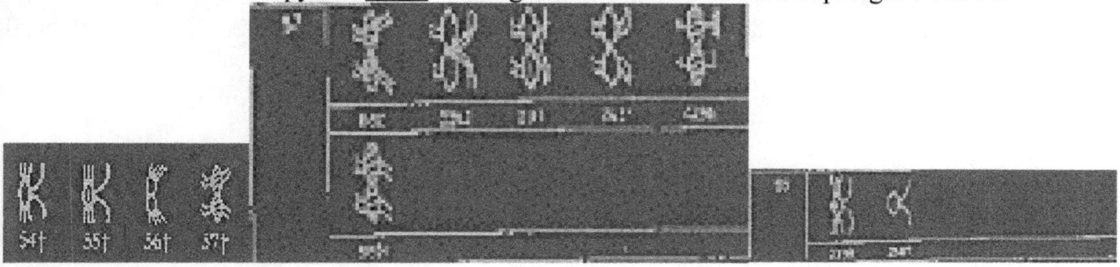

mákṣā f., *mákṣ* -- m. f. ' fly ' RV., *mákṣikā* -- f. ' fly, bee ' RV., *makṣika* -- m. Mn.Pa. *makkhikā* -- f. ' fly ', Pk. *makkhiā* -- f., *macchī* -- , °*chiā* -- f.; Gy. hung. *makh* ' fly ', wel. *makhī* f., gr. *makí* f., pol. *mačin*, germ. *mačlin*, pal. *mắki* ' mosquito ',*mắkī´la* ' sandfly ', *mắkī´li* ' house -- fly '; Ash. *mačī˜´* ' bee '; Paš.dar. *mēček* ' bee ', weg. *mečī´k* ' mosquito ', ar. *mučək, mučag* ' fly '; Mai. *mā̆çhī* ' fly '; Sh.gil. *mă̄ṣī´* f., (Lor.) *m**l*çī* ' fly ' (→ Ḍ. *m**l*çhi* f.), gur. *mă̄çhī´* ' fly ' (' bee ' in gur. *mă̄çhi̯kraṇ*, koh. *mă̄çhi -- gŭn* ' beehive '); K. *màchi* f. ' fly, bee, dark spot '; S. *makha, makhi* f. ' fly, bee, swarm of bees, sight of gun ', *makho* m. ' a kind of large fly '; L. (Ju.) *makhī* f. ' fly ', khet. *makkī´*; P. *makkh* f. ' horsefly, gnat, any stinging fly ', m. ' flies ', *makkhī*f. ' fly '; WPah.rudh. *makkhī* ' bee ', jaun. *mākwā* ' fly '; Ku. *mākho* ' fly ', gng. *mā̃kh*, N. *mākho*, A. *mākhi*, B. Or. *māchi*, Bi. *māchī*, Mth. *māchī, mā̃chī, makhī* (← H.?), Bhoj. *māchī*; OAw. *mākhī*, lakh. *māchī* ' fly ', *ma -- mākhī* ' bee ' (mádhu --); H. *māchī, mākhī, makkhī* f. ' fly ', *makkhā* m. ' large fly, gadfly '; G. *mākh, mākhī* f. ' fly ',*mākhɔ* m. ' large fly '; M. *mās* f. ' swarm of flies ', n. ' flies in general ', *māśī* f. ' fly ', Ko. *māsu, māśi*; Si. *balu -- mäkka*, st. -- *mäki* -- ' flea ', *mässa*, st. *mäsi* -- ' fly '; Md. *mehi* ' fly '. *makṣātara -- , *mākṣa -- , mākṣiká -- ; *makṣākiraṇa -- , *makṣācamara -- , *makṣācālana -- , *makṣikākula -- ; *madhumakṣikā -- .Addenda: mákṣā -- : S.kcch. *makh* f. ' fly '; WPah.kṭg. *mákkhɔ, máṅkhɔ* m. ' fly, large fly ', *mákkhi* (kc. *makhe*) f. ' fly, bee ', *máṅkhi* f., J. *mākhī* f.pl., Garh. *mākhi.*(CDIAL 9696)

*vartakara ' making turns (of the quail) '. [Pop. etym. for vártikā -- (*vartīra* -- m. Suśr., °*tira* -- m. lex.)? -- varta -- 1, kará -- 1]Ku. B. *baṭer* ' quail '; Or. *baṭara, batara* ' the grey **quail** '; Mth. H. *baṭer* f. ' quail '; -- → P. *baṭer*, °*rā* m., °*rī* f., L. *baṭērā* m., S. *baṭero* m.; K. *bāṭuru* m. ' a kind of quail ', *baṭēra* m. ' quail '.(CDIAL 11350) Rebus: vartalōha n. ' a kind of brass (i.e. *cup metal?) ' lex. [*varta -- 2 associated with lōhá -- by pop. etym.?]Pa. *vaṭṭalōha* -- n. ' a partic. kind of metal '; L.awāṇ. *valṭōā* ' metal pitcher ', P. *valṭoh, ba*° f., *vaṭlohā, ba*° m.; N. *baṭlohi* ' round metal vessel '; A. *baṭlahi* ' water vessel '; B. *bāṭlahi, bāṭulāi* ' round brass cooking vessel '; Bi. *baṭlohī* ' small metal vessel '; H. *baṭlohī*, °*loī* f. '

brass drinking and cooking vessel ', G. *vaṭloi* f.Addenda: vartalōha -- : WPah.kṭg. *bəlṭóɔ* m. ' large brass vessel '. (CDIAL 11357)

Mohenjodaro MIC, Pl. CVI,93

Alternative rebus readings: **baṭṭai[i]** quail (N.) vartaka = a duck (Skt.) batak = a duck (G.) vartikā = quail (RV.); wuwrc partridge (Ash.); barti = quail, partridge (Kho.); vaṭṭaka_ quail (Pali); vaṭṭaya (Pkt.) (CDIAL 11361). Rebus: vartaka 'merchant' (Skt.)

varta = *circular object; *turning round (Skt.); vaṭu = twist (S.)(CDIAL 11346)

baṭa = a quail, or snipe (Santali) baṭa = a quail, or snipe, coturuix coturnix cot; boṇḍe baṭa = a large quail; dak baṭa = the painted stripe, rostraluta benghalensis bengh; guṇḍri baṭa = a small type, coloured like a guṇḍri (quail); kũk baṭa = a medium-sized type; kheḍra baṭa = the smallest of all; laṇḍha baṭa = a small type (Santali.lex.) baṭai (Nag.); baṭer (Has.); [H. baṭai or bat.er perdix olivacea; Sad. baṭai] coturnix coromandelica, the blackbreasted or rain-quail; two other kinds of quail are called respectigely: hur.in bat.ai and gerea baṭai (Mundari.lex.) baṭer = quail (Ku.B.); baṭara, batara = the grey quail (Or.)(CDIAL 11350).Rebus: bhaṭa 'kiln, furnace' (H.)

This work is volume 5 of a quintet of studies of Bharatiya civilization. The quintet narrates the form and function of Indus Script and provides profiles of Samskrta Bharati, language of the civilization:

1. I*ndus Script Cipher -- Hieroglyhphs of Indian Linguistic Area* (2010)
2. *Indus Script: Meluhha metalwork hieroglyphs* (2014)
3. *Philosophy of Symbolic forms in Meluhha cipher* (2014)
4. *Cultural History of Bharatam Janam – Indus Script metalwork catalogs* (2016)
5. *Samskrta Bharati – Indus Script Dictionary, Epigraphia Mlecchita Vikalpa, 'Meluhha* cipher' (2016)

[Author: S. Kalyanaraman, Herndon, Sarasvai Research Center.]

Indus Script hieroglyphs are orthographic signifiers rendered as epigraphs and on iconographs to catalogue metalwork, lapidary work.

This fifth volume in the quintet presents a dictionary for Indus Script hieroglyphs -- both 'signs' and 'pictorial motifs' -- together with Prakrtam(Meluhha/Mleccha) lexis to signify lapidary crafts and metalwork of the Bronze Age.

Prakrtam provides the semantic foundation for metalwork lexis of Samskrta Bharati of Bhartiya civilization. The metalwork lexis evidenced by Indus Script decipherment is complimented by an *Indian lexicon* which records over 8000 semantic clusters of the Indian *sprachbund.* In most of these 8000 semantic clusters, the presence of Samskrtam glosses demonstrates the extraordinary efforts made to identify and document sememes in Samskrtam lexis which are defined as: dhātuḥ धातुः A verbal root; भूवादयो धातवः P.I.3.1; पश्चादध्ययनार्थस्य धातोरधिरिवाभवत् R.15.9. (Apte. Samskrtam). This linguistic revolution is unparalleled in the annals of civilization studies, matched only by the extraordinary documentation by Panini in Ashtadhyayi premised on the research methodologies of tantra-yukti. This dhātupātha was prefaced by the earliest etymological of Yaska's Nirukta which is "explanation or etymological interpretation of a word ChUp. viii , 3 , 3 MBh. i , 266 &c." With such a profound grammatical tradition which dates back to a period of ca. 6th century BCE the central role of Samskrta Bharati in is ubiquitous, in the formation and evolution of all languages and dialects of Indian *sprachbund.* An excellent documentation of the formation and evolution of Marathi language by Jules Bloch (1920) should provide the role model for similar studies of all languages which form part of Indian *sprachbund* (language union).

DhAtu, roots are grouped by the form of their stem in ten present tense classes:

1. *bhū-ādayaḥ* (root-full grade thematic presents)
2. *ad-ādayaḥ* (root presents)
3. *ju-ho-ti-ādayaḥ* (reduplicated presents)
4. *div-ādayaḥ* (*ya* thematic presents)
5. *su-ādayaḥ* (*nu* presents)
6. *tud-ādayaḥ* (root-zero grade thematic presents)
7. *rudh-ādayaḥ* (*n*-infix presents)
8. *tan-ādayaḥ* (*no* presents)
9. *krī-ādayaḥ* (*ni* presents)
10. *cur-ādayaḥ* (*aya* presents, causatives)

The concept of *sphoṭa* is central to the identification and documentation of dhAtu, roots because, *sphoṭa* remains unaffected by individual speaker differences (mlecchita vikalpa or phonetic variations). Bhartrhari extends the *sphoṭa in categories of*

1. *varṇa-sphoṭa*, at the syllable level,
2. *pada-sphoṭa*, at the word level, and
3. *vakya-sphoṭa*, at the sentence level.

sphoṭa, or *Śábda* at all these levels is indivisible (permanent), because it is the intention (cognition) behind the utterance, while 'sounds' or *dhvani* can be sequenced and hence divisible (ephemeral). *vācaka* as the signifier, and 'vācya' as the signified provide a sound basis for decipherment of meaning conveyed by mlecchita vikalpa (Meluhha cipher of Indus Script). Thus, elephant hieroglyph is the signifier while the signified is karba 'iron' and ib 'iron, because the sound variant of the signifiers denote Kariba 'elephant trunk' and ibha 'elephant'. The meaning is thus rendered unambiguously by the mlecchita vikalpa, Meluhha cipher.

George Coedes, the French epigraphist's *magnum opus* was titled: *Histoire ancienne des États hindouisés d'Extrême-Orient*, 1944? (Translation: Ancient History of Hinduised States of the Far East). Published by Imprimere d'extreme-orient, Hanoi (1944).

Professor George Coedes, 1866-1969, was the undisputed doyen of early Southeast Asian scholarship. His studies of the early history of the region embrace his rediscovery of the maritime empire of Srivijaya and numerous studies of the history of Cambodia, and in particular, the life of the great ruler Jayavarman VII.

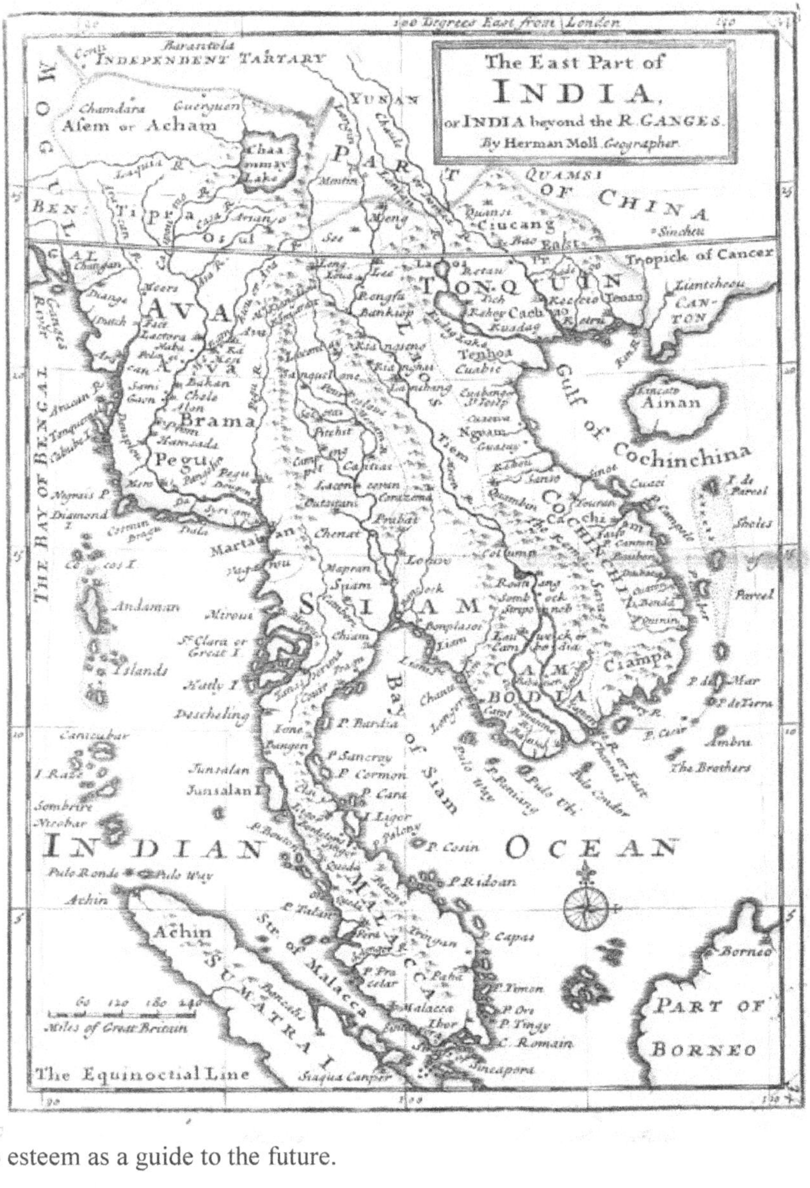

Coedes' major work of synthesis is his study *Les etats hindouises d'indochine et d'indonesie* that covers the period from approximately A. D. 1 to A. D. 1500. This work has been universally acclaimed and--the surest proof of its impact--heavily relied on by all later scholars. It is the basic text for all those who seek to understand Southeast Asia--not only its ancient past but also its immediate present--for the Southeast Asia of today cannotbe understood without a knowledge of the traditional values and institutions, which remain vital and which present leaders seem increasingly to esteem as a guide to the future.

Such a scientific and historical basis for linguistic performance finds its cultural presence in Greater Bharatam, in Indian Ocean Region, as exemplified by the history of Pulo Condor, an island in the Far East. This is also acknowledged by George Coedes.

Pulo Condor (Malay name) is an island off the coast of Vietnam. Vietnamese called it Con Son. Chinese Bauddham monk I-tsing refers to it as Pulo Condore. "Even in the island of Pulo Condore (in the south) and in the country of Suli (in the north), people praise the Sanskrit Sutras (of Panii). How much more then should people of the Divine Land (China) and the Celestial Store House (India), teach the real rules of the language." (I-tsing, A record of the Buddhist religion as practiced in India and the Malay Arhipelao, Tr. By J. Takakasu, Oxford, 1896, p. 169.) Just as I-tsing referred to China as Divine Land, a contemporary Dandin, the Samsktam poet said: Samskrtam nAma daivIvAk anvAkhyAtA maharshibhih 'Samskrtam is the divine language as expounded by the ancient sages). The region referred to as Suli by I-tsing connotes Sogdiana (which surrounds Samarkand of Uzbekistan in central Asia.) I-tsing reportedly stayed in Palembang (capital of Sri Vijaya in Sumatra) in 671 CE learning Samskrtam grammar. He then moved to Bharat where he lived for 14 years before returning to Palembang to translate the ancient texts collected from Bharatam. I-tsing also reports the presence of over 1000 monks in Sri Vijaya who 'lived by the same rules as those prevailing in India'. This is corroborated by the fact that most of the inscriptions of Greter India in the Indian Ocean Region (referred to by Geoerge Coedes, the French Epigraphist, as the Hinduised States of the Far East) including the Yupa insriptions of Mulavarman of East Borneo are in samskrtam. All 19 Yupa inscriptions including those of East Borneo are signifiers of Soma yaga. The practice of Yupa inscriptions dates back to the Sarasvati-Sindhu civilization days (ca. 2500 BCE) as evidenced by the octagonal yupa found in a yajnakunda of Binjor on the banks of Vedic River Sarasvati attesting to the performance of a Soma Yaga (perhaps Vajapeya) at that sacred place. An octagonal yupa signifies Vajapeya yajna according to the Taittiriya Samhita and Satapatha Brahmana texts which explain the significance of cashAla (signified by boar's snout, as also go-dhuma wheat chaff) as a process to carburize soft metal to produce alloys of metals to manufacture tools, implements and weapons. Samskrtam was the language of discourse pan-bharatam as evidenced by the presence of over 90% of words of Tamil language cognate with Samskrtam as noted in Madras University Tamil lexicon. The relationship between Samskrtam and vernaculars (spoken forms of Prakrtam) is best illustrated by the intensity of Vedic culture in Tamil-speaking regions as evidencedby ancient Tamil and Tamil Sangam literary texts.

பாரதம்[1] pāratam, n. < Bhārata. 1. India; இந்தியா தேசம். இமயகிரிக்குந் தென்கடற்கு மிடைப் பாகம் பாரதமே (சிவதரு. கோபுர. 51). 2. The great war of Kurukṣētra; பாரதப்போர். நீயன்றி மாபாரதமகற்ற மற்றார்கொல் வல்லாரே (பாரத. கிருட் டிணை. 34). 3. The Mahābhārata; மகாபாரதம். 4. A very long account; மிகவிரிவான செய்தி. பன்னி யுரைக்குங்காற் பாரதமாம் (திவ். இயற். பெரிய. ம. 72).

[quote]Among the interesting facts that emerge from a study of the progressive spread of vedic culture from the North-West to the other parts of India, is its infusion, with noticeable intensity, in the extreme south of India where, unlike in other parts, a well-developed Dravidian culture was already in vogue… Tolka_ppiyam which is the earliest available work of the sangam classics, is a technical text in 1610 aphorisms, divided into three sections, dealing respectively, with phonetics, grammar and poetics… The other available sangam works are three sets of collected poems, being, pattu-ppAṭṭu (Ten idylls), eṭṭu-ttokai (Eight collections) and patineki_ṟkaṇakku (eighteen secondary texts), which last appears to pertain to the late period of the saµgam age.

The ten poems are:

Tirumurukāṟṟuppaṭai,
Poruṇarāṟṟuppaṭai,
Ciṟupāṇāṟṟuppaṭai,
Perumpāṇāṟṟuppa,
Mullaippāṭṭu,

Maturaikkāñci,
Neṭunalvāṭai,
Kuṟiñcippāṭṭu,
Paṭṭiṉappālai and
Malaipaṭukaṭām.

All the above idylls are compositions of individual poets, and, except for the first, which is devotional and possibly, pertains to late sangam age, are centred round the royal courts of the Cera, Cola and Pāṇḍya kings, depicting the contemporary elite scholarly society and youthful life.

The second category consists of Eight collections:

Naṟṟiṇai, Kuṟuntokai, Aiṅkurunūṟu,
Patiṟṟuppattu, Paripāṭal, Kalittokai,
Akanaṉūṟu, Puṟanāṉūṟu

All these collections are highly poetic and self-contained stray verses of different poets put together in consideration of their contents. The third category consists of eighteen miscellaneous texts, some of them being collections of stray verses of different poets and some composed by individual authors.

ASCII Indic diacritics:
ñḍḷṇṭśṣṛ ṉ ṟ ṟ̤ ĩ ũã ũẽã āēīōū ṣṇ āṇḍ ṟṟ ṇṇ ēḷ

They are: tirukkuṟaḷ, nālaṭiyār, paṟamoṟi, tirikaṭukam, nāṉmaṇikkaṭṭikai, ciṟṟupañcamūlam, elāti, ācārakōvai, mutumoṟ̤ikkāñci, kalavaṟ̤i-nāṟpatu, initu-nāṟpatu, tiṇaimālainūṟṟaimpatu, aintiṇai-y-eṟ̤upatu, kainnilai, aintiṇai-yanpatu, tiṇaimoṟ̤i-y-aimpatu and kāṟnāṟpatu.
The verses in these works also refer to social customs and local sovereigns. The above works picture a well-knit and well-developed society having a distinct identity of its own. The frequent mention, in sangam poems, of the Cera, Cola and Pāṇḍya kings as the munificent patrons of the poets… and the archaeological evidence provided by 76 rock inscriptions in Tamil-Brāhmi script which corrobate the contents of the sangam works, in 26 sites in Tamilnadu (Mahadevan, I., Tamil Brāhmi inscriptions of the Sangam age, Proc. Second International Conference Seminar of Tamil Studies, I, Madras, 1971, pp. 73-106) help to fix the date of the classical sangam classics in their present form to between 100 B.C. and 250 CE… reference to the Pāṇḍyan kingdom by Megasthenes, Greek ambassador to the court of Candragupta Maurya (c. 324-

300 B.C.?) are also in point. On these and allied grounds, the sangam period of Tamil literature might be taken to have extended from about the 5th century B.C. to the 3rd century CE… It is highly interesting that sangam literature is replete with references to the vedas and different facets of vedic literature and culture, pointing to considerable appreciation, and literary, linguistic and cultural fusion of vedic-sanskrit culture of the north with the social and religious pattern of life in south India when the sangam classics were in the making… The vedas and their preservers, the brāhmans, are frequently referred to with reverence (Puṟanān u_ṟu 6, 15 and 166; Maturaikkāñci 468; tirukaṭukam 70, nāṉmaṇikkaṭikai 89, initu-nāṟpatu 8). The vedic mantra is stated as the exalted expressions of great sages (Tolka_ppiyam, Porul. 166, 176). While the great God śiva is referred as the source of the four vedas (Puṟa. 166), it is added that the twice-born (brāhman) learnt the four vedas and the six vedāngas in the course of 48 years (Tiru-murukāṟṟuppaṭai, 179-82). The vedas were not written down but were handed down by word of mouth from teacher to pupil (Kuṟuntokai 156), and so was called kel.vi (lit. what is heard, šruti)(Patiṟṟuppattu 64.4-5; 70.18-19; 74, 1-2; Puṟa. 361. 3-4). The brāhmans realized God through the Vedas (Paripāṭal 9. 12-13) and recited loftily in vedic schools (Maturaikkāñci 468- 76; 656)… the danger to the world if the brāhman discontinued the study of the veda is stressed in tirukkuṟal. 560. If the sangam classics are any criteria, the knowledge and practice of vedic sacrifices were very much in vogue in early south India. The sacrifices were performed by brāhmans strictly according to the injunctions of the vedic mantras (tirumurukāṟṟuppaṭai 94-96; kalittokai 36). The three sacred fires (gārhapatya, a_havani_ya and daks.ināgni) were fed at dawn and dusk by bràhmans in order to propitiate the gods (Kalittokai 1191 Puṟa. 2; 99; 122; Kuṟiñcippāṭṭu 225). Paripāṭal 2. 60-70 stipulates, in line with vedic sacrificial texts, that each sacrifice had a specific presiding deity, that paśus (sacrificial animals) were required for the sacrifice and that the sacrificial fire rose to a great height. The vedic practice of placing a tortoise at the bottom of the sacrificial pit is referred to in Akanāṉu_ṟu 361… Patiṟṟuppattu 64 and 70 glorify the Cera king Celvakkaṭunkovaṟiyātaṉ who propitiated the gods through a sacrifice performed by learned vedic scholars and distributed profuse wealth amongst them. Another Cera king, Perum-ceral Irumpoṟai is indicated in Patiṟṟuppattu 74 to have performed the Putrakāmes.ṭhi_ sacrifice for the birth of his son il.amceral irumpoṟai. The Cola ruler Peru-naṟkil.l.i was renowned as Rājasu_yam ve_ṭṭa co_ṟaṉ for his having performed the rājasu_ya sacrifice; another Cola ruler Naṟkil.l.i, too, was celebrated as a sacrificer (Puṟa. 363; 400). The Cola kings were also considered to have descended from the north Indian king śibi the munificent of Mahābhārata fame (Puṟa. 39; 43). The patronage accorded to vedic studies and sacrifices is illustrated also by the descriptive mention, in Puṟa. 166, of a great vedic scholar Viṇṇantāyaṉ of the Kauṇḍinya-gotra who lived at Pu_ñja_ṟṟu_r in the Co_ṟa realm under royal patronage. It is stated that Viṇṇantāyaṉ had mastered the four vedas and six vedāngas, denounced non-vedic schools, and performed the seven pākayajñas, seven Soma-yajñas and seven havir-yajñas as prescribed in vedic texts. The Pāṇḍyan kings equalled the Colas in the promotion of Vedic studies and rituals. One of the greatest of Pāṇḍya rulers, Mudukuṭumi Peruvaṟuti is described to have carefully collected the sacrificial materials prescribed in vedic and dharmašàstra texts and performed several sacrifices and also set up sacrificial posts where the sacrifices were performed (Puṟa. 2; 15). Maturaikkāñci (759- 63) mentions him with the appellation pal-śa_lai (pal-yāga-śālai of later Vēḷvikkuḍi and other inscriptions), 'one who set up several sacrificial halls'. The Pāṇḍya rulers prided themselves as to have descended from the Pāṇḍavas, the heroes of Mahābhārata (Puṟa. 3; 58; Akanān-u_ṟu 70; 342)… God

Brahmà is mentioned to have arisen, in the beginning of creation, with four faces, from the lotus navel of God Viṣṇu (Paripāṭal 8.3; Kalittokai 2; Perumpāṇāṟṟuppat.ai 402-04; Tirumurukāṟṟuppat.ai 164-65; Iniyavainārpatu 1). It is also stated that Brahma_ had the swan as vehicle (Innā-nārpatu 1). Viṣṇu is profusely referred to. He is the lord of the Mullai region (Tol. Akattiṇai 5) and encompasses all the Trinity (Paripāṭal 13.37). He is blue-eyed (Puṟa. 174), lotus-eyed (Paripāṭal 15.49), yellow-clothed (Paripāt.al 13.1-2), holds the conch and the discus in his two hands and bears goddess Laks.mì on his breast (Mullaippāṭṭu 1-3; Perumpāṇ 29-30; Kali. 104; 105; 145), was born under the asterism Tiru-o_ṇam (Maturai. 591), and Garuḍa-bannered (Puṟa. 56.6; Paripāṭal 13.4). Of Viṣṇuite episodes are mentioned his measuring the earth in three steps (Kali. 124.1), protecting his devotee Prahlāda by killing his father (Pari. 4. 12-21) and destroying the demon Keśin (Kali. 103.53-55). śiva has been one of the most popular vedic-purāṇic gods of the South. According to Akanāṉu_ṟu 360.6, śiva and Viṣṇu are the greatest gods. He is three-eyed (Puṟa. 6.18; Kali. 2.4), wears a crescent moon on his forehead (Puṟa. 91.5; Kali. 103.15), and holds the axe as weapon (Aka. 220.5; Puṟa. 56.2). He bears river Ganga_ in his locks (Kali. 38.1; 150.9) and is blue-necked (Puṟa. 91.6; Kali. 142). He is born under the asterism a_tirai (Skt. ārdra) (Kali. 150.20), has the bull for his vehicle (Paripāṭal 8.2) and is seated under the banyan tree (Aka. 181). Once, while sitting in Kaila_sa with Umā (Pārvati), his consort (Pari. 5.27-28; Paṟamoṟi 124), Rāvaṇa, the rāks.asa king shook the Kailāsa and śiva pressed the mountain down with his toe, crushing Ra_vaṇa and making him cry for mercy (Kali. 38). When the demon Tripura infested the gods, śiva shot through the enemy cities with a single arrow and saved the gods (Kali. 2; Puṟa. 55; Paripāṭal 5. 22-28). Puṟanān –u_ṟu (6. 16-17) refers also to śiva temples in the land and devotees walking round the temple in worship. God Skanda finds very prominent mention in saµgam classics, but as coalesced with the local deity Murukaṉ, with most of the purāṇic details of his birth and exploits against demons incorporated into the local tradition (Paripāṭal 5. 26-70; Tirumurukāṟṟuppaṭai, the whole work). Mention is also made of Indra. (Balarāma) is mentioned as the elder brother of Lord Kṛṣṇa, as fair in colour, wearing blue clothes, having the palmyra tree as his emblem and holding the ;lough as his weapon, all in line with the purāṇas (Paripāṭal 2. 20-23; Puṟa. 56. 3-4; 58.14; Kali. 104, 7-8). Tolkāppiyam (Akattiṇai iyal 5) divides the entire Tamil country into five, namely, Mullai (jungle) with Viṣṇu as its presiding deity, Kuṟiñji (hilly) with Murukaṉ as deity, Marutam (plains: cf. marusthali_ Skt.) with Indra as deity, Neytal (seashore) with Varuṇa as deity and Pālai (wasteland) with Koṟṟavai (Durgā) as deity… The sangam works are replete with references to the four castes into which the society was divided, namely, bra_hmanṇa, ks.atriya, vaiśya, and su_dra… brāhman antaṇa primarily concerned with books (Tol. Mara. 71), the ks.atriya (a-raśa, rāja) with the administration (Tol. Mara. 78) and śu_dra with cultivation (Tol. Mara. 81)… It is also stated that marriage before the sacred fire was prescribed only for the first three castes; but the author adds that the custom was adopted by the fourth caste also in due course (Tol. Kaṟpiyal 3)… one cannot fail to identify in sangam poetry the solid substratum of the distinct style, vocabulary and versification, on the one hand, and the equally distinct subject-matter, social setting and cultural traits, on the other, both of the Tamil genius and of vedic poetry. As far as the grammar of Dravidian is concerned, a detailed analytical study of Old Tamil as represented in Tolkāppiyam, with the vedic śiks.ās and prātiśākhyas, has shown that, 'Tolkāppiyaṉār clearly realized that Tamil was not related to Sanskrit either morphologically or genealogically… that he deftly exploited the ideas contained in the earlier grammatical literature, particularly in those works which dealt with vedic

etymology, without doing the least violence to the genius of the Tamil language'. (Sastri, P.S.S., *History of Grammatical Theories in Tamil and their relation to the Grammatical literature in Sanskrit*, Madras, 1934, p. 231)... It would be clear from the foregoing that during the sangam age there had already been intensive infusion of vedic culture in south India... Both the cultures coexisted, the additions often affecting only the upper layers of society... For novel names, concepts and ideas, the Sanskrit names were used as such, with minor changes to suit the Tamil alphabet (e.g. akiṉi for agni, vaicikaṉ for vaiśya, veta for veda, or translated (e.g. pāpāṉ for darśaka, kēḷvi for śruti). When, however, the concept already existed, in some form or other, the same word was used with extended sense (e.g. vēḷvi for yāga; māl or māyaṉ for Viṣṇu). Sometimes both the new vedic and extant Tamil words were used (e.g. ti_ for agni)... It is, however, important to note that the coming together of the two cultures, vedic and dravidian, was smooth, non-agressive and appreciative, as vouched for by the unobtrusive but pervasive presence of vedicism in the sangam works. The advent of vedic culture into South India was, thus, a case of supplementation and not supplantation... it is a moot question as to when vedic culture first began to have its impact on dravidian culture which already existed in south India... the age of this spread (of vedic culture) has to be much earlier than the times of the Rāmāyaṇa and Mahābhārata, both of which speak of vedic sages and vedic practices prevailing in the sub-continent. Literary and other traditions preserved both in north and south India attest to the part played by sage Agastya and Paraśurāma in carrying vedic culture to the south. On the basis of analytical studies of these traditions the identification of geographical situations and a survey of the large number of Agastya temples in the Tamil country, G.S. Ghurye points to the firm establishment of the Agastya cult in South India by the early centuries before the Christian era (Ghurye, G.S., *Indian acculturation: Agastya and Skanda*, Bombay, Popular Prakashan, 1977)... the considerable linguistic assimilation, in dravidian, of material of a pre-classical Sanskrit nature, it would be necessary to date the north-south acculturation in India to much earlier times.[unquote]
(Sharma, K.V. 1983, Spread of Vedic culture in ancient South India, *Adyar Library Bulletin* 47:1-1.)

Another node of the Vedic-Tamil network web is the Tamil-Munda network web which has yet to be unraveled. A beginning was made by the late Sudhibhushan Bhattacharjee (cf. Bibliography) with a number of works pointing to the possible etyma of Munda languages and some links with Dravidian glosses. This inquiry will certainly take us into the contacts along the Hindumahasagar rim (Indian Ocean Rim) regions explaining why as noted by George Coedes, there are many early Sanskrit Brahmi inscriptions in places such as Laos, Vietnam, Cambodia, Indonesia and Thailand, while the early epigraphs in Bharatam are in Prakrit Brahmi.

It will be apposite to recall the balanced views expressed by Maurice Winternitz in the context of Indian literary tradition in his work, A History of Indian Literature. "... The historical facts and hypotheses, such as mention of Vedic gods in the cuneiform inscriptions, and the relationship of Vedic antiquity to the A_ryan (Indo-Iranian) and Indo-European period, are so uncertain in themselves that the most divergent and contradictory conclusions have been drawn from them. Nevertheless, we have now such likely evidence of relations between ancient India and western Asia penetrating as far west as Asia Minor in the second
millennium B.C.E., that Vedic-culture can be traced back at least to the second millennium B.C... The linguistic facts, the near relationship between the language of the Veda and that of the Avesta on the one hand, and between the Vedic language and classical Sanskrit on the other, do not yield any positive results... As all the external evidence fails, we are compelled to rely on the evidence arising out of the history of Indian literature itself, for the age of the Veda. The surest evidence in this respect is still the fact

that Pa_rs'va, Maha_vi_ra and Buddha presuppose the entire Veda as a literature to all intents and purposes completed, and this is a limit which we must not exceed. We cannot, however, explain the development of the whole of this great literature, if we assume as late a date as round about 1200 BC or 1500 BC as its starting-point. We shall probably have to date the beginning of this development about 2000 or 2500 BC, and the end of it between 750 and 500 BC. The more prudent course, however, is to steer clear of any fixed dates, and to guard against the extremes of a stupendously ancient period or a ludicrously modern epoch." (Maurice Winternitz, 1907, Geschichte der Indischen Literatur, tr. A History of Indian Literature, 1981, Delhi, Motilal Banarsidass, pp. 287-288).

It is reasonable to hypothesise that Samskrtam in Prakrtam speech forms was the lingua franca of the civilization ca. 2500 BCE on the banks of Vedic River Sarasvati which is consistent with the assumption that Prkritam form of vAk evolved in the region from ca. 8th millennium BCE given the archaeological discoveries of cultural pointers. One pointer is the use of s'ankha turbinella pyrum bangles from ca. 6500 BCe. Another is the practice of sindhur on mang (parting of the hair) of married women as evidenced by the two terracotta toys found at Nausharo ca. 2500 BCE with sindhur painted red at hair partings, jewelry painted golden and hair painted black. A thir indicator is the practice of worship of S'ivalinga in Harappa with finds of six sivalingas at the site in addition to the stone bases with linga found in Mohenjodaro decorated with trefoil hieroglyphs on the bases and also on the uttariyam worn by the priest leaving the right shoulder bare. He was Potr Rigvedic purifier priest as was Potti the temple priest of later historical periods and Potedar, the Shroff or assessor of metal coins.

Three strands, *tri-dhātu* is an Indus Script hieroglyph on पोतृ *pōtṟ* 'purifier priest' to signify *dhăvaḍ, dhamaga* 'smelter, blacksmith' working in alloy of three mineral ores.

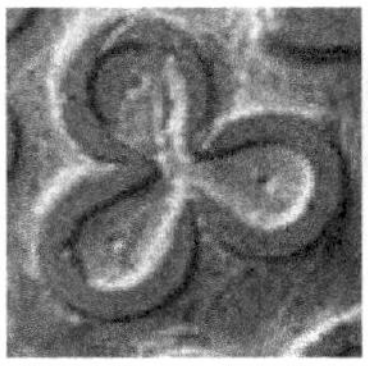

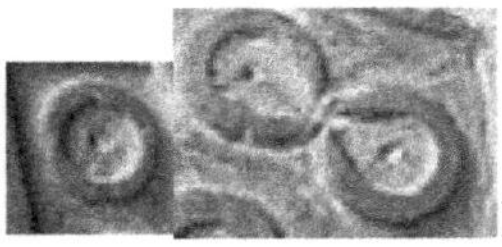

I suggest that a dotted circle is an orthographic signifier of one strand; two dotted circles joined together as orthographic signifiers of two strands; three dotted circles joined together as orthographic signifiers of three strands.

The cultural continuum of pōtṟ पोतृ as a priest of Vedic tradition is evidenced in the veneration of ancestors: போத்தி pōtti 'grandfather, Malabar priest'. In ancient times of Sarasvati-Sindhu civilization, he was priest of *dhăvaḍ* 'iron-smelters' (root: *dhāu* 'ore') with Indus script hieroglyphs signifiesपोतृ,'purifier' of dhātu, dhāū, dhāv 'red stone minerals'. This is evidenced by the Indus Script hieroglyphs signified on the limestone statue.

The cultural continuum of pōtṟ पोतृ as a priest of Vedic tradition is evidenced in the veneration of ancestors: போத்தி pōtti 'grandfather, Malabar priest'. In ancient times of Sarasvati-Sindhu civilization, he was priest of *dhăvaḍ* 'iron-smelters' (root: *dhāu* 'ore') with Indus script hieroglyphs signifiesपोतृ,'purifier' of dhātu, dhāū, dhāv 'red stone minerals'. This is evidenced by the Indus Script hieroglyphs signified on the limestone statue.

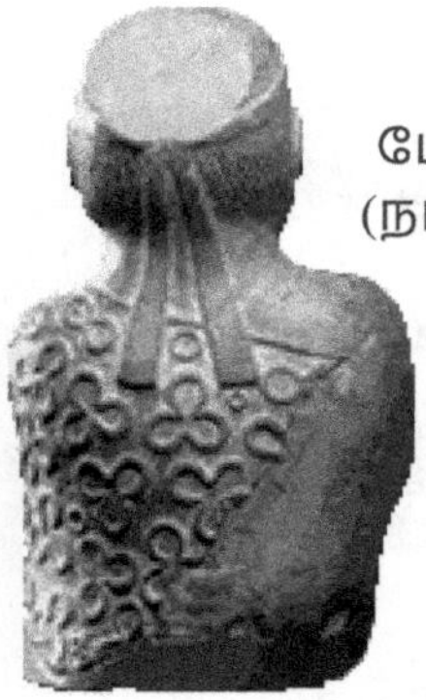

போற்றன் pōṟṟaṉ, *n*. prob. id. Grandfather; பாட்டன். (நாமதீப. 189.) போத்தி pōtti, *n*. < போற்றி. 1. Grandfather; பாட்டன். *Tinn*. 2. Brahman temple- priest in **Malabar;** மலையாளத்திலுள்ள கோயிலருச் சகன்.போற்றி pōṟṟi, < id. *n*. 1. Praise, applause, commendation; புகழ்மொழி. (W.) 2.Brahman temple-priest of Malabar; கோயிற் பூசைசெய்யும் மலையாளநாட்டுப் பிராமணன். (W.) 3. See போத்தி, 1.--*int*. Exclamation of praise; துதிச்சொல்வகை. பொய்தீர் காட்சிப் புரையோய் போற்றி (சிலப். 13, 92).போற்றுநர் pōṟṟunar, *n*. < போற்று-. 1. Relatives, kinsmen; சுற்றத்தார். போற்றா ருயிரினும் போற்றுந ருயிரினும் (பரிபா. 4, 52). 2. Those who understand; நன்குணர்வார். வேற்றுமை யின்றது போற்றுநர்ப் பெறினே (பரிபா. 4, 55).போற்று[1]-தல் pōṟṟu-, *5 v. tr*. 1. To praise, applaud; துதித்தல். (பிங்.) போற்று மடி யாருண்ணின்று நகுவேன் (திருவாச. 5, 60). 2. To worship; வணங்குதல். (பிங்.) 3. To protect, cherish, keep with great care; பாதுகாத் தல். போற்றி னரியவை போற்றல் (குறள், 693).

पोतृ pōtṟ Purifier Mohenjo-daro priest statue hieroglyphs and Harappa Indus Script tablet with 24 dots cartouche deciphered.

Dotted circle hieroglyph: पोत [pōta] *m f* A bead of glass and, sometimes, of gold and of stone. Rebus: पोतदार (p. 532) [pōtadāra] *m* (P) An officer under the native governments. His business was to assay all money paid into the treasury. He was also the village-silversmith.पोतदारी (p. 532) [pōtadārī] *f* (P) The office or business of पोतदार: also his rights or fees.पोतनिशी [pōtaniśī] *f* (P) The office or business of पोतनीस.पोतनीस [pōtanīsa] *m* (P) The treasurer or cash-keeper.पोतेचाल [pōtēcāla] *f* (Treasury-currency.) The currency in which the public revenue is received. 2 Used as *a* Of that currency; as पोतेचालीचा (रूपया-पैसा- नाणें &c.) Coin or money admitted into or issued from the Government-treasury; sterling money of the realm.पोतेझाडा [pōtējhāḍā] *m* Settlement of the accounts of the treasury.पोथी [pōthī] *f* A book, a pamphlet, a manuscript.

Potaraju legend in Andhra Pradesh is a recollection of the memories of metallurgical artificers' work. The word pota has a metallurgical connotation related to metalcasting in Telugu: పోత (p. 0823) [pōta] *pōta*. [Tel. from పోయు.] n. Pouring, పోయుట. Casting, as of melted metal. A hieroglyph to signify the expression is: *பொத்திரம் pottiram , n. < pōtra. Missile weapon; எறியாயுதம். பொத்திரம் பாய்ந்து மாய்ந் தீர் (சேதுபு. சங்கரபாண்டி. 41).* पोत्र the snout of a hog , R2it. Hcar.; a thunderbolt. (Samskrtam)

Discovery of the language of a civilization

Phonetic guide

a rut,at	m. mum	n- new

a_/ l*aw*	n: ki*ng*	r- cu*rl*
a~_ lo*ng*	*n~* *ny*et	r. *r*ug
/a~ *un-*	h-/k- w*h*at	r.. (*zsh*)
i it	c *ch*ange	s fu*s*e
i_ b*ee*	c. *s*o	s. *sh*ut
i~_ b*een*	d *th*en	s' *s*ugar
/i~ *in*	d. *d*ot	t bo*th*
u y*ou*	l. riva*lr*y	t. *t*oo
u_/ *oo*ze	n. a*n*d	
u~_ b*oon*		
/u~ j*une*		
e b*e*t		
e_ *a*te		
e~_ b*an*e		
/e~ wh*en,whey*		
o *o*bese		
o_ n*o*te		
o~_ b*one*,*one*		

Semantic clusters (1242 English words and Botanical species Latin)

- Economic Court: Flora and Products from Flora@
- Birds
- Insects
- Fauna

- Animate phenomena: birth, body, sensory perceptions and actions

- Visual phenomena, forms and shapes

- Numeration and Mensuration
- Economic Court: Natural phenomena, Earth formations, Products of earth (excluding flora clustered in a distinct category) @
- Building, Infrastructure
- Work, skills, products of labour and workers (fire-worker, potter/ smith/ lapidary, weaver, farmer, soldier)

- Language fields
- Kinship
- Social formations
- Other semantic clusters

Economic Court: Flora and Products from Flora

butter curdle flesh flour food grain honey liquor mahua molasses oil oilcake rice spice sugar supper tobacco wheat
bark cloth cotton drug flax fragrance fringe garland harvest granary glue hemp indigo itch kunda lac log medicine mouldy ointment peel poison pulp pungent raw reed resin root sandal scent seed sheaf sheath skein sow stick straw thorn thresh tip-cat
apple asparagus balsam bamboo banana barley basil basket betel bud camphor cardamom cashew celery chaff clearingnut clove bush cork coconut coffee creeper cucumber cumin ebony date fenugreek forest flower fruit garden garlic ginger gooseberry gourd hibiscus jackfruit jalap jujube leadwort leaf linseed lotus mango mushroom mustard palm orpiment pepper pericarp petal pomegranate raspberry saffron sago sprout tree tuber turmeric wax wood-apple

abies abrus acacia acalypha acampe acanthus achyranthes aconitum acorus adenanthera aegle
aeschynomena aeschynomene agaricus agathotes agati ageratum aglaia
aguilaria ailantus alangium aloe alosanthes alpinia amarantus albizzia amomum
andropogon anethum anodendron anogeissus anthocephalus anthriscus antiaris
areca aristolochia arka artemisia artocarpus arum atlantia averrhoea azima balanites
barleria barringtonia basella bassia bauhinia berberis betula bixa blyxa bombax boswellia
bryonia buchanania butea caesalpinia caesaria cajanus calamus calophyllum canarium cannabis cant
hium capparis carallia cardiospermum careya carissa carthamus carum caryota cassia cassytha cedr
ela cedrus celastrus celosia celtis cerbera ceropegia ceratonia chenopodium cicer cichorium cinnaba
r cinnamomum cinnamon citrus clarion cleistanthus clerodendrum clitoria
coccinia cocculus colocasia colosanthes
convolvulus cordia coriandrum costum costus cratraeva crocus crotalaria croton cucumis curculigo cur
cuma cyperus dalbergia datura desmodium
dichrostachys dillenia dioscorea diospyros dodonea dolichos eclipta elaeocarpus elettaria eleusine er
icybe erythrina erythroxylon eugenia eugenis euphorbia excoecaria feronia ferula ficus frankincense
flacourtia garcinia galangal gamboge gardenia gaultheria gendarussa gentiana gloria gmelina grewia
grislea gymnema gynandropsis gyrocarpus heliotropium hemidesmus hiptage holcus hopea hydnocarp
us ichnocarpus ilex indigofera ipomoea jasminum juniper justicia kaempferia lagenaria lagerstroemia
laurus lepidum leucas ligusticum linum lobellia lodhra luffa
luvunga macaranga mangifera marsilia melastoma meliosma memecyclon mentha mesua
millingtonia mimusops
momordica moringa morus mucuna myrica myristica myrobalan myrtus nardostachys nauclea nelu
mbium nerium nyctanthes nymphaea ochlandra ochre ocimum odina olea ophioxylon oryza palmyra
pandanus panicum papaver pavetta pavonia phaseolus phoenix phyllanthus physalis pimpinella
pinus piper plumbago pogostemon polygala polygonum premna
prunus psidium pterocarpus pterospermum pouzolzia prosopis quercus randia raphanus rauwofia r
hizophora ricinus rottleria rubia rumex saccharum sal salicornia salvadora salvinia
sandoricum santalum sapindus sarcostemma saussurea schleichera scirpus
semecarpus sesamum sesbana sesbania shorea sinapis solanum soymida sphaeranthus
spinachia sterculia stereospermum strobilanthes strychnos swertia
symplocos syzygium tabernaemontana tamarindus tectona tephrosia terminalia thespesia tinospora
tribulus tragia trapa trema
trichosanthes trigonella trophis unquis utrica vaccinium veronia vitex vulpes wrightia xylia zizyphus

Birds

bird bluejay cock crane crow cuckoo
dove duck eagle feather gizzard crest hawk heron kingfisher myna nest
owl parrot pheasant quail robin shrike skylark snipe sparrow teal weaver-bird

Insects

bat beehive caterpillar chameleon cockroach crab frog insect lizard mosquito scorpion snake spider

Fauna

animal antelope, goat, deer, markhor, ram alligator bear buffalo bull camel dog elephant fish hare herd horn horse ivory lair lion lowing mongoose monkey musk-deer octopus pony porpoise rat rhinoceros shoal squirrel tail tiger tortoise yak yak-tail

Animate phenomena: birth, body, sensory perceptions and actions

abortion age amazed anger anus arrive ask attack back bald bathe behind beard beat beg being belly bile birth bite blink blood blow body boil bone breath bristle butt buttock care cheek chest chignon chin climb come copulate creep cross cry cut dance death decay doubt dream dumb dwarf echo elbow end excrement eye faeces fall fat finger fist flee fly frolic front funeral genus give gore groan hair hand hatch head heel hear heart herpes hiccup hide hit hunt hurt idle intoxicate invite itch jaundice joint juggler jump kick lame laugh lift leap leg lip listen liver look male mane meet mole mouth movement muscle nail navel neck nerve noise nose numb old penis perish phlegm plague pour pregnant pudendum pull pus push put raise rattle recite reply repress restrain rinse roar roll run rush scab scar scatter seize senses separate serve silence sing sink sit shoulder shrink slander slap sleep speak splash spleen split sprain squeeze stammer standing stay stirring stop strength suck surprise swallow sweep swell swing syllable take tame taste throb throw tired toe trunk tumour turning turn-back tusk twist udder urine vault vomit vulva waist walk woman word wrinkle young

Visual phenomena, forms and shapes

ball beauty bend bit black braid brown bubble chequered circle colour crack curve dense dot endless entangled extremity fitting flow fork full green heap hole hollow hump incline invert knob knot leak left line long loose middle ooze red slack slant small square straight stripe white

Numeration and Mensuration

account agreement audit average balance (scales) banker big broad centre cheap coin collect collection contain counting deficient divide eight finger five four half high increase joint knot lightness load mark marked market marking numeration one remainder six seven ten two three twelve twenty measure weight zero

Economic Court: Natural phenomena, Earth formations, Products of earth (excluding flora clustered in a distinct category)

barren basin borax brass bright bronze burst clay cloud cold collyrium crystal darkness dawn desert dew dry extinguish fire frost gem glitter gold (including soma) goods earth hail heat hill island lapislazuli lightning moon mud night north ocean ore pearl planet pleiades rain rainbow river ruby sand salt sediment shell silk silver sky smoke soap solstice south star stone sun tank tin thunder water wave wet wind zodiac

Building, infrastructure

arch brick bridge building bund cave chisel chop churn corner door drain fence fencing ford fort house kitchen lattice loft parapet pillar rafter roof shelf space stable wall wattle way (path, road)

Work, skills, products of labour and workers (fire-worker, potter/ smith/ lapidary, weaver, farmer, soldier)

[The lexemes related to weapons and tools are so vivid and distinctive that the entire group has been clustered together to provide an overview of the skills developed which are reflected in semantic expansions related to weapon types and to wielding them. Thus, the clusters in the following list (e.g. awl, axe, bow, goad, razor, saw, sickle) are only to be treated as 'tool' samplers.]

Weapons and Tools (798kb.) awl axe bow goad razor saw sickle	assembly amulet army axle badge bead bed bellows blanket boat bolt bore bracelet brazier break broken butcher camp cart carve censer cloak comb commonwealth convey crucible cymbals deliver dent depart dice distill drill drive drum edge embark engrave enter entreat erect fan fasten fatigue fear fell ferry filter fire flag flute forge fry furnace furrow glove gong groove guard guild hammer indra jacket join kill kiln kubera labour ladder ladle lamp land landless lathe leash leather lid lever loom lute manger mill mirror mould necklace net occupation oil-press ornament pannier patrol perforate pin plait plough pole pot potsherd potter pressed produce profession pure purity raft rope screen seat sew shackle script sling (bearing/ carrying) snare soldier spike spinner (weaver) spy stake stampsteam stirrup stool stopper store tablet trap treasury trough uproot vessel warrior wash water-lift well well-digger wheel whip winnow write

Language fields

grammar (Etymology, linguistics, grammar, particles, prepositions, adverbs)	arab tamil telugu
	become near next now only other that there thus time until

	augment consonant name no prefix riddle sign signature yes

Kinship

ancestor bride brother companion family father friend gentleman girl lead love marriage mistress mother self single sister wife

Social formations

abuse ambush auction authenticbard bawd brahma bravo buy chief class commend confidence conflict confusion cruel country court dedicate deity demon disgrace doctrine evil exile faith festival fop fraud free freedom game get gift goblin good gratitude guilt hindu honour idol justice law learn lease lend life load loan malice manner market meditate memorial mercy miser mystic oppose painting penalty place play please pledge pomp poor post power prank pride principal procession protect regularity regulation rich rob rogue royal rule sacrifice safety salutation scheme sell send shame sindhu stupid support surplus tax teacher temple terror theft tomb town trade tribe unruly useless value violence virtuous vow wager wicked win witness worship

Other semantic clusters

(including cognisance and lexemes which may indicate semantic expansion and may span many other semantic clusters; e.g. 'mix' cluster may relate to animate and inanimate clusters)

adhere begin blocked bold bundle clean clever close coax commence dangle deceit defeat deliberate desire detached dip dirty disgust dull enclose endure false forget hard inferior know mark marked marking mass means medley mix narrow neat need new notch opportunity outside overflow part particle paste pit pitfall ponder purpose quick quit ready remember rise rot rough rub ruin section shade shake similar slow strip thin think trace tranquil trouble truth unripe upper vermillion

The author assumes full responsibility for the semantic and etymological judgements made and the errors that might have crept in with thousands of database iterations in organizing the semantic clusters found in the word lists (The lexicon includes over half-a-million Indian words). The author is indebted to Prof. Krishnamurthy who first observed from a review (1994) of an earlier draft of the Lexion (alphabetially sequenced) that the model of Carl Darling Buck's work for Indo-European languages may also be adapted. The author hopes that with the impossibility of 'dating' the origin of a word, all its inherent limitations, the omissions, intentional or otherwise and errors that will in due course be pointed out by scholars specialized in their fields, the Indian Lexicon will be a tentative, but bold start of a skeleton dictionary of the Indian linguistic area ca. 3000 B.C. and will be expanded further to include modern words.

Indian Lexicon

Organizing (Clustering) the lexemes of all Indian Languages

For a perspective on the philological issues see:

An introduction Discovering the language of India ca. 3000 B.C. (65 kb.)

This is a lexicon with a difference. It is a comparative semantic (sic) lexicon of synonyms from Indian languages. See list of the languages of India surveyed in the *Indian Lexicon.*

Indian Lexicon goes beyond the concept of a comparative lexicon or an etymological dictionary.

It is a search for synonyms in ancient forms of Indian languages. Hence, it may be called a semantic lexicon and not an etymological lexicon. This search has taken the compiler 20 years to accomplish using a powerful computer processor to compile the database of semantic clusters, working on an average, for 4 hours daily.

The lexemes of all Indian languages are organized in two major categories:

- Alphabetical sequence

The *Dravidian Etymological Dictionary* (DEDR) uses the order of the Tamil alphabet to seqauence etymological groups, assuming Proto-Dravidian phonemes in the reconstructed PDr roots or stems involved, with the order of the Tamil alphabet applied of these phonemes. Tamil phonemes do not serve as PD reconstructions in all cases. The Indian Lexicon is a first step towards the compilation of an Indian Etymological Dictionary. Proto-Indic construction of phonemes of Proto-Indic roots or stems involved has not been attempted. Lexemes from the Indian languages are clustered based primarily on 'semantics' and secondarily on 'phonetis'. The *Comparative Dictionary of Indo-Aryan Languages* (CDIAL) provides many reconstructions of Proto-Indo-Aryan phonemes prefixing the root or stem involved with an * as has beeen attempted, in superb other works in philology, for the reconstruction of Indo-European etyma.

- Semantic sequence

The semantic problem has been handled vigorously and the *Indian Lexicon* includes many borrowings among and between languages. This approach has resulted in clustering as many as over 3000 etymological groups of DEDR with the comparative groups of CDIAL, together with thousands of lexemes of Santali, Mundarica and other languages of the Austro-Asiatic linguistic group. There could be many opinions among linguists on semantic developments of a language. It is assumed that there were homophones in a Proto-Indic language which was the lingua franca of the Sarasvati-Sindhu civilization, ca. 2500 B.C.; this assumption, coupled with the Mesopotamian links, provides some hope for deciphering the inscriptions of the Sarasvati (Indus) Script.

A note is appended which recounts Prof. Emeneau's postulation of an Indian Linguistic Area, together with some briefs on the key dates related to the desiccation of the Sarasvati River.(Note on Key dates of the

Sarasvati River and the Indian Linguistic Area) This provides the underpinnings for a hypothesis that many entries in this *Indian Lexicon* are likely to provide the phonemes which were current for a millennium, starting circa 3000 B.C. This hypothesis will be tested by an attempt to decipher the inscriptions of the civilization which sustained the Indian Linguistic Area.

The semantic sequence provided in the *Indian Lexicon* is like a meta-index of English meanings, using synonyms or near-synonyms of basic English words, while trying to separate English homonyms or near-homonyms. Botanical names (primarily Latin) have been used ater Hooker to index flora, though some entries are also sequenced in the context of sememes related to cultural processes, for e.g. 'food'.

- Search facility

In addition to the alphabetic and semantic sequences, a general search facility is also provided. This search can be performed using ANY INDIAN WORD or ANY ENGLISH MEANING. While entering the Indian word (from any language), the simple transliteration rules have to be observed which will be obvious from a cursory review of the *Indian Lexicon* clusters.

There are over 8300 semantic clusters included in the *Indian Lexicon* from over 25 languages which makes the work very large. Hence, to render the search faster, a meta-index has been constructed.

For the purposes of the preliminary decipherment effort, a search within the Semantic sequence lists using the search facilities provided on the Browser tool bar (Netscape or Internet Explorer) should be adequate.

Munda lexemes in Sanskrit (After Kuiper, 37 kb.)

Sememes (213 kb.)

Etyma in Niruktam (25 kb.)

Roots (Dha_tupa_t.ha) (156 kb.)

Verb forms (After Whitney, 42 kb.)

Phonetic guide (Basic sounds of the language)

Abbreviations : Grammatical

Abbreviations used for linguistic categories and other languages

Bibliography (Textual sources of lexemes)

Lexemes of Epigraphy (281kb.)

Organizing (Clustering) the lexemes of Indian languages

Elucidates the method used to organize the synonyms in alphabetic, semantic sequences and to facilitate comprehensive searches for ANY INDIAN LANGUAGE WORD OR ANY ENGLISH MEANING.

An Overview and Objectives

This is a comparative study of the 'semantics' of lexemes of all the languages of India (which may also be referred to, in a geographical/ historical phrase, as the Indian linguistic area). The objective of the lexicon is to discover the semantic repertoire of India ca. 3000 B.C. to further facilitate efforts at deciphering the inscriptions and script of the Sarasvati-Sindhu civilization.

Indian Languages included in the Indian Lexicon

A.Assamese Ap.Apabhram.s'a Ash. Ashkun (As.ku~_--Kafiri) Aw. Awadhi_ B. Bengali (Ban:gla_) Bal. Balu_ci_ (Iranian) Bashg. Bashgali_ (Kafiri) Bel. Belari Bhoj. Bhojpuri_ Bi. Biha_ri_ Br. Bra_hui_ Brj. Brajbha_s.a_ Bshk. Bashkari_k (Dardic) Bur.Burushaski Chil. Chili_s (Dardic)	K. Ka_s'mi_ri_ Ka. Kannad.a Kaf. Kafiri Kal. Kalasha (Dardic) Kand. Kandia (Dardic) Kat.. Kat.a_rqala_ (Dardic) Kho. Khowa_r (Dardic) Khot. Khotanese (Iranian) Kmd. Ka_mdeshi (Kafiri) Ko. Kota Kod.. Kod.agu (Coorg)	L. Lahnda_ M. Mara_t.hi_ Ma.Malayalam Mai.Maiya~_ (Dardic) Malt.Malto Ma_lw.Ma_lwa_i_ Mand.. Mand.a Marw.Ma_rwa_r.i_ Md.Maldivian dialect of Sinhalese Mj. Munji_ (Iranian) Mth. Maithili_ Mu. Mun.d.a_ri (Munda) N. Nepa_li Nahali Nin:g. Nin:gala_mi (Dardic)	P. Punja_bi_ (Paja_bi_) Pa. Parji Pali Pah. Paha_r.i_ Pa_Ku. Pa_lu Kur-umba Pas'. Pas'ai (Dardic) Pe. Pengo Phal. Phalu_r.a (Dardic) Pkt. Prakrit S. Sindhi_ Sant. Santa_li_ (Mun.d.a_) Sh. Shina (S.in.a_.Dardic) Si. Sinhalese Sik. Sikalga_ri_ (Mixed Gypsy	Ta.Tamil Te.Telugu Tir.Tira_hi_ (Dardic) To. Toda Tor.To_rwa_li_ (Dardic) Tu. Tulu U. Urdu Werch.Werchikwa_r or Wershikwa_r (Yasin dialect of Burushaski) Wg. Waigali_ or Wai-ala_ (Kafiri) Wkh. Wakhi (Iranian) Wot..Wot.apu_ri_ (language of Wot.apu_r and Kat.a_rqala_. Dardic) WPah. West Paha_r.i_

D.. D.uma_ki Dm. Dame~d.i_ (Kafiri-Dardic) G. Gujara_ti_ Ga. Gadba Garh.Gar.hwa_li_ Gau. Gauro (Dardic) Gaw.Gawar-Bati (Dardic) Gmb. Gambi_ri_ (Kafiri) Go. Gondi Gy. Gypsy or Romani H. Hindi_ Ir. Irul.a	Koh. Kohista_ni_ (Dardic) Kol. Kolami Kon. Kon:kan.i_ Kond.a Kor. Koraga Kt. Kati or Katei (Kafiri) Ku. Kumauni_ Kui Kurub.Bet.t.a Kuruba Kur.Kur.ux (Oraon, Kurukh) Kuwi	Nk. Naikr.i (dialect of Kolami = LSI, Bhili of Basim; Naiki of Chanda) Or. Or.iya_	Language: LSI xi 167) Skt. Sanskrit Sv. Savi (Dardic)	

The Indian Lexicon establishes an Indian Linguistic Area, ca. 3000 B.C. by authenticating the use of the lexemes for inscriptions of the civilization of the ancient period.

This Indian lexicon seeks to establish a semantic concordance, across the languages or *numeraire facile* of the Indian linguistic area: from Brahui to Santali to Bengali, from Kashmiri to Mundarica to Sinhalese, from Marathi to Hindi to Nepali, from Sindhi or Punjabi or Urdu to Tamil. A semantic structure binds the languages of India, which may have diverged morphologically or phonologically as evidenced in the oral tradition of Vedic texts, or epigraphy, literary works or lexicons of the historical periods. This lexicon, therefore, goes beyond, the commonly held belief of an Indo-European language and is anchored on proto-Indian sememes.

The work covers over 8,300 semantic clusters which span and bind the Indian languages. The basic finding is that thousands of terms of the Vedas, the Munda languages (e.g., Santali, Mundarica, Sora; cf. Munda lexemes in Sanskrit)(37 kb.), the so-called Dravidian languages and the so-called Indo-Aryan languages have common roots. This belies the received wisdom of cleavage between, for example, the Dravidian or Munda and the Aryan languages.

The idea of a semantic dictionary

Carl Darling Buck, *A dictionary of selected synonyms in the principal Indo-European languages: a contribution to the history of ideas*, 1949, Univ. of Chicago Press. "The associations underlyng semantic changes are so complex that no rigid classification of the latter is possible. Many changes may be variously viewed. In a sense, each word has its individual semantic history... in the history of words for domestic animals the conspicuous feature is the frequent interchange between classes of the same species, as when words of the same cognate group denote in different languages 'bull', 'ox', or 'cow', and in another species 'ram, wether', or 'lamb', or show a shift from 'wether', through an intermediate generic use, to 'ewe'. "Semantic borrowing" refers to the borrowing not of the formal word but of some special meaning. There are, of course, great numbers of actual loanwords, some in Greek from pre-Greek sources, many in Latin from Greek, still more in most of the European languages from Latin or in many cases more specifically from Frenh; again from early Germanic and later from German in Balto-Slavic and from Slavic in Rumanian. But besides these there are "translation words". A special use of a familiar foreign word was adopted for the usually corresponding native word. Thus Lat. *na_vis* 'ship' came to be used in Christian times for the 'nave' of a church... Semantic word study may proceed from two opposite points of view, form or meaning. For example, on may study the history of Lat. di_cere 'say' and its cognates in Latin, or, with enlarged scope, its cognates in all the Indo-European languages; in other words the diverse uses of derivatives of the Indo-European root *deik- and its probable sense. Such is the material brought together in the etymological dictionaries of the usual type. Conversely, one may start from the notion 'say' and study the history of words used to express it in different languages... By the study of synonyms, their etymology and semantic history, one seeks to show the various sources of a given notion, the trails of its evolution... also presents an interesting picture of word distribution... Even for the Indo-European field anything like a complete semantic dictionary is beyond probable realization at present... The specialist can recognize these, and at the same time is aware of how of how large a proportion of the current etymologies, even in most of the best etymological dictionaries, are uncertain, with varying degrees of probability or plausibility... and it is best to let the facts speak for themselves in each case."

Sememes (213 kb.)

"Sememe [sememic(s)] is a term used in SEMANTIC theories to refer to a minimal UNIT of MEANING. For some, a sememe is equivalent to the meaning of a MORPHEME; for others it is a FEATURE of meaning, equivalent to the notion of 'semantic COMPONENT' or 'semantic feature' in some theories. The term sememics is used as part of the description of strata in STRATIFICATIONAL GRAMMAR; the 'sememic stratum', which handles the SYSTEMS of semantic relationship between LEXICAL ITEMS, is here distinguished from the HYPERSEMEMIC stratum, at which is analysed the relationship between LANGUAGE and the external world. SEMOTACTICS, in this approach, involves the study of SEQUENTIAL arrangement of sememes. See Robins 1980: Ch.8." (David Crystal, *A Dictionary of Linguistics and Phonetics*, Blackwell, 1991).

These sememes should be distinguished from dha_tus or verb roots since the radicals span both nouns and verbs and also include attributive thoughts connoted, for example, by adjectives.

Sememes are clustered in the Indian Lexicon more like classemes (a term used by some European linguists, e.g. Eugene Coseriu, to refer to the relatively abstract SEMANTIC FEATURES shared by LEXICAL items belonging to different semantic FIELDS, e.g. animate/inanimate, adult/child. The term contrasts with the irreducible semantic features (SEMES) which work, at a very particular level, within a particular semantic field, e.g. *table* being identified in terms of 'number of legs', 'shape', etc. (See Lyons 1977: Ch.9)

Many sememes are from Sanskrit which re-inforced the development of the literary structures of historical periods of all the languages flowing from proto-Indian lingua franca. CDIAL (with comparative etymological groups collected over a period of 40 years until 1966) provides thousands of possible derivations or phonological reconstructions of 'old Indo-aryan form' in Sanskrit, within its 14,845 head-words. A magnificent attempt was made in the past by linguists of unsurpassed erudition, to identify the sememes of Indian languages. A notable result was the formation and delineation of the grammatical rules of the Sanskrit language.

Indian Lexicon establishes that over 3000 etyma of the Dravidian Etymological Dictionary (DEDR) have concordant sememes in the lexemes of Indo-Aryan and Munda languages, thus negating the linguists' differentiation of the Dravidian tongues from the Indo-Aryan and Munda language streams.

The Indus (Sarasvati-Sindhu) Script decipherment problem

Many lexemes will be dated to circa 3000 B.C., when the most expansive civilization of the times flourished in thousands of settlement sites in the Sarasvati-Sindhu doab. This dating for the selected lexemes is based on a suggested rebus/semantic clustering method to decipher the script of the civilization. The underlying language may be called the *Indian*; hence, the lexicon is called "An Indian Lexicon".

A paradigm change is posited that circa 3000 B.C., the Indo-Aryan, Dravidian and Munda sub-families of languages had not been differentiated fully. This hypothesis has to be validated further through more linguistic/lexical studies.Etyma in Niruktam (25 kb.)

Roots (Dha_tupa_t.ha) (156 kb.)

Dha_tupa_t.ha (lit. a study of roots or verb forms) reputedly by Pa_n.ini provides a list of 2200 roots (in ten technical classes) with almost all irregular and noteworthy forms which can be expanded in the series of active, passive, casual desiderative and derivative groups.

The classification of verbal bases in the following ten classes is based on vikaran.a the inserted conjugational affix, the conjugational sign placed between the root and the terminations.Verb forms (Whitney) (42 kb.)

The roots, verb-forms, and primary derivatives of the Sanskrit language : A supplement to his Sanskrit grammar.

Whitney's work lists all the quotable roots of the Sanskrit language together with the tense and conjugation-systems made from them, the noun and adjective (infinitival and participal) formations that attach themselves most closely to the verb and with the other derivative noun and adjective-stems usually classed as primary. "... since etymology is from beginning to end a matter of balancing probabilities, and thick-set with uncertainties and chances of error. It has been my intention to err rather upon the side of liberality of inclusion than the opposite... main intent is to furnish the means of examining in their chronologic entirety the groups of words and forms that cluster about the so-called roots in Sanskrit, that they may be studied, and have their relations determined, witth more complete understanding... The meanings added after the roots by no means claim to be exhaustive; they are in general intended only to identify the root... The classes of (verb-)forms that contain the most puzzling problems are the reduplicated ones, and the present stems ending in ya..." (Whitney, 1885, pp. v to xiii).

Soma is a metaphor. It is NOT a herbal but a metal. 'Soma is a plant; the word is derived from (the root) su (to press): it is pressed again and again. Its character (as a deity) is mostly secondary and only rarely primary. In order to point out its (primary use) in the hymns relating to soma-juice while it is being purified, we shall quote...be pure with thy sweetest and most gladdening stream. O soma, thou art pressed for Indra to drink. The stanza is explained by the mere reading of it. Now here is another stanza addressed to him or to the moon, as follows. Because they grind the herbs together, one thinks that he has drunk the soma. Of the soma which the Bra_hman.as know, none whatsoever partakes...' (Nir. 11.2; 11.3; 11.4). cf. 'The meaning of expressions of the Vedic Sanskrit and of the popular speech is not different: va_kya_rtho_lo_kave_dayo_ravis'is.t.ah (Pu_. Mi_i.1.31)... abhidha_ne_ rthava_dah.: there is a figurative description in such expressions (of describing such lifeless things as grass, stones, and axe as if they were living beings)' (Sayan.a's preface, p.3);'There is no such contradiction, because even one Rudra by his greatness can take on a thousand forms...gun.a_davipratis.e_dhah. sya_t: 'on account of the figurative description, there will be no contradiction' (Pu_. Mi_. i.2.47)..

This is a comparative lexicon covering all the languages of India (which may also be referred to, in a geographical/historical phrase, as the Indian subcontinent).

This lexicon seeks to establish a semantic concordance, across the languages or numeraire facile of the Indian sub-continent.(Numerair facile or easy currency, to use the eloquent phrase of Mallarme; this phrase is comparable to another monetary (!) metaphor: 'borrowing' used in comparative linguistics. A superb example of 'easy currency' is provided by the Indian Epigraphical Glossary. Some selected terms used in epigraphy of Indian languages are listed in this lexicon. This list provides evidence of the degrees of freedom enjoyed by the writers of inscriptions to depict in a variety of scripts, the phonetics (or 'easy currency') underlying many economic transactions.) The language subcontinent ranges from Brahui to Santali to Bengali, from Kashmiri to Mundarica to Sinhalese, from Marathi to Hindi to Nepali, from Sindhi or Punjabi or Urdu to Tamil. A semantic structure binds the languages of India, which may have diverged morphologically or phonologically as evidenced in the oral tradition of Vedic texts, or epigraphy, literary works or lexicons of the historical periods. This lexicon,therefore, goes beyond, the commonly held belief of an Indo-European language2 and is anchored on proto-Indian sememes.

'A genetic relationship between the classical languages, Greek, Latin,and Sanskrit, was identified in the late eighteenth century by Sir WilliamJones, who correctly postulated a 'common source' for these three languages,and suggested that Celtic, Iranian and Germanic might well be connected. The genetic relationship was first scientifically codified and set out on a comparative basis by Franz Bopp, whose major work -- Vergleichende Grammatik des Sanskrit, Zend, Armenischen, Griechischen, Lateinischen, Lithauischen, Altslawischen, Gothischen und Deutschen-- was published in 1833. ('Zend' in Bopp's title refers to Avestan)...' (George L. Campbell, Compendium of the World's Languages, Routledge, London, 1991, p.610).

In philology, as in archaeology, the search for 'truth' is an extension of a researcher's imagination. Imagination is not an act of faith, but a statement of hypothesis based on relational entities in linguistic structures identified through painstaking lexical work. Two such entities in linguistic structures are: morpheme and *sememe* which bind an etymological group. *Sememe* may be defined as a phoneme imbued with 'meaning'. Morpheme is defined as a 'meaningful' linguistic unit. *Sememe* constitutes the semantic substratum of a morpheme or simply, 'meaning'. What is 'meaning'? It is a concept closely linked to a social compact for inter-personal communication. The 'private language' of a speaker's brain (with 'personal' experiences embedded in neural networks) is revealed through sounds uttered by the speaker. Language is formed if these uttered sounds echo the 'private language' of a listener. Such an echo constitutes meaning or the semantic sub-structure of a language. *Sememes* are the basic semantic structural units of a language which combine to yield morphemes or words. A *sememe* can, for example, be distinguished from a phoneme or a gesture which *does not communicate a message in a social compact.* Only those uttered sounds which are heard and accepted in a social compact can constitute the repertoire of a language. *Sememes* (or, dha_tupada's) are given a variety of phonemic and morphological forms in the *lingua franca* to constitute semantic expressions, or the vocabulary of an evolving and growing civilization.

The work covers over 8,000 semantic clusters which span and bind the Indian languages. The basic finding is that thousands of terms of the Vedas, the Munda languages (e.g., Santali, Mundarica, Sora), the so-called Dravidian languages and the so-called Indo-Aryan languages have common roots. This belies the received wisdom of cleavage between, for example, the Dravidian or Munda and the Aryan languages.

The lexicon seeks to establish an areal 'Indian' language type, by establishing semantic concordance among the so-called Indo-Aryan, Dravidian and Munda languages. The area spanned is a geographical region bounded by the Indian ocean on the south and the mountain ranges which insulate it from other regions of the Asian continent on the north, east and west.

This lexicon is a tribute to the brilliant work done by etymologists4 and scholars of Indian linguistics, and to a number of scholars who have contributed to unravelling the enigma of the Indus Script and to the study of ancient Indian science and technology. (Obscure speech or writing. The orthography of the Indus Script is vivid and symmetric and is used to convey cryptic messages. Each message on seals (many with cord holes, and probably worn visibly by their owners), tablets, copper plates, pottery, bangles etc. uses, generally, between one to about six signs. The sign sequences are frequently superimposed on a field symbol or pictograph. The signs include glyphs such as svastika _ , dotted circles, short and long linear strokes. The principal enigma is the speech which the script depicted!)

The author believes that the work can contribute to/strengthen the unifying elements of Indian common cultural heritage and counter divisive forces which occasionally hold sway. The author also realizes that language is an extraordinarily emotional issue and is subject to a variety of possible interpretations. Language is also a philosophical problem par excellence. The justification for this comparative lexicon of languages currently spoken by over a billion people of the world can be provided at a number of levels:

(1) to bring people closer to the ancient heritage of a Indian language family of which the extant Indian languages (Indo-Aryan, Dravidian and Munda language streams) are but dialectical forms; 4Etymology has been defined as the 'origin, formation, and development (of a word)...(and) as a branch of grammar dealing with forms...étumon (French) literal sense of a word, original form, primary or basic word.....' (The Oxford Lexicon of English Etymology, 1985).

(2) to generate further studies in the disciplines of (i) Indian archaeology, (ii) general semantics and comparative linguistics; (iii) design of fifth-generation computer systems6; and (3) to provide a basis for further studies in grammatical philosophy and neurosciences on the formation of semantic patterns or structures in the human brain -- neurosciences related to the study of linguistic competence which seems to set apart the humans from other living beings. The urgent warrant for this work is the difficulty faced by scholars in collating different lexicons and in obtaining works such as CDIAL (A Comparative Dictionary of Indo-Aryan Languages) even in eminent libraries. In tracing the etyma (lit. truth in Greek) of the Indian languages, it is adequate to indicate the word forms which can be traced into the mists of history7.

These computer systems are in the realm of artificial intelligence or approaches to the design of computer systems which can 'learn' from experience. It may be, hypothesized that sememes are recorded as 'ideographs' neuronally linking 'perceived images' or 'felt experiences' with 'phonetic formants'. It is notable that early scripts were 'ideographic'. It is also notable that the linguistic competence of a human child builds upon the linguistic faculties of the brain within one to two years after birth, with layers of inter-locked sensory perceptions including 'heard' sounds, until the vocal cords are developed to 'repeat' such sounds, as recollections of 'experiences' of the child's development. 7Some observations of ancient historians are instructive: "there are many nations among the Indians, and they don't speak the same language" (Herodotus, Historiae 3.98). Hsuan Tsang (602-664 A.D.): "The letters of their alphabet were arranged by the god Brahma _ , and their forms have been handed down from the first till now. They are forty-seven in number, and are combined so as to form words according to the object, and according to circumstances (of time or place): there are other forms (inflexions) used. This alphabet has spread in different directions and formed diverse branches, according to circumstances; therefore there have been slight modifications in the sounds of the words (spoken language); but in its great features there has been no change. Middle India preserves the original character of the language in its integrity. Here the pronunciation is soft and agreeable, and like the language of the Devas. The pronunciation of the words is clear and pure, and fit as a model for all men. The people of the frontiers have contracted several erroneous modes of pronunciation; for according to the licentious habits of the people, so also will be the corrupt nature of their language... (the young in India are instructed from the age of seven in five sciences (vidya _), of which)... thefirst is called the elucidation of sounds (s'abdavidya_). This treatise explains and illustrates the agreement (concordance) of words, and it provides an index for derivatives." (Beale, Samuel (trans.)(1885). Si-yu-ki. Buddhist Records.)

Hypotheses on Indian vocabulary

The following hypotheses govern the semantic clustering attempted in this lexicon.

It is possible to re-construct a proto-Indian idiom or *lingua franca* of circa the centuries traversed by the Indus valley civilization (c. 2500 to 1700 B.C.).

II. India is a linguistic area nurtured in the cradle of the Indus Valley civilization.

The hypotheses reject two earlier linguistic assertions: (i) Sir William Jones's assertion in 1786 of an Indo-European linguistic family and (ii) Francis Whyte Ellis's assertion in 1816 of a southern Indian family of languages. These two assertions have resulted in two comparative or etymological dictionaries of the so-called 'Indo-Aryan' and 'Dravidian' languages. This cleavage between the two language families is rejected. The exclusion of the so-called Austro-Asiatic or Munda (or Kherwa _ri) languages is also rejected. Instead, it is proposed that there was a proto-Indian linguistic area (c. 2500 B.C.) which included these three language groups. The underlying assumption is that the so-called Dravidian, Munda and Aryan the Western World, by Hsuan Tsang, Vol. 1, Boston). Abu_Raih-a_n al-Biru_ni (973-1048 A.D.): :"The Hindus and their like boast of this copiousness, whilst in reality it is one of the greatest faults of the language. For it is the task of language to give a name to everything in creation and to its effects, a name based on general consent, so that everybody, when hearing this name pronounced by another man, understands what he means. If therefore one and the same name or word means a variety of things, it betrays a defect of the language and compels the hearer to ask the speaker what he means by the word. And thus the word in question must be dropped in order to be replaced either by a similar one of a sufficiently clear meaning, or by an epithet describing what is really meant. If one and the same thing is called by many names, and this is not occasioned by the fact that every tribe or class uses a separate one of them, and if in fact, one single name would be sufficient, all other names save this one are to be classified as mere nonsense, as a means of keeping people in the dark, and throwing an air of mystery about the subject. And in any case this copiousness offers painful difficulties to those who want to learn the whole of the language, for it is entirely useless, and only results in a sheer waste of time... (another reason for the differences between Muslims and Hindus is that)... the (Hindus') language is divided into a neglected vernacular one, only in use among the common people, and a classical one, only in use among the upper and educated classes, which is much cultivated, and subject to the rules of grammatical inflection and etymology, and to all the niceties of grammar and rhetoric..." Sachau, Edward C. (trans.)(1910). Al-Bi_ru_ni's India. An Account of the Religion, Philosophy, Literature, Geography, Chronology, Astronomy, Customs, Laws and Astrology of India, Vols. I-II, London).

Languages can be traced to an ancient Indian family by establishing the unifying elements, in semantic terms. This echoes Pope's observations made in a different context: '... that between the languages of Southern India and those of the Aryan family there are many deeply seated and radical affinities; that the differences between the Dravidian tongues and the Aryan are not so great as between the Celtic (for instance) and the Sanskrit8; 8"The Sanskrit language, whatever may be its antiquity, is of a wonderful structure; more perfect than the Greek, more copious than the Latin, and more exquisitely refined than either, yet bearing to both of them a stronger affinity, both in the roots of a verb and in the forms of grammar, than could possibly have been produced by accident; so strong indeed that no philologer could examine them all three, without believing them to have sprung from some common source, which, perhaps no longer exists; there is a similar reason, though not quite so forcible, for supposing that both the Gothic and the Celtic, though blended with a very different idiom, had the same origin with the Sanskrit; and the old Persian might be added to the same family, if this were the place for discussing any question concerning the antiquities of Persia." (Jones, Sir W., 1786, reprint in Jones 1807, and in Lehmann 1967, pp. 7-20; 'Third Anniversary Discourse' to the Asiatic Society of Bengal).and that, by consequence, the doctrine that the place of the Dravidian dialects is rather with the Aryan than with the Turanian family of languages is still capable of defence... the resemblances (appeared) most frequently in the more uncultivated Dravidian dialects... the identity (was) most striking in the names of instruments, places, and acts connected with a simple life...' (G.U.Pope, Indian Antiquary; loc. cit. R. Swaminatha Aiyar, Dravidian Theories, 1922-23, repr., Delhi, Motilal Banarsidass, 1987, pp.11-12).

Methodology and limitations of the work

The methodology to test the hypotheses will be based on the design of a vocabulary super-set (in semantic terms). The governing principle of this lexicon is that phonetic and grammatical laws are subordinate to semantic laws within a language family. Cognates do not have to be concordant in phonetic and morphological forms; cognates have to be concordant in phonetic and semantic forms to suggest linguistic affinity among dialects of a language family. To quote, Tolka_ppiyam, "ella_c collum porul. kur-ittan-ave (Tol. Col.Peya. 1), i.e. all words are semantic indicators.

The compounded forms of *sememes* of the *lingua franca* of the Indus Valley civilization have been reconstructed from the following sources: * lexical entries of Indian languages found in the comparative, etymological dictionaries: CDIAL (A Comparative Dictionary of Indo-Aryan Languages) and DEDR (A Dravidian Etymological Lexicon); * etymological groups (as semantic super-sets) culled from (a) lists of ancient verb forms such as those found in the dha_tupa_t.ha, Niruktam, Whitney's lexicon, Vedic lexicon; (b) lists of ancient noun forms, such as materia medica found in nighan.t.u's and medical works, annotated with insights frombotanical works, pharmacopoeia and works on pharmacognosy ; (c) epigraphical records of many languages of the region which mainly record economic transactions; and (d) language dictionaries of Indian languages.

This lexicon is organized primarily on a comparative basis and secondarily on a historical basis (and not on a genealogical basis, i.e. not trying to trace the changes in phonetic forms of a sememe.

The vocabulary is presented in groups of etyma taken from CDIAL, DEDR, Tamil and other language lexicons of Dravidian, Aryan and Munda language streams. The etymological groups are put together as semantic cognates and it will be left for future research work to determine the nature of the interactions (or what linguists call, using a pecuniary term: 'borrowing') between and among the languages which constituted the proto-Indian linguistic area. The results of the research are restricted to the identification, in a comparative lexicon, of comparative *sememes* and morphemes, including many allomorphs (i.e. two or more forms of a morpheme). An attempt to conjecture or decipher the possible *proto-Indian* 'phonetic' forms will require further studies and research work. The results of these studies will help for e.g. (1) to eliminate duplicate semantic clusters included in this lexicon and (2) to re-group the clusters in a true syllabic sequence.

anantapa_ram kila s'abdas'a_stram. svalpam tatha_yur bhavas' ca vighna_h- sa_ram.

tato gra_hyam apa_sya phalgu ham.sair yatha_ks.i_ram iva_mbumadhya_t : boundless indeed is the science of language, but life is short and obstacles arenumerous; hence take what is good and leave what is worthless, as geese take ilk from the midst of water (From Pancatantra cf. Otto Boehtling's IndischeSpruche, St. Petersburg, 1870-73 (reprint Osnabruck, 1966), Vol. I, p.45, No.243).

The symbol * is used in etymological dictionaries as a prefix to reconstructions of ancient morphemes; these reconstructions are generally hypothetical, sometimes based on argued laws of 'phonetic change.' 11Each semantic cluster includes a number of words. Vowel sequencing is not rigidly followed for a string of semantic clusters with an initial consonant. Broadly, the sequences (of semantic clusters) are, generally, linked to the initial consonants in the following order: k, c, t, n, p/m/v. Thus, for example, kXc may include kac, ka~c, ka_c, ka~_c, kic, ki_c, kuc etc.vowel/nasal sequences. Choice of Sanskrit or Tamil, for example, for purposes of syllabic sequencing of the semantic clusters may be considered to be arbitrary. This is premised on the belief that it is incorrect to assume that anyone of the present-day languages of India preserves the proto-Indian phonemic structures. In many instances, this order is also ignored to place concordant 'image' clusters close to other semantic clusters or to place, for example c- or t- clusters with concordant meanings. Similarly, since there has been an extraordinary divergence of phonetics among v-, m-, b-, p- words, in many instances, such words are sequenced in close proximity. If an 'image' word (in particular, a word evoking a pictograph from the Indus script) was found only in one of the Indian languages, such a word is treated as a unique semantic cluster and included in the lexicon, even though this author has not been able to locate concordant words in other languages of the family.

For 'alphabetical` indexing or 'areal` (i.e. by geographical regions) sequencing, Turner's A Comparative Dictionary of Indo-Aryan Languages (CDIAL), Burrow and Emeneau's A Dravidian Etymological Lexicon (DEDR), Pali, Sanskrit, Kannada, Tamil, Munda, Santali and other lexicons of Indian languages are unsurpassed sources. DEDR solves the problem of sequencing by using Tamil morphemes as the reference base for the entire group in Tamil syllabic order. In effect, the vocabulary of this lexicon, include many CDIAL and DEDR entries as sub-sets12 and constitute a semantic index to both CDIAL and DEDR which will continue to provide the basic references to areal etyma. The primary justification for choosing a simple sequencing based on a limited number of initial vowels/consonants and consonantal combinations (with intervening vowels or nasals)13 is that each semantic cluster can be treated as a distinct monograph which may provide material for further study of the Indian language family in which there has apparently been an extraordinary semantic affinity between and among related languages. 12This work is dedicated to Pa_n.ini and Tolka_ppiyan-. Pa_n.ini is perhaps the earliest grammarian who created a super-set of morphemes based on phonologicaland morphological rules perceived by him for Sanskrit. The guidelines provided by him for analyzing the structure of a language are of unsurpassed excellence. So are the guidelines contained in the grammatical work of Tolka_ppiyan-, Tolka_ppiyam (of a later era) of great value in any attempt at semanticclustering of areal vocabulary.13The pratya_ha_ra su_tra of Pa_n.ini deals with grammatical symbols orabbreviations; a pratya_ha_ra is formed by taking any efficient letter andjoining it with a non-efficient letter. Such letters are listed in fourteenaphorisms: a i un.; r.lr.k; e on.g; ai auc; ha ya va rat.; lan.;n ma n.a n.a nam; jhabhan; gha d.ha dhas.; ja ba ga d.a das'; kha pha cha t.a tha ca t.a tav; ka pay; s'a s.a sar; hal : these fourteen groups of letters are called s'ivasu_tra_n.i or mahe_s'vara_n.i su_tra_n.i. In the s'ivasu_tras, the long vowels and the anusvara and visarga are omitted. The consonants are arranged in the following order: the aspirate,the semivowels, the nasals, the aspirated soft consonants, the unaspiratedsoft consonants, the aspirated hard consonants, the unaspirated hardconsonants, the sibilants, and the aspirate inserted a second time... The object of the scheme is to devise a plan by which several letters may be designated by a single syllable called a pratya_ha_ra, so that the necessity for naming them severally in a su_tra may be dispensed with. In this list of letters contained in the 14 aphorisms, the non-efficient letters may be identified as: n., k, n. etc. Some interpretations state that ac means all the vowels; hal means all the consonants; jas' means all soft unaspirated consonants; car means all hard unaspirated consonants. The pratya_ha_ras areelaborated into 42 starting rom _n. and ending with s'al.

One substantive problem in organizing the semantic clusters was the problem of 'alphabetical' or 'syllabic' sequencing. It has been difficult to follow a strict alphabetical ordering in this work. This is due to the author's inability to pin down the ancient 'phonetics' of a sememe or to construct a proto-Indian form. This limitation has resulted in some duplication of terms in more than one semantic cluster. The idiosyncratic sequencing14 is due to the limits of knowledge of the author; the result has been a number of semantic clusters included in the lexicon containing phonetic forms which may not always 14The clusters are in the following groups of initial word sounds: a-i-ue- o; k-kh-g-gh; c-ch-j-jh/s-s'-s.;n -n; t-th-d-dh/t.-t.h-d.-d.h; r-l; v-p-ph-b-bh-m. correspond with the etymological grouping.S amuel Johnson refers to a lexicographer as an harmless drudge15. What a pleasant and glorious drudge! An etymologist is also a drudge but may provoke, hopefully lively, linguistic disputes among the proponents of dialects of a language family, on issues such as 'true inheritance' or 'great antiquity'16! he disputes (or positive creative tensions), may also draw inspiration and guidance from the past linguistic studies of great scholars who have provided valuable insights into the phonological, grammatical and lexical aspects of a proto-Indian language family.

An English semantic index has been included. The index is composed of (i) English meanings, and (ii) flora (names of botanical species in Latin terms), plants and products of plants (in English and vernacular terms which have entered the English lexicon). As in DEDR, no attempt has been made to state the equivalence of Latin flora terms; DEDR entries in a group of etyma record the equivalence found in Hooker at the end of the numbered etymological group. The index is primarily based on the elegantly designed index of A Dravidian Etymological Lexicon (DEDR). To quote from DEDR: (p.773) "This is an index of the more important meanings recorded for words in the Dravidian languages. No attempt has been made to list all the English meanings given in the entries, since such a procedure would have swollen this index beyond all reason. In fact, in any attempt to keep it within bounds, usually only one of a group of synonyms or near-synonyms has been listed: e.g. *resemble* is listed, but not *similar* and *like*... The derivational system of English words, since it does not coincide with that of Dravidian, has in general been ignored..."

Organization of the work

The dominance of economic activities in the lives of ancient Indians will 15Given the limitations of linguistic competence of the author, this lexicon has taken over five years of the author's life, working on a powerful personal computer system, averaging about 4 hours daily -- a challenging drudgery. This work might, perhaps, have taken more than one lifetime, without the use of computer technology. The technology proved to be an efficient tool to sort and re-sort the text entries and to perform thousands of iterations in creating the semantic clusters.

The ancient economic court was dominated by plant products such as fragrances, incenses and exudations which were highly valued and in great demand. For example, the ancient Egyptian civilization records trans-continental expeditions18 to pw'nt (or punt) in search of such plant products which may be designated as Kube_ra's nava-nidhi or nine treasures of Kube_ra, in the yaks.atradition of great antiquity.

The inclusion of names of many plants and plant products in the lexicon, has a strong justification in terms of ancient life-styles. The etyma related to plants have been elaborated with cross-references on therapeutic effects described in works dealing with the subject of pharmacognosy and, in some instances, the references in pharmacopoeia of various countries have also been provided.

Plants and plant products (gums, gum-resins, fragrances, incenses, plant exudations, bark, in particular) had an extraordinary place in the cultural processes of ancient civilizations (particularly in the Indian linguistic area, in the ancient Egyptian civilization and in the Biblical areas), including for example, the depiction of the so-called nine treasures of Kube_ra, all of which may relate to plant products. (i) The existence of many nighan.t.us principally devoted to materia medica of the ancient medical systems and (ii) the archaeological finds of viha_ras such as the Ajanta and Ellora caves which might have been used by medicine-men and to stock plant products justify further studies on the economic importance of plant products in cultural history.

Vedic soma was comparable in economic importance to the plants and plant products. In an extraordinary process described eloquently in Vedic chants, 17"... language in the concrete sense... is... the sum of words and phrases by which any man expresses his thought." (Whitney, William D., Oriental and Linguistic Studies, New York, 1874, p. 372 cited in: Chomsky Current Issues in Linguistic Theory, The Hague, 1964, p. 22). 18"In year 8 of Sankhkare Mentuhotpe (2009-1998 B.C.) ... an expedition of 3,000 men, recruited from Upper Egypt and led by the Chief Steward Henenu, left the Nile valley near Kopptos and headed east across the desert towards the Red Sea, 90 miles away. Their orders were to re-establish commerce by sea with the fabulously rich land of Punt... unvisited by Egyptians since the days of the Sixth Dynasty... voyages to Byblos and Punt seem to be regular in the Sixth Dynasty (2345-2181 B.C.)... with references to building ships for an expedition to Punt... in the Twelfth Dynasty (1991-1786 B.C.), ships sailed southward from Red Sea ports to the incense-land of Punt... " (E.S. Edwards et al (eds.), The Cambridge Ancient History, Vol. I, Pt. 2, 1971, Cambridge, University Press, p. 491; p.183; p.194; p.495).

soma was purchased, and went through a process kept secret from the seller. Soma was washed in water (yad-adbhih paris.ichyase mr.jyama_no gabhastyoh- : RV.ix.65.6), then pounded either with stone or in a mortar (RV. 1.83.6; RV.1.28.4); it had am.s'u (RV. ix.67.28); it yielded andhas, rasa, pitu, pi_yu_s.a oramr.ta; it was purifed through a strainer (antah- pavitra a_ hitah- : RV. ix.12.5). It was not 'drunk' by mortals. Soma was the product of an activity using intense fire, and involving the participation of the entire household for days and nights. Soma was wealth. The dawn of urbanization and transition from agrarian economy to an economy dominated by artisans, are vividly reconstructed from the archaeological finds of the Indus Valley civilization which may also be called the Sarasvati_civilization. A pen picture with exquisite photographs is provided in the Age of God-Kings:"About 2500 BC, a people of unknown origin started constructing a series of cities as remarkable as any the world had yet seen. Artisans set to work, trade flourished and a system of writing evolved. At its apogee, the Indus civilization encompassed nearly 1.3 million square kilometers; its boundaries stretched from the foothills of the Himalayas to the Arabian Sea and from the Ganges watershed to the Gulf of Bombay, just to the north of what is now Bombay. It was the largest cultural domain of its era... This people also perfected the art of casting objects in bronze, a breakthrough in technology that ranks among humankind's greatest early achievements... The pictographic script of the Indus people has not yet been successfully deciphered. The Southeast Asian rice farmers seem not to have developed a system of writing... the Indus people... built grand cities, centers of production and trade... One of these cities... Harappa... around 2300 BC, Harappa was home to 35,000 people... Another great city took shape 550 kilometers to the south, on the lower Indus... Mohenjo-Daro -- 'Hill of the Dead' in Sindhi... Two gateways provided access through the wall. Within the citadel were assembly halls, administrative offices and a number of residences for various officials and functionaries. Only an enormous collective effort could have created these two great urban centers of the Indus culture... The huge complexes at Mohenjo-Daro and Harappa that are believed to be municipal granaries covered thousand upon thousand of square meters. They had raised brick floors... and strong, timbered roofs to protect against the weather. The apparent threshing areas nearby were paved in brick and included circular pits where workers pounded the kernels with wooden staves to remove the husks from the grain... The harvest was probably a state monopoly, and the granaries served, in effect, as state treasuries... They were the world's first people to grow cotton and to weave its fibre into textiles... Trading posts were established far beyond the valley's fringes. The Indus people founded a settlement at Sutkagen Dor, west of Baluchistan and within reach of the Persian Gulf. To the south of the valley, a large seaport took shape at Lothal on the Gulf of Cambay... From Lothal, high-prowed, double-ended sailing vessels carried the gold, gems and timber products of southern India along the coast to the Indus Valley and beyond. The richest trade route from the valley lay to the west, through the Persian Gulf to Mesopotamia. Starting about 2350 BC, traffic with the urban centers of Sumer and Akkad expanded to become a prime source of revenue... Merchants used sets of cubical stone weights that never varied in value throughout the Indus region. The basic unit was 16, equal to 14 grams. The larger weights were multiples of 16 -- 32,64,128, and so on up to 12,800 (11 kilograms); the smaller ones were all fractions of 16... The Indus merchants, like their Sumerian counterparts, developed a method of record keeping and used carved stone seals to stamp their property. Every mercantile family had its own device, and probably every important citizen did also. More than 2,000 examples have been found in the Indus cities, and others have turned up in Mesopotamia, left there by overseas traders... One popular motif appears to have been a unicorn sniffing at an incense burner. The unicorn is probably a bull in profile, so that one horn hides the other. But why the creature has been offered incense is a puzzlement. In a seal from Mohenjo-Daro, both the unicorn and the incense brazier are being carried aloft in some kind of procession... the Indus tongue is lost in antiquity and none of the signs (on seals) corresponds to any used by the Egyptians or Sumerians. The seal inscriptions are brief -- one or two lines... The Indus people left no surviving histories, no religious texts, no literary epics... (Harappan merchants used the seals as a kind of trademark impressing them on clay tags to label their goods)... after each catastrophe (earthquake or flood), the citizens picked up their lives again. Some sections of Mohenjo-Daro were rebuilt as many as eight times. In each reconstruction, the architects re-created the previous construction virtually brick for brick... Sometime during the nineteenth century BC, however, the Indus cities began to slip into permanent decline... Scribes in Mesopotamia recorded rich shipments from the Indus Valley until around 1800 BC, when they suddenly ceased... The urban heritage was passed on to the east... somber notes of Harappan ideology would continue to reverberate through the coming centuries." (The Age of God-kings, 3000-1500 B.C., Amsterdam, Time-Life Books, 1991, pp.129-141).

Archaeology and Language

One approach suggested by Colin Renfrew is a correlation, however hypothetically, of language changes with demographic and social changes recorded by archaeology. Decipherment of the script is important to bring the civilization within the bounds of history, and to establish that the civilization should not remain categorized as 'prehistoric'. For, 'prehistoric' would mean 'prior to the use of writing.' (cf. Colin Renfrew, Archaeology and Language: the Puzzle of Indo-European Origins, Penguin Books, 1987, p.2). If this lexicon has established that the Indian language family had closely related members, it should be reasonable to hypothesize that the Indus Script was related to one or more dialects of this language, though there is no direct evidence to prove precisely which language was spoken between 2500 to 1700 B.C. in the region traversed by this civilization. "... (Archaeology) is beginning to interest itself in the ideology of early communities: their religions, the way they expressed rank, status and group identity. The question of language is important here... modern linguistics and current processual archaeology offer the opportunity for a new synthesis... (Indus Valley Civilization) was a literate civilization... some four hundred signs were found, fifty-three of them used commonly... this suggests that it must be a mixed hieroglyphic and syllabic script rather than a pure syllabic script like Minoan Linear B... not enough (signs) for a true pictographic script like that of the Egyptian hieroglyphs or the Chinese script... are the Indus Valley sealstone inscriptions in an early form of Indo-European?.

There is no inherent reason why the people of the Indus Valley Civilization should not already have been speaking an Indo-European language, the ancestor of the Rigveda...

Hypothesis A, then, would carry the history of the Indo-European languages in north India and Iran back to the early neolithic period in those areas... (Hypothesis B) outlines an alternative... which accepts the likelihood of local farming origins... (and) a process ofe' lite dominance... by wellorganized and mobile tribal groups, with a chiefdom organization... while we cannot expect to find direct evidence in the archaeological record for a specific prehistoric language or language group, we can indeed study processes or demographic and social change. It is these processes of change which we may seek, however hypothetically, to correlate with language change in those areas... it is perfectly possible that the languages used in the Indus Valley civilization as early as 3000 BC were already Indo-European... We are talking here of simple peasant farmers, with a restricted range of domestic plants and animals and a limited range of crafts. These may generally have included weaving and pottery-making and other farming skills, but theirs were egalitarian societies... 'segmentary societies,' laying stress on the almost autonomous nature of individual village or neighborhood communities. Naturally there were links and marriage exchanges between these... three issues now remain that we should look at: language origins, language dispersals, and the relationship between archaeology and linguistic studies... " (Colin Renfrew, op cit., pp. 5,7, 183-185, 190-191, 197, 205, 264. 271, 73).

One approach to study *changes* in languages is to cluster the dialects of a language together. Such a clustering is attempted in this lexicon. These clusters provide the basis for further studies to correlate the *changes* in languages with the socio-economic changes established through archaeology.

Language and Script

An attempt to link the Indus Script to the Indian etyma, is a search for Indian linguistic roots. It is, in effect, a search for words which are 'as old as time`. Many scripts of the current Indian languages are syllabic in structure. It is notable that Tamil, in particular, utilizes a remarkably compact alphabet (syllabary derived via grantha forms from the Bra_hmi_script); for example, the script symbol for the syllable, ka connotes a phonetic spectrum of ka, kha,ga and gha. The use of a limited number of script symbols for syllables is perhaps an indication that, even if the phoneme (for a given morpheme) had a ka, kha, ga or gha, the semantic content remained unaltered. This extraordinary economy (yet, diversity) in script form is, therefore, an indication that for effective linguistic communication of a message, phonetic formants19 are subordinate to 19In phonetics, formants refer to banks of energy generated by an acoustic pattern and measured in cycles per second (cps);... formants are specified by their frequency and relative intensity... vowel formants, for example bend upwards, that is, they increase in frequency, before they reach their steady positions after a specific duration (of about a tenth of a second when the sound retains its plosive character)... changes of this kind in vowel the semantic structure of morphemes.20

Many ancient scripts were evolved on the principle of 'ideographs', i.e. depicting a word as an image (logo, on a seal, for example) using a homophone (i.e. a similar sounding word). The importance of 'images' in formulating 'meaning' (in neuronal structures) or for designing 'scripts', is paralleled formants are known as 'transitions'... for example, the explosion of (p) does not sound like that of (t)... its energy is distributed fairly evenly over all frequencies, whereas (t) has most energy between 2,000 and 4,000 cps if the following vowel is rounded, or between 3,500 and 6,000 cps if it is not rounded... for (d), for instance, this transition will always be related to a frequency of about 1,800 cps... (J. D. O'Connor, Phonetics, Pelican Books, 1973, pp. 87-90).

Some notes on phonetics and semantics

An ancient consonant: -mb- may explain the transition from -mb- to -m- or -b-/-bh- or -v-/-p- in many etyma.Possibly, the ancient consonant in many etyma was a compound consonant: tc- or ts-. In two linguistic streams, the accent oscillates between s-/c- and t-;cf. tagori, cakra potter's wheel. t- is preferred when the -c- intervenes in the following syllable as in tai-, teccu- (sewing) (Ta.) To smoothen the phonetic structure, -c- is either replaced by -d- or omitted, in semantic extensions, as in (cu_ci = u_ci =) su_di needle (Nk.); su_i_tailor (WPah.). Many etyma are notable with perhaps another compound consonant: ss'-, which, in two linguistic streams, evidences two phonetic transforms: > h-, > k-. ku sign of the dative case; connective particle as in ar.ikuve _ n; suffix added to verbs, nouns, etc., to form (a) abstract nouns, as in nanku; (b) verbal nouns, as po _ kku; finite verbs in 1st pers. sing. fut., as un.ku; prefix added to words in Sanskrit, as in kutar-k-kam, signifying badness, evil, unfairness; earth (Ta.lex.) gan.d.e, gen.d.iya, ken.t.ai carp (DEDR 1947) > kayal carp (DEDR 1252) This concordance (and possible phonetic change) finds a remarkable parallel in the homonymous etyma: 'ladle, spoon'. gen.t.e spoon, ladle (Te.)(DEDR 1267) > kailuladle, spoon (Tu.); kayyil id.(Ma.); ki_li ladle (Kurub.)(DEDR 1257).

A transposition of initial syllables ne_-/ve_-, ne-/ve- occurs in many etyma;for example, in one linguistic stream, for semant. 'weaving' syllable ve_-occurs; and in another, semant. 'weaving' syllable ne_- occurs: the actionsrelate to twisting and plaiting of cane (net.ru S.) or bamboo (ve_l.a Pali);[cf.ve_y (-v-, -nt-) to thatch (Ta.)(DEDR 5532)]; negad.u is a polypus thatentangles swimmers (Te.), vehar. is an octopus of the Ganges (P.)}.by a distinct semantic structural feature of Santali language in which words are not uniquely marked for specific functions such as noun or verb but most stems of words are multifunctional. There is no grammatical gender for nouns which may be lexically marked (using for example, herel for male; maejiu for female). There are no formal marks for grammatical class, a word can perform various functions: as noun, as adjective or as verb. In Santali, every stem or root (sememe) is potentially a verb. Qualifiers can be constructed by simply adding -n for e.g. kad.awa.n hor. a man who has buffaloes. (George L. Campbell, Compendium of the World's Languages, Routledge, London, 1991, p. 1199)21. "In Santali, any word may (in theory at least) be used as a verb simply by adding a, which is the verbal sign, and other signs to signify tense, mood etc. The a alone signifies the general or future tense in the active voice -- used to make general statements, or statements referring to the future... The verb generally comes at the end of a sentence or phrase... (Santali language) consists of rootwords and various infixes, suffixes and particles, joined together or agglutinated in such a way as to form phrases and sentences... dalgot'kedeae... dal the root word, meaning to strike or striking; got' an adverbial particle giving the sense of quickly or suddenly; ked the sign ket', denoting the past tense of the active voice, modified to ked... e ... signifying an animate object -- him, or her... a the verbal sign, showing that the idea of striking is used verbally; e the short form of the 3rd personal pronoun, singular... denoting the subject -- he, or she." (R.M. Macphail, An Introduction to Santali, 1953, p.2). Taking into account, this historical factor which governed the evolution of alphabets and the important part played by 'root word'22 in Santali (a member of the ancient Indian family of languages) this lexicon attempts to identify 'sememes' and also provide an aid to epigraphists or scholars interested in deciphering the Indus script. For this purpose (and based on the assumption that the Indus script may be related 21There is a concordant rule in Pa _n.ini: s'iva_dis'yo_n. (s'iva-a_dis'yah-, an.); avr.ddhas'yo_nadi_ma_nus.ibhyastanna_mika_jyah- (Bk. IV. Ch. I.112, 113), i.e. the affix or patronymic an. comes in the sense of a descendant, after the words s'iva etc.; the affix an. comes in the sense of a descent, after words which are the names of rivers, or women, when such words are not vriddham words; and when they are used as names and not as adjectives. Another set of aphorisms deals with 'collection': tasya samu _ hah-; bhiks.a_dis'yo_n. (Bk. IV. Ch. I.37, 38): an ffix is added to a word, when the sense is 'a collection thereof'; the affixan. comes, in the sense of 'collection thereof', after the words bhiks.a_(alms)etc. The affixes an. and an come after the words sindhu and apakara in the sense of 'produced therein' ajanau ca (Bk. IV. Ch. III.33).

For Sanskrit, the definition given by Pa_n.ini is : bhu_va_dayo_dha_tavah(Bk. I, Ch. III.1) i.e. the words beginning with bhu_'to become' and denoting action, are called dha_tu or verbal roots; ten classes identified by Sanskrit grammarians of such action verbs (about 2,000) are: bhu_, ad, hu, div, su, tud,rudh, tan, kri_, chur; this classification is based on modifications seen in these roots before specific terminations (parasmaipada or a_tmane_pada or both).

Dha_tu is a morpheme which may antedate Pa_n.ini and connotes a morphemeexpressing action, analogous to the Santali language tradition.to the Indian language family), many semantic clusters in this lexiconinclude, what are titled as, 'image' words, i.e. word forms which could havebeen represented graphically, as in the symbols and signs used in the as-yetundeciphered Indus script23. Such 'image' clusters are sequenced close23Of an unknown language! In dealing with an unknown language, twoinventories have to be made: a phonemic inventory and a semantic inventory andboth these inventories have to be presented in semantic clusters... In thislexicon, considering the distribution of sounds in words within a clustercontaining the same meaning, it may be noted that though different phoneticpreferences (for example: l or n; m or v; sa or ka; t.a or ta) occur indifferent members of the language family, they represent the same phoneme.Similarly, speakers of a given language of the Indian family have their own ideas on what constitutes a syllable (phoneme sequence). These ideas may differ from the ideas of speakers of other languages who may break the same sequence into two or three syllables. After all, society shapes language; and, language is a reflection of the society that shapes it. Semantic clustering may, therefore, be considered a linguistic technique which attempts to reconstruct the images of life-activities of a society. to the other substantive clusters which are related to life-activities of ancient civilizations as evidenced by archaeological finds and artifacts. The titles provided to many semantic clusters with the prefix 'image' refer to a number of images provided by the pictographs and signs of the seals and tablets containing Indus script. Such pictographs and signs will be clustered to aid those interested in deciphering the script. At this stage of the author's knowledge, it has not been possible to include some thoughts on 'alternative interpretations' of these 'ideographs' of the Indus script. A separate monograph will be presented providing an approach to breaking the deadlock of the decipherment problem. A start can be made assuming that each pictograph is a homonym (i.e. an image of a similar sounding 'substantive' word). Many 'substantives' are indeed based on the economic activities of an evolving civilization.

On the problem of the Indus Script, it is important to refer to one message on a sealing from Umma, since no bilingual script messages have so far been found: "...an imprint of (indus) seal upon the fragment of a clay label from a bale of cloth had also been published by Father Scheil (Revue d'Assyriologie, Vol. 22: 56), and this was said to come from the site of Umma, the neighbor city of Lagash...No.1. First among the seals discovered at Ur (in 1923) is the unique object ...in the British Museum...On the face stands, below, the figure of a bull with head bent down...the inscription...is in archaic cuneiform writing...of a period before 2500 B.C. There are three signs and very probably traces of a fourth, almost obliterated; the three preserved are themselves scratchy and rather worn, though not ill-formed. Hence their reading is doubtful--the choices are, for the first SAG(K) or KA, for the second KU or possibly LU, while the third is almost certainly S' I, and the fourth, it existed at all, is quite uncertain...using the commonest values of the signs, sak-ku-s'i--(with possible loss of something at the end) may be pronounced the best provisional reading...It does not, at least, seem to be any Sumerian or Akkadian name...(the seal is) probably, a product of some place under the influence both of Indus and of the Sumerian civilizations." (Gadd, 1932, pp.3-32.)

Adding an assumed syllable TU at the end, the value of the message reads: sakku-s'i-tu.

Hunter noted that three round seals with Harappan characters found in Mesopotamia may not be in Harappan language since there were marked differences in the sequence of letters. (Hunter, 1932, p.469.) Analogously, an Indus-type seal (squarish with a perforated button on the ridged back) with cuneiform characters may be surmised to relate to a non-Harappan language. The non-Harappan origin is surmised for a glazed steatite cylinder seal found at Tell Asmar, which shows an Indus motif: procession of an elephant, a rhinoceros and a crocodile.(Frankfort, 1933, pp.50-53; Asthana, 1979, p.40.) Ur III texts indicate the need for interpreters to translate the Meluhhan language. sak means 'head'. kusi_ tu is a 'king's garment' of the "Neo-Assyrian kings similar to those worn by images of the gods." (Oppenheim, 1964, p.98.) It is unclear if the s in the word should be pronounced s'. The semantic content of the entire message in archaic cuneiform script may be given the value: king's [head] garment. An alternative interpretation may be that, the kus'itu was a money-lender (cf. Vedic.lex.) ?sak = ?saha partner?24 sak meant probably, a principal (trading partner) in relation to an agent. Or, it could be sag, an archaic form of san.gha or society. Could the inscription mean : sag kos'a or the treasury of the society? These are tentative interpretations which will have to be further validated by an evaluation of the entire (though, very limited -- only a few thousands) sample of messages without committing what Gilbert Ryle calls a 'category mistake25.' An approach to a resolution of the decipherment problem will be sha_h a rich merchant, one who lends money on interest; a banker, a shopkeepeer, a trader; a king; a title assumed by faqirs; the principal in relation with an agent; sha_h, guma_shta_an affix to the names of Sayyads; sha_hdara_ the name of a village on the bank of the Ravi near Lahore containing the magnificent mausoleum of the Emperor Jahangir; sha_ hra_h a principal street, a public road; sha_h maksadi_a kind of marble from Yusufzai; sha_h nashin. A projecting platform erected on the roof of a house to sit on; sha _h bin. patnahin., guru_bin. gat nahin. no honour (credit) without banker, no salvation without a Guru; shahir a city; shahir pana_h the city walls; sa_hu_ka_r a great merchant, a rich person, a banker, a money-lender; honest, respectable; sa_huka_ra_the business of a sa_hu_ka_r, a banking and money business (P.lex.)

Ryle, the Oxford philosopher, expounds on the category mistake in contrasting the concepts of 'brain' and 'mind'. What socio-economic category do the Indus Script messages indicate? Are they names? Are they professional titles? Are they marriage badges with inscribed lists of presents? Are they deeds for transfer of landed property? Are they receipts for property stored in granaries? Are they commodities and their measures? Are they gum-resins? Are they grains, other plant products and their measures? Are they toll-stamps used by toll-collectors at ferries? Are they announcing ownership of property attempted in a separate monograph, using, mainly, the semantic and image clusters of this lexicon.

Semantics and Poets' search for the supreme language

To aid researchers in linguistics and neuro-scientists interested in the study of brain functions related to linguistic competence, some principal sememes of items like boats? Are they proof of duties paid to the temple? Are they bills of lading?]

ancient speech26 are listed in separate annexes of this lexicon. This is consistent with the principal focus of this lexicon which is to: cluster together word forms with comparable semantic content and establish the essential semantic unity among the Indian languages. In this process of semantic clustering, attention is paid to concordant phonetic forms. In evaluating the development of pronunciation and sense of words of the languages of the Indian linguistic area, an effort has been made to avoid duplicating the functions of lexicography. The focus is on 'meaning' of words,27 extensions of meaning and on phonetic transforms cognate with the basic words. Lexicographers have attempted to define the phonetic structure of a morpheme in a language, with care and integrity, given the constraints of the phonetic symbols used for the script of the chosen language. This lexicon proceeds on the assumption that the language lexicons which are its source books, are based on painstaking social surveys and provide a commonly accepted form (i.e. through social contract) of the phonetic variants of various dialects of any

anupa _ sita-vr.ddha _ na_m. vidya_na_tiprasi_dati : the Goddess of Learning does not smile on those who neglect the ancients (Bharttr.hari, Va_kyapadi_ya ii.493).

Tolka _ppiyam offers some words of caution while discussing a class ofwords called 'free morphemes' (uri-c-col)[as distinct from 'bound morpheme'(it.ai-c-col)]. These words of caution should be heeded by etymologists! porut.kup porul. teriyin- atuvaram pin-r-e_; porut.kut tiripillai un.arnta vallin; un.arcciva_yil un.arvo_r valitte_; mor. .ipporul. ka_ran.am vir. .ipput to_n-r-a_; er. .uttuppirinticaittal ivan.iyalpu in-r-e_: Tol. Col. 385-9, i.e. there will be no limit if one tries to know the meaning of the meaning; the meaning will not get confused if the listener gets the sense of the speaker; the meaning depends on the strength of the feelings conveyed; the origin of the meaning of a word is never certain; it is not in the nature of this morpheme to be divided into meaningful units. Such 'free morphemes' include: mannostalgia, wonder and irony; til great desire, time and implied meaning; konfear,uselessness, time and greatness; tancam easiness; el luminosity; empty morphs such as ya _,

ka_, pir-a, pir-akku, aro_. cf. On nouns (peyariyal): porun.mai teritalum con-maiteritalum collin- a_kum en-man-a_r pulavar; teripuve_r-u nilaiyalum kur-ippil to_n-ralumirupa_r-r-u en-pa porun.mai nilaiye_: Tol. Col. 153-4, i.e. scholars tell usthat words reveal the object that is indicated and their grammatical form; it is said that meaning is indicated directly and by suggestion.one language. Since the focus is on semantics, the author has exercised a degree of freedom to coalesce the phonetic variations and as necessary, repeated some etyma in more than one semantic cluster. Speakers of every language and poets, in particular, of every language do possess enormous degrees of freedom for verbal creativity to anchor life experiences, but subject to the social contract on *sememes* or the 'meaning' of morphemes used in inter-personal verbal or written communication. Take for instance, the rules of Sanskrit language, codified by the linguisticgenius, Pa_n.ini and obeyed through literary media for over a millennium. Pa_n.ini's phonological and morphological canons are hypostatized (attributed real identities to a concept) aphorisms. Pa_n.ini was held in such awe that later

linguists would not refer to what Pa_n.ini 'says' but use the verb 'pas'yati'referring to his aphorisms [i.e. referring to what Pa_n.ini 'sees', as a r.s.i orseer]. Pa_n.ini opposes the bha_s.a_, defined by him in an archaic chandah-(cf. S.Le'vi, J.A., 1891, II, p. 549; Me`moires de la Socie'te de Linguistic de Paris,XVI, p.278-279; loc. cit. Bloch, The Formation of the Mara_t.hi_Language, 1914,p.3). "... in the enumeration of Bharata (XVII, 48): ma_gadhyavantija_pra_cya_su_ryasenyardhama_gadhi_ba_hli_ka_da_ks.in.a_tya_ca sapta ha_s.a_h- praki_rtita_h-" six out ofseven are geographically determinable and three out of these four (ma_gadhi, s'auraseni_, maha_ra_s.t.ri) are mentioned by Vararuci. Later on Dan.d.in adds to these three La_t.i_'and similar other ones' (Ka_vya_dars'a, I,35)... Later on Vararuci situates the Pais'a_ci_on the same level as the three great Pra_krts with ageographical name... the language of braj is used for the cycle of Kr.s.n.a, thatof Bundelkhand for that of A_lha_-u_dal, that of Avadha for that of Ra_ma and generally speaking for the Epic... No region of India has imposed its language on the entire country... within each dialect there is a large quantity ofwords or series of words which have had a history independent of the dialects where they have been found in use. This history, which can be established with some difficulty even in the case of well-known languages as those of Europe,is altogether impossible, at least provisionally, in India... " (Bloch, op cit., pp. 11-12; p.45). In making bold to attempt this 'impossible' task through semantics, one dominant structural characteristic of the Indian language family can be noted with confidence: the use of 'echo words' identified as such in this lexicon. (Pa _ n.ini calls such words a _mred.ita orrepeated : Bk. VIII. Ch. 1.2). The endency to repeat words or with fine initial consonantal variations is a characteristic that runs across the entire family of languages, a characteristic that was also noted by Vararuci. The ancient linguists tried to delineate this 'refined' language as the 'perfect' language (whether divinely inspired smr.ti remembered or s'ruti heard); yet, the spoken word was governed by the inexorable laws of neurosciences and social contract -- as evidenced by the Pra _kr.ts (original or natural forms) which did ot obey these 'rules' of the grammarian though adored by the linguists. The ra_kr.ts (including Pali) continued to diverge from the 'perfection' of Sanskrit and were socio-linguistically accepted in Sanskrit drama in the early centuries of the Christian era, though not spoken by gods or heroes in the dramas, but only by the proletariat! Women sang in Maha _ra_s.t.ri_pra_kr.t, spoke inxxxiS'auraseni pra_kr.t and people in the lower rungs of the social ladder spoke ma_gadhi_pra_kr.t. Many pra_kr.ts were written in Kharo_s.t.hi script. Buddha (c. sixthcentury B.C.) perhaps preached in ardhama_gadhi_pra_kr.t (Pali), written in Bra_hmi_script. Mun.d.a_ri_and Santali (grouped as Kherwari or Austro-Asiatic)perhaps ante-date the Indo-European or the so-called Dravidian linguistic presence in India. The Indian language family also includes Gypsy (Romany; gypsy ~~ Egyptian; ethonym: roma). Gypsies popularly believed to have come from Egypt, emigrated from India towards the end of the first millennium A.D. via Iran into Anatolia, South Russia, and the Balkans, to reach western Europeby the fifteenth century, Britain by the sixteenth; via Iran, Syria and the Mediterranean into north Africa and the Iberian peninsula. (George L. Campbell, Compendium of the World's Languages, Routledge, London, 1991, p.1164).Ya_ska (6th-4th c. B.C.), Pa_n.ini 5th c. B.C.), Ka_tya_yana (3rd c. B.C.), Patanjali (c. 150 B.C.) have laid the foundations of anskrit etymology andgrammar. The su_tras of Pa_n.ini analyze Sanskrit into a system of roots, stems and suffixes.Ka_tya_yana's va_rttikas explain, criticize and supplement these rules. Patanjali's bha_s.ya explains the rules of Pa_n.ini and Ka_tya_yana and is often severelycritical of the latter. Kaiyat.a commends Patanjali of the three since he has observed more numbers of actual forms : (II.4.26) munidvaya_c ca bha_s.ayaka_rahprama_n.ataram adhikalaks.yadars'itva_t : the author of the commentary (i.e. Patanjali) has greater authority than the other two sages because he has observedmore linguistic usage. Grammatical rules were formulated, perhaps, for thebenefit of 'immigrants' or as teaching aids to students of a language. In this process of delineating grammatical rules, the phonetic and morphological structures of each of the Indian languages were codified and frozen as 'rules' of the language. (cf. the example of Tolka _ ppiyam for Tamil or As.t.a_dhya_yi forSanskrit). Pa_n.ini also called Gonadri_ya/ Gonika_putra) is perhaps the oldest grammarian of the world. After salutation to the supreme spirit, o _m parama_tmane namah-, the great work is invoked by Pa_n.ini as: atha s'abda_nus'a_sanam, i.e. now an explanatorysystem for words or a dissertation on the science (grammar and philology) of words. His As.t.a_dhya_yi (lit. 8 chapters with 3,996 mnemonic su_tras) and later critical evaluation/defence by Patanjali (also called, Da_ks.i_putra in his Maha_bha_s.ya or Great Prose Work) countering Ka_tya_yana's criticismin the Va_rttika_s (explanatory tracts of words) are unsurpassed ancient linguistic explorations into the etyma of and rules governing the Sanskrit language. Pa_n.ini traces with stunning precision and scholarly excellence, the individual phonetic and morphological changes throughout the language which may be called a language that spanned both Vedic and Classical Sanskrit. (For a good survey of works on Pa_n.ini.

Was there an ancient Aindra school of grammar? Taittiri_ya-sam.hita_6.4.7 connects Indra to the origin of grammar: "Speech indeed spoke formerly without manifestation (avya_kr.ta). The gods said to Indra: 'do manifest this speech for us'... Indra approaching it from the middle made it manifest (avya _kr.t).Therefore speech is manifest (vya_kr.ta)" : [From Patanjali's introduction to the Maha_bha_s.ya, quoted in Staal, J.F., "Sanskrit Philosophy of Language", Current Trends in Linguistics, 5, pp. 499-531, 1969].

"The Sanskrit is above all things an analyzable language, one admitting of the easy and distinct separation of ending from stem, and of derivative suffix from primitive word, back to the ultimate attainable elements, the socalled roots. Accordingly, in its perfected form (for all the preparatory stages are unknown to us), the Hindu grammar offers us an established body of roots, with rules for their conversion into stems and for the inflection of the latter, and also for the accompanying phonetic changes--this last involving and resting upon a phonetic science of extraordinary merit, which has called forth the highest admiration of modern scholars; nothing at all approaching it has been produced by any ancient people; it has served as the foundation in no small degree of our own phonetics; even as our science of grammar and of language has borrowed much from India... actually more than half (of the roots listed in Pa _n.ini)-- never have been met with, and never will be met with, in the Sanskrit literature of any age... Beyond allquestion, a certain number of cases are to be allowed for, of real roots, proved such by the occurrence of their evident cognates in other related languages, and chancing not to appear in the known literature; but they can go only a very small way indeed toward accounting for the eleven hundred unauthenticated roots... The skilled students of the native grammar, as it seems to me, have been looking at their task from the wrong point of view, and laboring in the wrong direction. They have been trying to put the non-existent grammarians' dialect in the place of the genuine Sanskrit..." (Whitney, William Dwight, "The Study of Hindu Grammar and the Study of Sanskrit", American Journal of Philology, 5, pp. 279-297, 1884).

Cf. George Cardona, Pa_n.ini : A Survey of Research, 1976; for an excellent reader on the Sanskrit grammarians, cf. Stall, J.F. (ed.), A Reader on the SanskritGrammarians, Cambridge, M.I.T. Press, 1972). It would be inappropriate to call Pa_n.ini's Sanskrit brahminical or Aryan; for he notes (Ch. VI, 62,58) that there were non-Aryan brahmins as well! The contributions made by ancientIndian linguists are echoes of the oral tradition of padapa_t.has (i.e. the word texts which give every word of the sam.hita_31 free from euphonic combinations and analyze compounds into their component morphemes) of the Vedic chants which are as old as civilization. There are other linguistic tracts, in particular in the so-called Dravidian family of languages and in the socalled Austro-Asiatic family of languages (exemplified in India by Mundarica and Santali languages), which preserve the echoes of the ancient speech which sustained ancient civilizations such as the Indus Valley civilization. Ya_ska is perhaps the first etymologist of the world. His Nirukta treats etymology as a complement of grammar (tad idam vidya_-stha_nam vya_karan.asya ka_rtsnyam : N. i.15) and is a principal aid to understanding Vedic texts. Ya_ska defines sam.hita_as the closest conjunction (of original words) by means of euphonic combination or as based on original words. In the padapa _t.ha,i.e. word-for-word analysis, the sandhi is dissolved; each pra_tis'a_khya foreach branch of the Veda specifies how the sam.hita_must be derived from thecorpus of utterances in continuous text. Thus Ya_ska provides an etymological complement to the word-for-word analysis. According to Ya_ska, grammatical rules are not universal; too much importance should not be attached to the grammatical form because, the complex formations (vr.ttayah-) have many exceptions; he is a bold etymologist who derives is.t.i(sacrifice) from □yaj (to sacrifice) based on the meanings of words in thecontext of their use. His principal rule is direct: 'If their meanings are thesame, their etymologies should be the same, if the meanings are different, theetymologies should also be different (N. ii.7); 'words are used to designate objects with regard to everyday affairs in the world, on account of their comprehensiveness and minuteness

(N. i.2)[Durga, the commentator, explains 'comprehensiveness' as a psychological process (manifest and unmanifest states of consciousness) to apprehend meaning through the instrumentality of the spoken word; the process is elaborated: manifest consciousness is expressed through an effort of exhalation of breath, modification of speech-organs to produce the word; the word pervades the unmanifest consciousness of the hearer, makes it manifest and the meaning is apprehended. Durga also comments on the term 'minuteness': movements of hands and the winking of the eyes etc. are also comprehensive; they will express the meaning and in this manner there will be no need to study grammar and the Vedic texts! But these are not minute, i.e. these communication modes are not definitive (or accurate) and are not economical in the effort in production.] Ya_ ska notes the four ordclasses,noun, verb, preposition and particle and adds:... S'a_kat.a_yana holds that nouns are derived from verbs. This, too, is the doctrine of the etymologists. 'Not at all,' says Gargya and some of the grammarians, 'but only those, the accent and grammatical form of which are regular and which are accompanied by an explanatory radical modification.' Those (nouns), such as cow, horse, man, elephant etc. are conventional (terms, and hence are underivable)(Ni. 1.12). Pa _n.ini combines particles (avyaya, 195 in number) and prepositions into one category, nipa _ta (Bk. I, Ch. IV, 56).

According to Ya_ska, particles are of three types: (i) of comparison (upama),(ii) of adding or putting together of the senses or ideas (karmopasam.graha or semantic sub-clusters), (iii) of expletives which do not express any meaning (kam, i_m, id, u and iva). Ya_ska notes that the verb has 'becoming' as its fundamental notion; and that the noun has 'being' as its fundamental notion and recalls that according to Audumbara _ yan.a speech is permanent in the organs only. This statement of Audumbara_yan.a is fundamental in understanding the neural bases of linguistic competence. Tamil (a primary member of the so-called Dravidian languages) is an ancient language. This lexicon contains a number of references from Tamil works,

According to R.gvedapra_tis'a_kya (xii.6.702) and Ya_ska, prepositions are twenty and combine with the noun and verb to express a meaning (these are: pra, abhi, a _, para, nih-, duh-, anu, vi, upa, apa, sam, pari, prati, ni, ati,adhi, su, ud, ava and api). Pa_n.ini: pra etc., are called prepositions(karmapravacani_ya) when joined with verbs.' (Bk.I. Ch. IV.58; 83-97). Va_jasaneyipra_tis'a_khya provides the most succinct definition (viii.54): 'A verb denotes an action, and a preposition makes that action specific.' (Pra_tis'a_kyasor pa_rs.adas are the oldest grammatical treatises of different schools based on the original forms of words). 33In Tamil grammar, vat.amor. .i or vat.a-col (Tol. Col. 401) refers to a Sanskrit word (centamir. .kkan. vanta vat.amor. .iyu ma_r-r-a_te_: Ya_pperun.kalam. Virutti.Pakkam. 461 i.e. Sanskrit seeded by refined Tamil does not compare) [kan. Seed as cause (Ci. Po_. 9,3,3); a_r-r-u-tal to be equal to, to compare with (Kur-al.,101); centamir. . is standard Tamil, free from all corruptive elements, opp. To kot.u-n-tamir. . : Tol. Col. 398; centamir. .na_t.u is said to be bounded by the acknowledging the antiquity of the language and its importance as a dominant member of the Indian language family. Similar references are provided from Vedic texts in many etyma groups. The rich ancient Tamil literature (which dates back to the San.gam age of c. the first millennium A.D.) includes Vaikai-ya _r-u, on the east by Maruvu_r, and on the west by Karuvu_r : Tol. Col.400, Urai.); kot.u-n-tamir. . is Tamil dialect current in regions surroundingcentamir. .na_t.u (Nan-. 273, Urai.) (Ta.lex.)

Any indication of derivatives or so-called 'borrowing' indicated by the sign < in lexicons, should be treated with great caution. No claim is sought to be made that a particular phonetic form was, in fact, derived from another language, just because the sign < has been used (only in a very few semantic clusters) in this lexicon. The sign should be taken to indicate a possible close affinity or geographical extension between the languages involved in the semantic relationship.Tolka _ppiyam35 (?c. 5th century A.D.), a grammar and socio-linguistic tract; the fifth-century work, Tiruval.l.uvar's Tirukkural., s'aiva religious works such as Tiruva _cakam and Tirumantiram; existential expositions such as Pur-ana_n-u_ru,Akana_n-u_ru (400 poems each on social and family lives); Pattuppa_t.t.u (ten songs) and Et.t.uttokai (eight anthologies) delineating love and war as facets of life.

To quote Caldwell who relates a study of this language to the comparative grammatical structures of a family of the so-called Dravidian languages: "Does there not seem to be reason for regarding the Dravidian family of languages, not only as a link of connection between the Indo-European and Scythian groups, but -- in some particulars, especially in relation to the pronouns -- as the best surviving representative of a period in the history of human speech older than the Indo-European stage, older than the Scythian and older than the separation of the one from the other... The orientalists who supposed the Dravidian languages to be derived from Sanskrit were not aware of the existence of uncultivated languages of the Dravidian family, in which Sanskrit words are not at all, or but very rarely, employed... Another evidence consists in the extraordinary copiousness of the Tamil vocabulary, and the number and variety of the grammatical forms of Shen-Tamil. The Shen-Tamil grammar is a crowded museum of obsolete forms, cast-off inflexions, and curious anomalies... It is a different question whether some of the Dravidian forms and roots may not have formed a portion of the linguistic inheritance, which appears to have descended to the earliest Dravidian from the fathers of the human race." (Caldwell's Comparative Grammar of the Dravidian Family of Languages, p.x, p.45, p.82). In Tolka_ppiyam, Tamil does include the so-called vat.acol (or northern words): vat.acor- kil.avi vat.a l.er. .ut tori_i er. .uttot.u pun.arntacolla_kumme : Tol. Col. 395, i.e. 'northern' words are those words which shed their scripts and are adapted; this is distinguished from 'dialectical' words (centamir. . ... ticai-c-cor- kil.avi) in vogue in the twelve territories of the Tamil land with regional variations and two other kinds of words: iyar--col,tiri-col (primitives and derivatives) used in poetry (ceyyul.).

The author is Tolka_ppiyan-, reputed to be a disciple of Agastya, as born in Ka_ppiya-k-kut.i (it.aiccan.kamirunta_r akattiyan-a_run tolka_ppiyan-a_rum : Ir-ai. 1,Pak. 5; tun-n-arun ci_rttit tolka_ppiyan-mutar- pan-n-irupulavarum : Pu. Ve. Cirappuppa_.); Civajna_n-a-mun-ivar provides an elaborate commentary on the pa_yiramand the first su_tra of Tolka_ppiyam, as tolka_ppiya-c-cu_ttiravirutti (Tamil lexicon.) This lexicon establishes the possibility of tracing the etyma for all three patterns of prefixing, agglutinative and inflexional types of morphology in languages. The inflexional languages such as Sanskrit and languages influenced significantly by Sanskrit show a myriad morphological variants. Unlike CDIAL which breaks out the inflexional variants under 'head words' based on assumed 'root words' with an *, this lexicon clusters the variants under semantic clusters. [Thus, for example, □vij (move suddenly) can be clustered with ve_ga speed and □vi_j or □vyaj fan and vizun to sift, winnow (K.) As far as practicable, only words listed in the language lexicons are included in the semantic clusters of this lexicon, without making any attempt to derive the ancient phonetic form of the Indian sememe or a proto-Indian reconstruction of a morpheme with an *.] This lexicon, as does R.L. Turner's A Comparative Dictionary of Indo-Aryan languages (CDIAL), includes a number of words from the Vedic texts37, attesting to the great antiquity of many semantic clusters which are also concordant with the archaeological artifacts unearthed from the Indus Valley civilization and other Indian archaeological explorations. An early attempt to trace the 'sememes' was made in works such as the Dha_tupa_t.ha for Sanskrit and in the brilliant work of the Vedic scholars of the nineteenth and twentieth centuries (following the tradition of Sa_yan.a in the R.gvedabha_s.yabhu_mika_ of an earlier century) who have successfully established the semantic contents of the Vedic texts,38 proving Ya_ska right: "Vedic stanzas are significant, because (their) words are identical (with those of the spoken language)..." (Nirukta 1.16). Sa_yan.a makes a similar comment in his preface to the R.gveda: va_kya_rtho_lo_kave_dayo_ravis'is.t.ah- (the meaning of expressions of the Vedic Sanskrit and of the popular speech is not different) and also notes: 'abhidha_ne_rthava_dah there Is a figurative description in such expressions... this is very frequently employed in poetical compositions. For instance, a river is described as having a pair of cakrava_ka birds for her breasts, a row of swans for her teeth, a ka_sa plant for her garment, and moss for her hair. Similarly, the Vedic texts invoking inanimate objects should be construed as implying praise...' It can be hypothesized that soma was a similar 'figurative description'.

Vedic texts (c. 1200 to 200 B.C.) include the corpus of the R.gveda, Yajurveda, Sa_ maveda, Atharvaveda (s'ruti) and a number of exegetical texts (smr. ti) including the bra_hman.as, a_ran.yakas, upanis.ads, dating from the latter parts of the first millennium B.C. Morphological divergences between classical Sanskrit and the Vedic texts are remarkable. The occurrence of many so-called Dravidian and Munda idioms in and the dialectical heterogeneity of the Vedas are reflected in a number of parallel forms of the texts which were later unified through oral traditions. 38An exception to this statement is the unresolved problem of soma. A variety of interpretations are provided for this word which is the principal process or life-activity elaborated in the R.gveda. The author of this lexicon has interpreted soma as electrum or silver-gold ore, in a separate work in the context of a study of the history of ancient Indian alchemy. This lexicon provides etymological evidence in support of this interpretation. Soma as perhaps, a major process involving the lives of ancients of the Indian language family.

Grammatical philosophy

Some leads are available to explore further the concept of 'meaning' in philosophical and linguistic terms. "homo foneticus indicus was no mere crosssectioned larynx sited under an empty cranium... on the contrary, the whole man, belly, heart and head, produced voice" (J.E.B. Gray 1959, "An Analysis of Nambudiri R.gvedic Recitation and the Nature of the Vedic Accent", Bulletin of the School of Oriental and African Studies 22, pp. 499-530) A word points to an external object, as a semantic indicator; it also refers to the intention of the speaker. One technical term is 'artha' which may be a synonym of 'meaning'. "For xlii the grammarian, 'artha' does not mean the external reality but whatever the word brings to the mind. Artha does not mean vastvarttha but s'abda _ rtha, not reality, but, the meaning of words. Individual words bring something to the mind and the sentence as a whole also brings something to the mind. But these things are included in the expression 's'abda_rtha'. Grammar studies both these things in order to evolve notions which will explain the forms of the language. Grammar is satisfied if these notions conform to what we understand from words, no matter whether they conform to reality or not. Grammar does not look at reality directly in the face. As Hela_ra_ja puts it: s'abdaprama_n.aka_na_m.hi s'abda eva hi yatha_rtham abhidhatte athaiva tasya_bhidha_nam upapannam; na tuvastumukhapraks.ataya_ : for to those whose authority is the word, the word designates what it corresponds to, and its designation is accordingly appropriate; but it is not for looking reality directly in the face (Hela_ra_ja on Va_kyapadi_ya III. Sam.. verse 66)... Thus while explaining the different conceptions of Time mentioned by Bharttr.hari in the Ka_lasamuddes'a such as that it is an entity which exists apart from the mind or that it is a mere construction of the human mind, Hela_ra_ja says that Bharttr.hari is not really concerned with what time is philosophically, but that he is anxious to examine and analyze that something which is responsible for our putting the Sanskrit verb in different tenses as in abhu _t (was), asti (is) and bhavis.yat (will be).That something may not be able to stand close philosophical scrutiny, but if it serves the purpose of explaining the different tenses, one would have to accept it (Hela_ra_ja on Va_kyapadi_ya. III. Ka_. 58). Similarly in the kriya_samuddes'a, the question is: What is action? The answer given by Bharttr.hari on the basis of the Bha_s.ya passages is that it is a process, something having parts arranged in a temporal sequence. It is not directly perceptible, but it is to be inferred... These parts may be further subdivided and the smaller parts will also be actions. There will come a time when the part cannot be further sub-divided. It cannot then be called action at all. Only that can be called action which has parts arranged in a temporal sequence. After having clearly explained all this, Hela_ra_ja adds that for grammarians the real question is not whether an action has actually parts or not, but whether the verb presents it as such. The answer is that verbs do present action, however momentary, in nature, as something having parts which cannot co-exist but are arranged in a temporal sequence. And Vaiya _karan.as go by what the words present to us. (Hela _ ra _ ja on Va _ kyapadi _ya. III. Kri. 10)." (Subramania Iyer, K.A., "The Point of View of the Vaiya _karan.as", Journal of Oriental Research, 18, pp.84-96, 1948).Vya_d.i (Sarvadars'ana-sam.graha, Bibliographica Indica, pp. 140-4) notes that since letters by themselves cannot convey meaning, a unifying factor can be hypothesized; the factor (sphot.a) which is all-pervading and exists independent of letters. sphot.a is the idea which bursts out or flashes on the mind when a sound is uttered, the impression produced on the mind at hearing a sound: budhairvaiya _karan.ah- pradha_na bhu_ta sphot.a ru_pavyan.gyanjakasya s'abdasyadhaviniriti vyavaha_rah kr.tah (Ka_vyapraka_s'a. 1; it is also the eternal sound recognized by the Mi_ma_m.sakas or inquirers (Skt. lex.) It connotes he relationship between sounds and meaningful words. sphut.ati praka_s'ate'rtho' sma_d iti sphot.o va_caka iti ya_vat (Kon.d.abhat.t.a, Vya_karan.a-bhu_s.an.a (Bombay, 1915, p.236); Na_ges'abhat.t.a, Sphot.ava_da (Adyar Library, 1946), p.5). Ma_dhava, Sarvadars'anasam.graha (ed. Abhyankar, p. 300), gives the double explanation that the sphot.a is revealed by the letters, and itself reveals the meaning: sphut.yate vyajyate varn.air iti sphot.ovarn.a_bhivyan.gyah-, sphut.ati sphut.i_bhavaty asma_d artha iti sphot.o' rthapratya_yakah-. "The sphot.a then is simply the linguistic sign in its aspect of meaning-bearer (bedeutungstrager). The term sphot.a occurs first in the Maha _bha_s.ya, Na_ges'a ascribed the doctrine to Sphot.a_yana, who is quoted by Pa_n.ini(vi.1.123) on a point of morphology... the sphot.a (the unchanging substratum)is the word, the sound is merely an attribute of the word. How? Like a drumbeat.

When a drum is struck, one drum-beat may travel twenty feet, another thirty, another forty. But the sphot.a is of precisely such and such a size, the increase in length is caused by the sound... Patanjali's sphot.a (except in so far as it is for him the meaning-bearer) is really comparable to Bharttr.hari's pra_kr.ta-dhvani. The commentators, being acquainted with the later theory, naturally point out that the speed of utterance belongs to the vaikr.ta-dhvani... Bharttr.hari (Va_kya-padi_ya i.44 : dva_v upa_da_nas'abdes.u s'abdau s'abdavido viduh- eko nimittam. s'abda_na_m aparo'rthe prayujyate : in meaningful language, linguists recognize two (entites which can be called) words: one is the underlying cause of words, the other is attached to the meaning... The Nya_ya philosophers for example, held that the meaning of a word was presented to the mind by the last sound, aided by the memory-impression of the preceding sounds... Va_kyapadi_ya i. 75-8: sphot.asya_bhinnaka_lasya dhvanika_la_nupa_tinahgrahan.opa_dhibhedena vr.ttibhedam. pracaks.ate; svabha_vabheda_n nityatve hrasva-di_rgha-pluta_dis.u pra_kr.tasya dhvaneh-ka_lah- s'abdasyety upacaryate; varn.asya grahan.e hetuh- pra_kr.to dhvanir is.yate vr.ttibhede nimittatvam. vaikr.tah- pratipadyate; s'abdasyordhvam abhivyakter vr.ttibhede tu vaikr.ta_h- dhvnayah- samupohante sphot.a_tma_tair na bhidyate: According to the differences in the specific cause of its comprehension (in individual instances), men attribute differences in speed of utterance (vr.tti) to the sphot.a which is not divided in time, and merely reflects the time of the sound. Similarly, in the case of the short, long, and prolate vowels-- since, on the view that these are permanent, they are intrinsically distinct-- it is the time-pattern of the primary sound which is metaphorically attributed to the word (the sphot.a) itself. The 'primary sound' (pra_kr.ta-dhvani) is defined as the cause of the perception of the letters (phonemes), the 'secondary sound' (vaikr.ta-dhvani, literally 'modified') is the causal factor underlying differences of diction. But it is only after the word has been revealed that the secondary sounds are presented to the mind as differences of diction; hence (a fortiori) the essential nature of the sphot.a is not disrupted by these... Ma_dhava's statement : varn.a_tiriktovarn.a_bhivyan.gyo' rthapratya_yako nityah- s'abdah- sphot.a iti tadvido vadanti may be translated as 'the abiding word which is the conveyor of the meaning... is called the sphot.a by the grammarians'..." (Brough, John "Theories of General Linguistics in the Sanskrit Grammarians", Transactions of the PhilologicalSociety, pp. 27-46, 1951). The padapa_t.has break down the sam.hita_ into its constituent words; Ya_ska's Nirukta studies the meaning of some of such words.

Thus the phonetics of a word and its meaning are integral components of Vedic studies. Va_rttika defines a grammatical sentence as eka-tin. i.e. possessing one verb. (Va_kyapadi_ya ii.3). "The Bha_t.t.a school (of the later Mi_ma_m.sa) on the whole seems to preserve the more primitive attitude. According to them words have in themselves meanings, and as the words are uttered in a sentence, each word performs its task of expressing its meaning, and the sentence is the summation of these meanings. The Pra_bha_kara school, on the other hand, held the more sophisticated theory that the individual words did not express any meaning until they were united together into a sentence. This was upheld by an appeal to the method whereby a child learns its own mother tongue. They pointed out that it was by hearing sentences 'fetch the cow', 'fetch the horse', and so forth, that the child came gradually to understand that the animal which he saw on each several occasion was, in fact, either a cow or a horse and that the action performed by his elders was the act of fetching. These two views were named respectively abhihita_nvaya-va_da and anvita_bhidha_nava_da, terms which are troublesome to translate by concise English expressions.

Roughly speaking, the first is the theory that the sentence is 'a series of expressed word-meanings', and the second is that the sentence is 'the expressed meaning of a series (of words)' ... At the beginning of the second book of the Va_kyapadi_ya, Bharttr.hari gives a list of definitions and quasidefinitions of a sentence. Five of these are grouped by the commentator under the traditional Mima_m.sa_designations. Thus the view that the sentence is a unified collection (sam.gha _ta) and the view that it is an ordered series(krama) are aspects of the abhihita_nvaya-va_da; while the other three belong to the anvita_bhidha_na-va_da. These are, that the sentence is defined by a verbal expression (a_khya_ta-s'abda) or by the first word (padam a_dyam) or by all the words taken separately with the feature of mutual requirement or expectancy superadded (pr.thak sarvapadam. sa_ka_n.ks.am). All these views, of course, imply the feature of expectancy39, and the first and second are to be explained with reference to this feature, since the verb or the first word is only what it is in view of its ties with the other words in its own sentence. All these theories are adversely criticized by Bharttr.hari... The occurrence of homophones in a language has always provided grammarians with an interesting problem... Bharttr.hari gives a list of such factors, of which the most important are va_kya, sentence-context, and prakaran.a, situational context...historical and comparative studies frequently enable us to glean from texts in related languages useful hints towards this understanding (of meaning)... In the end the utmost that can be said of the meaning of a sentence according to Bharttr.hari is that it is grasped by an instantaneous flash of insight (pratibha_)(Va_kyapadi_ya, ii.119,145)... And when we have understood a sentence,we cannot explain to another the nature of this understanding. (Va_kyapadi_ya,ii.146: idam. ad iti sa_nyes.am ana_khyeya_katham.cana : pratya_tmavr.ttisiddha_sa_kartra_pi na hiru_pyate : This (pratibha_) cannot in any way be explained to others in terms such as 'it is this'; its existence is ratified only in the individual's experience of it, and the experiencer himself cannot describe it)." (Brough, John, "Some Indian Theories of Meaning", Transactions of the Philological Society, 1953, pp. 161-176)40. There is no supreme language; all languages are personal and social experiences of a community. Yet, every language is governed by an extraordinary phonetic repertoire orchestrated by 'neuronal laws' of the human brain. 40 cf. Kunjunni Raja, K., Indian Theories of Meaning, Madras, 1963. In neurosciences, an axiom is that the brain 'perceives' what it wants to perceive. At another level of analysis or 'brain theory', it may be stated that the brain is a 'variance machine', selectively recording only changes or 'variances' from the 'previously recorded experiences or perceptions'.

The neuronal structures in which verbal creativity is embedded are the common substratum; they are language-neutral. This means, that irrespective of the language used by a speaker, or the language heard by a listener, the neurons and neuronal networks pulsate, governed by the as-yet undefined semantic laws of neurosciences. Man can create poetry; if the poem has to convey meaning to the audience, the poet has to abandon his search for the 'perfect' language and bow to the superior wisdom of the common parlance which is,in effect, the linguistic social contract for which words are but social memory-markers, or '*nume'raire facile.*' The private memory-markers in the private language of a speaker's or listener's brain are the product of his life-history which can be 'emotionally' or 'neuronally' experienced.

No scientific technique is relevant, no language is adequate and no poet is competent to communicate the emotions of the 'private language' of the brain.

Abbreviations : Grammatical

* hypothetical	dat. dative	lex. lexicographical works or Kos'as	redup. reduplicated
< (is) derived from	dist.fr.distinct from	lit. literature	ref. reference(s)
> (has) become	du. dual	loc. locative	S South
? doubtful	E East	m. masculine	sb./subst.substantive
Xinfluenced by	e.g. example	M Middle	semant. semantically
+ extended by	etym. etymology	metath. metathesis (of)	st. stem
~ parallel with	expr.expression	N North	subj. subjunctive
acc.accusative	f./fem. feminine	Na_ Na_ci Na_t.u usage	syn. synonym
adj. adjective	fig. figuratively	Naut. Nautical	Tinn. Tinnevelly usage
adv. adverb	fr. from	nom.nominative	Tj. Tanjore usage
aor. aorist	fut. future	nom.prop. nomen proprium (proper name)	usu. usual(ly)
caus. causative	gen. genitive	num.numeral(s)	vais.n..vais.n.ava usage
cent. century	hon. honorific	NWNorth-west	vb. verb
cf. confer (compare)	id. idem (having the same meaning)	O Old	viz. videlicet (namely)
cmpd.compound(ed)	imper.imperative	obl. oblique case	W West
com. commentary, t.i_ka_	incl. including	onom.onomatopoeic	
conj.conjunction	inf.infinitive	p. page	

	inj.injunctive inscr.inscription	part. participle pass. passive perf. perfect perh. perhaps phonet.phonetically pl. plural pp. past participle (passive) pres. present pron. pronoun Pudu. Pudukkottai usage	

Abbreviations used for linguistic categories and other languages

As'. As'okan inscriptions Austro-as. Austro-asiatic (cf. Munda) BHSkt. Buddhist Hybrid Sanskrit (Franklin Edgerton, Buddhist Hybrid Sanskrit Grammar and Dictionary, Newhaven, 1953) Dard. Dardic Dhp. Ga_ndha_ri or Northwest Prakrit (as recorded in the Dharmapada ed. J. Brough, Oxford 1962) Drav. Dravidian IA. Indo-aryan IE. Indo-european Ind. Indo-aryan of India proper excluding Kafiri and Dardic (as classified by R.L. Turner)	Ar.Arabic Aram.Aramaic Arm.Armenian Av. Avestan (Iranian) E. English Gk. Greek Goth. Gothic Ishk. Ishka_shmi_ (Iranian) Kurd. Kurdish (Iranian)

KharI. Kharos.t.hi_ inscriptions; Middle Indo-aryan forms occurring in Corpus Inscriptionum Indicarum Vol. II Pt.I, Calcutta, 1929 MIA Middle Indo-aryan NiDoc. Language of 'Kharos.t.hi_ Inscriptions discovered by Sir Aurel Stein in Chinese Turkestan' edited by A.M. Boyer, E.J. Rapson, and E. Senart	Lat. Latin Lith.Lithuanian OHG. Old High German Orm. O_rmur.i_ (Iranian) OSlav. Old Slavonic Par. Para_ci_ (Iranian) Pahl. Pahlavi (Iranian) Pers. Persian (Iranian) Port. Portuguese Pr. Prasun (Kafiri) Psht. Pashto (Iranian) Tib. Tibetan Toch. Tocharian Turk. Turkish Yid. Yidgha (Iranian)

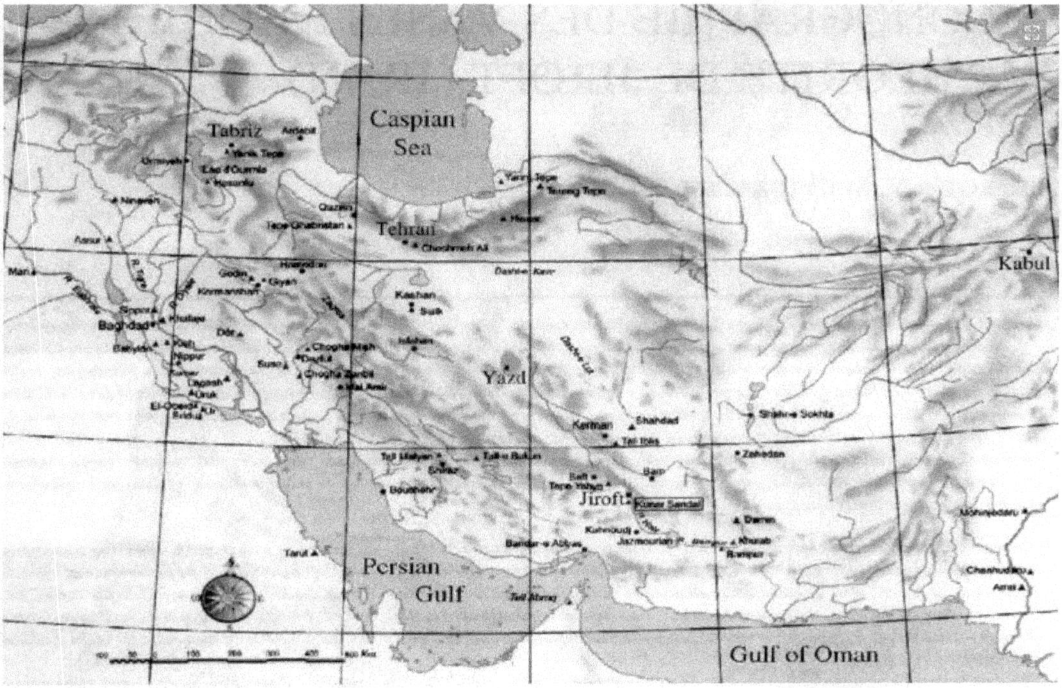

3rd millennium BCE sites along Persian Gulf: Jiroft, Konar Sandal with chlorite vessels close to Chanhudaro

vidyā samuddeśa lit. objective of schooling or eduation included *mlecchita vikalpa* to be learned by youth

- *mlecchita vikalpa* (lit. Meluhha cipher) was identified as one of the 64 arts (including two allied communication arts called *akṣára muṣṭika kathanam* and *deśabhāṣā jñānam* – lit. fist-finger gesture narrations and knowledge of spoken language) to be learned by the youth.
- Source: Vātsyāyana's *Kāmasūtra* वात्स्यायन कामसूत्र in a section titled: *vidyā samuddeśa* lit. objective of schooling or eduation.

Gallery of hieroglyphs from chlorite vessels of Jiroft and Konar Sandal:

a

e

b

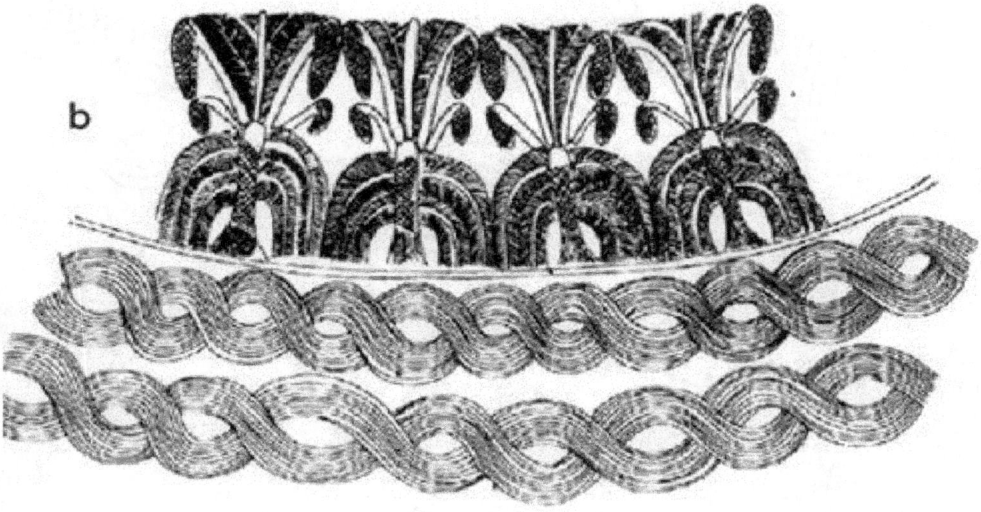

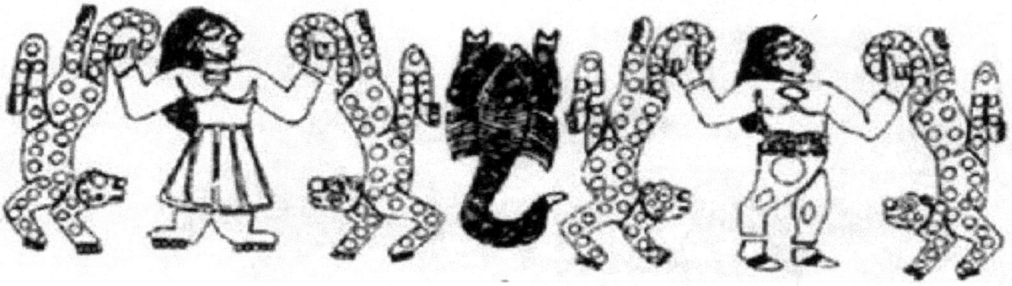

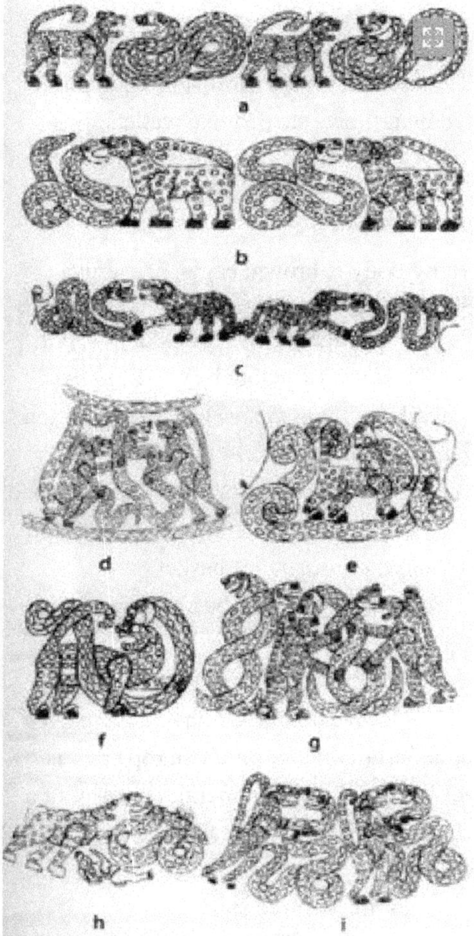

Eagle, scorpion (woman), strands of rope, ibexes, zebu. Man with claws/bull man playing with cheeta, scorpion in middle, man with claws holding hoos of snakes. Cheetas fighting snakes, handbags.

Meluhha and Jiroft

A dominant hieroglyph depicted on Jiroft artifacts is a 'wallet'. The Meluhha word for this hieroglyph is *dhokra. Meluhha h*ieroglyphs related to metalwork are depicted on artifacts shaped like wallets.

Prakrtam lexis

Hieroglyph: *Ta.* eruvai a kind of kite whose head is white and whose body is brown; eagle. *Ma.* eruva eagle, kite.(DEDR 818) rebus: eraka 'moltencast, copper' (Kannada.Tulu)
Hieroglyph: wallet: *dhōkkal ' sacking, matting '. 2. *dhōkha -- . 3. *dhōṅga -- 2. 4. *ḍhōkka -- 1. [Cf. *ṭōkka -- 1]1. Ext. -- *ḍ* -- : N. *dhokro* ' large jute bag ', B. *dhokaṛ*; Or. *dhokaṛa* ' cloth bag '; Bi. *dhŏkrā* ' jute bag '; Mth. *dhokṛā* ' bag, vessel, receptacle '; H. *dhukṛī* f. ' small bag '; G. *dhokṛũ* n. ' bale of cotton '; -- with -- *ṭṭ* -- : M. *dhokṭī* f. ' wallet '; -- with -- *n* -- : G. *dhokṇũ* n. ' bale of cotton '; -- with -- *s* -- : N. (Tarai) *dhokse* ' place covered with a mat to store rice in '.2. L. *dhohẽ* (pl. *dhūhī̃*) m. ' large thatched shed '.3. M. *dhõgḍā* m. ' coarse cloth ', *dhõgṭī* f. ' wallet '.4. L. *ḍhok* f. ' hut in the fields '; Ku. *ḍhwākā* m. pl. ' gates of a city or market '; N. *ḍhokā* (pl. of **ḍhoko*) ' door '; -- OMarw. *ḍhokaro* m. ' basket '; -- N. *ḍhokse* ' place covered with a mat to store rice in, large basket '.(CDIAL 6880) Rebus: *dhokra kamar* 'cire perdue, lost-wax casting metalworker'.

Hieroglyph: dhā´tu n. *strand of rope ' (cf. *tridhā´tu* -- ' threefold ' RV.,*ayugdhātu* -- ' having an uneven number of strands ' KātyŚr.). [√dhā] S. *dhāī* f. ' wisp of fibres added from time to time to a rope that is being twisted ', L. *dhāī̃* f. Rebus: ' substance ' RV., m. ' element ' MBh., ' metal, mineral, ore (esp. of a red colour) ' Mn., ' ashes of the dead ' lex., ' Pa. *dhātu* -- m. ' element, ashes of the dead, relic '; KharI. *dhatu* ' relic '; Pk. *dhāu* -- m. ' metal, red chalk '; N. *dhāu* ' ore (esp. of copper) '; Or. *ḍhāu* ' red chalk, red ochre ' (whence *ḍhāuā* ' reddish '; M. *dhāū*, *dhāv* m.f. ' a partic. soft red stone ' (whence *dhā̆vaḍ* m. ' a caste of iron -- smelters ', *dhāvḍī* ' composed of or relating to iron '); -- Si. *dā* ' relic ' (CDIAL 6773)

Hieroglyph: vṛ́ścika m. (*vṛścana* -- m. lex.) ' scorpion ' RV., ' cater- pillar covered with bristles ' lex. [Variety of form for ' scorpion ' in MIA. and NIA. due to taboo? <-> √vraśc?]Pa. *vicchika* -- m. ' scorpion ', Pk. *vicchia* -- , *viṁchia* -- m., Sh.koh. *bičh* m. (< **vṛści* -- ?), Ku. *bichī*, A. *bisā* (also ' hairy caterpillar ': -- *ī* replaced by m. ending -- *ā*), B. Or. *bichā*, Mth. *bīch*, Bhoj. Aw.lakh. *bīchī*, H. poet. *bīchī* f., *bīchā* m., G. *vīchī*, *vīchī* m.; -- **vicchuma* -- : Paš.lauṛ. *uċúm*, dar. *učum*, S. *vichũ* m., (with greater deformation) L.mult. *vaṭhũhā*, khet. *vaṭṭhũha*; -- Pk. *vicchua* -- ,*viṁchua* -- m., L. *vichū* m., awāṇ. *vicchū*, P. *bicchū* m., Or. (Sambhalpur) *bichu*, Mth. *bīchu*, H. *bicchū*, *bīchū* m., G. *vīchu* m.; -- Pk. *viccu* -- , °*ua* -- , *viṁcua* -- m., K. *byucu* m. (← Ind.), P.bhaṭ.*biccū*, WPah.bhal. *biċċū* m., cur. *biccū*, bhiḍ. *biċċoṭū* n. ' young scorpion ', M. *vīċũ*, *vīċū* m. (*vīċḍā* m. ' large scorpion '), *vīċvī*, °*ċvīṇ*, °*ċīṇ* f., Ko. *viccu*, *viṁcu*, *iṁcu*. -- N. *bacchiũ* ' large hornet '? (Scarcely < **vapsi* -- ~ *vaspi --). vṛścikapattrikā -- . Addenda: vṛ́ścika -- : Garh. *bicchū*, °*chī* ' scorpion ', A. also *bichā* (phonet. -- *s* --) (CDIAL 12081) rebus: *bicha, meRed bicha* 'iron stone ore'

Hieroglyph: miṇḍā'l ‘ markhor ’ Rebus: meD 'iron' (Ho.Munda)
Hieroglyph: karada ‘leopard’ rebus: karada ‘hard alloy’

kulā ‘ winnowing fan, hood of a snake ’(Assamese)(CDIAL 3350) kola ‘woman’ (Nahali) rebus: kol ‘working in iron’ kolle ‘blacksmith’ kolhe ‘smelter. nAga ‘snake’ rebus: nAga ‘lead’.

Hieroglyph: poLa 'zebu' Rebus: poLa 'magnetite'

Stairs of Konar Sandal Ziggurat

The main part of the Konar Sandal Ziggurat of the Jiroft ancient site, located in the southern Iranian province of Kerman.

The objects discovered at Jiroft date from between the fourth and third millennium BC. Many are made of chlorite, a soft stone from local quarries. They are finely worked and engraved with images of animals, flowers and trees

Jiroft artifacts with Meluhha hieroglhyphs referencing *dhokra kamar* working with metals.

Dark grey steatite bowl carved in relief. Zebu or brahmani bull is shown with its hump back; a male figure with long hair and wearing akilt grasps two sinuous objects, representing running water, which flows in a continuous stream. Around the bowl, another similar male figure stands between two lionesses with their head turned back towards him; he grasps a serpent in each hand. A further scene (not shown) represents a prostrate bull which is being attacked by a vulture and a lion.

The zebu is reminiscent of Sarasvati Sindhu seals. The stone used, steatite, is familiar in Baluchistan and a number of vessels at the Royal Cemetery at Ur were made out of this material.

The bowl dates from c. 2700-2500 B.C. and the motif shown on it resembles that on a fragment of a green stone vase from one of the Sin Temples at Tell Asmar of almost the same date.

Khafajeh bowl; a man sitting, with his legs bent underneath, upon two zebu bulls. This evokes the proto-Elamite bull-man; the man holds in his hands streams of water and issurrounded by ears of corn. He has a crescent beside his head. On the other side of the bowl, a man is standing upon two lionesses and grasping two serpents.

An Early Dynastic II votive plaque from the Inanna temple at Nippur VIII (after Pritchard, 1969: 356, no. 646). "It has something very Harappan about it also in the lower part depicting two 'unicorn' bulls around a tree. The six dots around the head of the Harappan hero, clearly visible in one seal (Mohenjodaro, DK 11794; cf. Mackay, 1937: II, pl. 84:75) may be compared to the six locks of hair characteristic of the Mesopotamian hero from Jemdet Nasr to Akkadian times (cf. Calmeyer, 1957-71: 373). From the Early Dynastic period onwards the scene usually comprises a man fighting with one or two bulls, and a bull-man fighting with one or two lions....North-west India of the third millennium BC can be considered as an integral, if marginal, part of the West Asian cultural area." (Parpola, A., New correspondences between Harappan and Near Eastern glyptic art, in: Bridget Allchin (ed.), *South Asian Archaeology, 1981*, Cambridge, Cambridge University Press, 1984).

Kolom ‘rice plant’ rebus: kolimi ‘smithy, forge’.

Hieroglyph: Garh. *ṭokṇu* ‘ to hinder, check ’(CDIAL 5476) rebus: A. *ṭokan* ‘ heavy stick, club ’; K. *ṭŏkh* (dat. *°kas*) m. ‘ hammering ’; Ash. *ṭoká* ‘ nail, peg ’(CDIAL 5476) This orthographic signifier is thus a semantic determinantof a forge where a metalsmith hammers ingots to the desired shape of implements, pots and pans. The heavy stick carried by the s’ilpi on Sanchi stupa torana is a signifier of a forge, together with smelting and metal mint work of coinage. The pair of animals: dula ‘pair’ rebus: dul ‘cast metal’.

Lapis lazuli stamp seal. Behind the man, drummer, are a stream, a long-horned, bearded goat above a zebu. Mountain range with a line of over 15 notches and a circle on top register.

Bronze Age, about 2400-2000 BCE
From the ancient Near East British Museum.

Height: 3.100 cm

Thickness: 2.500 cm

Width: 4.000 cm

ME 1992-10-7,1

Room 52: Ancient Iran

This stamp seal was originally almost square, but because of damage one corner is missing. Originally two figures faced each other. The one on the left has largely disappeared. On the right is a man with his legs folded beneath him. It is suggested that at the top are rain clouds and rain or a fenced enclosure. Behind the man are a long-horned goat above a zebu. This last animal is related in style to similar creatures depicted on seals from the Indus Valley civilization, which was thriving at this time. There were close connections between the Indus Valley civilization and eastern Iran. One of the prized materials that was traded across the region was lapis lazuli, the blue stone from which this seal is made.

The Sar-i Sang mines in the region of Badakhshan in north-east Afghanistan were probably the source for all lapis lazuli used in the ancient Near East. From here it was carried across Iran, where several lapis working sites have been discovered, and on to Mesopotamia and Egypt. Another source for lapis lazuli exists in southern Pakistan (a region of the Indus Valley civilization) but it is unclear if they were mined at the time of this seal.

D. Collon, 'Lapis lazuli from the east: a stamp seal in the British Museum', *Ancient Civilizations from Scy*, 5/1 (1998), pp. 31-39

http://www.britishmuseum.org/explore/highlights/highlight_objects/me/l/lapis_lazuli_stamp_seal.aspx

See: http://bharatkalyan97.blogspot.in/2014/09/catalogs-of-pola-kuntha-gota-bichi.html

The hieroglyph: mountain-range signifies: *ḍā̃ro* 'blacksmith' (Nepali)(CDIAL 5524) dhangar, 'blacksmith' (Hindi) Or. dhāṅgaṛ ' young servant, herdsman, name of a Santal tribe ', dhāṅgaṛā ' unmarried youth ', °ṛī ' unmarried girl ', dhāṅgarā ' youth, man '; H. dhaṅgar m. ' herdsman ', dhā̃gaṛ, °ar m. ' a non-- Aryan tribe in the Vindhyas, digger of wells and tanks ' (CDIAL 5524)

S. ṭakuru m. ' mountain ', ṭakirī f. ' hillock ', ṭākara f. ' low hill ', ṭākirū m. ' mountaineer '; N. ṭākuro, °ri ' hill top ' K. ḍáki f. ' hill, rising ground '. -- Ext. -- r -- : K. ḍakürü f. ' hill on a road '. Ext. -- r -- : Pk. ḍaggara -- m. ' upper terrace of a house '; M. ḍagar f. ' little hill, slope '. Ku. ḍā̃g, ḍā̃k ' stony land '; B. ḍāṅ ' heap ', ḍāṅgā ' hill, dry upland '; H. ḍā̃g f. ' mountain -- ridge '; M. ḍā̃g m.n., ḍā̃gaṇ, °gāṇ, ḍāgāṇ n. ' hill -- tract '. -- Ext. -- r -- : N. ḍaṅgur ' heap '. M. ḍũg m. ' hill, pile ', °gā m. ' eminence ', °gī f. ' heap '. -- Ext. -- r -- : Pk. ḍuṁgara -- m. ' mountain '; Ku. ḍũgar, ḍũgrī; N. ḍuṅgar ' heap '; Or. ḍuṅguri ' hillock ', H.

ḍũgar m., G. ḍũgar m., ḍũgrī f. S. ḍũgaru m. ' hill ', H. M. ḍõgar m. Pa. tuṅga -- ' high '; Pk. tuṁga -- ' high ', tuṁgīya -- m. ' mountain '; K. tŏng, tọ̆ngu m. ' peak ', P. tuṅg f.; A. tuṅg ' importance '; Si. tuňgu ' lofty, mountain '. -- Cf. uttuṅga -- ' lofty ' MBh. K. thọ̆ngu m. ' peak '. H. dā̃g f. ' hill, precipice ', dā̃gī ' belonging to hill country '. S.kcch. ḍūṅghar m. ' hillock '.(CDIAL 5423)

Rebus: Mth. ṭhākur ' blacksmith '; N. ḍāṅro ' term of contempt for a blacksmith '(Nepali)(CDIAL 5524) ṭhakkura m. ' idol, deity (cf. ḍhakkārī --), ' lex., ' title ' Rājat. [Dis- cussion with lit. by W. Wüst RM 3, 13 ff. Prob. orig. a tribal name EWA i 459, which Wüst considers nonAryan borrowing of śākvará -- : very doubtful] Pk. ṭhakkura -- m. ' Rajput, chief man of a village '; Kho. (Lor.) takur ' barber ' (= ṭ° ← Ind.?), Sh. ṭhăkŭr m.; K. ṭhôkur m. ' idol ' (← Ind.?); S. ṭhakuru m. ' fakir, term of address between fathers of a husband and wife '; P. ṭhākar m. ' landholder ', ludh. ṭhaukar m. ' lord '; Ku. ṭhākur m. ' master, title of a Rajput '; N. ṭhākur ' term of address from slave to master ' (f. ṭhakurāni), ṭhakuri ' a clan of Chetris ' (f. ṭhakurni); A. ṭhākur ' a Brahman ', ṭhākurānī ' goddess '; B. ṭhākurāni, ṭhākrān, °run ' honoured lady, goddess '; Or. ṭhākura ' term of address to a Brahman, god, idol ', ṭhākurāṇī ' goddess '; Bi. ṭhākur ' barber '; Mth. ṭhākur ' blacksmith '; Bhoj. Aw.lakh. ṭhākur ' lord, master '; H. ṭhākur m. ' master, landlord, god, idol ', ṭhākurāin, ṭhā̃kurānī f. ' mistress, goddess '; G. ṭhākor, °kar m. ' member of a clan of Rajputs ', ṭhakrāṇī f. ' his wife ', ṭhākor ' god, idol '; M. ṭhākur m. ' jungle tribe in North Konkan, family priest, god, idol '; Si. mald. "tacourou" ' title added to names of noblemen ' (HJ 915) prob. ← Ind. Garh. ṭhākur ' master '; A. ṭhākur also ' idol ' (CDIAL 5488)

Two hieroglyphs on the lapis-lazuli stamp seal are: zebu and markhor.

Hieroglyph: poLa 'zebu' Rebus: poLa 'magnetite'

Hieroglyph: miṇḍā'l ' markhor ' Rebus: meD 'iron' (Ho.Munda)

Hieroglyph: Bi. mẽṛhwā ' a bullock with curved horns like a ram's '; M. mẽḍhrū̃ n. ' sheep '.(CDIAL 10311) mēṇḍha2 m. ' ram ', °aka -- , mēṇḍa -- 4, miṇḍha -- 2, °aka -- , mēṭha -- 2,mēṇḍhra -- , mēḍhra -- 2, °aka -- m. lex. 2. *mēṇṭha- (mēṭha -- m. lex.). 3. *mējjha -- . [r-- forms (which are not attested in NIA.) are due to further sanskritization of a loan -- word prob. of Austro -- as. origin (EWA ii 682 with lit.) and perh. related to the group s.v. bhēḍra --] Pa. meṇḍa -- m. ' ram ', °aka -- ' made of a ram's horn (e.g. a bow) '; Pk. meḍḍha -- ,meṁḍha -- (°ḍhī -- f.), °ṁḍa -- , miṁḍha -- (°dhiā -- f.), °aga -- m. ' ram ', Dm. Gaw. miṇKal.rumb. amŕn/aŕə ' sheep ' (a -- ?); Bshk. minā'l ' ram '; Tor. miṇḍ ' ram ', miṇḍā'l ' markhor '; Chil. mindh*ll ' ram ' AO xviii 244 (dh!), Sv. yēṛo -- miṇ; Phal. miṇḍ, miṇ ' ram ',miṇḍṓl m. ' yearling lamb, gimmer '; P. mẽḍhā m., °ḍhī f., ludh. mīḍḍhā, mī̃ḍhā m.; N. meṛho,meṛo ' ram for sacrifice '; A. mersāg ' ram ' (-- sāg < *chāgya -- ?), B. meṛā m., °ṛi f., Or.meṇḍhā, °ḍā m., °ḍhi f.,H. meṛh, meṛhā, mẽḍhā m., G. mẽḍhɔ, M. mẽḍhā m., Si. mäḍayā.2. Pk. meṁṭhī -- f. ' sheep '; H. meṭhā m. ' ram '.3. H. mejhukā m. ' ram '.(CDIAL 10310) <menDa>(A) {N} ``^sheep''. *Des.<meNDa>(GM) `sheep'.
#21810<meD>(:) <arij=meD>(Z),

<ari?=me?n>(A) {N} ``^female ^kid''. ^goat. #3022.<kin=meD>(Z) {N} ``^male ^goat, billy goat''. |<kin> `prefix used in names of male animals'. #17072. <auG kinme?n>(A) {N} ``^nanny ^goat''. |<auG> `mother'. #3729.(Gorum)

I suggest an alternative possibility that the gloss 'med' is an adaptation of the Meluhhan gloss vividly identified in Munda languages. meḍ ‘body’ Rebus: meḍ ‘iron’ (Ho.), mRdu ‘iron’ (Samskrtam)

Chanhudaro 23a *miṇḍāl* ‘markhor’ (Tōrwālī) *meḍho* a ram, a sheep (Gujarati)(CDIAL 10120) Rebus: *mẽṛhẽt, meḍ* ‘iron’ (Mu.Ho.) Traceable to the Samskrtam gloss: mRdu ‘iron’, i.e. soft malleable metal ore.

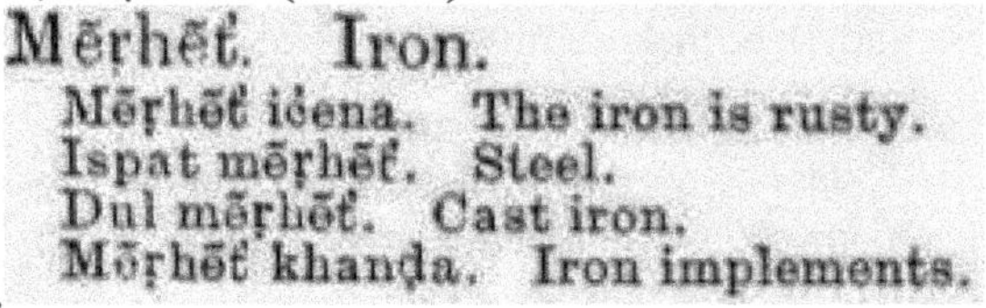

Mẽṛhẽť. Iron.
Mẽṛhẽť icena. The iron is rusty.
Ispat mẽṛhẽť. Steel.
Dul mẽṛhẽť. Cast iron.
Mẽṛhẽť khanḍa. Iron implements.

Wilhelm von Hevesy wrote about the Finno-Ugric-Munda kinship, like "Munda-Magyar-Maori, an Indian link between the antipodes new tracks of Hungarian origins" and "Finnisch-Ugrisches aus Indien". (DRIEM, George van: Languages of the Himalayas: an ethnolinguistic handbook. 1997. p.161-162.) Sumerian-Ural-Altaic language affinities have been noted. Given the presence of Meluhha settlements in Sumer, some Meluhha glosses might have been adapted in these languages. One etyma cluster refers to 'iron' exemplified by meD (Ho.). The alternative suggestion for the origin of the gloss med 'copper' in Uralic languages may be explained by the word meD (Ho.) of Munda family of Meluhha language stream:

Sa. <i>mE~R~hE~'d</i> `iron'. ! <i>mE~RhE~d</i>(M).

Ma. <i>mErhE'd</i> `iron'.

Mu. <i>mERE'd</i> `iron'.

~ <i>mE~R~E~'d</i> `iron'. ! <i>mENhEd</i>(M).

Ho <i>meD</i> `iron'.

Bj. <i>merhd</i>(Hunter) `iron'.

KW <i>mENhEd</i>

@(V168,M080)

http://www.ling.hawaii.edu/austroasiatic/AA/Munda/ETYM/Pinnow&Munda

— Slavic glosses for 'copper'

Мед [Med]Bulgarian

Bakar Bosnian

Медзь [medz']Belarusian

Měď Czech

Bakar Croatian

KòperKashubian

Бакар [Bakar]Macedonian

Miedź Polish

Медь [Med']Russian

Meď Slovak

BakerSlovenian

Бакар [Bakar]Serbian

Мідь [mid'] Ukrainian[unquote]

http://www.vanderkrogt.net/elements/element.php?sym=Cu

Miedź, med' (Northern Slavic, Altaic) 'copper'.

One suggestion is that corruptions from the German "Schmied", "Geschmeide" = jewelry. Schmied, a smith (of tin, gold, silver, or other metal)(German) result in med 'copper'.

In this hieroglyph multiplex on the lapis-lazuli stamp seal, there are three hieroglyph components: 1. roundish ball; 2. notches (over 15 short strokes down a line); 3. mountain range.

Kur. goṭā any seed which forms inside a fruit or shell. *Malt.* goṭa a seed or berry(DEDR 069) N. *goṭo* ' piece ', *goṭi* ' chess piece '; A. *goṭ* ' a fruit, whole piece ', *°ṭā* ' globular, solid ', *guṭi* ' small ball, seed, kernel '; B. *goṭā* ' seed, bean, whole '; Or. *goṭā* ' whole, undivided ', M. *goṭā* m. ' roundish stone ' (CDIAL 4271) <gOTa>(P) {ADJ} ``^whole". {SX} ``^numeral ^intensive suffix". *Kh., Sa., Mu., Ho<goTA>,B.<goTa> `undivided'; Kh.<goThaG>(P), Sa.<goTAG>,~<gOTe'j>, Mu.<goTo>; Sad.<goT>, O., Bh.<goTa>; cf.Ju.<goTo> `piece', O.<goTa> `one'. %11811. #11721. <goTa>(BD) {NI} ``the ^whole". *@. #10971. (Munda etyma)

Rebus: <gota> {N} ``^stone". @3014. #10171. Note: The stone may be gota, laterite mineral ore stone. *khoṭ* m. 'base, alloy' (Punjabi) Rebus: koṭe 'forging (metal)(Mu.) Rebus: goṭī f. 'lump of silver' (G.) goṭi = silver (G.) koḍ 'workshop' (Gujarati).

Rebus: P. *goṭṭā* ' gold or silver lace ', H. *goṭā* m. ' edging of such ' (→ K. *goṭa* m. ' edging of gold braid ', S. *goṭo* m. ' gold or silver lace '); M. *goṭ* ' hem of a garment, metal wristlet '(CDIAL 4271)

Rebus: *goṭa 'laterite'.* Laterites are rusty soil types with iron oxides rich in iron and aluminium. They are formed in hot and wet tropical areas. Laterites can be easily cut with a spade into regular-sized blocks.

Hieroglyph: *dhollu* 'drummer' (Western Pahari) Rebus: dul 'cast metal'.

The 'drummer' hieroglyph thus announces a cast metal. ḍhōla m. ' large drum ' Rudray. 2. *ḍhōlla -- . [Only OAw. definitely attests -- l --] 1. Gy. pal. daul ' drum ', Paš. ḍūl (← Par. ḍuhūl IIFL iii 3, 65), Kho. (Lor.) dol, K. ḍōl m., kash. ḍhōl, L. P. Ku. N. A. B. ḍhol, OAw. ḍhora m., H. ḍhol m. -- Ext. -- kk -- : L. ḍholkī f. ' small drum ', Ku. ḍholko, H. ḍholak f.2. Pk. ḍholla -- m., Or. ḍhola, Mth. Bhoj. Aw. lakh. Marw. G. M. ḍhol m.*ḍhōlayati ' makes fall ' see *ḍhulati. *ḍhōlla -- : S.kcch. ḍholkī f. ' small drum '; WPah.kṭg. ḍhō`l m. ' large drum ', ḍhòlki f. ' small drum ', ḍhòlkɔ m. ' drum '; -- WPah.kṭg. ḍhòllu ' drummer '.(CDIAL 5608)

meḍho a ram, a sheep (G.)(CDIAL 10120); mRdu 'iron' Rebus: *muṇḍa* 'iron' (Sanskrit) mRdu, 'soft iron' *adar ḍangra* 'zebu'
H. *muḍḍhā* m. ' shoulder ', *mū̃ḍhā* m. ' lump, hump, shoulder ' Or. *muṇḍā* ' lump '.(CDIAL 10189)
Rebus: *muṇḍa* 'iron' (Sanskrit) mRdu, 'soft', *kuṇṭha*, 'hard', *kadāra* 'brittle' are three varieties of *muṇḍa loha*(Vagbhata, *Rasaratnasamuccaya*, 69-74). *muṇḍitam, muṇḍa loham* 'iron'; *muṇḍajam* 'steel' (Sanskrit) Thus, zebu reads rebus: *kuṇṭha munda (loha),* a type of iron native metal. (Vagbhata,

Rasaratnasamuccaya, 69-74).
पोळी [pōḷī] dewlap. Rebus: Russian gloss, *bulat* is cognate *pola* 'magnetite' iron in Asuri (Meluhha). Magnetite is the most magnetic of all the naturally occurring igneous and metamorphic rocks with black or brownish-black with a metallic luster. These magnetite ore stones could have been identified as *pola* iron by Meluhha speakers. Kannada gloss *pola* meaning 'point of the compass' may link with the characteristic of magnetite iron used to create a compass.*pŏlāduwu* made of steel; *pŏlād* प्वलाद् or *phōlād* फोलाद् मृदुलोहविशेषः] m. steel (Gr.M.; Rām. 431, 635, *phōlād*). *pŏlödi pōlödi phōlödi* लोहविशेषमयः adj. c.g. of steel, steel (Kashmiri) urukku what is melted, fused metal, steel.(Malayalam); ukk 'steel' (Telugu)(DEDR 661) This is cognate with famed 'wootz'steel. "Polad, Faulad" for steel in late Indian languages is traceable to Pokkhalavat, Polahvad. Pokkhalavat is the name of Pushkalavati, capital of Gandhara famed for iron and steel products. पोळें [pōḷēṃ] 'honeycomb' (shown as a pictorial motif on Lothal Seal 51).

Lothal Seal 51

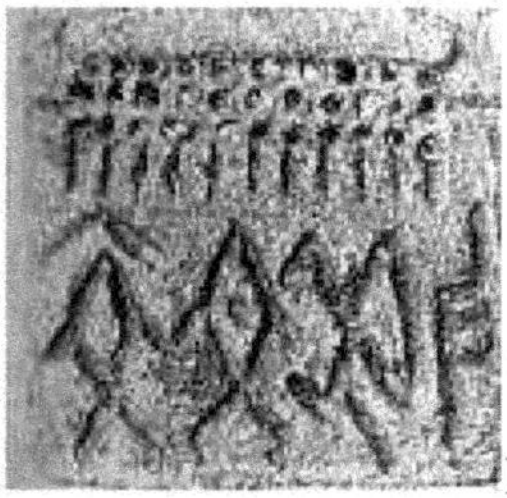

Lothal seal 51 Hieroglyph: *pōḷī,* 'dewlap, honeycomb' *pola, 'zebu' Rebus: pola,* 'magnetite'

ibha 'elephant' (Skt.); rebus: ib 'iron' (Ko.)
kolo 'jackal' (Kon.)

pola (magnetite), *gota* (laterite), *bichi* (hematite), three types of ferrite ores are signified by hieroglyphs:

pola 'zebu', *gota* 'round object', *bichi* 'scorpion'.

(a)

(b)

(c)

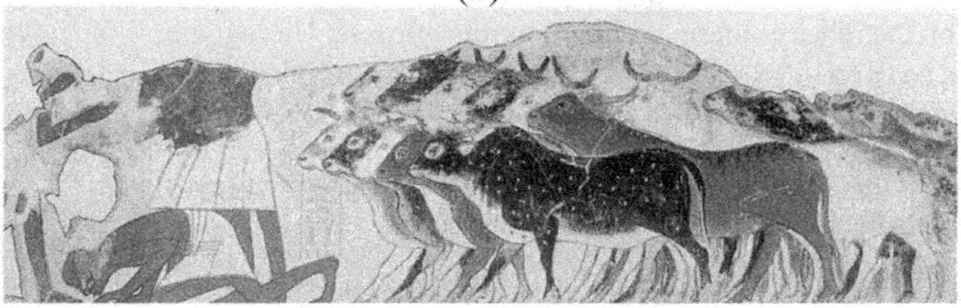

(d)

Pictorial evidence of the origin and dispersal of zebu. (a) Harappa seal (National Museum, India, [70]), 5000–3500 BP; (b) detail of cylindrical chlorite vessel (Mesopotamia (mid-5th millennium BP, The British Museum, London); (c) detail of conic object from Tarut Island near the Eastern coast of the Arabian peninsula (Metropolitan Museum, NY) and (d) detail of a painting: inspection of cattle belonging to Nebamun, Thebes,*ca.* 3400 BP, The British Museum, London).

http://www.mdpi.com/1424-2818/6/4/705/htm Marleen Felius et al, 2014, On the history of cattle genetic resources, *Diversity* 2014, 6(4), 705-750 "Around 2000 years after the taurine domestication, zebu was domesticated in the Indus Valley at the edge of the Indian Desert. Fossil remains attributed to zebu have been found in Mehrgarh, a proto-Indus culture site in Baluchistan in southwest Pakistan and were dated at 8000 BP."

Zebu, archaeometallurgy legacy of India. Zebu signifies magnetite, ferrous-ferric oxide Fe_3O_4 on Indus Script corpora metalwork catalogues.

That zebu, *bos indicus*, is an exclusive legacy of South Asia is proven by genetic studies.

Nausharo: céramique de la période I (c. 2500 BCE) cf. Catherine Jarrige

http://www.waa.ox.ac.uk/XDB/tours/indus6.asp

After the domestication of the zebu, *bos indicus*, deployment of the hierolyph of zebu on Indus Script Corpora is a significant advance in archaeometallurgy documentation.

The writing system depicting a hieroglyph multiplex of a zebu tied to a post with a bird perched on top is based on the rebus rendering of the Prakrtam glosses: Hieroglyph: पोळ [*pōḷa*], 'zebu' Rebus: magnetite, citizen. baTa 'quail' Rebus: baTha 'furnace'. The messaging on Nausharo pots of a magnetite furnace for metalwork continues on seals and tablets including copper plates as metalwork catalogues.

The Prakrtam gloss पोळ [*pōḷa*], 'zebu' as hieroglyph is read rebus: *pōḷa*, 'magnetite, ferrous-ferric oxide';*poliya* 'citizen, gatekeeper of town quarter'.

Zebu also signifies a native metal blacksmith: another gloss for zebu: *ad.ar d.an:gra* (Santali); rebus: *aduru* 'native metal' (Ka.) *d.han:gar* 'blacksmith' (WPah.) *aduru* = *gan.iyinda tegadu karagade iruva aduru* = ore taken from the mine and not subjected to melting in a furnace (Kannada. Siddha_nti Subrahman.ya' S'astri's new interpretation of the*Amarakos'a*, Bangalore, Vicaradarpana Press, 1872, p. 330). *Ta. ayil* iron. *Ma. ayir, ayiram*any ore. *Ka. aduru* native metal. *Tu. ajirda karba* very hard iron. (DEDR 192). *ayas* 'metal' (Rigveda); *aya*'iron' (Gujarati)
Note: *karba* 'iron' is signified by hieroglyphs: *karibha* 'trunk of elephant' (Pali); *ibha*'elephant' (Samsritam). Thus, *ajirda karba* (Tulu) = *aduru (aya) karba* 'native metal iron' in semantic expansion of Prakrtam in tune with archaeometallurgy advances in smelting, alloying and *cire perdue*metalcastings.

On a hieroglyph multiplex (hypertext), both zebu and elephant are signified by hieroglyph component: horn of zebu, trunk of elephant (together with other hieroglyph components such as tiger, snake, bovine, scarf, pannier):

m0301 Mohenjo-daro

Hieroglyph: पोळ [pōḷa] *m* A bull dedicated to the gods, marked with a trident and discus, and set at large. பொலியெருது poli-y-erutu , *n.* < பொலி- +. 1. Bull kept for covering; பசுக்களைச் சினையாக்குதற் பொருட்டு வளர்க்கப்படும் காளை. (பிங்.) கொடிய பொலியெருதை யிருமூக்கிலும் கயி றொன்று கோத்து (அறப். சத. 42). 2. The leading ox in treading out grain on a threshing-floor; களத்துப் பிணையல்மாடுகளில் முதற்செல்லுங் கடா. (W.) பொலி முறைநாகு poli-murai-nāku, *n.* < பொலி + முறை +. Heifer fit for covering; பொலியக்கூடிய பக்குவமுள்ள கிடாரி. (S. I. I. iv, 102.)

Rebus 1: pōḷa 'magnetite, ferrous-ferric oxide Fe3O4'.

Rebus 2: pol m. 'gate, courtyard, town quarter with its own gate': Ka. poṟal town, city. Te. prōlu, (inscr.) pṟōl(u) city. ? (DEDR 4555) पोवळ or पोंवळ [pōvaḷa or pōṃvaḷa] f पोवळी or पोंवळी f The court-wall of a temple. (Marathi) *pratōlika ' gatekeeper '. [pratōlī --] H. pauliyā, pol°, pauriyā m. ' gatekeeper ', G. poḷiyɔ m.(CDIAL 8632) pratōlī f. ' gate of town or fort, main street ' MBh. [Cf. tōlikā -- . -- Perh. conn. with tōraṇa -- EWA ii 361, less likely with *ṭōla --] Pk. paōlī -- f. ' city gate, main street '; WPah. (Joshi) prauḷ m., °ḷi f., pauḷ m., °ḷi f. ' gateway of a chief ', proḷ ' village ward '; H. paul, pol m. ' gate, courtyard, town quarter with its own gate ', paulī f. ' gate '; OG. poli f. ' door '; G. poḷi f. ' street '; M. pauḷ, poḷ f. ' wall of loose stones '. -- Forms with -- r -- poss. < *pradura -- : OAw. paüri ' gatepost '; H. paur, °rī, pãwar, °rī f. ' gate, door '.WPah.poet. prɔ̃ḷ m., prɔḷo m., prɔḷe f. ' gate of palace or temple '.(CDIAL 8633) Porin (adj.) [fr. pora=Epic Sk. paura citizen, see pura. Semantically cp. urbane>urbanus>urbs; polite= poli/ths>po/lis. For pop. etym. see DA i.73 & 282] belonging to a citizen, i. e. citizenlike, urbane, polite, usually in phrase porī vācā polite speech D i.4, 114; S i.189; ii.280=A ii.51; A iii.114; Pug 57; Dhs 1344; DA i.75, 282; DhsA 397. Cp. BSk. paurī vācā MVastu iii.322. Porisa2 (nt.) [abstr. fr. purisa, *pauruṣyaŋ, cp. porisiya and poroseyya] 1. business, doing of a man (or servant, cp. purisa 2), service, occupation; human doing, activity M i.85 (rāja°); Vv 6311 (=purisa -- kicca VvA 263); Pv iv.324 (uṭṭhāna°=purisa -- viriya, purisa -- kāra PvA 252). -- 2. height of a man M. i.74, 187, 365.(Pali) పౌరము [pauramu] *pauramu*. [Skt. from పురి.] adj. Belonging to a city or town (పురము.) పౌరసతులు the ladies of the place: citizens' wives. పౌరలోకము *paura-lōkamu*. n. The townsfolk, a body of citizens. పౌరుడు *pauruḍu*. n. A citizen. పౌరులు citizens, townsfolk.(Telugu)

वृषः 1 A bull; असंपदस्तस्य वृषेण गच्छतः Ku.5.8; Me.54; R.2.35; Ms.9.123. -2 The sign *Taurus* of the zodiac. -3 The chief or best of a class, the best of its kind; (often at the end of comp.); मुनिवृषः, कपिवृषः &c. -उत्सर्गः setting free a bull on the occasion of a funeral rite, or as a religious act generally; एकादशाहे प्रेतस्य यस्य चोत्सृज्यते वृषः । प्रेतलोकं परित्यज्य स्वर्गलोकं च गच्छति (Samskrtam. Apte)

वृषोत्सर्ग [p=1012,2] *m.* letting loose a bull (or accord. to some , a bull and four heifers , as a work of merit esp. on the occasion of a श्राद्ध in honour of deceased ancestors) Gr2S. Pan5cat. RTL. 319 (Monier-Williams. Samskrtam)

"The letting loose of a bull (vRshotsarga) stamped with Siva's trident -- in cities like Benares and Gaya is fraught with the highest merit. This setting free of a bull to roam about at will often takes place at zrAddhas." (Monier Monier-Williams, 1891, *Brahmanism and Hinduism: or religious thought and life in Asia*, Macmillan, p.319). In Hindu tradition, GRhyasUtra prescribe procedures for vRshotsarga.

"It is note-worthy that the details of the ceremony of setting a bull at liberty viz. the 'Vrshotsarga' in the

Grhya-Sutras viz. S & P, in which it is described are almost identical (mutual borrowing or a common source are possibilities). On the Karttika full-moon day or on the day of the Asvayuja month falling under the Nakshtra RevatI, the fire is made to blaze in the midst of cows and Ajya oblations are sacrificed with ap propriate Mantras. Then he sacrifices from the Sthalipaka be longing to Pushan with an invocation to Pushan. Then he selects a bull of one, two or three colours or a red bull or one that leads the herd or is loved by the herd, perfect in all limbs and the finest in the herd, mumuring the Rudra-hymns. Then that bull is adorned, as also four of the finest young cows of the herd and then he says "This young bull, I give you as your husband; sporting with him, your lover, walk about etc." When the bull is in the midst of the cows, he recites over them the Rig-Verses X, 169. With the milk of all those cows he should cook milk-rice and feed the Brahmins with it. In the opinion of some (P) an animal is sacrificed in this rite, in which case the ritual is the same as that of the *sula-gava*."
http://dli.gov.in/rawdataupload/upload/0113/986/RTF/00000141.rtf

Hieroglyph: eagle పోలడు [pōlaḍu] , పోలిగాడు or దూడలపోలడు *pōlaḍu*. [Tel.] n. An eagle. పసులపోలిగాడు the bird called the Black Drongo. *Dicrurus ater*. (F.B.I.)(Telugu)

Rebus: पोळ [pōḷa] 'magnetite', ferrous-ferric oxide Fe3O4 (Asuri)

Rebus: cattle festival: पोळा [pōḷā] *m* (पोळ) A festive day for cattle,--the day of new moon of श्रावण or of भाद्रपद. Bullocks are exempted from labor; variously daubed and decorated; and paraded about in worship. "Pola is a bull-worshipping festival celebrated by farmers mainly in the Indian state of Maharashtra (especially among the Kunbis). On the day of Pola, the farmers decorate and worship their bulls. Pola falls on the day of the *Pithori Amavasya* (the new moon day) in the month of Shravana (usually in August)." https://en.wikipedia.org/wiki/Pola_(festival) Festival held on the day after Sankranti (= kANum) is called pōlāla paNDaga (Telugu).

Bemrose, Collo., Derby.

FIGURES OF ANIMALS MADE FOR POLA FESTIVAL.

Toy animals made for the Pola festival especially celebrated by the Dhanoje Kunbis. (Bemrose, Colo. Derby - Russell, Robert Vane (1916). The Tribes and Castes of the Central Provinces of India: volume IV. Descriptive articles on the principal castes and tribes of the Central Provinces. London: Macmillan and Co., limited. p. 40).

Some artifacts of Sarasvati-Sindhu Civilization point to the possibility that the celebration of pola cattle festival may be traced to the cultural practices of 3rd millennium BCE.

Copper chariot was found by M.S. Vats, the Director of the ASI, at Harappa. Dates back to 3000 BCE "(Vats) found several pieces of a small copper chariot, about two inches in height. Hreconstructed it from those several pieces or parts. The wheels are missing, so are the yoke and the axle. The man sitting inside has braided his long hair into a knot. Mr. Vats claims this to be the first miniature model of a chariot in the worlld." https://aryaninvasionmyth.wordpress.com/2012/10/01/3/

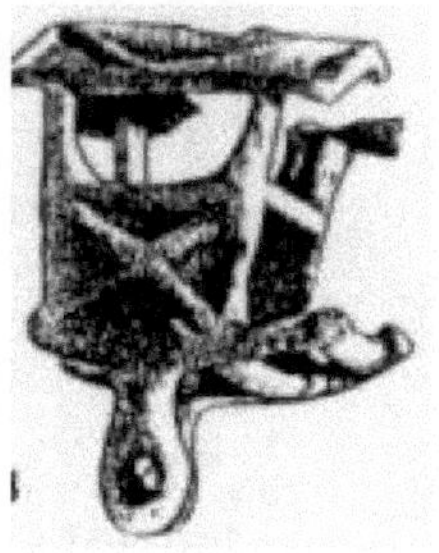

Copper model of a passenger box on a cart, Chanhudaro, ca. 2,000 BCE http://bharatkalyan97.blogspot.in/2011/07/ancient-chariots-in-indian-civilization.html

Harappan Chariot toy kept at the Brooklyn University Museum

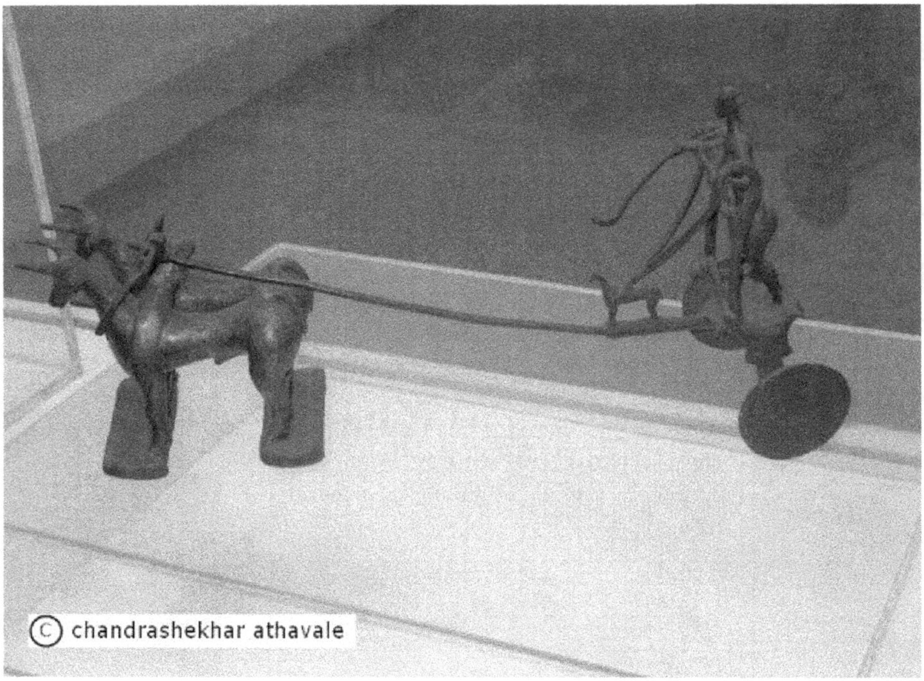

Oxen pulled Bronze chariot found at Daimabad in Maharshtra

chandrashekharasandprints.wordpress.com

Daimabad bronze chariot. c. 1500 BCE. 22X52X17.5 cm.

Buffalo. Daimabad bronze. Prince of Wales Museum, Mumbai.

Daimabad bronzes. Buffalo on four-legged platform attached to four solid wheels 31X25 cm.; elephanton four-legged platform with axles 25 cm.; rhinoceros on axles of four solid wheels 25X19 cm. (MK Dhavalikar, 'Daimabad bronzes' in: Harappan civilization, ed. by GL Possehl, New Delhi, 1982, pp. 361-6; SA Sali, Daimabad 1976-1979, New Delhi, 1986).

Hieroglyph: पोळ [pōḷa]*n* C (Or पोळें) A honeycomb. (Marathi)

पोळा [pōḷā]The cake-form portion of a honeycomb. A kindled portion flying up from a burning mass, a flake. पोळींव [pōḷīṃva] *p* of पोळणें Burned, scorched, singed, seared.पोळणें [pōḷaṇēṃ] *v i* To catch, burn, singe; to be seared or scorched.

This note demonstrates that the hieroglyph read rebus in Meluhha signifies a unique archaeometallurgy legacy of ancient India and Ancient Near East including the Levant.

Zebu when deployed as a hieroglyph multiplex on Indus Script corpora signifies magnetite Fe3O4 metalwork catalogues.

"Magnetite is a mineral, ferrous-ferric oxide, one of the three common naturally occurring iron oxides (chemical formula Fe3O4) and a member of the spinel group. Magnetite is the most magnetic of all the naturally occurring minerals on Earth.[Harrison, R. J.; Dunin-Borkowski, RE; Putnis, A (2002). "Direct imaging of nanoscale magnetic interactions in minerals". Proceedings of the National Academy of Sciences 99 (26): 16556–16561] Naturally magnetized pieces of magnetite, called lodestone, will attract small pieces of iron, and this was how ancient people first noticed the property of magnetism...Magnetite reacts with oxygen to produce hematite, and the mineral pair forms a buffer that can control oxygen fugacity."

"Magnetite is a mineral, one of the three common naturally occurring iron oxides (chemical formula Fe3O4) and a member of the spinel group. Magnetite is the most magnetic of all the naturally occurring minerals on Earth.[Harrison, R. J.; Dunin-Borkowski, RE; Putnis, A (2002). "Direct imaging of nanoscale magnetic interactions in minerals". Proceedings of the National Academy of Sciences 99 (26): 16556–16561.] Naturally magnetized pieces of magnetite, called lodestone, will attract small pieces of iron, and this was how ancient people first noticed the property of magnetism."

http://www.pnas.org/content/99/26/16556.full.pdf loc.cit. *https://en.wikipedia.org/wiki/Magnetite*

Magnetite and pyrite from Piedmont, Italy

https://en.wikipedia.org/wiki/Magnetite

Magnetite is a common mineral, an important ore of iron, ferromagnetic, that is, it is a natural magnet strongly attracted to magnetic fields. Heavily striated crystals with growth layers come from Parachinar, Pakistan. http://www.minerals.net/mineral/magnetite.aspx

"The process by which lodestone is created has long been an open question in geology. Only a small amount of the magnetite on Earth is found magnetized as lodestone. Ordinary magnetite is attracted to a magnetic field like iron and steel is, but does not tend to become magnetized itself; it has too low a magnetic coercivity (resistance to demagnetization) to stay magnetized for long...The leading theory suggests that lodestones are magnetized by the strong magnetic fields surrounding lightning bolts."

https://en.wikipedia.org/wiki/Lodestone See: http://www.phy6.org/earthmag/lodeston.htm

[quote] Magnetite, a ferrimagnetic mineral with chemical formula Fe3O4, one of several iron oxides, is one of the more common meteor-wrongs. Magnetite displays a black exterior and magnetic properties.

magnetite

Magnetite can be a found in a meteorite's crust. When a meteor enters the earth's atmosphere the rock's surface is ablated by ultra high temperatures. Before it hits the ground, the molten surface solidifies into a thin glassy coating, called fusion crust. Crystals of magnetite color the thin fusion crust black. (Magnetite streaks black - see photo below)

lodestone
A piece of intensely magnetic magnetite was used as an early form of magnetic compass. Iron, steel and ordinary magnetite are attracted to a magnetic field, including the Earth's magnetic field. Only magnetite with a particular crystalline structure, lodestone, can act as a natural magnet and attract and magnetize iron. The name "magnet" comes from lodestones found in a place called Magnesia. [unquote] http://meteorite-identification.com/Hot%20Rocks/magnetite.html

Ancient Blacksmiths: ukku pola (steel from magnetite)?

Magnetite var. lodestone 5.0x4.5x3.5cm With nails and metal dust attached to it.

Superb, mirror-like crystals of lustrous Magnetite covering one side of block of matrix. These Magnetite crystals are exceptionally sharp and well formed. 5 x 4 x 2 cm.A tool to use the magnetic qualities of iron is a lodestone (which is a natural magnetic iron oxide mineral). Such a tool could have enabled ancient blacksmiths to identify and distinguish a type if iron ore called 'magnetite' called in Meluhha: *pola* (which yields the Russian *bulat* steel) made from Latin *wootz* (Meluhha *ukku*).

"In the Muslim world of the 9th-12th centuries CE, the production of fuladh, a Persian word, has been described by Al-Kindi, Al-Biruni and Al-Tarsusi, from *narm-ahan*and *shaburqan*, two other Persian words representing iron products obtained by direct reduction of the ore. *Ahan* means iron. *Narm-ahan* is a soft iron and shaburqan a harder one or able to be quench-hardened. Old nails and horse-shoes were also used as base for *fuladh* preparation. It must be noticed that, according to Hammer- Purgstall, there was no Arab word for steel, which explain the use of Persian words. Fuladh prepared by melting in small crucibles can be considered as a steel in our modem classification, due to its properties (hardness, quench hardened ability, etc.). The word *fuladh* means "the purified" as explained by Al-Kindi. This word can be found as *puladh*, for instance in Chardin (1711 AD) who called this product; *poulad jauherder*, *acier onde*, which means "watering steel", a characteristic of what was called Damascene steel in Europe."

http://bharatkalyan97.blogspot.in/2014/02/identity-of-ancient-meluhha-blacksmiths.html

Known to ancient Greeks, magnetite was so-called because it was found in the lands of the Magnetes (Magnesia) in Thessaly. Ancient Indians (Bharatam Janam) called it पोळ [pōḷa] which gave the root for the famed crucible wootz steel called पोलाद [pōlāda] *n* (or P) पोलादी 'steel'.
पोलाद [pōlāda] *n* (or P) Steel. पोलादी *a* Of steel. (Marathi) bulad 'steel, flint and steel for making fire' (Amharic); fUlAd 'steel' (Arabic)

The Marathi gloss pōlāda may be formed with pōḷa+hlād = magnetite ore + rejoice.

[HLĀD ' rejoice ': āhlādayati,āhlādayati ' refreshes, gladdens ' MBh. [*āhlāda* -- m. ' joy ', Pk. *alhāya* -- m.: √hlād] H. *āhlānā*, *aihl*°, *alhānā* intr. ' to rejoice '.(CDIAL 1549) प्रह्ला prahrā (ह्ला hlā) दः dḥ प्रह्ला (ह्ला) दः 1 Great joy, pleasure, delight, happi- ness. प्रह्ला (ह्ला) दन *a.* Gladdening, delighting; प्रह्लादनं ज्योतिरजन्यनेन R.13.4. अग्निः agniḥ -प्रस्तरः [अग्निं प्रस्तृणाति अग्नेः प्रस्तरो वा] a flint, a stone producing fire.]

pola 'magnetite ore' (Munda. Asuri)

See: http://bharatkalyan97.blogspot.in/2014/02/ancient-blacksmiths.html Three mineral ores: *pola* (magnetite), *gota* (laterite), *bichi* (hematite) -- all three Meluhha glosses -- are three varieties of minerals with sources for alloying metals. The importance of *bichi* (hematite) as a hieroglyph has been detailed.

See: http://bharatkalyan97.blogspot.in/2014/09/catalogs-of-pola-kuntha-gota-bichi.html Catalogs of *pola*, *kuṇṭha*, *goṭa*, *bichi* native metalwork in Meluhha Indus script hieroglyphs

Socio-cultural context in which pola and gota were recognized by early metalworkers (blacksmiths):

While we do not know where this piece was found, the zebu bull motif ("the essence of civilization" according to the Italian exhibitors) is similar to a pot found at Nausharo in Balochistan and dated to roughly 2600-2500 BCE. The archaeologist Ute-Franke-Vogt writes about the Kulli culture from which it may stem "This late Kulli occupation to which the largest number of sites in southern Balochistan belong, co-existed with the Indus Civilization (Kanri Buthi). http://balochhistory11.blogspot.in/2014/12/brilliantly-painted-pottery-vessels.html

Nausharo, Mehrgarh: ceramique c. 2500 BCE, C. Jarrige. Nausharo was inhabited later than Mehrgarh, probably first from about 2800 BCE C. Jarrige

http://www.guimet.fr/La-mission-archeologique-de-l,636

loc. cit. http://www.waa.ox.ac.uk/XDB/tours/indus6.asp

https://www.academia.edu/14548989/Bhirrana_to_Mehrgarh_and_beyond_in_the_civilization_contact_areas_from_8th_millennium_BCE

Slippainted cylindrical jar. Kulli.

Indus Valley Terracotta Vessel - LO.1329
Origin: Pakistan/Western India
Circa: 3500 BC to 2000 BC Dimensions: 11.1" (28.2cm) high x 12.9" (32.8cm) wide
Collection: Asian Art
Medium: Terracotta http://barakatgallery.com/store/Index.cfm/FuseAction/ItemDetails/UserID/catalogue/ItemID/23292/CFID/9319250/CFTOKEN/12663335.htm

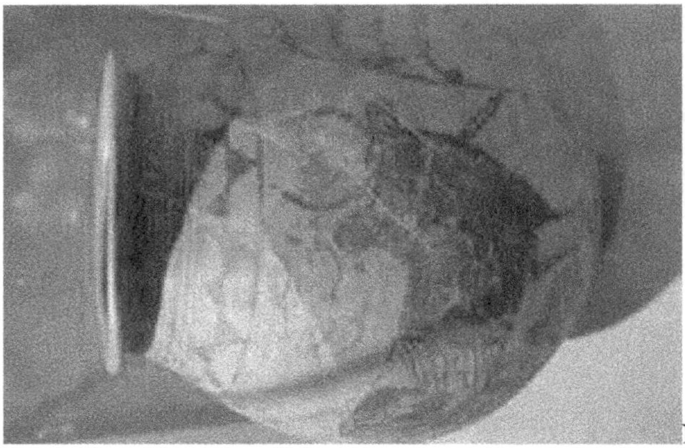
Nausharo. Pot

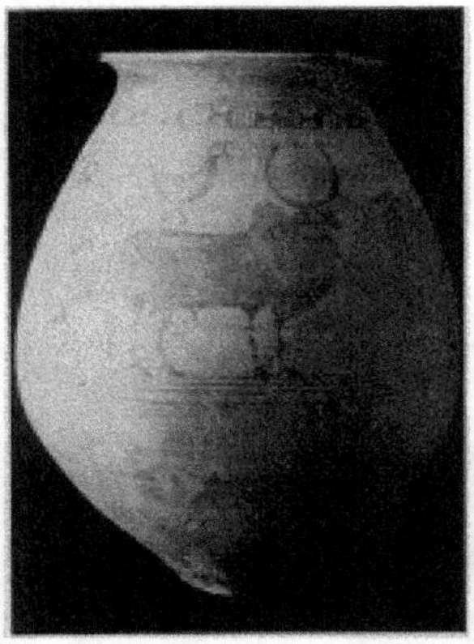

A zebu bull tied to a post; a bird above. Large painted storage jar discovered in burned rooms at Nausharo, ca. 2600 to 2500 BCE. Cf. Fig. 2.18, J.M. Kenoyer, 1998, Cat. No. 8. Bos indicus motif on a pot from the Mehrgarh period (ca. 7000-5500 BCE) Hieroglyph: baṭa 'quail'; bhaṭa 'furnace' (G.); baṭa 'a kind of iron' (Gujarati.)

Hypertexts signifying a tiger or zebu tied by a rope to a post are signified on some examples from Indus Script Corpora.

Pl. XXII B. Terracotta cake with incised figures on obverse and reverse, Harappan. On one side is a human figure wearing a head-dress having two horns and a plant in the centre; on the other side is an animal-headed human figure with another animal figure, the latter being dragged by the former.

Decipherment of hieroglyphs on the Kalibangan terracotta cake:

bhaTa 'warrior' rebus: bhaTa 'furnace'

kolmo 'rice plant' rebus: kolimi 'smithy, forge'

koD 'horn' rebus: koD 'workshop'

kola 'tiger' rebus: kolle 'blacksmith', kolhe 'smelter' kol 'working in iron'

The tiger is being pulled to be tied to a post, pillar.

Hieroglyph: *Ka.* kunda a pillar of bricks, etc. *Tu.* kunda pillar, post. *Te.* kunda id. *Malt.* kunda block, log. ? Cf. Ta. kantu pillar, post. (DEDR 1723) Rebus: (agni)kuNDA 'fire-altar, vedi'.

Hieriglyph: *meṛh* rope tying to post, pillar: mēthí m. ' pillar in threshing floor to which oxen are fastened, prop for supporting carriage shafts ' AV., °*thī* -- f. KātyŚr.com., *mēdhī* -- f. Divyāv. 2. mēṭhī -- f. PañcavBr.com., *mēḍhī* -- , *mēṭī* -- f. BhP.1. Pa. *mēdhi* -- f. ' post to tie cattle to, pillar, part of a stūpa '; Pk. *mēhi* -- m. ' post on threshing floor ', N. *meh(e)*, *miho*, *miyo*, B. *mei*, Or. *maï* -- *dāṇḍi*, Bi. *mēh*, *mēhā* ' the post ', (SMunger) *mehā* ' the bullock next the post ', Mth. *meh*, *mehā* ' the post ', (SBhagalpur)*mīhā̃* ' the bullock next the post ', (SETirhut) *mẽhi bāṭi* ' vessel with a projecting base '.2. Pk. *mēḍhi* -- m. ' post on threshing floor ', *mēḍhaka*<-> ' small stick '; K. *mīr*, *mīrü* f. ' larger hole in ground which serves as a mark in pitching walnuts ' (for semantic relation of ' post -- hole ' see kūpa -- 2); L. *meṛh* f. ' rope tying oxen to each other and to post on threshing floor '; P. *mehṛ* f., *mehaṛ* m. ' oxen on threshing floor, crowd '; OA *meṛha*, *mehra* ' a circular construction, mound '; Or. *meṛhī,meri* ' post on threshing floor '; Bi. *mẽṛ* ' raised bank between irrigated beds ', (Camparam) *mẽṛhā* ' bullock next the post ', Mth. (SETirhut) *mẽṛhā* ' id. '; M. *meḍ(h)*, *meḍhī* f., *meḍhā* m. ' post, forked stake '.mēthika -- ; mēthiṣṭhá -- . mēthika m. ' 17th or lowest cubit from top of sacrificial post ' lex. [mēthí --]Bi. *mẽhiyā* ' the bullock next the post on threshing floor '.mēthiṣṭhá ' standing at the post ' TS. [mēthí -- , stha --] Bi. (Patna) *mĕhṭhā* ' post on threshing floor ', (Gaya) *mehṭā*, *mẽhṭā* ' the bullock next the post '.(CDIAL 10317 to, 10319) Rebus: meD 'iron' (Ho.); med 'copper' (Slavic)

Note the Isapur yupa which show ropes in the middle and on the top to tie an animal as shown on the Kaibangan terracotta cake. In the case of the Kalibangan terracotta cake, the hieroglyph shows a kola, 'tiger' tied to the rope. The rebus reading is kol 'working in iron'. The work in iron is signified by the post, yupa: *meḍ(h)*, 'post, stake' rebus: *meḍ* 'iron', med 'copper' (Slavic).

Thus, the terracotta cake inscription signifies a iron workshop smelter/furnace and smithy.

Kulli. Plate. Two tigers tied to a meshed axle. Stars. Fish.

Decipherment:

dula 'pair' rebus: *dul* 'cast metal'

kola 'tiger' rebus: *kolhe* 'smelter' kol 'working in iron' *kolle* 'blacksmith'. http://www.harappa.com/figurines/index.html kola 'tiger' kola 'woman' Rebus: kol 'working in iron'. Ta. kol working in iron, blacksmith; kollaṉ blacksmith. Ma. kollan blacksmith, artificer. Ko. kole·l smithy, temple in Kota village. To. kwala·l Kota smithy. Ka.kolime, kolume, kulame, kulime, kulume, kulme fire-pit, furnace; (Bell.;.P.U.) konimi blacksmith

(Gowda) kolla id. Koḍ. kollë blacksmith. Te. kolimi furnace. Go.(SR.) kollusānā to mend implements; (Ph.) kolstānā, kulsānā to forge; (Tr.) kōlstānā to repair (of ploughshares); (SR.) kolmi smithy (Voc. 948). Kuwi (F.) kolhali to forge(DEDR 2133).

मेढ (p. 662) [mēḍha] the polar star (Phonetic determinant); *meḍ(h)*, *meḍhī* f., *meḍhā* m. 'post, forked stake' rebus: *meD*'iron' (Ho.); *med* 'copper'

kāṇḍa 'water' rebus: *kāṇḍa* 'tools, pots and pans and metal-ware'.

Thus, the inscription on the Kulli plate signifies iron smelting, cast iron (metal) implements.

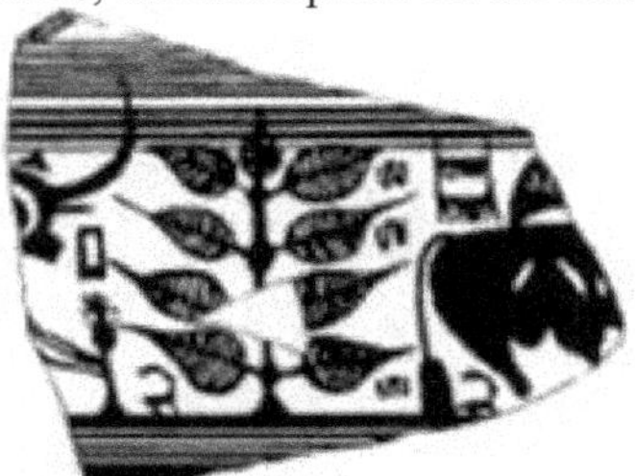

Zebu and leaves. In front of the standard device and the stylized tree of 9 leaves, are the black buck antelopes. Black paint on red ware of Kulli style. Mehi. Second-half of 3rd millennium BCE. [After G.L. Possehl, 1986, *Kulli: an exploration of an ancient civilization in South Asia*, Centers of Civilization, I, Durham, NC: 46, fig. 18 (Mehi II.4.5), based on Stein 1931: pl. 30.

Decipherment:

adar ḍangra 'zebu' (Santali); Rebus: aduru 'native metal' (Ka.);ḍhan:gar 'blacksmith' (WPah.) ayir = iron dust, any ore (Ma.) aduru = *gan.iyinda tegadu karagade iruva aduru* = ore taken from the mine and not subjected to melting in a furnace (Ka. Siddha_nti Subrahman.ya' S'astri's new interpretation of the Amarakos'a, Bangalore, Vicaradarpana Press, 1872, p. 330) EDR 192 *Ta.* ayil iron. *Ma.* ayir, ayiram any ore. *Ka.* aduru native metal. *Tu.* ajirda karba very hard iron.

Hieroglyph: *lo* = nine (Santali); *no* = nine (B.) *on-patu* = nine (Ta.)

[Note the count of nine fig leaves on m0296] Rebus: loa = a species of fig tree, *ficus glomerata*, the fruit of *ficus glomerata* (Santali.lex.)(Phonetic determinant)

   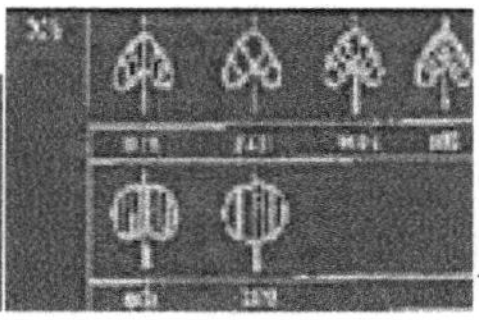

V326 (Orthographic variants of Sign 326)

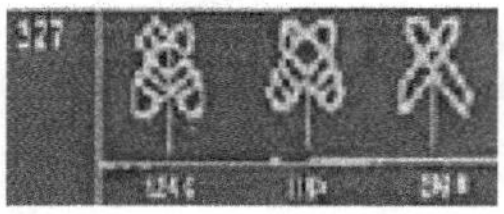

V327 (Orthographic variants of Sign 327)

loa = a species of fig tree, *ficus glomerata*, the fruit of *ficus glomerata* (Santali) Rebus: lo 'iron' (Assamese, Bengali); loa 'iron' (Gypsy) lauha = made of copper or iron (Gr.S'r.); metal, iron (Skt.); lo_haka_ra = coppersmith, ironsmith (Pali); lo_ha_ra = blacksmith (Pt.); lohal.a (Or.); lo_ha = metal, esp. copper or bronze (Pali); copper (VS.); loho, lo_ = metal, ore, iron (Si.) loha lut.i = iron utensils and implements (Santali.lex.)

The hypertext signifies iron or copper metal work, with particular reference to magnetite ore: lo 'iron or copper' PLUS poLa 'zebu' rebus: poLa 'magnetite (ferrite ore)' PLUS *meṛh* f. 'rope tying oxen to each other and to post on threshing floor' rebus: meD 'iron', med 'copper'.

Shahdad plates signifying zebu and tiger as catalogues of metalwork:

Shahdad.Plates 5 & 6. Chlorite incised vessel Grave No. 001.

Object No. 0004 (p.26) Hakemi, Ali, 1997, *Shahdad, archaeological excavations of a bronze age center in Iran*, Reports and Memoirs, Vol. XXVII, IsMEO, Rome. 766 pp.

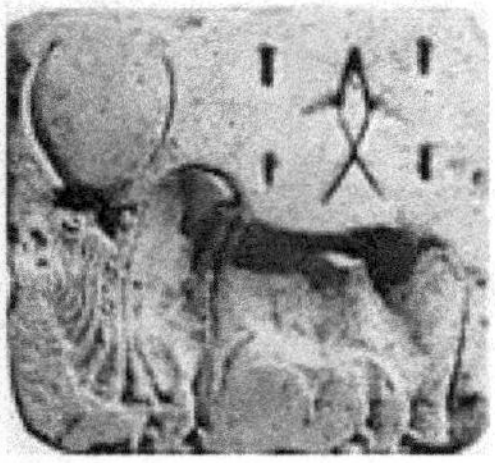

Mohenjo-daro Seals m1118 and Kalibangan 032, glyphs used are: Zebu (*bos taurus indicus*), fish, four-strokes (allograph: arrow).*ayo* 'fish' (Mu.) + *kaṇḍa* 'arrow' (Skt.) *ayaskāṇḍa* 'a quantity of iron, excellent iron' (Pāṇ.gaṇ) aya = iron (G.); ayah, ayas = metal (Skt.) *gaNDa*, 'four' (Santali); Rebus: *kaṇḍ* 'fire-altar', 'furnace'), arrow read rebus in mleccha (Meluhhan) as a reference to a guild of artisans working with *ayaskāṇḍa* 'excellent quantity of iron' (Pāṇini) is consistent with the primacy of economic activities which resulted in the invention of a writing system, now referred to as Indus Writing.

काण्डः kāṇḍḥ ण्डम् ṇḍam The portion of a plant from one knot to another. काण्डात्काण्ड- त्प्ररोहन्ती Mahānār.4.3. A stem, stock, branch; लीलोत्खातमृणाल काण्डकवलच्छेदे U.3.16; Amaru.95; Ms. 1.46,48, Māl.3.34. కాండము [kāṇḍamu] *kāṇḍamu*. [Skt.] n. Water. నీళ్లు (Telugu) kaṇṭhá -- : (b) ' water -- channel ': Paš. *kaṭā´* ' irrigation channel ', Shum. *xāṭṭä.* (CDIAL 14349).

Chanhu-darho in Sindh in 1935-36. Steatite, Height: 3.20 Width: 3.20 cm (h:1 1/4 w:1 1/4 inches). Courtesy of The Cleveland Museum of Art, J. H. Wade Fund 1973.160.

poLa 'zebu' rebus: poLa 'magnetite'

kaNDa 'square/divisions' rebus: kANDa 'implements' dula 'pair' rebus: dul 'cast metal' PLUS meD 'body' rebus: meD 'iron or copper' Thus, metal implements.

Parenthesis may be orthographically a split rhombus, shaped like an ingot: Hieroglyph: *mūhā* 'ingot' rebus: mũhẽ = the quantity of iron produced at one time in a native smelting furnace of the Kolhes; iron produced by the Kolhes and formed like a four-cornered piece a little pointed at each end; *kolhe tehen me~ṛhe~t mūhā akata* = the Kolhes have to-day produced pig iron (Santali) PLUS karaNDava 'aquatic bird' rebus: karaDa 'hard alloy' thus, hard alloy ingot.

khareḍo = a currycomb (Gujarati) खरारा [kharārā] m (H) A currycomb. 2 Currying a horse. (Marathi) Rebus: 1. करडा [karaḍā] Hard from alloy--iron, silver &c. (Marathi) 2. kharādī ' turner' (Gujarati) The hypertext message is thus a metalwork catalogue of a metals turner working with iron, hard alloy ingots and magnetite (ferrite ore).

http://bharatkalyan97.blogspot.in/2016/01/octagonal-yupo-bhavati-satapatha.html

Decipherment of Sibri cylinder seal:

खांडा [khāṇḍā] *m* A jag, notch, or indentation (as upon the edge of a tool or weapon). (Marathi) Rebus: *khāṇḍā* 'tools, pots and pans, metal-ware'. poLa 'zebu' rebus: poLa 'magnetite ore'. Thus magnetite (iron) metal tools/implements.

M-264 a

Mohenjodaro seal (M-264) dula 'pair' rebus: dul 'cast metal' adar 'lid' rebus: aduru 'native metal'

खांडा [khāṇḍā] *m* A jag, notch, or indentation (as upon the edge of a tool or weapon). (Marathi) Rebus: *khāṇḍā* 'tools, pots and pans, metal-ware'.karNIka 'rim of jar' Rebus: karNI 'supercargo' karNIka 'scribe'.

M-262 A

Mohenjodaro seal (M-262) poLa 'zebu' rebus: poLa 'magnetite ore'

meD 'body' rebus: meD 'iron' med 'copper' gaNDa 'four' rebus: khaNDa 'implements'. Thus iron implements.

M-328 a

Mohenjodaro seal (M-328) poLa 'zebu' rebus: poLa 'magnetite ore'

meD 'body' rebus: meD 'iron' med 'copper' koDa 'one' rebus: koD 'workshop' kuTi 'water-carrier' rebus: kuThi 'smelter' karNIka 'rim of jar' Rebus: karNI 'supercargo' karNIka 'scribe'.

A Munda gloss for fish is 'aya'. Read rebus: *aya* 'iron' (Gujarati) *ayas* 'metal' (Vedic).

The script inscriptions indicate a set of modifiers or ligatures to the hieroglyph indicating that the metal, *aya*, was worked on during the early Bronze Age metallurgical processes -- to produce *aya* ingots, *aya* metalware ,*aya* hard alloys.

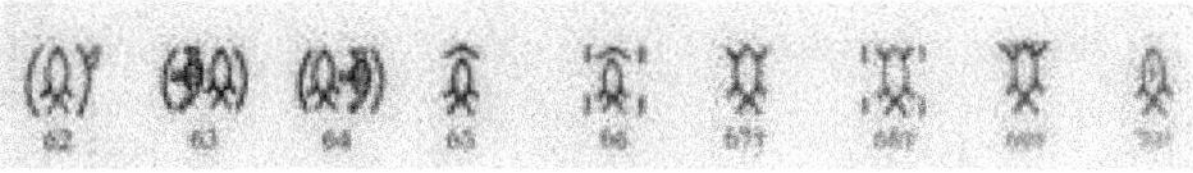

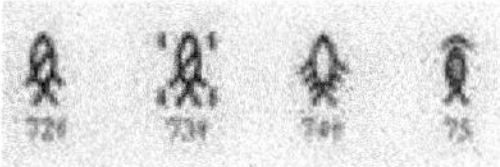

Fish hieroglyph in its vivid orthographic form is shown in a Susa pot which contained metalware – weapons and vessels.

Context for use of 'fish' glyph. This photograph of a fish and the 'fish' glyph on Susa pot are comparable to the

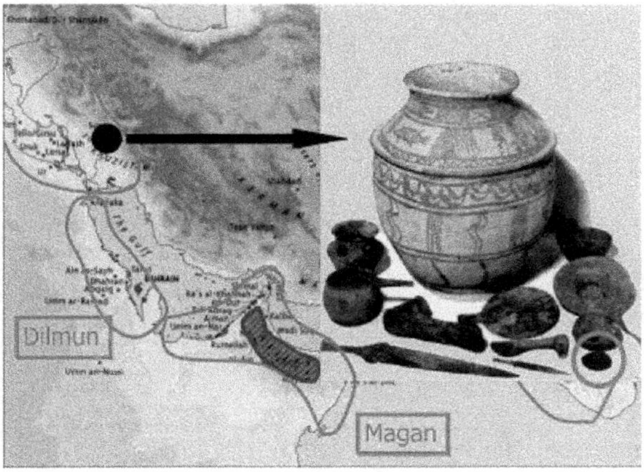

'fish' glyph on Indus inscriptions.The modifiers to the 'fish' hieroglyph which commonly occur together are: slanted stroke, notch, fins, lid-of-pot ligatured as superfix: 

For determining the semantics of the messages conveyed by the script. Positional analysis of 'fish' glyphs has also been Presented in: *The Indus Script: A Positional-statistical Approach*

By Michael Korvink, 2007, Gilund Press.

Table from: The Indus Script: A Positional-statistical Approach By Michael Korvink, 2007, Gilund Press.

Mahadevan notes (Para 6.5 opcit.) that 'a unique feature of the FISH signs is their tendency to form clusters, often as pairs, and rarely as triplets also. This pattern has fascinated and baffled scholars from the days of Hunter posing problems in interpretation.' One way to resolve the problem is to interpret the glyptic elements creating ligatured fish signs and read the glyptic elements rebus to define the semantics of the message of an inscription.

karaṇḍa 'duck' (Sanskrit) *karaṛa* 'a very large aquatic bird' (Sindhi) Rebus: करडा [*karaḍā]*

Hard from alloy--iron,

silver &c. (Marathi) Rebus: fire-god: @B27990. #16671. Remo <*karandi*>E155 {N} ``^fire-^god".(Munda) Rebus:. *kharādī* ' turner' (Gujarati)

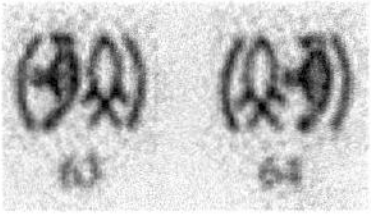

The 'parenthesis' modifier is a circumfix for both 'fish' and 'duck' hieroglyphs, the semantics of () two parenthetical modifiers are: kuṭilá— 'bent, crooked' KātyŚr., °*aka*— Pañcat., n. 'a partic. plant' [√kuṭ 1] Pa.*kuṭila*— 'bent', n. 'bend'; Pk. *kuḍila*— 'crooked', °*illa*— 'humpbacked', °*illaya*— 'bent'DEDR 2054

(*a*) *Ta.* koṭu curved, bent, crooked; koṭumai crookedness, obliquity; koṭukki hooked bar for
(*b*) fastening doors,
(*c*) clasp of an ornament. A pair of curved lines: *dol* 'likeness, picture, form' [e.g., two tigers, two bulls,
(*d*) sign-pair.] Kashmiri. dula दुल । युग्मम् m.

a pair, a couple, esp. of two similar things (Rām. 966). Rebus: dul meṛeḍ cast iron (Mundari. Santali) *dul* 'to cast metal in a mould' (Santali) pasra meṛed, pasāra meṛed = syn. of koṭe meṛed = forged iron, in contrast to dul meṛed, cast iron (Mundari.) Thus, *dul kuṭila* 'cast bronze'.

The parenthetically ligatured fish+duck hieroglyphs thus read rebus: *dul kuṭila ayas karaḍā* 'cast bronze *Ayas*or cast alloy metal with *ayas* as component to create *karaḍā* ''hard alloy with *ayas*'.

 Ligatures to fish: parentheses + snout *dul kuṭila ayas* 'cast bronze *ayas* alloy with *tuttha*, copper sulphate'

Modifier hieroglyph:could be a fish fin or a 'snout' . If 'fish fin' the reading is: khambhaRA 'fish fin' rebus: kampaTTa 'mint, coiner, coinage'. If read as hieroglyph: WPah.kṭg. *ṭōṭ* ' mouth ' .WPah.kṭg. *thótti* f., *thótthəṛ* m. ' snout, mouth ', *ṭhõt* (phonet. *thõt*) (CDIAL 5853). Semantics, Rebus: tutthá n. (m. lex.), *tutthaka* -- n. ' blue vitriol (used as an eye ointment) ' Suśr., B. *tuth*.2. K. *thŏth*, dat. °*thas* m., P. *thothā* m.3. S.*tūtio* m., A. *tutiyā*, B. *tũte*, Or. *tutiā*, H. *tūtā*, *tūtiyā* m., M. *tutiyā* m.4. M. *totā* m.(CDIAL 5855) *Ka.* tukku rust of iron; tutta, tuttu, tutte blue vitriol. *Tu.* tukků rust; mair(ů)suttu, (*Eng.-Tu. Dict.*) mairůtuttu blue vitriol. *Te.* t(r)uppu rust; (*SAN*)

A. trukku id., verdigris. / Cf. Skt. tuttha- blue vitriol (DEDR 3343).

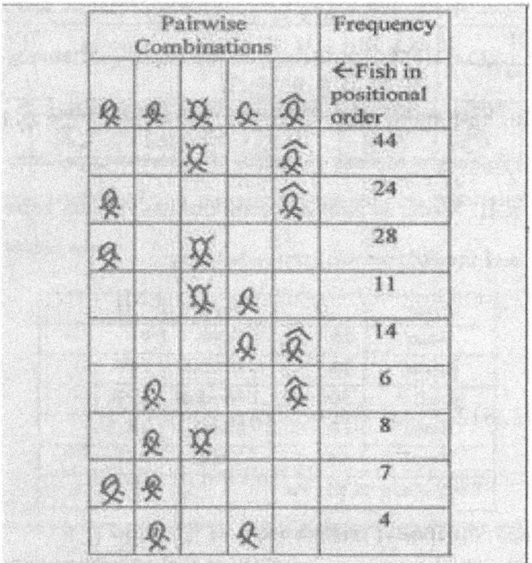

Pairwise Combinations
Frequency
←Fish in positional order
44
24
28
11
14
6
8
7
4

Figure 20: Positional Order of the "Fish" Signs

Fish, *aya* 'metal'

Fish + corner, *aya koṇḍa*, 'metal turned or forged'

Fish PLUS fins: aya 'fish' rebus: aya, ayas 'iron, metal'

PLUS L. *khabbh* m., mult. *khambh* m. ' shoulder –

blade, wing,

feather ', khet. *khamb* ' wing ', mult. *khambhaṛā* m. ' fin ';

P. *khambh* m. ' wing,

feather '; G. *khā̆m* f., *khabhɔ* m. ' shoulder '. (CDIAL 13640)

rebus: *Ta.* kampaṭṭam coinage, coin. *Ma.* kammaṭṭam,

kammiṭṭam coinage, mint.

Ka. kammaṭa id.; kammaṭi a coiner.(DEDR 1236).

Fish + scales , *aya ãs (amśu)* 'metallic stalks of stone ore'.

Vikalpa: *badhoṛ* 'a species of fish with many bones' (Santali)

Rebus: *baḍhoe* 'a carpenter, worker in wood'; *badhoria*

'expert in working in wood'(Santali)

Fish + splinter, *aya aduru* 'smelted native metal'

Fish + sloping stroke, *aya ḍhāḷ* 'metal ingot'

Fish + arrow or allograph, Fish + circumscribed four short strokes

This indication of the occurrence, together, of two or more 'fish' hieroglyphs with modifiers is

an assurance that the modifiers ar semantic indicators of how aya 'metal' is worked on by the artisans.

ayakāṇḍa ''large quantity of stone (ore) metal' or *aya kaṇḍa,* 'metal fire-altar'. *ayo, hako* 'fish'; *ãs* = scales of fish (Santali); rebus: *aya* 'metal, iron' (G.); *ayah, ayas* = metal (Skt.) Santali lexeme, *hako* 'fish'

is concordant with a proto-Indic form which can be identified as *ayo* in many glosses, Munda,

Sora glosses in particular, of the Indian linguistic area.

beḍa hako (ayo) 'fish' (Santali); *beḍa* 'either of the sides of a hearth' (G.) Munda: So. *ayo* `fish'. Go.

ayu `fish'. Go <ayu> (Z), <ayu?u> (Z),, <ayu?> (A) {N} ``^fish''. Kh. kaDOG `fish'. Sa. Hako `fish'. Mu. hai (H) ~ haku(N) ~ haikO(M) `fish'. Ho haku `fish'. Bj. hai `fish'. Bh.haku `fish'. KW haiku ~ hakO |

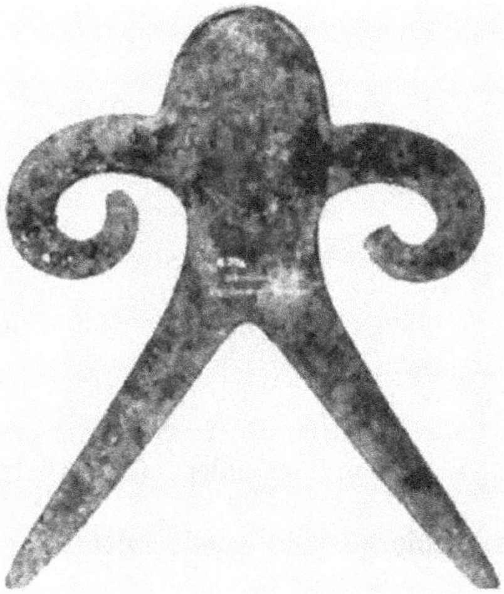

Analyzed hai-kO, ha-kO (RDM). Ku. Kaku`fish'

.@(V064,M106) Mu. ha-i, haku `fish' (HJP). @(V341)

ayu>(Z), <ayu?u> (Z) <ayu?>(A) {N} ``^fish''. #1370

. <yO>\\<AyO>(L)

{N} ``^fish''. #3612. <kukkulEyO>,,<kukkuli-yO>(LMD) {N} ``prawn''.

!Serango dialect. #32612. <sArjAjyO>,,<sArjAj>(D) {N} ``prawn''. #32622. <magur-yO>(ZL) {N} ``a kind of ^fish''. *Or.<>. #32632. <ur+GOl-Da-yO>(LL) {N} ``a kind of ^fish''. #32642.

<bal.bal-yO>(DL) {N} ``smoked fish''. #15163. Vikalpa: Munda:

<aDara>(L) {N} ``^scales of a fish, sharp bark of a tree''.#10171.

So<aDara>(L) {N} ``^scales of a fish, sharp bark of a tree''.

Indian mackerel Ta. *ayirai, acarai, acalai* loach, sandy colour, *Cobitis thermalis*; *ayilai* a kind of fish. Ma.*ayala* a fish, mackerel, scomber; *aila, ayila* a fish; *ayira* a kind of small fish, loach (DEDR 191)

aduru native metal (Ka.); ayil iron (Ta.) ayir, ayiram any ore (Ma.); ajirda karba very hard iron (Tu.)(DEDR 192)

. Ta. ayil javelin, lance, surgical knife, lancet.Ma. ayil javelin, lance; ayiri surgical knife, lancet. (DEDR 193).

aduru = gan.iyinda tegadu karagade iruva aduru = ore taken from the mine and not subjected to melting in a furnace (Ka. Siddhānti Subrahmaṇya' Śastri's new interpretation of the AmarakoŚa, Bangalore, Vicaradarpana Press, 1872, p.330);

adar = fine sand (Ta.); ayir – iron dust, any ore (Ma.) Kur. adar the waste of pounded rice, broken grains, etc. Malt. adru broken grain (DEDR 134). Ma. aśu thin, slender;ayir, ayiram iron dust.Ta. ayir subtlety, fineness, fine sand, candied sugar; ? atar fine sand, dust. அய.ற[3] ayir, n. 1. Subtlety, fineness; நணசம. (த_வ_.) 2.

[M. ayir.] Fine sand; நுண்மணல். (மலசலப. 92.) ayiram, n. Candied sugar; ayil, n. cf. ayas. 1. Iron; 2. Surgical knife, lancet; Javelin, lance; ayilavan̲, Skanda, as bearing a javelin (DEDR 341).

Tu. gadarů a lump (DEDR 1196)

kadara— m. 'iron goad for guiding an elephant' lex. (CDIAL 2711). अयोगू: A blacksmith; Vāj.3.5.

अयस् a. [इ-गतौ-असुन्] Going, moving; nimble. n. (-यः) 1 Iron (एति चलति अयस्कान्तसंनिकर्षं इति तथात्वम्; नायसोल्लिख्यते रत्नम् Śukra 4.169. अभितप्तमयो$पि मार्दवं भजते कैव कथा शरीरिषु R.8.43. -2 Steel. -3 Gold. -4 A metal in general. ayaskāṇḍa 1 an iron-arrow. -2 excellent iron. -3 a large quantity of iron. -क_ नत_(अयसक_नत_) 1 'beloved of iron', a magnet, load-stone; 2 a precious stone; °मजण_ a loadstone; ayaskāra 1 an iron-smith, blacksmith (Skt.Apte) ayas-kāntamu. [Skt.] n. The load-stone, a magnet. ayaskāruḍu. n. A black smith, one who works in iron. ayassu. n. ayō-mayamu. [Skt.] adj. made of iron (Te.) áyas— n. 'metal, iron' RV. Pa. ayō nom. sg. n. and m., aya— n. 'iron', Pk. aya— n., Si. ya. AYAŚCŪRṆA—, AYASKĀṆḌA—, *AYASKŪṬA—. Addenda: áyas—: Md. da 'iron', dafat 'piece of iron'. ayaskāṇḍa— m.n. 'a quantity of iron, excellent iron' Pāṇ. gaṇ. viii.3.48 [ÁYAS—, KAA´ṆḌA—]Si.yakaḍa 'iron'.*ayaskūṭa— 'iron hammer'. [ÁYAS—, KUU´ṬA—1] Pa. ayōkūṭa—, ayak m.; Si. yakuḷa'sledge —hammer', yavuḷa (< ayōkūṭa) (CDIAL 590, 591, 592). cf. Lat. aes , aer-is for as-is ; Goth. ais , Thema aisa; Old Germ. e7r , iron ;Goth. eisarn ; Mod. Germ. Eisen.

Note on *(amśu)* 'metallic stalks of stone ore'. An uncertain meaning of *soma* in Rigveda though the entire samhita holds the processing of soma in a nutshell, can be resolved in the context of modifers to 'fish' hieroglyph to denote 'fins or scales'.

The vedic texts provide an intimation treating *amśu* as a synonym of *soma.*

George Pinault has found a cognate word in Tocharian, *ancu* which means 'iron'. I have argued in my book , *Indian alchemy, soma in the Veda*, that *Soma* was an allegory, 'electrum' (gold-silver compound). See: http://bharatkalyan97.blogspot.in/2011/10/itihasa-and-eagle-narratives.html for Pinault's views on *ancu, amśu* concordance.

The link with the Tocharian word is intriguing because *Soma* was supposed to come from Mt. Mujavant.

A cognate of Mujavant is Mustagh Ata of the Himalayan ranges in Kyrgystan.

Is it possible that the *ancu* of Tocharian from this mountain was indeed *Soma*?

The referemces to *Anzu* in ancient Mesopotamian tradition parallels the legends of *śyena* 'falcon' which is used in Vedic tradition of *Soma yajña* attested archaeologically in Uttarakhand with a *śyenaciti*, 'falcon-shaped' fire-altar.

http://bharatkalyan97.blogspot.in/2011/11/syena-orthography.html śyena, orthography, Sasanian iconography.

Continued use of Indus Script hieroglyphs.

Comparing the allegory of soma and the legend of Anzu, the bird which stole the tablets of destiny, I posit a hypothesis that the tablets of destiny are paralleled by the Indus writing corpora which constitute a veritable catalog of stone-, mineral- and

metal-ware in the bronze age evolving from the chalcolithic phase of what constituted an 'industrial' revolution of ancient times creating

ingots of metal alloys and weapons and tools using metal alloys which transformed the relation of communities with nature and resulted

in the life-activities of lapidaries transforming into miners, smiths and traders of metal artefacts.
I suggest that ayas of bronze age created a revolutionary transformation in the lives of people of these bronze age times.

Maybe, Tocharian ancu had the same meaning as Rigvedic gloss, *amśu.* If so, *ancu* might have denoted electrum, 'gold-silver compound' which was subjected to reduction, by oxidation of impurities, by incessant firing for five days and nights to create the shining wealth of gold. The old Egyptian gloss for electrum was*assem*, cognate *soma.*

"The earliest animal figurines from Harappa are Early Harappan (Ravi Phase, Period 1 and Kot Diji Phase, Period 2) zebu figurines. They are typically very small with joined legs and stylized humps. A few of these zebu figurines have holes through the humps that may have allowed them to be worn as amulets on a cord or a string. One Early Harappan zebu figurine was found with the remains of a copper alloy ring still in this hole. Approximate dimensions (W x H (L) x D) of the uppermost figurine: 1.2 x 3.3 x 2.8

cm." https://www.harappa.com/figurines/32.html
http://bharatkalyan97.blogspot.in/2014/09/ayas-vedic-gloss-in-hieroglyph.html

Indus Script signboards: Bharhut, Sanchi, Dholavira. Bharatam was Sheffield of Ancient Bronze Age. Date palm spathe sippi yields the cipher.
Mirror: https://www.academia.edu/s/abeef0b49e

Bharatam was Sheffield of Ancient Bronze Age. Three monolithic hoardings of Bharhut, Sanchi and Dholavira are discussed in this monograph.

The idiom 'Sheffield of Ancient Bronze Age' is taken and adapted from the Illustrated Weekly News of Nov. 21, 1936 which reported the discovery of Chanhudaro by Ernest Mackay and called the site 'Sheffield of Ancient India.'

Sanchi stupa Northern Gateway Torana Hieroglyph multiplex, showing date palm spathes, hanging down the pair of sippi, 'shells'. The spathe of datepalm is also sippi, as a phonetic determinant of the word sippi which the artisan wants to convey through the hoarind on the torana welcoming prospective customers who want to acquire the metal and s'ankha artifacts made by the Sanchi artisans. The fins of fish are also hieroglyphs read rebus: .khambhaṛā 'fin', 'wing' Rebus: kammaṭa 'coiner, coinage, mint' . Thus the hieroglyph multiplex as hypertext signifies a mint and artificers' metalwork at the workshops of Sanchi.

Date palm spathe is called *sippi.* This Prakrtam gloss yields the Indus Script cipher. The word signifies *sippi* 'artisan, craftsman'.(Old Awadhi). The hieroglyph of sippi, spathe of date palm adorns the signboard on Sanchi and Bharhut stupa toranas. The proclamation is to invite prospective buyers to witness the handicrafts of the Bronze Age sculpted, forged by the artisans of the Sarasvati_Sindhu civilizational continuum.

The tradition of creating signboards as proclamations of artifice dates back to Sarasvati-Sindhu civilization, exemplified by the monolithic Dholavira Signboard with 10 Indus Script Hieroglyphs. Size of each hieroglyph on the Dholavira signboard measures 35 to 37 cm. high and 25 to 27 cm.wide. This signboard could have been seen by seafaring merchants coming on their boats from the Ancient Near East navigating through the Persian Gulf.

Dholavira Gateway

Dholavira Signboard on gateway. A reconstruction.

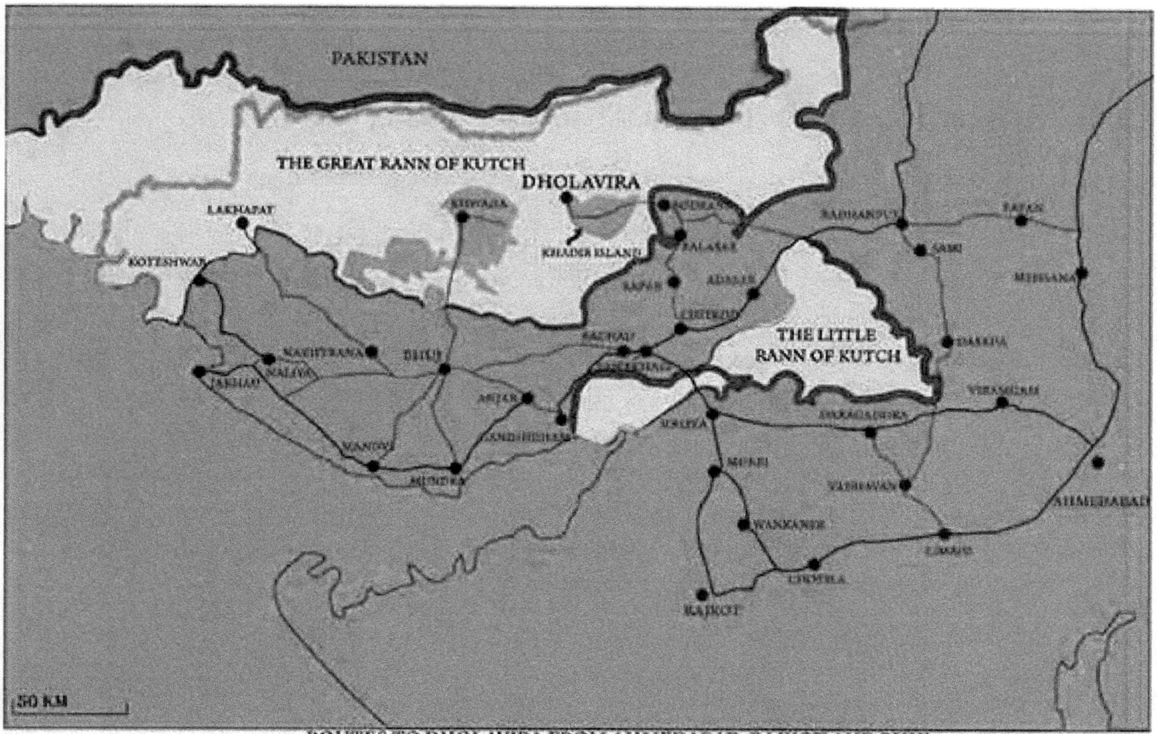

ROUTES TO DHOLAVIRA FROM AHMEDABAD, RAJKOT AND BHUJ

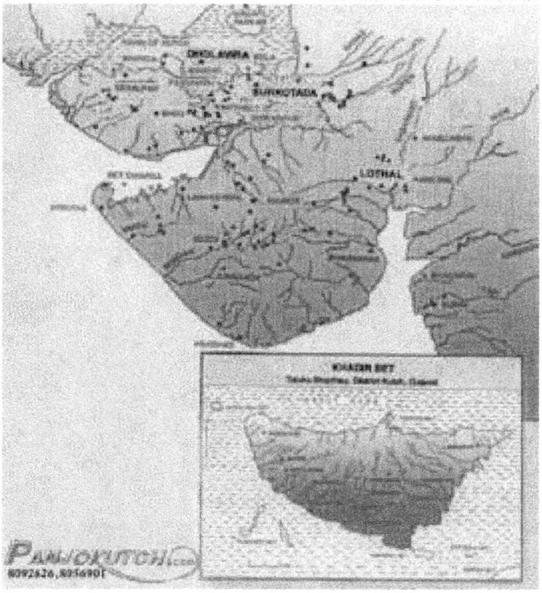

This pictorial motif gets normalized in Indus writing system as a hieroglyph sign:

Hieroglyph: *karaṁḍa* -- m.n. ' bone shaped like a bamboo ', *karaṁḍuya* -- n. ' backbone ' (Prakrit) Rebus: करडा [*karaḍā*] Hard from alloy--iron, silver &c. (Marathi)

Pk. *karaṁḍa* -- m.n. ' bone shaped like a bamboo ', *karaṁḍuya* -- n. ' backbone '. *kaṇṭa3 ' backbone, podex, penis '. 2. *kaṇḍa -- . 3. *karaṇḍa -- 4. (Cf. *kāṭa -- 2, *ḍākka -- 2: poss. same as káṇṭa -- 1] 1. Pa. *piṭṭhi -- kaṇṭaka* -- m. ' bone of the spine '; Gy. eur. *kanro* m. ' penis ' (or < káṇṭaka --); Tir. *mar -- kaṇḍḗ* ' back (of the body) '; S. *kaṇḍo* m. ' back ', L. *kaṇḍ* f., *kaṇḍā* m. ' backbone ', awāṇ. *kaṇḍ*, °*ḍī* ' back '; P. *kaṇḍ* f. ' back, pubes '; WPah. bhal. *kaṇṭ* f. ' syphilis '; N. *kaṇḍo* ' buttock, rump, anus ', *kaṇḍeulo* ' small of the back '; B. *kā̃ṭ* ' clitoris '; Or. *kaṇṭi* ' handle of a plough '; H. *kā̃ṭā* m. ' spine ', G. *kā̃ṭɔ* m., M. *kā̃ṭā* m.; Si. *äṭa -- kaṭuva* ' bone ', *piṭa -- k°* ' backbone '. 2. Pk. *kaṁḍa* -- m. ' backbone '.(CDIAL 2670) مركنديي *mar-kanḏḏa'ī*, s.f. (6th) The throat, the windpipe, the gullet. 2. The end of the backbone where the neck joins. Sing. and Pl.(Pushto)

खरडा [kharaḍā] A leopard. खरड्या [kharaḍyā] *m* or खरड्यावाघ *m* A leopard (Marathi).

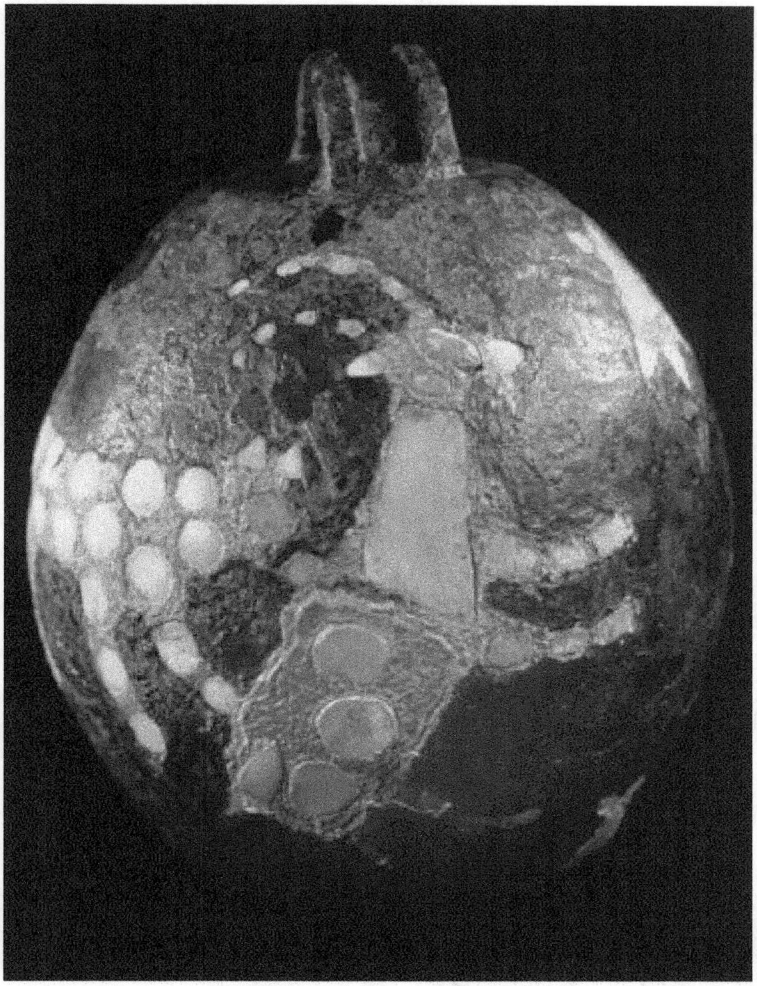

Leopard weight. Shahi Tump. H.16.7cm; dia.13.5cm; base dia 6cm; handle on top. Lead, cire perdue.

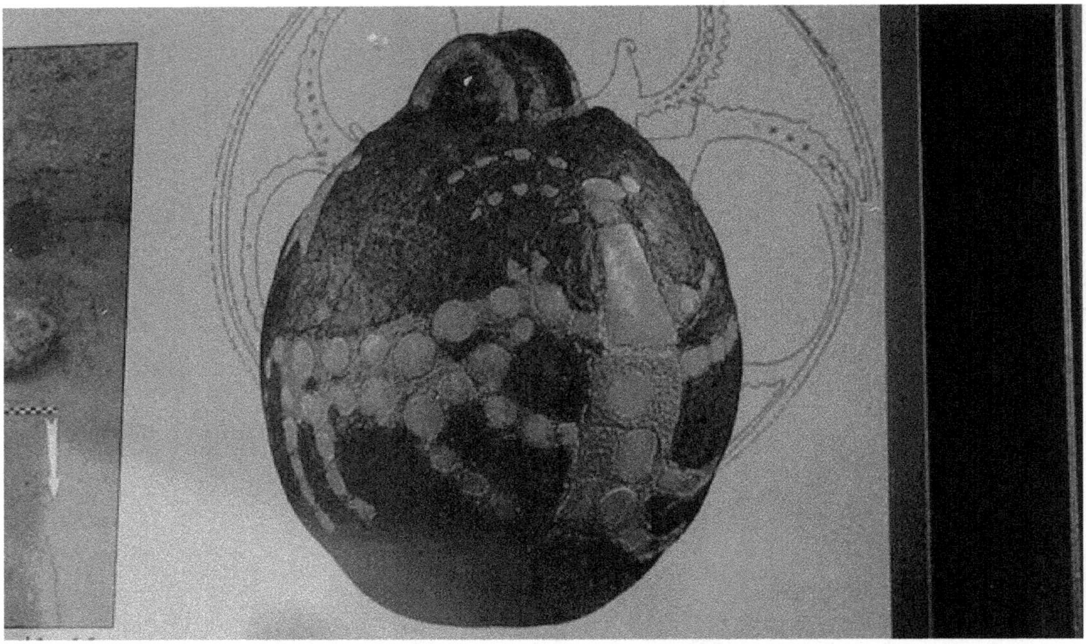

http://bharatkalyan97.blogspot.in/2015/10/indus-script-corpora-of-lost-wax.html?view=classic

Lead filling in copper shell. Seashells for hieroglyphs. *karaḍa*'panther' Rebus:*karaḍa*'hard alloy'.

miṇḍāl'markhor' (Tōrwālī) *meḍho*a ram, a sheep (Gujarati)(CDIAL 10120) Rebus:*mẽṛhẽt, meḍ*'iron' (Mu.Ho.) Vikalpa: mlekh'goat' Rebus: milakkhu'copper' (Pali) mleccha-mukha 'copper' (Samskrtam)

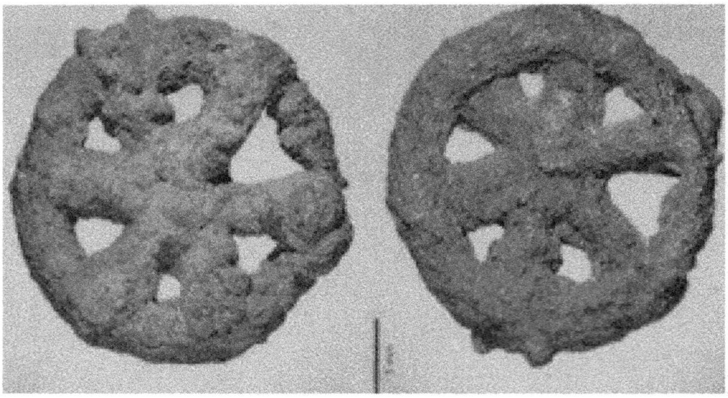

Earliest lost-wax castings? 2.2 cm dia. Wheels w/spokes. Mehergarh BourgaritD., Mille B. 2007. Les premiers objetsmétalliquesont-ilsétéfabriquéspar des métallurgistes?*L'actualitéChimique*. Octobre-Novembre2007 -n°312-313:54-60. Earliest lost-wax castings? 2.2 cm dia. Wheels w/spokes. Mehergarh BourgaritD., Mille B. 2007. Les premiers objetsmétalliquesont-ilsétéfabriquéspar des métallurgistes?*L'actualitéChimique*. Octobre-Novembre2007 -n°312-313:54-60.

arā'spokes' Rebus:*āra 'brass'*.cf.erka= ekke(Tbh. of arka) aka (Tbh. of arka) copper(metal); crystal (Kannada) Glyph: *eraka*'naveof wheel' Rebus: eraka'copper'; cf.erka= ekke(Tbh. of arka) aka (Tbh. of arka) copper(metal); crystal (Kannada) *eraka*'moltencastcopper' Duplicated: dula'pair' Rebus: dul'cast metal' Thus cast copper, brass casting.

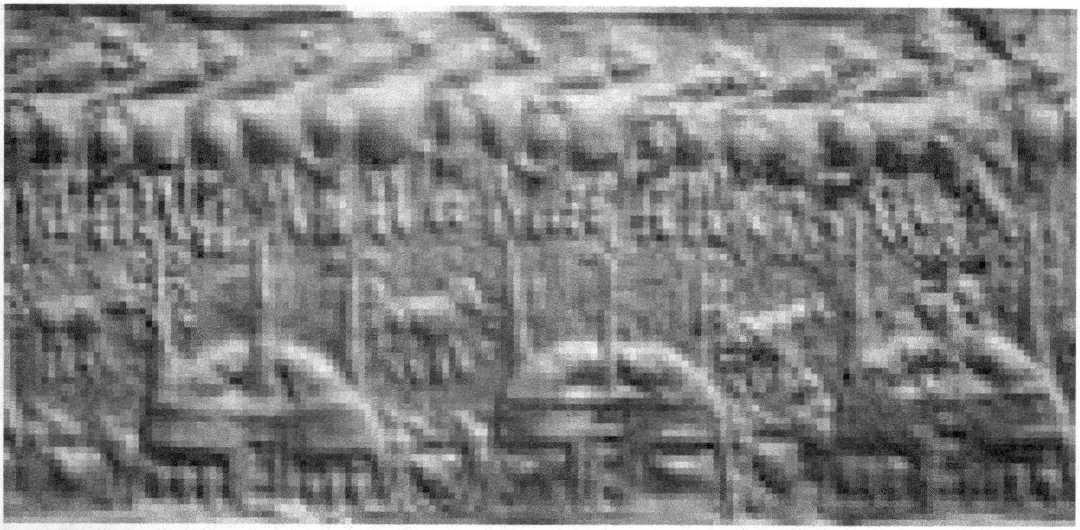

Recumbent ram. Silver. Lost-wax casting. Mounted on pins and dowelled into the center of cylinder seal. Ashmolean Museum, Oxford. Uruk. c. 3200 BCE pasaramu, pasalamu = an animal, a beast, a brute, quadruped (Telugu) Rebus: pasra = a smithy, a place where a blacksmith works; to do a blacksmith's work; *kamar pasrat.hene sen akantalea* = our man has gone to the smithy; pasrao lagao (or ehop) akata = he (the blacksmith) has started his work (Santali).

Steatite pendant. m1656A

Metalware. Turner. Joinery

खोंड [khōṇḍa] m A young bull, a bullcalf. (Marathi) Rebus: kõdār 'turner' (Bengali); कोंद kōnda 'engraver, lapidary setting or infixing gems' (Marathi) G. sãghāṛɔ m. 'lathe' ; संघाट joinery; M. sãgaḍ 'double-canoe' Rebus: sangataras. संगतराश lit. 'to collect stones, stone-cutter, mason.'

lo 'pot to overflow' *kāṇḍa* 'water'.

Rebus: *lokhaṇḍ* (overflowing pot) 'metal tools, pots and pans, metalware' (Marathi).

<kanda> {N} ``large earthen water ^pot kept and filled at the house''. @1507. #14261. (Munda) Rebus: khanda 'a trench used as a fireplace when cooking has to be done for a large number of people' (Santali) kand 'fire-altar' (Santali)

karaḍakum 'a streamlet' (Gujarati); [*karaḍamu* 'a wave' (Telugu) Rebus: करडा [*karaḍā*] Hard from alloy--iron, silver &c. (Marathi) *kharādī* ' turner'

There are two glosses in Samskrtam which signify मृदु mṛdu 'soft metal of iron' and पोळ pōḷa 'magnetite (a ferrite ore)'. मृदा--कर [p= 830,2] *m.* a thunderbolt W.

Schmidt or Schmitz occupational surname in German is cognate with Smith 'blacksmith'. The root embedded is: mṛdu This reinforces the Meluhha lexis glosses *mẽṛhẽt, meḍ* to signify 'iron, metal' -- together with the Indus Script hieroglyphs deployed to connote these glosses: *mẽṛhẽt, meḍ* In addition to the hieroglyphs detailed in http://bharatkalyan97.blogspot.in/2015/12/an-array-of-indus-script-hieroglyphs-to.html to additional hieroglyphs which signify the semantics rebus of 'iron, metal' are:

मेढा (p. 665) [mēḍhā] A twist or tangle arising in thread or cord, a curl or snarl.

Examples of six मेढा [mēḍhā] curls of hair on cylinder seals

Ibni-Sharrum cylinder seal shows a kneeling person with six curls of hair.Cylinder seal of Ibni-sharrum, a

scribe of Shar-kali-sharri (left) and impression (right), ca. 2183–2159 B.C.; Akkadian, reign of Shar-kali-sharri.
http://bharatkalyan97.blogspot.in/2013/08/ancient-near-east-bronze-age-heralded.html

rāngo 'water buffalo bull' (Ku.N.)(CDIAL 10559) Rebus: rango 'pewter'. ranga, rang pewter is an alloy of tin, lead, and antimony (anjana) (Santali).

baTa 'six' Rebus: bhaTa 'furnace', baTa 'iron'. मेढा [mēḍhā] curls Rebus: mẽṛhẽt, meḍ 'iron (metal)'. Thus, together, iron furnace.

Four standard-bearers with six curls of hair. http://bharatkalyan97.blogspot.in/2015/08/ancient-near-east-jasper-cylinder-seal.html

Hieroglyph: मेढा [mēḍhā] 'a curl or snarl; twist in thread' (Marathi) Rebus: mẽṛhẽt, *meḍ* 'iron' (Mu.Ho.) Thus, the four Akkadian standard bearers are *meḍ bhaṭa* iron-furnace metal- workers producing alloy implements, moltencast metalcastings, crucible ingots. The hooded snake reinforces the semantic determinative: kulA 'hooded serpent' Rebus: kolle 'blacksmith' kol 'working in iron'.

The proclamation (sangara) is that four types of furnaces are announced: for aya 'fish' rebus: ayas 'metal'; lokhANDa 'overflowing pot' Rebus: lokhANDa 'metal implements'; arka 'sun' Rebus: eraka 'moltencast copper'; koThAri 'crucible' ebus: Or. *koṭhārī* ' treasurer '; Bhoj. *koṭhārī* ' storekeeper ', H. *kuṭhiyārī* m. kōṣṭhāgārika -- : G. *koṭhārī* m. ' storekeeper '.(CDIAL 3551)kulA 'hood of serpent' Rebus: kolle 'blacksmith'. Rebus representation is indicated by a determinative: a conical jar containing ingots. Thus, the reference to the 'crucible' may be a message related to ingots of alloys produced from the crucible, the way the traditions evolved to produce crucible steel.

http://bharatkalyan97.blogspot.in/2015/09/spinner-kati-lady-rebus-khati.html

Example of मेढा [mēḍhā]twist (rope) on a Bogazkoy seal

मेढा [mēḍhā] twist Rebus: mẽṛhẽt, meḍ 'iron (metal)' dula 'pair' rebus: dul 'cast metal' Thus, cast iron
eruvai 'kite, eagle' rebus: eruvai 'copper'

.

Copper and arsenic ores

Ore name	Chemical formula
Arsenopyrite	$FeAsS$
Enargite	Cu_3AsS_4
Olivenite	$Cu_2(AsO_4)OH$
Tennantite	$Cu_{12}As_4S_{13}$
Malachite	$Cu_2(OH)_2CO_3$
Azurite	$Cu_3(OH)_2(CO_3)_2$

Sulfide deposits frequently are a mix of different metal sulfides, such as copper, zinc, silver, lead, arsenic and other metals. (Sphalerite (ZnS2), for example, is not uncommon in copper sulfide deposits, and the metal smelted would be brass, which is both harder and more durable than bronze.)The metals could theoretically be separated out, but the alloys resulting were typically much stronger than the metals individually.

http://bharatkalyan97.blogspot.in/2015/12/evolution-of-brahmi-script-syllable-ma.html?view=timeslide

मेढ (p. 662) [mēḍha] The polar star.मेढेमत (p. 665) [mēḍhēmata] *n* (मेढ Polar star, मत Dogma or sect.) A persuasion or an order or a set of tenets and notions amongst the Shúdra-people. Founded upon certain astrological calculations proceeding upon the North star. Hence मेढेजोशी or डौरीजोशी.

Seal impression, Ur (Upenn; U.16747); dia. 2.6, ht. 0.9 cm.; Gadd, PBA 18 (1932), pp. 11-12, pl. II, no. 12; Porada 1971: pl.9, fig.5; Parpola, 1994, p. 183; water carrier with a skin (or pot?) hung on each end of the yoke across his shoulders and another one below the crook of his left arm; the vessel on the right end of his yoke is over a receptacle for the water; a star on either side of the head (denoting supernatural?). The whole object is enclosed by 'parenthesis' marks. The parenthesis is perhaps a way of splitting of the ellipse (Hunter, G.R., *JRAS*, 1932, 476). An unmistakable example of an 'hieroglyphic' seal. kuṭi 'water-carrier' (Telugu); Rebus: kuṭhi 'smelter furnace' (Santali) kuṛī f. 'fireplace' (H.); krvṛI f. 'granary (WPah.); kuṛī, kuṛo house, building'(Ku.)(CDIAL 3232) kuṭi 'hut made of boughs' (Skt.) guḍi temple (Telugu) मेढ (p. 662) [mēḍha] 'polar' star' Rebus: mẽṛhẽt, meḍ 'iron' (Ho.Munda)

मृदु mṛdu '(soft) iron'

मृदु mṛdu : (page 1287) A kind of iron.-कार्ष्णायसम्,-कृष्णायसम् soft-iron, lead. (Apte. Samskrtam) This gloss could link with the variant lexis of Indian sprachbund with the semantics 'iron': Bj. <i>merhd</i>(Hunter) `iron'. Sa. <i>mE~R~hE~'d</i> `iron'. ! <i>mE~RhE~d</i>(M).

Metonymy as an organizing principle for the writing system of Indus Script Corpora

Three artefacts with Indus writing are remarkable for their definitive intent to broadcast the metallurgical message: 1. Dholavira signboard on a gateway; 2. Shahdad standard; and 3. Tablets showing processions of three standards: scarf hieroglyph, one-horned young bull hieroglyph and standard-device hieroglyph. Thus, the three artifacts embody metonymy as an organizing principle for a writing system.

Rebus readings of the inscriptions relate to and document the metallurgical competence of Meluhhan lapidaries-artisans. Some other select set of inscriptions from the wide, expansive area stretching from Haifa to Rakhigarhi, from Altyn Depe (Caucus) to Daimabad (Maharashtra) are presented to show the area which had evidenced the use of Meluhha (Mleccha) language of Indian *sprachbund.*

Hieroglyphs deployed on Indus inscriptions have had a lasting effect on the glyptic motifs used on hundreds of cylinder seals of the Meluhha contact regions. The glyptic motifs continued to be used as a logo-semantic writing system, together with cuneiform texts which used a logo-syllabic writing system, even after the use of complex tokens and bullae were discontinued to account for commodities. The Indus writing system of hieroglyphs read rebus matched the Bronze Age revolutionary imperative of minerals, metals and alloys produced as surplus to the requirements of the artisan communities and as available for the creation and sustenance of trade-networks to meet the demand for alloyed metal tools, weapons, pots and pans, apart from the supply of copper, tin metal ingots for use in the smithy of nations, *harosheth hagoyim* mentioned in the Old Testament (Judges). This term also explains the continuum of Aramaic script into the cognate *kharoṣṭī* 'blacksmith-lip' *goya* 'communities'.

Indus-Sarasvatī Signboard Text. Read rebus as Meluhha (Mleccha) announcement of metals repertoire of a smithy complex in the citadel. The 'spoked wheel' is the semantic divider of three segments of the broadcast message. Details of readings, from r. to l.:

Segment 1: Working in ore, molten cast copper, lathe (work)

ḍato ‘claws or pincers of crab’ (Santali) rebus: *dhatu* ‘ore’ (Santali)

eraka ‘knave of wheel’ Rebus: *eraka* ‘copper’ (Kannada) *eraka* ‘molten cast (metal)(Tulu). *sangaḍa* 'pair' Rebus: *sangaḍa*‘lathe’ (Gujarati

Segment 2: Native metal tools, pots and pans, metalware, engraving (molten cast copper)

खांडा [khāṇḍā] *m* A jag, notch, or indentation (as upon the edge of a tool or weapon). (Marathi) Rebus: *khāṇḍā* ‘tools, pots and pans, metal-ware’.

H-73 a

Harappa seal (H-73)[Note: the ‘water carrier’ pictogram]
Hieroglyph: fish + notch: aya 'fish' + khāṇḍā *m* A jag, notch Rebus: aya 'metal'+ *khāṇḍā* ‘tools, pots and pans, metal-ware’. kuTi 'water-carrier' Rebus: kuThi 'smelter'.

aḍaren, ḍaren lid, cover (Santali) Rebus: *aduru* ‘native metal’ (Ka.) *aduru* = gan.iyinda tegadu karagade iruva aduru = ore taken from the mine and not subjected to melting in a furnace (Kannada) (Siddhānti *Subrahmaṇya’ śāstri’s new interpretation of the Amarakośa*, Bangalore, Vicaradarpana Press, 1872, p. 330) *koṇḍa* bend (Ko.); Tu. Kōḍi corner; kōṇṭu angle, corner, crook. Nk. kōnṭa corner (DEDR 2054b) G. khũ̆ṭrī f. 'angle' Rebus: *kõdā* 'to turn in a lathe'(B.) कोंद kōnda 'engraver, lapidary setting or infixing gems' (Marathi) koḍ 'artisan's workshop' (Kuwi) koḍ = place where artisans work (G.) ācāri koṭṭya 'smithy' (Tu.) कोंडण [kōṇḍaṇa] f A fold or pen. (Marathi) B. kõdā 'to turn in a lathe'; Or.kũnda 'lathe', kũdibā, kũd 'to turn' (→ Drav. Kur. Kũd ' lathe') (CDIAL 3295) A. kundār, B. kũdār, ri, Or.Kundāru; H. kũderā m. 'one who works a lathe, one who scrapes', rī f., kũdernā 'to scrape, plane, round on a lathe'; kundakara— m. 'turner' (Skt.)(CDIAL 3297). कोंदण [kōndaṇa] n (कोंदणें) Setting or infixing of gems.(Marathi) খোদকার [khōdakāra] n an engraver; a carver. **খোদকারি** n. engraving; carving; interference in other's work. খোদাই [khōdāi] n engraving; carving. **খোদাই করা** v. to engrave; to carve. **খোদানো** v. & n. en graving; carving. খোদিত [khōdita] a engraved. (Bengali) खोदकाम [khōdakāma] n Sculpture; carved work or work for the carver. खोदगिरी [khōdagirī] f Sculpture, carving, engraving: also sculptured or carved work. खोदणावळ [khōdaṇāvaḷa] f (खोदणें) The price or cost of sculpture or carving. खोदणी [khōdaṇī] f (Verbal of खोदणें) Digging, engraving &c. 2 fig. An exacting of money by importunity. V लाव, मांड. 3 An instrument to scoop out and cut flowers and figures from paper. 4 A goldsmith's die. खोदणें [khōdaṇēṃ] v c & i (H) To dig. 2 To engrave. खोद खोदून विचारणें or –पुसणें To question minutely and searchingly, to probe. खोदाई [khōdāī] f (H.) Price or cost of digging or of sculpture or carving. खोदींव [khōdīṃva] p of खोदणें Dug. 2 Engraved, carved, sculptured. (Marathi)

eraka 'knave of wheel' Rebus: *eraka* 'copper' (Kannada) *eraka* 'molten cast (metal)(Tulu).

Segment 3:  Coppersmith mint, furnace, workshop (molten cast copper)

loa 'fig leaf; Rebus: loh '(copper) metal' *kamaḍha* 'ficus religiosa' (Skt.); *kamaṭa* = portable furnace for melting precious metals (Te.); *kampaṭṭam* = mint (Ta.) The unique ligatures on the 'leaf' hieroglyph may be explained as a professional designation: *loha-kāra* 'metalsmith'; *kāruvu* [Skt.] n. 'An artist, artificer. An agent'.(Telugu).

khuṇṭa 'peg'; khũṭi = pin (M.) rebus: kuṭi= furnace (Santali) kūṭa 'workshop' kuṇḍamu 'a pit for receiving and preserving consecrated fire' (Te.) kundār turner (A.); kũdār, kũdāri (B.)

eraka 'knave of wheel' Rebus: *eraka* 'copper' (Kannada) *eraka* 'molten cast (metal)(Tulu).

Size matters. Archaeological context matters. How could one interpret the utility for the people of Dholavira, of 10 large glyphs (35 to 37 cm. high and 25 to 27 cm.wide) carefully laid out, in sequence, using gypsum pieces on an inscription which was a Signboard mounted on a gateway? Maybe, the Signboard text was visible from a distance for seafaring merchants and artisans from Dilmun or Magan or Elam. How can one assume it to be oral literature, for the guidance of tourists or merchants entering the citadel or even for the people of Dholavira (Kotda)? Why should any pundit conceive of the text, arbitrarily, to be non-linguistic? The glyphs are not randomly drawn but are repetitions from several tablets and seals which carry one or more of nearly 500 such distinct glyphs on nearly 7000 inscriptions of Indus writing. Why can't the glyphs be read rebus as hieroglyphs as a cypher code for the underlying sounds & semantics of words in Meluhha (Mleccha) language -- comparable to the rebus reading of N'r-M'r palette which used N'r 'cuttle-fish' and M'r 'awl' hieroglyphs to be read together as Narmer, the name of an Egyptian emperor?

Dholavira Gateway as seen from the citadel. "The first quake hit the township around 2800 BC, the second around 2500 BC, and the third around 2000 BC," said Bisht.

One gateway had a signboard. "It is believed that the stone signboard was hung on a wooden plank in front of the gate. This could be the oldest signboard known to us," said Bisht. http://tinyurl.com/l3cszrr

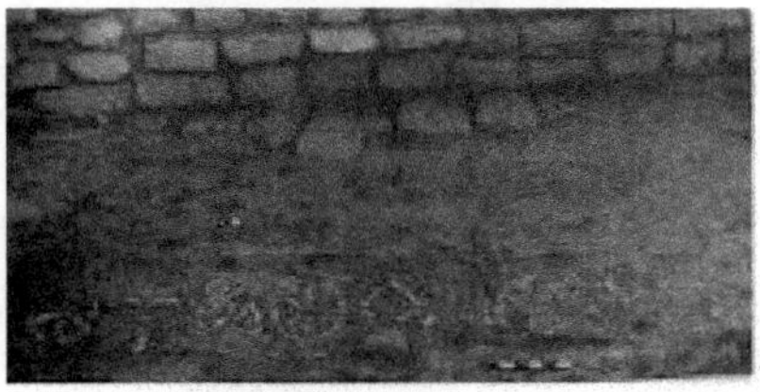

Dholavira Signboard on GatewayThe citadel had two gateways: one on the northern and the other on the eastern side. Each gateway had an elaborate staircase. The landing of the staircase was at a depth of 2.3 m. After ten steps and a further descent of 2 m., the staircase led to a passage way which was 7 m. long On either side of the passage, there was a chamber which had a roof resting on stone pillars. In one of the chambers, a unique inscription was discovered. The ten letters of the inscription had a height of about 35 to 37 cm. and a width of 25 to 27 cm. The letters wee made of sliced pieces of some 'crystalline material, maybe rock, mineral or paste'. Perhaps mounted on a wooden board, the inscription might have constituted a sign-board. Ring-stones were used to support the pillars.

[quote] RS Bisht opined that the Harappans were a literate people. The commanding height at which the 10-sign board had been erected showed that it was meant to be read by all people.Besides, seals with Indus signs were found everywhere in the city – in the citadel, middle town, lower town, annexe, and so on. It meant a large majority of the people knew how to read and write. The Indus script had been found on pottery as well. Even children wrote on potsherds. Bisht said: "The argument that literacy was confined to a few people is not correct. You find inscriptions on pottery, bangles and even copper tools. This is not graffiti, which is child's play. The finest things were available even to the lowest sections of society. The same seals, beads and pottery were found everywhere in the castle, bailey, the middle town and the lower town of the settlement at Dholavira, as if the entire population had wealth.
[unquote] http://varnam.nationalinterest.in/2010/06/the-sign-board-at-dholavira/

The Dholavira Gateway Signboard text is perhaps the world's first advertisement hoarding by any artisan or merchant.

Indus Scrip hieroglyphs: tāmrapaṭṭī ताम्र-पट्टी, 'copper-city, copper-town' Bharhut भरहुत; kammaṭa dhāvḍā 'Mint, smelter', Besanagara बेसनगर
Mirror: http://tinyurl.com/gwh9zj6

This monograph demonstrates the continuum of Indus Script writing system in both Sanchi and Bharhut as evidenced by the hieroglyph-multiplexes as hypertexts on sculptures and friezes.

The hieroglyph components on Sanchi stupa and Bharhut stupa are:
1. lotus; 2. mollusc; 3. spathe (of palms); 4. fish fins, wings on lions; 5. rope tying pair of fishes; garland 6. elephant; 7. tiger; 8. lion; 9. spoked wheel; 10. tree.

Hieroglyph: tAmarasa 'red lotus' Rebus: tAmra 'copper
Hieroglyph: sangi, hangi 'mollusc' Rebus: sangin 'shell-cutter'

Hieroglyph: *sippī* f. 'spathe of date palm' Rebus: *sippi* 'artificer, craftsman'. śilpin ' skilled in art ', m. ' artificer '
Hieroglyph: khambhaṛā 'fin', 'wing' Rebus: kammaṭa 'coiner, coinage, mint'
Hieroglyph: daũrā 'rope' Rebus dhāvḍā 'smelter';
Hieroglyph: aya 'fish' rebus: aya, ayas 'iron, metal'; dula 'pair' rebus: dul 'cast metal'
Hieroglyph: ibha 'elephant' kariba 'trunk of elephant' Rebus: ib 'iron' karba 'iron'
Hieroglyph: kola 'tiger' Rebus: kol 'working in iron' kolle 'blacksmith' kolhe 'smelter
Hieroglyph: arya 'lion' (Akkadian) Rebus: Ara 'brass' PLUS hambhaṛā 'wing' Rebus: kammaṭa 'coiner, coinage, mint'

Hieroglyph: eraka 'knave of wheel' Rebus: eraka 'moltencast, copper' Hieroglyph: arAm 'spokes' Rebus:

Ara 'brass'.

Hieroglyph: kuTi 'tree' Rebus: kuThi 'smelter'Hieroglyph: daürā, dāman 'garland' Rebus dhāvḍā 'smelter'.

The galleries signifying these hieroglypha are presented in the context of continued use of Indus Script cipher tradition of rebus rendering of Prakrtam words to compile metalwork catalogues.
si
The torana (gateways) of Sanchi and Bharhut which are adorned with one or more of these hieroglyph-complexes are a proclamation of the metalwork rendered at these worskhop sites. Bharhut, for example, displays a frieze declaring it to be a copper city, copper town.

Not far from Sanchi and Bharhut are Eran and Vidisha which were mint towns, where thousands of punch-marked and cast coins of various metals have been found. The artisans and artists who had created the Begram ivory bronzes with Indus Script hieroglyphs had contributed to the building of the Sanchi and Bharhut stupas and related artifacts and sculptures as proclamations of their artisanal competence and metal workshops.

Why was the hieroglyph-multiplex signifying two fins of a pair of fishes called s'rivatsa, 'child of wealth'? The metallurgical excellence achieved by the Sarasvati-Sindhu civilization artisans was indeed a celebration in metalwork as children of wealth. So it is that VAgdevi claims in the Devi Sukta of Rigveda
वाग्देवी सूक्तम् ऋग्वेद 10.125

अहं राष्ट्री संगमनी वसूनां चिकितुषी प्रथमा यज्ञियानाम् ।
तां मा देवा व्यदधुः पुरुत्रा भूरिस्थात्रां भूर्यावेशयन्तीम् ॥ 3 ॥

I am the sovereign queen, the collectress of treasures, cognizant (of the Supreme Being), the chief of objects of worship; as such the gods have put me in many places, abiding in manifold conditions, entering into numerous (forms.

Vagdevi (Divinity of Speech) is a signifier metaphor of wealth, vasu as may be seen from the following Rigveda Sukta based on Sayana bhashya.

वाग्देवी सूक्तम् ऋग्वेद 10.125

ऋषि वागाम्भृणी; devata: वागाम्भृणी (atmastuti); chanda: त्रिष्टुप्, 2 जगती

ऋषिः वाक् आम्भृणी	छन्दः त्रिष्टुप् 1,3-8, जगती 2	देवता आत्मा

अहं रुद्रेभिर्वसुभिश्चराम्यहमादित्यैरुत विश्वदेवैः ।
अहं मित्रावरुणोभा बिभर्म्यहमिन्द्राग्नी अहमश्विनोभा ॥ 1 ॥
अहं सोममाहनसं बिभर्म्यहं त्वष्टारमुत पूषणं भगम् ।
अहं दधामि द्रविणं हविष्मते सुप्राव्ये३ यजमानाय सुन्वते ॥ 2 ॥
अहं राष्ट्री संगमनी वसूनां चिकितुषी प्रथमा यज्ञियानाम् ।
तां मा देवा व्यदधुः पुरुत्रा भूरिस्थात्रां भूर्यावेशयन्तीम् ॥ 3 ॥
मया सो अन्नमत्ति यो विपश्यति यः प्राणिति य ईं शृणोत्युक्तम् ।
अमन्तवो मां त उप क्षियन्ति श्रुधि श्रुत श्रद्धिवं ते वदामि ॥ 4 ॥
अहमेव स्वयमिदं वदामि जुष्टं देवेभिरुत मानुषेभिः ।
यं कामये तंतमुग्रं कृणोमि तं ब्रह्माणं तमृषिं तं सुमेधाम् ॥ 5 ॥
अहं रुद्राय धनुरा तनोमि ब्रह्मद्विषे शरवे हन्तवा उ ।
अहं जनाय समदं कृणोम्यहं द्यावापृथिवी आ विवेश ॥ 6 ॥
अहं सुवे पितरमस्य मूर्धन्मम योनिरप्स्व१न्तः समुद्रे ।
ततो वि तिष्ठे भुवनानु विश्वोतामूं द्यां वर्ष्मणोप स्पृशामि ॥ 7 ॥
अहमेव वातइव प्र वाम्यारभमाणा भुवनानि विश्वा ।
परो दिवा पर एना पृथिव्यैतावती महिना सं बभूव ॥ 8 ॥

RV_10,125.01a ahaṃ rudrebhir vasubhiś carāmy aham ādityair uta viśvadevaiḥ |
RV_10,125.01c aham mitrāvaruṇobhā bibharmy aham indrāgnī aham aśvinobhā||
RV_10,125.02a ahaṃ somam āhanasam bibharmy ahaṃ tvaṣṭāram uta pūṣaṇam bhagam |
RV_10,125.02c ahaṃ dadhāmi draviṇaṃ haviṣmate suprāvye yajamānāya sunvate ||
RV_10,125.03a ahaṃ rāṣṭrī saṃgamanī vasūnāṃ cikituṣī prathamā yajñiyānām |
RV_10,125.03c tām mā devā vy adadhuḥ purutrā bhūristhātrām bhūry āveśayantīm ||
RV_10,125.04a mayā so annam atti yo vipaśyati yaḥ prāṇiti ya īṃ śṛṇoty uktam |
RV_10,125.04c amantavo māṃ ta upa kṣiyanti śrudhi śruta śraddhivaṃ te vadāmi ||
RV_10,125.05a aham eva svayam idaṃ vadāmi juṣṭaṃ devebhir uta mānuṣebhiḥ|
RV_10,125.05c yaṃ kāmaye taṃ-tam ugraṃ kṛṇomi tam brahmāṇaṃ tam ṛṣiṃ taṃ sumedhām ||
RV_10,125.06a ahaṃ rudrāya dhanur ā tanomi brahmadviṣe śarave hantavā u |
RV_10,125.06c ahaṃ janāya samadaṃ kṛṇomy ahaṃ dyāvāpṛthivī ā viveśa ||
RV_10,125.07a ahaṃ suve pitaram asya mūrdhan mama yonir apsv antaḥ samudre |
RV_10,125.07c tato vi tiṣṭhe bhuvanānu viśvotāmūṃ dyāṃ varṣmaṇopa spṛśāmi||
RV_10,125.08a aham eva vāta iva pra vāmy ārabhamāṇā bhuvanāni viśvā |
RV_10,125.08c paro divā para enā pṛthivyaitāvatī mahinā sam babhūva ||

10.125.01 I proceed with the Rudras, with the Vasus, with the A_dityas, and with the Vis'vedeva_s; I support both Mitra and Varun.a, Agni and Indra, and the two As'vins.[Deity Prama_tma_: the word, or first of creatures].
10.125.02 I support the foe-destroying Soma, Tvas.t.a_, Pu_s.an and Bhaga; I bestow wealth upon the institutor of the rite offering the oblation, deserving of careful protection, pouring forth the libation.
10.125.03 I am the sovereign queen, the collectress of treasures, cognizant (of the Supreme Being), the chief of objects of worship; as such the gods have put me in many places, abiding in manifold conditions, entering into numerous (forms.
10.125.04 He who eats food (eats) through me; he who sees, who breathes, who hears what is spoken, does so through me; those who are ignorant of me perish; hear you who have hearing, I tell that which is

deserving of belief.
10.125.05 I verily of myself declare this which is approved of by both gods and men; whomsoever I will, I render formidable, I make him a Brahma_, a r.s.i, or a sage. [A Brahman: Brahma_, the creator].
10.125.06 I bend the bow of Rudra, to slay the destructive enemy of the Bra_hman.as, I wage war with (hostile) men. I pervade heaven and earth.
10.125.07 I bring forth the paternal (heaven) upon the brow of this (Supreme Being), my birthplace is in the midst of the waters; from thence I spread through all beings, and touch this heaven with my body.
10.125.08 I breathe forth like the wind giving form to all created worlds; beyond the heaven, beyond this earth (am I), so vast am I in greatness.

Phoenix dactylifera

Phoenix dactylifera fruit - dates. Spathe of date palm

Sanchi stupa torana, Northern gateway.

Hieroglyph-multiplex atop Sanchi torana, Northern gateway. The spathe of palm hang down the pair of molluscs which tie into a rope holding two fins of fish.\

Hieroglyph: Pali sippī- pearl oyster, Pkt. sippī- id., etc. (DEDR 2535). *sippī* f. 'spathe of date palm' Rebus: *sippi* 'artificer, craftsman'. śilpin ' skilled in art ', m. ' artificer ' Gaut., *śilpika*<-> ' skilled ' MBh. [śílpa --] Pa. *sippika* -- m. ' craftsman ', NiDoc. *śilpiǵa*, Pk. *sippi* -- , °*ia* -- m.; A. *xipini* ' woman clever at spinning and weaving '; OAw. *sīpī* m. ' artizan '; M. *śĩpī* m. ' a caste of tailors '; Si. *sipi* -- *yā* ' craftsman '.(CDIAL 12471) சிற்பியர். (சூடா.) *சிற்பம்*[1] *ciṟpam* , *n.* < *šilpa*. 1. Artistic skill; தொழிலின் திறமை. செருக்கயல் சிற்பமாக (சீவக. 2716). 2. Fine or artistic workmanship; நுட்பமான தொழில். சிற்பந் திகழ்தரு திண்மதில் (திருக்கோ. 305). சிற்பர் ciṟpar , *n.* < *šilpa*. Mechanics, artisans, stone-cutters; சிற்பிகள். (W.)*சிற்பி ciṟpi*, *n.* < *šilpin*. Mechanic, artisan, stone-cutter; கம்மியன். (சூடா.)*சிற்பியல் ciṟpiyal* , *n.* < சிற்பம்[1] + இயல். Architecture, as an art;

சிற்பசாஸ்திரம். மாசில் கம் மத்துச் சிற்பியற் புலவர் (பெருங். இலாவாண. 4, 50).

Sanchi stupa. Eastern gateway

Sanchi stupa. Western gateway.

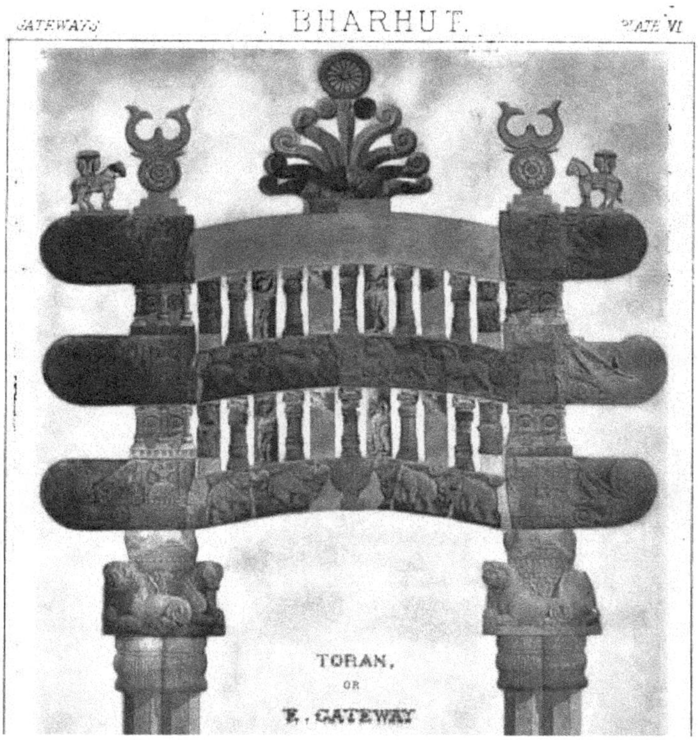

Bharhut Stupa. Eastern gateway. Centrepiece: sippi 'shell' rebus: sippi 'artisan' eraka 'nave of wheel' rebus: eraka 'moltencast copper'. tAmarasa 'lotus' rebus: tAmra 'copper'. kola 'tiger' rebus: kol 'working in iron' kolle 'blacksmith' kolimi 'smithy, forge'. For reading of 'srivatsa' hieroglyph, see details of Sanchi Stupa torana with identical hieroglyph components.

ताम्र-पट्टी on Bharhut frieze on a coping rail.

tāmrapaṭṭI 'copper-town, copper-city'.

Square seal (silver) from Karur, with symbols like the Srivatsa and legend "Kuravan". Ist century B.C.E Source: http://www.frontline.in/static/html/fl2013/stories/20030704000207100.htm

A kuravan is one of 5 kurava who are teachers, upadhyaya; the word also connotes a basket maker: குரவன் kuravaṉ , *n.* < *guravahguru.* 1. Elderly person qualified by age, family connection, respectability, knowledge or authority, to give advice and exercise control; any one of*aiṅ-kuravar*; அரசன், உபாத்தியாயன் அல்லது குரு, தாய், தந்தை, தமையன் என்ற ஐங்குர வருள் ஒருவர். நிகரில் குரவரிவர் (ஆசாரக். 17). 2. Minister; மந்திரி. (பிங்.) 3. Brahmā, as the father of all; பிரமன். (திவா.)குறவன் kuṟavaṉ

, n. < id. [T. korava, K. koṟava, M. kuṟavan.] 1. Inhabitant of the hilly tract; குறிஞ்சிநிலமகன். குறவரு மருளுங் குன் றத்து (மலைபடு. 275). 2. Inhabitant of the desert tract; பாலைநிலமகன். (பிங்.) 3. Kuṟava, a caste of fowlers, snake-catchers, basket-makers and fortune-tellers; வலைவைத்தல் பாம்புபிடித்தல் கூடைமுடைதல் குறிசொல்லுதல் முதலிய தொழில்கள் செய்யும் சாதியினன். 4. Pretender, cringing hypocrite; பாசாங்குபண்ணுகிறவன். Colloq. 5. Mercury, quicksilver; பாதரசம். (மூ. அ.)

Note on rebus reading of svastika hieroglyph on Sanchi stupa and Jaina Ayagapata

Pali etyma point to the use of 卐 with semant. 'auspicious mark'; on the Sanchi stupa; the cognate gloss is: *sotthika, sotthiya* 'blessed'.

Or. *ṭaü* ' zinc, pewter '(CDIAL 5992). *jasta* 'zinc' (Hindi) sathya, *satva* 'zinc' (Kannada) The hieroglyph used on Indus writing consists of two forms: 卐卍. Considering the phonetic variant of Hindi gloss, it has been suggested for decipherment of Meluhha hieroglyphs in archaeometallurgical context that the early forms for both the hieroglyph and the rebus reading was: *satya*.

The semant. expansion relating the hieroglyph to 'welfare' may be related to the resulting alloy of brass achieved by alloying zinc with copper. The brass alloy shines like gold and was a metal of significant value, as significant as the tin (cassiterite) mineral, another alloying metal which was tin-bronze in great demand during the Bronze Age in view of the scarcity of naturally occurring copper+arsenic or arsenical bronze.

I suggest that the Meluhha gloss was a phonetic variant recorded in Pali etyma: *sotthiya.* This gloss was represented on Sanchi stupa inscription and also on Jaina *ayagapata* offerings by worshippers of ariya, ayira dham*ma*, by the same hieroglyph (either clockwise-twisting or anti-clockwise twisting rotatory symbol of svastika). Linguists may like to pursue this line further to suggest the semant. evolution of the hieroglyph over time, from the days of Sarasvati-Sindhu civilization to the narratives of Sanchi stupa or Ayagapata of Kankali Tila.

स्वस्ति [svasti] *ind* S A particle of benediction. Ex. राजा तुला स्वस्ति असो O king! may it be well with thee!; रामाय स्वस्ति रावणाय स्वस्ति! 2 An auspicious particle. 3 A term of sanction or approbation (so be it, amen &c.) 4 Used as *s n* Welfare, weal, happiness.स्वस्तिक [svastika] *n m* S A mystical figure the inscription of which upon any person or thing is considered to be lucky. It is, amongst the जैन, the emblem of the seventh deified teacher of the present era. It consists of 卍. 2 A temple of a particular form with a portico in front. 3 Any auspicious or lucky object.(Marathi)

svasti f. ' good fortune ' RV. [su -- 2, √as1]Pa. *suvatthi* -- , *sotthi* -- f. ' well -- being ', NiDoc. *śvasti*; Pk. *satthi* -- , *sotthi* -- f. ' blessing, welfare '; Si. *seta* ' good fortune ' < **soti* (H. Smith EGS 185 < *sustha* --). svastika ' *auspicious ', m. ' auspicious mark ' R. [svastí --]Pa. *sotthika* -- , *°iya* -- ' auspicious '; Pk. *satthia* -- , *sot°* m. ' auspicious mark '; H. *sathiyā, sati°* m. ' mystical mark of good luck '; G. *sāthiyɔ* m. ' auspicious mark painted on the front of a house '.(CDIAL 13915, 13916)

Nibbānasotthi (welfare). saccena suvatthi hotu nibbānaŋ Sn 235.Sotthi (f.) [Sk. svasti=su+asti] well -- being, safety, bless ing A iii.38=iv.266 ("brings future happiness"); J i.335; s. hotu hail! D i.96; sotthiŋ in safety, safely Dh 219 (=anupaddavena DhA iii.293); Pv iv.64(=nirupaddava PvA 262); Sn 269; sotthinā safely, prosperously D i.72, 96; ii.346; M i.135; J ii.87; iii.201. suvatthi the same J iv.32. See sotthika & sovatthika. -- kamma a blessing J i.343. -- kāra an utterer of blessings, a herald J vi.43. -- gata safe wandering, prosperous journey Mhvs 8, 10; sotthigamana the same J i.272. -- bhāva well -- being, prosperity, safety J i.209; iii.44; DhA ii.58; PvA 250. -- vācaka utterer of blessings, a herald Miln 359. -- sālā a hospital Mhvs 10, 101.Sotthika (& °iya) (adj.) [fr. sotthi] happy, auspicious, blessed, safe VvA 95; DhA ii.227 (°iya; in phrase dīgha° one who is happy for long [?]).Sotthivant (adj.) [sotthi+vant] lucky, happy, safe Vv 8452.Sovatthika (adj.) [either fr. sotthi with diaeresis, or fr. su+atthi+ka=Sk. svastika] safe M i.117; Vv 187 (=sotthika VvA 95); J vi.339 (in the shape of a svastika?); Pv iv.33 (=sotthi -- bhāva -- vāha PvA 250). -- âlankāra a kind of auspicious mark J vi.488. (Pali)

[quote]Cunningham, later the first director of the Archaeological Survey of India, makes the claim in: The Bhilsa Topes (1854). Cunningham, surveyed the great stupa complex at Sanchi in 1851, where he famously found caskets of relics labelled 'Sāriputta' and 'Mahā Mogallāna'. [1] The

Bhilsa Topes records the features, contents, artwork and inscriptions found in and around these stupas. All of the inscriptions he records are in Brāhmī script. What he says, in a note on p.18, is: "The swasti of Sanskrit is the suti of Pali; the mystic cross, or swastika is only a monogrammatic symbol formed by the combination of the two syllables, su + ti = suti." There are two problems with this. While there is a word suti in Pali it is equivalent to Sanskrit śruti'hearing'. The Pali equivalent ofsvasti is sotthi; and svastika is either sotthiya or sotthika. Cunningham is simply mistaken about this. The two letters su + ti in Brāhmī script are not much like thesvastika. This can easily been seen in the accompanying image on the right, where I have written the word in the Brāhmī script. I've included the Sanskrit and Pali words for comparison. Cunningham's imagination has run away with him. Below are two examples of donation inscriptions from the south gate of the Sanchi stupa complex taken from Cunningham's book (plate XLX, p.449).

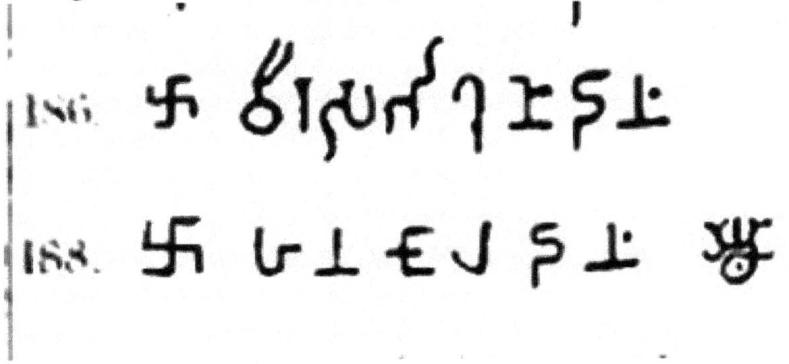

"Note that both begin with a lucky svastika. The top line reads 卐 vīrasu bhikhuno dānaṃ - i.e. "the donation of Bhikkhu Vīrasu." The lower inscription also ends with dānaṃ, and the name in this case is perhaps pānajāla (I'm unsure about jā). Professor Greg Schopen has noted that these inscriptions recording donations from bhikkhus and bhikkhunis seem to contradict the traditional narratives of monks and nuns not owning property or handling money. The last symbol on line 2 apparently represents the three jewels, and frequently accompanies such inscriptions...Müller [in Schliemann(2), p.346-7] notes that svasti occurs throughout 'the Veda' [sic; presumably he means the Ṛgveda where it appears a few dozen times]. It occurs both as a noun meaning 'happiness', and an adverb meaning 'well' or 'hail'. Müller suggests it would correspond to Greek εὐστική (eustikē) from εὐστῶ (eustō), however neither form occurs in my Greek Dictionaries. Though svasti occurs in the Ṛgveda, svastika does not. Müller traces the earliest occurrence of svastika to Pāṇini's grammar, the Aṣṭādhyāyī, in the context of ear markers for cows to show who their owner was. Pāṇini discusses a point of grammar when making a compound using svastika and karṇa, the word for ear. I've seen no earlier reference to the word svastika, though the symbol itself was in use in the Indus Valley civilisation.[unquote]

1. Cunningham, Alexander. (1854) The Bhilsa topes, or, Buddhist monuments of central India : comprising a brief historical sketch of the rise, progress, and decline of Buddhism; with an account of the opening and examination of the various groups of topes around Bhilsa. London : Smith, Elder. [possibly the earliest recorded use of the word swastika in English].
2. Schliemann, Henry. (1880). Ilios : the city and country of the Trojans : the results of researches and discoveries on the site of Troy and through the Troad in the years 1871-72-73-78-79. London : John Murray.
http://jayarava.blogspot.in/2011/05/svastika.html

Bharhut sculptural relief. The center-piece is the slab with hieroglyphs (sacred writing) held on the platform which holds a pair of 'srivatsa' hieroglyph compositions. The artist is conveying the key interpretative message that the composition contains inscribed, engraved, written symbols (hieroglyphs). The hieroglyphs are read rebus using Meluhha glosses to explain the veneration of *ayira-ariya dhamma.* A related life-activity reading: *ayira* 'fish' rebus: *aya* 'metal alloy'; *karada* 'saffower' rebus: *karada* 'hard alloy of metal'. This is work done in kole.l 'smithy' rebus: kole.l 'temple'.

The central hieroglyphs flanked by two 'srivatsa' hieroglyphs are a pair of spathes:

Hieroglyph: दळ (p. 406)[daḷa] दल (p. 404) [dala] *n* (S) A leaf. 2 A petal of a flower. *dula* 'pair'

Rebus: metalcast: ढाळ [ḍhāḷa] Cast, mould, form (as of metal vessels, trinkets &c.) *dul* 'cast metal'. The three 'x' on this frame are also hieroglyphs: *kolmo* 'three' Rebus: *kolami* 'smithy' *dATu* 'cross' rebus: *dhatu* 'mineral'. Thus, the sculptural composition is a narrative of work in a Meluhha smithy.

Many reliefs depict life-activities of people. Many symbols are hieroglyphs read rebus, related to dharma and archaeometallurgy, lapidary work on semiprecious stones and work with sea-shells (*turbinella pyrum*).

Fire altar. Smith at work. In front of the hut, smithy. Tree on field. Swan or goose on field. kanda 'fire-altar' (Santali)

Sanchi sculptural relief: What is the fire altar flanked by two roofed huts?

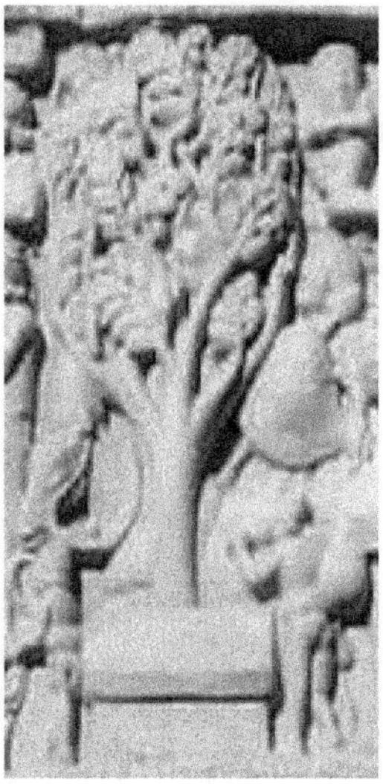

Veneration of the tree, surrounded by dwarfs, gaNa. kuTi 'tree' Rebus: kuThi 'smelter'

Hieroglyph composition of spathe+ molluscs clanked by elephants.

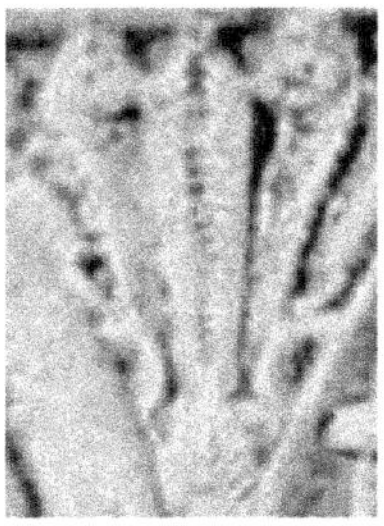

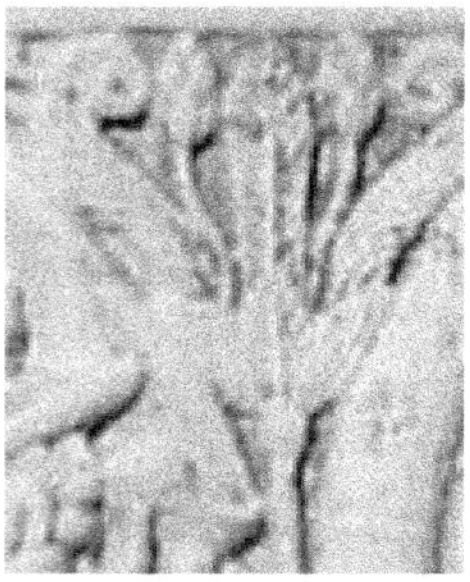

Hieroglyph: spathe, buds flanked by molluscs -- atop a ring flanked by two petas, dala 'petal'. DhALako 'ingot'

Venerated tree, garlanded. gaNa and worshippers. Tree atop ingot slab.

Lakshmi flanked by elephants. Divinity of wealth. Hieroglyphs: *ibha* 'elephant' rebus: *ib* 'iron' (Santali) kariba 'trunk of elephant' rebus: karba 'iron' (Kannada) *dula* 'pair' rebus:*dul* 'cast metal'. Hence, *dul ib* 'cast iron'.

Ayagapata

Foliage motif. Fish tied in a pair of molluscs, flanking two arches 'M' shaped enshrining two slabs (with script) hangi 'molusc' Rebus: sanghi 'member of sangha, community' dAma 'tying' Rebus: dhamma 'dharma, consciousness-cosmic ordering'. ayira 'fish' rebus: ayira, ariya 'person of noble character, dharmin'.

Sanchi relief. Monkeys, tree, archer.

Sanchi reliefs. Adoration of tree with garlands.

Source: http://personal.carthage.edu/jlochtefeld/buddhism/sanchi/wginterior.html Thanks to James G. Lochtefeld

Buffalo heads on field of sculptural relief together with tree, bulls, antelopes, archers. Sanchi relief.Western gateway. Top right: a fire altar is flanked by two huts, smithies, brick-kilns.

Bharhut. Cock on tree and lion (tiger?) in front of smithy brick-kiln. kola 'tiger' rebus: kol 'working in iron' kolhe 'smelters' (Santali)

A smith at work. Relief also shows roof of smithy with a base or bricks. On the left is the pair of inerted fish-tails. Bharhut coping from stupa, Cleveland Museum, Sunga, India, 2nd Century, B.C., Sculpture and painting- The Cleveland Museum, ACSA

Mounted as a pair of 'srivatsa' symbols atop two pillars of the Sanchi stupa torana (north gate), the proclamation is: aya kammaṭa 'metal mint' PLUS dhāvḍā 'smelter', the two components of the message are signified by: daüṛā 'rope' tying the fins of fishes khambhaṛā 'fin'. dula 'pair' rebus: dul 'cast metal'.

It should be noted that the orthography of Sanchi and Bharhut is comparable to that of Begram ivories. There is evidence of an inscription in Sanchi stupa that dantakara 'irovy workers' had donated for the construction of the stupa. The ivory worker guilds had shown their artificer competence in working with copper and metal by the proclamations announced with Indus Script hieroglyph signifiers on Sanchi and Bharhut Stupa toranas.

The continuum from Binjor octagonal brick (aSTAzri skamba or Yupa) continues in Begram and Sanchi/Bharhut Bharatam Janam artificers' works and also on thousands of punch-marked and cast coins in mints of historical periods in an extended region stretching from Taxila to Eran, Vidisha, Karur, Sri Lanka.

This remarkable hypertext is thus a continuum of Indus Script cipher and Prakrtam used by Bharatam janam, 'metalcaster people'.

There are two hieroglyph components in the hieroglyph-multiplex (hypertext) atop Sanchi stupa. They are: 1. fin (tail) of a pair of fishes; 2. rope tying the two fishes together. These components are clearly seen in the orthographic variants signified on Jaina Ayagapattas.

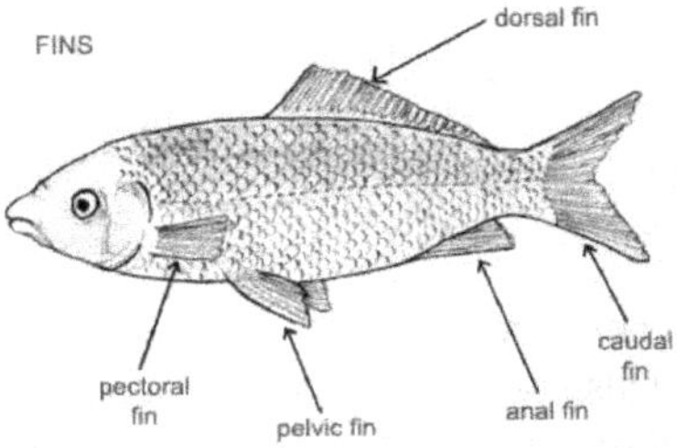

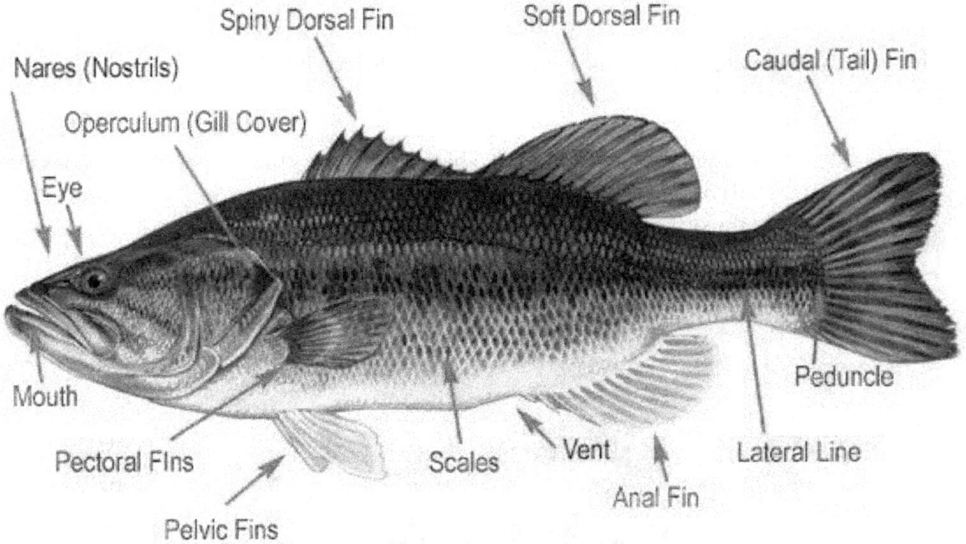

Hieroglyph: *khambhaṛā* m. ' fin ' (Lahnda):*skambha2 ' shoulder -- blade, wing, plumage '. [Cf. **skapa* -- s.v. *khavaka --] S. *khambhu*, °*bho* m. ' plumage ', *khambhuṛi* f. ' wing '; L. *khabbh* m., mult. *khambh* m. ' shoulder -- blade, wing, feather ', khet. *khamb* ' wing ', mult. *khambhaṛā* m. ' fin '; P. *khambh* m. ' wing, feather '; G. *khā̆m* f., *khabhɔ* m. ' shoulder '.(CDIAL 13640)

Rebus: *Ta.* kampaṭṭam coinage, coin. *Ma.* kammaṭṭam, kammiṭṭam coinage, mint. *Ka.* kammaṭa id.; kammaṭi a coiner. (DEDR 1236)

skambhá1 m. ' prop, pillar ' RV. 2. ' *pit ' (semant. cf. kū´pa -- 1). [√skambh]
1. Pa. *khambha* -- m. ' prop '; Pk. *khaṁbha* -- m. ' post, pillar '; Pr. *iškyöp*, *üšköb* ' bridge ' NTS xv 251; L. (Ju.) *khabbā* m., mult. *khambbā* m. ' stake forming fulcrum for oar '; P. *khambh*, *khambhā*, *khammhā* m. ' wooden prop, post '; WPah.bhal. *kham* m. ' a part of the yoke of a plough ', (Joshi) *khāmbā* m. ' beam, pier '; Ku. *khāmo* ' a support ', gng. *khām* ' pillar (of wood or bricks) '; N. *khā̃bo* ' pillar, post ', B. *khām*, *khāmbā*; Or. *khamba* ' post, stake '; Bi. *khāmā* ' post of brick -- crushing machine ', *khāmhī* ' support of betel -- cage roof ', *khamhiyā* ' wooden pillar supporting roof '; Mth. *khāmh*, *khāmhī* ' pillar, post ', *khamhā* ' rudder -- post '; Bhoj. *khambhā* ' pillar ', *khambhiyā* ' prop '; OAw. *khāṁbhe* m. pl. ' pillars ', lakh. *khambhā*; H. *khām* m. ' post, pillar, mast ', *khambh* f. ' pillar, pole '; G. *khām*m. ' pillar

', *khā̃bhi*, °*bi* f. ' post ', M. *khā̃b* m., Ko. *khāmbho*, °*bo*, Si. *kap* (< **kab*); -- X gambhīra -- , sthāṇú -- , sthū´ṇā -- qq.v.
2. K. *khambürü* f. ' hollow left in a heap of grain when some is removed '; Or. *khamā* ' long pit, hole in the earth ', *khamiā* ' small hole '; Marw. *khā̃baṛo* ' hole '; G.*khā̃bhũ* n. ' pit for sweepings and manure '. *skambhaghara -- , *skambhākara -- , *skambhāgāra -- , *skambhadaṇḍa -- ; *dvāraskambha -- . Addenda: skambhá -- 1: Garh. *khambu* ' pillar '.(CDIAL 13639)

Hieroglyph: *daürā* 'rope' Rebus: *dhāvḍā* 'smelter'

Hieroglyph: *daü̃rā, daürā* ' rope '(Oriya): dā´man1 ' rope ' RV. 2. *dāmana -- , *dāmanī* -- f. ' long rope to which calves are tethered ' Hariv. 3. *dāmara -- . [**dāmara* -- is der. fr. *n*/*r* n. stem. -- √dā2]1. Pa. *dāma* -- , inst. °*mēna* n. ' rope, fetter, garland ', Pk. *dāma* -- n.; Wg. *dām* ' rope, thread, bandage '; Tir. *dām* ' rope '; Paš.lauṛ. *dām* ' thick thread ', gul. *dūm* ' net snare ' (IIFL iii 3, 54 ← Ind. or Pers.); Shum. *dām* ' rope '; Sh.gil. (Lor.) *dōmo* ' twine, short bit of goat's hair cord ', gur. *dōm* m. ' thread ' (→ Ḍ. *dōṅ* ' thread '); K. *gu -- dômu* m. ' cow's tethering rope '; P. *dā̃u, dāvā̃* m. ' hobble for a horse '; WPah.bhad. *daũ* n. ' rope to tie cattle ', bhal. *daõ* m., jaun. *dā̃w;* A. *dāmā* ' peg to tie a buffalo -- calf to '; B. *dām, dāmā* ' cord '; Or. *duā̃* ' tether ', *dāī̃* ' long tether to which many beasts are tied '; H. *dām* m.f. ' rope, string, fetter ', *dāmā* m. ' id.,garland '; G. *dām* n. ' tether ', M. *dāvẽ* n.; Si. *dama* ' chain, rope ', (SigGr) *dam* ' garland '. -- Ext. in Paš.dar. *damaṭā´*, °*ṭī´*, nir. weg. *damaṭék* ' rope ', Shum.*ḍamaṭik*, Woṭ. *damṓṛ* m., Sv. *dåmoṛī´*; -- with -- *ll* -- : N. *dāmlo* ' tether for cow ', *dā̃wali, dāũli, dāmli* ' bird -- trap of string ', *dā̃wal, dāmal* ' coeval ' (< ' tied together '?); M. *dā̃vlī* f. ' small tie -- rope '.
2. Pk. *dāvaṇa* -- n., *dāmaṇī* -- f. ' tethering rope '; S. *ḏāvaṇu, ḏāṇu* m. ' forefeet shackles ', *ḏāviṇī, ḏāṇī* f. ' guard to support nose -- ring '; L. *ḍā̃vaṇ* m., *ḍā̃vaṇī, ḍāuṇī*(Ju. *ḏ* --) f. ' hobble ', *dāuṇī* f. ' strip at foot of bed, triple cord of silk worn by women on head ', awāṇ. *dāvuṇ* ' picket rope '; P. *dāuṇ, dauṇ*, ludh. *daun* f. m. ' string for bedstead, hobble for horse ', *dāuṇī* f. ' gold ornament worn on woman's forehead '; Ku. *dauṇo* m., °*ṇī* f. ' peg for tying cattle to ', gng. *dɔ̃ṛ* ' place for keeping cattle, bedding for cattle '; A. *dan* ' long cord on which a net or screen is stretched, thong ', *danā* ' bridle '; B. *dāmni* ' rope '; Or. *daaṇa* ' string at the fringe of a casting net on which pebbles are strung ', *dāuṇi* ' rope for tying bullocks together when threshing '; H. *dāwan* m. ' girdle ', *dāwanī* f. ' rope ', *dā̃wanī* f. ' a woman's orna<-> ment '; G. *dāmaṇ, ḍā°* n. ' tether, hobble ', *dāmṇũ* n. ' thin rope, string ', *dāmṇī* f. ' rope, woman's head -- ornament '; M. *dāvaṇ* f. ' picket -- rope '. -- Words denoting the act of driving animals to tread out corn are poss. nomina actionis from *dāmayati2.3. L. *ḍā̃varāvaṇ*, (Ju.) *ḏā̃v°* ' to hobble '; A. *dāmri* ' long rope for tying several buffalo -- calves together ', Or. *daü̃rā, daürā* ' rope '; Bi. *daũrī* ' rope to which threshing bullocks are tied, the act of treading out the grain ', Mth. *dā̃mar, daũraṛ* ' rope to which the bullocks are tied '; H. *dā̃wrī* f. ' id., rope, string ', *dā̃wrī* f. ' the act of driving bullocks round to tread out the corn '. Addenda: dā´man -- 1. 1. Brj. *dā̃u* m. ' tying '. 3. *dāmara -- : Brj. *dā̃wrī* f. ' rope '.(CDIAL 6283)

Rebus: *dhāvḍī* ' composed of or relating to iron ' (Marathi) धवड [dhavaḍa] *m* (Or धावड) A class or an individual of it. They are smelters of iron.धावड [dhāvaḍa] *m* A class or an individual of it. They are smelters of iron. धावडी [dhāvaḍī] *a* Relating to the class धावड. Hence 2 Composed of or relating to iron. (Marathi) dhā´tu n. ' substance ' RV., m. ' element ' MBh., ' metal, mineral, ore (esp. of a red colour) ' Mn., ' ashes of the dead ' lex., ' *strand of rope ' (cf.*tridhā´tu* -- ' threefold ' RV., *ayugdhātu* -- ' having an uneven number of strands ' KātyŚr.). [√dhā]Pa. *dhātu* -- m. ' element, ashes of the dead, relic '; KharI. *dhatu* ' relic '; Pk. *dhāu* -- m. ' metal, red chalk ';

N. *dhāu* ' ore (esp. of copper) '; Or. *ḍhāu* ' red chalk, red ochre ' (whence *ḍhāuā* ' reddish '; M. *dhāū, dhāv* m.f. ' a partic. soft red stone ' (whence *dhā̆vaḍ* m. ' a caste of iron -- smelters ', *dhāvḍī* ' composed of or relating to iron '); -- Si. *dā* ' relic '; -- S. *dhāī* f. ' wisp of fibres added from time to time to a rope that is being twisted ', L. *dhāī̃* f. (CDIAL 6773)

Srivatsa with *kanka*, 'eyes' (Kui).

Begram ivories. Plate 389 Reference: Hackin, 1954, fig.195, no catalog N°. According to an inscription on the southern gate of Sanchi stupa,

it has been carved by ivory carvers of Vidisha.Southern Gateway panel information:West pillar Front East Face has an inscription. *Vedisakehi dantakarehi rupa-kammam katam* - On the border of this panel – Epigraphia Indica vol II – written in Brahmi, language is Pali – the carving of this sculpture is done by the ivory carvers of Vedisa (Vidisha). http://puratattva.in/2012/03/21/sanchi-buddham-dhammam-sangahm-5-1484

Ta. kaṇ eye, aperture, orifice, star of a peacock's tail. *Ma.* kaṇ, kaṇṇu eye, nipple, star in peacock's tail, bud. *Ko.* kaṇ eye. *To.* koṇ eye, loop in string. *Ka.* kaṇ eye, small hole, orifice. *Koḍ.* kaṇṇï id. *Pe.* kaṇga (*pl.* -ŋ, kaṇku) id. *Manḍ.* kan (*pl.* -ke) id. *Kui* kanu (*pl.* kan-ga), (K.) kanu (*pl.* kaṛka) id. *Kuwi* (F.) kannū (S.) kannu (*pl.* kanka), (Su. P. Isr.) kanu (*pl.* kaṇka) id. (DEDR 1159).

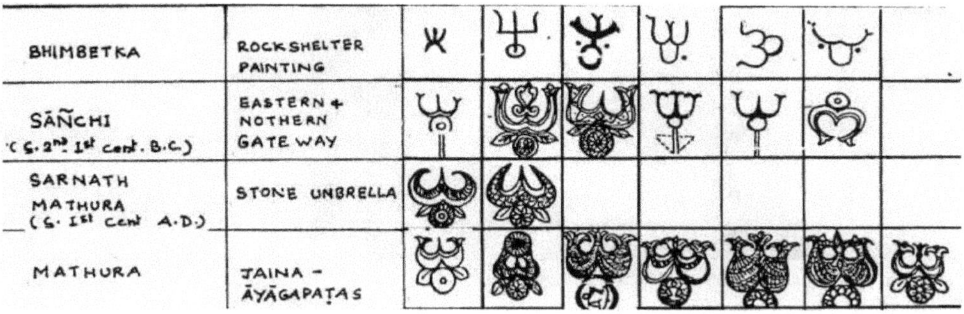
BHIMBETKA
ROCKSHELTER PAINTING
SĀÑCHI
(S. 2nd 1st cent. B.C.)
EASTERN + NOTHERN GATE WAY
SARNATH
MATHURA
(S. 1st cent A.D.)
STONE UNBRELLA
MATHURA
JAINA - ĀYĀGAPAṬAS

śrivatsa symbol [with its hundreds of stylized variants, depicted on Pl. 29 to 32] occurs in Bogazkoi (Central Anatolia) dated ca. 6th to 14th cent. BCE on inscriptions Pl. 33, Nandipāda-Triratna at: Bhimbetka, Sanchi, Sarnath and Mathura] Pl. 27, Svastika symbol: distribution in cultural periods] The association of śrivatsa with 'fish' is reinforced by the symbols binding fish in Jaina āyāgapaṭas (snake-hood?) of Mathura (late 1st cent. BCE). śrivatsa symbol seems to have evolved from a styli□ed glyph showing 'two fishes'. In the Sanchi stupa, the fish-tails of two fishes are combined to flank the 'śrivatsa' glyph. In a Jaina āyāgapaṭa, a fish is ligatured within the śrivatsa glyph, emphasizing the association of the 'fish' glyph with śrivatsa glyph.

(After Plates in: Savita Sharma, 1990, Early Indian symbols, numismatic evidence, Delhi, Agama Kala Prakashan; cf. Shah, UP., 1975, Aspects of Jain Art and Architecture, p.77)

Khandagiri caves (2nd cent. BCE) Cave 3 (Jaina Ananta gumpha). Fire-altar?, śrivatsa, svastika

(hieroglyphs) (King Kharavela, a Jaina who ruled Kalinga has an inscription dated 161 BCE) contemporaneous with Bharhut and Sanchi and early Bodhgaya.

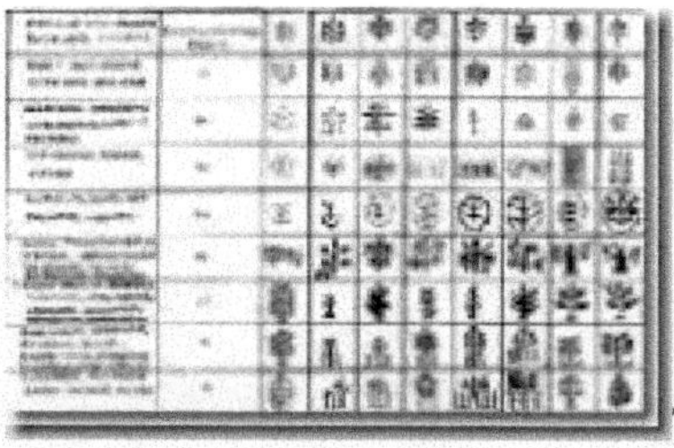

Tree shown on a tablet from Harappa.

[Pl. 39, Savita Sharma, opcit. Tree symbol (often on a platform) on punch-marked coins; a symbol recurring on many tablets showing Sarasvati hieroglyphs].

Kushana period, 1st century C.E.From Mathura Red Sandstone 89x92cm
books.google.com/books?id=evtIAQAAIAAJ&q=In+the+image...

Ayagapatta, Kankali Tila, Mathura.

Two Indus script hieroglyphs sangi 'mollusc' Rebus: sangin 'shell-cutter; sippī 'spathe of date palm' Rebus: sippi 'artificer, craftsman'
Mirror: http://tinyurl.com/gr9qpmo

The two hieroglyph-multiplexes signified by s'ankha 'mollusc or shell' and by sippi 'spathe of date palm' are signifiers of 1. shell-cutter; 2. artisan, artificer. Thus the multiplex shown on Bharhut and Sanchi sculptural panels are a celebration of the artisan's competence in communicating the message of metalwork and shell-work by craftsmen, Bharatam Janam.
See: http://bharatkalyan97.blogspot.in/2016/02/indus-scrip-hieroglyphs-tamrapatti.html

Indus Scrip hieroglyphs: tāmrapaṭṭī ताम्र-पट्टी, 'copper-city, copper-town' Bharhut भरहुत; kammaṭa dhāvḍā 'Mint, smelter', Besanagara बेसनगर The name Besanagara may relate to yuechi, vais'ya traders who had their domain of seafaring mercantile activity across Eurasia.

Zoom: 52996 (cf. John Huntington database) Standard carried by horse-rider. In Indian tradition, kinnara is a celestial musician. Possibly, the s'ankha shown as a mollusc on the standard is a semantic reinforcement of the s'ankha as a trumpet. Sippi 'snail' rebus: sippi 'artificer'.

Procession on Horseback

Bharhut, c. 100 BCE

Indian Museum, Calcutta

Hackin 1954, p.169, figs.18 Ivory? Size: 10.6 x 15.8 x 0.4 cm Begram rectangular plaque depicting three palmettos with curled-up ends, held together by rings made up of lotus petals. Between the palmettos elongated fruit is shown . This scene is bordered by a band depicting a series of four-leaved flowers set in a square frame. In this hieroglyhphic multiplex, there are three distinct orthographic components:

Mollusc 1. mollusc (snail) pair depicted by a pair of antithetical S curved lines: *sā̃khī*
Rebus: sā̃kh 'conch-shell-cutter' சிப்பி[1] cippi , *n*. < Pkt. *šippīšukti*. 1. Shell; முத்து முதலியவற்றைப் பொதிந்திருக்கும் ஓடு. 2. Shell-fish; சிப்பியோடுகூடிய நீர்வாழ்ப ராணி. நண்டு சிப்பி வேய்கதவி (நல்வழி, 36).
Rebus: sipi 'artifier'.
Palmetto or Spathe 2. spathe of a palm or palmetto: *sippī* f. 'spathe of date palm'
Rebus: *sippi* 'artificer, craftsman'. It could also be seen as a chisel:śaṅkula Rebus: sangin 'shell-cutter'.
Tied together, cord 3. a thread or cord that ties the mollusc pair and spath in the centre together into a composite orthographic unit. *dām* 'rope' Rebus: dhamma 'dharma' *dhamা̃a* 'employment in the royal administration'. http://bharatkalyan97.blogspot.in/2015/06/deciphering-indus-script-meluhha.html

The Meluhha gloss which signifies the series is: ధోరణి [dhōraṇi] dhōraṇi. [Skt.] n. A series, line, range; వరుస. A way, style, tradition. పద్ధతి dhorani [dhoranî] f. uninterrupted series (Samskrtam) The semantics of this gloss is demonstrated by a series of hieroglyphs on the Begram ivory plaque and on Bharhut and Sanchi Stupa Toranas (Architraves on gateways). See also: దోరణ [dōraṇa] or దోరణము Same as తోరణము. (q. v.) దోరపాక or ఒరపాక a shed with a pent roof. (Telugu)

From a Jaina AyAgapatta. Fish tied with a rope and a pair of molluscs. aya 'fish'

rebus: ayas, ayas 'iron, metal' sangi 'mollusc' rebus: sangi 'shell-cutter'; dAman 'rope, garland' rebus: dhAvaD 'smelter'. sippi 'shell' rebus: sippi 'artisan'.

Ganesha, Indus Script tradition. significance of hieroglyphs on Dholkal, Bastar, Chattisgarh Ganesha with metal chain and pine cone
Mirror: https://www.academia.edu/s/32bd84b1b4

There are two unique hieroglyphs on Ganesha seated statue of Dholkal, Bastar, Chattisgarh: The*yajnopavitam* worn by Ganesha is a chain of three stranded metal chain (iron or steel) wires. Ganesha carries on his left hand a pine cone.

Both hieroglyphs, together with the trunk of elephant in iconographs are related to metalwork catalogues of Indus Script corpora. Veneration of Ganesha dates back to Rigvedic times (See RV 2.23 sukta *gaṇānāṃ tvā gaṇapatiṃ havāmahe kaviṃ kavīnām upamaśravastamam* -- with translation appended). In the tradition of Bharatam Janam, gana are related to *kharva*, dwarfs as part of Kubera's nidhi; rebus: *karba* 'iron'.

Evidence for Sivalinga is provided in other sites (Mohenjodaro and Harappa) of the civilization:

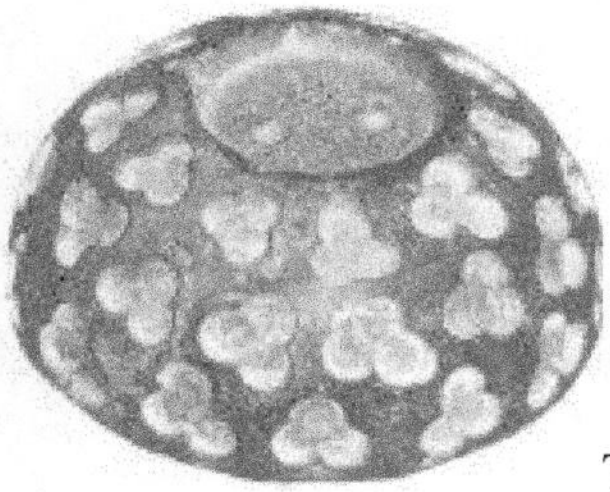

Tre-foil inlay decorated base (for linga icon?); smoothed, polished pedestal of dark red stone; National Museum of Pakistan, Karachi; After Mackay 1938: I, 411; II, pl. 107:35; Parpola, 1994, p. 218.

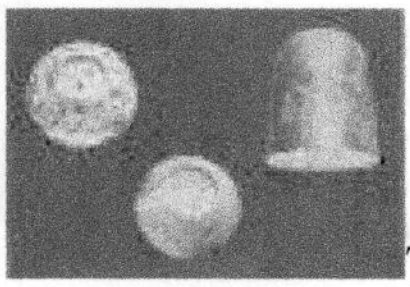

Two decorated bases and a lingam, Mohenjodaro.

Lingam, grey sandstone *in situ*, Harappa, Trench Ai, Mound F, Pl. X (c) (After Vats). "In an earthenware jar, No. 12414, recovered from Mound F, Trench IV, Square I... in this jar, six lingams were found along with some tiny pieces of shell, a unicorn seal, an oblong grey sandstone block with polished surface, five stone pestles, a stone palette, and a block of chalcedony..." (Vats,MS, *Excavations at Harappa*, p. 370).

A Terracotta Linga from Kalibangan (2600 BCE).

The two Dholavira pillars evoke the imageries of a festival which is celebrated even today by Lingavantas, particularly in Karnataka.

These pillars at Dholavira could be a depiction of fiery pillars of light as Sivalinga. (cf. Atharvaveda Skambha Sukta 10.7).

Just above the pillars is an 8-shaped stone structure with Yupa, signifying a *yajna kunda*.

Veneration of S'ivalinga has been noted with the discovery of 6 sivalingas in Harappa, a terracotta S'ivalinga in Kalibangan, and two decorated bases with one S'ivalinga in Mohenjodaro.

Ganesha of Dholkal, Bastar is an emphatic evidence for the thesis of Sandhya Jain in her path-breaking monograph: 'Adi Deo Arya Devata- A Panoramic View of Tribal-Hindu Cultural Interface'. Ganesha is a defining hieroglyph/metaphor of the cultural history of Bharatam Janam. (Bharatam janam, 'metalcaster folk', an expression defining the identity of Bharatiya by Rishi Viswamitra in RV 3.53.12).

Hieroglyph: kariba 'trunk of elephant' rebus: karba 'iron' ibha 'elephant' rebus: ib 'iron.

Hieroglyph: *dhāu* 'strand of rope' Rebus: *dhāv* 'red ore' (ferrite) ti-*dhāu* 'three strands' Rebus: *ti-dhāv* 'three ferrite ores: magnetite, hematite, laterite'.
Hieroglyph: Ash. piċ -- kandə ' pine ', Kt. pṳ̄ċi, piċi, Wg. puċ, püċ (pṳ̄ċ -- kəŕ ' pine -- cone '), Pr. wyoċ, Shum. lyēwič (lyē -- ?).(CDIAL 8407). Cf. Gk. peu/kh f. ' pine ', Lith. pušìs, OPruss. peuse NTS xiii 229. The suffix –kande in the lexeme: Ash. piċ-- kandə ' pine ' may be cognate with the bulbous glyphic related to a mangrove root: Koḍ. kaṇḍe root-stock from which small roots grow; ila·ti kaṇḍe sweet potato (ila·ti England). Tu. kaṇḍe, gaḍḍè a bulbous root; Ta. kaṇṭal mangrove, Rhizophora mucronata; dichotomous mangrove, Kandelia rheedii. Ma. kaṇṭa bulbous root as of lotus, plantain; point where branches and bunches grow out of the stem of a palm; kaṇṭal what is bulb-like, half-ripe jackfruit and other green fruits; R. candel. (DEDR 1171). Rebus: *kaṇḍa* 'tools, pots and pans of metal'.

Hieroglyph: కండె [kaṇḍe] *kaṇḍe*. [Telugu] n. A head or ear of millet or maize. జొన్నకంకి.

Rebus:*Tu.* kandůka, kandaka ditch, trench. *Te.* kandakamu id. *Konḍa* kanda trench made as a fireplace during weddings. *Pe.* kanda fire trench. *Kui* kanda small trench for fireplace. *Malt.* kandri a pit. (DEDR 1214).

http://bharatkalyan97.blogspot.in/2013/11/maize-and-pine-cone-meluhha-hieroglyphs.html

m0301 Indus Script Seal shows a trunk of elephant ligatured to a human face and other animal-related hieroglyphs.

That the veneration of Ganesha is a phenomenon traceable to the Bronze Age is signified by the remarkable hieroglyph-multiplex orthographically combining the trunk of elephant with the horns of a buffalo and a segment of the feline. This unique orthographic feature of Indus Script leads to the iconography of Ganesha with a human body and the head and trunk of an elephant

Material: terra cotta

Dimensions: 4.8 cm height, 5.4 cm width, 4.6 cm breadth

Harappa, Lot 800-01

Harappa Museum, H87-348

Elephant, trunk of elephant: kar-ibha, ib; rebus: karba 'iron'; ib 'iron'.

Fig. 1. La tête d'éléphant (Nausharo, période III : NS 91023201), côté gauche (photo C. Jarrige).

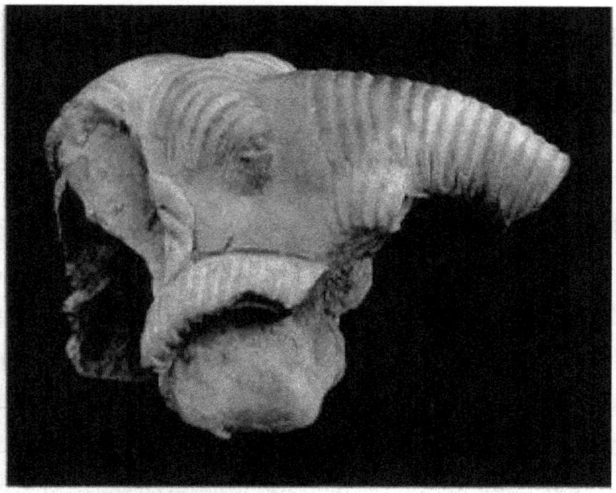

Fig. 2. La tête d'éléphant, côté droit (photo C. Jarrige).

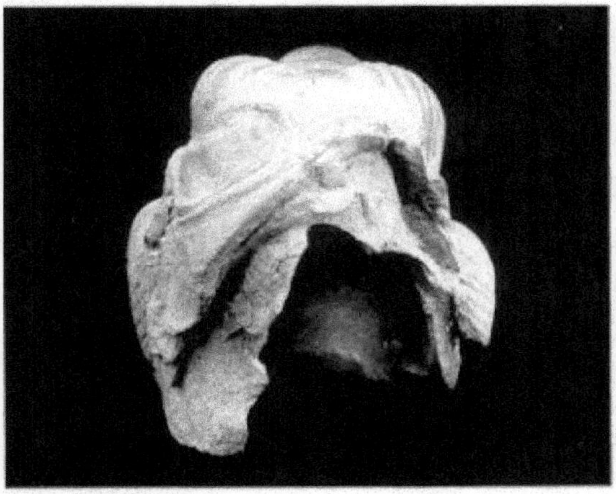

Fig. 3. Vue arrière (photo C. Jarrige).

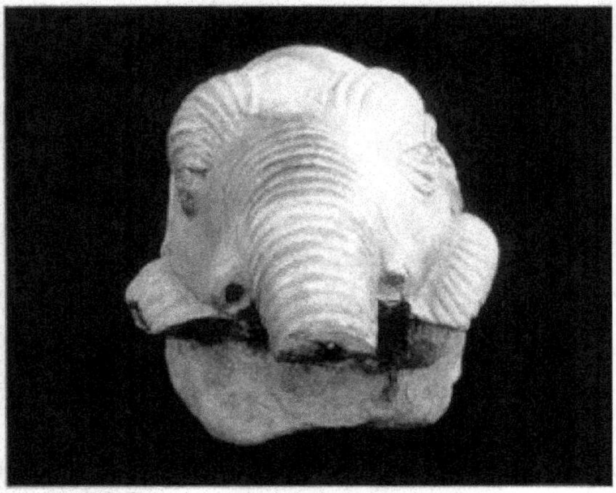

Fig. 4. Vue de face (photo C. Jarrige).

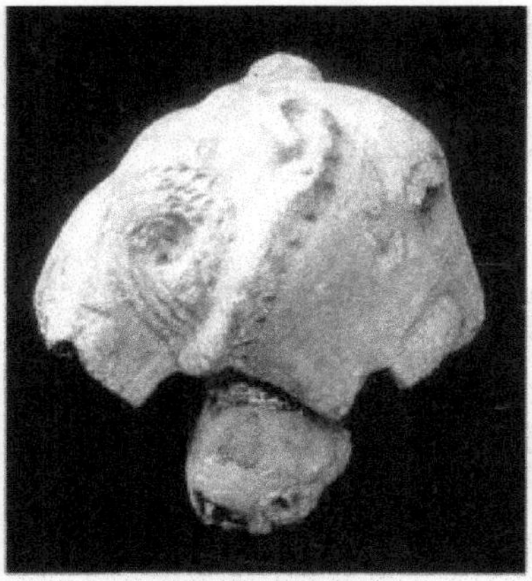

Fig. 6. L'objet composite zoomorphe (Nausharo, période III : NS 92027004) : vue de profil (photo C. Jarrige).

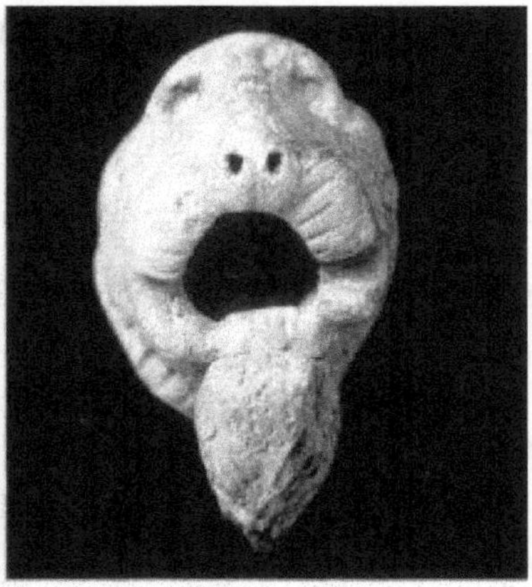

Fig. 7. La tête de félin vue de face (photo C. Jarrige).

Une tête d'éléphant en terre cuite de Nausharo (Pakistan)

In: Arts asiatiques. Tome 47, 1992. pp. 132-136. Jarrige Catherine

http://www.persee.fr/web/revues/home/prescript/article/arasi_0004-3958_1992_num_47_1_1330

The elephant head ligatured with a buffalo at Nausharo is a curtain-raiser for the practice of ligaturing in Indian tradition for *utsava bera* 'idols carried on processions'. The phrase *utsava bera* denotes that processions of the type shown on Mesopotamian cylinder seals or Mohenjo-daro tablets are trade processions for *bera* 'bargaining, trade'. Thus, the processions with hieroglyphs may be part of trade-exchange fairs of ancient times. It is significant that the utsava bera of Ganesa is shown together with a rat or mouse -- as *vāhana*: *ibha* 'elephant' Rebus: ib 'iron'. *mūṣa* 'rat, mouse' Rebus: *mūṣa* 'crucible'. Thus both rat/mouse and elephant face ligatured to a body, are Meluhha hieroglyphs related to metallurgical processes.

Dance step of *Gaṇeśa* shown on a sculptural friezed of Candi Sukuh:

Forge scene stele. Forging of a keris or kris (the iconic Javanese dagger) and other weapons. The blade of the keris represents the khaNDa. Fire is a purifier, so the blade being forged is also symbolic of the purification process central theme of the consecration of gangga sudhi specified in the inscription on the 1.82 m. tall, 5 ft. dia. lingga hieroglyph, the deity of Candi Sukuh.

http://bharatkalyan97.blogspot.in/2015/01/sekkizhar-periya-puranam-candi-sukuh.html

The scene in bas relief The scene depicted Bhima as the blacksmith in the left forging the metal, Ganesa in the center, and Arjuna in the right operating the tube blower to pump air into the furnace.

Candi Sukuh temple was consecrated by Bhre Daha in 1440 CE celebrating Bhima, an embodiment of the philosophy of life alternating between death and rebirth in an eternal cycle, a cosmic dance. King Kertanagara's role in unifying Majapahit Empire, founded on Dharma-Dhamma is recorded in history. Some refer to Candi Sukuh as a temple venerating Tantrik Saivism as 'Bhima cult'. Bhre Daha belonged to the tradition of royal purohita Bhagawan Ganggasudhi, associated with the royal house of Girindrawardhana. Gangga sudhi is rebus for kanga sudhi ‘purification by brazier, kanga’.

The dance step of the male torso of Harappa and the dance step of the elephant-headed Ganesa on Candi Sukuh frieze are explained in a remarkable hieroglyph on a Bhirrana potsherd and a Mohenjodaro tablet:

Dance-step in a cire perdue bronze statue, Mohenjodaro replicated on a Bhirrana potsherd. The red potsherd with the engraving resembling the Dancing Girl bronze figurine of Mohenjodaro, found at Bhirrana.

m0493Bt Pict-93: Three dancing figures in a row. Text 2843 Glyph: Three dancers. Kolmo ‘three’; meD ‘to dance’ Rebus: kolami ‘furnace, smithy’; meD ‘iron’

1000-yr-old Dholkal idol awaits survey report

TNN | Feb 1, 2013, 11.10 PM IST

RAIPUR: Chhattisgarh archaeology and culture department claims to have done a survey, on a unique discovery of 1000-year-old Ganesha idol, located on the zenith of Dholkal mountain in the interiors of Maoist hotbed south Bastar, in January this year.

This age old six-foot idol of the 10th century was discovered by a local journalist in September 2012, following which the archaeology department had formed a committee, ensuring that a researched survey was conducted on the place.

Talking to TOI, in-charge curator (Jagdalpur) J R Bhagat, said: "The survey was done on January 17, but the report is not yet ready, it would be submitted to the department soon. He added that the idol is located at a height of 13,000 feet, amid dense forest. It is presumed that the idol was made long ago during the time of Nagvanshi dynasty in the 9th or 10th century. We have also found traces of early man and few of their stone weapons, which means the place hasn't had frequent visitors and remained isolated all these years, Bhagat said.

According to Rajeev Ranjan Prasad, a local author and researcher, the idol is located on the zenith of a huge dhol shaped mountain, which seems like a place, impossible to reach. This place was discovered for the first time by an English geologist Crookshank in 1934 at the time when Bailadila mining was under survey.

After studying Crookshank's geological report of south Bastar, "I matched the historical evidences of the place and compiled the photographs. Though this idol is located high above, it remained unnoticed due to dense forest and tough routes.

Moreover, the Maoists dominance in the region, hushes away the population, Ranjan told TOI. He said that as the place is on the top of a mountain, about 13km high, it is a tough terrain to reach or to hang around for long. He said that evidences of ancient colonies existing around the mountain have also come to light.

Researching for years now, Ranjan said that Bastar has many such places that need attention and conservation but due to lack of enthusiasm, they remain ignored. "There were many important idols, temples, which have been excavated off their existence or destroyed forever. The ancient place initially doomed with backwardness and now with Maoists, calls for attention and grooming from the government," he said.

Bastar has been considered a place of scenic beauty with thousands of archaeological and historical secrets hidden in its torso. "Few locals, who chance upon new findings, bring it to the notice of officials but many put a curtain, assuming that revealing it would disturb the ambience of their place with archaeologists, media and foreigners digging all over," an archaeologist remarked.

http://timesofindia.indiatimes.com/city/raipur/1000-yr-old-Dholkal-idol-awaits-survey-report/articleshowprint/18296857.cms

Ganesha. Pine cone on left hand. Provinience unknown.

Ganesha. Patan. Nepal.

Ganesha. Hampi. Karnataka.

Ganesha. Umananda. Guwahati. Assam.

10th century Ganesha idol discovered on Dholkal mountain
South Bastar, Dantewada, Chhatisgarh, India

RAIPUR: Chhattisgarh archaeology and culture department claims to have done a survey, on a unique discovery of 1000-year-old Ganesha idol, located on the zenith of Dholkal mountain in the interiors of Maoist hotbed south Bastar, in January this year.

This age old six-foot idol of the 10th century was discovered by a local journalist in September 2012, following which the archaeology department had formed a committee, ensuring that a researched survey was conducted on the place. (via indiatimes.com)

http://hinducosmos.tumblr.com/post/96687841632/10th-century-ganesha-idol-discovered-on-dholkal

Ganesha idols from Barsur, Chattisgarh.

Ganesha. Khajuraho temple.

Ganesha. Kelaniya temple. Sri Lanka

Ganesha. Teakwood. Chiang mai. North Thailand.

Chachoengsao, Thailand. World's tallest bronze Ganesh statue. (39 m)

Ganesha and the Sacred Trees in Wailua, Hawaii.

Sandstone Ganesha. Cambodia, 7th century. Cleveland Museum of Art.

Ganesha, Champa art from Vietnam

Skanda, Ganesha. Sanstone Danang, Cham Museum. Vietnam

Ganesha. Danang, Cham Museum, Vietnam

Arca Ganesha at rumah makan babi guling bu oka,ubud

Ganesha. Volcanic Stone. Central Java. Indonesia. ca. 9th century.

Ganesha, Bali, Indonesia.

Ganesha. Bali. Indonesia

Ganesha, Mohan Temple, Landa Bazaar, Rawalpindi.

Ganesha. Thailand.

Inscription on Vinayaka, Cambodia

Among the old inscriptions of the vinAyaka temples in the far-East are the following

1) The Angkor Borei inscription of 611 AD, which mentions the construction of a shrine to mahAgaNapati.

2) 660 AD the jayavarman II inscription describing a temple built to shrIgaNapati.

3) 817 AD inscription at Po Nagar in Vietnam of harivarman, the Champa King mentioning the temple built to shrI gaNapati (vinAyaka).

4) 890 AD inscription of yashovarman I mentioning the building of two tantric Ashramas for the worship of vinAyaka known as chandanAdri gaNesha (sandal mountain gaNesha).

The most mysterious inscription is from Prasat Prei Kuk shrine in Cambodia to vinAyaka built by king ishAnavarman I.

ya kaschid dAnavendra paraviShaya-haro nirjito nyena shaktyA

The chief of the dAnavas capturing others territory was conquered by the might of another

baddho vai sR^inkalAbhis chiram iha patito yaM stuva~N chaila-ruddhaH

bound with chains after having fallen here for a long time shut up in the mountain praises him

tan dR^iShTvA kinnarAbhish shatagaNasahitas svapnashoShe himAdrer

Having seen that, with a 100 gaNas and kinnaras, having woken up, from the Himalayan peak,

AyAto mokShanArthA~N jayati gaNapatis tvad-dhitAyeva so yaM

comes this gaNapati who for your welfare conquers for the purpose of liberating.

https://manasataramgini.wordpress.com/2005/09/07/the-odd-cambodian-inscription-of-vinayaka/

kandə 'pine cone' Rebus, signified metalwork: *khaṇḍa*. A portion of the front hall, in a temple; *kaṇḍ* 'fire-altar' (Santali) *kāṇḍa* 'tools, pots and pans and metal-ware' (Marathi)

लोखंड (p. 723) [lōkhaṇḍa] *n* (लोह S) Iron लोखंडकाम (p. 723) [lōkhaṇḍakāma] *n* Iron work; that portion (of a building, machine &c.) which consists of iron. 2 The business of an ironsmith.

लोखंडी (p. 723) [lōkhaṇḍī] *a* (लोखंड) Composed of iron; relating to iron लोहोलोखंड (p. 723) [lōhōlōkhaṇḍa] *n* (लोह & लोखंड) Iron tools, vessels, or articles in general.

http://bharatkalyan97.blogspot.in/2014/10/pine-cone-is-meluhha-metalwork.html

Temple de Serapis

This temple was built for the Egyptian merchants. It was located on the Commercial Agora near the western gate. There is also another entrance into the temple from the south-west corner of the Agora through stairs.

There are certain indications that suggest the temple was never finished fully. It is estimated that the construction of the temple was started in the 2nd century CE.

There is a statue found inside the temple made by using the Egyptian granite. Also some inscriptions found inside the temple indicate that the temple was constructed for those who believe in Serapis. In Ephesus Museum there is a monument on which the main Goddess of Ephesians, Artemis, and the principal god of Egypt, Serapis, take place together with garland as a symbol of peace.

It is well documented fact that Ephesus had a very strong commercial link with the influential port city of Egypt, Alexandria. During these ancient times Egypt was the biggest producer of wheat. They exchanged wheat with other commercial items from Ephesus and other Ionian cities.

It was converted to a church during the following Christian period. There are remains of a baptisterium in the eastern corner of the temple.

http://www.ephesus.us/ephesus/temple_of_serapis.htm

Temple of Isis, Pompeii. "the original building built under Augustan was damaged in an earlier earthquake of 62 CE...The cult of Isis is thought to arrived in Pompeii around 100 BCE."

http://www.crystalinks.com/isis.html

A detailed archaeological excursus on the roots of the pine-cone and peacock bronzes in the Vatican is warranted to further substantiate the hypothesis of Meluhha metalwork.

The original pine cone. Pigna (Fir cone) is the name of the quarter of Rome where this bronze sculpture was found; it was part of a fountain and it spouted water from holes on its top. It was probably placed in front of a Temple to Isis in Iseo Campense; the gilded peacocks decorated one of the entrances to Hadrian's Mausoleum. The Egyptian lions were added by Pope Gregory XVI; they came from Mostra dell'Acqua Felice and were replaced by copies. http://www.romeartlover.it/Vasi181.html

Pigna Vatican Museum Courtyard gilt bronze. Rome.
Originally a Roman fountain dating from 1st or 2nd century CE

The bronze pine cone (`Pigna`) at the Cortile della Pigna square. Peacocks from Hadrians Mausoleum (Castel Sant'Angelo) http://pictify.com/130116/pigna-vatican-museum-courtyard Pine cone at the Vatican, flanked by two peacocks.

It was at Campus Martius prior to it being moved to the Court of the Pigna.

*glyph-type symbols below the animal (Courtyard of the Pinecone)*

One version of the pine-cone origins: "Publius Cincius Slavius, whose name appears on the base of the sculpture, built the Pine Cone statue that now resides in the Court of the Pine Cone (Cortile della Pigna) in the Vatican, in the 1st century AD. The piece was originally a fountain that resided in the Temple of Isis in Campo Martius next to the Pantheon. The site of the Temple of Isis is now occupied by the Biblioteca Casanatense but the area is still to this day called Pigna. The fountain is described as having water gushing from the holes in the scales of the cone similar to the Meta Sudans (the sweating rock that was also topped by a pine cone according to some) that still stands outside the Coliseum. The Pine Cone was then moved to the hall of St Peter's Basilica in the 8th century in the time of Popes John VI, John VII or Zachary (Pope Zachary seems the most likely as he did more than the other two to "Christianize" Rome by building churches over the old Roman temples). One of them moved the Pine Cone from the Temple of Isis to St Peter's Basilica (the original built by Constantine the Great) where it was covered by a baldachin (it is recreated in this state in the game Assassin's Creed: Brotherhood where it houses a Piece of Eden). In 1608, when St Peters was being enlarged to its present form the Pine Cone was moved to its current location by Pope Paul V...The bronze peacocks, however, were not part of the original sculpture but are thought to be originally taken from Hadrian's mausoleum (now Rome's fortress, the Castel St. Angelo)." http://thedailybeagle.net/2013/09/08/the-pigna-and-the-apollo-belvedere-two-treasures-of-the-vatican/

Another version of the pine cone origins:

[quote]The Huge statue known as the Pigna (pine) or the Fontana Della Pigna depicts a giant Pine Cone. It is located in St. Peter's, in an area called the court of the Pigna.The Court of the Pigna is the northern part of the grand renaissance Belvedere Courtyard that stretches between the Papal Palaces to the "palazzetto" which belonged to Innocent VII's . The courtyard was segmented into three parts after the construction of Sixtus V's Library and the Braccio Nuovo of Pius VII. The present courtyard derived its name form the beautiful pine cone statue set into the "nicchone", borders on the south side with the Braccio Nuovo, and on the east it borders with the Chiaromonti Gallery. To its north you can find Innocent VIII's Palazzetto and on the west the galleries of the Apostolic Library are located.

The pine cone was cast out of bronze in the 1st or 2nd century by the sculptor Publius Cincius Slavius. He was identified as its creator because his name was written on the base of the huge pine. The Statue's height is almost 4 meters and on both sides of the pine cone there are bronze peacocks which are copies of the ones in Hadrian's tomb.

Before it was moved to its current location, known as the Court of the Pigna, the statue of the Pine was situated in the Campus Martius. This area is still known today as "Pigna" after this statue. At its previous location it was used as a fountain with the water pouring from holes pierced in the scales of the cone. At the 8th century it was transferred to the entrance hall of the medieval basilica of St. Peter. It was placed decoratively in the middle of the fountain covered by ornate baldachin. We know this because the statue was identified in Renaissance drawings of the hall. Eventually, during the construction of the current basilica, in 1608, the giant pine cone fountain was moved and situated in its current location.

This statue is a beautiful and ancient one and it's definitely worth stopping by and admiring it as it has been part of Rome's landscape for almost 2000 years! [unquote]

http://vatican.com/photos/gallery/court_of_the_pigna-p45

Technical information
Blessing genius Neo-Assyrian period, circa 721-705 BCE (reign of Sargon II)
Third gate of the palace of Sargon II, Khorsabad (ancient Dur-Sharrukin), Iraq

Bas-relief of gypseous alabaster
H. 4.09 m; L. 2.36 m; D. 0.75 m
Victor Place excavations, 1852-54

AO 19863
Near Eastern Antiquities [see: Musée du Louvre]

Blessing genius

Protective genii are supernatural beings who watch over humans or buildings and ward off evil spirits. This winged genius, along with one directly opposite, guarded the gates of the city of Khorsabad. It blessed all those who passed by it with water sprinkled from a pine cone.

Description

A protective and blessing genius

The site of Khorsabad (called Dur-Sharrukin in antiquity), which was excavated between 1843 and 1854 by Paul-Emile Botta and Victor Place, yielded orthostats, carved slabs of stone that protected and adorned the bases of brick walls. This monumental winged genius, represented frontally, was placed in the inner passage of one of the city gates. Another genius was located directly opposite. Both stood immediately behind the pair of winged bulls with human heads that guarded the gate. Like other genii placed at certain entrances to the palace, this one has a protective role. However it also performed a blessing function: from the pine cone, which could be shaken, liquid drawn from a little bucket was sprinkled over the passageway and those who passed along it.

A monumental sculpture

This colossal figure carved in high relief depicts a winged, bearded genius, shown frontally as far as the waist and in profile below. He holds a pine cone in his right hand and a small metal vessel (or situla) in his left hand. The face, framed by a curly beard, is surmounted by a tiara adorned with two pairs of horns. Over the figure's short tunic is a fringed cape, which covers the right shoulder and left leg. Two pairs of wings emerge from the back and spread symmetrically on either side of the body. His arms and forearms are adorned with rings and bracelets. He wears sandals, which cover his heels. On the base of this sculpture is a game of tick-tack-toe, scratched into it in ancient times, probably by sentries passing the time while on duty at the gate.

Genii: between the human and the divine?

Genii, depicted as bulls with human heads, men with birds' heads, and winged men, figure prominently in Assyrian mythology. They are creatures endowed with powers superior to those of human beings, yet they are not great deities, although they are sometimes represented with some of their attributes, for example, the horned tiara here. These supernatural beings had the power to ward off evil spirits. The genius seen here had an essentially protective role: it defended the gates and walls of the city. However, it was also a blessing genius, which held holy water and sprinkled it on visitors with a pine cone. Genii are often depicted in Assyrian art, especially in ceremonial scenes where they are shown pollinating the sacred palm tree. [see: Mesopotamia | Louvre Museum]
http://www.geocities.ws/leinad.trotta/prophecies.html

Somnathpur, Halebid. Lakshmi. Divinity of wealth holding maize cob or pine-cone.

Hieroglyphs: *kandə* 'pine', 'ear of maize'. Rebus: *kaṇḍa* 'tools, pots and pans of metal'. Rebus: kāḍ 'stone'. Ga. (Oll.) kanḍ, (S.) kanḍu (pl. kanḍkil) stone (DEDR 1298).

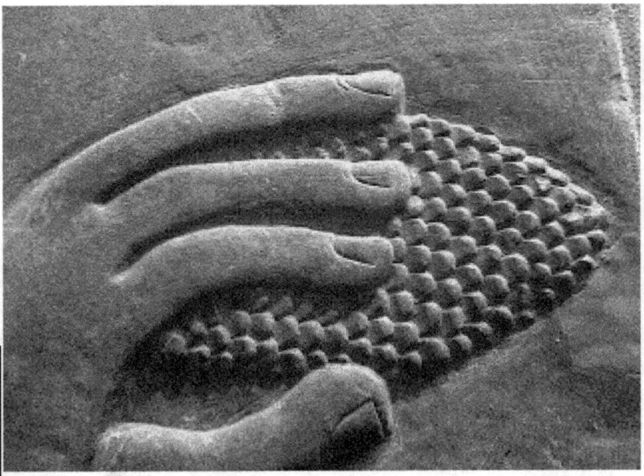

[quote] Detail of pine cone. Standard Inscription.Palace of Ashurnasirpal, priest of Ashur, favorite of Enlil and Ninurta, beloved of Anu and Dagan, the weapon of the great gods, the mighty king, king of the world, king of Assyria; son of Tukulti-Ninurta, the great king, the mighty king, king of Assyria, the son of Adad-nirari, the great king, the mighty king of Assyria; the valiant man, who acts with the support of Ashur, his lord, and has no equal among the princes of the four quarters of the world; the wonderful shepherd who is not afraid of battle; the great flood which none can oppose; the king who makes those who are not subject to him submissive; who has subjugated all mankind; the mighty warrior who treads on the neck of his enemies, tramples down all foes, and shatters the forces of the proud; the king who acts with the support of the great gods, and whose hand has conquered all lands, who has subjugated all the mountains and received their tribute, taking hostages and establishing his power over all countries. [unquote]

Halebid."Maize breeders in India, China, United States, and Great Britain, who have seen extensive collections of the illustrations, concur...only sculptors with abundant ears of maize as models could have created these illustrations of maize"(Click to enlarge). Photo by Carl L. Johannessen.

'Maize' and 'pine-cone' are two hieroglyphs depicted, respectively, on Indian sculptures at Somnathpur (Lakshmi, divinity of wealth) and on sculptures and reliefs of Ashur (Nimrud). Rebus readings are evidence of presence of Meluhha speakers in the Ancient Near East who participated in the bronze-age inventions of tin-bronzes and created the writing systems of deploying hieroglyphs together with cuneiform and Indus texts.

Hieroglyphs: *kandə* 'pine', 'ear of maize'. Rebus: *kaṇḍa* 'tools, pots and pans of metal'. Rebus: kāḍ 'stone'. Ga. (Oll.) kanḍ, (S.) kanḍu (pl. kanḍkil) stone (DEDR 1298).

Hieroglyph: Ash. pić -- kandə ' pine ', Kt. pṳ̄ći, piċi, Wg. puć, püć (pṳ̄ć -- kəŕ ' pine -- cone '), Pr. wyoć, Shum. lyēwič (lyē -- ?).(CDIAL 8407). Cf. Gk. peu/kh f. ' pine ', Lith. pušìs, OPruss. peuse NTS xiii 229. The suffix –kande in the lexeme: Ash. pić-- kandə ' pine ' may be cognate with the bulbous glyphic related to a mangrove root: Koḍ. kaṇḍe root-stock from which small roots grow; ila·ti kaṇḍe sweet potato (ila·ti England). Tu. kaṇḍe, gaḍḍè a bulbous root; Ta. kaṇṭal mangrove, Rhizophora mucronata; dichotomous mangrove, Kandelia rheedii. Ma. kaṇṭa bulbous root as of lotus, plantain; point where branches and bunches grow out of the stem of a palm; kaṇṭal what is bulb-like, half-ripe jackfruit and other green fruits; R. candel. (DEDR 1171). Rebus: *kaṇḍa* 'tools, pots and pans of metal'.
Hieroglyph: కండె [kaṇḍe] *kaṇḍe*. [Telugu] n. A head or ear of millet or maize. జొన్నకండె.

Allograph: *Kur.* kaṇḍō a stool. *Malt.* kanḍo stool, seat. (DEDR 1179). Rebus:*Tu.* kandůka, kandaka ditch, trench. *Te.* kandakamu id. *Koṇḍa* kanda trench made as a fireplace during weddings. *Pe.* kanda fire trench. *Kui* kanda small trench for fireplace. *Malt.* kandri a pit. (DEDR 1214).

[quote] Detail of pine cone. Standard Inscription.Palace of Ashurnasirpal, priest of Ashur, favorite of Enlil and Ninurta, beloved of Anu and Dagan, the weapon of the great gods, the mighty king, king of the world, king of Assyria; son of Tukulti-Ninurta, the great king, the mighty king, king of Assyria, the son of Adad-nirari, the great king, the mighty king of Assyria; the valiant man, who acts with the support of Ashur, his lord, and has no equal among the princes of the four quarters of the world; the wonderful shepherd who is not afraid of battle; the great flood which none can oppose; the king who makes those who are not subject to him submissive; who has subjugated all mankind; the mighty warrior who treads on the neck of his enemies, tramples down all foes, and shatters the forces of the proud; the king who acts with the support of the great gods, and whose hand has conquered all lands, who has subjugated all the mountains and received their tribute, taking hostages and establishing his power over all countries.

When Ashur, the lord who called me by my name and has made my kingdom great, entrusted his merciless weapon to my lordly arms, I overthrew the widespread troops of the land of Lullume in battle. With the assistance of Shamash and Adad, the gods who help me, I thundered like Adad the destroyer over the troops of the Nairi lands, Habhi, Shubaru, and Nirib. I am the king who had brought into submission at his feet the lands from beyond the Tigris to Mount Lebanon and the Great Sea [the Mediterranean], the whole of the land of Laqe, the land of Suhi as far as Rapiqu, and whose hand has conquered from the source of the river Subnat to the land of Urartu.

The area from the mountain passes of Kirruri to the land of Gilzanu, from beyond the Lower Zab to the city of Til-Bari which is north of the land of Zaban, from the city of Til-sha-abtani to Til-sha-Zabdani, Hirimu and Harutu, fortresses of the land of Karduniash [Babylonia], I have restored to the borders of my land. From the mountain passes of Babite to the land of Hashmar I have counted the inhabitants as peoples of my land. Over the lands which I have subjugated I have appointed my governors, and they do obeisance.

I am Ashurnasirpal, the celebrated prince, who reveres the great gods, the fierce dragon, conqueror of the cities and mountains to their furthest extent, king of rulers who has tamed the stiff-necked peoples, who is crowned with splendor, who is not afraid of battle, the merciless champion who shakes resistance, the glorious king, the shepherd, the protection of the whole world, the king, the word of whose mouth destroys mountains and seas, who by his lordly attack has forced fierce and merciless kings from the rising to the setting sun to acknowledge one rule.

The former city of Kalhu [Nimrud], which Shalmaneser king of Assyria, a prince who preceded me, had built, that city had fallen into ruins and lay deserted. That city I built anew, I took the peoples whom my hand had conquered from the lands which I subjugated, from the land of Suhi, from the land of Laqe, from the city of Sirqu on the other side of the Euphrates, from the furthest extent of the land of Zamua, from Bit-Adini and the land of Hatte, and from Lubarna, king of the land of Patina, and made them settle there.

I removed the ancient mound and dug down to the water level. I sank the foundations 120 brick courses deep. A palace with halls of cedar, cypress, juniper, box-wood, meskannu-wood, terebinth and tamarisk, I founded as my royal residence for my lordly pleasure for ever.

Creatures of the mountains and seas I fashioned in white limestone and alabaster, and set them up at its gates. I adorned it, and made it glorious, and set ornamental knobs of bronze all around it. I fixed doors of cedar, cypress, juniper and meskannu-wood in its gates. I took in great quantities, and placed there, silver, gold, tin, bronze and iron, booty taken by my hands from the lands which I had conquered. [unquote]

http://www.flickr.com/photos/brankoab/7673434338/

New York city Art museum. Ashurnasirpal. Kalhu Ear-ring and pendant with a pine cone glyph

Pine cone glyphs adorn the side stools and is atop the 'altars' or 'standards'. [quote]Description: The 'Garden Party' relief from the North Palace of Ashurbanipal at Nineveh. This carved stone picture hides a gory secret. King Ashurbanipal and his Queen are enjoying a party in their garden. Can you see the Queen sitting down facing her husband? A harpist on the left plays music while they eat and drink. But in the tree beside him is the severed head of King Teumann, a local ruler who had tried to fight against Ashurbanipal. The picture was on the wall in the royal palace, to warn any visitors not to try the same thing. It should also be noted that depictions of women are rare in Assyrian art. (Source: British Museum website) Date: c.645 BCE [unquote]

Assyrian Period, reign of King Ashurnasirpal 11 (883 -- 859 BCE) Alabastrous Limestone Height 110.5 cm. Width 183 cm. Depth 6.4 -- 9.6 cm. Miho Museum http://www.shumei.org/art/miho/miho.html

Marduk, winged, holding the pine-cone. Bracelet has safflower hieroglyph. Annunaki, Sumerian.

Pine cones helod by eagle-divinities flanking tree of life. The divinities also hold wallets.

Masonic cadueceus with pine cone.

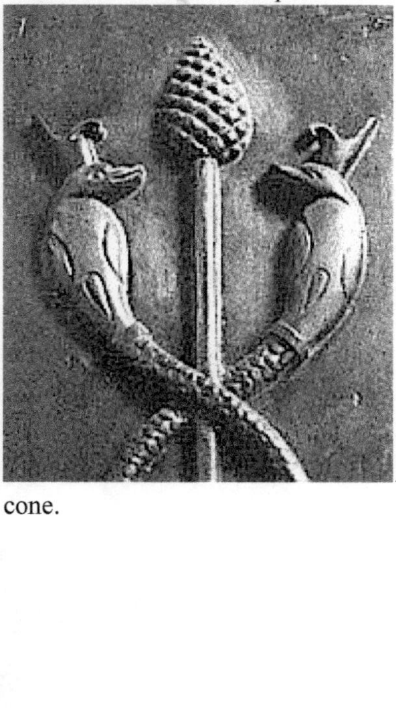
A pair of eagle-headed Annunak flanking a staff capped with a pine-cone.

Assyrian) alabaster Height: 236.2 cm (93 in). Width: 135.9 cm (53.5 in). Depth: 15.2 cm (6 in). This relief decorated the interior wall of the northwest palace of King Ashurnasirpal II at Nimrud. On his right hand, he holds a pine cone. Examples of reliefs of king ashur-nasir-pal II

The Egyptian Staff of Osiris, dating back to approximately 1224 BC, depicts two intertwining serpents rising up to meet at a pinecone. (Photo: Egyptian Museum, Turin, Italy).

Myths in Vatican to invent explanations for the pine-cone and peacocks and the context of Temples for Isis

Jenny Uglow has rendered a remarkable historical account. (Uglow, Jenny, 2012, The Pinecone, Faber & Faber). The book narrates the story of the builder Sarah Losh of the magical church in Wreay, near Carlisle, Victorian England. She was heiress to an industrial fortune. Everywhere in this church are pinecones, her signature in stone, making the church a rendering of the power of myth 'and the great natural cycles of life and death and rebirth'. The book provides Sarah's travel to Rome: "Death, as well as beauty, marched the streets. And the processions were matched by the panoply of symbols, on ancient columns and new buildings, in temples and market squares. Among these were plenty of pinecones: the Pope carried a carved cone on his staff; a pinecone fountain stood outside the old church of St Mrco, and the largest cone in the world, flanked by two peacocks, was found at the Vatican. This was the only original Roman fountain remaining in Rome, the Fontana della Pigna, dating from the first century AD, which had once stood next to the Temple of Isis in the Forum, spouting water from the top."

Isis was worshipped in the entire Greco-Roman world.

The Temple of Isis in Pompeii. The cult of Isis is said to have arrived in Pompeii ca. 100 BCE. (Nappo, Salvatore. "*Pompey: Guide to the Lost City*", White Star, 2000, p.89) "Its role as a Hellenized Egyptian temple in a Roman colony was fully confirmed with an inscription detaled by Francisco la Vega on July 20, 1765." This was the second structure. Original structure under Augustan was damaged in an earthquake of 62 CE.

http://en.wikipedia.org/wiki/Temple_of_Isis_(Pompeii)

Peacocks. Braccio Nuovo Museum, Vatican.

Pigna is the name of rione IX of Rome. "Pigna ("pine-cone") refers to a famous bronze sculpture of Roman origin, in the shape of a huge pine-cone. It likely acted as a fountain in the Baths of Agrippa, the first establishment of this kind opened in Rome (late 1st century BC), at the back of the Pantheon's site."

http://roma.andreapollett.com/S5/rione09.htm

Logo of the Rione.

"Pigna. There used to be a tradition, wholly unfounded, but deeply rooted in the Roman mind, to the effect that the great bronze pine-cone, eleven feet high, which stands in one of the courts of the Vatican, giving it the name c Garden of the Pine-cone,' was originally a sort of stopper which closed the round aperture in the roof of the Pantheon. The Pantheon stands at one cornerof the Region of Pigna, and a connection between the Region, the Pantheon, and the Pine-cone seems vaguely possible, though altogether unsatisfactory. The truth about the Pine-cone is perfectly well known; it was part of a fountain in Agrippa's artificial lake in the Campus Martius, of which Pigna was a part, and it was set up in the cloistered garden of Saint Peter's by Pope Symmachus about fourteen hundred years ago. The lake may have been near the Pantheon." (Crawford, Francis Marion, *Ave Roma Immortals*, 1898, London, Macmillan & Co. Ltd., p.345)

http://www.cristoraul.com/ENGLISH/BIBLIOGRAPHICA/HTML-Library/ROMANIKA/Ave-Roma-Immortalis.htm

"Composed of a large bronze pine cone almost four meters high which once spouted water from the top, the Pigna originally stood near the Pantheon next to the Temple of Isis. It was moved to the courtyard of the old St. Peter's Basilica during the Middle Ages and then moved again, in 1608, to its present location." -- Official history on the Vatican website.

The bronze peacocks on either side of the fountain are copies of those decorating the tomb of the Emperor Hadrian, now the Castel Sant' Angelo. http://en.wikipedia.org/wiki/Fontana_della_Pigna. The peacocks decorated the Mausoleum or the tomb of Hadrian erected between 134 and 139 CE. Copies of "Bronze peacocks" maybe from the Mausoleum of Hadrian. The originals are in the New Wing of the Chiaramonti Museum (Braccacio Museum)

Detail of the water holes on the bronze pine-cone.

Water holes on the pine-cone can be seen.

http://projectavalon.net/forum4/showthread.php?17959-Pining-for-the-truth

Thanks to Roger-Pears who found online on February 16th, 2015, the following copy of a drawing of the fountain, itself taken from Huelsen. (A. van den Hoek & John H. Herrmann Jr, "Paulinus of Nola, courtyards and canthari: a second look", In: A. van den Hoek &c, *Pottery, Pavements, and Paradise: Iconographic and Textual Studies on Late Antiquity*, Brill (2013), p.45, fig. 13; C. Huelsen, "Der Cantharus von Alt-St. -Peter und die antiken Pignen-Brunnen,", *Romische Mitteilungen* 19 (1904), 88-102. Plate 5a. Online at Archive.org here.)

Water installation with bronze pine-cone in the atrium of Old St Peter's Basilica, Rome. Drawing by Cronaca (1457-1505). Uffizi, Florence, 1572.

Further drawings in Heulsen article:

Andrea della Vaccaria, “Ornamenti di fabriche antichi e moderni dell’alma citta di Roma”, 1600, quarto.

Another image from a manuscript, Ms. Brussels 17872, fol. 56v, by Philipp de Winghe, and made around 1591-2.

http://www.roger-pearse.com/weblog/2015/02/16/the-fountain-of-the-pine-cone-outside-old-st-peters-in-rome/

Drawing of St.Peter's fountain by

Francisco de Hollanda (early 1500s)

St. Peter's fountain, in a pen drawing by anonymous (c. 1525) "Medieval chronicles such as the famous Mirabilia Urbis Romae (12th century) mentioned St. Peter's fountain among the city's noticeable features. The water gushed from hundreds of tiny holes on its surface...Scarce Renaissance drawings feature the fountain standing in the center of a square basin, covered by a canopy that rested over eight columns (originally they were four) and richly decorated with marbles of various types; in particular on its top parts were bronze peacocks; maybe from the mausoleum of Hadrian, which in the description provided by the chronicle are referred to as 'griffons' covered with a gold leaf...When St. Peter's was completely rebuilt (1506-1614), the fountain and the canopy were dismantled, and most of the precious materials were reused for other purposes. The only parts spared were the peacocks and the pine-cone, which around 1565 Pirro Ligorio set in the large niche of the Courtyard of Belvedere,, later renamed of the Pine-cone. The peacocks now on display in the courtyard are copies; the original ones, which still shine as gold (as the old chronicle says), are kept indoors, in the Braccio Nuovo (new wing) of the Chiaramonti Museum (Vatican Museums)." http://roma.andreapollett.com/S3/roma-ft1b.htm

❝ *These pine-cones were a customary feature of the classic fountain, as the scales of the cone present natural and graceful outlets for the falling water. Symmachus's fountain was one of the beauties of Rome in the days when the great Gothic King Theodoric ruled and loved the city. Three hundred years later it captivated the fancy of Charlemagne, crowned Emperor in St. Peter's on Christmas Day, 800; and the fountain afterward erected before his great cathedral at Aix [now Aachen Cathedral] is ornamented with a huge pine-cone like the one which he and his Franks had seen in the exquisite fountain of St. Peter's.*

http://www.garden-fountains.us/fount...rs-fountain/5/

One of the original bronze peacocks.

One of the original peacocks now in Braccacio Museum. Two bronze peacocks are from Hadrian's Mausoleum (tomb).

Bronze peacocks lent by Vatican to be shown in British Museum. http://www.standard.co.uk/arts/walltowall-hadrian-7408277.html

The present Pigna in the Vatican seems to be a left-over from the original Basilica of St. Peter. The left-over may be two bronze artifacts: 1. bronze pine-cone in original; 2. replicas of two bronze peacocks originals of which ar kept in Braccacio Nuovo Museum. The question is: how did the two bronze artifacts, the pine-cone and the pair of peacocks get lodged in St. Peter's Basilica. Some answers and some conjectures are discussed.

[quote]"Bronze Pine Cone" signed Publius Cincius Salvio from the area of the Baths of Agrippa, maybe fountain in the Temple of Isis (Note: Possible location discussed in Annex A).

It was eventually placed in the atrium of the old Basilica of St. Peter.

It gave the name to the central neighborhood called Rione Pigna, where the Temple of Isis was originally located. [unquote]

http://romapedia.blogspot.in/2014/10/vatican-museums-courtyard-of-pine-cone.html

One surmise is that the pinecone acted as a fountain in the Baths of Agrippa dated to 1st century BCE. http://roma.andreapollett.com/S5/rione09.htm

The surmise is based on the following evidence:

Pine-cone and sivalingas as a fountain of water found in a large archaeological complex dating back to the 3rd century BCE in largo di Torre Argentina of Palazzetto Venezia.

See: http://en.wikipedia.org/wiki/Largo_di_Torre_Argentina

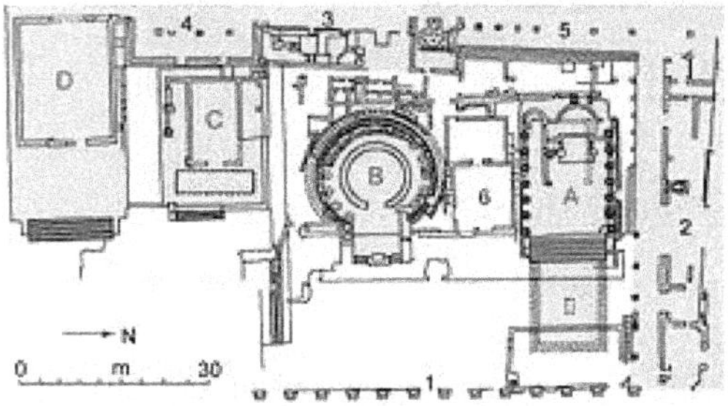

Map of the archaeological complex: Largo di Torre Argentina, Rome, Italy

This complex had 4 temples dated to A) 3rd cent BCE (Temple of Juturna), B) 101 BCE (Fortuna Huiusce Diei), C) 4th or 3rd cent. (Feronia), D) 2nd cent. BCE (Lares Permarini) devoted to various divinities revered by Gaius Lutalius Catulus, Quintus Lutalius Catulus . Further excavations may perhaps explain the reason for the fountain with the pine-cone surrounded by 4 sivalingas. In Meluhha archaeometallurgical tradition, the sivalingas were stambhas or pillars of light/fire used as ekamukha linga in smelter structures and metalwork areas (as shown in Bhuteshwar relief).

Temple: खंडेराव [khaṇḍērāva] *m* (खंड Sword, and राव) An incarnation of Shiva. Popularly खंडेराव is but dimly distinguished from भैरव. खंडोबा [khaṇḍōbā] *m* A familiar appellation of the god खंडेराव. खंडोबाचा कुत्रा [khaṇḍōbācā kutrā] *m* (Dog of खंडोबा. From his being devoted to the temple.) A term for the वाघ्या or male devotee of खंडोबा.

Hieroglyph: खंडोबाची काठी [khaṇḍōbācī kāṭhī] *f* The pole of खंडोबा. It belongs to the temples of this god, is taken and presented, in pilgrimages, at the visited shrines, is carried about in processions &c. It is covered with cloth (red and blue), and has a plume (generally from the peacock's tail) waving from its top.

The cultural link of metalwork with Rudra-Siva iconically denoted by 1) orthographic variants of *linga,* 2) ekamukhalinga evidences of Ancient Far East and 3) the presence of *linga* in the context of a metal smelter in a Bhuteshwar artifact of 2nd cent. BCE is thus an area for further detailed investigation in archaeometallurgy and historical linguistics of Indian *Sprachbund.*

http://tinyurl.com/qz56u27

Bera Utsav is a regional festival celebrated in the Murshidabad district of the state of West Bengal. The annual event is organized at the historical and picturesque location of Lalbagh, which at one time was the home of the Nawabs and is located on the banks of River Bhagirathi. People throng the district of Murshidabad to witness this magnificent event. The event is held on the last Thursday of the Bhadra month of the traditional Bengali calendar.

utsavá m. ' enterprise ' RV., ' festival ' MBh. [√sū] Pa. *ussava* -- m. ' festival ', Pk. *ucchava* -- , °*chaa* -- , *ussava* -- , *ūsa*°, *ōsa*° m., K. *wŏċhav*, °*ċhuwu* m.; S. *uchaü*, *och*°, *ocho* m. ' feast given to brahmans '; Or. *ucha* ' festival ', *osā* ' festival, vow '. dīpōtsava -- , mahōtsava -- .(CDIAL 1876) 9979 mahōtsava m. ' great festival ' MBh. [mahā -- , utsavá --]Pk. *mahocchava* -- , °*hōsava* -- , °*hussava* -- , °*hūsava* -- m.; P. *mahocchā* m. ' celebration, appointment of a new mahout '; H. *mahochā* m. ' great festival ', OG.*mochava* m.(CDIAL 9979)dīpōtsava m. ' festival of lights ' BhavP. [dīpa -- , utsavá --]

Pk. *dīvūsava* -- m. ' new moon of Kārtik '; N. *deusi* ' festival beginning on the 5th day of Diwāli '.(CDIAL 6359)

In the Vaikhanasa temple, the immovable (Dhruva-bimba or dhruva-bera) main idol that is installed in the sanctum and to which main worship is offered (archa-murti) represents the primary aspect of the deity known as Vishnu (Vishnu-tattva). The other images in the temple which are worshipped each day during the ritual sequences are but the variations of the original icon (adi-murti). These other forms are emanations of the main idol, in successive stages. And, within the temple complex, each form is accorded a specific location; successively away from the Dhruva bera.

Just as the Vishnu of Rig-Veda takes three strides (trini pada vi-chakrama Vishnuh), the main idol (Dhruva – bera) installed in the temple too takes three forms which are represented by Kautuka-bera, Snapana-bera and Utsava-bera.

The Kautuka –bera (usually made of gems, stone, copper, silver, gold or wood and about 1/3 to 5/9 the size of the Dhruva-bera)receives all the daily worship(nitya-archana); the Snapana-bera (usually made of metal and smaller than Kautuka) receives ceremonial bath (abhisheka) and the occasional ritual- worship sequences(naimitta-archana); and, the Utsava-bera (always made of metal) is for festive occasions and for taking out in processions . To this, another icon is added .This is Bali – bera (always made of shiny metal) taken out , daily , around the central shrine when food offerings are made to Indra and other devas, as well as to Jaya and Vijaya the doorkeepers of the Lord ; and to all the elements.

And, on occasions when a movable icon is used for daily worship, special rituals, and processions and for food-offering, it is known as Bhoga-bera.

These five forms together make Pancha bera or Pancha murti.

And again it is said, Purusha is symbolized by Kautuka bera; Satya by Utsava bera; Acchuta by Snapana bera; and Aniruddha by Bali bera.

To put these together in a combined form:

- The main idol (Dhruva-bera) which is immovable represents Vishnu (Vishnu-tattva).
- Purusha symbolized by Kautuka-bera is an emanation of the Dhruva-bera. Kautuka-bera is next in importance, and is an exact replica of the Dhruva-bimba. it is placed in the sanctum very close to Dhruva bera.
- Satya symbolized by Utsava-bera (processional deity) emanates from Purusha represented Kautuka-bera. And, Utsava-bera is placed in the next pavilion outside the sanctum.
- Achyuta symbolized by Snapana-bera emanates from Satya represented by Utsava-bera. Snapana-bera receives Abhisheka, the ceremonial bath; and, it is placed outside the sanctum in snapana-mantapam enclosure.
- Aniruddhda symbolized by Bali-bera emanates from Achyuta represented by Snapana-bera. The food offerings are submitted to Balibera. And, it is placed farthest from the Dhruva-bhera residing in the sanctum.

These different icons are not viewed as separate or independent deities; but are understood as emanations from the original icon, Dhruva–bimba.

Symbolisms

The symbolisms associated with the four murtis (chatur-murti) are many; and are interesting. As said earlier; the four are said to compare with the strides taken by Vishnu/Trivikrama. The main icon represents Vishnu who is all-pervasive, but, does not move about. When the worship sequences are conducted, the spirit (tejas) of the main idol moves into the Kautuka,-bera, which rests on the worship pedestal (archa-pitha). This is the first stride of Vishnu.Again, at the time of offering ritual bath, the tejas of the main idol moves into the Snapana-bera which is placed in the bathing-enclosure (snapana –mantapa). This is the second stride taken by Vishnu. And, the third stride is that when the Utsava-bera is taken out in processions. This is when the tejas of the Main idol reaches out to all.

In Marichi's Vimana-archa-kalpa the five forms, five types of icons, the pancha-murti (when Vishnu is also counted along with the other four forms) are compared to five types of Vedic sacred fires (pancha-agni): garhapatya; ahavaniya; dakshinAgni; anvaharya; and sabhya. These in turn are compared to the primary elements (earth, water, fire, air, and space). And, the comparison is extended to five vital currents (prana, apana, vyana, udana and samana).

Further it is explained; the Vaikhanasa worship-tradition retained the concept of Pancha-Agni, but transformed them into five representations of Vishnu (pancha –murthi): Vishnu, Purusha, Satya, Achyuta and Aniruddha. And, that again was rendered into five types of temple deities as pancha-bera: Dhruva, Kautuka, Snapana, Utsava and Bali.

[The Vaikhanasa concept of five forms of Godhead parallels with that of Pancharatara which speaks of: Para, Vyuha, Vibhava, Antaryamin and Archa. Of these, Para is the absolute form, the cause of all existence and it is beyond intellect. Vyuha are the emanations from Para for sustaining creation. The Vyuha, in turn, assumes five worship-worthy forms: Vishnu, Purusha, Satya, Achyuta and Aniruddha. Vibhava represent the Avatars for destroying the evil, uplifting the virtuous and maintain balance in the world. Antaryamin is the inbeing who resides as jiva in all creatures. And, Archa is the most easily accessible form; the form which protects the devotees and eliminates their sorrows. This is the form that is worshipped in the temples.]

http://creative.sulekha.com/tantra-agama-part-four-vaikhanasa-continued_591617_blog

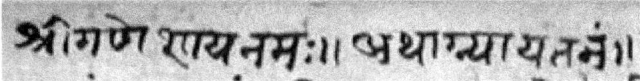

Source: agnyāyatanaṁ and agnihotrahomaḥ colophon: punarādheyam

http://muktalib5.org/VEDIC_ROOT/TEXTS/JOGLEKAR/JOGLEKAR-PDF/J0045.pdf

गणा *f.* N. of one of the mothers in स्कन्द's retinue MBh. ix , 2645 (cf. अहर्- , मर्/उद्- , व्/ऋष- , स्/अ- , सप्त्/अ- , स्/अर्व- ; देव-,महा- ,andविद-गण्/अ.) गण [p=343,1] *m.* a flock , troop , multitude , number , tribe , series , class (of animate or inanimate beings) , body of followers or attendants RV. AV.&c troops or classes of inferior deities (especially certain troops of demi-gods considered as शिव's attendants and under the special superintendence of the god गणे*श ; cf. -देवता) Mn. Ya1jn5. Lalit. &c a single attendant of शिव VarBr2S. Katha1s. Ra1jat. iii , 270N. of गणे*श W.a company , any assemblage or association of men formed for the attainment of the same aims Mn. Ya1jn5. Hit.*m.* a particular group of सामन्s La1t2y. i , 6 , 5 VarYogay. viii , 7

Source: http://muktalib5.org/VEDIC_ROOT/vedic_library.htm

ॐ गणानां त्वा गणपतिं हवामहे
कविं कवीनामुपमश्रवस्तमम् ।
ज्येष्ठराजं ब्रह्मणाम् ब्रह्मणस्पत
आ नः शृण्वन्नूतिभिःसीदसादनम् ॥
ॐ महागणाधिपतये नमः ॥

RV_2,023.01a gaṇānāṃ tvā gaṇapatiṃ havāmahe kaviṃ kavīnām upamaśravastamam |
RV_2,023.01c jyeṣṭharājam brahmaṇāṃ brahmaṇas pata ā naḥ śṛṇvann ūtibhiḥ sīda sādanam ||
RV_2,023.02a devāś cit te asurya pracetaso bṛhaspate yajñiyam bhāgam ānaśuḥ |
RV_2,023.02c usrā iva sūryo jyotiṣā maho viśveṣām ij janitā brahmaṇām asi ||
RV_2,023.03a ā vibādhyā parirāpas tamāṃsi ca jyotiṣmantaṃ ratham ṛtasya tiṣṭhasi |
RV_2,023.03c bṛhaspate bhīmam amitradambhanaṃ rakṣohaṇaṃ gotrabhidaṃ svarvidam ||
RV_2,023.04a sunītibhir nayasi trāyase janaṃ yas tubhyaṃ dāśān na tam aṃho aśnavat |

RV_2,023.04c brahmadviṣas tapano manyumīr asi bṛhaspate mahi tat te mahitvanam ||
RV_2,023.05a na tam aṃho na duritaṃ kutaś cana nārātayas titirur na dvayāvinaḥ |
RV_2,023.05c viśvā id asmād dhvaraso vi bādhase yaṃ sugopā rakṣasi brahmaṇas pate ||
RV_2,023.06a tvaṃ no gopāḥ pathikṛd vicakṣaṇas tava vratāya matibhir jarāmahe |
RV_2,023.06c bṛhaspate yo no abhi hvaro dadhe svā tam marmartu ducchunā harasvatī ||
RV_2,023.07a uta vā yo no marcayād anāgaso 'rātīvā martaḥ sānuko vṛkaḥ |
RV_2,023.07c bṛhaspate apa taṃ vartayā pathaḥ sugaṃ no asyai devavītaye kṛdhi ||
RV_2,023.08a trātāraṃ tvā tanūnāṃ havāmahe 'vaspartar adhivaktāram asmayum |
RV_2,023.08c bṛhaspate devanido ni barhaya mā durevā uttaraṃ sumnam un naśan ||
RV_2,023.09a tvayā vayaṃ suvṛdhā brahmaṇas pate spārhā vasu manuṣyā dadīmahi |
RV_2,023.09c yā no dūre taḷito yā arātayo 'bhi santi jambhayā tā anapnasaḥ ||
RV_2,023.10a tvayā vayam uttamaṃ dhīmahe vayo bṛhaspate papriṇā sasninā yujā |
RV_2,023.10c mā no duḥśaṃso abhidipsur īśata pra suśaṃsā matibhis tāriṣīmahi ||
RV_2,023.11a anānudo vṛṣabho jagmir āhavaṃ niṣṭaptā śatrum pṛtanāsu sāsahiḥ |
RV_2,023.11c asi satya ṛṇayā brahmaṇas pata ugrasya cid damitā vīḷuharṣiṇaḥ ||
RV_2,023.12a adevena manasā yo riṣaṇyati śāsām ugro manyamāno jighāṃsati |
RV_2,023.12c bṛhaspate mā praṇak tasya no vadho ni karma manyuṃ durevasya śardhataḥ ||
RV_2,023.13a bhareṣu havyo namasopasadyo gantā vājeṣu sanitā dhanaṃ-dhanam |
RV_2,023.13c viśvā id aryo abhidipsvo mṛdho bṛhaspatir vi vavarhā rathāṃ iva ||
RV_2,023.14a tejiṣṭhayā tapanī rakṣasas tapa ye tvā nide dadhire dṛṣṭavīryam |
RV_2,023.14c āvis tat kṛṣva yad asat ta ukthyam bṛhaspate vi parirāpo ardaya ||
RV_2,023.15a bṛhaspate ati yad aryo arhād dyumad vibhāti kratumaj janeṣu |
RV_2,023.15c yad dīdayac chavasa ṛtaprajāta tad asmāsu draviṇaṃ dhehi citram ||
RV_2,023.16a mā na stenebhyo ye abhi druhas pade nirāmiṇo ripavo 'nneṣu jāgṛdhuḥ |
RV_2,023.16c ā devānām ohate vi vrayo hṛdi bṛhaspate na paraḥ sāmno viduḥ ||
RV_2,023.17a viśvebhyo hi tvā bhuvanebhyas pari tvaṣṭājanat sāmnaḥ-sāmnaḥ kaviḥ |
RV_2,023.17c sa ṛṇacid ṛṇayā brahmaṇas patir druho hantā maha ṛtasya dhartari ||
RV_2,023.18a tava śriye vy ajihīta parvato gavāṃ gotram udasṛjo yad aṅgiraḥ |
RV_2,023.18c indreṇa yujā tamasā parīvṛtam bṛhaspate nir apām aubjo arṇavam ||
RV_2,023.19a brahmaṇas pate tvam asya yantā sūktasya bodhi tanayaṃ ca jinva |
RV_2,023.19c viśvaṃ tad bhadraṃ yad avanti devā bṛhad vadema vidathe suvīrāḥ ||

| (19) | **23** | (म. 2, अनु. 3) |

ऋषिः गृत्समदः भार्गवः शौनकः   छन्दः जगती 1-14,16-18, त्रिष्टुप् 15,19
देवता ब्रह्मणस्पतिः 1,5,9,11,17,19 बृहस्पतिः 2-4,6-8,10,12-16,18

गणानां॑ त्वा ग॒णप॑तिं हवामहे क॒विं क॑वी॒नामु॑प॒मश्र॑वस्तमम् ।
ज्ये॒ष्ठ॒राजं॒ ब्रह्म॑णां ब्रह्मणस्पत॒ आ नः॑ शृ॒ण्वन्नू॒तिभिः॑ सीद॒ साद॑नम् ॥ 1 ॥
दे॒वाश्चि॑त्ते असुर्य॑ प्रचेत॒सो बृह॑स्पते य॒ज्ञियं॑ भा॒गमा॑नशुः ।
उ॒स्रा इ॑व॒ सूर्यो॒ ज्योति॑षा म॒हो विश्वे॑षा॒मिज्ज॑नि॒ता ब्रह्म॑णामसि ॥ 2 ॥
आ वि॒बाध्या॑ परि॒रापस्त॒मांसि॑ च॒ ज्योति॑ष्मन्तं॒ रथ॑मृ॒तस्य॑ तिष्ठसि ।
बृह॑स्पते भी॒ममि॑मि॒त्रद॑म्भनं रक्षो॒हणं॑ गो॒त्रभिदं॒ स्व॑र्वि॒दम् ॥ 3 ॥
सु॒नी॒तिभि॑र्नयसि॒ त्राय॑से॒ जनं॒ यस्तुभ्यं॒ दाशा॒न्न त॒मंहो॑ अश्नवत् ।
ब्र॒ह्म॒द्विष॑स्तपनो मन्यु॒मीर॑सि॒ बृह॑स्पते॒ महि॒ तत्ते॑ महि॒त्व॑नम् ॥ 4 ॥
न तमंहो॒ न दु॑रि॒तं कुत॑श्च॒न नारा॑तय॒स्तित॑रु॒र्न द्व॒याविनः॑ ।
विश्वा॒ इद॑स्माद्धुर॒सो वि बा॑ध॒से यं सु॒गोपा॒ रक्ष॑सि ब्रह्मणस्पते ॥ 5 ॥
त्वं नो॑ गो॒पाः प॑थि॒कृद्वि॑चक्ष॒णस्तव॑ व्र॒ताय॑ म॒तिभि॑र्जरामहे ।
बृह॑स्पते॒ यो नो॒ अ॒भि ह्व॒रो द॒धे स्वा तं म॑र्मर्तु दु॒च्छुना॒ हर॑स्वती ॥ 6 ॥
उ॒त वा॒ यो नो॑ म॒र्चया॒दना॑गसो॒ऽरातीवा॒ मर्तः॑ सानु॒को वृकः॑ ।
बृह॑स्पते॒ अप॒ तं व॑र्तया प॒थः सु॒गं नो॑ अ॒स्यै दे॑व॒वीत॑ये कृधि ॥ 7 ॥

बृहस्पते देवनिदो नि बर्हय मा दुरेवा उत्तरं सुम्नमुन्नशन् ‖ 8 ‖
त्वया वयं सुवृधा ब्रह्मणस्पते स्पार्हा वसु मनुष्या ददीमहि ।
या नो दूरे तळितो या अरातयोऽभि सन्ति जम्भया ता अनप्रसः ‖ 9 ‖
त्वया वयमुत्तमं धीमहे वयो बृहस्पते पप्रिणा सस्निना युजा ।
मा नो दुःशंसो अभिदिप्सुरीशत प्र सुशंसा मतिभिस्तारिषीमहि ‖ 10 ‖
अनानुदो वृषभो जग्मिराहवं निष्टप्ता शत्रुं पृतनासु सासहिः ।
असि सत्य ऋणया ब्रह्मणस्पत उग्रस्य चिद्दमिता वीळुहर्षिणः ‖ 11 ‖
अदेवेन मनसा यो रिषण्यति शासामुग्रो मन्यमानो जिघांसति ।
बृहस्पते मा प्रणक्तस्य नो वधो नि कर्म मन्युं दुरेवस्य शर्धतः ‖ 12 ‖
भरेषु हव्यो नमसोपसद्यो गन्ता वाजेषु सनिता धनंधनम् ।
विश्वा इदर्यो अभिदिप्स्वो३मृधो बृहस्पतिर्वि ववर्हा रथाँइव ‖ 13 ‖
तेजिष्ठया तपनी रक्षसस्तप ये त्वा निदे दधिरे दृष्टवीर्यम् ।
आविस्तत्कृष्व यदसत्त उक्थ्यं१ बृहस्पते वि परिरापो अर्दय ‖ 14 ‖
बृहस्पते अति यदर्यो अर्हाद्द्युमद्विभाति क्रतुमज्जनेषु ।
यद्दीदयच्छवस ऋतप्रजात तदस्मासु द्रविणं धेहि चित्रम् ‖ 15 ‖
मा नः स्तेनेभ्यो ये अभि द्रुहस्पदे निरामिणो रिपवोऽन्नेषु जागृधुः ।
आ देवानामोहते वि व्रयो हृदि बृहस्पते न परः साम्नो विदुः ‖ 16 ‖
विश्वेभ्यो हि त्वा भुवनेभ्यस्परि त्वष्टाजनत्साम्नःसाम्नः कविः ।
स ऋणचिदृणया ब्रह्मणस्पतिर्द्रुहो हन्ता मह ऋतस्य धर्तरि ‖ 17 ‖
तव श्रिये व्यजिहीत पर्वतो गवां गोत्रमुदसृजो यदङ्गिरः ।

इन्द्रेण युजा तमसा परीवृतं बृहस्पते निरपामौब्जो अर्णवम् ॥ 18 ॥
ब्रह्मणस्पते त्वमस्य यन्ता सूक्तस्य बोधि तनयं च जिन्व ।
विश्वं तद्भद्रं यदवन्ति देवा बृहद्वदेम विदथे सुवीराः ॥ 19 ॥
। इति द्वितीयाष्टके षष्ठोऽध्यायः समाप्तः ।

r.s.i: gr.tsamada (a_n:girasa s'aunahotra pas'ca_d) bha_rgava s'aunaka; devata_: br.haspati, 1-5,9,11,17,19 brahman.aspati; chanda: jagati_, 15,19 tris.t.up; Anuva_ka III

2.023.01 We invoke the Brahman.aspati, chief leaderof the (heavenly) bands; a sage of sage; abounding beyond measure in (every kind of) food;best lord of prayer; hearing our invocations, come with your protections, and sit down in the chamber of sacrifice. [Brahman.aspati = brahman.o annasya parivr.d.hasya karman.o va_ pa_layita_, the protector or cherisher of food,or of any great or solemn acts of devotion; he has other attributes in the text, as, gan.a_na_m gan.apatih, chief of the gan.as (inferior deities); jyes.t.hara_jam brahman.a_m, the best lord of mantras, or prayers: pras'asyam sva_minam mantra_n.a_m].
2.023.02 Br.haspati, destroyer of the asuras, through you the intelligent gods have obtained the sacrificialportion; in like manner as the adorable sun generates the (solar) rays by his radiance, so are you the generator of all prayers. [Br.haspati = Brahman.aspati; perhaps Br.haspati is of a more martial character; his protection is souhght for against enemies and evil spirits; perhaps, br.hata_m veda_na_m pa_lakah: br.hat = mantra, br.hato mantrasya, sva_min].
2.023.03 Having repelled revilers and (dispersed) the darkness you stand Br.haspati, on the radiant chariot of sacrifice, (which is) formidable (to foes), the humiliator of enemies, the destroyer of evil spirits, the cleaver of the clouds, the attainer of heaven.
2.023.04 You lead men, Br.haspati, by virtuous instructions; you preserve them (from calamity); sin will never overtake him who presents (offerings) to you; you are the afflicter of him who hates (holy) prayers; you are the punisher of wrath; such is your great mightiness. [Him who hates holy prayers: brahmadvis.ah = those who hate either the bra_hman.as,or the mantras or prayers].
2.023.05 The man whom you, Brahman.aspati, a kind protector, defend, neither sorrow nor sin, nor adversaries nor dissemblers ever harm, for you drive away from him all injurious (things).
2.023.06 You, Br.haspati, are our protector and the guide of (our) path; (you are) the discerner (of all things); we worship with praises for your adoration; may his own precipitate malice involve him (in destruction) who practises deceit against us.
2.023.07 Turn aside from (the true) path, Br.haspati, the arrogant and savage man who advances to injure us, although unoffending and keep us in the right way for (the completion of) this offering to the gods.
2.023.08 Br.haspati, defender (from calamity), we invoke you, the protector of our persons, the speaker of encouraging words and well disposed towards us; do you destroy the revilers of the gods; let not the malevolent attain supreme felicity.
2.023.09 Through you, Brahman.aspati, (our) benefactor, may we obtain desirable wealth from men destroy those (our) unrighteous enemies, whether nigh or far off, who prevail against us.

2.023.10 Through you, Br.haspati, (who are) the fulfiller of our desires; pure, and associated (with us), we possess excellent food; let not the wicked man who wishes to deceive us be our master; but let us, excelling in (pious) praises, attain (prosperity).
2.023.11 You, Brahman.aspati, who have no requiter (of your bounty), who are the showerer (of benefits), the repairer to combat, the consumer of foes, the victor in battles, you are true, the discharger of debts, the humiliator of the fierce and of the exulting.
2.023.12 Let not, Br.haspati, the murderous (weapon) of that man reach us, who, with unrighteous mind, seeks to harm us; who, fierce and arrogant, designs to kill (your) worshippers; may we baffle the wrath of the strong evil-doer].
2.023.13 Br.haspati is to be invoked in battles; he is to be approached with reverence; he who moves amidst combats, the distributor of repeated wealth; the lord Br.haspati has verily overturned all the assailing malignant (hosts), like chariots (overturned in battle).
2.023.14 Consume with your brightest (weapon) the ra_ks.asas, who have held your witnessed prowess in disdain; manifest, Br.haspati, your glorified (vigour), such as it was (of old), and destroy those who speak against you.
2.023.15 Br.haspati, born of truth, grant us that wonderful treasure, wherewith the pious man may worship exceedingly; that (wealth) which shines amongst men; which is endowed with lustre, (is) the means of (performing holy) rites, and invogirates (its possessor) with strength. [dravin.am citram = lit., various or wonderful wealth; in the Bra_hman.as it is interpreted as brahma varcas or tejas, brahmanical virtue or energy (cf. Yajus. 26.3; dravin.am = dhanam (Aitareya Bra_hman.a 4.11)].
2.023.16 Deliver us not to the thieves, the enemies delighting in violence, who seize ever upon the food (of others); those who cherish in their hearts the abandonment (of the gods); (they), Br.haspati, who do not know the extent of (your) power (against evil spirits). [Who do not know the extenf of your power: na parah sa_mno viduh = ye puma_msah sa_mnah sa_maya_t tvattah parah parasta_d anyadukr.s.t.am sa_ma yad raks.oghnam na ja_nanti, those men who do not know anything greater than the faculty of destroying ra_ks.asas, derived from you made up of that faculty; sa_ma vai raks.oha = sa_ma is the killer of ra_ks.asas].
2.023.17 Tvas.t.a_ engendered you (chief) amongst all beings, (whence) you are the reciter of many a holy hymn: Brahman.aspati acknowledges a debt to the performer of a sacred rite; he is the acquitter (of the debt), and the destoyer of the oppressor. [When you are the reciter: sa_mnah sa_mnah kavih, the reicter or another of every sa_ma, sarvasya sa_mnah ucca_rayita_ karta_si; or kavi refers to tvas.t.a_, further explained as the sage who created Brahman.aspati by the efficacy of the sa_ma: sa_mnah sa_ren.a tvam aji_janat; acknowledges a debt: r.n.acit stotr.ka_mam r.n.am iva cinoti, he takes the intention of the praiser as if it was a debt, or obligation; acquitter of the debt: r.n.aya is explained as the discharger or remover of the debt which is of the nature of sin: pa_paru_pasya r.n.asya pr.thak karta_].
2.023.18 When Br.haspati, descendant of An:giras, for your glory, Parvata had concealed the herd o fkine, you did set them free, and with thine associate, Indra, did send down the ocean of water which had been enveloped by darkness.
2.023.19 Brahman.aspati, who are the regulator of this (world), understand (the purport) of (our) hymn, and grant us posterity; for all is prosperous that the gods protect; (and therefore) may we blessed with excellent

descendants, glorify you at this sacrifice. [Yajus. 34.58; vadema = may we declare or glorify you; or, let us speak, let what we ask be given to us;let it be enjoyed by us: di_yata_m bhujyata_m ucca_rayema].

Meaning:
1: Om, O Ganapati, To You Who are the Lord of the Ganas (Celestial Attendants or Followers), weOffer our Sacrificial Oblations,
2: You are the Wisdom of the Wise and the Uppermost in Glory,
3: You are the Eldest Lord (i.e. ever Unborn) and is of the Nature of Brahman (Absolute Consciousness); You are the Embodiment of the Sacred Pranava (Om),
4: Please come to us by Listening to our Prayers and be Present in the Seat of this Sacred Sacrificial Altar.
5: Om, our Prostrations to the Mahaganadhipati (the Great Lord of the Ganas).

http://www.greenmesg.org/mantras_slokas/sri_ganesha-gananam_tva_ganapatim.php

Making of Indus Script Dictionary

--Indus Script Hieroglyph Sign List-together with orthographic variants of signs to decipher the writing system

Orthographic methods of encryption are used to signify additional specific or technical attributes t of the base hieroglyph to record meaning. Hieroglyph-multiplexes are the method used to Prakrtam metlwork lexis. This lexis or vocabulary was referred to as Meluhha on cuneiform texts and on a cylinder seal of Shu-Ilishu. Meluhha is cognate with mleccha a grammatical category of mispronunciations in spoken forms of vAk, 'speech'. The writing system is designated as mlecchita vikalpa (meluhha cipher) by Vatsyayana who lists in Vidyasamuddesa (objective of education) 64 arts including three arts related to language studies: akshara mushtika kathanam, des'abhASA jnaanam, and mlecchita vikalpa: messaging with hand and finger gestures, knowledge of dialects or vernacular or lingua franca and cipher writing.:

Almost all Indus Script hieroglyphs of the Sign list and hieroglyph-multiplexes presented as pictorial motifs on Indus Script Corpora have been deciphered, thus providing the tools and resources for making an Indus Script Dictionary. Thousands of Persian Gulf seals and inscriptions, Ancient Near East cylinder seals and artefacts also also convey metalwork messages signified by Indus Script hieroglyphs. These have been demonstrated in the quintet of books related to Indus Script decipherment: The quintet narrates the form and function of Indus Script and provides profiles of Samskrta Bharati, language of the civilization:

1. *Indus Script Cipher -- Hieroglyhphs of Indian Linguistic Area* (2010)
2. *Indus Script: Meluhha metalwork hieroglyphs* (2014)
3. *Philosophy of Symbolic forms in Meluhha cipher* (2014)
4. *Cultural History of Bharatam Janam – Indus Script metalwork catalogs* (2016)
5. *Samskrta Bharati – Indus Script Dictionary, Epigraphia Mlecchita Vikalpa, 'Meluhha* cipher' (2016)

[Author: S. Kalyanaraman, Herndon, Sarasvai Research Center.]

For example, the body hieroglyph in Sign 1 signifies meD 'body' rebus: meD 'iron

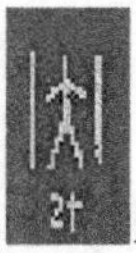
Additional attributes are signified on Sign 2 by use of a circumscript of two linear strokes: koDa 'one' dula 'two' rebus: koD 'workshop' dul 'cast metal'. Thus the hieroglyph multiplex of hypertext of Sign 2 signifies meD 'iron' koD 'workshop' dul 'metal casting'.

Aother method of encryption is to combine hieroglyphs to signify two or more distinct material categories:

For example, the fish hieroglyph in aya 'fish' rebus: aya 'iron' ayas 'metal'.

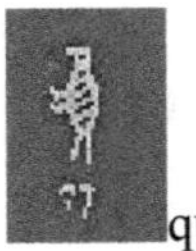quail: baTa ‘quail’ rebus: bhaTa ‘furnace’

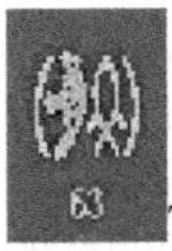Together, the hieroglyphs fish and quail circumscribed by parentheses signifies: bhaTa ‘furnace’ (for) aya ‘iron’ ayas ‘metal’. The split oval may result in split parentheses; the split oval may signify an oval-shaped bun ingot. Thus, the furnace of iron/metal is for casting metal ingots.

Such orthographic combinations of hieroglyph components is exemplified by the sign

This combines: fish, water-carrier, rim of jar, hole, harrow hieroglyph components. Aya ‘fish’ rebus: aya ‘iron’ ayas ‘metal’; kuTi ‘water-carrier’ rebus: kuThi ‘smelter’; dula ‘hole’ rebus: dul ‘cst metal’; adar ‘harrow’ rebus: aduru ‘unsmelted metal’. Thus the hieroglyph-multiplex as hypertext signifies: aya kuThi, dul aduru ‘iron smelter cast unsmelted metal’.

Another method used in encryption is to add a hieroglyph component as a semantic-phonetic determinant.

This is exemplified by the following variants of Signs 180 and 181 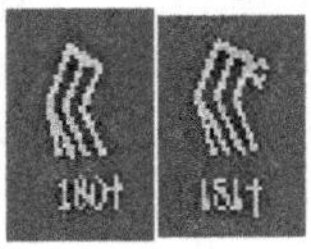

The ligature hieroglyph component is ‘claws’. The word which signifies this orthography is daTo ‘claws’ rebus: datu ‘mineral ore’. In this context of a semantic determinant, the three strand component of the hieroglyph-multiplex or hypertext signifies: dhau ‘strand of rope’ rebus: dhav ‘smelter’. Thus the hypertext signifies smelting of mineral ore. (See alternative orthography signifying strands of rope (semantics: smelter) on the robe of Purifier priest, Potr.

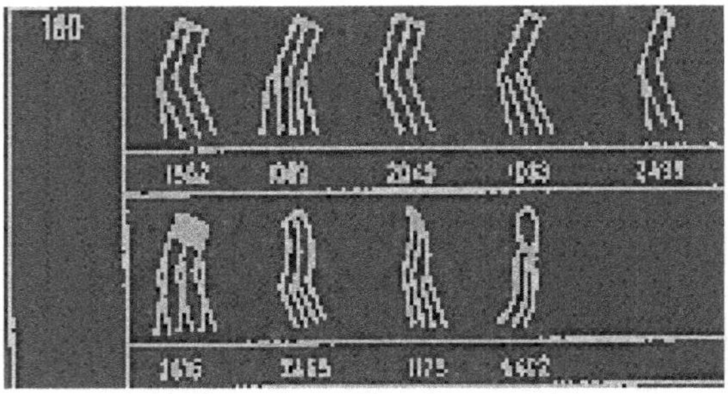

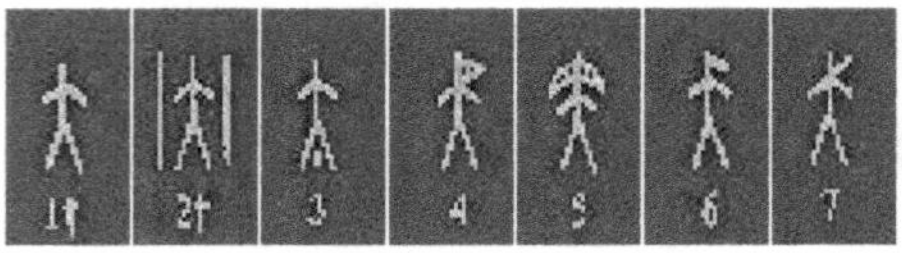

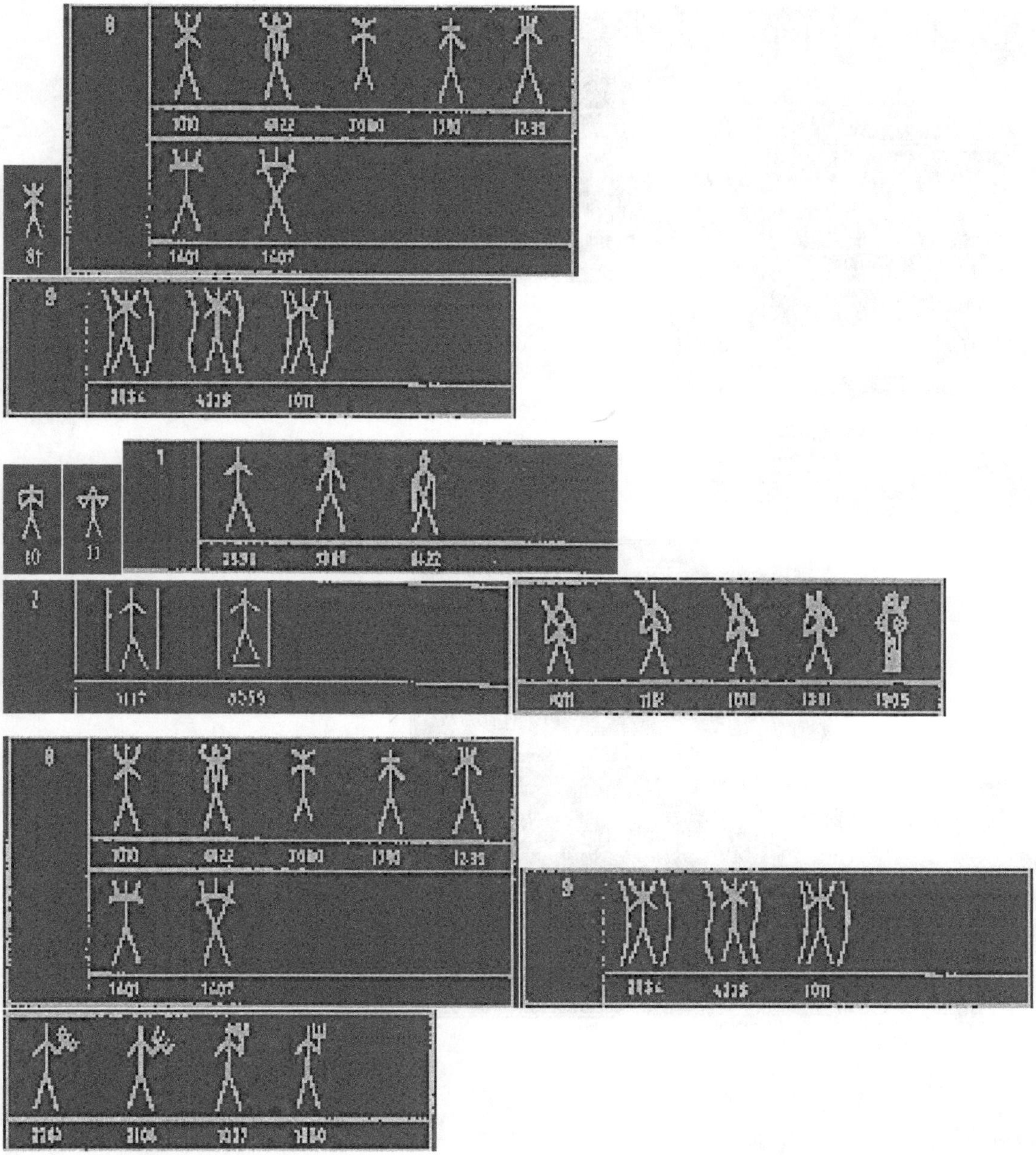

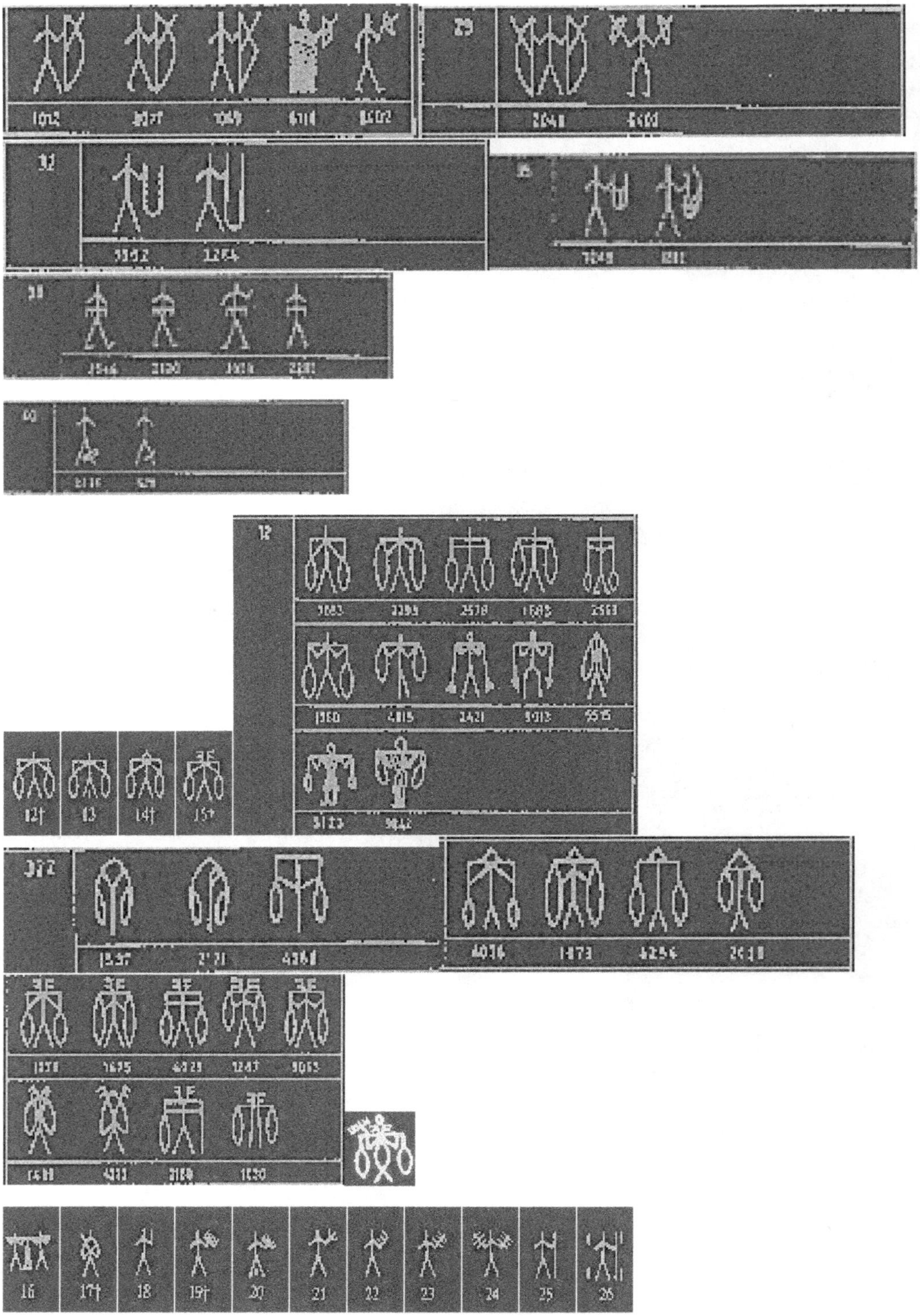

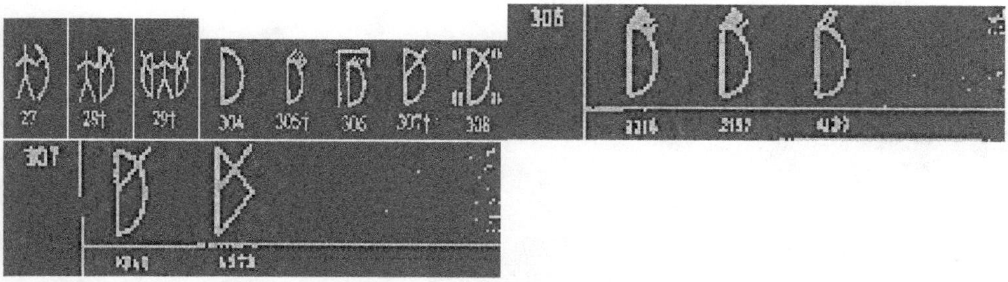
27
28†
29†
304
305†
306
307†
308
306
307

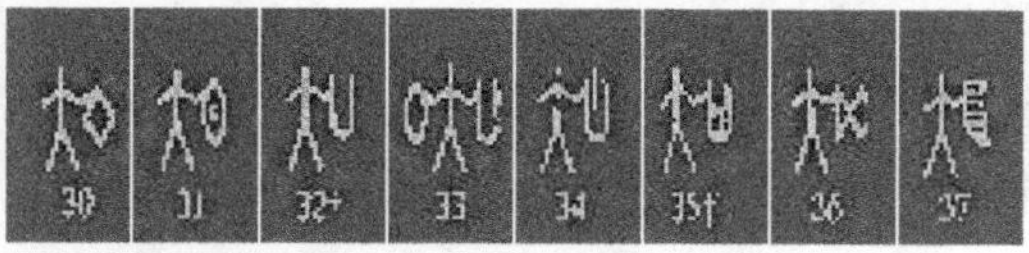
30
31
32†
33
34
35†
36
37

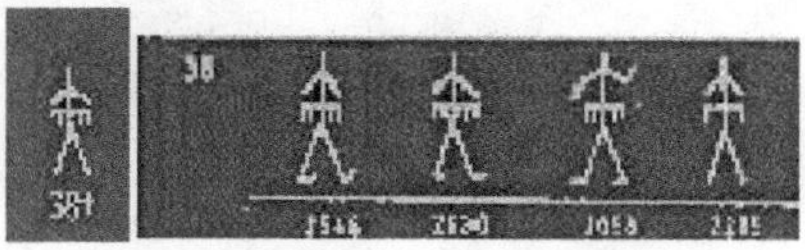
38†
38

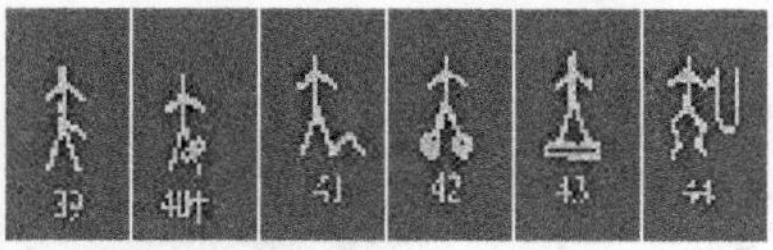
39
40†
41
42
43
44

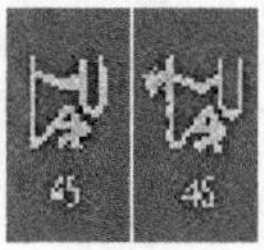
45
46

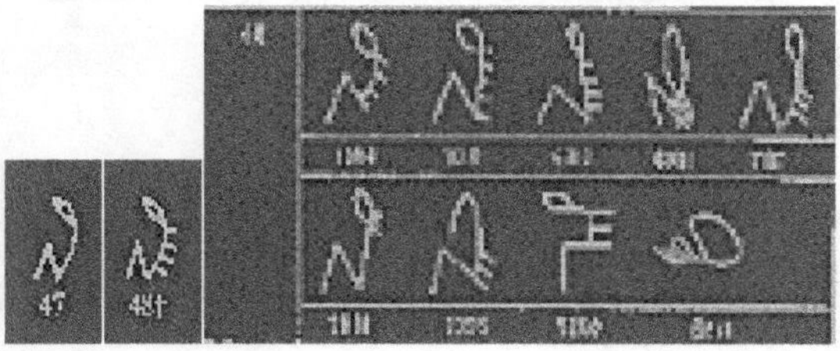
47
48†
48

49†

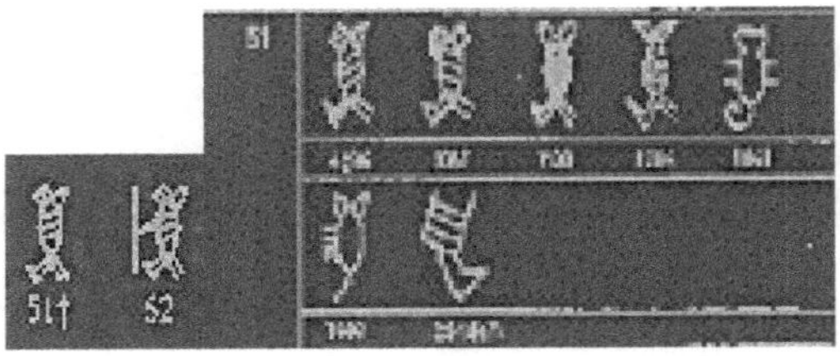
51† 52

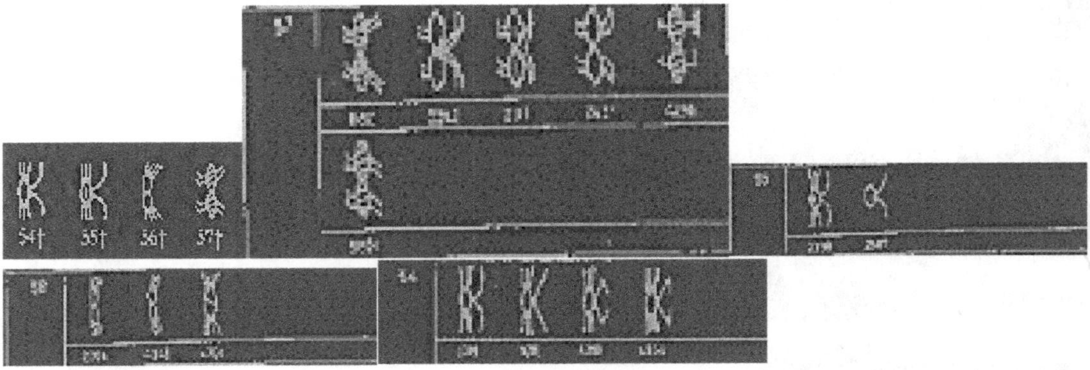
54† 55† 56† 57†

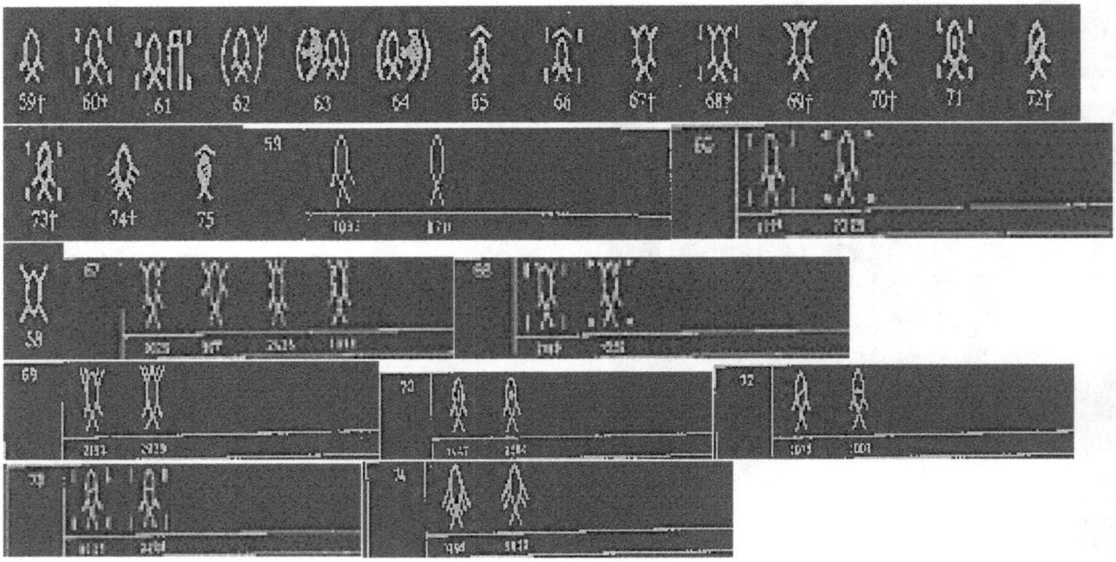
59† 60† 61 62 63 64 65 66 67† 68† 69† 70† 71 72†
73† 74† 75
58

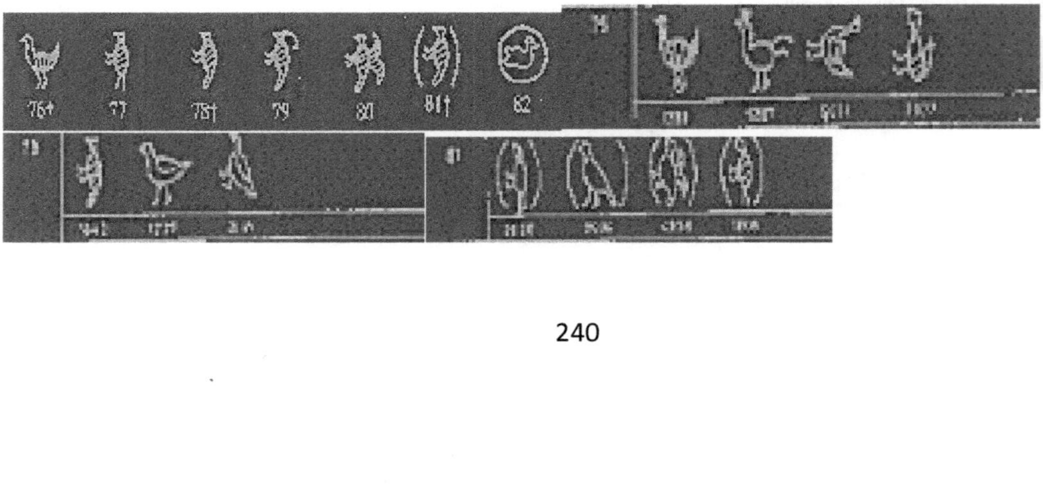
76† 77 78† 79 80 81† 82

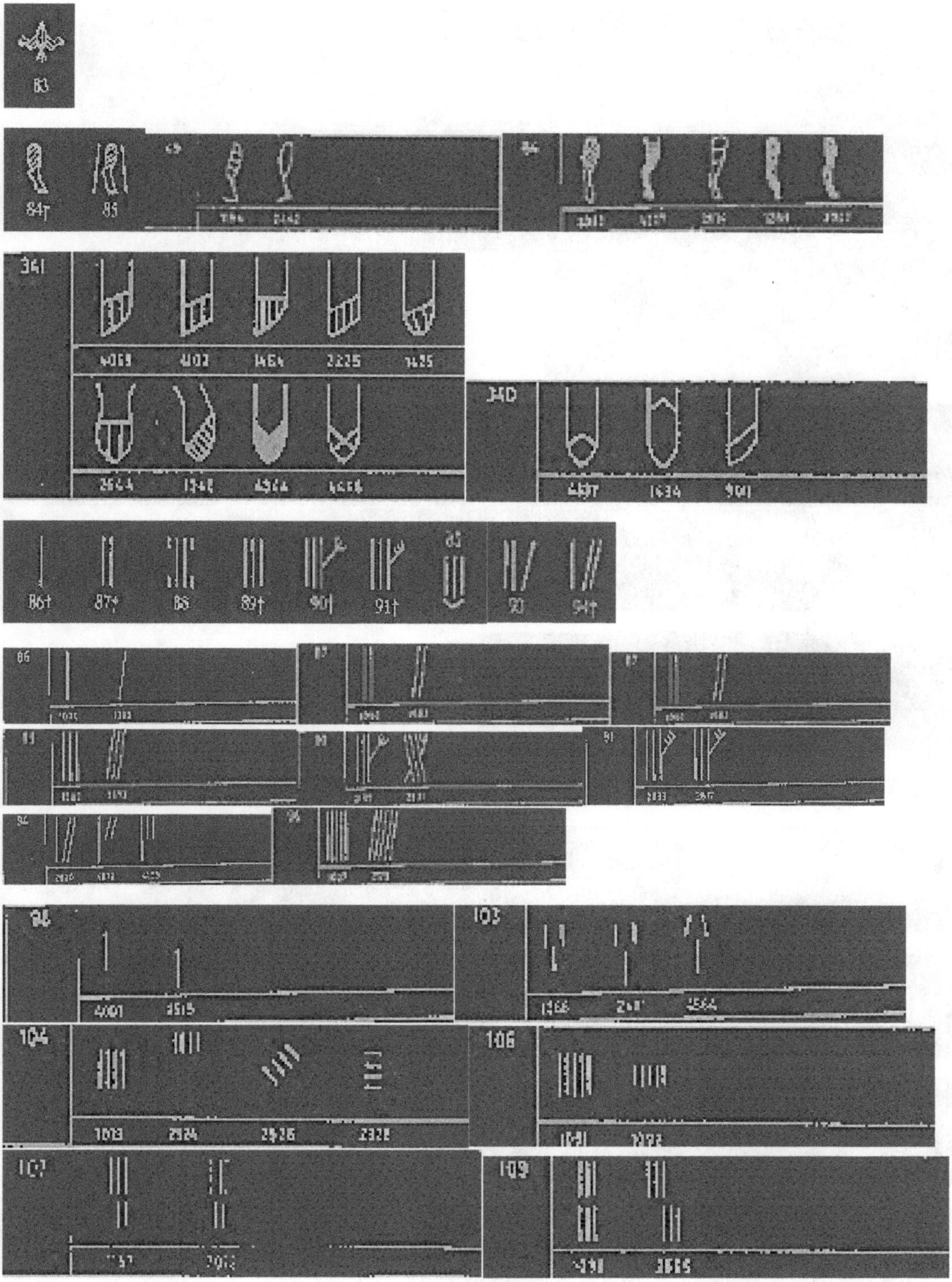
83
84†
85
341
86†
87†
88
89†
90†
91†
94†
103
104
106
107
109

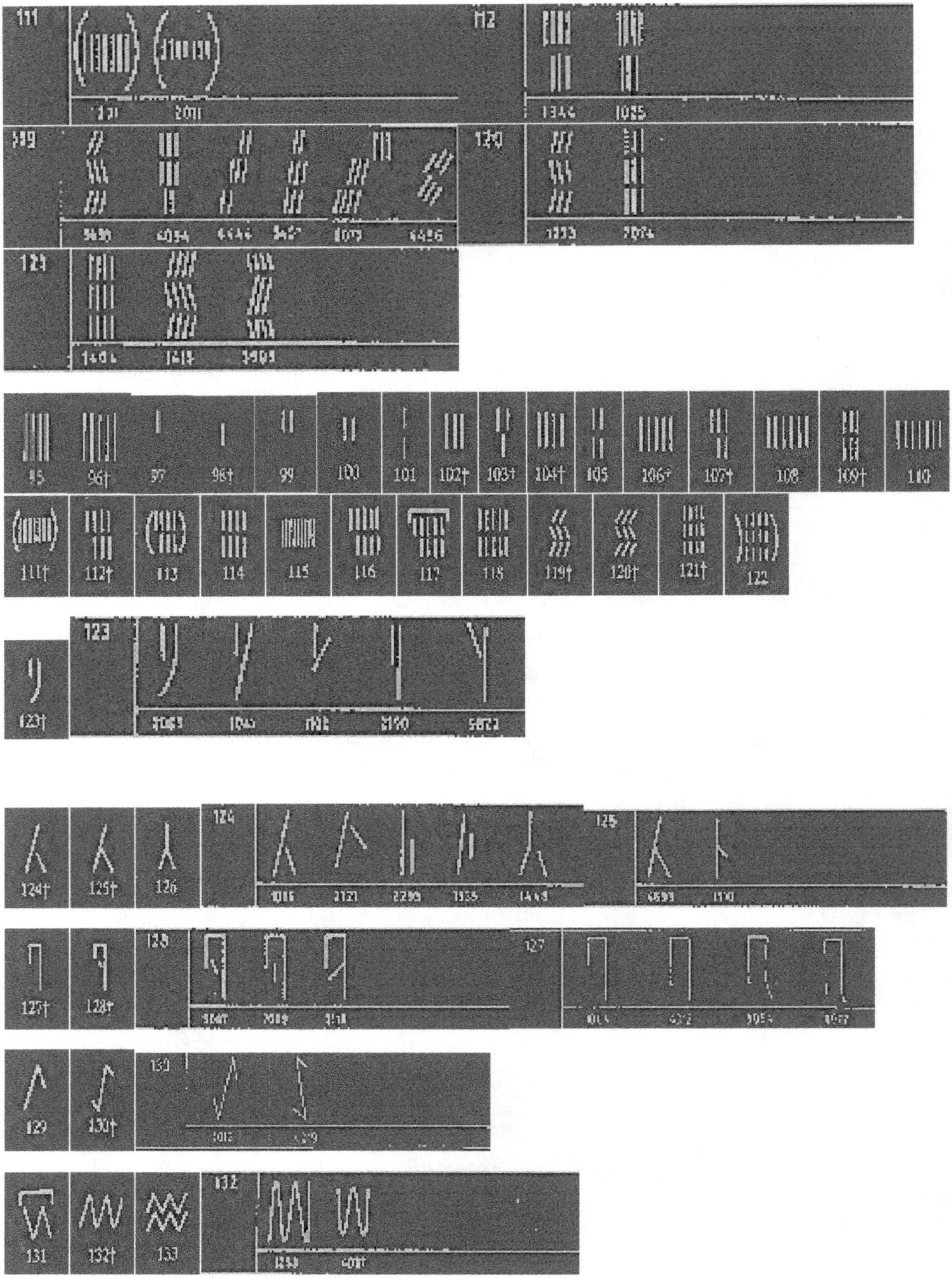
111
112
119
120
121
95
96†
97
98†
99
100
101
102†
103†
104†
105
106†
107†
108
109†
110
111†
112†
113
114
115
116
117
118
119†
120†
121†
122
123
123†
124
125
124†
125†
126
128
127
127†
128†
129
130†
130
131
132†
133
132

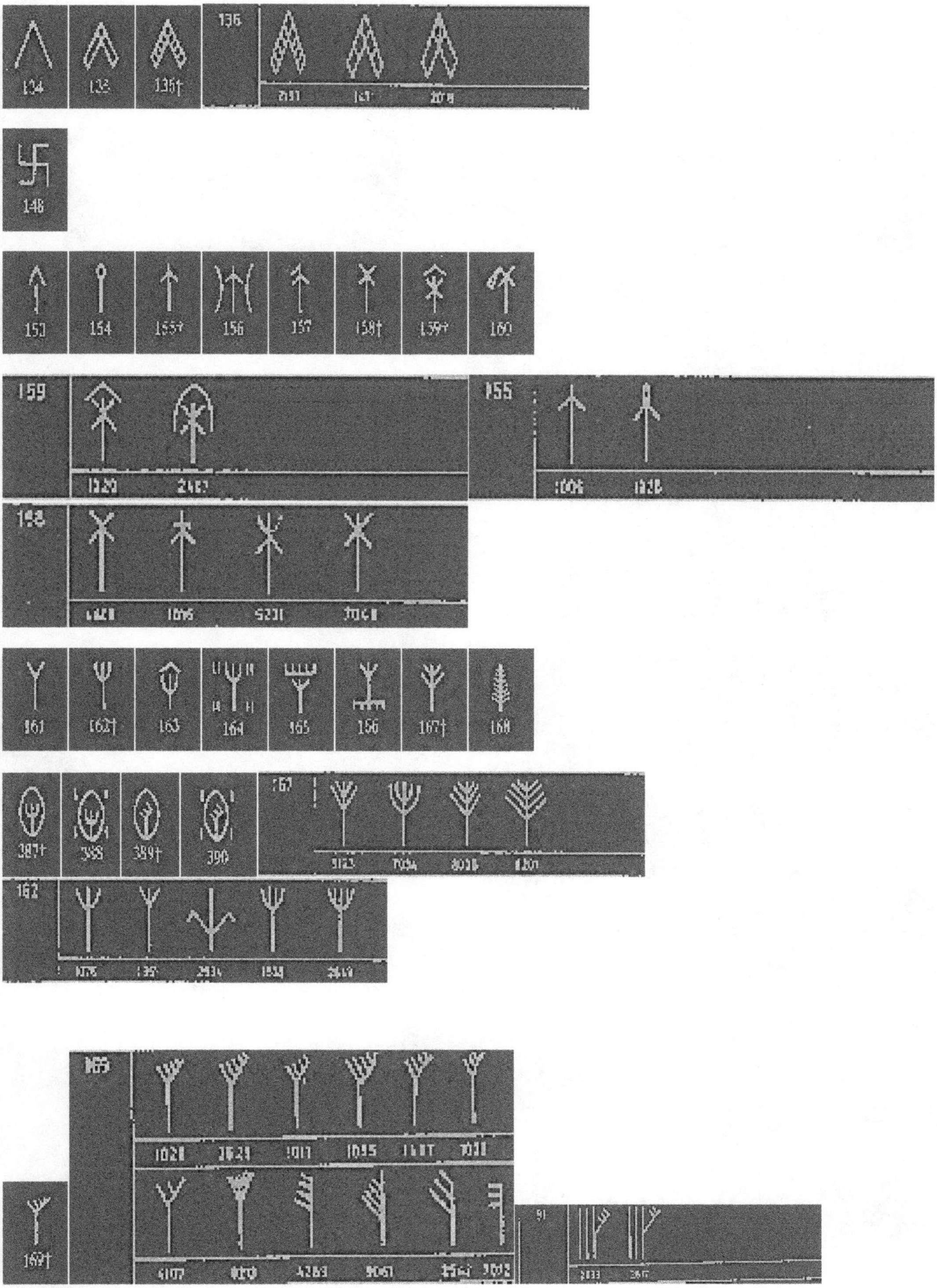

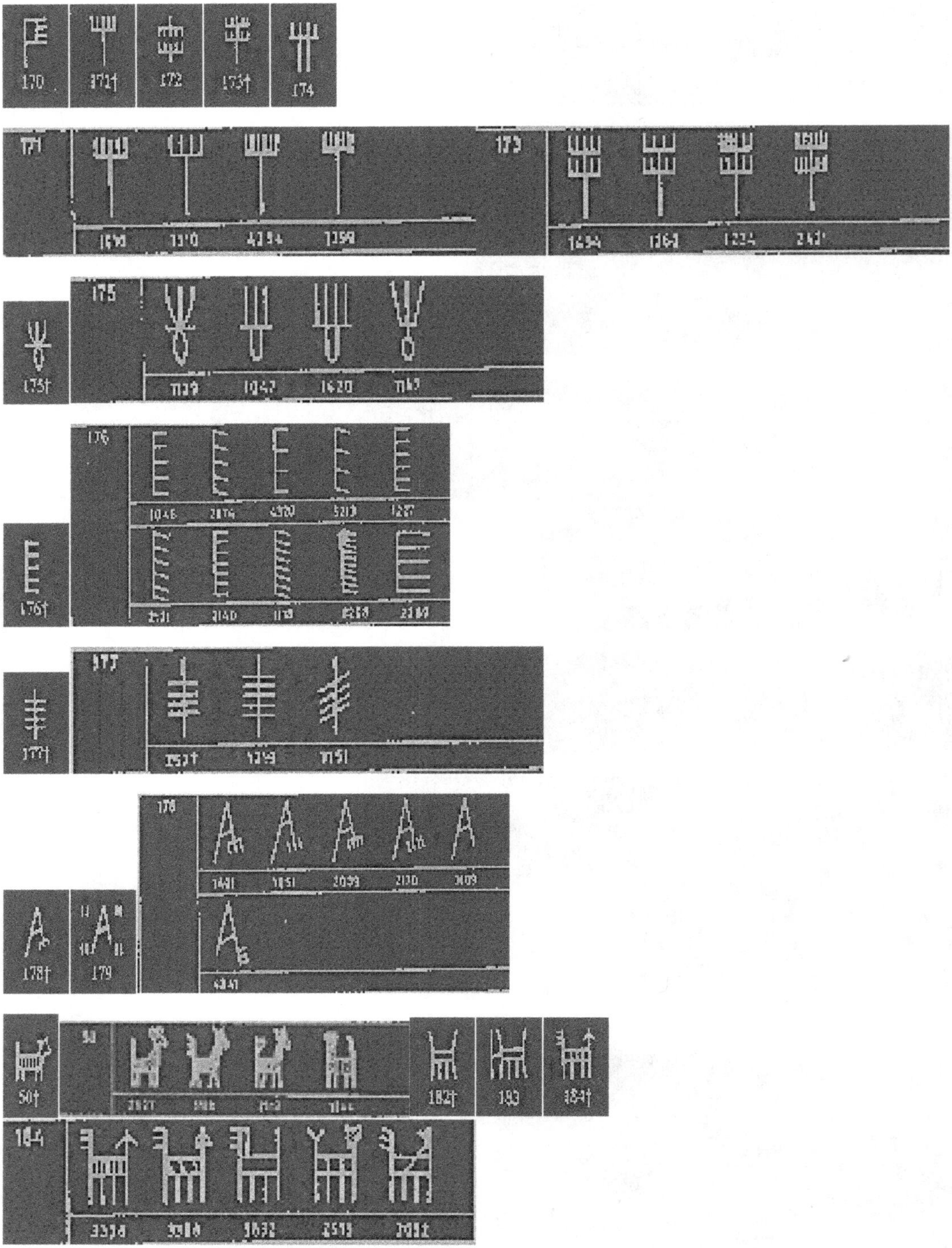
170
171†
172
173†
174
171
173
175
175†
176
176†
177
177†
178
178†
179
50†
182†
183
184†
184

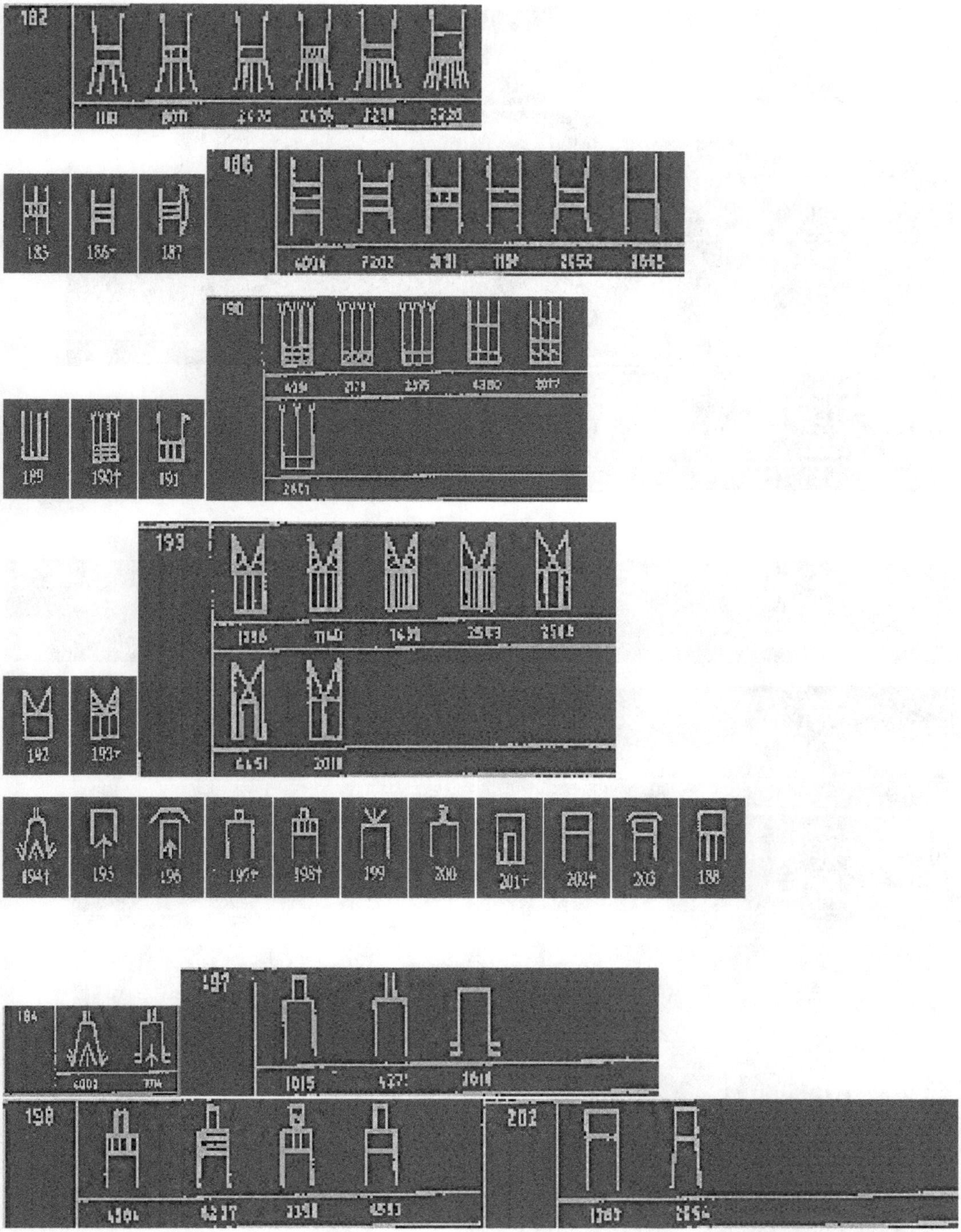

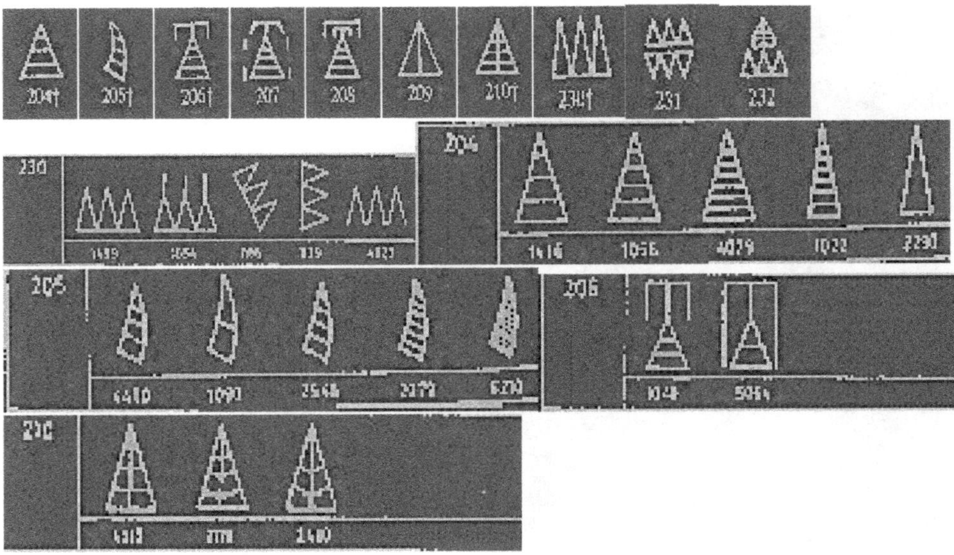
204†
205†
206†
207
208
209
210†
230†
231
232
230
204
205
206
210

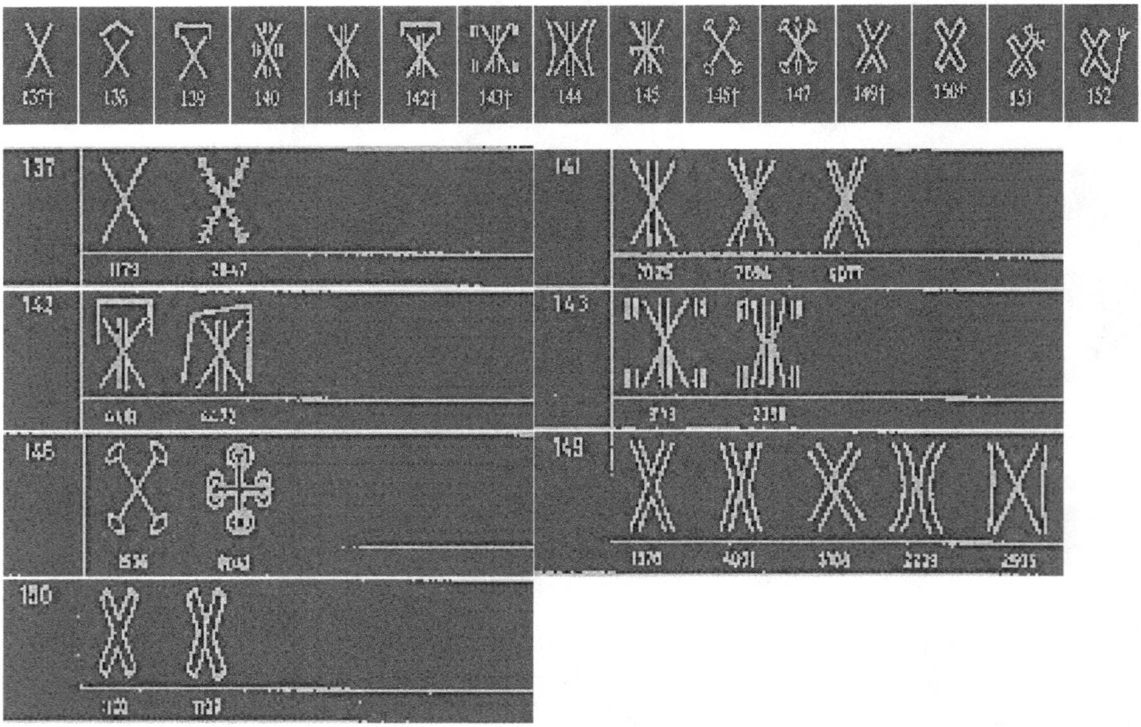
137†
138
139
140
141†
142†
143†
144
145
146†
147
149†
150†
151
152
137
141
142
143
146
149
150

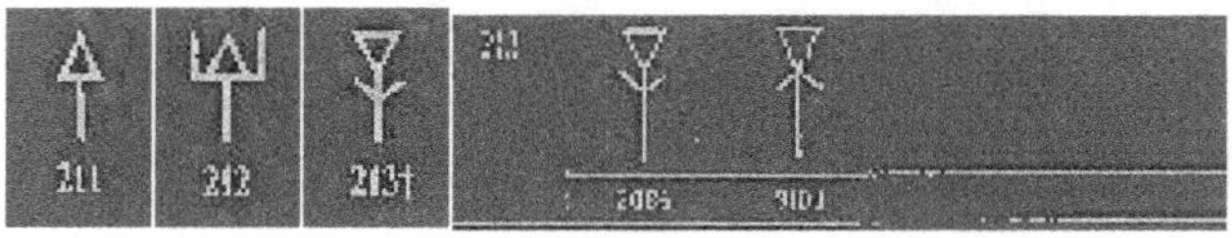
211
212
213†
213

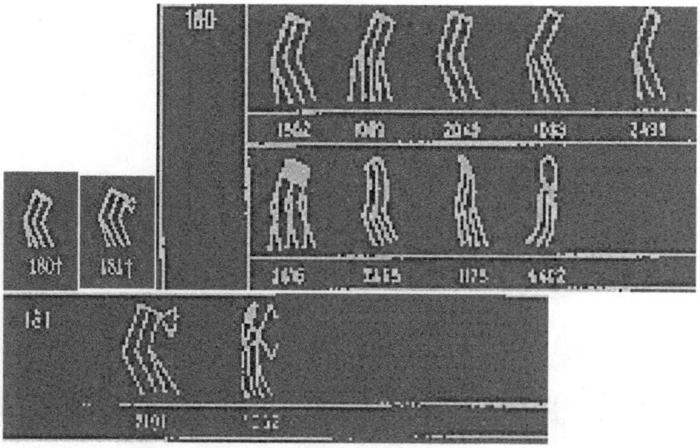
180†
181†
180
181

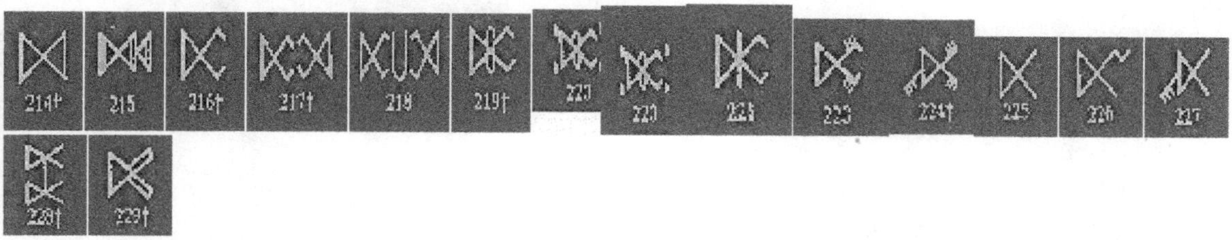
214†
215
216†
217†
218
219†
220
221
222
223
224†
225
226
227
228†
229†

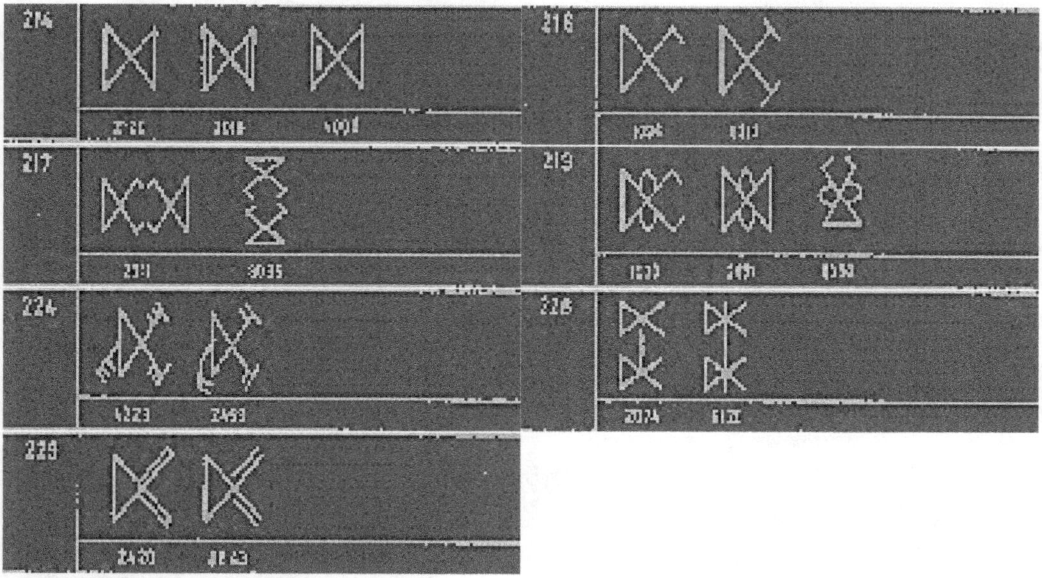
214
216
217
219
224
228
229

233
234
235

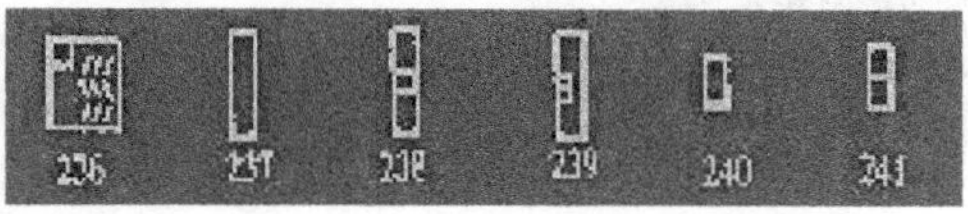
236
237
238
239
240
241

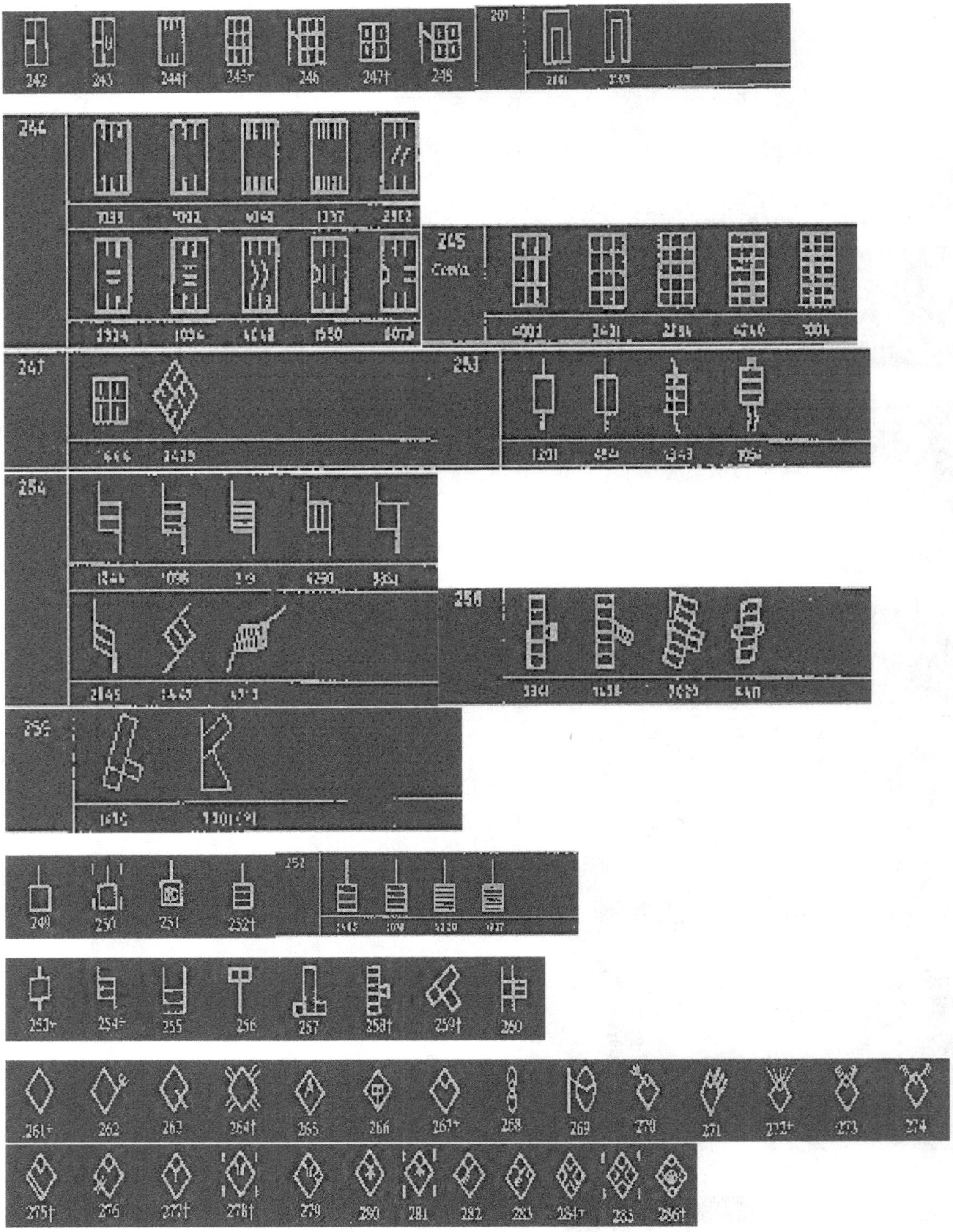
242 243 244† 246 247† 248
244
245
Ceni
247†
253
254
258
259
252
249 250 251 252†
255 256 257 258† 259† 260
262 263 264† 265 266 268 269 270 271 273 274
275† 276 277† 278† 279 280 281 282 283 285 286†

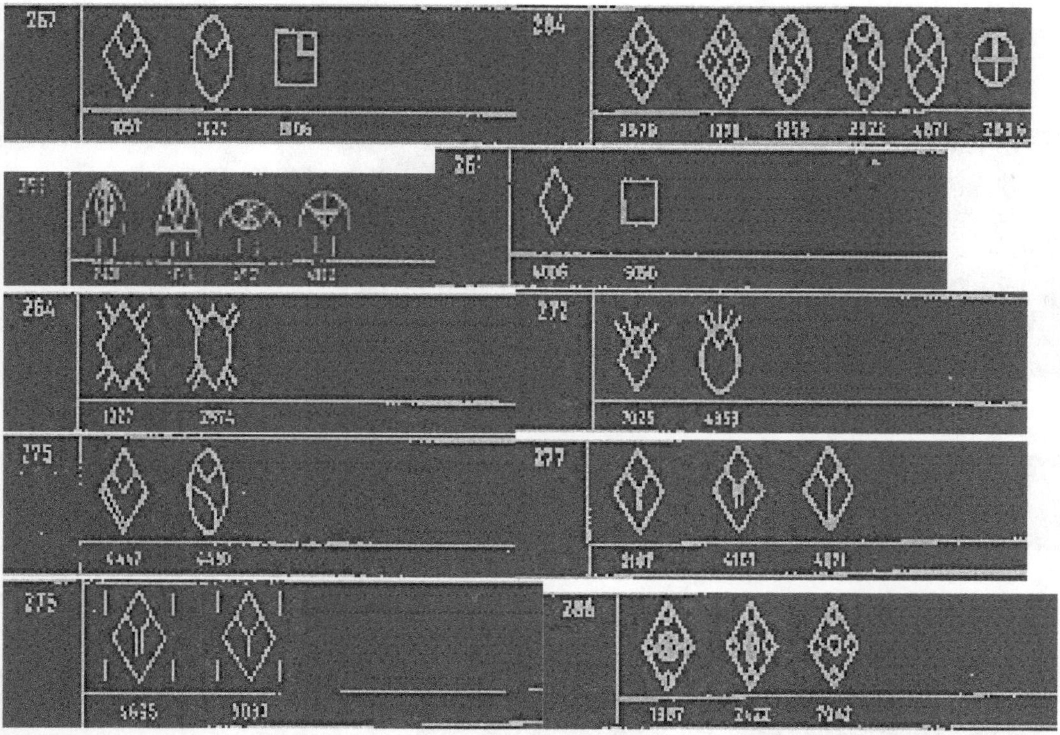

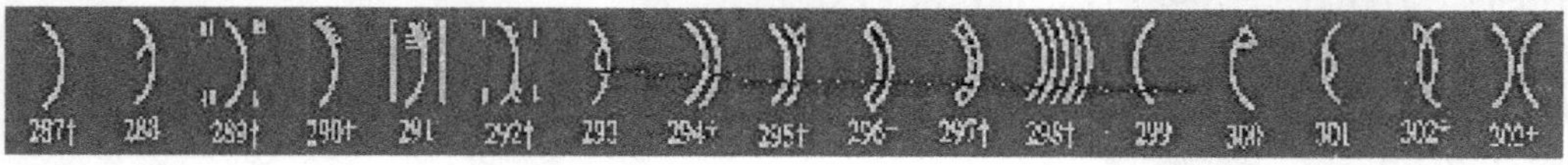

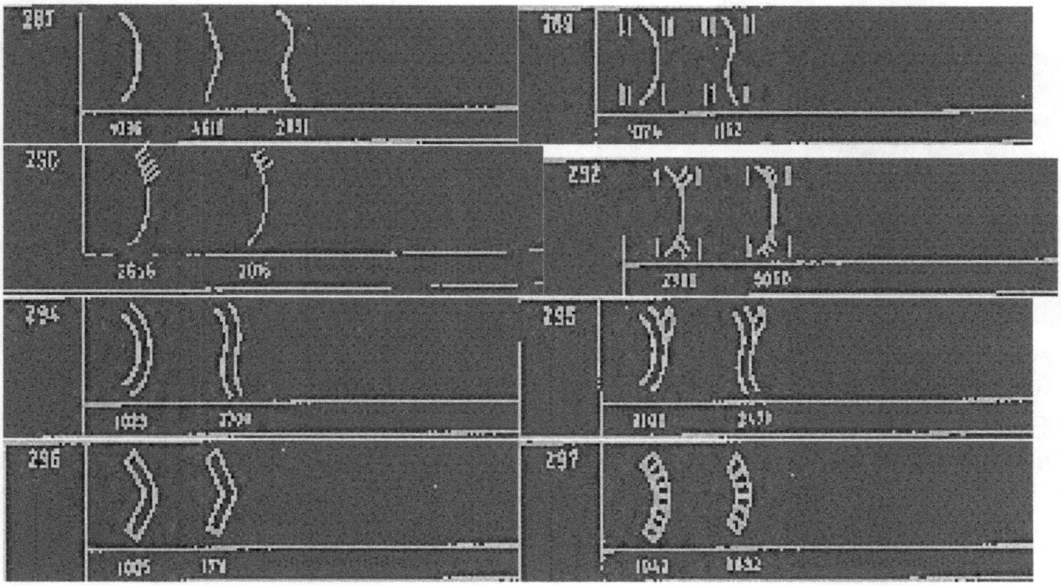

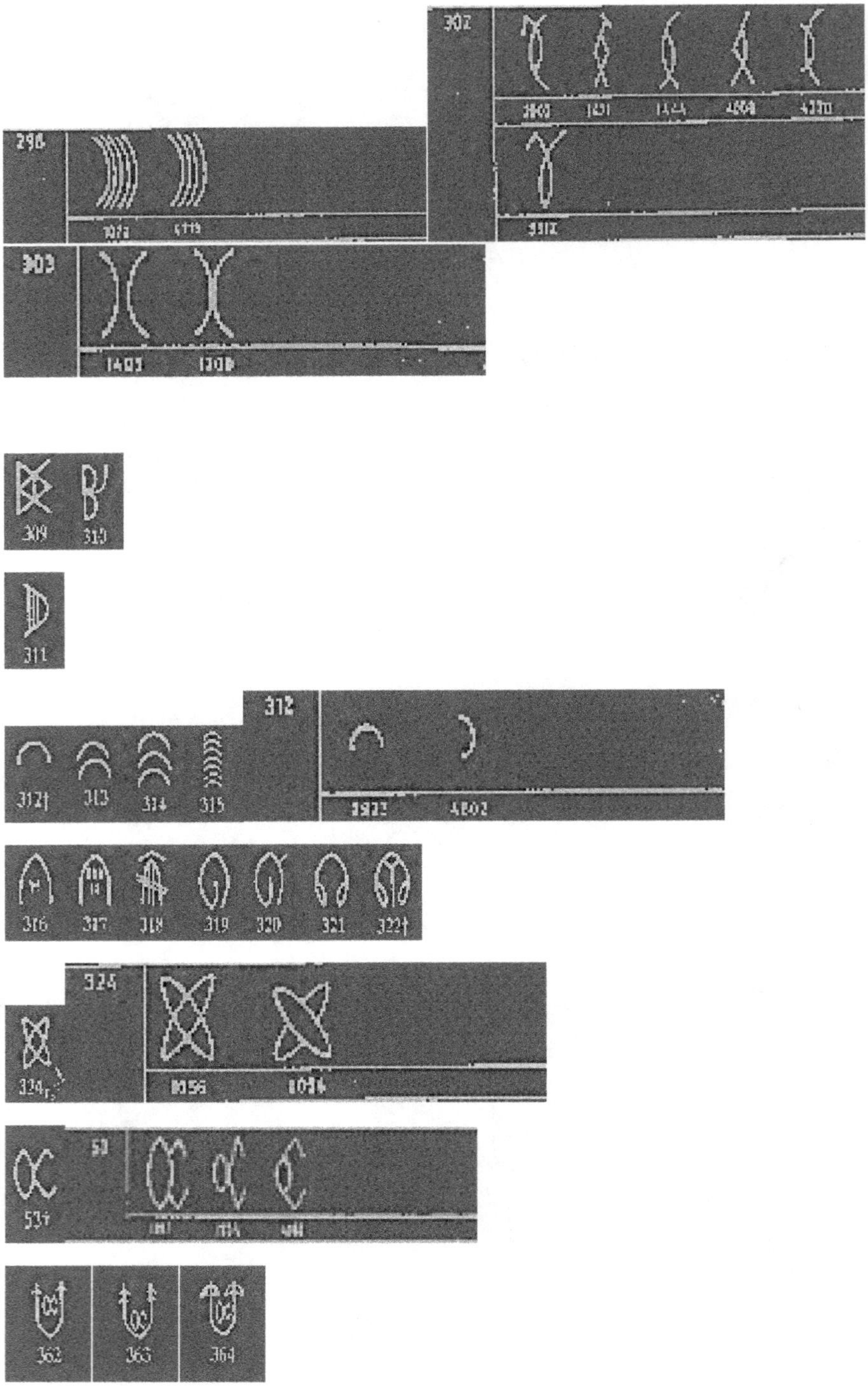
298
302
303
309
310
311
312
313
314
315
316
317
318
319
320
321
324
53
362
363
364

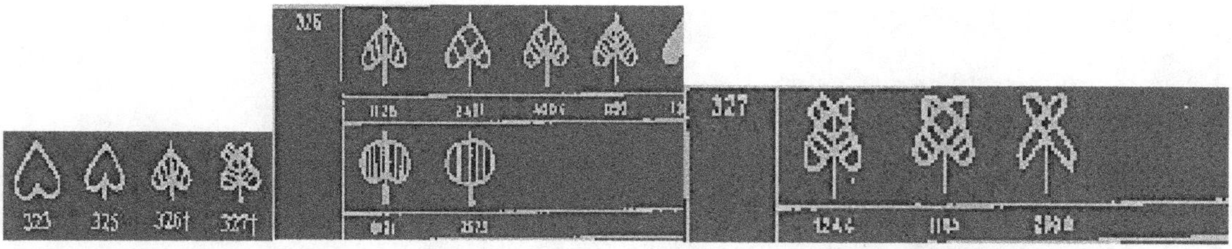
323 325 326† 327†
326
327

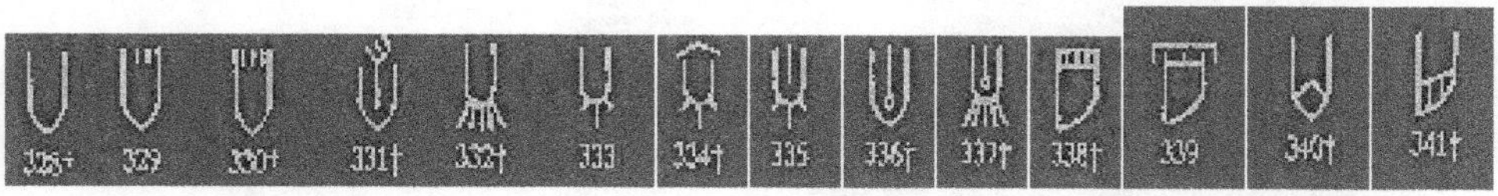
328† 329 330† 331† 332† 333 334† 335 336† 337† 338† 339 340† 341†

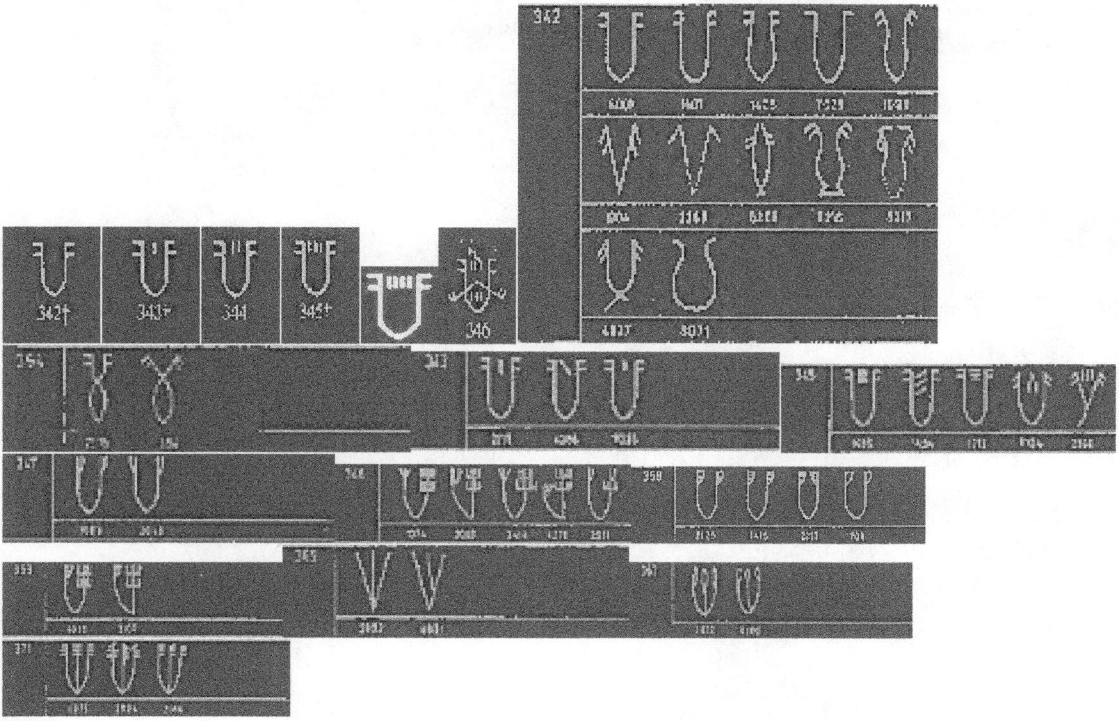
342
342† 343† 344 345† 346

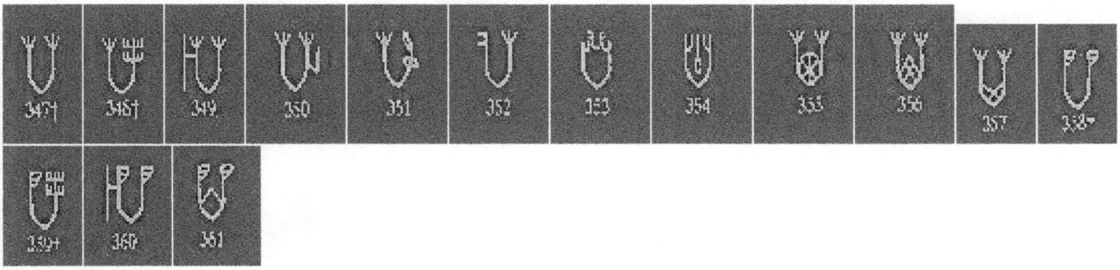
347† 348† 349 350 351 352 353 354 355 356 357 358†
359† 360 361

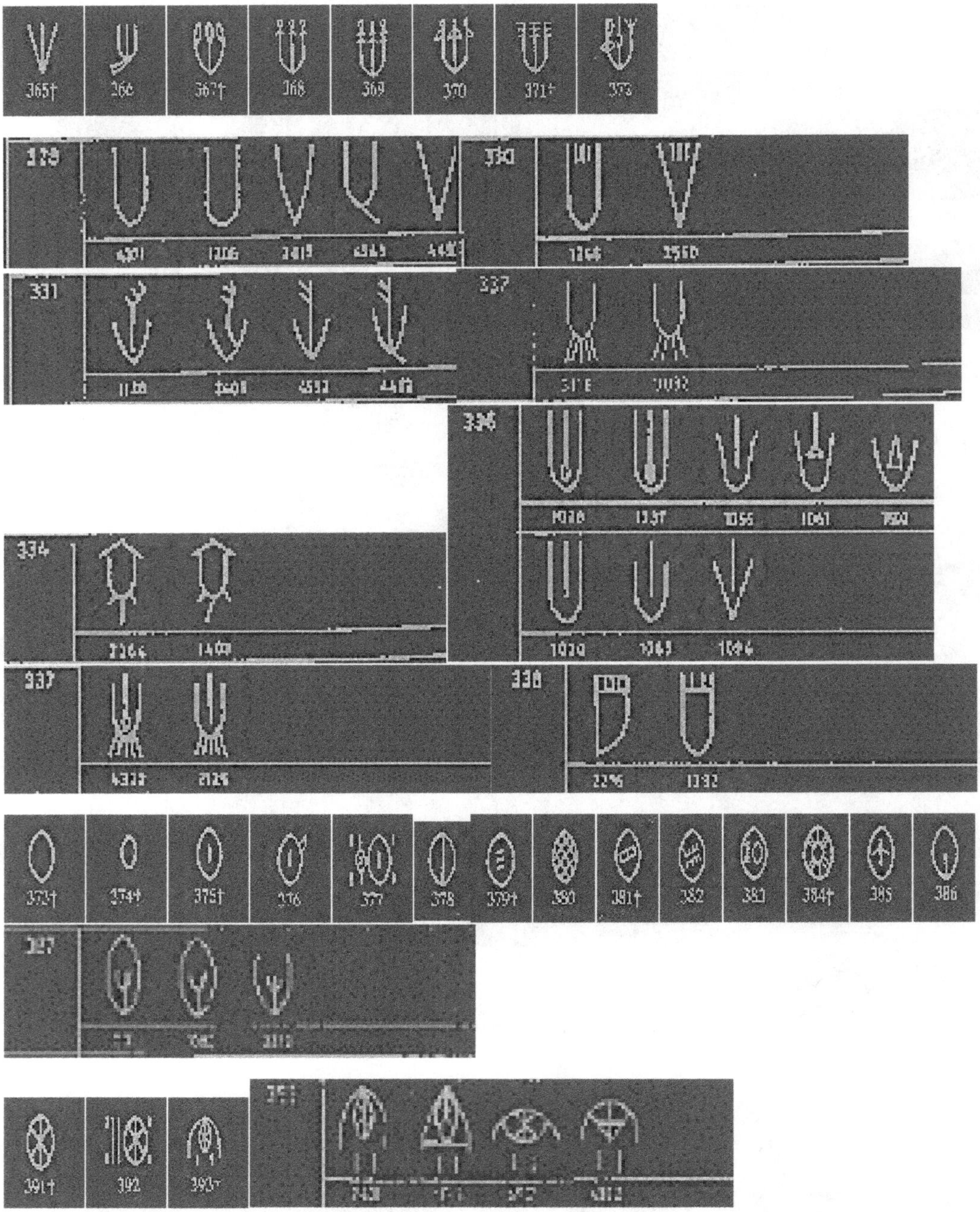

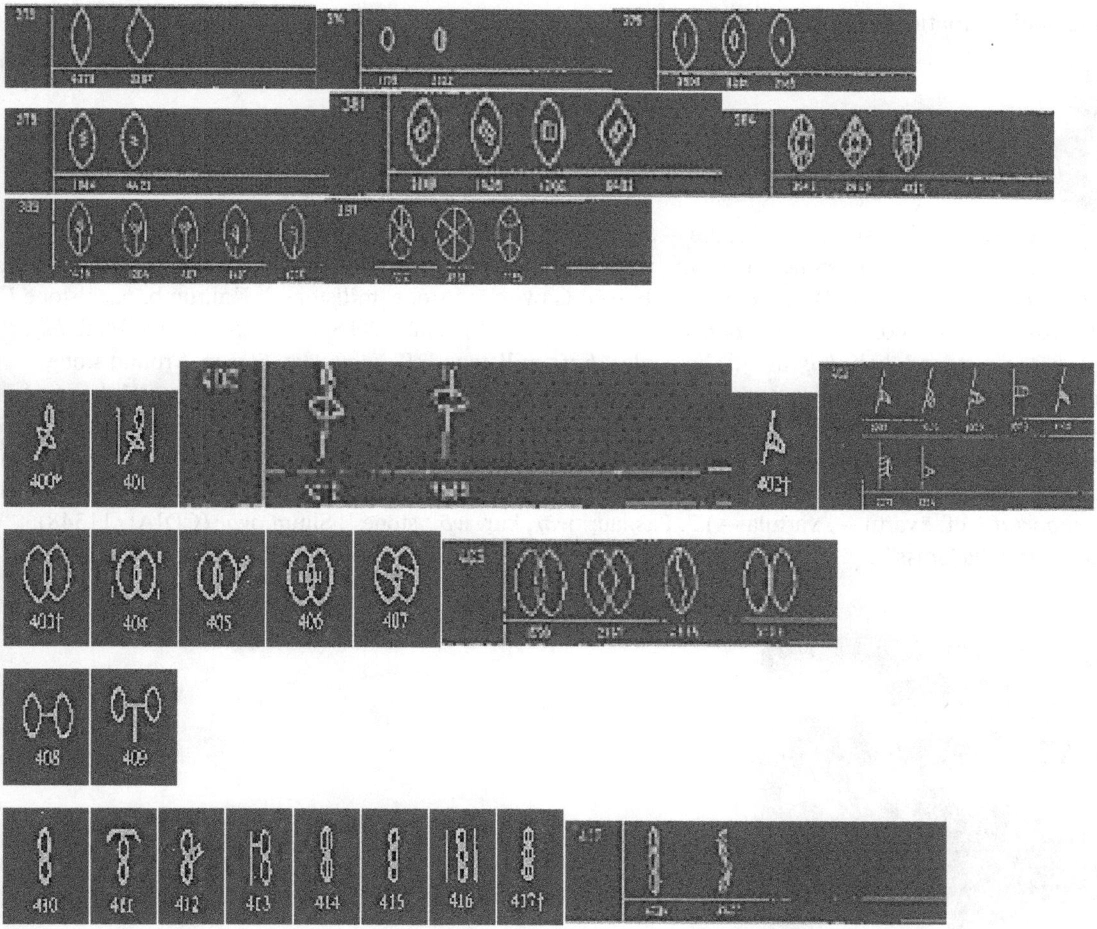
401
404
405
406
407
408
409
410
412
413
414
415
416

***varta3** ' round stone '. 2. ***vārta -- .** [Cf. Kurd. *bard* ' stone '. -- √vr̥t1]
1. Gy. eur. *bar*, SEeur. *baṛ* ' stone ', pal. *wăṭ*, *wŭṭ* ' stone, cliff '; Ḍ. *boṭ* m. ' stone ', Ash. Wg. *wāṭ*, Kt. *woṭ*, Dm. *bɔ̄̆ṭ*, Tir. *baṭ*, Niṅg. *bōṭ*, Woṭ. *baṭ* m., Gmb. *wāṭ*; Gaw. *wāṭ* ' stone, millstone '; Kal.rumb. *bat* ' stone ' (*bad -- váṣ* ' hail '), Kho. *bort*, Bshk. *baṭ*, Tor. *bāṭ*, Mai. (Barth) "*bhāt*" NTS xviii 125, Sv. *bāṭ*, Phal. *bā̆ṭ*; Sh.gil. *băṭ* m. ' stone ', koh. *băṭṭ* m., jij. *baṭ*, pales. *baṭ* ' millstone '; K. *waṭh*, dat. *°ṭas* m. ' round stone ', *vüṭü* f. ' small do. '; L. *vaṭṭā* m. ' stone ', khet. *vaṭ* ' rock '; P. *baṭṭ* m. ' a partic. weight ',*vaṭṭā*, *ba°* m. ' stone ', *vaṭṭī* f. ' pebble '; WPah.bhal. *baṭṭ* m. ' small round stone '; Or. *bāṭi* ' stone '; Bi. *baṭṭā* ' stone roller for spices, grindstone '. -- With unexpl. -- *ṭṭh* -- : Sh.gur. *baṭṭh* m. ' stone ', gil. *baṭhā´* m. ' avalanche of stones ', *baṭhúi* f. ' pebble ' (suggesting also an orig. **vartuka* -- which Morgenstierne sees in Kho. place -- name*bortuili*, cf. *vartu -- , vartula --).2. Paš.lauṛ. *wāṛ*, kuṛ. *wō* ' stone ', Shum. *wāṛ*.(CDIAL 11348).
Rebus: vartaloha 'brass''

Mohenjo-daro. m1457 Copper plate with 'twist' hieroglyph. Mohejodaro, tablet in bas relief (M-478) The first hieroglyph-multiplex on the left (twisted rope):

m478a tablet

கோலம்[1] kōlam, *n.* [T. *kōlamu*, K. *kōla*, M. *kōlam*.] 1. Beauty, gracefulness, hand- someness; அழகு. கோலத் தனிக்கொம்பர் (திருக் கோ. 45). 2. Colour; நிறம். கார்க்கோல மேனி யானை (கம்பரா. கும்பக. 154). 3. Form, shape, external or general appearance; உருவம். மானுடக் கோலம். 4. Nature; தன்மை. 5. Costume; appropriate dress; attire, as worn by actors; trappings; equipment; habiliment; வேடம். உள்வரிக் கோலத்து (சிலப். 5, 216). 6. Ornament, as jewelry; ஆபரணம். குறங்கிணை திரண்டன கோலம் பொறாஅ (சிலப். 30, 18). 7. Adornment, decoration, embellishment; அலங்காரம். புறஞ்சுவர் கோலஞ்செய்து (திவ். திருமாலை, 6). 8. Ornamental figures drawn on floor, wall or sacrificial pots with rice-flour, white stone-powder, etc.; மா,

கற்பொடி முதலியவற்றாலிடுங் கோலம். தரை மெழுகிக் கோலமிட்டு (குமர. மீனாட். குறம். 25).

The hieroglyphs on m478a tablet are read rebus:

kuTi 'tree'Rebus: kuThi 'smelter'

bhaTa 'worshipper' Rebus: bhaTa 'furnace' baTa 'iron' (Gujarati) This hieroglyph is a phonetic deterinant of the 'rimless pot': baṭa = rimless pot (Kannada) Rebus: baṭa = a kind of iron (Gujarati) bhaṭa 'a furnace'. Hence, the hieroglyph-multiplex of an adorant with rimless pot signifies: 'iron furnace' bhaTa.

bAraNe ' an offering of food to a demon' (Tulu) Rebus: baran, bharat (5 copper, 4 zinc and 1 tin) (Punjabi. Bengali) The narrative of a worshipper offering to a tree is thus interpretable as a smelting of three minerals: copper, zinc and tin.

Numeral four: gaNDa 'four' Rebus: kand 'fire-altar'; Four 'ones': *koḍa* 'one' (Santali) Rebus: *koḍ* 'artisan's workshop'. Thus, the pair of 'four linear strokes PLUS rimless pot' signifies: 'fire-altar (in) artisan's wrkshop'.

Circumscript of two linear strokes for 'body' hieroglyph: dula 'pair' Rebus: dul 'cast metal' *koḍa* 'one'(Santali) Rebus: *koḍ* 'artisan's workshop'. Thus, the circumscript signifies 'cast metal workshop'. meD 'body' Rebus: meD 'iron'.

khareḍo = a currycomb (G.) Rebus: kharādī 'turner' (Gujarati)

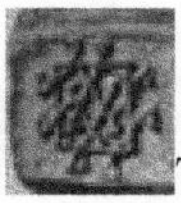The hieroglyph may be a variant of a twisted rope.

dhāu 'rope' rebus: dhāu 'metal' PLUS मेढा [mēḍhā] 'a curl or snarl; twist in thread' rebus: mẽṛhẽt, meḍ 'iron'. Thus, metallic ore.

kōlam, *n.* [T. *kōlamu*, K. *kōla*, M. *kōlam*.] 'ornamental figure' Rebus: *kol* 'working in iron'

The inscription on m478 thus signifies, reading hieroglyphs from r.:

Tree: kuThi 'smelter'

Worshipper: bhaTa 'furnace'

Four linear strokes + rimless pot: kanda baTa 'fire-altar for iron'

Circumscript two linear strokes + body: meD koDa 'metal workshop'Currycomb:khareḍo 'currycomb' rebus: kharādī 'turner'; dhāu 'metal' PLUS mẽṛhẽt, meḍ 'iron'; kol 'working in iron'. Together, the two hieroglyphs

signify metalworker, ironsmith turner.

m0478b tablet

erga = act of clearing jungle (Kui) [Note image showing two men carrying

uprooted trees] thwarted by a person in the middle with outstretched hands

Aḍaru twig; aḍiri small and thin branch of a tree; aḍari small branches (Ka.); aḍaru twig (Tu.)(DEDR 67). Aḍar = splinter (Santali); rebus: aduru = native metal (Ka.) Vikalpa: kūtī = bunch of twigs (Skt.) Rebus: kuṭhi = furnace (Santali) *ḍhaṁkhara* — m.n. 'branch without leaves or fruit' (Prakrit) (CDIAL 5524)

Hieroglyph: *era* female, applied to women only, and generally as a mark of respect, wife; hopon era a daughter; era hopon a man's family; manjhi era the village chief's wife; gosae era a female Santal deity; bud.hi era an old woman; era uru wife and children; nabi era a prophetess; diku era a Hindu woman (Santali)

•Rebus: er-r-a = red; eraka = copper (Ka.) erka = ekke (Tbh. of arka) aka (Tbh. of arka) copper (metal); crystal (Ka.lex.) erako molten cast (Tu.lex.) agasa_le, agasa_li, agasa_lava_d.u = a goldsmith (Te.lex.)

kuTi 'tree' Rebus: kuṭhi = (smelter) furnace (Santali)

heraka = spy (Skt.); eraka, hero = a messenger; a spy (Gujarati); er to look at or for (Pkt.); er uk- to play 'peeping tom' (Ko.) Rebus: erka = ekke (Tbh. of arka) aka (Tbh. of arka) copper (metal); crystal (Ka.lex.) cf. eruvai = copper (Ta.lex.) eraka, er-aka = any metal infusion (Ka.Tu.) eraka 'copper' (Kannada)

kōṭu branch of tree, Rebus: खोट [khōṭa] f A mass of metal (unwrought or of old metal melted down); an ingot or wedge.

Hieroglyph: Looking back: *krammara* 'look back' (Telugu) *kamar* 'smith, artisan' (Santali)

kola 'tiger, jackal' (Kon.); rebus: *kol* working in iron, blacksmith, 'alloy of five metals, panchaloha' (Tamil) kol 'furnace, forge' (Kuwi) kolami 'smithy' (Telugu)

^ Inverted V, m478 (lid above rim of narrow-necked jar) The rimmed jar next to the tiger with turned head has a lid. Lid 'ad.aren'; rebus: aduru 'native metal' karnika 'rim of jar' Rebus: karni 'supercargo' (Marathi) Thus, together, the jar with lid composite hieroglyhph denotes 'native metal supercargo'. karn.aka = handle of a vessel; ka_n.a_, kanna_ = rim, edge; kan.t.u = rim of a vessel; kan.t.ud.iyo = a small earthen vessel; kan.d.a kanka = rim of a water-pot; kan:kha, kankha = rim of a vessel

Comparable hieroglyph of kneeling adorant with outstretched hands occurs on a Mohenjo-daro seal m1186, m478A tablet and on Harappa tablet h177B:

Rebus readings: *maṇḍa* ' some sort of framework (?) '. [In *nau - maṇḍḗ* n. du. ' the two sets of poles rising from the thwarts or the two bamboo covers of a boat (?) ' ŚBr. Rebus: M. *mā̃ḍ* m. ' array of instruments &c. '; Si. *maḍa -- ya* ' adornment, ornament '. (CDIAL 9736) *kamaḍha* 'penance' (Pkt.)Rebus: *kampaṭṭam* 'mint' (Tamil) *battuḍu*. n. A worshipper (Telugu) Rebus: *pattar* merchants (Tamil), perh. Vartaka (Skt.)

Mohenjo-daro seal. m0301 baradh 'bull' (Gujarati); baddi (Nahali)
Sign 48: baraḍo = spine, the backbone, back (Gujarati)
Glyph: baraḍo = spine; backbone; the back; baraḍo thābaḍavo = lit. to strike on the backbone or back; hence, to encourage; baraḍo bhāre thato = lit. to have a painful backbone, i.e. to do something which will call for a severe beating (G.lex.) man.uk.o a single vertebra of the back (G.)

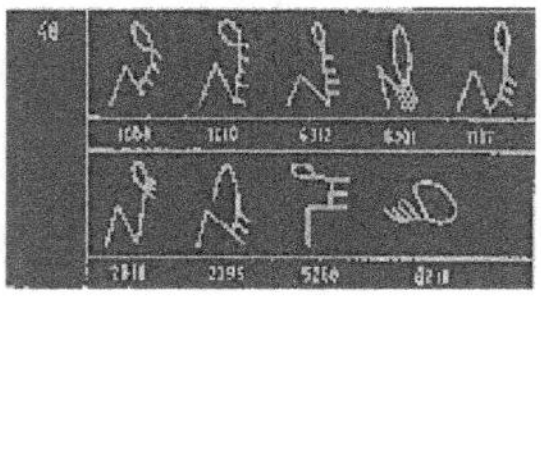

Rebus: baraḍo (vardhaki). Rebus: baraḍo, vardhaka 'carpenter, mason' (Santali. Sanskrit) *baḍhi* 'a caste who work both in iron and wood' (Santali)barduga = a man of acquirements, a proficient man (Ka.) Rebus: bharatiyo = a caster of metals, a brazier; bharatar, bharatal, bharatal. = moulded; an article made in a mould (G.) bharata = casting metals in moulds; bharavum = to fill in; to put in; to pour into (G.lex.) bhart = a mixed metal of copper and lead; bhartīyā = a barzier, worker in metal; bhaṭ, bhrāṣṭra = oven, furnace (Skt.)

maruḍiyo = one who makes and sells wristlets, and puts wristlets on the wrists of women (G.lex.) maraḍa = twisting; a twist; a turn; marad.avum = to twist, to turn; maraḍāvum = to bend; maroḍa = a twist, a turn; writhing, a bend; maroḍavum = to writhe, to twist, to contort; to bend (Gujarati)

bhāraṇ = to bring out from a kiln (G.) bāraṇiyo = one whose profession it is to sift ashes or dust in a goldsmith's workshop (G.lex.) baran, bharat (5 copper, 4 zinc and 1 tin)(P.B.) In the Punjab, bharata = a factitious metal compounded of copper, pewter, tin (M.) In Bengal, an alloy called bharan or toul was created by adding some brass or zinc into pure bronze. bharata = casting metals in moulds; bharavum = to fill in; to put in; to pour into (G.lex.) Bengali. ভরন [bharana] n an inferior metal obtained from an alloy of coper, zinc and tin.

bharaḍo a devotee of Śiva; a man of the bharaḍā caste in the brāhman.as (G.) baraṛ = name of a caste of jat- around Bhaṭiṇḍa; baraṛaṇḍā melā = a special fair held in spring (Punjabi) bharāḍ = a religious service or entertainment performed by a bharāḍī; consisting of singing the praises of some idol or god with playing on the ḍaur (drum) and dancing; an order of aṭharā akhāḍe = 18 gosāyī group; bharāḍ and bhāratī are two of the 18 orders of gosāyī (M.lex.) bārṇe, bāraṇe = an offering of food to a demon; a meal after fasting, a breakfast (Tu.lex.) barada, barda, birada = a vow (Gujarati) vrata id. (Sanskrit) Rebus: bhāraṇ = to bring out from a kiln (G.) bāraṇiyo = one whose profession it is to sift ashes or dust in a goldsmith's workshop (G.lex.) baran, bharat (5 copper, 4 zinc and 1 tin)(P.B.) In the Punjab, bharata = a factitious metal compounded of copper, pewter, tin (M.) In Bengal, an alloy called bharan or toul was created by adding some brass or zinc into pure bronze. bharata = casting metals in moulds; bharavum = to fill in; to put in; to pour into (G.lex.) Bengali. ভরন [bharana] n an inferior metal obtained from an alloy of coper, zinc and tin.

m1186 seal. *kaula*— m. ‘worshipper of Śakti according to left—hand ritual’, *khōla*—3 ‘lame’; Khot. *kūra*— ‘crooked’ BSOS ix 72 and poss. Sk. *kōra*— m. ‘movable joint’ Suśr.] Ash. *kṓlƏ* ‘curved, crooked’; Dm. *kōla* ‘crooked’, Tir. *kṓolƏ*; Paš. *kōlā́* ‘curved, crooked’, Shum. *kolā́ṇṭa*; Kho. *koli* ‘crooked’,

(Lor.) also ‘lefthand, left’; Bshk. *kōl* ‘crooked’; Phal. *kūulo*; Sh. *kōl̥u* ‘curved, crooked’ (CDIAL 3533).

Rebus: kol ‘pancaloha’ (Tamil)

bhaTa 'worshipper' Rebus: bhaTa 'furnace' baTa 'iron' (Gujarati)

saman 'make an offering (Santali) samanon 'gold' (Santali)

minDAl 'markhor' (Torwali) meDho 'ram' (Gujarati)(CDIAL 10120) Rebus: me~Rhet, meD 'iron' (Mu.Ho.Santali)

heraka 'spy' (Samskrtam) Rebus:eraka 'molten metal, copper'

maNDa 'branch, twig' (Telugu) Rebus: maNDA 'warehouse, workshop' (Konkani)\karibha, jata kola Rebus: karba, ib, jasta, 'iron, zinc, metal (alloy of five metals)

maNDi 'kneeling position' Rebus: mADa 'shrine; mandil 'temple' (Santali)

dhatu 'scarf' Rebus: dhatu 'mineral ore' (Santali)

The rice plant adorning the curved horn of the person (woman?) with the pig-tail is kolmo; read rebus, kolme ‘smithy’. Smithy of what? Kol ‘pancaloha’. The curving horn is: kod.u = horn; rebus: kod. artisan’s workshop (Kuwi)

The long curving horns may also connote a ram on h177B tablet:

h177B

4316 Pict-115: From R.—a person standing under an ornamental arch; a kneeling adorant; a ram with long curving horns.

The ram read rebus: me~d. ‘iron’; glyph: me_n.d.ha ram; min.d.a_l markhor (Tor.); meh ram (H.); mei wild goat (WPah.) me~r.hwa_ a bullock with curved horns like a ram’s (Bi.) me~r.a_, me~d.a_ ram with curling horns (H.)

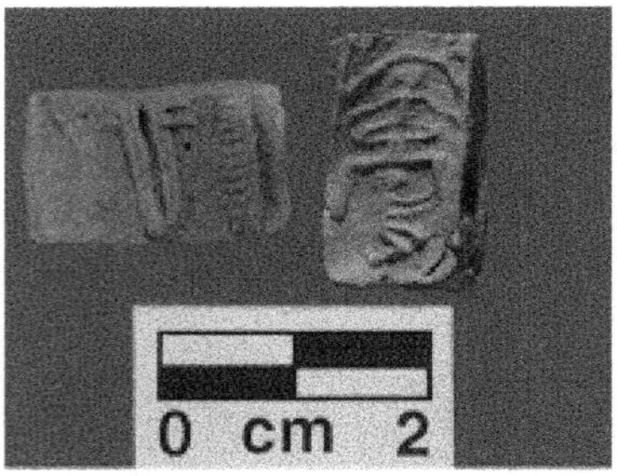

Ganweriwala tablet. Ganeriwala or Ganweriwala (Urdu: گنے ریوالا Punjabi: گنیریوالا) is a Sarasvati-Sindhu civilization site in Cholistan, Punjab, Pakistan.

Glyphs on a broken molded tablet, Ganweriwala. The reverse includes the 'rim-of-jar' glyph in a 3-glyph text. Observe shows a person seated on a stool and a kneeling adorant below.

Hieroglyph: kamadha 'penance' Rebus: kammata 'coiner, mint'.

Reading rebus three glyphs of text on Ganweriwala tablet: brass-worker, scribe, turner:

1. kuṭila ‘bent’; rebus: kuṭila, katthīl = bronze (8 parts copper and 2 parts tin) [cf. āra-kūṭa, ‘brass’ (Skt.) (CDIAL 3230)

2. Glyph of 'rim of jar': kárṇaka m. ' projection on the side of a vessel, handle ' ŚBr. [kárṇa --]Pa. kaṇṇaka -- ' having ears or corners '; (CDIAL 2831) kaṇḍa kanka; Rebus: furnace account (scribe). kaṇḍ = fire-altar (Santali); kan = copper (Tamil) khanaka m. one who digs , digger , excavator Rebus: karanikamu. Clerkship: the office of a Karanam or clerk. (Telugu) káraṇa n. ' act, deed ' RV. [√kṛ1] Pa. karaṇa -- n. 'doing'; NiDoc. karana, kaṁraṁna 'work'; Pk. karaṇa -- n. 'instrument'(CDIAL 2790)

3. khareḍo = a currycomb (G.) Rebus: kharādī ' turner' (G.)

Hieroglyph: मेढा [mēḍhā] A twist or tangle arising in thread or cord, a curl or snarl (Marathi). Rebus: meḍ 'iron, copper' (Munda. Slavic) mẽṛhẽt, meD 'iron' (Mu.Ho.Santali)

med' 'copper' (Slovak)

Santali glosses:

Mẽṛhẽt. Iron.
Mẽṛhẽt icena. The iron is rusty.
Ispat mẽṛhẽt. Steel.
Dul mẽṛhẽt. Cast iron.
Mẽṛhẽt khanḍa. Iron implements.

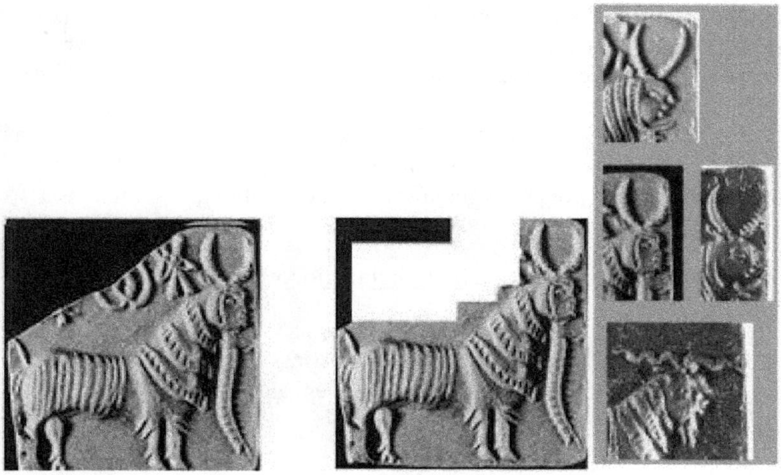

m1186 (DK6847) [Pleiades, scarfed, framework, *ficus religiosa* , scarfed person, worshipper, twigs (on head), horn, markhor, human face ligatured to markhor, stool, ladle, frame of a building]

Mohenjo-daro seal. Ligaturing components: horns of zebu, human face, tail-hood of serpent, elephant tusk, scarves on neck, bovine forelegs, feline hind legs.

paṭa 'hood of snake'. *Rebus: padm* 'tempered, sharpness (metal)'. nāga 'serpent' Rebus: nāga 'lead (alloy)'

mũh 'face' Rebus: *mũhe* 'ingot'. *khũṭ* 'zebu'.khũṭ 'community, guild' (Munda)

ibha 'elephant' Rebus: ib 'iron'. Ibbo 'merchant' (Gujarati).

ḍhangar 'bull' Rebus: *dhangar* 'blacksmith' (Maithili) *ḍangar* 'blacksmith' (Hindi)

kol 'tiger' Rebus: kol 'working in iron'.

dhaṭu m. (also *dhaṭhu*) m. 'scarf' (WPah.) Rebus: *dhatu* 'mineral (ore)'

Rebus reading of the 'face' glyph: mũhe 'face' (Santali) mũh opening or hole (in a stove for stoking (Bi.); ingot (Santali) mũh metal ingot (Santali) mũhã = the quantity of iron produced at one time in a native smelting furnace of the Kolhes; iron produced by the Kolhes and formed like a four-cornered piece a little pointed at each end; mūhā mẽṛhẽt = iron smelted by the Kolhes and formed into an equilateral lump a little pointed at each of four ends; kolhe tehen mẽṛhẽt ko mūhā akata = the Kolhes have to-day produced pig iron (Santali.lex.) kaula mengro 'blacksmith' (Gypsy) mleccha-mukha (Skt.) = milakkhu 'copper' (Pali) The Sanskrit loss mleccha-mukha should literally mean: copper-ingot absorbing the Santali gloss, mũh, as a suffix

The composite animal (bovid) is re-configured by Huntington. http://huntington.wmc.ohio-state.edu/public/index.cfm

In a scintillating study of the orthography of Indus Script, Dennys Frenez & Massimo Vidale provide an insight comparing two hieroglyph components on Indus Script corpora: 1. elephant trunk and 2. hand of a person seated in penance

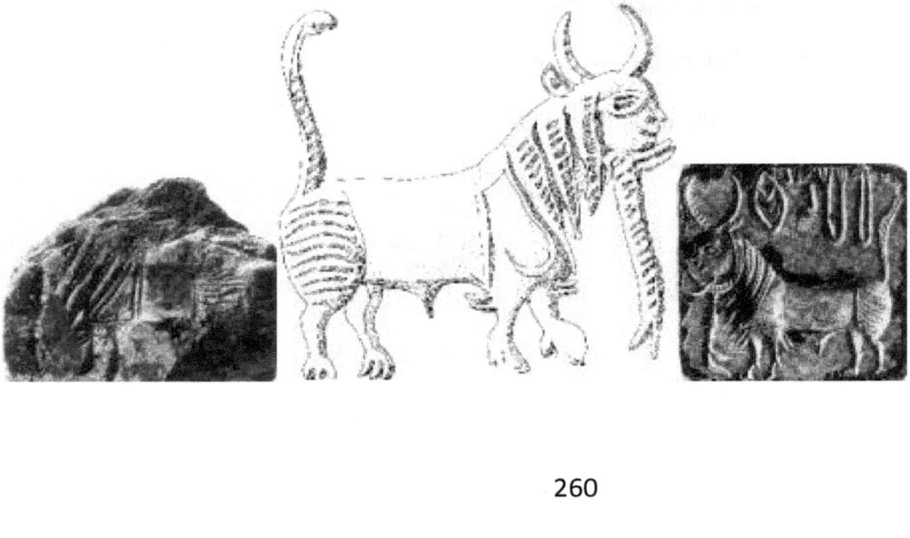

m1177, m1175, m300

Metalwork provides a framework for defined meaning of words used in the vernacular and continued use of such words in writing systems using what Frenez and Vidale call 'symbolic hypertexts' as on Indus Script provide the evidence for Indus Script decipherment of Indus Script Corpora as *catalogus catalogorum* of metalwork. (Dennys Frenez & Massimo Vidale, 2012,Harappa Chimaeras as 'Symbolic Hypertexts'. Some Thoughts on Plato, Chimaera and the Indus Civilization in: *South Asian Studies* Volume 28, Issue 2, pp. 107-130).

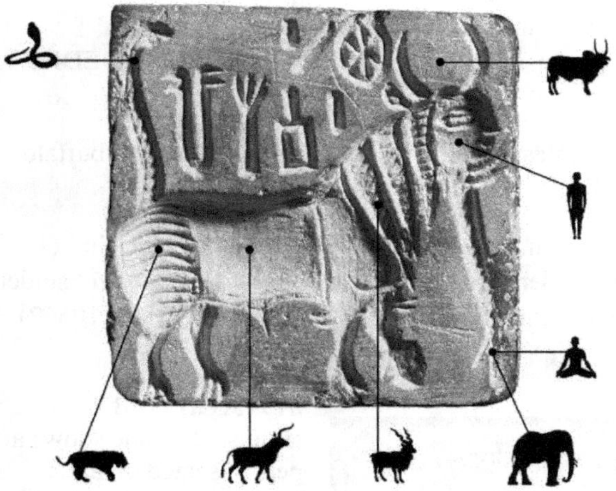

Meluhha (Prakrtam) glosses which decipher the hieroglyph components are consistent with this insight of Frenez and Vidale comparing the snout of the elephant's trunk with the hands of the person seated in penance: karabha 'trunk of elephant' (Pali) kara 'hand' (Rigveda). Gujarati gloss expands the semantics of 'hand' to include *karā̃* 'wristlets, bangles'.

It is remarkable that samples of orthography on seated persons in penance on Indus seals, the hands are decorated with wristlets and bangles. Obviously, the artisan is conveying the gloss: *karā̃* 'wristlets, bangles' while signifying the hand: kara (Rigveda. Prakrtam. Pali)

Hieroglyph: karabha 'trunk of elephant' (Pali) 2803 karin m. ' elephant '. [See karabhá --]Pa. *karin* -- m., Pk. *kari* -- , °*iṇa* -- m., °*iṇī* -- , °*iṇiyā* -- f.; <-> Si. *kiriyā* ← Pa.(CDIAL 2803)

Hieroglyph: hand: karál ' doing, causing ' AV., m. ' hand ' RV. [√kr̥1]

Pa. Pk. *kara* -- m. ' hand '; S. *karu* m. ' arm '; Mth. *kar* m. ' hand ' (prob. ← Sk.); Si. *kara* ' hand, shoulder ', inscr. *karā* ' to ' < *karāya.* -- Deriv. S. *karāī* f. ' wrist '; G. *karā̃* n. pl. ' wristlets, bangles '.(CDIAL 2779)

Rebus: karba, ajirda karba 'iron' (Tulu) (Note: cognate of *ajirda* is *ayas* 'metal', aduru 'native metal').

The 'ram' glyph shows the animal with curved, long horns and sometimes also gets ligatured with a human face on some Indus script inscriptions. The human face is also read rebus in mleccha (meluhha): *mũhe* 'face' (Santali); rebus:*mũh* ingot (Santali); opening or hole (in a stove for stoking (Bi.)mũhā̃ = the quantity of iron produced at one time in a native smelting furnace of the Kolhes; iron produced by the Kolhes and formed like a four-cornered piece a little pointed at each end; mūhā mĕṛhĕt = iron smelted by the Kolhes and formed into an equilateral lump a little pointed at each of four ends; kolhe tehen mĕṛhĕt ko mūhā akata = the Kolhes have to-day produced pig iron (Santali.lex.) kaula mengro 'blacksmith' (Gypsy) mleccha-mukha (Skt.) = milakkhu 'copper' (Pali) The Sanskrit loss mleccha-mukha should literally mean: copper-ingot absorbing the Santali gloss, mu~h, as a suffix. See used in cmpds.

(Telugu): మ్లేచ్ఛముఖము mlēchha-mukhamu. n. Copper, రాగి. మ్లేచ్ఛము mlēchhamu. n. Cinnabar. ఇంగిలీకము.

Thus, a 'ram' glyph ligatured with 'human face' glyph reads: mũh meḍh 'ram face'; rebus: (metal) ingot merchant. It is notable that *meḍ, meḍho* has two rebus meanings: 1. iron (metal); 2. merchant.

Elephant, trunk of elephant: kar-ibha, ib; rebus: karba 'iron'; ib 'iron'.

Ka. bisu (becc-), besu, bese to unite firmly, solder; join, be united; bisu soldering; bisuge, besage, besavu, besike, besige, besuge id., state of being soldered or firmly united, close connexion, composition; beccu state of being soldered or united. *Tu.* besigè soldering gold or other metal. (DEDR 5468)

Hieroglyph: *rā̃go* 'buffalo': raṅku m. ' a species of deer ' Vās., °*uka* -- m. Śrīkaṇṭh.Ku. N. *rā̃go* ' buffalo bull '? (CDIAL 10559)

raṅga3 n. ' tin ' lex. [Cf. nāga -- 2, vaṅga -- 1]Pk. *raṁga* -- n. ' tin '; P. *rā̃g* f., *rā̃gā* m. ' pewter, tin ' (← H.); Ku. *rāṅ* ' tin, solder ', gng. *rā̃k*; N. *rāṅ, rāṅo* ' tin, solder ', A. B. *rāṅ*; Or. *rāṅga* ' tin ', *rāṅgā* ' solder, spelter ', Bi. Mth. *rā̃gā*, OAw. *rāṁga*; H. *rā̃g* f., *rā̃gā* m. ' tin, pewter '; Si. *raṅga* ' tin '.(CDIAL 10562)

h1973B h1974B Two tablets. One side shows a person seated on a tree branch, a tiger looking up, a crocodile on the top register and other animals in procession in the bottom register. kāru 'crocodile' (Telugu). Rebus: artisan (Marathi) Rebus: khar 'blacksmith' (Kashmiri) kola 'tiger' Rebus: kol 'working in iron'. Hieroglyph: heraka 'spy' Rebus: eraka 'copper'. khōṇḍa 'leafless tree' (Marathi). Rebus: *kõdār* 'turner' (Bengali) kuTi 'tree' rebus: kuThi 'smelter'. Hieroglyph: barad, balad, 'ox' Rebus: baran, bharat (5 copper, 4 zinc and 1 tin)(Punjabi.Bengali). भरत (p. 603) [bharata] *n* A factitious metal compounded of copper, pewter, tin &c.भरतखंड (p. 603) [bharatakhaṇḍa] *n* (S) भरतवर्ष *n* S A division of the globe,--that from the Himálaya range to the ocean, India.भरतशास्त्र (p. 603) [bharataśāstra] *n* S The shástra of the drama, the authoritative treatise upon dramatic composition and representation. 2 Used freely in the sense of The *laws* of the drama and of scenic exhibition.भरताचें भांडें (p. 603) [bharatācē mbhāṇḍēṃ] *n* A vessel made of the metal भरत. 2 See भरिताचें भांडें.भरती (p. 603) [bharatī] *a* Composed of the metal भरत. A hieroglyph to signify भरत (p. 603) [bharata] is: barad, balad 'ox'.

Looking back: krammara 'look back' Rebus: kamar 'smith, artisan'.

One side of a molded tablet m 492 Mohenjo-daro (DK 8120, NMI 151. National Museum, Delhi. A person places his foot on the horns of a buffalo while spearing it in front of a cobra hood.

kulā ''hooded serpent' Rebus: kol 'working in iron' kolle 'blacksmith' kolhe 'smelter' *kulā* ' winnowing fan, hood of a snake ' (Assamese)(CDIAL 3350)

Hieroglyph: kolsa = to kick the foot forward, the foot to come into contact with anything when walking or running; kolsa pasirkedan = I kicked it over (Santali.lex.)mēṛsa = v.a. toss, kick with the foot, hit with the tail (Santali)

kol 'furnace, forge' (Kuwi) kol 'alloy of five metals, pancaloha' (Ta.) •kolhe (iron-smelter; kolhuyo, jackal) kol, kollan-, kollar = blacksmith (Ta.lex.)•kol'to kill' (Ta.)•sal 'bos gaurus', bison;

rebus: sal 'workshop' (Santali)me~ṛhe~t iron; ispat m. = steel; dul m. = cast iron; kolhe m. iron manufactured by the Kolhes (Santali); meṛed (Mun.d.ari); meḍ (Ho.)(Santali.Bodding)

nAga 'serpent' Rebus: nAga 'lead'

Hieroglyph: rã̄go ' buffalo bull '

Rebus: Pk. raṅga 'tin' P. rã̄g f., rã̄gā m. ' pewter, tin ' Ku. rāṅ ' tin, solder 'Or. rāṅga ' tin ', rāṅgā ' solder, spelter ', Bi. Mth. rã̄gā, OAw. rāṁga; H. rã̄g f., rã̄gā m. ' tin, pewter 'raṅgaada -- m. ' borax ' lex.Kho. (Lor.) ruṅ ' saline ground with white efflorescence, salt in earth ' *raṅgapattra ' tinfoil '. [raṅga -- 3, páttra --]B. rāṅ(g)tā ' tinsel, copper -- foil '.

paTa 'hood of serpent' Rebus: padanu 'sharpness of weapon' (Telugu)

Hieroglyph: kunta1 ' spear '. 2. *kōnta -- . [Perh. ← Gk. konto/*s* ' spear ' EWA i 229]1. Pk. *kuṁta* -- m. ' spear '; S. *kundu* m. ' spike of a top ', °*dī* f. ' spike at the bottom of a stick ', °*diṛī*, °*dirī* f. ' spike of a spear or stick '; Si. *kutu* ' lance '.

2. Pa. *konta* -- m. ' standard '; Pk. *koṁta* -- m. ' spear '; H. *kõt* m. (f.?) ' spear, dart '; -- Si. *kota* ' spear, spire, standard ' perh. ← Pa.(CDIAL 3289)

Rebus: kuṇṭha munda (loha) 'hard iron (native metal)'

Allograph: कुंठणें [kuṇṭhaṇēṃ] *v i* (कुंठ S) To be stopped, detained, obstructed, arrested in progress (Marathi)

Tablet. Crocodile above. Peson kicking and spearing a bison, near a seated,horned (with twig) person.Harappa. Harappa Museum, H95-2486 Meadow and Kenoyer 1997

karA 'crocodile' Rebus: khAr 'blacksmith' (Kashmiri)
kamaDha 'penance' (Prakrtam) Rebus: kammaTa 'mint, coiner'
kUtI 'twigs' Rebus: kuThi 'smelter'
muh 'face' Rebus: muhe 'ingot' (Santali)

poliya 'citizen, gatekeeper of town quarter' Hieroglyph: *pola 'zebu'*

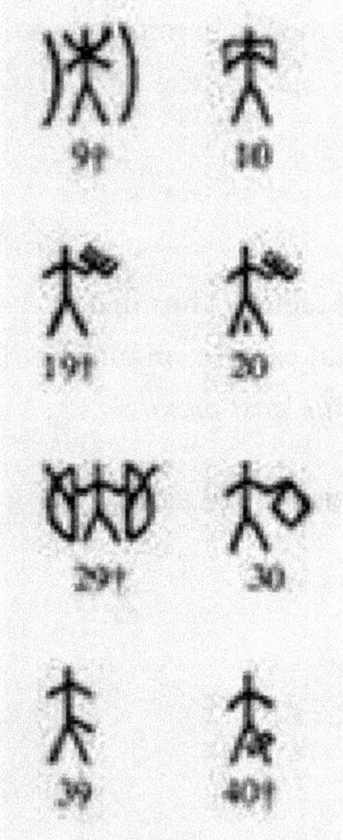

mēd ‘body’ (Kur.)(DEDR 5099) Rebus: meḍ ‘iron’ (Ho.) खांडा [*khāṇḍā*] *m* A jag, notch, or indentation (as upon the edge of a tool or weapon)(Marathi). Rebus: *kāṇḍa* ‘tools, pots and pans and metal-ware’ (Marathi) Thus, *meḍ kāṇḍa 'iron implements'.*

Ligature: Stool or plank/seat

Sign 43: Kur. *kaṇḍō* a stool. Malt. *kanḍo* stool, seat. (DEDR 1179) Rebus: kaṇḍ 'fire-altar' (Santali) *kāṇḍa* ‘tools, pots and pans and metal-ware’ (Marathi) + *kāṭi* 'body stature; Rebus: fireplace trench. Thus, furnace for metals in mint. Thus, fire-altar metalware furnace.

Alternative: PLUS mēd ‘body’ (Kur.)(DEDR 5099) Rebus: meḍ ‘iron’ (Ho.) Thus, *meḍ kāṇḍa 'iron implements'.*

Ligature: crab, claws

Sign 36: : mēd ‘body’ (Kur.)(DEDR 5099); meḍ ‘iron’ (Ho.) Thus,

meḍ dhātu 'iron ore'

Alternative Sign 36: *kāṭi* 'body stature; Rebus: fireplace trench. Thus, furnace for metals in mint + *kamaḍha* 'crab' Rebus: *kammaṭa* 'mint, coiner'. *ḍato* = claws of crab (Santali) Rebus: *dhātu* 'mineral ore'. Thus mineral ore mint, coiner.

kamaḍha 'archer, bow' Rebus: *kammaṭa* 'mint, coiner'. dula 'two' Rebu: dul 'cast metal'. Thus metal castings mint. + kāṭi 'body stature; Rebus: fireplace trench. Thus, furnace for metal castings in mint. Alternative reading could be: *mēd 'body' (Kur.) Rebus: meḍ 'iron' (Ho.) PLUS dul 'cast metal' PLUS kammaṭa 'mint' Thus, together, cast iron mint.*

Similarly, in all the following hieroglyph-multiplexes, the 'body' hieroglyph can be deciphere and explained:as

mēd 'body' (Kur.) Rebus: *meḍ* 'iron' (Ho.)

Sign 28: Archer. Ligature one bow-and-arrow hieroglyph

kamaḍha 'archer, bow' Rebus: *kammaṭa* 'mint, coiner'. + *kāṭi* 'body stature; Rebus: fireplace trench. Thus, furnace for metals in mint. 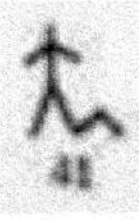 Ligature hieroglyph: 'lid of pot'

aḍaren
'lid of pot' Rebus: aduru 'unsmelted, native metal' + kāṭi 'body stature; Rebus: fireplace trench. Thus furnace for aduru, unsmelted, native metal.Ligatures: water-carrier + lid of pot

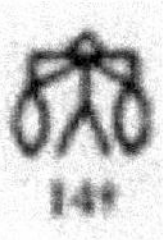
Sign 14: *kuṭi* 'water-carrier' Rebus*: kuṭhi*

'smelter/furnace'+
kāṭi 'body stature; Rebus: fireplace trench +
aḍaren'lid of pot' Rebus: aduru 'unsmelted, native metal' + kāṭi 'body stature; Rebus: fireplace trench. Thus furnace for aduru, unsmelted, native metal. Thus, furnace-smelter for unsmelted, native metal.

Ligatures: water-carrier + notch

Sign 13: *kuṭi* 'water-carrier' Rebus*: kuṭhi* 'smelter/furnace'+ kāṭi 'body stature; Rebus: fireplace trench. + खांडा [*khāṇḍā*] *m* A jag, notch, or indentation (as upon the edge of a tool or weapon)(Marathi). Rebus: *kāṇḍa* 'tools, pots and pans and metal-ware' (Marathi) + kāṭi 'body stature; Rebus: fireplace trench. + kāṭi 'body =stature; Rebus: fireplace trench. Thus, smelter-furnace metalware.

Ligature: water-carrier

Sign 12: *kuṭi* 'water-carrier' Rebus*: kuṭhi* 'smelter/furnace'+ kāṭi 'body stature; Rebus: fireplace trench. Thus, smelter furnace.

Seal impression, Ur (Upenn; U.16747); dia. 2.6, ht. 0.9 cm.; Gadd, PBA 18 (1932), pp. 11-12, pl. II, no. 12; Porada 1971: pl.9, fig.5; Parpola, 1994, p. 183; water carrier with a skin (or pot?) hung on each end of the yoke across his shoulders and another one below the crook of his left arm; the vessel on the right end of his yoke is over a receptacle for the water; a star on either side of the head (denoting supernatural?). The whole object is enclosed by 'parenthesis' marks. The parenthesis is perhaps a way of splitting of the ellipse (Hunter, G.R., *JRAS*, 1932, 476). An unmistakable example of an 'hieroglyphic' seal. kuṭi 'water-carrier' (Telugu); Rebus: kuṭhi 'smelter furnace' (Santali) kuṛī f. 'fireplace' (H.); krvṛI f. 'granary (WPah.); kuṛī, kuṛo house, building'(Ku.)(CDIAL 3232) kuṭi 'hut made of boughs' (Skt.) guḍi temple (Telugu) मेढ (p. 662) [mēḍha] 'polar' star' Rebus: mẽṛhẽt, meḍ 'iron' (Ho.Munda)

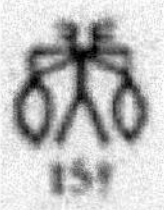

Ligatures: water-carrier (as in Sign 12) + rim of jar

Ligature: rim of jar Rebus: *kanda kanka* 'fire-trench account, *karṇi* supercargo' *Tu.* kandůka, kandaka ditch, trench. *Te.* kandakamu id. *Koṇḍa* kanda trench made as a fireplace during weddings. *Pe.*kanda fire trench. *Kui* kanda small trench for fireplace. *Malt.* kandri a pit. (DEDR 1214).

'rim-of-jar' hieroglyph Rebus: *kanka* (Santali) karṇika 'scribe'(Sanskrit) *kuṭi* 'water-carrier' Rebus*: kuṭhi* 'smelter/furnace'.+*kāṭi*'body stature; Rebus: fireplace trench. Thus, smelter furnace account, supercargo.

h073  4617 [An orthographic representation of a water-carrier].

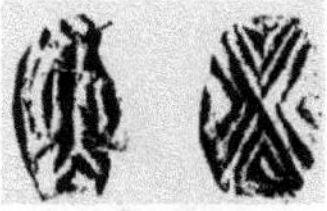

Chanhudaro Seal obverse and reverse. 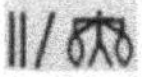 6118 The 'water-carrier' and X signs of this so-called Jhukar culture seal are comparable to other inscriptions. Fig. 3 and 3a of Plate L. After Mackay, 1943.

Ligature 'two spoked wheels'

Spokes-of-wheel, nave-of-wheel *āra* 'spokes' Rebus: *āra 'brass'*. cf. erka = ekke (Tbh. of arka) aka (Tbh. of arka) copper (metal); crystal (Kannada) Glyph: *eraka*'nave of wheel' Rebus: eraka 'copper'; cf. erka = ekke (Tbh. of arka) aka (Tbh. of arka) copper (metal); crystal (Kannada) *dula* 'two' Rebus: *dul* 'cast metal'. Thus, moltencast copper castings ++ kāṭi 'body stature; Rebus: fireplace trench. Thus, furnace for copper metal castings.

Ligature hieroglyph 'corner'

kanac 'corner' Rebus: *kañcu* 'bronze' + *kāṭi* 'body stature; Rebus: fireplace trench. Thus, furnace for bronze castings.

Ligatures: corner + notch

Sign 31: *kana, kanac* = corner (Santali); Rebus: *kañcu* = bronze (Telugu) PLUS खांडा [*khāṇḍā*] *m* A jag, notch, or indentation (as upon the edge of a tool or weapon). Rebus: *kāṇḍa* 'tools, pots and pans and metal-ware' Thus, bronze metalware. + *kāṭi*'body stature; Rebus: fireplace trench. Thus, furnace bronze metalware castings.

Ligature hieroglyph: 'stick' or 'one'

Sign1 Hieroglyph: काठी [kāṭhī] *f* (काष्ट S) (or शरीराची काठी) The frame or structure of the body: also (viewed by some as arising from the preceding sense, Measuring rod) stature (Marathi) B. *kāṭhā* ' measure of length '(CDIAL 3120).
H. *kāṭhī 'wood'* f. G. *kāṭh* n. ' wood ', °*ṭhī* f. ' stick, measure of 5 cubits '(CDIAL 3120). + kāṭi 'body stature; Rebus: fireplace trench.The 'stick' hieroglyph is a phonetic reinforcement of 'body stature' hieroglyph. Alternatively, koḍ 'one' Rebus: koḍ 'workshop'+ kāṭi 'body stature; Rebus: fireplace trench.. Thus, workplace of furnace fire-trench.
Rebus: G. *kāṭɔṛɔ* m. ' dross left in the furnace after smelting iron ore '.(CDIAL 2646)
Rebus: kāṭi , *n.* < U. *ghāṭī*. 1. Trench of a fort; அகழி. 2. A fireplace in the form of a long ditch; கோட்டையடுப்பு காடியடுப்பு kāṭi-y-aṭuppu , *n.* < காடி&sup6; +. A fireplace in the form of a long ditch used for cooking on a large scale; கோட்டையடுப்பு.
Rebus: S.kcch. *kāṭhī* f. ' wood 'Pa. Pk. *kaṭṭha* -- n. ' wood '(CDIAL 3120).
Sign 37 Hieroglyph: WPah.kṭg. *ṭōṭ* ' mouth '.WPah.kṭg. *thótti* f., *thótthər* m. ' snout, mouth ', A. *ṭhõt*(phonet. *thõt*) (CDIAL 5853).
Rebus:

tutthá n. (m. lex.), *tutthaka* -- n. ' blue vitriol (used as an eye ointment) ' Suśr., *tūtaka* -- lex. 2. *thōttha -- 4. 3. *tūtta -- . 4. *tōtta -- 2. [Prob. ← Drav. T. Burrow BSOAS xii 381; cf. *dhūrta* -- 2 n. ' iron filings ' lex.]1. N. *tutho* ' blue vitriol or sulphate of copper ', B. *tuth*.2. K. *thŏth*, dat. °*thas* m., P. *thothā* m.3. S.*tūtio* m., A. *tutiyā*, B. *tũte*, Or. *tutiā*, H. *tūtā*, *tūtiyā* m., M. *tutiyā* m.
4. M. *totā* m.(CDIAL 5855) *Ka.* tukku rust of iron; tutta, tuttu, tutte blue vitriol. *Tu.* tukků rust;

mair(ů)suttu, (*Eng.-Tu. Dict.*) mairůtuttu blue vitriol. *Te.* t(r)uppu rust; (*SAN*) trukku id., verdigris. / Cf. Skt. tuttha- blue vitriol (DEDR 3343).
Sign 2: dula 'pair' Rebus: dul 'cast metal' + kāṭi 'body stature; Rebus: fireplace trench. Thus furnace for metal casting. koḍ 'one' Rebus: koḍ 'workshop'. Thus, furnace workshop.

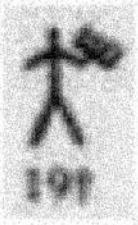 Ligature: harrow

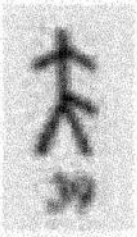

 Ligatures: harrow + notch (between legs) Allographs: Signs 18, 39 

Sign 18: खांडा [*khāṇḍā*] *m* A jag, notch, or indentation (as upon the edge of a tool or weapon)(Marathi). Rebus: *kāṇḍa* 'tools, pots and pans and metal-ware' (Marathi) + kāṭi 'body stature; Rebus: fireplace trench. Thus, furnace for metalware castings of unsmelted, native metal.

Ligature component in hieroglyph 'harrow'

Sign 19: *aḍar* 'harrow'; rebus: *aduru* 'native unsmelted metal' (Kannada) + kāṭi 'body stature; Rebus: fireplace trench. Thus, furnace for native metal.

Sign 20: खांडा [*khāṇḍā*] *m* A jag, notch, or indentation (as upon the edge of a tool or weapon)(Marathi). Rebus: *kāṇḍa* 'tools, pots and pans and metal-ware' (Marathi) + kāṭi 'body stature; Rebus: fireplace trench. Thus, furnace for metalware castings of unsmelted, native metal.

 Ligature hieroglyph 'currycomb'

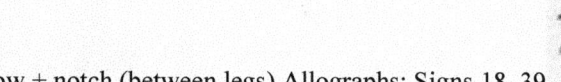

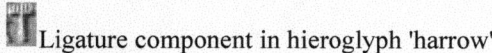

kSign 38: *hareḍo* = a currycomb (Gujarati) खरारा [*kharārā*] *m* (H) A currycomb. 2 Currying a horse. (Marathi) Rebus: करडा [*karaḍā*] Hard from alloy--iron, silver &c. (Marathi) *kharādī* ' turner' (Gujarati) kāṭi 'body stature; Rebus: fireplace trench. Thus, fireplace for hard alloy metal.

 Ligature hieroglyph 'foot, anklet'

Sign 40: toṭi bracelet (Tamil)(DEDR 3682). Jaina Skt. (*IL* 20.193) toḍaka- an

anklet (Sanskrit) *khuṭo* ' leg, foot ', °ṭī ' goat's leg ' Rebus: *khōṭā* 'alloy' (Marathi) Rebus: tuttha 'copper sulphate' + kāṭi 'body stature; Rebus: fireplace trench. Thus smelted copper sulphate alloy.

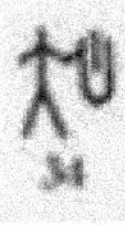
Ligature hieroglyph 'rimless pot + ladle'

Sign 34:
muka 'ladle' (Tamil)(DEDR 4887) Rebus: *mũh* 'ingot' (Santali) *baṭa* = a kind of iron (G.) *baṭa* = rimless pot (Kannada) Thus, iron ingot.+ kāṭi 'body stature; Rebus: fireplace trench. Thus, iron ingot furnace.

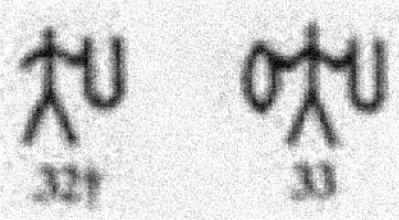
Ligatures: rimless pot + hollow or ingot

Sign 32: *baṭa* = rimless pot (Kannada) Rebus: *baṭa* = a kind of iron (G.)+ *kāṭi* 'body stature; Rebus: fireplace trench. Thus, iron furnace
Sign 33: As for Sign 32 + dulo 'hole' Rebus: dul 'cast metal' Thus, furnace iron castings.

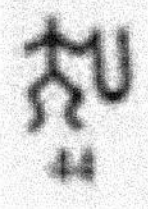
Ligatures: rimless pot + dance step

Sign 44: meṭ sole of foot, footstep, footprint (Ko.); meṭṭu step, stair, treading, slipper (Te.)(DEDR 1557). Rebus: *meḍ* 'iron'(Munda); मेढ meḍh'merchant's helper'(Pkt.) *meḍ* iron (Ho.) *meṛed-bica* = iron stone ore, in contrast to bali-bica, iron sand ore (Munda) + *kāṭi* 'body stature; Rebus: fireplace trench. Thus, iron furnace.

Ligatures: rimless pot + wire mesh

Sign 35: *baṭa* = rimless pot (Kannada) Rebus: *baṭa* = a kind of iron (G.)+ *kāṭi* 'body stature; Rebus: fireplace trench + *akho* m. 'mesh of a net' Rebus: L. P. *akkhā* m. ' one end of a bag or sack thrown over a beast of burden '; Or. *akhā* ' gunny bag '; Bi. *ākhā*, *ā̃khā* ' grain bag carried by pack animal '; H. *ākhā* m. ' one of a pair of grain bags used as panniers '; M. *ā̃khā* m. ' netting in which coco -- nuts, &c., are carried ', *ā̆khẽ* n. ' half a bullock -- load ' (CDIAL 17) అంకెము [aṅkemu] *ankemu*. [Telugu] n. One pack or pannier, being half a bullock load. Thus, a consignment or packload of furnace iron castings.

Ligature: warrior + *ficus religiosa*

Sign 17: *loa* '*ficus religiosa*' Rebus: *lo* 'iron' (Sanskrit) PLUS unique ligatures: लोखंड [lōkhaṇḍa] *n* (लोह S) Iron. लोखंडाचे चणे खावविणें or चारणें To oppress grievously.लोखंडकाम [lōkhaṇḍakāma] *n* Iron work; that portion (of a building, machine &c.) which consists of iron. 2 The business of an ironsmith.लोखंडी [lōkhaṇḍī] *a* (लोखंड) Composed of iron; relating to iron. (Marathi)*bhaṭa* 'warrior' (Sanskrit) Rebus: *baṭa* a kind of iron (Gujarati). Rebus: *bhaṭa* 'furnace' (Santali) Thus, together, th ligatured hieroglyph reads rebus: *loa bhaṭa* 'iron furnace'

Ligature 'armed body stature' or 'horned body stature'

Sign 8:*bhaṭa* 'warrior' (Sanskrit) Rebus: *baṭa* a kind of iron (Gujarati). Rebus: *bhaṭa* 'furnace' (Santali) + kāṭi 'body stature; Rebus: fireplace trench. Thus, furnace for a kind of iron.

Ligatures: two curved lines

Sign 9: Read rebus as for Sign 8 PLUS Ligature hieroglyphs of two curved lines
dula 'pair' Rebus: dul 'cast metal + ()kuṭila 'bent' CDIAL 3230 kuṭi— in cmpd. 'curve', *kuṭika*— 'bent' MBh. Rebus: *kuṭila, katthīl* = bronze (8 parts copper and 2 parts tin) [cf. *āra-kūṭa*, 'brass' (Sanskrit) +*bhaṭa* 'warrior' (Sanskrit) Rebus: *baṭa* a kind of iron (Gujarati). Rebus: *bhaṭa* 'furnace' (Santali) + kāṭi 'body stature; Rebus: fireplace trench. Thus, furnace bronze castings.

Ligature hieroglyph: 'roof' Allograph: Sign 10

Sign 5: *mūdh* ' ridge of roof ' (Assamese)(CDIAL 10247) Rebus: *mund* 'iron' + *kāṭi* 'body stature;

Rebus:fireplace trench. Thus, furnace for iron  Ligature hieroglyph 'flag'

Sign 4; *koḍi* 'flag' (Ta.)(DEDR 2049). Rebus 1: *koḍ* 'workshop' (Kuwi) Rebus 2: *khŏḍ* m. 'pit', *khŏḍü* f. 'small pit' (Kashmiri. CDIAL 3947). + kāṭi 'body stature; Rebus: fireplace trench. Thus, furnace workshop.

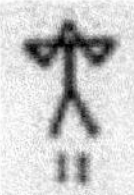

Sign 16:dula 'two' Rebus: dul 'cast metal' + + kāṭi 'body stature; Rebus: fireplace trench +*koḍi* 'summit of mountain' (Tamil). Thus, furnace for metal casting. *mēḍu* height, rising ground, hillock (Kannada) Rebus: *mẽṛhẽt, meḍ* 'iron' (Munda.Ho.) Thus, iron metal casting. The ligaured hieroglyph of Sign 11 is a ligature with two mountain peaks. Hence *dul meḍ* 'iron casting'

 Ligature hieroglyph 'paddy plant' or 'sprout'

kolmo 'paddy plant' Rebus: *kolami* 'smithy, forge' Vikalpa: *mogge* 'sprout, bud' Rebus: *mũh* 'ingot' (Santali) dolu 'plant of shoot height' Rebus: dul 'cast metal' + kāṭi 'body stature; Rebus: fireplace trench. Thus furnace smithy or ingot furnace.

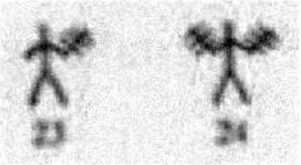 Ligature hieroglyph: 'three short strokes on a slanted stroke'

Signs 23, 24: dula 'two' Rebus: dul 'cast metal' *dhāḷ* 'a slope'; 'inclination of a plane' (G.); *ḍhāḷiyum* = adj. sloping, inclining (G.) Rebus: *ḍhālako* = a large metal ingot (G.) *ḍhālakī* = a metal heated and poured into a mould; a solid piece of metal; an ingot (Gujarati) + kāṭi 'body stature; Rebus: fireplace trench' Thus ingot furnace for castings. Three short strokes: kolom 'three' Rebus: kolami 'smithy, forge'. Thus it is a place where artisans work with furnace for metal castings.

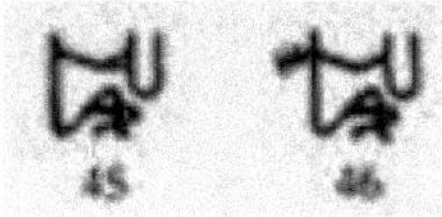 Ligatures: Worshipper + rimless pot + scarf (on pigtail)

Signs 45, 46: A variant of 'adorant' hieroglyph sign is shown with a 'rimless, broad-mouthed pot' which is *baṭa* read rebus:*bhaṭa* 'furnace'. If the 'pot' ligature is a phonetic determinant, the gloss for the 'adorant' is *bhaṭa* 'worshipper'. If the 'kneeling' posture is the key hieroglyphic representation, the gloss is *eragu* 'bow' Rebus: *erako* 'moltencast copper'. Thus moltencast copper furnace. + *dhaṭu* m. (also dhaṭhu) m. 'scarf' (Western Pahari) (CDIAL 6707) Rebus*: dhatu* 'minerals' (Santali). Thus Sign 46 read rebus: moltencast copper minerals furnace.

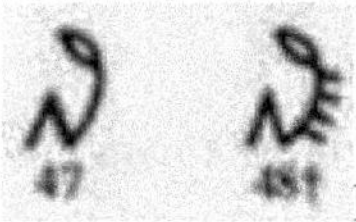 Hieroglyphs: backbone + four short strokes

Signs 47, 48: *baraḍo* = spine; backbone (Tulu) Rebus: *baran, bharat* 'mixed alloys' (5 copper, 4 zinc and 1 tin) (Punjabi) +

gaṇḍa 'four' Rebus: *kaṇḍ* 'fire-altar'. Thus, Sign 48 reads rebus: *bharat kaṇḍ* 'fire-altar', furnace for mixed alloy called *bharat*(copper, zinc, tin alloy),

'Backbone, spine' hieroglyph: *baraḍo* = spine; backbone; the back; baraḍo thābaḍavo = lit. to strike on the backbone or back; hence, to encourage; baraḍo bhāre thato = lit. to have a painful backbone, i.e. to do something which will call for a severe beating (Gujarati)bārṇe, bāraṇe = an offering of food to a demon; a meal after fasting, a breakfast (Tulu) barada, barda, birada = a vow (Gujarati)bharaḍo a devotee of S'iva; a man of the bharaḍā caste in the bra_hman.as (Gujarati) baraṛ = name of a caste of jat- around Bhaṭiṇḍa; bararaṇḍā melā = a special fair held in spring (Punjabi) bharāḍ = a religious service or entertainment performed by a bharāḍi_; consisting of singing the praises of some idol or god with playing on the d.aur (drum) and dancing; an order of aṭharā akhād.e = 18 gosāyi_ group; bharād. and bhāratī are two of the 18 orders of gosāyi_ (Marathi).

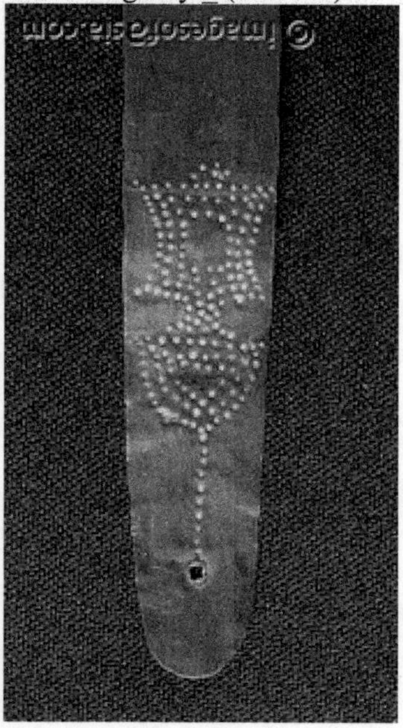

Gold fillet. Punctuated design on both ends.

Mohenjodaro. http://www.imagesofasia.com/html/mohenjodaro/gold-fillet.html

Gold fillet. Punctuated design on both ends.

Mohenjodaro. http://www.imagesofasia.com/html/mohenjodaro/gold-fillet.html

Hieroglyph: Endless knot

dhAtu 'strand of rope' Rebus: dhAtu 'mineral, metal, ore'धातु [p= 513,3] *m.* layer , stratum Ka1tyS3r. Kaus3. constituent part , ingredient (esp. [and in RV. only] ifc. , where often = " fold " e.g. त्रि-धा/आतु , threefold &c ; cf.त्रिविष्टि- , सप्त- , सु-) RV. TS. S3Br. &c (Monier-Williams) dhā´tu *strand of rope ' (cf. *tridhā´tu* -- ' threefold ' RV., *ayugdhātu* -- ' having an uneven number of strands ' KātyŚr.).; S. *dhāī* f. ' wisp of fibres added from time to time to a rope that is being twisted ',

L. *dhāī̃* f.(CDIAL 6773) tántu m. ' thread, warp ' RV. [√tan] Pa. *tantu* -- m. ' thread, cord ', Pk. *taṁtu* -- m.; Kho. (Lor.) *ton* ' warp ' < **tand* (whence *tandeni* ' thread between wings of spinning wheel '); S. *tandu* f. ' gold or silver thread '; L. *tand* (pl. °*dū̃*) f. ' yarn, thread being spun, string of the tongue '; P. *tand* m. ' thread ', *tanduā*, °*dūā* m. ' string of the tongue, frenum of glans penis '; A. *tā̃t* ' warp in the loom, cloth being woven '; B. *tā̃t* ' cord '; M. *tā̃tū* m. ' thread '; Si. *tatu*, °*ta* ' string of a lute '; -- with -- *o*, -- *ā* to retain orig. gender: S. *tando* m. ' cord, twine, strand of rope '; N. *tā̃do* ' bowstring '; H. *tā̃tā* m. ' series, line '; G. *tā̃tɔ* m. ' thread '; -- OG. *tāṁtaṇaü* m. ' thread ' < **tāṁtaḍaü*, G.*tā̃tṇɔ* m.(CDIAL 5661)

मेढा [mēḍhā] A twist or tangle arising in thread or cord, a curl or snarl.(Marathi)(CDIAL 10312).L. meṛh f. 'rope tying oxen to each other and to post on threshing floor'(CDIAL 10317) Rebus: *meḍ*'iron'. *mẽṛhet* 'iron' (Mu.Ho.)

Thus, together, a strand and a curl, the hieroglyph-multiplex of endless-knot signifies iron mineral. mRdu dhAtu (iron mineral).

h1018copperobject Head of one-horned bull ligatured with a four-pointed star-fish (Gangetic octopus?).

kodiyum 'rings on neck' kod `horn' (Kuwi); rebus: kod `artisan's workshop' (Gujarati). खोंड [khōṇḍa] m A young bull, a bullcalf.(Marathi) Rebus: kõdā 'to turn in a lathe'(B.) कोंद kōnda 'engraver, lapidary setting or infixing gems' (Marathi). The joined animal is a Gangetic octopus.veṛhā octopus, said to be found in the Indus (Jaṭki lexicon of A. Jukes, 1900) Rebus: . *vēḍa* 'boat'(Prakrtam) Alternative:

Rebus: beṛhī 'warehouse';

beṛā building with a courtyard (WPah.)

9308 bēḍā f. ' boat ' lex. 2. vēḍā, *vēṭī* -- f. lex. 3. bhēḍa -- 3 m., *bhēla* -- 1, °*aka* -- m.n. lex.1. Pk. *bēḍa* -- , °*aya* -- m., *bēḍā* -- , °*ḍiyā* -- f. ' boat ', Gy. eur. *bero*, S. *ḇeṛo* m., °*ṛī* ' small do. '; L. *bēṛā* (Ju. *ḇ* --) m. ' large cargo boat ', *bēṛī* f. ' boat ', P. *beṛā* m., °*ṛī* f.; Ku. *beṛo* ' boat, raft ', N. *beṛā*, OAw. *beḍā*, H. *beṛā* m., G. *beṛɔ* m., *beṛi* f., M.*beḍā* m.2. Pk. *vēḍa* -- m. ' boat '.3. Pk. *bhēḍaka* -- , *bhēlaa* -- m., *bhēlī* -- f. ' boat ';

B. *bhelā* ' raft ', Or. *bheḷā.*
*bēḍḍa -- , *bēṇḍa -- ' defective ' see *biḍḍa -- .Addenda: bēḍā -- . 1. S.kcch. *beṛī* f. ' boat ', *beṛo* m. ' ship '; WPah.poet. *beṛe* f. ' boat ', J. *beṛī* f.3. bhēḍa -- 3: A. *bhel* ' raft ' (phonet. *bhel*) ' raft ' AFD 89.

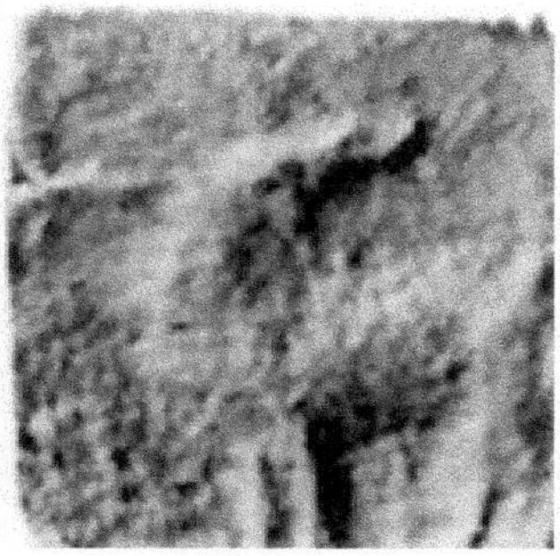

m0438 copper tablet

krammara 'look back' (Telugu) rebus: kamar 'blacksmith' mlekh 'goat' rebus: milakkhu 'copper' mleccha 'copper'. thus, coppersmith.

dhollu 'drummer' (Western Pahari) Rebus: dul 'cast metal'

kola 'tiger' Rebus: kolle 'blacksmith' kol 'working in iron'

kolimi 'smithy, forge' *jasta, dasta 'five' (Kafiri) jasta, sattva 'zinc'*

Zinc (Pewter)

jasta'h, Pewter, Pl. ئي *ey*. جس *jas*, s.m. (6th) Pewter. Sing. and Pl. See also HI جست *jast*, s.m. (6th) Pewter. Sing. and Pl.(Pashto) These glosses are cognate with jasta 'zinc' (Hindi) *svastika* pewter (Kannada); jasta = zinc (Hindi) yasada (Jaina Prakrtam)

hasta 'hand' (Rigveda); Kafiri. **dasta* -- < **jasta* -- is a Meluhha homonym. The semantics 'hand' and 'five' are meanings signified by *hath*, *ath* ' hand, five '(Gypsy). Thus, it is reasonably deduced that Proto-Prakrtam (Meluhha) *jasta* signified numeral 'five'.

I suggest that it reads *sattva*. Its rebus rendering and meaning is *zastas* 'spelter or sphalerite or sulphate of zinc.'

Zinc occurs in sphalerite, or sulphate of zinc in five colours.

The Meluhha gloss for 'five' is: *taṭṭal* Homonym is: ṭhaṭṭha 'brass'(i.e. alloy of copper + zinc).

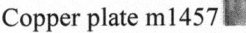

Copper plate m1457  The set of hieroglyphs deciphered as: 1. zinc-pewter and 2. bronze:1. *jasta, sattva* and 2. *kuṭila*

Hieroglyph: *sattva* 'svastika hieroglyph'; *jasta, dasta 'five'* (Kafiri) Rebus: *jasta, sattva 'zinc'*

Hieroglyph: *kuṛuk* 'coil' Rebus: *kuṭila, katthīl* = bronze (8 parts copper and 2 parts tin) cf. āra-kūṭa, 'brass' Old English *ār* 'brass, copper, bronze' Old Norse *eir* 'brass, copper', German *ehern* 'brassy, bronzen'. kastīra n. ' tin ' lex. 2. *kastilla -- .1. H. *kathīr* m. ' tin, pewter '; G. *kathīr* n. ' pewter '.2. H. (Bhoj.?) *kathīl, °lā* m. ' tin, pewter '; M. *kathīl* n. ' tin ', *kathlẽ* n. ' large tin vessel '.(CDIAL 2984)

as shown on c5a, c5b, c6, c9 copper plate types with hieroglyph-multiplex kamaṭha= fig leaf, religiosa(Samskrtam)dula 'two' Rebus: dul 'cast metal 'Thus, cast loh 'copper casting' in furnace:baṭa= wide-mouthed pot; baṭa= kiln (Te.) kammaṭa=portable furnace(Te.) kampaṭṭam 'coiner,mint' (Tamil) kammaṭa (Malayalam) loa 'ficus' rebus: loh 'copper'

-

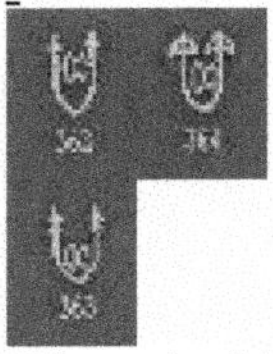

Thus, the hieroglyph-multiplexes (Signs 362, 363, 364 variants) signify: cast copper mint. Thus the multiplex as hypertext is an example of data mining technique to precisely delineate the processes involved and ancient professions of metalwork delineated.

Indus Script hieroglyph multiplexes signify mint; scorpion, ficus glomerata, fish signify bica 'hematite ore', loa 'copper ore', ayas 'native metal'

meRed bica 'iron stone ore', lo 'copper ore'

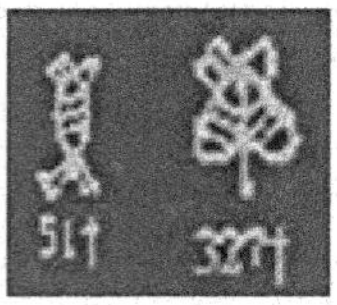

These are two glyphs of the script with unique superscripted ligatures; this pair of ligatures does not occur on any other ligatured glyph in the entire corpus of Indus script inscriptions. Orthographically, Sign 51 glyph is a 'scorpion'; Sign 327 glyph is a 'ficus glomerata leaf'. The glosses for the 'sound values' are, respectively: bica 'scorpion' (Santali), lo 'ficus' (Santali).

It is assumed that locks of hair are superscripted on the scorpion hieroglyhph. Hieroglyph: *mēṇḍhī ' lock of hair, curl '. [Cf. **mēṇḍha* -- 1 s.v. *miḍḍa --]S. *mĩ̄ḍhī* f., *°ḍho* m. ' braid in a woman's hair ', L. *mẽ̄ḍhī* f.; G. *mī̃ḍlɔ, miḍ°* m. ' braid of hair on a girl's forehead '; M. *meḍhā* m. ' curl, snarl, twist or tangle in cord or thread '.(CDIAL 10312). Thus, the message is : *meṛed-bica* = 'iron (hematite) stone ore'. Hieroglyph: Superscript of a curl to the scorpion hieroglyph: मेढा (p. 665) [mēḍhā] A twist or tangle arising in thread or cord, a curl or snarl.(Marathi) Rebus: *mẽṛhẽt, meḍ* 'iron' (Mu.Ho.)

Hook hieroglyph which sometimes follows the 'scorpion' hieroglyhph:

M. *mẽḍhā* m. ' crook or curved end (of a horn, stick, &c.) '.Thus, the 'crook' hieroglyph is a semantic determinant of the hieroglyph-multiplex composed of the 'curl PLUS crook PLUS scorpion'.
Hence, Rebus: *mẽṛhẽt, meḍ* 'iron' (Mu.Ho.) PLUS bicha; that is, the compound phrase *meṛed-bica* = 'iron (hematite) stone ore' (Santali)

Similarly, the ligature superscript on 'ficus' hieroglyph is a determinative of 'metal, mineral': मेढा (p. 665) [mēḍhā] A twist or tangle arising in thread or cord, a curl or snarl.(Marathi) Rebus: *mẽṛhẽt, meḍ* 'iron' (Mu.Ho.) Thus, it appears that the metallic nature of the copper was signified by a gloss which signified a ferrite ore.

The inscription on the seal starts with 'scorpion' hieroglyph on modern impression of seal M-414 from Mohenjo-daro. After CISI 1:100. This sign is followed by a hieroglyph multiplex signifyinjg: rimledss pot PLUS ficus leaves PLUS infixed crab hieroglyphs. The terminal sign is 'fish' hieroglyph.

Rebus-metonymy readings in Meluhha cipher (mlecchita vikalpa) are of the three sets of hieroglyph multipexes: 1. *meṛed-bica* 'iron (hematite) stone ore' 2. *bhaTa loh kammaṭa* 'furnace copper mint, coiner' 3. *aya* 'alloy metal'.

Note: The 'ficus' hieroglyph is signified by two glosses: *vaTa* 'banyan' *loa* 'ficus glomerata'. Rebus: bhaTa 'furnace' loha 'copper, iron'.

m-857 Seal. Mohenjo-daro The four hieroglyph multiplex on Mohenjo-daro seal m-857 signifies: 1. *meṛed-bica* = 'iron (hematite) stone ore' 2. *dhatu karava karNI* 'supercargo of mineral ore', scribed. (The one-horned young bull PLUS standard device is deciphered as: kondh 'young bull' Rebus: kondh 'turner'; koD 'horn' Rebus: koD 'workshop'; sangaDa 'lathe' Rebus: sangAta 'collection of materials, i.e. consignment or boat load.

On Mohenjo-daro seal m-414, the 'scorpion' sign is followed by a hieroglyph multiplex which is explained by Asko Parpola:

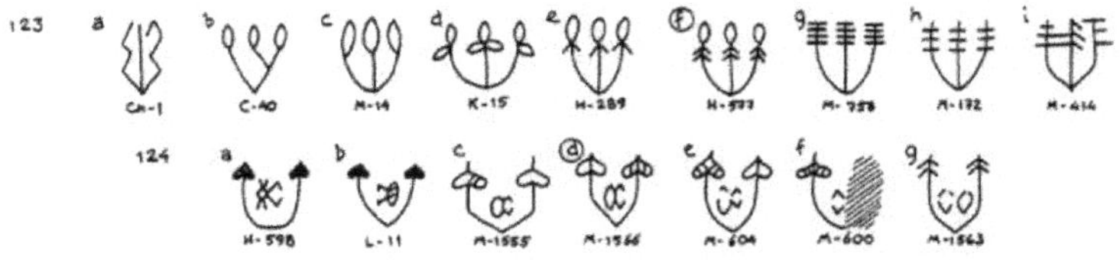

Many variants of Sign 123 (Parpola corpus) are identified signifying, according to Parpola [quote] a three-branched 'fig-tree' and of its ligature with the 'crab' sign, where the middlemost branch has been omitted to accommodate the inserted 'crab' sign. (After Parpola, Asko, 1994, Deciphering the Indus Script, Cambridge, Cambridge University Press: 235).

Parpola illustrates the 'crab' hieroglyhph with the following examples from copper plate inscriptions (Note: there are 240 copper plates with inscriptions from Mohenjo-daro):

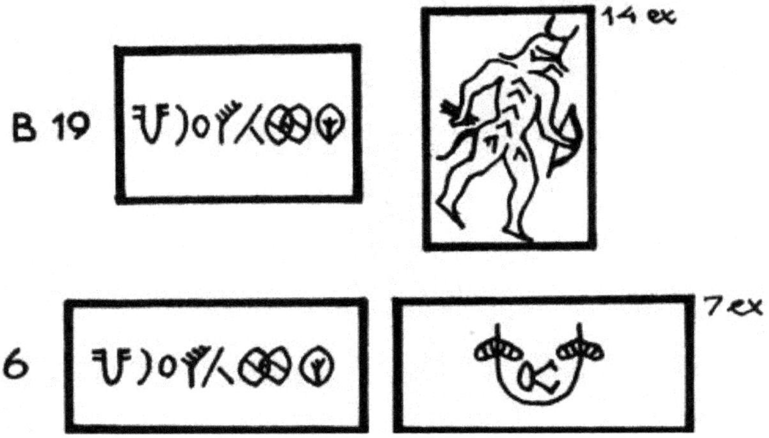

Copper tablets from Mohenjo-daro providing a 'pictorial translation' of the Indus sign 'crab inside fig tree' (After Parpola 1994: 234, fig. 13.13)

Variants of 'crab' hieroglyph (After Parpola 1994: 232, cf. 71-72)

The hieroglyph-multiplex, thus orthographically signifies two ficus leaves ligatured to the top edge of a wide rimless pot and a crab hieroglyph is inscripted. In this hieroglyph-multiplex three hieroglyph components are signified: 1. rimless pot, 2. two ficus leaves, 3. crab. baTa 'rimless pot' Rebus: bhaTa 'furnace'; loa 'ficus' Rebus: loha 'copper, iron'; kamaDha 'crab' Rebus: kammaTa 'coiner, mint'.

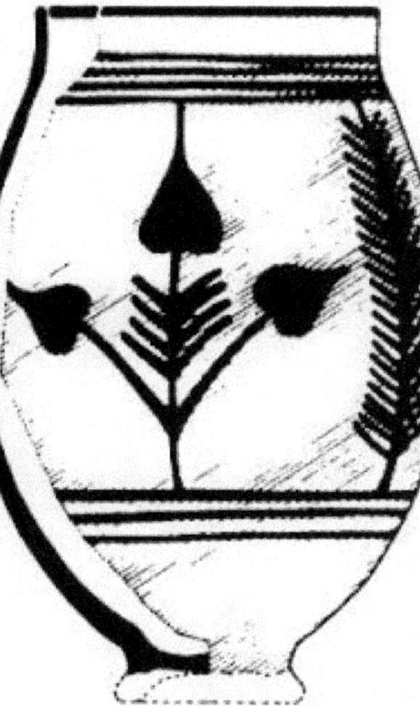

Examples are:

Modern impression of Harappa Seal h-598

Modern impression of seal L-11 Lothal

The third sign is a 'fish' hieroglyph.

(http://www.harappa.com/script/script-indus-parpola.pdf Asko Parpola, 2009k,'Hind leg' + 'fish': towards further understanding of the Indus Script, in: SCRIPTA, volume 1 (September 2009): 37-76, The Hummn Jeongeum Society)

Annex A: loa 'ficus glomerata' Rebus: loha 'copper, iron'

Parpola also presents a figure of a pot with ficus leaves hieroglyph. A painted goblet with the 'three-branched fig tree' motif from Nausharo I D, transitional phase between the Early and Mature Harappan periods (c. 2600-2550 BCE) (After Samzun 1992: 250, fig.29.4 no.2)

vaṭa1 m. ' the banyan Ficus indica ' MBh. Pa. *vaṭa* -- m. ' banyan ', Pk. *vaḍa* -- , °*aga* -- m., K. *war* in *war* -- *kulu* m., S. *baṛu* m. (← E); P. *vaṛ*, *baṛ* m., *vohṛ*, *bohṛ* f. ' banyan ', *vaṛoṭā*, *ba°* m. ' young banyan ' (+?); N. A. *bar* ' banyan ', B. *baṛ*, Bi. *bar* (→ Or. *bara*), H. *baṛ* m. (→ Bhoj. Mth. *baṛ*), G. *vaṛ* m., M. *vaḍ* m., Ko. *vaḍu*. *vaṭapadra -- , *vaṭapātikā -- .Addenda: vaṭa -- 1: Garh. *baṛ* ' fig tree '. 11215 *vaṭapātikā ' falling from banyan '. [vaṭa -- 1, pāta --] G. *vaṛvāī* f. ' hanging root of banyan tree '. (CDIAL 11211)

Allograph: vaṭa 'string': vaṭa2 ' string ' lex. [Prob. ← Drav. Tam. *vaṭam*, Kan. *vaṭi*, *vaṭara*, &c. DED 4268] N. *bariyo* ' cord, rope '; Bi. *barah* ' rope working irrigation lever ', *barhā* ' thick well -- rope ', Mth. *barahā* ' rope '.vaṭāraka -- , *varāṭaka* -- m. ' string ' MBh. [vaṭa -- 2]Pa. *sa* -- *vaṭākara* -- ' having a cable '; Bi. *baral* -- *rassī* ' twisted string '; H. *barrā* m. ' rope ', *barārā* m. ' thong '. (CDIAL 11212, 11217)

lo 'nine', loa 'ficus religiosa' Rebus: loh 'copper'; kunda 'young bull' Rebus: kundār, kũdār 'turner'; firs hieroglph from r. on the text: eraka 'nave of wheel' Rebus: eraka 'moltencast'; arA 'spoke' Rebus: Ara 'brass'; kanac 'corner' Rebus: kancu 'bronze'.

lo = nine (Santali) [Note the count of nine fig leaves on m0296]

loa = a species of fig tree, ficus glomerata, the fruit of ficus glomerata (Santali.lex.)

loha lut.i = iron utensils and implements (Santali.lex.)

lauha = made of copper or iron (Gr.S'r.); metal, iron (Skt.); lo_haka_ra = coppersmith, ironsmith (Pali); lo_ha_ra = blacksmith (Pt.); lohal.a (Or.); lo_ha = metal, esp. copper or bronze (Pali); copper (VS.); loho, lo_ = metal, ore, iron (Si.)

Ficus glomerata: loa, kamat.ha = ficus glomerata (Santali); rebus: loha = iron, metal (Skt.) kamat.amu, kammat.amu = portable furnace for melting precious metals (Te.) kammat.i_d.u = a goldsmith, a silversmith (Te.) kampat.t.tam coinage coin (Ta.);*kammat.t.am kammit.t.am* coinage, mint (Ma.); *kammat.a* id.; *kammat.i* a coiner (Ka.)(DEDR 1236)

Sumerian cylinder seal showing flanking goats with hooves on tree and/or mountain. Uruk period. (After Joyce Burstein in: Katherine Anne Harper, Robert L. Brown, 2002, The roots of tantra, SUNY Press, p.100)Hence, two goats + mountain glyph reads rebus: meḍ kundār 'iron turner'. Leaf on mountain: kamaṛkom 'petiole of leaf'; rebus: kampaṭṭam 'mint'. loa = a species of fig tree, ficus glomerata, the fruit of ficus glomerata (Santali) Rebus: lo 'iron' (Assamese, Bengali); loa 'iron' (Gypsy). The glyphic composition is read rebus: meḍ loa kundār 'iron turner mint'. kundavum = manger, a hayrick (G.) Rebus: kundār turner (A.); kũdār, kũdāri (B.); kundāru (Or.); kundau to turn on a lathe, to carve, to chase; kundau dhiri = a hewn stone; kundau murhut = a graven image (Santali) kunda a turner's lathe (Skt.)(CDIAL 3295) This rebus reading may explain the hayrick glyph shown on the sodagor 'merchant, trader' seal surrounded by four animals.Two antelopes are put next to the hayrick on the platform of the seal on which the horned person is seated. mlekh 'goat' (Br.); rebus: milakku 'copper' (Pali); mleccha 'copper' (Skt.) Thus, the composition of glyphs on the platform: pair of antelopes + pair of hayricks read rebus: milakku kundār 'copper turner'. Thus the seal is a framework of glyphic compositions to describe the repertoire of a brazier-mint, 'one who works in brass or makes brass articles' and 'a mint'.

Ta. meṭṭu mound, heap of earth; mēṭu height, eminence, hillock; muṭṭu rising ground, high ground, heap. Ma. mēṭu rising ground, hillock; māṭu hillock, raised ground; miṭṭāl rising ground, an alluvial bank; (Tiyya) maṭṭa hill. Ka. mēḍu height, rising ground, hillock; miṭṭu rising or high ground, hill; miṭṭe state of being high, rising ground, hill, mass, a large number; (Hav.) muṭṭe heap (as of straw). Tu. miṭṭè prominent, protruding; muṭṭe heap. Te. meṭṭa raised or high ground, hill; (K.) meṭṭu mound; miṭṭa high ground, hillock, mound; high, elevated, raised, projecting; (VPK) mēṭu, mēṭa, mēṭi stack of hay; (Inscr.) meṇṭa-cēnu dry field (cf. meṭṭu-nēla, meṭṭu-vari). Kol. (SR.) meṭṭā hill; (Kin.) meṭṭ, (Hislop) met mountain. Nk. meṭṭ hill, mountain. Ga. (S.3, LSB 20.3) meṭṭa high land. Go. (Tr. W. Ph.) maṭṭā, (Mu.) maṭṭa mountain; (M. L.) meṭā id., hill; (A. D. Ko.) meṭṭa, (Y. Ma. M.) meṭa hill; (SR.) meṭṭā hillock (Voc. 2949). Konḍa meṭa id. Kuwi (S.) metta hill; (Isr.) meṭa sand hill. (DEDR 5058) kamaṛkom = fig leaf (Santali.lex.) kamarmaṛā (Has.), kamaṛkom (Nag.); the petiole or stalk of a leaf (Mundari.lex.)Rebus: kampaṭṭam coinage, coin (Ta.)(DEDR 1236) kampaṭṭa- muḷai die, coining stamp (Ta.) Vikalpa: lo 'iron' (Assamese, Bengali); loa 'iron' (Gypsy)

Etyma from Indo-Aryan languages: lōhá 'copper, iron'

11158 lōhá ' red, copper -- coloured ' ŚrS., ' made of copper ' ŚBr., m.n. ' copper ' VS., ' iron ' MBh. [*rudh --] Pa. *lōha* -- m. ' metal, esp. copper or bronze '; Pk. *lōha* -- m. ' iron ', Gy. pal. *li*°, *lihi*, obl. *elhás*, as. *loa* JGLS new ser. ii 258; Wg. (Lumsden) "*loa*" ' steel '; Kho. *loh* ' copper '; S. *lohu* m. ' iron ', L. *lohā* m., awāṇ. *lō`ā*, P. *lohā* m. (→ K.rām. ḍoḍ. *lohā*), WPah.bhad. *lɔ̄u* n., bhal. *lòtilde;* n., pāḍ. jaun. *lōh*, paṅ. *luhā*, cur. cam. *lohā*, Ku. *luwā*, N. *lohu*, °*hā*, A. *lo*, B. *lo*, *no*, Or. *lohā*, *luhā*, Mth. *loh*, Bhoj. *lohā*, Aw.lakh. *lōh*, H. *loh*, *lohā* m., G. M. *loh* n.; Si. *loho*, *lō* ' metal, ore, iron '; Md. *ratu* -- *lō* ' copper '. *lōhala -- , *lōhila -- , *lōhiṣṭha -- , lōhī -- , laúha -- ; lōhakāra -- , *lōhaghaṭa -- , *lōhaśālā -- , *lōhahaṭṭika -- , *lōhōpaskara -- ; vartalōha -- .Addenda: lōhá -- : WPah.kṭg. (kc.) *lóɔ* ' iron ', J. *lohā* m., Garh. *loho*; Md. *lō* ' metal '.†*lōhaphāla -- or †*lōhahala -- . lōhakāra 11159 lōhakāra m. ' iron -- worker ', °*rī* -- f., °*raka* -- m. lex., *lauhakāra* -- m. Hit. [lōhá -- , kāra -- 1] Pa. *lōhakāra* -- m. ' coppersmith, ironsmith '; Pk. *lōhāra* -- m. ' blacksmith ', S. *luhā̆ru* m., L. *lohār* m., °*rī* f., awāṇ. *luhār*, P. WPah.khaś. bhal. *luhār* m., Ku. *lwār*, N. B. *lohār*, Or. *lohaḷa*, Bi.Bhoj. Aw.lakh. *lohār*, H. *lohār*, *luh*° m., G. *lavār* m., M. *lohār* m.; Si. *lōvaru* ' coppersmith '. Addenda: lōhakāra -- : WPah.kṭg. (kc.) *lhwā`r* m. ' blacksmith ', *lhwàri* f. ' his wife ', Garh. *lwār* m.

lōhaghaṭa 11160 *lōhaghaṭa ' iron pot '. [lōhá -- , ghaṭa -- 1] Bi. *lohrā*, °*rī* ' small iron pan '. 11160a †*lōhaphāla -- ' ploughshare '. [lōhá -- , phā'la -- 1] WPah.kṭg. *lhwā`ḷ* m. ' ploughshare ', J. *lohāl* m. ' an agricultural implement ' Him.I 197; -- or < †*lōhahala -- . lōhala 11161 lōhala ' made of iron ' W. [lōhá --] G. *lohar*, *lohariyɔ* m. ' selfwilled and unyielding man '.

lōhaśālā 11162 *lōhaśālā ' smithy '. [lōhá -- , śā'lā --] Bi. *lohsārī* ' smithy '. lōhahaṭṭika 11163 *lōhahaṭṭika ' ironmonger '. [lōhá -- , haṭṭa --] P.ludh. *lōhṭiyā* m. ' ironmonger '. 11163a †*lōhahala -- ' ploughshare '. [lōhá -- , halá --] WPah.kṭg. *lhwā`ḷ* m. ' ploughshare ', J. *lohāl* ' an agricultural instrument '; rather < †*lōhaphāla -- . lōhi 11164 lōhi ' *red, blood ' (n. ' a kind of borax ' lex.). [~ rṓhi -- . -- *rudh --] Kho. *lei* ' blood ' (BelvalkarVol 92 < **lōhika* --), Kal.rumb. *lū˘i*, urt. *lhɔ̄̃i*. lṓhita 11165 lṓhita ' red ' AV., n. ' any red substance ' ŚBr., ' blood ' VS. [< rṓhita -- . -- *rudh --] Pa. *lōhita* -- in cmpds. ' red ', n. ' blood ', °*aka* -- ' red '; Pk. *lōhia* -- ' red ', n. ' blood '; Gy. eur. *lolo* ' red ', arm. *nəxul* ' blood, wound ', pal. *lúḥrä* ' red ', *inhī'r* ' blood ', as. *lur* ' blood ', *lohri* ' red ' Miklosich Mund viii 8; Ḍ. *lōya* ' red '; Ash. *leu* ' blood ', Wg. *läi*, Kt. *lūi*, Dm. *lōi*; Tir. *ləwī*, (Leech) *luhī* ' red ', *lǭ̄i* ' blood '; Paš. *lū* f. ' blood ', Shum. *lúī*, Gmb. *lūi*, Gaw. *lō*; Bshk. *lōu* ' red ' (AO xviii 241 < **lohuta* --); S. *lohū* m. ' blood ', L. *lahū* m., awāṇ. *làū*; P. *lohī* ' red ', *lohū*, *lahū* m. ' blood '; WPah.jaun. *loī* ' blood ', Ku. *loi*, *lwe*, B. *lau*, Or. *lohu*, *nohu*, *la*(*h*)*u*, *na*(*h*)*u*, *laa*, Mth. *lehū*, OAw. *lohū* m., H. *lohū*, *lahū*, *lehū* m., G. *lohī* n.; OM.*lohivā* ' red ' Panse Jñān 536; Si. *lehe*, *lē* ' blood ', *le* ' red ' SigGr ii 460; Md. *lē* ' blood '. -- Sh. *lēl* m. ' blood ', *lōlyŭ* ' red ' rather < *lōhila -- . lōhitaka -- . Addenda: lṓhita -- : Kho. *lei* ' blood ' BKhoT 70, WPah.kṭg. *lóu* m., Garh. *loi*, Md. *lei*, *lē*.

lōhitaka 11166 lōhitaka ' reddish ' Āpast., n. ' calx of brass, bell- metal ' lex. [lṓhita --] K. *lōy* f. ' white copper, bell -- metal '. lōhittara 11167 *lōhittara ' reddish '. [Comp. of **lōhit* -- ~ rōhít -- . - *rudh --] Woṭ. *latúr* ' red ', Gaw. *luturá*: very doubtful (see úparakta --) lōhila 11168 *lōhila ' red '. [lōhá --] Wg. *lailäi* -- *štä* ' red '; Paš.chil. *lēle* -- *šiṓl* ' fox '; Sv. *lohīló* ' red ', Phal. *lohílu*, *ləhōilo*; Sh.gil. jij. *lēl* m. ' blood ', gil. *lōlyŭ*, (Lor.)*loilo* ' red, bay (of horse or cow) ', pales. *lēlo swā̃ṛə* ' (red) gold '. -- X nī'la -- : Sh.gil. *līlo* ' violet ', koh. *līlụ*, pales. *lī'lo* ' red '. -- Si. *luhul*, *lūlā* ' the dark -- coloured river fish Ophiocephalus striatus '? -- Tor. *lohūr*, *laūr*, f. *lihīr* ' red ' < **lōhuṭa*<-> AO xviii 241? lōhiṣṭha 11169 *lōhiṣṭha ' very red '. [lōhá --] Kal.rumb. *lohíṣṭ*, urt. *liūṣṭ* ' male of Himalayan pheasant ', Phal. *lōwīṣṭ* (f. *šām* s.v. śyāmá --); Bshk. *lōī'ṭ* ' id., golden oriole '; Tor.*lawēṭ* ' male golden oriole ', Sh.pales. *lēṭh*.

lōhī 11170 lōhī f. ' any object made of iron ' Kāv., ' pot ' Divyāv., *lōhikā* -- f. ' large shallow wooden bowl bound with iron ',*lauhā* -- f. ' iron pot ' lex. [lōhá --]
Pk. *lōhī* -- f. ' iron pot '; P. *loh* f. ' large baking iron '; A. *luhiyā* ' iron pan '; Bi. *lohiyā* ' iron or brass shallow pan with handles '; G.*lohiyũ* n. ' frying pan '.

lōhōpaskara 11171 *lōhōpaskara ' iron tools '. [lōhá -- , upaskara -- 1]
N. *lokhar* ' bag in which a barber keeps his tools '; H. *lokhar* m. ' iron tools, pots and pans '; -- X lauhabhāṇḍa -- : Ku. *lokhaṛ* ' iron tools '; H. *lokhaṇḍ* m. ' iron tools, pots and pans '; G. *lokhãḍ* n. ' tools, iron, ironware '; M. *lokhãḍ* n. ' iron ' (LM 400 < -- *khaṇḍa* --). laúkika -- , laukyá -- see *lōkíya -- . laulāha 11172 laulāha m. ' name of a place ' Stein RājatTrans ii 487.

K. *lōlav* ' name of a Pargana and valley west of Wular Lake '.

11172a laúha -- ' made of copper or iron ' GṛŚr., ' red ' MBh., n. ' iron, metal ' Bhaṭṭ. [lōhá --] Pk. *lōha* -- ' made of iron '; L. *lohā* ' iron -- coloured, reddish '; P. *lohā* ' reddish -- brown (of cattle) '. lauhabhāṇḍa -- , *lauhāṅga -- .
lauhakāra -- see lōhakāra -- . Addenda: laúha -- [Dial. *au* ~ *ō* (in *lōhá* --) < IE. *ou* T. Burrow BSOAS xxxviii 74]

lauhabhāṇḍa 11173 lauhabhāṇḍa n. ' iron pot, iron mortar ' lex. [laúha -- , bhāṇḍa -- 1] Pa. *lōhabhaṇḍa* -- n. ' copper or brass ware '; S. *luhā̃ḍiṛī* f. ' iron pot ', L.awāṇ. *luhā̃ḍā*; P. *luhā̃ḍā, lohṇḍā*, ludh. *lō̃hḍā* m. ' frying pan '; N. *luhũṛe* ' iron cooking pot '; A. *lohorā* ' iron pan '; Bi. *lohãṛā* ' iron vessel for drawing water for irrigation '; H. *lohaṇḍā, luh°* m. ' iron pot '; G. *loḍhũ* n. ' iron, razor ', pl. ' car<-> penter's tools ', *loḍhī* f. ' iron pan '. -- X *lōhōpaskara<-> q.v.

lauhāṅgika 11174 *lauhāṅgika ' iron -- bodied '. [láuha -- , áṅga -- 1]
P. *luhā̃gī* f. ' staff set with iron rings ', H. *lohā̃gī* f., M. *lohā̃gī, lavh°, lohãgī* f.; -- Bi. *lohãgā, lahaũgā* ' cobbler's iron pounder ', Mth.*lehõgā.*

A variant orthography for *sãghāṛɔ* 'lathe' is displayed on m0296 Mohenjo-daro seal.

m0296 Decoding of a very remarkable set of glyphs and a 5-sign epigraph on a seal, m0296, together with a review of few other pictographs used in the writing system of Indus script. This seal virtually defines and prefaces the entire corpus of inscriptions of mleccha (cognate meluhha) artisans of smithy guild, caravan of Sarasvati-Sindhu civilization. The center-piece of the orthography is a stylized representation of a 'lathe' which normally is shown in front of a one-horned young bull on hundreds of seals of Indus Script Corpora. This stylized sãghāṛɔ 'lathe' is a layered rebus-metonymy to denote 'collection of implements': sangāṭh संगाठ् । सामग्री m. (sg. dat. sangāṭas संगाटस्), a collection (of implements, tools, materials, for any object), apparatus, furniture, a collection of the things wanted on a journey, luggage, and so on. This device of a stylized 'lathe' is ligatured with a circular grapheme enclosing 'protuberances' from which emanate a pair of 'chain-links'. These hieroglyphs are also read as rebus-metonymy layers to represent a specific form of lapidary or metalwork: *goṭī 'lump of* silver' (Gujarati); *goṭa* m. ' edging of gold braid '(Kashmiri). Thus, a collection of hieroglyphs are deployed as rebus-metonymy layered encryptions, to convey a message in Meluhha (mleccha) speech form.

Hieroglyph: gõṭh 1 अर्गलम्, चिन्हितग्रन्थिः f. (sg. dat. gõṭhi गाँ&above;ठि), a bolt, door-chain; a method of tying up a parcel with a special knot marked or sealed so that it cannot be opened by an unauthorized person. Cf. gā̃ṭh and gõṭhü. -- dyunu -- m.inf. to knot, fasten; to bolt, fasten (a door) (K.Pr. 76). *gōṭṭa ' something round '. [Cf. guḍá -- 1. -- In sense ' fruit, kernel ' cert. ← Drav., cf. Tam. *koṭṭai* ' nut, kernel ', Kan. *goṟaṭe* &c. listed DED 1722] K. *goṭh* f., dat. *°ṭi* f. ' chequer or chess or dice board '; S. *goṭu* m. ' large ball of tobacco ready for hookah ', *°ṭī* f. ' small do. '; P. *goṭ* f. ' spool on which gold or silver wire is wound, piece on a chequer board '; N. *goṭo* ' piece ', *goṭi* ' chess piece '; A. *goṭ* ' a fruit, whole piece ', *°ṭā* ' globular, solid ', *guṭi* ' small ball, seed, kernel '; B. *goṭā* ' seed, bean, whole '; Or. *goṭā* ' whole, undivided ', *goṭi* ' small ball, cocoon ', *goṭāli* ' small round piece of chalk '; Bi. *goṭā* ' seed '; Mth. *goṭa* ' numerative particle '; H.*goṭ* f. ' piece (at chess &c.) '; G. *goṭ* m. ' cloud of smoke ', *°ṭɔ* m. ' kernel of coconut, nosegay ', *°ṭī* f. ' lump of silver, clot of blood ', *°ṭilɔ* m. ' hard ball of cloth '; M. *goṭā*m. ' roundish stone ', *°ṭī* f. ' a marble ', *goṭuḷā* ' spherical '; Si. *guṭiya* ' lump, ball '; -- prob. also P. *goṭṭā* ' gold or silver lace ', H. *goṭā* m. ' edging of such ' (→ K. *goṭa* m. ' edging of gold braid ', S. *goṭo* m. ' gold or silver lace '); M. *goṭ* ' hem of a garment, metal wristlet '. Rebus: *°ṭī* f. ' lump of silver*gōḍḍ -- ' dig ' see *khōdd -- .Ko. *gōṭu* ' silver or gold braid '.(CDIAL 4271).Rebus: *goṭī* f. ' lump of silver (Gujarati).

Hieroglyph: kaḍī a chain; a hook; a link (G.); kaḍum a bracelet, a ring (G.) Rebus: kaḍiyo [Hem. Des. kaḍaio = Skt. sthapati a mason] a bricklayer; a mason; kaḍiyaṇa, kaḍiyeṇa a woman of the bricklayer caste; a wife of a bricklayer (Gujarati)

Why nine leaves? lo = nine (Santali); no = nine (Bengali) [Note the count of nine 'ficus' leaves depicted on the epigraph.]
lo, no 'nine' phonetic reinforcement of Hieroglyph: *loa* 'ficus' *loa* = a species of fig tree, ficus glomerata (Santali) Rebus*:* *lo* 'copper' (Samskrtam) loha lut.i = iron utensils and implements (Santali) lauha = made of copper or iron (Gr.S'r.); metal, iron (Skt.); lo_haka_ra = coppersmith, ironsmith (Pali); lo_ha_ra = blacksmith (Pt.); lohal.a (Or.); lo_ha = metal, esp. copper or bronze (Pali); copper (VS.); loho, lo_ = metal, ore, iron (Si.)

Interlocking bodies: ca_li (IL 3872); rebus: s'lika (IL) village of artisans. [cf. sala_yisu = joining of metal (Ka.)]
kamaḍha = *ficus religiosa* (Skt.); kamar.kom 'ficus' (Santali) rebus: kamaṭa = portable furnace for melting precious metals (Te.); kampaṭṭam = mint (Ta.) Vikalpa: Fig leaf 'loa'; rebus: loh '(copper) metal'. loha-kāra 'metalsmith' (Sanskrit). *loa* 'fig leaf; Rebus: loh '(copper) metal' The unique ligatures on the 'leaf' hieroglyph may be explained as a professional designation: *loha-kāra* 'metalsmith'; *kāruvu* [Skt.] n. 'An artist, artificer. An agent'.(Telugu).

sãghāṛɔ 'lathe' is a signifier and the signified is: सं-घात sãghāta 'caravan consignment' [an assemblage, aggregate of metalwork objects (of the turner in workshop): metals, alloys]. sangāṭh संगाठ् । सामग्री m. (sg. dat. sangāṭas संगाटस्), a collection (of implements, tools, materials, for any object), apparatus, furniture, a collection of the things wanted on a journey, luggage, and so on. -- karun -- करुन् । सामग्रीसंग्रहः m.inf. to collect the ab. (L.V. 17).(Kashmiri).
Hieroglyph: one-horned young bull: खोंड (p. 216) [khōṇḍa] m A young bull, a bullcalf. Rebus: कोंद kōnda 'engraver, lapidary setting or infixing gems' (Marathi)
kot.iyum = a wooden circle put round the neck of an animal; kot. = neck (G.lex.) [cf. the orthography of rings on the neck of one-horned young bull]. ko_d.iya, ko_d.e = young bull; ko_d.elu = plump young bull; ko_d.e = a. male as in: ko_d.e du_d.a = bull calf; young, youthful (Te.lex.)

Glyph: ko_t.u = horns (Ta.) ko_r (obl. ko_t-, pl. ko_hk) horn of cattle or wild animals (Go.); ko_r (pl. ko_hk), ko_r.u (pl. ko_hku) horn (Go.); kogoo a horn (Go.); ko_ju (pl. ko_ska) horn, antler (Kui)(DEDR 2200). Homonyms: kohk (Go.), gopka_ = branches (Kui), kob = branch (Ko.) gorka, gohka spear (Go.) gorka (Go)(DEDR 2126).
kod. = place where artisans work (Gujarati) kod. = a cow-pen; a cattlepen; a byre (G.lex.) gor.a = a cow-shed; a cattleshed; gor.a orak = byre (Santali.lex.) got.ho [Skt. kos.t.ha the inner part] a warehouse; an earthen
Rebus: kõdā'to turn in a lathe'(B.) कोंद kōnda 'engraver, lapidary setting or infixing gems' (Marathi) koḍ 'artisan's workshop' (Kuwi) koḍ = place where artisans work (G.) ācāri koṭṭya 'smithy' (Tu.) कोंडण [kōṇḍaṇa] f A fold or pen. (Marathi) B. kõdā 'to turn in a lathe'; Or.kŭnda 'lathe', kũdibā, kũd 'to turn' (→ Drav. Kur. Kũd ' lathe') (CDIAL 3295) A. kundār, B. kũdār, ri, Or.Kundāru; H. kũderā m. 'one who works a lathe, one who scrapes', rī f., kũdernā 'to scrape, plane, round on a lathe'; kundakara—m. 'turner' (Skt.)(CDIAL 3297). कोंदण [kōndaṇa] n (कोंदणें) Setting or infixing of gems.(Marathi) খোদকার [khōdakāra] n an engraver; a carver. খোদকারি n. engraving; carving; interference in other's work. খোদাই [khōdāi] n engraving; carving. খোদাই করা v. to engrave; to carve. খোদানো v. & n. en graving; carving. খোদিত [khōdita] a engraved. (Bengali) खोदकाम [khōdakāma] n Sculpture; carved work or work for the carver. खोदगिरी [khōdagirī] f Sculpture, carving, engraving: also sculptured or carved work. खोदणावळ [khōdaṇāvaḷa] f (खोदणें) The price or cost of sculpture or carving. खोदणी [khōdaṇī] f (Verbal of खोदणें) Digging, engraving &c. 2 fig. An exacting of money by importunity. V लाव, मांड. 3 An instrument to scoop out and cut flowers and figures from paper. 4 A goldsmith's die. खोदणें [khōdaṇēṃ] v c & i (H) To dig. 2 To engrave. खोद खोदून विचारणें or –पुसणें To question minutely and searchingly, to probe. खोदाई [khōdāī] f (H.) Price or cost of digging or of sculpture or carving. खोदींव [khōdīṃva] p of खोदणें Dug. 2 Engraved, carved, sculptured. (Marathi)

A more precise understanding of the gloss 'ayas' comes from the frequent use of a hieroglyph on Indus Script inscriptions.

A Munda gloss for fish is 'aya'. Read rebus: *aya* 'iron' (Gujarati) *ayas* 'metal' (Vedic).

The script inscriptions indicate a set of modifiers or ligatures to the hieroglyph indicating that the metal, *aya*, was worked on during the early Bronze Age metallurgical processes -- to produce *aya* ingots, *aya* metalware,*aya* hard alloys.

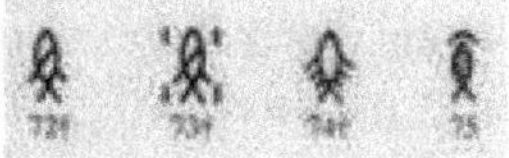

Fish hieroglyph in its vivid orthographic form is shown in a Susa pot which contained metalware -- weapons and vessels.

Context for use of 'fish' glyph. This photograph of a fish and the 'fish' glyph on Susa pot are comparable to the 'fish' glyph on Indus inscriptions.

The modifiers to the 'fish' hieroglyph which commonly occur together are: slanted stroke, notch, fins, lid-of-pot ligatured as superfix: 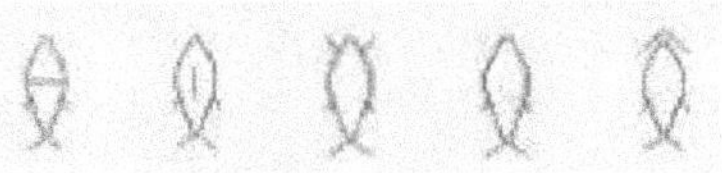 For determining the semantics of the messages conveyed by the script. Positional analysis of 'fish' glyphs has also been presented in: *The Indus Script: A Positional-statistical Approach* By Michael Korvink, 2007, Gilund Press.

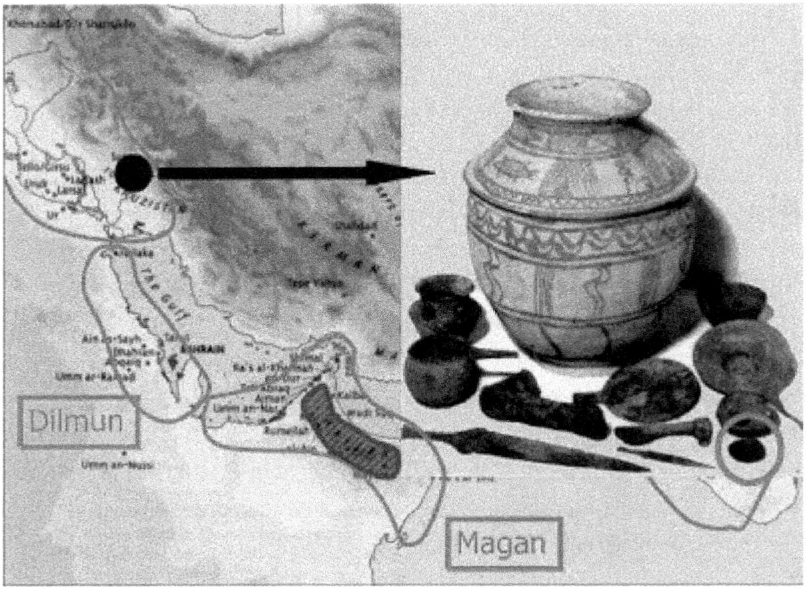

Table from: The Indus Script: A Positional-statistical Approach By Michael Korvink, 2007, Gilund Press. Mahadevan notes (Para 6.5 opcit.) that 'a unique feature of the FISH signs is their tendency to form clusters, often as pairs, and rarely as triplets also. This pattern has fascinated and baffled scholars from the days of Hunter posing problems in interpretation.' One way to resolve the problem is to interpret the glyptic elements creating ligatured fish signs and read the glyptic elements rebus to define the semantics of the message of an inscription.

karaṇḍa 'duck' (Sanskrit) *karaṛa* 'a very large aquatic bird' (Sindhi) Rebus: करडा *[karaḍā]* Hard from alloy--iron, silver &c. (Marathi) Rebus: fire-god: @B27990. #16671. Remo <*karandi*>E155 {N} ``^fire-^god".(Munda) Rebus:. *kharādī* ' turner' (Gujarati)

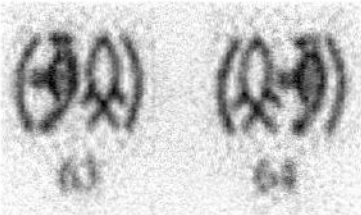

The 'parenthesis' modifier is a circumfix for both 'fish' and 'duck' hieroglyphs, the semantics of () two parenthetical modifiers are: kuṭilá— 'bent, crooked' KātyŚr., °*aka*— Pañcat., n. 'a partic. plant' [√kuṭ 1] Pa. *kuṭila*— 'bent', n. 'bend'; Pk. *kuḍila*— 'crooked', °*illa*— 'humpbacked', °*illaya*— 'bent'DEDR 2054 *(a) Ta.* koṭu curved, bent, crooked; koṭumai crookedness, obliquity; koṭukki hooked bar for fastening doors, clasp of an ornament. A pair of curved lines: *dol* 'likeness, picture, form' [e.g., two tigers, two bulls, sign-pair.] Kashmiri. dula दुल । युगमम् m. a pair, a couple, esp. of two similar things (Rām. 966). Rebus: dul meṛeḍ cast iron (Mundari. Santali) *dul* 'to cast metal in a mould' (Santali) pasra meṛed, pasāra meṛed = syn. of koṭe meṛed = forged iron, in contrast to dul meṛed, cast iron (Mundari.) Thus, *dul kuṭila* 'cast bronze'.

The parenthetically ligatured fish+duck hieroglyphs thus read rebus: *dul kuṭila ayas karaḍā* 'cast bronze *ayas*or cast alloy metal with *ayas* as component to create *karaḍā* ''hard alloy with *ayas*'.

Ligatures to fish: parentheses + snout *dul kuṭila ayas* 'cast bronze *ayas* alloy with *tuttha*, copper sulphate'

Modifier hieroglyph: 'snout' Hieroglyph: WPah.kṭg. *ṭōṭ* ' mouth '.WPah.kṭg. *thótti* f., *thótthəṛ* m. ' snout, mouth ', A. *ṭhõt*(phonet. *thõt*) (CDIAL 5853). Semantics, Rebus:

tutthá n. (m. lex.), *tutthaka* -- n. ' blue vitriol (used as an eye ointment) ' Suśr., *tūtaka* -- lex. 2. *thōttha -- 4. 3. *tūtta -- . 4. *tōtta -- 2. [Prob. ← Drav. T. Burrow BSOAS xii 381; cf. *dhūrta* -- 2 n. ' iron filings ' lex.]1. N. *tutho* ' blue vitriol or sulphate of copper ', B. *tuth*.2. K. *thŏth*, dat. °*thas* m., P. *thothā* m.3. S.*tūtio* m., A. *tutiyā*, B. *tũte*, Or. *tutiā*, H. *tūtā*, *tūtiyā* m., M. *tutiyā* m.
4. M. *totā* m.(CDIAL 5855) *Ka.* tukku rust of iron; tutta, tuttu, tutte blue vitriol. *Tu.* tukků rust; mair(ů)suttu, (*Eng.-Tu. Dict.*) mairůtuttu blue vitriol. *Te.* t(r)uppu rust; (*SAN*) trukku id., verdigris. / Cf. Skt. tuttha- blue vitriol (DEDR 3343).

Fish + corner, *aya koṇḍa*, 'metal turned or forged'

Fish, *aya* 'metal'

Binjor seal. Fish + scales, *aya ãs (amśu)* 'metallic stalks of stone ore'. Vikalpa: *badhoṛ* 'a species of fish with many bones' (Santali)
Rebus: *baḍhoe* 'a carpenter, worker in wood'; *badhoria* 'expert in working in wood'(Santali) It is possible that the orthography signifies Fish + fins. The gloss for fins is *skambha2 ' shoulder -- blade, wing, plumage '. [Cf. **skapa* -- s.v. *khavaka --]
S. *khambhu*, °*bho* m. ' plumage ', *khambhuṛi* f. ' wing '; L. *khabbh* m., mult. *khambh* m. ' shoulder -- blade, wing, feather ', khet. *khamb* ' wing ', mult. *khambhaṛā* m. ' fin '; P. *khambh* m. ' wing, feather ';
G. *khā̆m* f., *khabhɔ* m. ' shoulder '.(CDIAL 13640) It is significant that this ligatured fish hieroglyph-multiplex is used on Binjor seal associated with the performance of Soma Yaga (signified by the octagonal yupa on the yajna kunda).

Aya 'fish' rebus: aya, ayas 'iron metal' PLUS *khambhaṛā* m. ' fin ' (Lahnda) rebus: kammaTa 'mint, coiner'. Thus, this unique fish ligature is seen to signify metal used by the coiner in a mint.

Fish + splinter, *aya aduru* 'smelted native metal'

Fish + sloping stroke, *aya ḍhāḷ* 'metal ingot'

Fish + arrow or allograph, Fish + circumscribed four short strokes

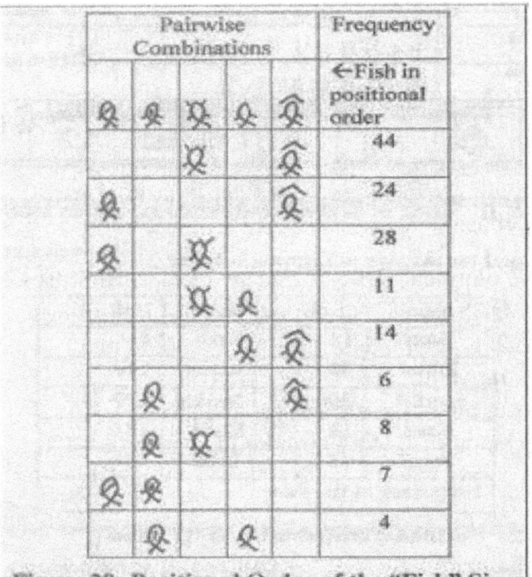
Pairwise Combinations
Frequency
←Fish in positional order
44
24
28
11
14
6
8
7
4

Figure 20: Positional Order of the "Fish" Signs

This indication of the occurrence, together, of two or more 'fish' hieroglyphs with modifiers is an assurance that the modifiers ar semantic indicators of how aya 'metal' is worked on by the artisans.

ayakāṇḍa ''large quantity of stone (ore) metal' or *aya kaṇḍa,* 'metal fire-altar'. *ayo, hako* 'fish'; *ãs* = scales of fish (Santali); rebus: *aya* 'metal, iron' (G.); *ayah, ayas* = metal (Skt.) Santali lexeme, *hako* 'fish' is concordant with a proto-Indic form which can be identified as *ayo* in many glosses, Munda, Sora glosses in particular, of the Indian linguistic area.

beḍa hako (ayo) 'fish' (Santali); *beḍa* 'either of the sides of a hearth' (G.) Munda: So. *ayo* `fish'. Go. ayu `fish'. Go <ayu> (Z), <ayu?u> (Z),, <ayu?> (A) {N} ``^fish''. Kh. kaDOG `fish'. Sa. Hako `fish'. Mu. hai (H) ~ haku(N) ~ haikO(M) `fish'. Ho haku `fish'. Bj. hai `fish'. Bh.haku `fish'. KW haiku ~ hakO |Analyzed hai-kO, ha-kO (RDM). Ku. Kaku`fish'.@(V064,M106) Mu. ha-i, haku `fish' (HJP). @(V341) ayu>(Z), <ayu?u> (Z) <ayu?>(A) {N} ``^fish''. #1370. <yO>\\<AyO>(L) {N} ``^fish''. #3612. <kukkulEyO>,,<kukkuli-yO>(LMD) {N} ``prawn''. !Serango dialect. #32612. <sArjAjyO>,,<sArjAj>(D) {N} ``prawn''. #32622. <magur-yO>(ZL) {N} ``a kind of ^fish''. *Or.<>. #32632. <ur+GOl-Da-yO>(LL) {N} ``a kind of ^fish''. #32642.<bal.bal-yO>(DL) {N} ``smoked fish''. #15163. Vikalpa: Munda: <aDara>(L) {N} ``^scales of a fish, sharp bark of a tree''.#10171. So<aDara>(L) {N} ``^scales of a fish, sharp bark of a tree''.

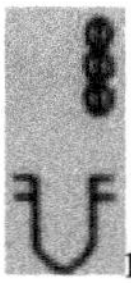

m1406 Seal using three-stranded rope: dhAtu Rebus: iron ore.

Hieroglyph: धातु [p= 513,3] *m.* layer , stratum KaltyS3r. Kaus3. constituent part , ingredient (esp. [and in RV. only] ifc. , where often = " fold " e.g. त्रि-धु्/आतु , threefold &c ; cf.त्रिविष्टि- , सप्त- , सु-) RV. TS. S3Br. &c (Monier-Williams) dhā´tu *strand of rope ' (cf. *tridhā´tu* -- ' threefold ' RV., *ayugdhātu* -- ' having an uneven number of strands ' KātyŚr.).; S. *dhāī* f. ' wisp of fibres added from time to time to a rope that is being twisted ', L. *dhāī̃* f.(CDIAL 6773)

Rebus: M. *dhāū, dhāv* m.f. ' a partic. soft red stone ' (whence *dhā̆vaḍ* m. ' a caste of iron -- smelters ', *dhāvḍī* ' composed of or relating to iron '); dhā´tu n. ' substance ' RV., m. ' element ' MBh., ' metal, mineral, ore (esp. of a red colour) '; Pk. *dhāu* -- m. ' metal, red chalk '; N. *dhāu* ' ore (esp. of copper) '; Or. *ḍhāu* ' red chalk, red ochre ' (whence *ḍhāuā* ' reddish '; (CDIAL 6773) धातु primary element of the earth i.e. metal , mineral, ore (esp. a mineral of a red colour) Mn. MBh. &c element of words i.e. grammatical or verbal root or stem Nir. Pra1t. MBh. &c (with the southern Buddhists धातु means either the 6 elements [see above] Dharmas. xxv ; or the 18 elementary spheres [धातु-लोक] ib. lviii ; or the ashes of the body , relics L. [cf. -गर्भ]) (Monier-Williams. Samskrtam)

Banawali10 9204 xolā = tail (Kur.); qoli id. (Malt.)(DEDR 2135). Rebus: kol 'pañcalōha' (Ta.) கொல் kol, n. Iron. (Tamil) Dm. *mraṅ* m. 'markhor' *Wkh. merg f. 'ibex'* (CDIAL 9885) Tor. *miṇḍ* 'ram', *miṇḍā́l* 'markhor' (CDIAL 10310) Rebus: meḍ 'iron' (Ho.) kolom 'sprout' Rebus: kolami 'smithy/forge'. eae 'seven' (Santali); rebus: eh-ku 'steel' (Ta.) gaṇḍa 'four' (Santali) Rebus: kaṇḍ fire-altar, furnace' (Santali) tagaraka 'tabernae montana' Rebus: tagaram 'tin'.

Courtyard with turners' workshops

h1018 copper plate. Star-fish? Gangetic octopus?

m297a. seal. 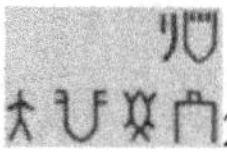2641

veṛhā octopus, said to be found in the Indus (Jaṭki lexicon of A. Jukes, 1900) Rebus: L. *veṛh, vehṛ* m. fencing; Mth. *beṛhī* granary; L. *veṛhā, vehṛā* enclosure containing many houses; *beṛā* building with a courtyard (WPah.) (CDIAL 12130)

koḍ 'horn' Rebus: koḍ = artisan's workshop (Kuwi)

खोंड [khōṇḍa] m A young bull, a bullcalf (Marathi) Rebus: *kõdār* 'turner' (Bengali)

मेड [mēḍa] f (Usually मेढ q. v.) मेडका m A stake (Marathi) meḍa 'pillar' (Go.) Rebus: meḍ 'iron' (Ho.)

kāṭhī = body, person; *kāṭhī* the make of the body; the stature of a man (Gujarati) Rebus: *khātī* 'wheelwright' (H.)

117 antelope; sun motif. Dholavira seal impression. arka 'sun' Rebus: araka, eraka 'copper, moltencast' PLUS करडूं karaḍū 'kid' Rebus: karaḍā 'hard alloy'. Thus, together, the rebus message: hard alloy of copper.

On arka in compound expressions: அருக்கம்[1] *arukkam, n.* < *arka.* (நாநார்த்த.) 1. Copper; செம்பு (Tamil) అగసాలి (p. 0023) [agasāli] or అగసాలెవాడు *agasāli*. [Tel.] n. A goldsmith. కంసాలివాడు.(Telugu) Kannada (Kittel lexicon):

ಅಕಸಾಲ aka2-sâla. = ಅಕ್ಕಸಾಲ, ಅಗಸಾಲ. A gold or silver smith (C.).
ಅಕಸಾಲಿಕೆ aka2-sâlikĕ. = ಅಕ್ಕಸಾಲಿಕೆ. The business of a gold or silver smith (C.).
ಅಕಸಾಲಿಗ aka2-sâliga. = ಅಕ್ಕಸಾಲಿಗ, ಅಗಸಾಲಿಗ. A gold or silver smith (C.).
ಅಕಸಾಲೆ aka-sâlĕ. = ಅಕ್ಕಸಾಲೆ q. v., ಅಗಸಾಲೆ. The workshop of a goldsmith. 2, a goldsmith (C.).

Bet Dwaraka turbinella pyrum seal. करडूं karaḍū 'kid' Rebus: karaḍā 'hard alloy'. barad 'ox' Rebus: bharata 'alloy of copper, pewter, tin' khond 'young bull' koD 'horn' Rebus: khond 'turner' koD 'workshop'. Thus workshop of hard alloys of copper, pewter, tin.

Bhirrrna seal. ASI karNika 'rim of jar' rebus: karNI 'supercargo'; karNaka 'account'; Alternative: kanka 'rim of jar' rebus: kanga 'brazier'. A variant of Signs is seen on the

Bhirrana seal: 47 481 *karaṁḍa* -- m.n. ' bone shaped like a bamboo ', *karaṁḍuya* -- n. ' backbone ' (Prakrit) Rebus: करडा [*karaḍā*] Hard from alloy--iron, silver &c. (Marathi)

40 Three-headed animal, plant; sun motifDholavira. Seal. Readings as above. PLUS kolmo 'rice plant' Rebus: kolami 'smithy, forge'. Thus, the message of the hieroglyph-multiplex is: smithy/forge for moltencast coper and hard alloys of copper, pewter, tin.

Hieroglyph: करडूं or करडें (p. 137) [karaḍū or karaḍēṃ] *n* A kid. कराडूं (p. 137) [karāḍūṃ] *n* (Commonly करडूं) A kid. (Marathi) Rebus: करडा (p. 137) [karaḍā] Hard from alloy--iron, silver &c. (Marathi. Molesworth).

Thanks to Benoy Behl for disseminating the photograph of an exquisite gold disc now in al-Sabah collection of Kuwait National Museum. This gold disc is a veritable metalwork catalogue, consistent with the entire Indus Script Corpora as catalogus catalogorum of metalwork. The uniqueness of the collection of hieroglyph-multiplexs on this gold disc is that a large number of metalwork catalogue items (more than 12) have been presented on a circular space with 9.6 cm diameter validating the Maritime Tin Route which linked Hanoi to Haifa through the Persian Gulf.

"Gold disc. al-Sabah Collection, Kuwait National Museum. 9.6 cm diameter, which was obviously from the Indus Valley period in India. Typical of that period, it depicts zebu, bulls, human attendants, ibex, fish, partridges, bees, pipal free an animal-headed standard." Benoy K. Behl https://www.facebook.com/BenoyKBehlArtCulture

Hieroglyph: kunda = a pillar of bricks (Ka.); pillar, post (Tu.Te.); block, log (Malt.); kantu = pillar, post (Ta.)(DEDR 1723).

Rebus: kun.d. = a pit (Santali) kun.d.amu = a pit for receiving and preserving consecrated fire; a hole in the ground (Te.) kun.d.am, kun.d.a sacrificial fire pit (Skt.) kun.d.a an altar on which sacrifices are made (G.)[i] gun.d.amu fire-pit; (Inscr.)

The hieroglyphs on the Kuwait Museum gold disc can be read rebus:
1. A pair of *tabernae montana* flowers *tagara* 'tabernae montana' flower; rebus: *tagara* 'tin'
2. A pair of rams *tagara* 'ram'; rebus: *damgar* 'merchant' (Akkadian) Next to one ram: kuTi 'tree' Rebus: kuThi 'smelter' Alternative: kolmo 'rice plant' Rebus: kolimi 'smithy, forge'.

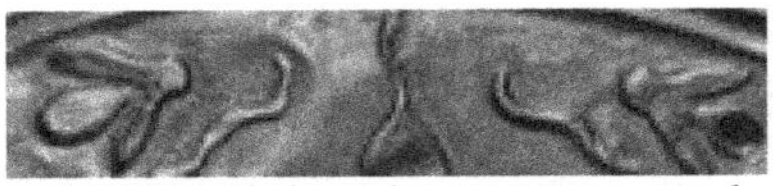

3. Ficus religiosa leaves on a tree branch (5) *loa* 'ficus leaf'; rebus: *loh* 'metal'. *kol* in Tamil means *pancaloha*'alloy of five metals'. PLUS flanking pair of lotus flowers: tAmarasa 'lotus' Rebus: tAmra 'copper' dula 'pair' Rebus: dul 'cast metal' thus, denoting copper castings.

4. A pair of bulls tethered to the tree branch: barad, barat 'ox' Rebus: bharata 'alloy of copper, pewter, tin' (Marathi) PLUS kola 'man' Rebus: kolhe 'smelter' kur.i 'woman' Rebus: kol 'working in iron' Alternative: *ḍhangar* 'bull'; rebus *ḍhangar* 'blacksmith' poLa 'zebu' Rebus: poLa 'magnetite'. Two persons touch the two bulls: *meḍ* 'body' (Mu.) Rebus: *meḍ* 'iron' (Ho.) Thus, the hieroglyph composition denotes ironsmiths.
5. A pair of antelopes looking back: *krammara* 'look back'; rebus: *kamar* 'smith' (Santali); *tagara* 'antelope'; rebus: *damgar* 'merchant' (Akkadian) Alternative: *melh, mr..eka* 'goat' (Brahui. Telugu) Rebus: milakkhu 'copper' (Pali), mleccha-mukha 'copper' (Samskrtam)
6. A pair of antelopes *mē̃ḍh* 'antelope, ram'; rebus: *mē̃ḍ 'iron' (Mu.)*
7. A pair of combs *kāṅga* 'comb' Rebus: *kanga* 'brazier, fireplace'

Phal. *kāṅga* ' combing ' in *ṣiṣ k° dūm* 'I comb my hair' *khyḗṅgia, kēṅgī* f.; *kaṅghā* m. ' large comb (Punjabi) káṅkata m. ' comb ' AV., n. lex., *°tī* -- , *°tikā* -- f. lex. 2. *kaṅkaṭa -- 2. 3. *kaṅkaśa -- . [Of doubtful IE. origin WP i 335, EWA i 137: aberrant -- *uta* -- as well as -- *aśa* -- replacing -- *ata* -- in MIA. and NIA.]1. Pk. *kaṁkaya* -- m. ' comb ', *kaṁkaya* -- , *°kaï* -- m. ' name of a tree '; Gy. eur. *kangli* f.; Wg. *kuṇi -- přũ* ' man's comb ' (for *kuṇi* -- cf. *kuṇälík* beside *kuṅälík*s.v. kṛmuka -- ; -- *přũ* see prapavaṇa --); Bshk. *kēṅg* ' comb ', Gaw. *khēṅgī´*, Sv. *khḗṅgiā*, Tor. *kyäṅg* ' comb ' (Dard. forms, esp. Gaw., Sv., Phal. but not Sh., prob. ← L. P. type < **kaṅgahiā* -- , see 3 below); Sh. *kōṅyi̯* f. (→ Ḍ. *k*lṅi* f.), gil. (Lor.) *kõī* f. ' man's comb ', *kõũ* m. ' woman's comb ', pales. *kōgō* m. ' comb '; K. *kanguwu* m. ' man's comb ', *kangañ* f. ' woman's '; WPah. bhad. *kā̃´kei* ' a comb -- like fern ', bhal. *kā̃kei* f. ' comb, plant with comb -- like leaves '; N. *kāṅiyo, kāĩyo* ' comb ', A. *kā̃kai*, B. *kā̃kui;* Or. *kaṅkāi, kaṅkuā* ' comb ', *kakuā* ' ladder -- like bier for carrying corpse to the burning -- ghat '; Bi. *kakwā* ' comb ', *kakahā, °hī*, Mth. *kakwā*, Aw. lakh. *kakawā*, Bhoj. *kakahī* f.; H. *kakaiyā* ' shaped like a comb (of a brick) '; G. (non -- Aryan tribes of Dharampur)*kākhāī* f. ' comb '; M. *kaṅkvā* m. ' comb ', *kā̃kaī* f. ' a partic. shell fish and its shell '; -- S. *kaṅgu* m. ' a partic. kind of small fish ' < **kaṅkuta* -- ? -- Ext. with --*l* -- in Ku. *kā̃gilo, kāĩlo* ' comb '.2. G. (Soraṭh) *kā̃gaṛ* m. ' a weaver's instrument '?3. L. *kaṅghī* f. ' comb, a fish of the perch family ', awāṇ. *kaghī* ' comb '; P. *kaṅghā* m. ' large comb ', *°ghī* f. ' small comb for men, large one for women ' (→ H. *kaṅghā* m. ' man's comb ', *°gahī, °ghī* f. ' woman's ', *kaṅghuā* m. ' rake or harrow '; Bi. *kā̃gahī* ' comb ', Or. *kaṅgei*, M. *kaṅgvā*); -- G. *kā̃gsī* f. ' comb ', with metath. *kā̃sko* m., *°kī* f.; WPah. khaś. *kāgśī*, śeu. *kāśkī* ' a comblike fern ' or < **kaṅkataśikha* -- .WPah.kṭg. *kaṅgi* f. ' comb '; J. *kā̃gṛu* m. ' small comb '.(CDIAL 2598)

Rebus: large furnace, fireplace: kang कंग् । आवसथ्यो &1;ग्निः m. the fire-receptacle or fire-place, kept burning in former times in the courtyard of a Kāshmīrī house for the benefit of guests, etc., and distinct from the three religious domestic fires of a Hindū; (at the present day) a fire-place or brazier lit in the open air on mountain sides, etc., for the sake of warmth or for keeping off wild beasts. nāra-kang, a fire-receptacle; hence, met. a shower of sparks (falling on a person) (Rām. 182). kan:gar `portable furnace' (Kashmiri)Cf. kā̃gürü, which is the fem. of this word in a dim. sense (Gr.Gr. 33, 7). kā̃gürü काँग्ॗ or kā̃gürü काँग or kā̃gar काँग्ॗर्ॗ । हसब्तिका f. (sg. dat. kā̃grĕ काँग्र्य or kā̃garĕ काँगर्य, abl. kā̃gri काँग्रि), the portable brazier, or *kāngrī,* much used in Kashmīr (K.Pr. *kángár,* 129, 131, 178; *káṅgrí,* 5, 128, 129). For particulars see El. s.v. *kángri;* L. 7, 25, *kangar;*and K.Pr. 129. The word is a fem. dim. of kang, q.v. (Gr.Gr.

37). kā̃gri-khŏphürükā̃gri-khŏphürü काँग्रि-ख्वफ्◌&above;रू&below; । भग्ना काष्ठाङ्गारिका f. a worn-out brazier. -khôru -खोरु&below; । काष्ठाङ्गारिका<-> र्धभागः m. the outer half (made of woven twigs) of a brazier, remaining after the inner earthenware bowl has been broken or removed; see khôru. -kŏnḍolu -कंड । हसन्तिकापात्रम् m. the circular earthenware bowl of a brazier, which contains the burning fuel. -kőñü -का&above;ञू&below; । हसन्तिकालता f. the covering of woven twigs outside the earthenware bowl of a brazier.

It is an archaeometallurgical challenge to trace the Maritime Tin Route from the tin belt of the world on Mekong River delta in the Far East and trace the contributions made by seafaring merchants of Meluhha in reaching the tin mineral resource to sustain the Tin-Bronze Age which was a revolution unleashed ca. 5th millennium BCE

8. A pair of fishes ayo 'fish' (Mu.); rebus: ayo 'metal, iron' (Gujarati); ayas 'metal' (Sanskrit)

9.A pair of buffaloes tethered to a post-standard kāṛā 'buffalo' கண்டி kaṇṭi buffalo bull (Tamil); rebus: *kaṇḍ* 'stone ore'; *kāṇḍa* 'tools, pots and pans and metal-ware'; *kaṇḍ* 'furnace, fire-altar, consecrated fire'.

10. A pair of birds Rebus 1: *kōḍi*. [Tel.] n. A fowl, a bird. (Telugu) Rebus: *khōṭ* 'alloyed ingots'. Rebus 2: *kol* 'the name of a bird, the Indian cuckoo' (Santali) *kol* 'iron, smithy, forge'. Rebus 3: baṭa = quail (Santali) Rebus: baṭa = furnace, kiln (Santali) bhrāṣṭra = furnace (Skt.) baṭa = a kind of iron (G.) bhaṭa 'furnace' (Gujarati)

11. The buffaloes, birds flank a post-standard with curved horns on top of a stylized 'eye' PLUS 'eyebrows' with one-horn on either side of two faces

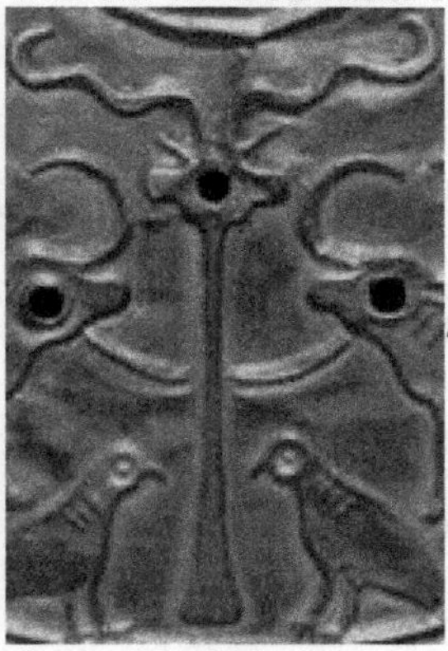

mũh 'face'; rebus: *mũh* 'ingot' (Mu.)

ṭhaṭera 'buffalo horns'. *ṭhaṭerā* 'brass worker' (Punjabi)

Pe. kaṇga (*pl.* -ŋ, kaṇku) eye. Rebus: kanga ' large portable brazier, fire-place' (Kashmiri).

Thus the stylized standard is read rebus: Hieroglyph components:*kanga* + *ṭhaṭerā* 'one eye + buffalo horn' Rebus: *kanga* 'large portable barzier' (Kashmiri) + *ṭhaṭerā* 'brass worker' (Punjabi)

Ta. kaṇ eye, aperture, orifice, star of a peacock's tail. *Ma.* kaṇ, kaṇṇu eye, nipple, star in peacock's tail, bud. *Ko.* kaṇ eye. *To.* koṇ eye, loop in string.*Ka.* kaṇ eye, small hole, orifice. *Koḍ.* kaṇṇï id. *Tu.* kaṇṇů eye, nipple, star in peacock's feather, rent, tear. *Te.* kanu, kannu eye, small hole, orifice, mesh of net, eye in peacock's feather. *Kol.* kan (*pl.* kanḍl) eye, small hole in ground, cave. *Nk.* kan (*pl.* kanḍḷ) eye, spot in peacock's tail. *Nk. (Ch.)* kan (*pl.* -l) eye. *Pa.*(S. only) kan (*pl.* kanul) eye. *Ga.* (Oll.) kaṇ (*pl.* kaṇkul) id.; kaṇul maṭṭa eyebrow; kaṇa (*pl.* kaṇul) hole; (S.) kanu (*pl.* kankul) eye. *Go.* (Tr.) kan (*pl.*kank) id.; (A.) kaṛ (*pl.* kaṛk) id. *Konḍa* kaṇ id. *Pe.* kaṇga (*pl.* -ŋ, kaṇku) id. *Manḍ.* kan (*pl.* -ke) id. *Kui* kanu (*pl.* kan-ga), (K.) kanu (*pl.* kaṛka) id. *Kuwi*(F.) kannū (*pl.* kar&nangle;ka), (S.) kannu (*pl.* kanka), (Su. P. Isr.) kanu (*pl.* kaṇka) id. *Kur.* xann eye, eye of tuber; xannērnā (of newly born babies or animals) to begin to see, have the use of one's eyesight (for ērnā, see 903). *Malt.* qanu eye. *Br.* xan id., bud. (DEDR 1159) kāṇá ' one -- eyed ' RV. Pa. Pk. *kāṇa* -- ' blind of one eye, blind '; Ash. *kā̃ṛa*, °*ṛī* f. ' blind ', Kt. *kā̃ŕ*, Wg. *kŕāmacrdotdot;*, Pr. *k&schwatildemacr;*, Tir. *kā´na*, Kho. *kāṇu* NTS ii 260,*kánu* BelvalkarVol

91; K. *kônu* ' one -- eyed ', S. *kāṇo*, L. P. *kāṇā̃*; WPah. rudh. śeu. *kāṇā* ' blind '; Ku. *kāṇo*, gng. *kā&rtodtilde;* ' blind of one eye ', N. *kānu;*A. *kanā* ' blind '; B. *kāṇā* ' one -- eyed, blind '; Or. *kaṇā*, f. *kāṇī* ' one -- eyed ', Mth. *kān*, *°nā, kanahā*, Bhoj. *kān*, f. *°ni, kanwā* m. ' one -- eyed man ', H. *kān,°nā*, G. *kāṇũ*; M. *kāṇā* ' one -- eyed, squint -- eyed '; Si. *kaṇa* ' one -- eyed, blind '. -- Pk. *kāṇa* -- ' full of holes ', G. *kāṇũ* ' full of holes ', n. ' hole ' (< ' empty eyehole '? Cf. *ā̃dhḷũ* n. ' hole ' < andhala --).S.kcch. *kāṇī* f.adj. ' one -- eyed '; WPah.kṭg. *kaṇɔ* ' blind in one eye ', J. *kāṇā*; Md. *kanu* ' blind '.(CDIAL 3019) Ko. *kāṇso* ' squint -- eyed '.(Konkani)

Paš. ainċ -- gánik ' eyelid '(CDIAL 3999) Phonetic reinforcement of the gloss: *Pe.* kaṇga (*pl.* -ŋ, kaṇku) eye.

See also: *nimišta kanag* 'to write' (SBal): *nipēśayati ' writes '. [√piś] Very doubtful: Kal.rumb. Kho. nivḗš -- ' to write ' more prob. ← EPers. Morgenstierne BSOS viii 659. <-> Ir. pres. st. *nipaiš -- (for *nipais -- after past *nipišta --) in Yid. nuviš -- , Mj. nuvuš -- , Sang. Wkh. nəviš -- ; -- Aś. nipista<-> ← Ir. *nipista -- (for *nipišta -- after pres. *nipais --) in SBal. novīsta or nimišta kanag ' to write '.(CDIAL 7220) *Alternative: dol* 'eye'; Rebus: *dul* 'to cast metal in a mould' (Santali) *Alternative: kandi* 'hole, opening' (Ka.)[Note the eye shown as a dotted circle on many Dilmun seals.]; *kan* 'eye' (Ka.); rebus: *kandi* (pl. –l) necklace, beads (Pa.);*kaṇḍ* 'stone ore' Alternative: *kā̃gsī* f. 'comb' (Gujarati); rebus 1: *kangar* 'portable furnace' (Kashmiri); rebus 2: *kamsa* 'bronze'.
khuṇḍ 'tethering peg or post' (Western Pahari) Rebus: *kūṭa* 'workshop'; *kuṭi*= smelter furnace (Santali); Rebus 2: *kuṇḍ 'fire-altar'*

Why are animals shown in pairs?

dula 'pair' (Kashmiri); rebus: dul 'cast metal' (Mu.)
Thus, all the hieroglyphs on the gold disc can be read as Indus writing related to one bronze-age artifact category: metalware catalog entries.

Oxford English Dictionary defines anthropomorphic: "a. treating the deity as anthropomorphous, or as having a human form and character; b. attributing a human personality to anything impersonal or irrational."

The copper anthropomorph of Haryana is comparable to and an elaboration of a copper anthropomorph of Sheorajpur, Uttar Pradesh. Both deploy Meluhha hieroglyphs using rebus-metonymy layered cipher of Indus writing.

The hieroglyhs of the anthropomorphs are a remarkable archaeological evidence attesting to the evidence of an ancient Samskrtam text, *Baudhāyana śrautasūtra.*

Baudhāyana śrautasūtra 18.44 which documents migrations of Āyu and Amavasu from a central region:

pran Ayuh pravavraja. tasyaite Kuru-Pancalah Kasi-Videha ity. etad Ayavam pravrajam. pratyan amavasus. tasyaite Gandharvarayas Parsavo 'ratta ity. etad Amavasavam

Trans. Ayu went east, his is the Yamuna-Ganga region (Kuru-Pancala, Kasi-Videha). Amavasu went west, his is Gandhara, Parsu and Araṭṭa.

Ayu went east from Kurukshetra to Kuru-Pancala, Kasi-Videha. The migratory path of Meluhha artisand in the lineage of Ayu of the Rigvedic tradition, to Kasi-Videha certainly included the very ancient temple town of Sheorajpur of Dist. Etawah (Kanpur), Uttar Pradesh.

Haryana anthropormorph (in the Kurukshetra region on the banks of Vedic River Sarasvati) deploys hieroglyphs of markhor (horns), crocodile and one-horned young bull together with an inscription text using Indus Script hieroglyphs. The Sheorajpur anthropomorph deploys hieroglyphs of markhor (horns) and fish. The astonishing continuity of archaeo-metallurgical tradition of Sarasvati-Sindhu (Hindu) civilization is evident from a temple in Sheorajpur on the banks of Sacred River Ganga. This temple dedicated to Siva has metalwork ceilings !!!

Both anthropomorph artefacts in copper alloy are metalwork catalogs of *dhokara kamar* '*cire perdue*(lost-wax) metal casters'.

Hieroglyhph: *eraka* 'wing' Rebus: *eraka, arka* 'copper'.In 2003, Paul Yule wrote a remarkable article on metallic anthropomorphic figures derived from Magan/Makkan, i.e. from an Umm an-Nar period context in al-Aqir/Bahla' in the south-western piedmont of the western Hajjar chain. "These artefacts are compared with those from northern Indian in terms of their origin and/or dating. They are particularly interesting owing to a secure provenance in middle Oman...The anthropomorphic artefacts dealt with...are all the more interesting as documents of an ever-growing body of information on prehistoric international contact/influence bridging the void between south-eastern Arabia and South Asia...Gerd Weisgerber recounts that in winter of 1983/4...al-Aqir near Bahla' in the al-Zahirah Wilaya delivered prehistoric planoconvex 'bun' ingots and other metallic artefacts from the same find complex..."

In the following plate, Figs. 1 to 5 are anthropomorphs, with 'winged' attributes. The metal finds from the al-Aqir wall include ingots, figures, an axe blade, a hoe, and a cleaver (see fig. 1, 1-8), all in copper alloy.

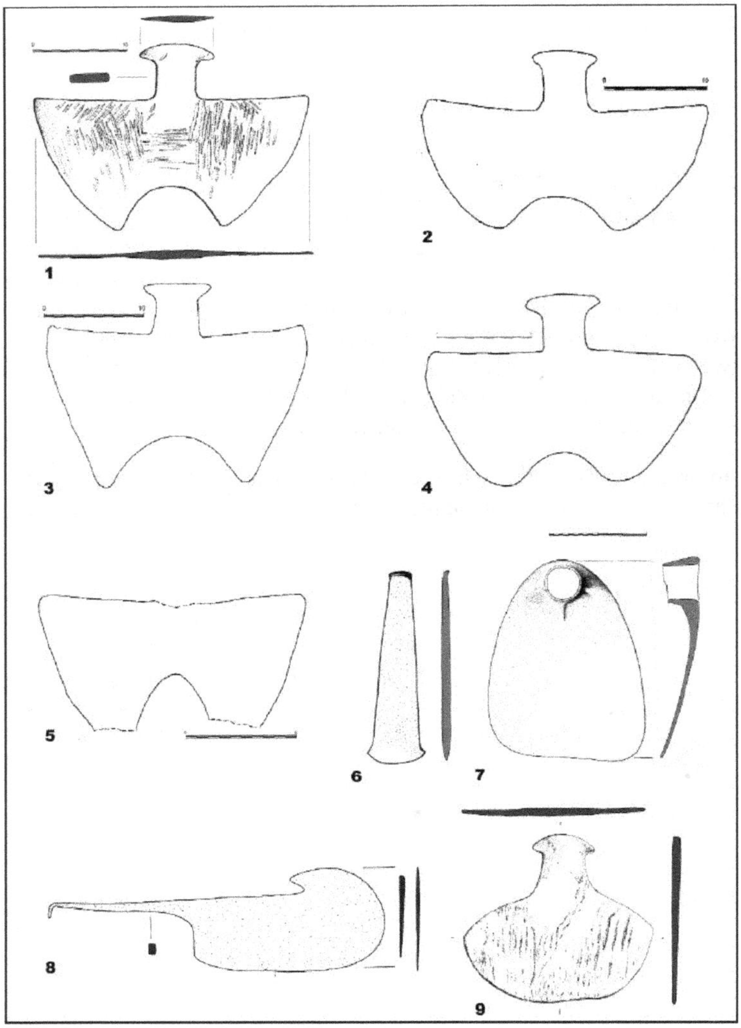

Fig. 1: Prehistoric metallic artefacts from the Sultanate of Oman: 1-8 al-Aqir/Bahla'; 9 Ra's al-Jins 2, building vii, room 2, period 3 (DA 11961) "The cleaver no. 8 is unparalleled in the prehistory of the entire Near East. Its form resembles an iron coco-nut knife from a reportedly subrecent context in Gudevella (near Kharligarh, Dist. Balangir, Orissa) which the author examined some years ago in India...The dating of the figures, which command our immediate attention, depends on two strands of thought. First, the Umm an-Nar Period/Culture dating mentioned above, en-compasses a time-space from 2500 to 1800 BC. In any case, the presence of "bun" ingots among the finds by nomeans contradicts a dating for the anthropomorphic figures toward the end of the second millennium BC. Since these are a product of a simple form of copper production, they existed with the beginning of smelting in Oman. The earliest dated examples predate this, i.e. the Umm an-NarPeriod. Thereafter, copper continues to be produced intothe medieval period. Anthropomorphic figures from the Ganges-Yamuna Doab which resemble significantly theal-Aqir artefacts (fig. 2,10-15) form a second line of evidence for the dating. To date, some 21 anthropomorphsfrom northern India have been published." (p. 539; cf. Yule, 1985, 128: Yule et al. 1989 (1992) 274: Yule et al 2002. More are known to exist, particularly from a large hoard deriving from Madarpur.)

Prehistoric metallic artefacts from al-Aqir (excepting ingots)

No.	cm	Inventory No.	description
1	29.5 x 19.5 x 0,9	DA 15499	anthropomorph
2	29.0 x 20.3	DA 15496	anthropomorph
3	27.7 x 17.4	DA 15497	anthropomorph
4	26.1 x 20.4	DA 15495	anthropomorph
5	30.1 x 15.2 (pres.)	DA 15713	anthropomorph
6	5.4 x 18.7 x 0.9	DA 11783	palstave
7	16.5 x 21.0 x 3.8	DA 11782	hoe
8	40.0 x 12.2 x 0.4	DA 15498	cleaver

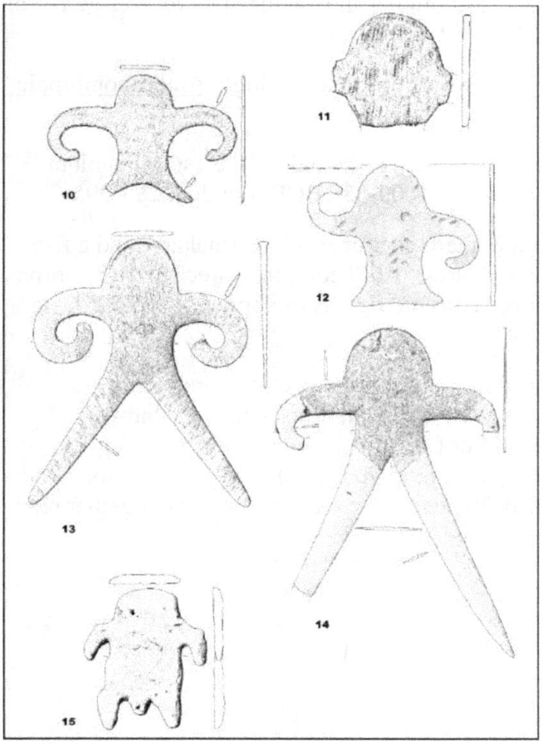

Fig. 2: Anthropomorphic figures from the Indian Subcontinent. 10 type I, Saipai, Dist. Etawah, U.P.; 11 type I, Lothal, Dist. Ahmedabad,Guj.; 12 type I variant, Madarpur, Dist. Moradabad, U.P.; 13 type II, Sheorajpur, Dist. Kanpur, U.P.; 14 miscellaneous type, Fathgarh,
Fig. 2: Anthropomorphic figures from the Indian Subcontinent. 10 type I, Saipai, Dist. Etawah, U.P.; 11 type I, Lothal, Dist. Ahmedabad,Guj.; 12 type I variant, Madarpur, Dist. Moradabad, U.P.; 13 type II, Sheorajpur, Dist. Kanpur, U.P.; 14 miscellaneous type, Fathgarh,Dist. Farrukhabad, U.P.; 15 miscellaneous type, Dist. Manbhum, Bihar.

The anthropomorph from Lothal/Gujarat (fig. 2,11), from a layer which its excavator dates to the 19 th century BCE. Lothal, phase 4 of period A, type 1. Some anthropomorphs were found stratified together with Ochre-Coloured Pottery, dated to ca. 2nd millennium BCE. Anthropomorph of Ra's al-Jins (Fig. 1,9) clearly reinforces the fact that South Asians travelled to and stayed at the site of Ra's al-Jins. "The excavators date the context from which the Ra's al-Jins copper artefact derived to their period III, i.e. 2300-2200 BCE (Cleuziou & Tosi 1997, 57), which falls within thesame time as at least some of the copper ingots which are represented at al-Aqir, and for example also in contextfrom al-Maysar site M01...the Franco-Italian teamhas emphasized the presence of a settled Harappan-Peri-od population and lively trade with South Asia at Ra's al-Jins in coastal Arabia. (Cleuziou, S. & Tosi, M., 1997, Evidence for the use of aromatics in the early Bronze Age of Oman, in: A. Avanzini, ed., *Profumi d'Arabia*, Rome 57-81)."

"In the late third-early second millennium, given the presence of a textually documented 'Meluhha village' in Lagash (southern Mesopotamia), one cannot be too surprised that such colonies existed 'east of Eden' in south-eastern Arabia juxtaposed with South Asia. In any case, here we encounter yet again evidence for contact between the two regions -- a contact of greater intimacy and importance than for the other areas of the Gulf."(Paul Yule, 2003, Beyond the pale of near Eastern Archaeology: Anthropomorphic figures from al-Aqir near Bahla' In: Stöllner, T. (Hrsg.): Mensch und Bergbau Studies in Honour of Gerd Weisgerber on Occasion of his 65th Birthday. Bochum 2003, pp. 537-542).

https://www.academia.edu/1043347/Beyond_the_Pale_of_Near_Eastern_Archaeology_Anthropomorphic_Figures_from_al-Aqir_near_Bahl%C4%81_Sultanate_of_Oman)

See: Weisgerber, G., 1988, Oman: A bronze-producing centre during the 1st half of the 1st millennium BCE, in: J. Curtis, ed., *Bronze-working centres of western Asia*, c. 1000-539 BCE, London, 285-295.

With curved horns, the 'anthropomorph' is a ligature of a mountain goat or *markhor* (makara) and a fish incised between the horns. Typical find of Gangetic Copper Hoards. At Sheorajpur, three anthropomorphs in metal were found. (Sheorajpur, Dt. Kanpur. Three anthropomorphic figures of copper. *AI*, 7, 1951, pp. 20, 29).

One anthropomorph had fish hieroglyph incised on the chest of the copper object, Sheorajpur, upper Ganges valley, ca. 2nd millennium BCE, 4 kg; 47.7 X 39 X 2.1 cm. State Museum, Lucknow (O.37) Typical find of Gangetic Copper Hoards. miṇḍāl markhor (Tor.wali) meḍho a ram, a sheep (G.)(CDIAL 10120) Rebus: meḍh 'helper of merchant' (Gujarati) meḍ iron (Ho.) meṛed-bica = iron stone ore, in contrast to bali-bica, iron sand ore (Munda) ayo 'fish' Rebus: ayo, ayas 'metal. Thus, together read rebus: *ayo meḍh* 'iron stone ore, metal merchant.'

A remarkable legacy of the civilization occurs in the use of 'fish' sign on a copper anthropomorph found in a copper hoard. This is an apparent link of the 'fish' broadly with the profession of 'metal-work'. The 'fish' sign is apparently related to the copper object which seems to depict a 'fighting ram' symbolized by its in-curving horns. The 'fish' sign may relate to a copper furnace. The underlying imagery defined by the style of the copper casting is the pair of curving horns of a fighting ram ligatured into the outspread legs (of a warrior).

The center-piece of the makara symbolism is that it is a big jhasa, big fish, but with ligatured components (alligator snout, elephant trunk, elephant legs and antelope face). Each of these components can be explained (alligator: manger; elephant trunk: sunda; elephant: ibha; antelope: ranku; rebus: mangar 'smith'; sunda 'furnace'; ib 'iron'; ranku 'tin'); thus the makara jhasa or the big composite fish is a complex of metallurgical repertoire.)

One nidhi was makara (syn. Kohl, antimony); the second was makara (or, jhasa, fish) [bed.a hako (ayo)(syn. bhed.a 'furnace'; med. 'iron'; ayas 'metal')]; the third was kharva (syn. karba, iron).

Title / Object: anthropomorphic sheorajpur
Fund context: Saipai, Dist. Kanpur
Time of admission: 1981
Pool: SAI South Asian Archaeology
Image ID: 213 101
Copyright: Dr Paul Yule, Heidelberg
Photo credit: Yule, Metalwork of the Bronze in India, Pl 23 348 (dwg)

Saipal, Dist. Etawah, UP. Anthropomorph, type I. 24.1x27.04x0.76 cm., 1270 gm., both sides show a chevron patterning, left arm broken off (Pl. 22, 337). Purana Qila Coll. Delhi (74.12/4) -- Lal, BB, 1972, 285 fig. 2d pl. 43d

http://heidicon.ub.uni-heidelberg.de/heidicon/239/213101.html

http://katalog.ub.uni-heidelberg.de/cgi-bin/titel.cgi?katkey=900213101

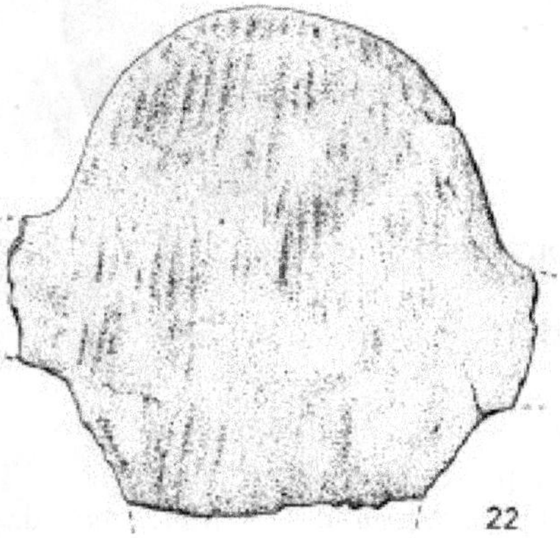
22

From Lothal was reported a fragmentary Type 1 anthropomorph (13.0 pres. X 12.8 pres. X c. 0.08 cm, Cu 97.27%, Pb 2.51% (Rao), surface ptterning runs lengthwise, lower portion slightly thicker than the edge of the head, 'arms' and 'legs' broken off (Pl. 1, 22)-- ASI Ahmedabad (10918 -- Rao, SR, 1958, 13 pl. 21A)

The extraordinary presence of a Lothal anthropomorph of the type found on the banks of River Ganga in Sheorajpur (Uttar Pradesh) makes it apposite to discuss the anthropomorph as a Meluhha hieroglyph, since Lothal is reportedly a mature site of the civilization which has produced nearly 7000 inscriptions (what may be called Meluhha epigraphs, almost all of which are relatable to the bronze age metalwork of India).

"Anthropomorphs occur in a variety of shapes and sizes (Plate A). The two basic types dominate, as defined by the proportions in combination with certain morphological features. All show processes suggestive of a human head, arms and legs. With one exception (no. 539) all are highly geometricising and flat. Fashioned from thick metal sheeting, these artifacts have stocky proportions and are patterned on both sides with elongated gouches or dents which usually are lengthwise oriented. Sometimes, however, the patterning is chevroned or cross-hatched. Significantly, the upper edge of the 'head' shows no thickening, as is the case of type H anthropomorphs. Examples have come to light at mid doab and a broken anthropomorph from distant Lothal as well. The only stratified example derives from Lothal, level IV. height range. 23.2-24.1cm; L/W: 0.65 - 0.88: 1; weight mean: 1260 gm." (Yule, Paul, pp.51-52). "Conclusions..."To the west at Harappa Lothal in Gujarat the presence of a fragmentary import type I anthropomorph suggests contact with the doab." "(p.92)

PLATE A

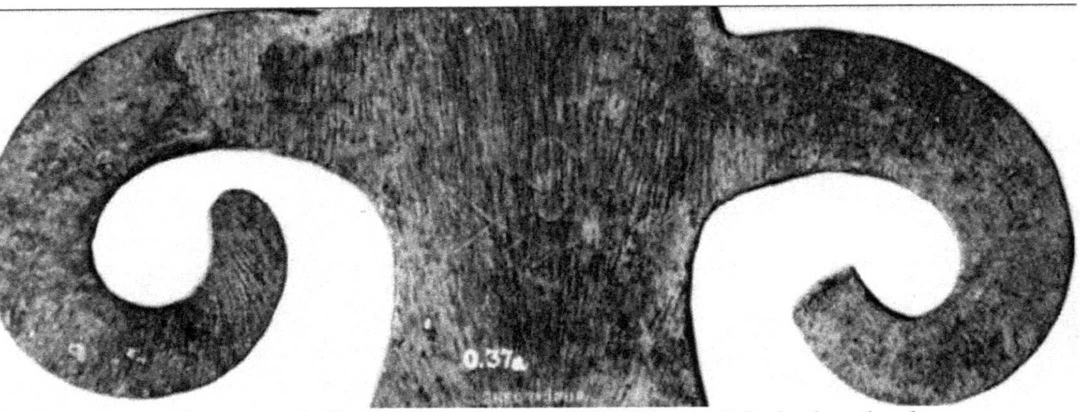

The Sheorajpur anthropomorph (348 on Plate A) has a 'fish' hieroglyph incised on the chest

Hieroglyphs: t*agara* 'ram' (Kannada) Rebus: *damgar* 'merchant' (Akk.) Rebus: *tagara* 'tin' (Kannada)

Ta. *takar* sheep, ram, goat, male of certain other animals (yāḷi, elephant, shark). பொருநகர் தாக்கற்குப் பேருந் தகைத்து (குறள், 486).Ma. *takaran* huge, powerful as a man, bear, etc. Ka. *tagar, ṭagaru, ṭagara, ṭegaru* ram. Tu. *tagaru, ṭagarů* id. Te. *tagaramu, tagaru* id. / Cf. Mar. *tagar* id. (DEDR 3000). Rebus 1:*tagromi* 'tin, metal alloy' (Kuwi) *takaram* tin, white lead, metal sheet, coated with tin (Ta.); tin, tinned iron plate (Ma.); tagarm tin (Ko.); tagara, tamara, tavara id. (Ka.) tamaru, tamara, tavara id. (Ta.): tagaramu, tamaramu, tavaramu id. (Te.); ṭagromi tin metal, alloy (Kuwi); tamara id. (Skt.)(DEDR 3001). trapu tin (AV.); tipu (Pali); tau, taua lead (Pkt.); *tū̃* tin (P.); ṭau zinc, pewter (Or.); tarūaum lead (OG.);*tarvũ* (G.); tumba lead (Si.)(CDIAL 5992). Rebus 2: *damgar* 'merchant'.

ṭhākur 'blacksmith': ṭhakkura m. ' idol, deity (cf. *ḍhakkārī* --), ' lex., ' title ' Rājat. [Dis- cussion with lit. by W. Wüst RM 3, 13 ff. Prob. orig. a tribal name EWA i 459, which Wüst considers nonAryan borrowing of *śākvará* -- : very doubtful]Pk. *ṭhakkura* -- m. ' Rajput, chief man of a village '; Kho. (Lor.) *takur* ' barber ' (= *ṭ*° ← Ind.?), Sh. *ṭhăkŭr* m.; K. *ṭhôkur* m. ' idol ' (← Ind.?); S. *ṭhakuru* m. ' fakir, term of address between fathers of a husband and wife '; P. *ṭhākar* m. ' landholder ', ludh. *ṭhaukar* m. ' lord '; Ku. *ṭhākur* m. ' master, title of a Rajput '; N. *ṭhākur* ' term of address from slave to master ' (f. *ṭhakurāni*), *ṭhakuri* ' a clan of Chetris ' (f. *ṭhakurni*); A. *ṭhākur* ' a Brahman ', *ṭhākurānī* ' goddess '; B. *ṭhākurāni, ṭhākrān,* °*run* ' honoured lady, goddess '; Or. *ṭhākura* ' term of address to a Brahman, god, idol ', *ṭhākurāṇī* ' goddess '; Bi. *ṭhākur* ' barber '; Mth. *ṭhākur* ' blacksmith '; Bhoj. Aw.lakh.*ṭhākur* ' lord, master '; H. *ṭhākur* m. ' master, landlord, god, idol ', *ṭhākurāin, ṭhā̆kurānī* f. ' mistress, goddess '; G. *ṭhākor,* °*kar* m. ' member of a clan of Rajputs ',*ṭhakrāṇī* f. ' his wife ', *ṭhākor* ' god, idol '; M. *ṭhākur* m. ' jungle tribe in North Konkan, family priest, god, idol '; Si. mald. "*tacourou*" ' title added to names of noblemen ' (HJ 915) prob. ← Ind.
Addenda: ṭhakkura -- : Garh. *ṭhākur* ' master '; A. *ṭhākur* also ' idol '(CDIAL 5488)

Hieroglyphs, allographs: ram, tabernae montana coronaria flower: तगर [tagara] *f* A flowering shrub, Tabernæ montana coronaria. 2 *n* C The flower of it. 3 *m* P A ram. (Marathi)

*tagga ' mud '. [Cf. Bur. *t**lg**ly̥* ' mud '] Kho. (Lor.) *toq* ' mud, quagmire '; Sh. *tăgā´* ' mud '; K. *tagöri* m. ' a man who makes mud or plaster '; Ku. *tāgaṛ* ' mortar '; B. *tāgāṛ* ' mortar, pit in which it is prepared '.(CDIAL 5626). (Note: making of mud or plaster is a key step in dhokra kamar's work of *cire perdue* (lost-wax) casting.)
krəm back'(Kho.) karmāra 'smith, artisan' (Skt.) kamar 'smith' (Santali)

Cylinder seal with kneeling nude heroes, ca. 2220–2159 b.c.; Akkadian Mesopotamia Red jasper H. 1 1/8 in. (2.8 cm), Diam. 5/8 in. (1.6 cm) Metropolitan Museum of Art – USA

bhaṭā 'brick kiln' (Assamese) بټ *baṯṯ*, s.m. (2nd) A large iron pan or cauldron for roasting grain, a furnace, a kiln.(Pashto)

baTa 'six' (see six locks of hair) rebus: bhaTa 'furnace'. meDa 'coil' rebus: meD 'iron'

bhuvɔ m. ' worshipper in a temple ' (Gujarati) rather < bhr̥ta --(CDIAL 9554) Yājñ.com., Rebus: *bhaṭā*'kiln, furnace' Pk. *bhuaga* -- m. ' worshipper in a temple 'Pk. *bhayaga* -- m. ' servant ', *bhaḍa* -- m. ' soldier '(CDIAL 9558) भट्ट[p= 745,1] *m.* (fr. भर्तृ) lord , my lord (also pl. and -पाद *m.* pl. ; according to Das3ar. ii , 64, a title of respect used by humble persons addressing a prince ; but also affixed or prefixed to the names of learned Brahmans , e.g. केदार- , गोविन्द-भ° &c , or भट्ट-केदार &c , below , the proper name being sometimes omitted e.g. भट्ट = कुमारिल-भ° ; also any learned man = doctor or philosopher) Ra1jat. Vet. &c. N. of a partic. mixed caste of hereditary panegyrists , a bard , encomiast L.

Yupa as flagpost, Indus Script evidences of proclamation from Girsu, Ancient Near East to Candi Sukuh, Ancient Far East

I suggest that yupa inscriptions and yupa found in archaeological sites of Kalibangan and Binjor (in fact, in almost every single site of the civilization) are flags hoisted as proclamations of metalwork signified by Somayaga in the Vedic tradition.

This Vedic tradition exemplified by flasposts is seen in an extensive civilizational contact area from Haifa, Israel to Hanoi, Vietnam which is, in effect, the Ancient Maritime Tin Road which preceded by 2 millennia, the Ancient Silk Road. The Tin Road linked the tin belt of the world with the regions which demanded tin to create tin-bronzes during the urban revolution unleashed by the Bronze Age.

A flagpost is proclamation. sangaDa 'lathe' 'portable furnace' as a device in front of the one-horned young bull is also sangara 'proclamation'.

The significance of the yupa with caSAla in a somayaga gets replicated, as an abiding Indus Script hieroglyph-multiplex hypertext, on many artifacts from an extensive contact zone from the Ancient Near East to Ancient Far East.

The tradition of processions of flagposts with hieroglyphs atop continued in Sumer/ Mesopotamia as may be seen from the following example:

Cylinder seal with kneeling nude heroes, ca. 2220–2159B.C.; Akkadian
Mesopotamia Red jasper; H. 1 1/8 in. (2.8 cm), Diam. 5/8 in. (1.6 cm) (L.1992.23.5)

"Four representations of a nude hero with six sidelocks of hair appear on this cylinder seal. Each wears a three-strand belt with a tassel. In all cases, the hero kneels on one knee and with both hands holds up a gatepost standard in front of his raised leg. Two vertical lines of inscription, one placed before a hero and another placed behind a second hero, give the name as Shatpum, son of Shallum, but do not provide an official title. Placed vertically in the field, a serpent appears behind one hero. In the spaces between the tops of the standards are four symbols: a sun disk, a lunar crescent, a fish, and a vase with flowing streams of water."

http://www.metmuseum.org/toah/works-of-art/L.1992.23.5

The heroes carrying the standard are signified by six curls on hair.

baTa 'six' rebus: bhaTa 'furnace' meDh 'curl' rebus: meD 'iron (metal)'.

Cylinder seal with kneeling nude heroes, ca. 2220–2159 b.c.; Akkadian Mesopotamia Red jasper H. 1 1/8 in. (2.8 cm), Diam. 5/8 in. (1.6 cm) Metropolitan Museum of Art - USA

Four flag-posts(reeds) with rings on top held by the kneeling persons define the four components of the iron smithy/forge.

The key hieroglyph is the hood of a snake seen as the left-most hieroglyph on this rolled out cylinder seal impression. I suggest that this denotes the following Meluhha gloss:

Hierogyph: A. kulā 'hood of serpent' Rebus: kolle 'blacksmith'; kolhe 'smelter' kol 'working in iron'

Alternative: *paṭam* , *n.* < *phaṭa*. ‘cobra's hood’ phaṭa n. ‘ expanded hood of snake ’ MBh. 2. *phēṭṭa -- 2. [Cf. *phuṭa* -- m., °*ṭā* -- f., *sphuṭa* -- m. lex., °*ṭā* -- f. Pañcat. (Pk. *phuḍā* -- f.), *sphaṭa* -- m., °*ṭā*-- f., *sphōṭā* -- f. lex. and phaṇa -- 1. Conn. words in Drav. T. Burrow BSOAS xii 386]1. Pk. *phaḍa* -- m.n. ‘ snake's hood ’, °*ḍā* -- f., M. *phaḍā* m., °*ḍī* f.2. A. *pheṭ*, *phẽṭ*. (CDIAL 9040). Rebus: ‘sharpness of iron’: *padm* (obl.*padt*-) temper of iron (Kota)(DEDR 3907); *patam* ‘sharpness, as of the edge of a knife’ (Tamil) Alternative complementary reading: <naG bubuD>(Z) {N} ``^cobra". |<naG> `?'. ^snake. *IA<naG>. ??is IA form <naG> or <nag>? #23502. nāgá1 m. ‘ snake ’ ŚBr. 2. ‘ elephant ’ BhP. [As ‘ ele- phant ’ shortened form of **nāga* -- *hasta* -- EWA ii 150 with lit. or extracted from *nāga* -- *danta* -- ‘ elephant tusk, ivory ’ < ‘ snake -- shaped tusk ’].
1. Pa. *nāga* -- m. ‘ snake ’, NiDoc. *nāǵa* F. W. Thomas AO xii 40, Pk. *ṇāya* -- m., Gy. as. *nâ* JGLS new ser. ii 259; Or. *naa* ‘ euphem. term for snake ’; Si. *nay*, *nā,nayā* ‘ snake ’. -- With early nasalization **nāṅga* -- : Bshk. *nāṅg* ‘ snake ’. -- Kt. Pr. *noṅ*, Kal. *nhoṅ* ‘ name of a god < *nā´ga* -- or ← Pers. *nahang* NTS xv 283. 2. Pa. *nāga* -- m. ‘ elephant ’, Pk. *ṇāya* -- m., Si. *nā.* śiśunāka -- . (CDIAL 7039) Rebus: nāga2 n. ‘ lead ’ Bhpr. [Cf. raṅga -- 3] Sh. *naṅ* m. ‘ lead ’ (< **nāṅga* -- ?), K. *nāg* m. (< **nāgga* -- ?).(CDIAL 7040) cf. annaku, anakku 'tin' (Akkadian) நாகம் nākam Black lead; காரீயம். (பிங்.) 9. Zinc; துத்தநாகம். (பிங்.) 10. A prepared arsenic; பாஷாணவகை (Tamil).

There is a possibility that the hieroglyph was intended to convey the message of an alloying metal like lead or tin or zinc which had revolutionised the bronze age with tin-bronzes, zinc-copper brass and other alloys to substitute for arsenical copper to make hard weapons and tools. It is instructive that zinc was called *tuthunāg which might have referred to the* sublimate of zinc and calamine collected in the furnaces in Zawar.

The leftmost hieroglyph shows ingots in a conical-bottom storage jar (similar to the jar shown on Warka vase, delivering the ingots to the temple of Inanna). Third from left, the overflowing pot is similar to the hieroglyph shown on Gudea statues. Fourth from left, the fish hieroglyph is similar to the one shown on a Susa pot containing metal tools and weapons. (Picture credit for the Susa pot with 'fish' hieroglyph: Maurizio Tosi).

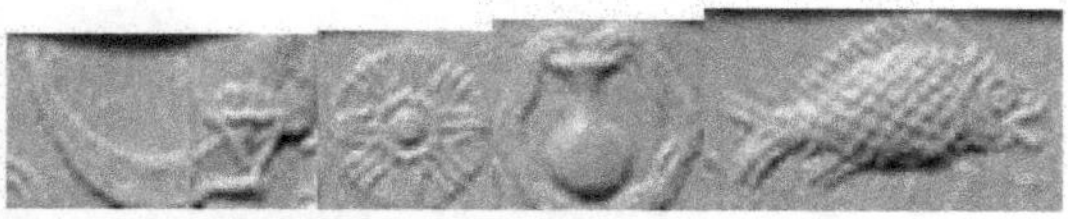

The leftmost hieroglyph shows ingots in a conical-bottom storage jar (similar to the jar shown on Warka vase (See Annex: Warka vase), delivering the ingots to the temple of Inanna). Third from left, the overflowing pot is similar to the hieroglyph shown on Gudea statues. Fourth from left, the fish hieroglyph is similar to the one shown on a Susa pot containing metal tools and weapons. (See Susa pot hieroglyphs of bird and fish: Louvre Museum) Hieroglyph: *meṇḍā* 'lump, clot' (Oriya) On mED 'copper' in Eurasian languages see Annex A: Warka vase).

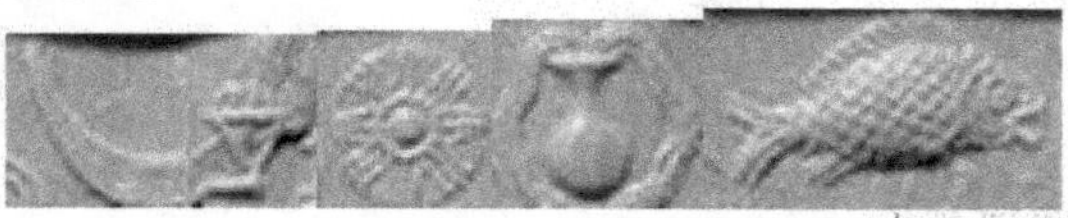

The leftmost hieroglyph shows ingots in a conical-bottom storage jar (similar to the jar shown on Warka vase (See Annex: Warka vase), delivering the ingots to the temple of Inanna). Third from left, the overflowing pot is similar to the hieroglyph shown on Gudea statues. Fourth from left, the fish hieroglyph is similar to the one shown on a Susa pot containing metal tools and weapons. (See Susa pot hieroglyphs of bird and fish: Louvre Museum) Hieroglyph: *meṇḍā* ‘lump, clot’ (Oriya)

On mED 'copper' in Eurasian languages:

Wilhelm von Hevesy wrote about the Finno-Ugric-Munda kinship, like "Munda-Magyar-Maori, an Indian link between the antipodes new tracks of Hungarian origins" and "Finnisch-Ugrisches aus Indien". (DRIEM, George van: Languages of the Himalayas: an ethnolinguistic handbook. 1997. p.161-162.) Sumerian-Ural-Altaic language affinities have been noted. Given the presence of Meluhha settlements in Sumer, some Meluhha glosses might have been adapted in these languages. One etyma cluster refers to 'iron' exemplified by meD (Ho.). The alternative suggestion for the origin of the gloss med 'copper' in Uralic languages may be explained by the word meD (Ho.) of Munda family of Meluhha language stream:

Sa. <i>mE~R~hE~'d</i> `iron'. ! <i>mE~RhE~d</i>(M).

Ma. <i>mErhE'd</i> `iron'.

Mu. <i>mERE'd</i> `iron'.

~ <i>mE~R~E~'d</i> `iron'. ! <i>mENhEd</i>(M).

Ho <i>meD</i> `iron'.

Bj. <i>merhd</i>(Hunter) `iron'.

KW <i>mENhEd</i>

@(V168,M080)

http://www.ling.hawaii.edu/austroasiatic/AA/Munda/ETYM/Pinnow&Munda

— Slavic glosses for 'copper'

Мед [Med]Bulgarian

Bakar Bosnian

Медзь [medz']Belarusian

Měď Czech

Bakar Croatian

KòperKashubian

Бакар [Bakar]Macedonian

Miedź Polish

Медь [Med']Russian

Meď Slovak

BakerSlovenian

Бакар [Bakar]Serbian

Мідь [mid'] Ukrainian[unquote]

http://www.vanderkrogt.net/elements/element.php?sym=Cu

Miedź, med' (Northern Slavic, Altaic) 'copper'.

One suggestion is that corruptions from the German "Schmied", "Geschmeide" = jewelry. Schmied, a smith (of tin, gold, silver, or other metal)(German) result in med 'copper'.

Four flag-posts(reeds) with rings on top held by the kneeling persons define the four components of the iron smithy/forge.

Hieroglyph: staff: మేడెము [mēḍemu] or మేడియము *mēḍemu*. [Tel.] n. A spear or dagger. ఈటె, బాకు. The rim of a bell-shaped earring, set with ems.రాళ్లుచెక్కిన□మికీ అంచుయొక్క పనితరము. "క ఒడితినన్నన్ వారక మేడెముపొడుతురె." BD. vi. 116.

Hieroglyph: meṇḍa 'bending on one knee': మండి [maṇḍi] or మండీ *manḍi*. [Tel.] n. Kneeling down with one leg, an attitude in archery, ఒక కాలితో నేలమీద మోకరించుట, ఆలీఢపాదము. मेट [mēṭa] *n* (मिटणें) The knee-joint or the bend of the knee. मेटेंखुंटीस बसणें To kneel down. *Ta.* maṇṭi kneeling, kneeling on one knee as an archer. *Ma.* maṇṭuka to be seated on the heels. *Ka.* maṇḍi what is bent, the knee. *Tu.* maṇḍi knee. *Te.* maṇḍī kneeling on one knee. *Pa.* maḍtel knee; maḍi kuḍtel kneeling position. *Go.* (L.) meṇḍā, (G. Mu. Ma.) minḍa knee (*Voc.* 2827). *Konḍa* (BB) meḍa,
meṇḍa id. *Pe.* menḍa id. *Manḍ.* menḍe id. *Kui* menḍa id. *Kuwi* (F.) menda, (S. Su. P.) menḍa, (Isr.) meṇḍa id. Cf. 4645 Ta. maṭaṅku (maṇi-forms). / ? Cf. Skt. maṇḍūkī- part of an elephant's hind leg; Mar. meṭ knee-joint. (DEDR 4677) Rebus: mẽṛhẽt, meḍ 'iron' (Mu.Ho.)

Hieroglyph: எருவை eruvai European bamboo reed. See கொறுக்கச்சி. (குறிஞ்சிப்.)
Rebus: 817 *Ta.* eruvai blood, (?) copper. *Ka.* ere a dark-red or dark-brown colour, a dark or dusky colour; (Badaga) erande sp. fruit, red in colour. *Te.* rēcu, rēcu-kukkaa sort of ounce or lynx said to climb trees and to dęstroy tigers; (B.) a hound or wild dog. *Kol.* resn a·te wild dog (i.e. *res na·te; see 3650). *Pa.* iric netta id. *Ga.*(S.3) rēs nete hunting dog, hound. *Go.* (Ma.) erm ney, (D.) erom nay, (Mu.) arm/aṛm nay wild dog (*Voc.* 353); (M.) rac nāī, (Ko.) rasi ney id. (*Voc.* 3010). For 'wild dog', cf. 1931 Ta. ce- red, esp. the items for 'red dog, wild dog'.

patākā f. ' flag ' MBh. 2. paṭākā -- f. lex. 3. *phaṭākā -- . [Prob. ← a non -- Aryan word containing *p(h)aṭ* aryanized with *t* EWA ii 200] 1. Pa. *patākā* -- f. ' flag '. 2. Pa. *paṭāka* -- n., Pk. *paḍāga* -- m., *paḍāyā* -- , *paḍāiā* -- f., mh. *paḍāha* -- m.; G. *paṛāi* f. ' paper kite '.
3. Kal.rumb. *phŕā* ' flag '; Or. *phaṛkā* (perh. influenced by Or. *phaṛa -- phaṛa* ' with a sudden movement ' s.v. *phaṭ --). Addenda: patākā -- . 2. paṭākā -- : S.kcch. *paṛāī* f. ' paper kite '.(CDIAL 7726)

mūhā mẽṛhẽt 'iron smelted by the Kolhes and formed into an equilateral lump a little pointed at each of four ends.' (Note ingots in storage pot superfixed on the crucible hieroglyph).

paTam 'snake hood' Rebus: padm 'sharpness' *paṭa* 'hood of snake'. *Rebus: padm* 'tempered, sharpness (metal)'. nāga 'serpent' Rebus: nāga 'lead (alloy)'

Ta. paṭam instep. *Ma.* paṭam flat part of the hand or foot. *Pe.* paṭa key palm of hand. *Manḍ.* paṭa kiy id.; paṭa kāl sole of foot. *Kuwi.* (Su.) paṭa nakipalm of hand. (DEDR 3843)

పదును (p. 0710) [padunu] or పదను *padunu*. [Tel. పది+ఉను.] Temper, sharpness, whetting, *Go.* (ASu.) padnā sharpness. *Konḍa* padnu being ready for use (as oilseed being preparèd for pressing), sharpening (of knife by heating and hammering). *Ta.* patamsharpness (as of the edge of a knife),*Ko.* padm (*obl.* padt-) temper of iron.(DEDR 3907)

Ta. patam cobra's hood. *Ma.* paṭam id. *Ka.* peḍe id. *Te.* paḍaga id. *Go.* (S.) paṛge, (Mu.) baṛak, (Ma.) baṛki, (F-H.) biṛki hood of serpent (*Voc.* 2154). / Turner, *CDIAL*, no. 9040, Skt. (s)phaṭa-, sphaṭā- a serpent's expanded hood, Pkt. phaḍā- id. For IE etymology, see Burrow, *The Problem of Shwa in Sanskrit*, p. 45.(DEDR 45 Appendix) phaṭa n. ' expanded hood of snake ' MBh. 2. *phēṭṭa -- 2. [Cf. *phuṭa* -- m., °*ṭā* -- f., *sphuṭa* -- m. lex., °*ṭā* -- f. Pañcat. (Pk. *phuḍā* -- f.), *sphaṭa* -- m., °*ṭā* -- f., *sphōṭā* -- f. lex. and phaṇa -- 1. Conn. words in Drav. T. Burrow BSOAS xii 386] 1. Pk. *phaḍa* -- m.n. ' snake's hood ', °*ḍā* -- f., M. *phaḍā* m., °*ḍī* f. 2. A. *pheṭ*, *phẽṭ*.(CDIAL 9040)

Hieroglyph: मेढा (p. 665) [mēḍhā] A twist or tangle arising in thread or cord, a curl or snarl.(Marathi. Molesworth)Rebus: mẽṛhẽt, meḍ 'iron' (Mu.Ho.)

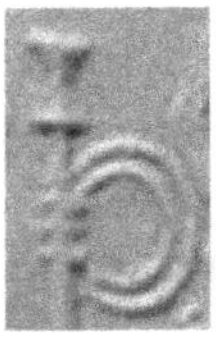

The top of each of the four posts is signified by an 'octagonal' (?) vajra rebus: 'thunderbolt weapon'. The flagpost also has a ring comparable to the ring described for a Somayaga Yupa in Satapatha Brahmana. Somayaga is a Soma सं-√ स्था a [p=1121,2]*A1.* -तिष्ठते (Pa1n2. 1-3 , 22 ; ep. and mc. also *P.* -तिष्ठति ; Ved. inf. -स्थातोस् A1pS3r.) , to stand together , hold together (pf. p. du. -तस्थान्/ए , said of heaven and earth) RV. ; to build (a town) Hariv. ; to heap , store up (goods) VarBr2S. occupation , business , profession W.

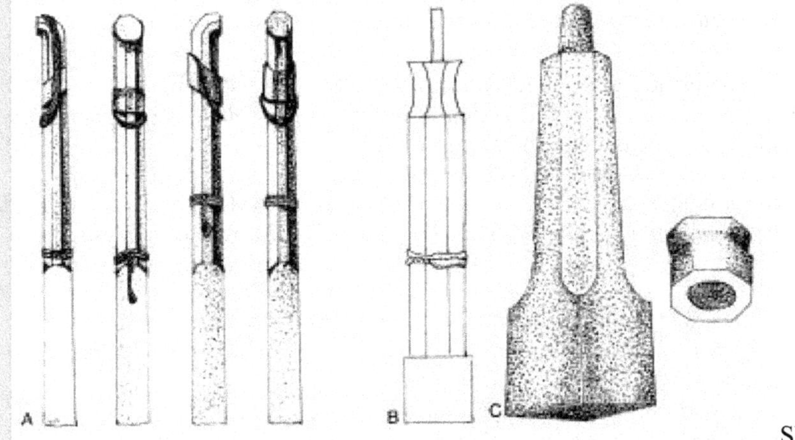

Shapes of Yupa: A. Commemorative stone yupa, Isapur – from Vogel, 1910-11, plate 23; drawing based on Vedic texts – from Madeleine Biardeau, 1988, 108, fig. 1; cf. 1989, fig. 2); C. Miniature wooden yupa and caSAla from Vaidika Samsodana Mandala Museum of Vedic sacrificial utensils – from Dharmadhikari 1989, 70) (After Fig. 5 in Alf Hiltebeitel, 1988, The Cult of Draupadi, Vol. 2, Univ. of Chicago Press, p.22)

Isapur Yupa inscription (102 CE, dated in year 24 in Kushana king Vasishka's reign) indicates performance of a sattra (yajna) of dvadasarAtra, 'twelve nights'. (Vogel, JP, The sacrificial posts of Isapur, *Annual Report of the Archaeological Survey of India, 1910-11*: 40-8).The Isapur yupa is comparable to the ring and vajra atop the flagpost of Jasper cylinder seal. (See the comparable orthography of the vajra carried by Vajrapani on a sculptural frieze from Peshawar).

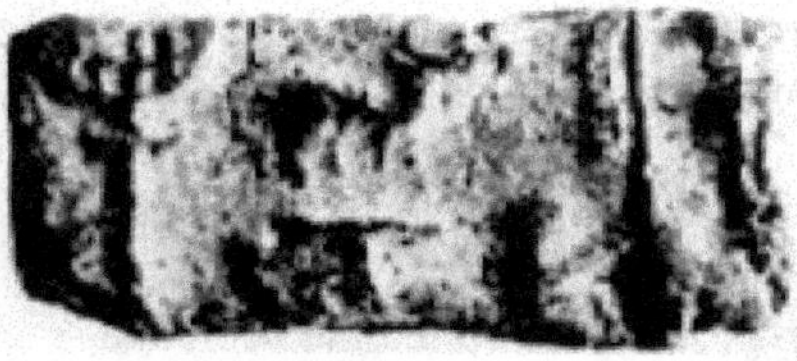
m0490, m0491
Stone-smithy guild on a Meluhha standard

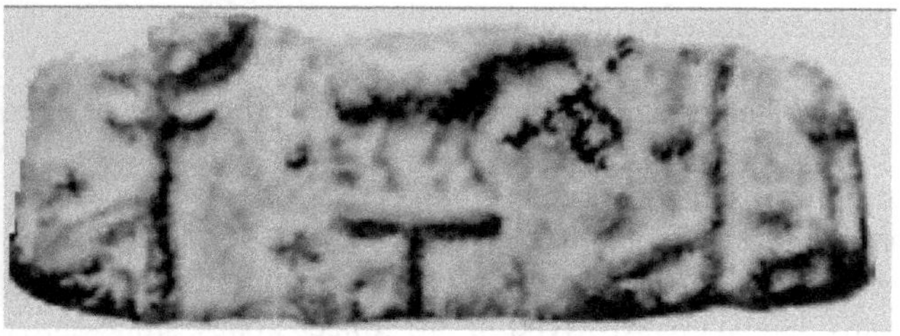

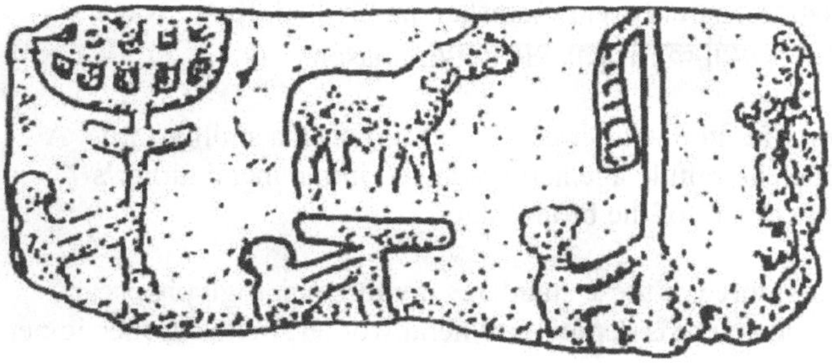

Harappa Tablet. Pict-91 (Mahadevan) m0490At m0490B Mohenjodaro Tablet showing Meluhha combined standard of three standards carried in a procession, comparable to Tablet m0491.

'Raised hand' hieroglyph on Pict-91 Harappa tablet: er-aka 'upraised hand' (Tamil) Rebus: eraka 'copper'.

m0491 Tablet. Line drawing (right). This tablet showing three hieroglyphs may be called the Meluhha standard.Combined reading for the joined or ligatured glyphs

Rebus reading is: dhatu kõdā sangaḍa 'mineral, turner, stone-smithy guild'.

Dawn of the bronze age is best exemplified by this Mohenjo-daro tablet which shows a procession of three hieroglyphs carried on the shoulders of three persons. The hieroglyphs are: 1. Scarf carried on a pole (dhatu Rebus: mineral ore); 2. A young bull carried on a stand kõdā Rebus: turner; 3. Portable standard device (Top part: lathe-gimlet; Bottom part: portable furnace sā̃gāḍ Rebus: stone-cutter sangatarāśū). sanghāḍo (Gujarati) cutting stone, gilding (Gujarati); sangsāru karaṇu = to stone (Sindhi) sanghāḍiyo, a worker on a lathe (Gujarati) sangataras. संगतराश lit. 'to collect stones, stone-cutter, mason.' संगतराश संज्ञा पुं० [फ़ा०] पत्थर काटने या गढ़नेवाला मजदूर । पत्थरकट । २. एक औजार जो पत्थर काटने के काम में आता है । (Dasa, Syamasundara. Hindi sabdasagara. Navina samskarana. 2nd ed. Kasi : Nagari Pracarini Sabha, 1965-1975.) पत्थर या लकडी पर नकाशी करनेवाला, संगतराश, 'mason'.

The procession is a celebration of the graduation of a stone-cutter as a metal-turner in a smithy/forge. A sangatarāśū 'stone-cutter' or lapidary of neolithic/chalolithic age had graduated into a metal turner's workshop (koḍ), working with metallic minerals (dhatu) of the bronze age.

Three professions are described by four standards; three of these standards are three hieroglyphs: scarf, young bull, standard device dhatu kõdāsā̃gāḍī Rebus words denote: ' mineral worker; metals turner-joiner (forge); worker on a lathe' – associates (guild).

Vāk and Mlecchita Vikalpa (Select inscriptions from Indus Script Corpora)

Note: Vāk refers to *sprachbund* (speech area) of ancient India on the banks of Rivers Sarasvati and Sindhu, two river basins of Himalayan glacial-fed rivers of ancient times.

A writing system is an intersection of speech and orthography. Speech is venerated in Rigveda as वाग्देवी, 'divinity of speech'. She declares, in a monologue that she is Rashtri, the lighted path for abhyudayam, for acquisition and movement of wealth by the first performers of yajna. The technological processes of yajna, Soma yaga, in particular, are signified by a writing system, Indus Script. This is called mlecchita vikalpa by Vatsyayana, to mean an alternative representation by mleccha (copper, metal) workers who documented their work. Each inscription is a metalwork catalogue rendering the entire corpora *catalogus catalogorum* of metalwork.

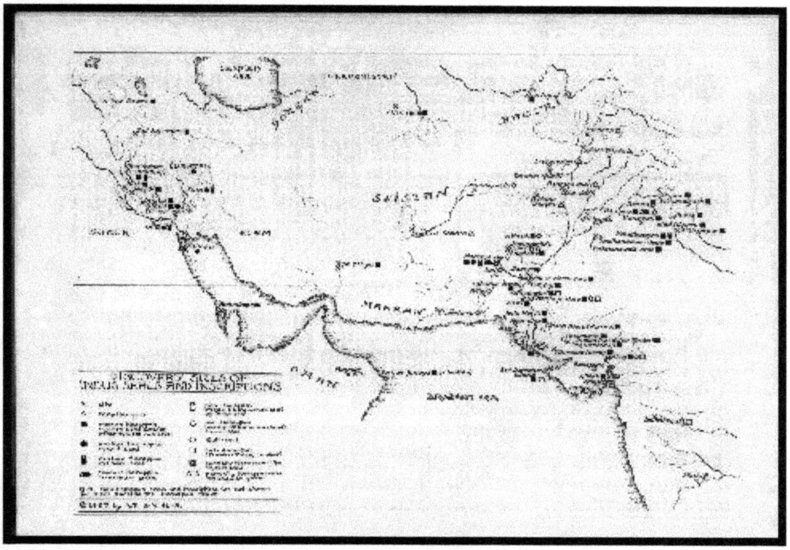

Discovery sites: Indus Script inscriptions

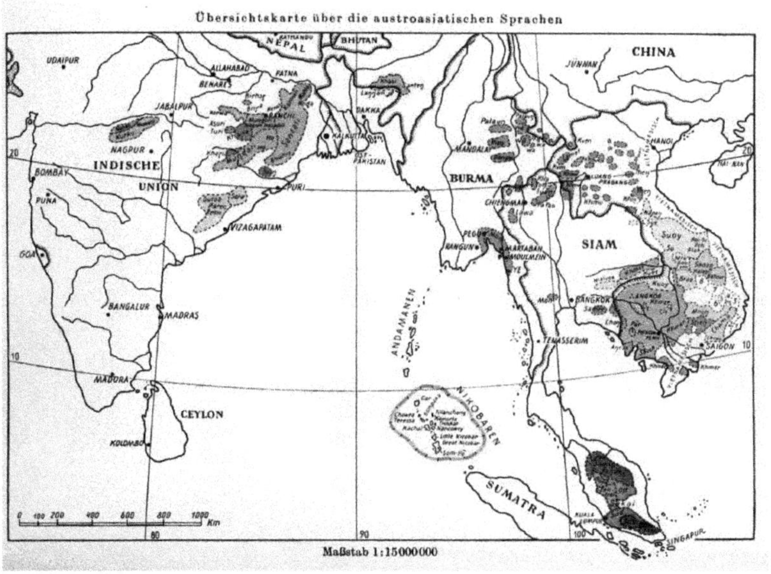

Pinnow's map of Austro-AsiaticLanguage speakers correlates with bronze age sites.[i] The areal map of Austric (Austro-Asiatic languages) showing regions marked by Pinnow correlates with the bronze age settlements in Bharatam or what came to be known during the British colonial regime as 'Greater India'. The bronze age sites extend from Mehrgarh-Harappa (Meluhha) on the west to Kayatha-Navdatoli (Nahali) close to River Narmada to Koldihwa- Khairdih-Chirand on Ganga river basin to Mahisadal – Pandu Rajar Dhibi in

Jharia mines close to Mundari area and into the east extending into Burma, Indonesia, Malaysia, Laos, Cambodia, Vietnam, Nicobar islands. A settlement of Inamgaon is shown on the banks of River Godavari.

Bronze Age sites of eastern India and neighbouring areas: 1. Koldihwa; 2.Khairdih; 3. Chirand; 4. Mahisadal; 5. Pandu Rajar Dhibi; 6.Mehrgarh; 7. Harappa;8. Mohenjo-daro; 9.Ahar; 10. Kayatha; 11.Navdatoli; 12.Inamgaon; 13. Non PaWai; 14. Nong Nor;15. Ban Na Di andBan Chiang; 16. NonNok Tha; 17. Thanh Den; 18. Shizhaishan; 19. Ban Don Ta Phet [After Fig. 8.1 in: Charles Higham, 1996, The Bronze Age of Southeast Asia, Cambridge University Press].

Background

Seafaring meluhhan merchants used Indus Writing in trade transactions; artisans created metal artifacts, lapidary artificats of terracotta, ivory for trade. Glosses of the proto-Indic or Indus language are used to read rebus the Indus script inscriptions. The Indus Script Corpora appended in the book, Cultural History of Bharatam Janam is principally based on the finds in India and Pakistan (together called Bharatam of ancient times). It is essential to include inscriptions from neighbouring areas with which Bharatam Janam had contacts and which included Indus Script hieroglyphs. Hence, the addendum.

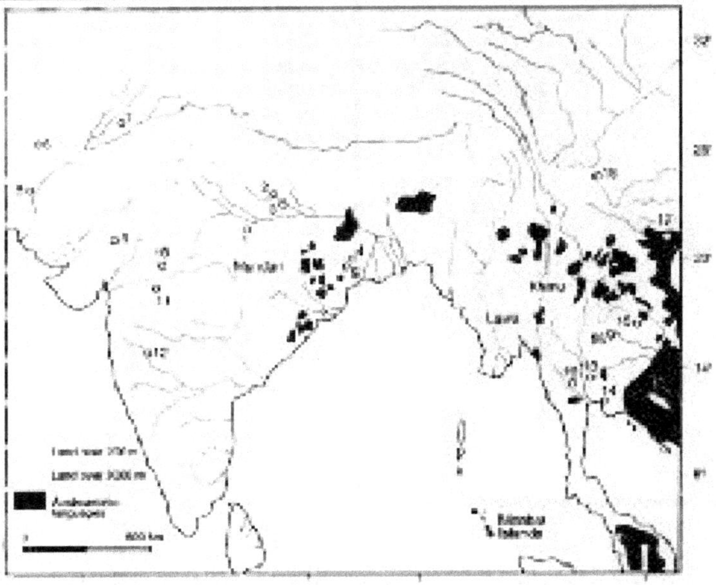

Addenda to Indus Script Corpora

Thumbnail images of over 4000 inscriptions have been included in: *Cultural History of Bharatam Janam – Indus Script metalwork catalogs* (2016). Characteristic signifiers of hieroglyphs are found in hundreds of inscriptions outside the River basins of Sarasvati and Sindhu, along the Persian Gulf and in sites of Ancient Near East.

Many scholars have noted the contacts between the Mesopotamian and Sarasvati Sindhu (Indus) Civilizations, in terms of cultural history, chronology, artefacts (beads, jewellery), pottery and seals found from archaeological sites in the two areas.

Cylinder seal impression. British Museum (Reg. No. OA 1960.7-18.1). Found in Seistan. Called the MacMahon cylinder seal. The end of the cylinder shows a combination of triangles (like a range of mountains) reminiscent of a Mohenjo-daro seal (M-443B). The inscription has six signs: a human figures ligatured to three rows of four vertical lines (total count of 12).. Next is a human figure holding in his left hand a rectangular device filled with single hatching (see Marshall 1931, II: 446, no. 196b).

"...the four examples of round seals found in Mohenjodaro show well-supported sequences, whereas the three from Mesopotamia show sequences of signs not paralleled elsewhere in the Indus Script. But the

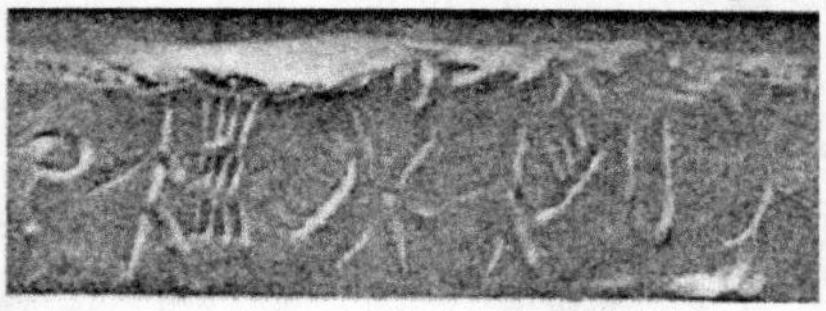

ordinary square seals found in Mesopotamia show the normal Mohenjodaro sequences. In other words, the square seals are in the Indian language, and were probably imported in the course of trade; while the circular seals, although in the Indus script, are in a different language, and were probably manufactured in Mesopotamia for a Sumerian- or Semitic-speaking person of Indian descent..." [G.R. Hunter,1932. Mohenjodaro--Indus Epigraphy, *JRAS*: 466-503]

The acculturation of Meluhhans (probably, Indus people) residing in Mesopotamia in the late third and early second millennium BC, is noted by their adoption of Sumerian names (Parpola, Parpola and Brunswig 1977: 155-159). "The adaptation of Harappan motifs and script to the Dilmun seal form may be a further indication of the acculturative phenomenon, one indicated in Mesopotamia by the adaptation of Harappan traits to the cylinder seal." (Brunswig et al, 1983, p. 110).

[Robert H. Brunswig, Jr. et al, New Indus Type and Related Seals from the Near East, 101-115 in: Daniel T. Potts (ed.), *Dilmun: New Studies in the Archaeology and Early History of Bahrain*, Berlin, Dietrich Reimer Verlag, 1983.]

Mountain topped by a leaf gets stylized as an important motif. Pro-elamite glyptics. Leaf motif. 1-c, After Legrain,L., 1921, Empreintes de cachets elamites, *Mem. Mission Arch. De Perse* 16, Paris: 62-654; d. After Amiet, P., 1961, *La glyptique mesopotamienne archaique*, Paris: 497; Mundigak IV.3; 3. After Casal, J.M., 1961, Fouilles de Mundigak I-II. *Mem. Delegation Arch. Franaise en Afthanistan* 17, Paris: fig. 102: 485; f. Early Harappan. Kalibangan. After Sankalia, 1974: 346, fig. 88d, A. H-L; cf. Fig. 23.45 Asko Parpola, 1996, fig. 23.45. Two goats eating from a tree on a mountain top in proto-Elamite seals from Susa [After Amiet, P., 1972, Glyptique susienne I-II, *Mem. Delegation Arch. En Iran* 43, Paris: 978 and Legrain, L., 1921, Emprientes de cachets elamites, *Mem. Mission Arch. De Perse* 16, Paris: 316].

Nude Bearded Hero Wrestling with Water Buffalo; Bull Man Fighting Lion Cylinder seal and impression Mesopotamia, Akkadian period (ca. 2334–2154 B.C.)
Serpentine 36 x 25 mm
Seal no. 159

http://www.themorgan.org/collections/collections.asp?id=193

Texts related to West Asian inscriptions (either not illustrated or not linked):

9801Susa

9811Djoka (Umma)

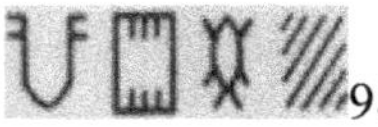
9821 Kish

9822 Kish

9834 Ur

9842 Ur

9852 Telloh

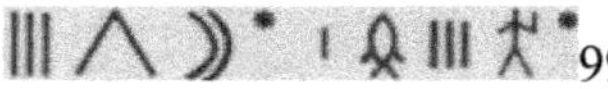
9903 Prob. West Asian find

9904 Prob. West Asian find

Indus script. H.2.3 cm; Harappan inscription,

Susa, Iran; steatite cylinder seal . A bison with head lowered, feeding from a basin. A second bison figure is seen. Inscription on top. Jacques de Morgan Excavatins. Louvre Sb 2425, Delaporte, 1920, s.299 and cf. T.24 from Tello, Iraq; Collon, 1987, Fig. 608.Musee du Louvre and Pierre and Maurice Chuzeville; Legend: dia. 1.6 cm. C. 2600 – 1700 BCE. This cylinder seal, carved with a originated in the Indus Valley. It is made of fired steatite, a material widely used by craftsmen in Harappa. The animal - a bull with no hump on its shoulders - is also widely attested in the region. The seal was found in Susa, reflecting the extent of commercial links between Mesopotamia, Iran, and the Indus.

[Pierre de talc. Louvre, AO 9036. P. Amiet, Bas-relliefs imaginaries de l'Orient ancien, Paris, 1973, p. 94, no. 274...ils proviendrait de Tello, l'ancienne Girsu, une des cites de l'Etat sumerien de Lagash. Musee National De Arts Asiatiques Guimet, 1988-1989, *Les cites oubliees de l'Indus Archeologie du Pakistan*.]

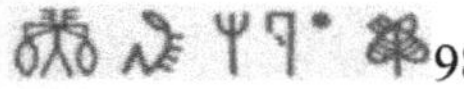9851 Telloh

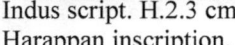

A seal made in Meluhha

The language of the inscription on this cylinder seal found in Susa reveals that it wasmade in Harappa in the Indus Valley. In Antiquity, the valley was known as Meluhha.

The seal's chalky white appearance is due to the fired steatite it is made of. Craftsmen in the Indus Valley made most of their seals from this material, although square shapes were usually favored. The animal carving is similar to those found in Harappan works. The animal is a bull with no hump on its shoulders, or possibly a short-horned gaur. Its head is lowered and the body unusually elongated. As was often the case, the animal is depicted eating from a woven wicker manger.

Trading links between the Indus, Iran, and Mesopotamia

This piece can be compared to another circular seal carved with a Harappan inscription, also found in Susa. The two seals reveal the existence of trading links between this region and the Indus valley. Other Harappan objects have likewise been found in Mesopotamia, whose sphere of influence reached as far as Susa.

The manufacture and use of the seals

Cylinder seals were used mainly to protect sealed vessels and even doors to storage spaces against tampering. The surface of the seal was carved. Because the seals were so small, the artists had to carve tiny scenes on a material that allowed for fine detail. The seal was then rolled over clay to produce a reverse print of the carving. Some cylinder seals also had handles.

Bibliography

Amiet Pierre, L'Âge des échanges inter-iraniens : 3500-1700 av. J.-C., Paris, Éditions de la Réunion des musées nationaux, 1986, coll. "Notes et documents des musées de France", p. 143 et p. 280, fig. 93.
Borne interactive du département des Antiquités orientales.

Les cités oubliées de l'Indus : archéologie du Pakistan, cat. exp. Paris, Musée national des arts asiatiques, Guimet, 16 novembre 1988-30 janvier 1989, sous la dir. de Jean-François Jarrige, Paris, Association française d'action artistique, 1988, pp. 194-195, fig. A5.

http://www.louvre.fr/en/oeuvre-notices/cylinder-seal-carved-elongated-buffalo-and-harappan-inscription

Louvre Museum; Luristan; unglazed, gray steatite; short-honed bull and 4 pictograms

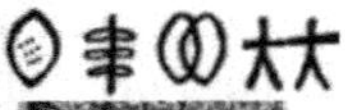

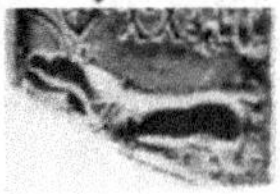

Iraq museum; glazed steatite; perhaps from an Iraqi site; the one-horned bull, the standard are below a six-sign inscription.

4 Foroughi collection; Luristan; medium gray steatite; bull, crescent, star and net square; of the Dilmun seal type.

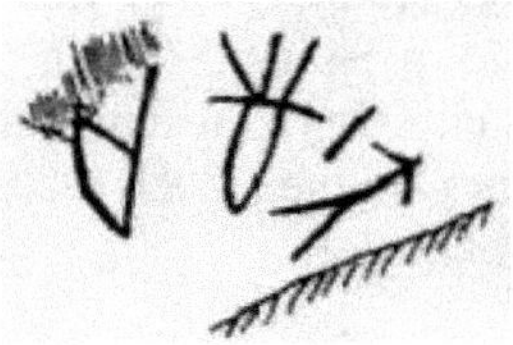

TextFailaka; unglazed steatite; an arc of four pictograms above the hindquarter of a bull.

Textseal, impression, inscription; Failaka; brownish-grey unglazed steatite; Indus pictograms above a short-horned bull.

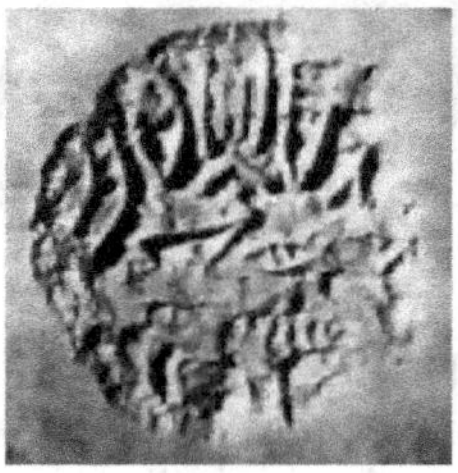

seal, impression; Qala'at al-Bahrain; green steatite; short-horned bull and five pictograms.

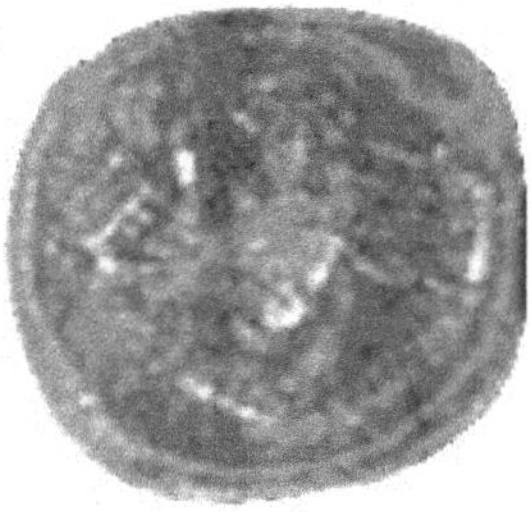

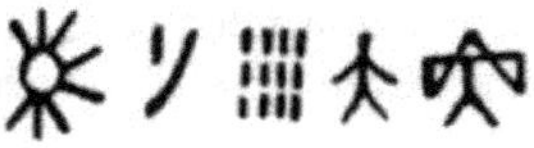

Found in association with an Isin-Larsa type tablet bearing three Amorite names.

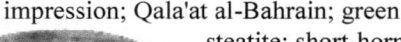

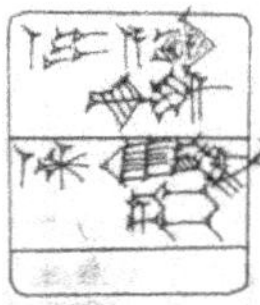

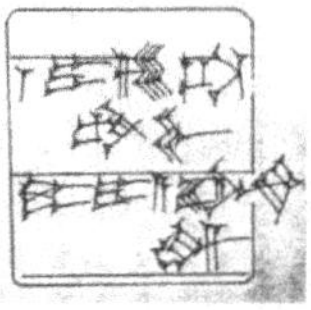

Qala'at al-Bahrain; ca. 2050-1900 BC; tablet, found in the same level where 8 Dilmun seals and six Harappan type weights were found. Three Amorite names are: Obverse. Janbi-naim; Ila-milkum; Reverse. Jis.i-tambu (son of Janbi-naim). The script is dated to c. 2050-1900 BCE.

Qala'at al-Bahrain; light-grey steatite; hindquarters of a bull and two pictograms.

urseal2 9832 Ur Seal; BM 122187; dia. 2.55; ht. 1.55 cm. Gadd PBA 18 (1932), pp. 6-7, pl. 1, no. 2

urseal39833 Ur Seal; BM 122946; Dia. 2.6; ht. 1.2cm.; Gadd PBA 18 (1932), p. 7, pl. I, no.3; Legrain, Ur Excavations, X (1951), no. 629.

urseal8Seal; BM 118704; U. 6020; Gadd PBA 18 (1932), pp. 9-10, pl. II, no.8; two figures carry between them a vase, and one presents a goat-like animal (not an antelope) which he holds by the neck. Human figures wear early Sumerian garments of fleece.

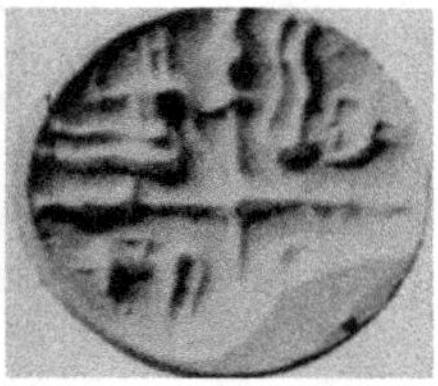

urseal9Seal; BM 122945; U. 16181; dia. 2.25, ht. 1.05 cm; Gadd PBA 18 (1932), p. 10, pl. II, no. o; each of four quadrants terminates at the edge of the seal in a vase; each quadrant is occupied by a naked figure, sitting so that, following round the circle, the head of one is placed nearest to the feet of the preceding; two figures clasp their hands upon their breasts; the other two spread out the arms, beckoning with one hand.

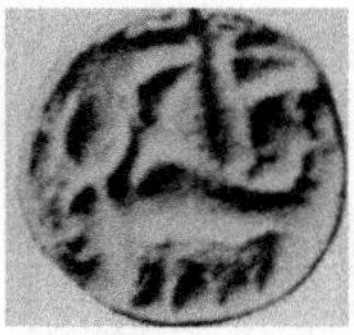

urseal10 Seal; BM 120576; U. 9265; Gadd, PBA 18 (1932), p. 10, pl. II, no. 10; bull with long horns below an uncertain object, possibly a quadruped and rider, at right angles to the ox (counter clockwise); "...there is, below, a bull with long horns roughly depicted, but above is a rather uncertain addition, which is perhaps an attempt to show one (possibly two) more, in a couching position, as viewed by turning the seal round until the face of the standing bull is downwards. If this is intended, the head of the second bull is turned back, and it is not, perhaps, quite impossible that the remaining part of the design is meant for a bird, such as is fairly often seen perched upon the back of a bull in Sumerian art, a device which has not yet been certainly explained." (C.J. Gadd, Seals of Ancient Indian Style Found at Ur', in: G.L. Possehl, ed., 1979, *Ancient Cities of the Indus*, Delhi, Vikas Publishing House, p. 118).

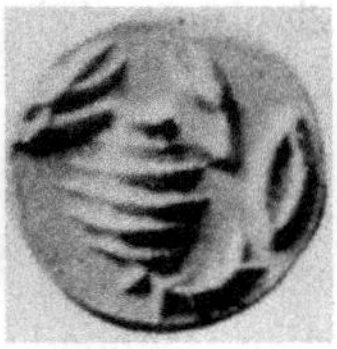

urseal11Seal; UPenn; a scorpion and an elipse [an eye (?)]; U. 16397; Gadd, PBA 18 (1932), pp. 10-11, pl. II, no. 11 [Note: Is the 'eye' an oval representation of a bun ingot made from bica_, sand ore?]

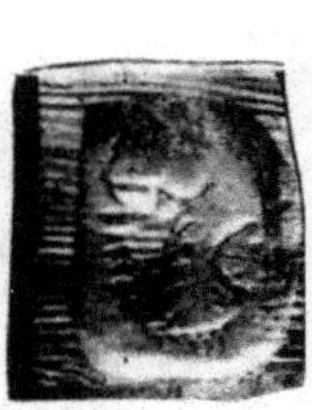

Rectangular stamp seal of dark steatite; U. 11181; B.IM. 7854; ht. 1.4, width 1.1 cm.; Woolley, Ur Excavations, IV (1956), p. 50, n.3. Scorpion.

Seal impression, Ur (Upenn; U.16747); dia. 2.6, ht. 0.9 cm.; Gadd, PBA 18 (1932), pp. 11-12, pl. II, no. 12; Porada 1971: pl.9, fig.5; Parpola, 1994, p. 183; water carrier with a skin (or pot?) hung on each end of the yoke across his shoulders and another one below the crook of his left arm; the vessel on the right end of his yoke is over a receptacle for the water; a star on either side of the head (denoting supernatural?). The whole object is enclosed by 'parenthesis' marks. The parenthesis is perhaps a way of splitting of the ellipse (Hunter, G.R., JRAS, 1932, 476). An unmistakable example of an 'hieroglyphic' seal.

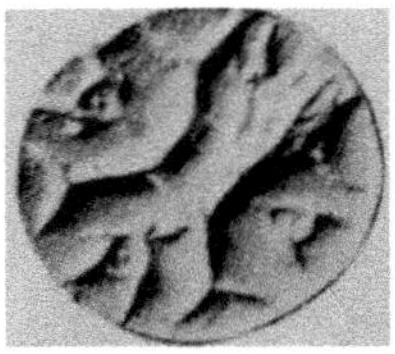

urseal13 Seal; BM 122841; dia. 2.35; ht. 1 cm.; Gadd PBA 18 (1932), p. 12, pl. II, no. 13; circle with center-spot in each of four spaces formed by four forked branches springing from the angles of a small square. Alt. four stylised bulls' heads (bucrania) in the quadrants of an elaborate quartering device which has a cross-hatched rectangle in the center.

urseal14Seal; UPenn; cf. Philadelphia Museum Journal, 1929; ithyphallic bull-men; the so-called 'Enkidu' figure common upon Babylonian cylinders of the early period; all have horned head-dresses; moon-symbols upon poles seem to represent the door-posts that the pair of 'twin' genii are commonly seen supporting on either side of a god; material and shape make it the 'Indus' type while the device is Babylonian.

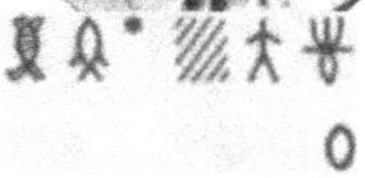

urseal159845 Ur [The first sign looks like an animal with a long tail – as seen from the back and may have been the model for the orthography of Sign 51 as noted in Mahadevan corpus].

Variants of Sign 51. Seal impression; UPenn; steatite; bull below a scorpion; dia. 2.4cm.; Gadd, PBA 18 (1932), p. 13, Pl. III, no. 15; Legrain, MJ (1929), p. 306, pl. XLI, no. 119; found at Ur in the cemetery area, in a ruined grave .9 metres from the surface, together with a pair of gold ear-rings of the double-crescent type and long beads of steatite and carnelian, two of gilt copper, and others of lapis-lazuli, carnelian, and banded sard. The first sign to the left has the form of a flower or perhaps an animal's skin with curly tail; there is a round spot upon the bull's back.

urseal16 9846 UrSeal impression; BM 123208; found in the filling of a tomb-shaft (Second Dynasty of Ur). Dia. 2.3; ht. 1.5 cm.; Gadd, PBA 18 (1932), pp. 13-14, pl. III, no. 16; Buchanan, JAOS 74 (1954), p. 149.

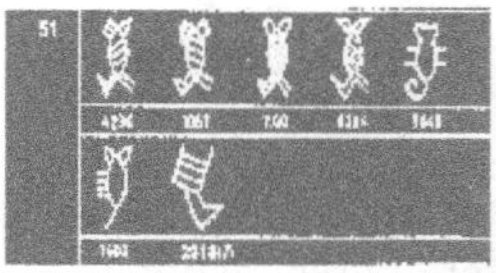

urseal179901 Prob. West Asian find Seal impression, Mesopotamia (?) (BM 120228); cf. Gadd 1932: no.17; cf. Parpola, 1994, p. 132. Note the doubling of the common sign, 'jar'.

urseal18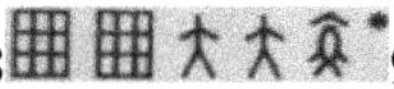9902 Prob. West Asian find Pictorial motif: Pict-45 Bull mating a cow. Seal and impression (BM 123059), from an antique dealer, Baghdad; script and motif of a bull mating with a cow; the tuft at the end of the tail of the cow is summarily shaped like an arrow-head; inscription is of five characters, most prominent among them the two 'men' standing side by side. To the right of these is a damaged 'fish' sign.cf. Gadd 1932: no.18; Parpola, 1994, p.219.

urseal6 Cylinder seal; BM 122947; U. 16220 (cut down into Ur III

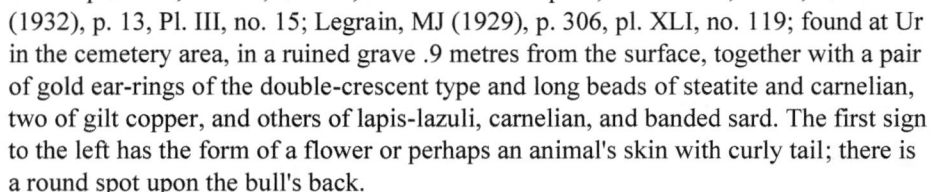

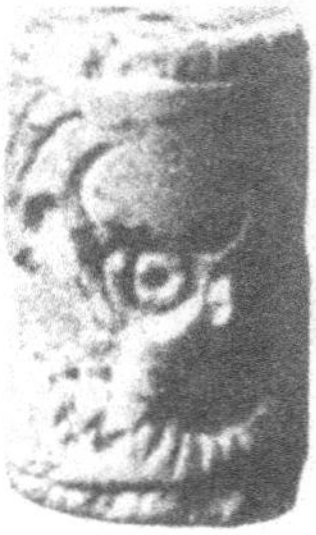

mausolea from Larsa level; U. 16220), enstatite; Legrain, 1951, No. 632; Collon, 1987, Fig. 611.Humped bull stands before a plant, feeding from a round manger or a bundle of fodder (or, probably, a cactus); behind the bull is a scorpion and two snakes; above the whole a human figure, placed horizontally, with fantastically long arms and legs, and rays about his head.

A symbolism of a woman spreading her legs apart, which recurs on an SSVC inscribed object. Cylinder-seal impression from Ur showing a squatting female. L. Legrain, 1936, *Ur excavations, Vol. 3, Archaic Seal Impressions*. [cf. Nausharo seal with two scorpions flanking a similar glyph with legs apart – also looks like a frog].

Mohenjo-daro. Sealing. Surrounded by fishes, lizard and snakes, a horned person sits in 'yoga' on a throne with hoofed legs. One side of a triangular terracotta amulet (Md 013); surface find at Mohenjo-daro in 1936. Dept. of Eastern Art, Ashmolean Museum, Oxford.

A zebu bull tied to a post; a bird above. Large painted storage jar discovered in burned rooms at Nausharo, ca. 2600 to 2500 BCE. Cf. Fig. 2.18, J.M. Kenoyer, 1998, Cat. No. 8.

A fish over a short-horned bull and a bird over a one-horned bull; cylinder seal impression, (Akkadian to early Old Babylonian).

Gypsum. 2.6 cm. Long 1.6 cm. Dia. [Drawing by Larnia Al-Gailani Werr. Cf. Dominique Collon 1987, *First impressions: cylinder seals in the ancient Near East*, London: 143, no. 609] Tell Suleimeh (level IV), Iraq; IM 87798; (al-Gailani Werr, 1983, p. 49 No. 7).

Cylinder-seal impression; a griffin and a tiger attack an antelope with its head turned back. The upper register shows two scorpions and a frog; the lower register shows a scorpion and two fishes.Syro-Mitannian, fifteenth to fourteenth centuries BCE, Pierpont Morgan Library, New York. [After Fig. 9 in: Jack M. Sasson (ed.), *Civilizations of the Ancient Near East*, p.2705].

Rhinoceros, elephant, lizard.Tell Asmar (Eshnunna), Iraq. IM 14674; glazed steatite; Frankfort, 1955, No. 642; Collon, 1987, Fig. 610.

Seal from Shortugai incised with an antelope and two other pictographs. "...Shortugai in Oxus basin, on the Kokcha-Amu Darya doab, has revealed the existence of a Harappan colony for carrying out trade in lapis lazuli. Apart form typical Harappan pottery, a seal bearing the script has also been found to confirm the trading character of the colony." (Six decades of Indus Studies in: BB Lal and SP Gupta, eds., *Frontiers of the Indus Civilization*, Fig. .8, p. 9].

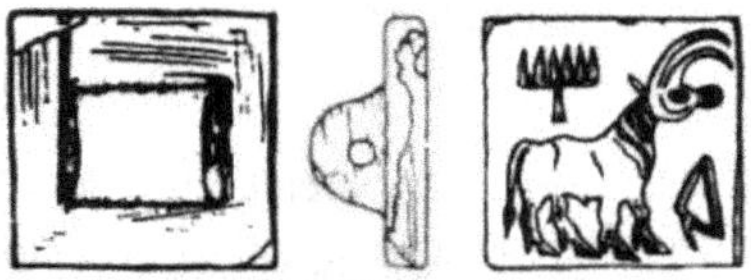

Ur, Iraq; BM 123195; clay, half missing; Collon, 1987, Fig. 613. Probably originated in the east (exact location unknown).

A person with a vase with overflowing water; sun sign. C. 18th cent. BCE. [E. Porada,1971, Remarks on seals found in the Gulf states, *Artibus Asiae*, 33, 31-7].

"The main importance of a seal found in 1980 in Maysar-1 (Weisgerber, 1980), is the fact that the Makan/Oman civilisation used seals, as did the great cultures of the Nile, Euphrates/Tigris and Indus. But it is also a convincing proof of contact between Meluhha and Makan. On three sides six animals are engraved: two caprides, an ibex and a wild goat; a zebu cow and a scorpion; a dog and again a wild goat. In our context the zebu cow is the most important. Together with the humped bull painted on a jar from Umm an-Nar (Bibby, 1970: 280) it demonstrates the presence of these animals in the Oman peninsula during the third millennium BCE. This again proves contact with India.

(Not illustrated) "A new seal from Hajjar in Bahrain now gives the same evidence, its shape being nearly identical with the Maysar-1 seal. Among its three engravings are a short-horned bull and an insription in Indus Valley script (Weisgerber, 1981: 218, fig. 54)." (Gerd Weisgerber, Makkan and Meluhha--third millennium BCE copper production in Oman and the evidence of contact with the Indus Valley, in: Parpola, Asko and Petteri Koskikallio (eds.), *South Asian Archaeology 1993,* Helsinki, Suomalainen Tiedeakatemia, 1994).

(Not illustrated) "(At Padri, Gujarat) A of the most significant discoveries is a copper fish-hook, which is 14 cm long and weights 41 gm. A copper fish-hook of such a magnitude has not been reported from any other site so far... The other material equipment include a seal on a stud handle engraved with fish motif, Harappan letters engraved on pot-sherds, cubical chert weights, micro steatite beads, beads of terracotta, carnelian, agate, etc."

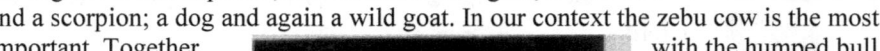

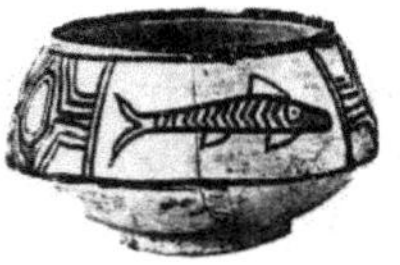

Early Harappan bowl. Fish. [After Fig. 23.35 in, Asko Parpola, New correspondences between Harappan and near Eastern glyptic art, in: in B. Allchin, ed., *South Asian Archaeology*, 1981, Cambridge].

Seal impression; Dept. of Antiquities, Bahrain; three Harapan-style bulls

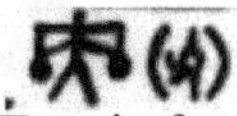

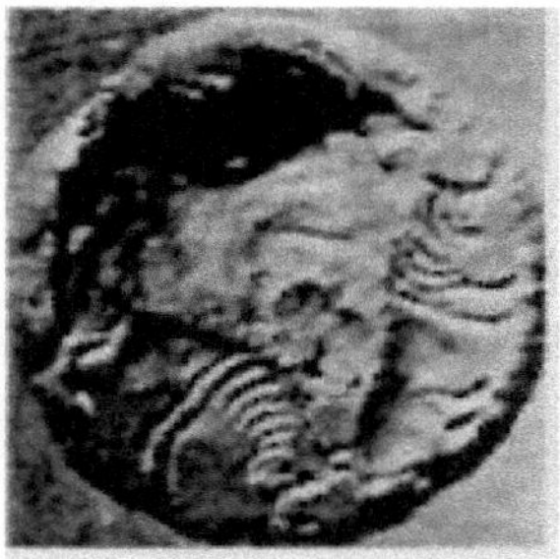

Nippur; ca. 13th cent. BC; white stone; zebu bull and two pictograms

Tree in front. Fish in front of and above a one-horned bull. Cylinder seal impression (IM 8028), Ur, Mesopotamia. White shell. 1.7 cm. High, dia. 0.9 cm. [Cf. Mitchell 1986 Indus and Gulf type seals from Ur: 280-1, no.8 and fig. 112; Shaikha Haya Ali Al Khalifa and Michael Rice, 1986, *Bahrain through the ages: the archaeology*, London: 280-1, no.8 and fig. 112]. cf. Gadd, PBA 18 (1932), pp. 7-8, pl. I, no.7;; Parpola, 1994, p. 181; fish vertically in front of and horizontally above a unicorn; trefoil design

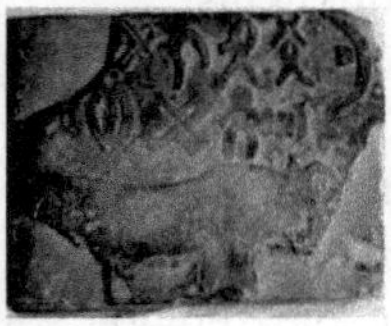

Terracotta sealing depicting an inscription, 2600 BCE, Western UP, Saharanpur (After Manoj Kumar Sharma). [Source: Page 32 in: Deo Prakash Sharma, 2000, *Harappan seals, sealings and copper tablets*, Delhi, National Museum].

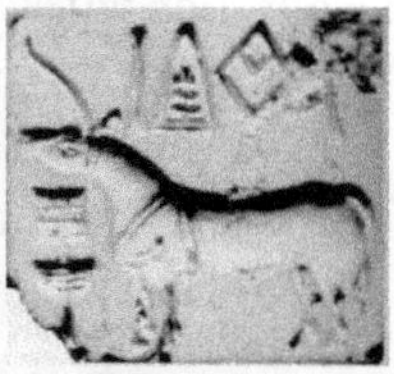

Stamp seals in Metropolitan Museum of Art, New York. 49.40.1 to 3. All three samples show a bull.

"Rendered in strict profile, standing before what might be an altar, the bull is by far the most popular motif in the Indus Valley glyptic art; there is virtually no v ariation in either the style or the iconographic details among the individual examples. The shoulder of the bull is emphasized by an upside-down doubly outlined heart shape that has been interpreted as painted decoration on the body of the bull, but is more likely an artistic convention for representing the muscles of the bull's shoulder."[After Fig. 38 in Holly Pittman, 1984, p. 84].

Mohenjo-daro. Silver seal (After Mackay 1938, vol. 2, Pl. XC,1; XCVI, 520). Two silver seals at Mohenjo-daro, two copper seals at Lothal and at Ras al-Junayz in Oman are rare uses of metal for making seals.

Stamp seal and a modern impression: unicorn or bull and inscription,, Mature Harappan period, ca. 2600–1900 B.C. Indus Valley Burnt steatite; 1 1/2 x 1 1/2 in. (3.8 x 3.8 cm)

http://www.metmuseum.org/toah/ho/02/ssa/ho_49.40.1.htm

Manuscripts in Schoyen Collection

Some manuscripts available in the Schoyen Collection. Located mainly in London and Oslo. URL

http://www.nb.no/baser/schoyen/contentnew3.html "The Schøyen Collection comprises most types of manuscripts from the whole world spanning over 5000 years. It is the largest private manuscript collection formed in the 20th century. The whole collection, MSS 1-5245, comprises 13,010 manuscript items, including 2,172 volumes. 6,510 manuscript items are from the ancient period, 3300 BCE – 500 CE. For scholarly research and access the collection is a unique source, uniting materials usually scattered world wide to two locations only. These MSS are the world's heritage, the memory of the world. They are felt not really to belong to The Schøyen Collection and its owner, who only is the privileged, respectful and humble keeper, neither do they belong to a particular nation, people, religion, culture, but to mankind, being the property of the entire world. In the future The Schøyen Collection will have to be placed in a public context that can fulfil these visions…The Schøyen Collection is located mainly in Oslo and London. Scholars are always welcome, and are strongly encouraged to do research and to publish material."

Source:http://www.nb.no/baser/schoyen/intro.html#1.1

Included in the 6,510 manuscripts from the ancient period, 3300 BCE - 500 CE are the following epigraphs which are closely associated with the script of the Sarasvati Civilization.

MS 249 Unidentified Minoan text. Knossos, Crete, 16th cent. BCE, Linear A script?

MS in Minoan on clay, Knossos, Crete, 16th c. BC, 1 black roundel, 3,0x2,7 cm, 4 characters of late Minoan I Linear A script, 2 impressions (1,6x1,0 cm) on opposite edges by an amygdaloid seal with head of papyrus plant.

Provenance: 1. Possibly the archive in the West Wing of the Knossos Palace (16th c. BC - ca. 1950); 2. Erlenmeyer Collection, Basel, CMS no. 120 (until 1981); 3. Erlenmeyer Foundation, Basel (1981-1988); 4. Christie's 5.6.1989:99.

Commentary: The famous Linear B script of the Mycenean kings, consisting of syllabic signs, ideograms and numerals, resisted decipherment for a generation. When Michael Ventris deciphered it in 1952, the achievement was called the "Everest" in classical archaeology. The language was archaic Greek. Linear A, the earliest script of Europe, has so far resisted all attempts of decipherment, partly because the language is unknown, and the material small, ca. 700 copies only, while Linear B is known in 12,000 - 13,000 examples. This roundel is the only one in private ownership. Outside the Greek museums, they are, in fact, represented in 2 Italian museums only. KN Wc 26 in Erik Hallager: The Knossos roundels, BSA 82(1987).

This MS has signs which are comparable with the signs on epigraphs of Sarasvati-Sindhu Civilization.

MS 4625 Cylinder seal with a scene of drinking from a straw, Pakistan ca. 1500-500 BCE

Seal of hard red stone, Coast between Indus and the Persian Gulf, Pakistan, ca. 1500-500 BC, 1 cylinder seal matrix, diam. 1,3x3,2 cm, figure sitting left, holding a long straw from his mouth to a pot with bulbous body and narrow neck, resting on a stand; behind him a servant holding up a fan; behind the servant another standing person grasping a small quadruped. Above and below him 3 other quadrupeds. Between the 2 main figures a solar disc with rays and a crescent and a full moon combined.

Provenance: 1. Found in Baluchistan?, Pakistan (1965); 2. The Waria Collection, Dadu, Pakistan (ca. 1965-2001).

Commentary: Drinking beer from a straw is known from Sumer ca. 2700 BC on, but usually a big pot from which a number of persons are all drinking through their own straws. The fan is known in Iranian seals of ca. 1300-1100 BC. While the scene as a whole is Near Eastern, the dress and anklets of the servant is clearly of Indian type. The iconography combined is thus unique.

MS 4602 Indus Valley cylinder seal, ca. 3000 BCE depicting a palm tree and a man between two lions with wings and snakeheads, holding one arm around each, two long fish below, and one fish jumping after one lion's tail or the tail of a sitting monkey above it

Seal matrix on creamy stone or shell, Indus Valley, Pakistan, ca. 3000 BC, 1 cylinder seal, diam. 2,0x3,7 cm, in fine execution influenced by the Jemdet Nasr style of Sumer.

Provenance: 1. Found in Mehrgarh, Pakistan; 2. The Waria Collection, Dadu, Pakistan (-2001).

Commentary: Similar fish can be found on Indus Valley pottery from the period and later http://www.nb.no/baser/schoyen/5/5.6/index.html#4602

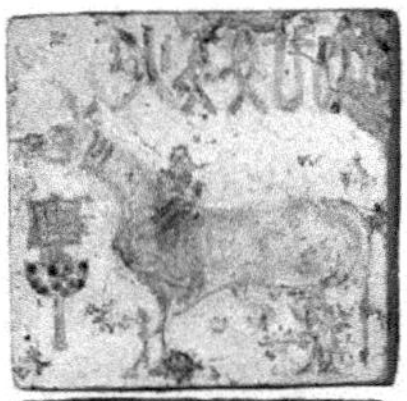

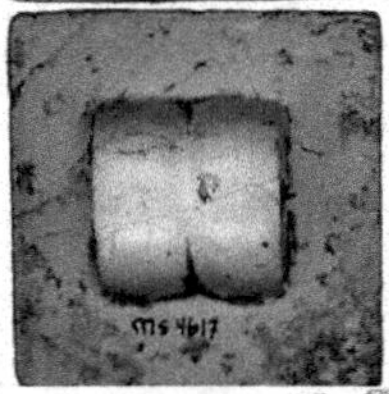

MS 4617 Pakistan, ca. 2200-2000 BCE

White steatite, 1 square seal matrix, 4,3x4,3x1,9 cm, 6 Indus Valley signs in a formal script of high quality, unicorn standing left facing an altar, with loop handle.

Provenance: 1. The Waria Collection, Dadu, Pakistan (-2001).

Commentary: This seal is among the largest extant. The execution is representing Indus art at its best. The Indus script is still undeciphered, as is the Linear A script from Crete and the Rongo-Rongo script from Easter Island, which has numerous signs in common with the Indus script.

MS 4619, Pakistan, ca. 2200-1800 BCE

White coated grey steatite, Mohenjo-Daro?, Indus Valley, Pakistan, ca. 2200-1800 BC, 1 round seal matrix, diam. 2,3x1,5 cm, 5 Indus Valley signs, bison left eating from a trough, with double loop handle.

Context: Only 2 more round seals with inscriptions are known, both with bison and from Mohenjo-Daro (M-415 and M-416).

Provenance: 1. The Waria Collection, Dadu, Pakistan (1960'ies-2001).

MS5059 Pakistan, ca. 2200-1800 BCE

White steatite, Mohenjo-Daro, Indus Valley, 2200-1800 BC, 1 square stamp seal matrix, 3,4x3,4x1,7 cm, 9 Indus valley signs

Provenance: 1. Found in Mohenjo-Daro (ca. 1950-1970); 2. The Waria Collection, Dadu, Pakistan (-2001).

MS5061 Pakistan, ca. 2200-1800 BCE

White steatite, Mohenjo-Daro, Indus Valley, 2200-1800 BC, 1 square stamp seal matrix, 2,4x2,5x1,2 cm, 3 Indus valley signs

Provenance: 1. Found in Mohenjo-Daro (ca. 1950-1970); 2. The Waria Collection, Dadu, Pakistan (-2001).

MS5062 Pakistan, ca. 2200-1800 BCE

White steatite, Mohenjo-Daro, Indus Valley, 2200-1800 BC, 1 square stamp seal matrix, 2,7x2,7x1,6 cm, 4 Indus valley signs

Provenance: 1. Found in Mohenjo-Daro (ca. 1950-1970); 2. The Waria Collection, Dadu, Pakistan (-2001).

MS5065 Pakistan, ca. 1800 BCE

MS Indus Valley language on copper, Mohenjo-Daro, Indus Valley, ca. 1800 BC, 1 square stamp seal matrix, 1,3x1,3x0,9 cm, 3 Indus valley signs in script

Provenance: 1. Found in Mohenjo-Daro (ca. 1950-1970); 2. The Waria Collection, Dadu, Pakistan (-2001).

Commentary: There is only one similar seal known, from Lothal (L-44).

Kuwait gold disc. Al-Sabah Museum.

Kuwait cylinder seal. Gold. Possibly southeastern Iran, mid 3rd millennium BCE. Ht. 2.21 cm. dia. 2.74 cm. Fabricated from gold sheet with chased decoration. Inv. No. LNS 4517J

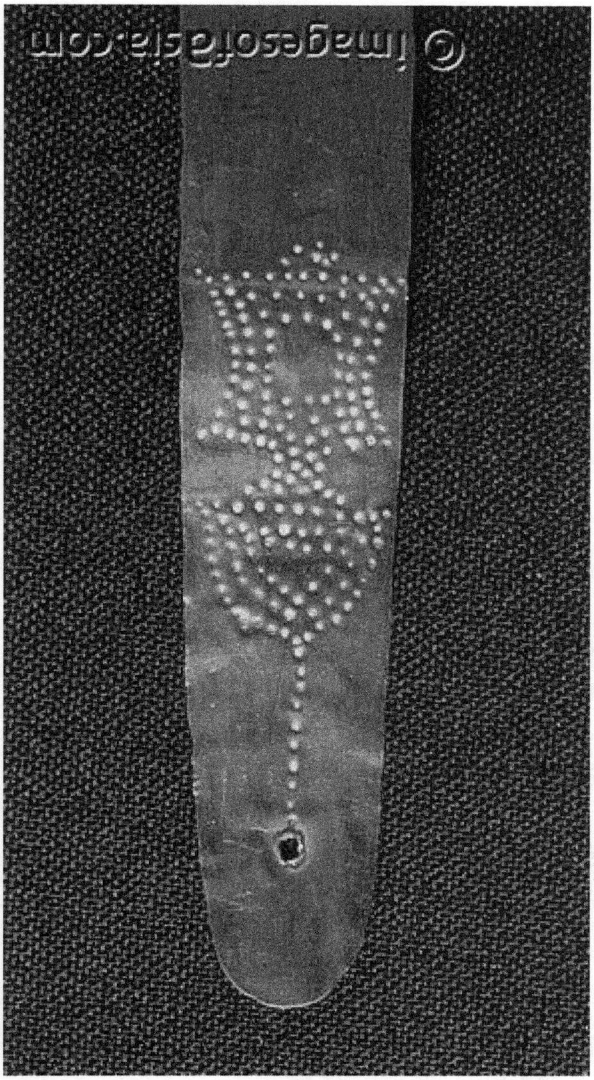

Gold fillet. Punctuated design on both ends. Mohenjodaro.
http://www.imagesofasia.com/html/mohenjodaro/gold-fillet.html

Gold fillet. Punctuated design on both ends. Mohenjodaro.
http://www.imagesofasia.com/html/mohenjodaro/gold-fillet.html

The gold pendant is made from a hollow cylinder with soldered ends and perforated point. Museum No. MM 1374.50.271; Marshall 1931: 521, pl. CLI, B3. [After Fig. 4.17a, b in: JM Kenoyer, 1998, p. 196]. A fish sign, preceded by seven short numeral strokes, also appears on a gold Golden pendant with inscription from jewelry hoard at Mohenjo-daro. Drawing of inscription that encircles the gold ornament. Needle-like pendant with cylindrical body. Two other examples, one with a different series of incised signs were found together. The pendant is made from a hollow cylinder with soldered ends and perforated point. Museum No. MM 1374.50.271; Marshall 1931: 521, pl. CLI, B3. [After Fig. 4.17a, b in: JM Kenoyer, 1998, p. 196]. Parallels from Mesopotamia , Anatolia and other contact areas

Seal impression, Ur (Upenn; U.16747); dia. 2.6, ht. 0.9 cm.; Gadd, PBA 18 (1932), pp. 11-12, pl. II, no. 12; Porada 1971: pl.9, fig.5; Parpola, 1994, p. 183; water carrier with a skin (or pot?) hung on each end of the yoke across his shoulders and another one below the crook of his left arm; the vessel on the right end of his yoke is over a receptacle for the water; a star on either side of the head (denoting supernatural?). The whole object is enclosed by 'parenthesis' marks. The parenthesis is perhaps a way of splitting of the ellipse (Hunter, G.R., *JRAS*, 1932, 476). An unmistakable example of an 'hieroglyphic' seal.

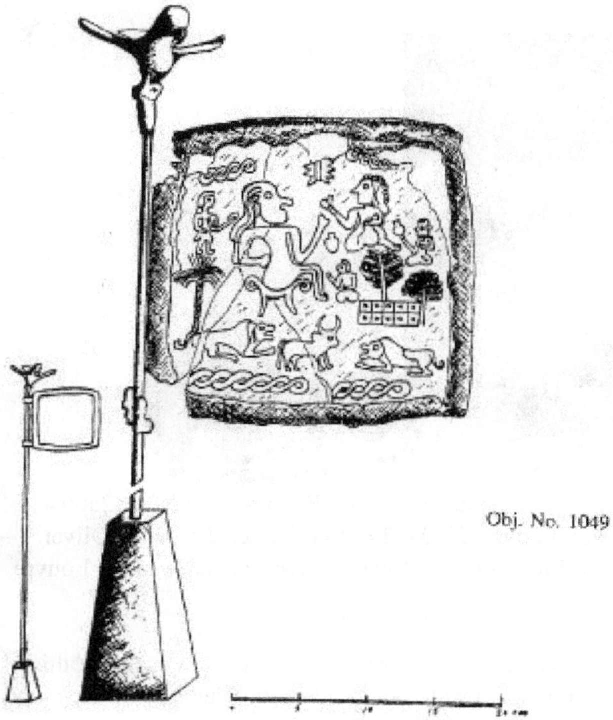

Shahdad Standard. Bronze. Drawing.

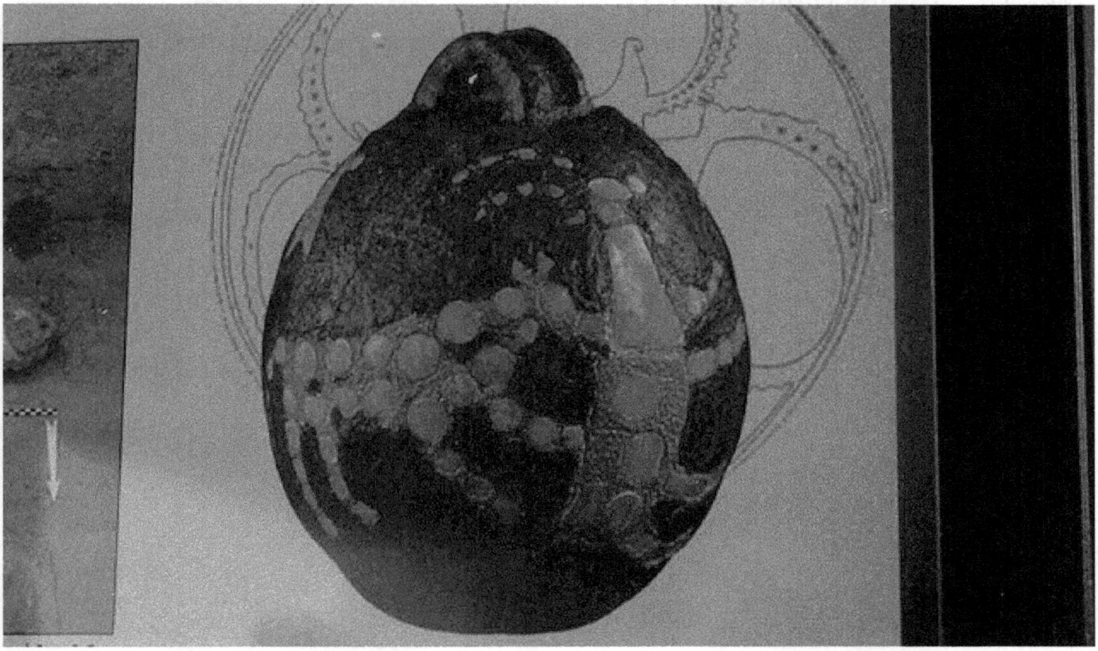

Lead weight. Shahi Tump. Ornamental ball (lead weight) discovered from Shahi Tump, Makran. It is 15 cm high and 15 kg in weight made by pure lead and wrapped in copper using cire perdue technique of casting.

The *vase a la cachette*, shown with its contents. Acropole mound, Susa. Old Elamite period, ca. 2500 - 2400 BCE. Clay. H 201/4 in. (51 cm) Paris. Musee du Louvre. Sb 2723 (After Harper, Prudence Oliver, Joan Aruz, Francoise Tallon, 1992, The Royal city of Susa: Ancient Near Eastern Treasures in the Louvre, Metropolitan Musem of Art, New York.

Two large clay jars were discovered in 1907 on the Susa Acropole. Known as the vase a la cachette, this find included eleven alabaster vessels, tools, and weapos; gold rings and beads; a tiny lapis lazuli frog; and six cylinder seals. Only one of the two containers is now preserved, painted and covered by a second painted bowl (fig. 35) MDP 13 (1912), pp. 144 f.,, pl. 24. Tallon (1987, pp. 328 ff.) explains that a second unpainted vessel containing some of his material is no longer preserved. For stratified parallels for the surviving container, see Steve and Gasche, 1971, p. 90.

The *vase a la cachette* find, consisting of objects made over a five-hundred year span and of diverse origins, was deposited no earlier than about 2400 BCE. Amiet (1986, p. 127) compares the alabaster material of the stone vases in the deposit with examples from Shahr-i-Sokhta.

Warka vase.

Louvre Excerpt

Fragment of the bas-relief called "The spinner"
Susa
Neo-Elamite period
Bitumen mastic
Remarkable condition

H 9.3 cm; L 13 cm

Sb 2834

Administrative tablet with cylinder seal impression of a male figure, hunting dogs, and boars, 3100–2900 B.C.; Jemdet Nasr period (Uruk III script)

Mesopotamia Clay; H. 2 in. (5.3 cm) The seal impression depicts a male figure guiding two dogs on a leash and hunting or herding boars in a marsh environment.

The rollout of Shu-ilishu's Cylinder seal. Courtesy of the Department des Antiquites Orientales, Musee du Louvre, Paris.

A Mesopotamian cylinder seal referring to the personal translator of the ancient Indus or Meluhan language, Shu-ilishu, who lived around 2020 BCE during the late Akkadian period. The late Dr. Gregory L. Possehl, a leading Indus scholar, tells the story of getting a fresh rollout of the seal during its visit to the Ancient Cities Exhibition at the Metropolitan Museum of Art in New York in 2004.

Cylinder seal and modern impression: hunting scene, 2250–2150 B.C.; late Akkadian period Mesopotamia Chert; H. 1 1/16 in. (2.8 cm) This seal, depicting a man hunting an ibex in a mountain forest, is an early attempt to represent a landscape in Mesopotamian art. It was made during the Akkadian period (ca. 2350–2150 B.C.), during which the iconographic repertory of the seal engraver expanded to include a variety of new mythological and narrative subjects. The owner of the seal was Balu-ili, a high court official whose title was Cupbearer. http://www.metmuseum.org/toah/ho/02/wam/hod_41.160.192.htm

Shaft-hole axhead with a bird-headed demon, boar,and dragon, late 3rd–early 2nd millennium BCE Central Asia (Bactria-Margiana) Silver, gold foil; 5 7/8 in. (15 cm) “Western Central Asia, now known as Turkmenistan, Uzbekistan, and northern Afghanistan, has yielded objects attesting to a highly developed civilization in the late third and early second millennium B.C. Artifacts from the region indicate that there were contacts with Iran to the southwest. Tools and weapons, especially axes, comprise a large portion of the metal objects from this region. This shaft-hole axhead is a masterpiece of three-dimensional and relief sculpture. Expertly cast in silver and gilded with gold foil, it depicts a bird-headed hero grappling with a wild boar and a winged dragon. The idea of the heroic bird-headed creature probably came from western Iran, where it is first documented on a cylinder seal impression. The hero's muscular body is human except for the bird talons that replace the hands and feet. He is represented twice, once on each side of the ax, and consequently appears to have two heads. On one side, he grasps the boar by the belly and on the other, by the tusks. The posture of the boar is contorted so that its bristly back forms the shape of the blade. With his other talon, the bird-headed hero grasps the winged dragon by the neck. The dragon, probably originating in Mesopotamia or Iran, is represented with folded wings, a feline body, and the talons of a bird of prey.”

Stamp seal, quatrefoil/maltese cross with infill, whip or snake

MS on grey steatite, North Syria/North Iraq/Iran, 5th millennium BC, 1 square stamp seal, 3,0x3,5x0,6 cm, 1 pictographic sign on reverse, pierced through.

Provenance: 1. Erlenmeyer Collection, Basel (before 1958-1981); 2. The Erlenmeyer Foundation, Basel (1981-1997); 3. Sotheby's 12.6.1997:6.

Stamp seal, standing male figure between two horned quadrupeds back to back and head to end

MS on speckled dark-olive steatite or chlorite, North Syria/Iraq/Iran, 5th-4th millennium BC, 1 circular stamp seal, diam. 8,4x1,3 cm, pierced through.

Provenance: 1. Erlenmeyer Collection, Basel (before 1958-1981); 2. The Erlenmeyer Foundation, Basel (1981-1997); 3. Sotheby's 12.6.1997:10.

Commentary: The earliest stamp seals of Sumer had various geometric patterns, later more elaborate designs and illustrations like the present seal, as a proof of identity and ownership. These can, together with the counting tokens, possibly be considered forerunners to the pictographic script of ca. 3200 BC.
http://www.nb.no/baser/schoyen/5/5.6/#2411

Stamp seal, large ibex walking left

MS on black steatite or chlorite, North Syria or Anatolia, 4th millennium BC, 1 rectangular gabled stamp seal, 4,7x5,1x1,3 cm, pierced through.

Provenance: 1. Erlenmeyer Collection, Basel (before 1958-1981); 2. The Erlenmeyer Foundation, Basel (1981-1997); 3. Sotheby's 12.6.1997:8.

MS 4631 Bulla-envelope with 11 plain and complex tokens inside, representing an account or agreement, tentatively of wages for 4 days' work, 4 measures of metal, 1 large measure of barley and 2 small measures of some other commodity

ι in clay, Adab, Sumer, ca. 3700-3200 BC, 1 spherical bulla-envelope nplete), diam. ca. 6,5 cm, cylinder seal impressions of a row of men walking t; and of a predator attacking a deer, inside a complete set of plain and complex okens: 4 tetrahedrons 0,9x1,0 cm (D.S.-B.5:1), 4 triangles with 2 incised lines 2,0x0,9 (D.S.-B.(:14), 1 sphere diam. 1,7 cm (D.S.-B.2:2), 1 cylinder with 1 grove 2,0x0,3 cm (D.S.-B.4:13), 1 bent paraboloid 1,3xdiam. 0,5 cm (D.S.-B.8:14).

Context: MSS 4631-4646 and 5114-5127are from the same archive. Only 25 more bulla-envelopes are known from Sumer, all excavated in Uruk. Total number of bulla-envelopes worldwide is ca. 165 intact and 70 fragmentary.

Commentary: While counting for stocktaking purposes started ca. 8000 BC plain tokens of the type also represented here, more complex accounting and recording of agreements started about 3700 BC using 2 systems: a) a string of complex tokens with the ends locked into a massive rollsealed clay bulla (see MS 4523), and b) the present system with the tokens enclosed inside a hollow bulla-shaped rollsealed envelope, sometimes with marks on the outside representing the hidden contents. The bulla-envelope had to be broken to check the contents hence the very few surviving intact bulla- envelopes. This complicated system was superseded around 3500-3200 BCE by counting tablets giving birth to the actual recording in writing, of various number systems (see MSS 3007 and 4647), and around 3300-3200 BC the beginning of pictographic writing. *Exhibited:* The Norwegian Intitute of Palaeography and Historical Philology (PHI), Oslo, 13.10.2003-06.2005.

MS 2963

ACCOUNT OF MALE AND FEMALE SLAVES

MS in Old Sumerian on clay, Sumer, ca. 3300-3200 BC, 1 nearly cubic tablet, 5,2x6,2x4,5 cm, 5 compartments in primitive pictographic script, fine cylinder seal impressions on all sides made prior to writing of 2 men walking left, carrying ostriches, a basket between them and wine amphorae above.

Context The tablets MSS 2963, 3149-3151, 4510 and 4511, are all nearly cubic in form, MS 4511 being 4,8x4,8x4,5 cm. There is nothing similar in any public collection apart from 1 in Berlin. They possibly derive from the bulla-envelopes with counting tokens inside (cf. MSS 4631-4632, 4638, ca. 3700-3200 BC). The cubic tablets might represent the next logical step, the adding of pictographs representing the commodities involved, and adapted from the spherical shape of the bullas, to cubic shape, before being reduced to a thinner and more handy tablet. The 2 earliest cubic tablets (MSS 4510 and 3151) are ideonumerographical from Uruk V period, ca. 3400 BC, next to the protopictographical texts Uruk VI, the earliest continous writing know, predating the Tell Brak and Kish tablets (ca. 3200 BC, and the Uruk IV tablets (ca. 3200-3100 BC).

Commentary: The present tablet is the earliest written evidence of slavery, see collection 24.13

MS 2645 Indus valley script, and old akkadian illustration. North West Afghanistan, ca. 21st cent.

This seal links Indus Valley and Old Akkadian civilizations. The seal is of blue stone, North West Afghanistan, ca. 23rd-21st c. BC, 1 cylinder seal, 3,9x2,7 cm, 5 Indus valley signs, illustration standing archer aiming his bow at a falling boar, in the style of the best Old Akkadian art in Sumer.

Harappa, potsherd.

Experts believe that this seal may have been used by a merchant from the Indus Valley who was living in Bahrein or Babylon. This seal was found in the Mesopotamian city of Babylon. The seal shows a bull and has a short inscription in the Indus Valley script. However, it is not square like seals from the Indus Valley. It is round with a knob on the back, which is more like seals from the Gulf island of Bahrein which date from about 2000 B.C. Other seals like this were found in the Sumerian city of Ur. A copy of a square, Indus-type seal with a picture of a bull was also found at Ur. However, this seal had an inscription in cuneiform script rather than in the Indus Valley script.

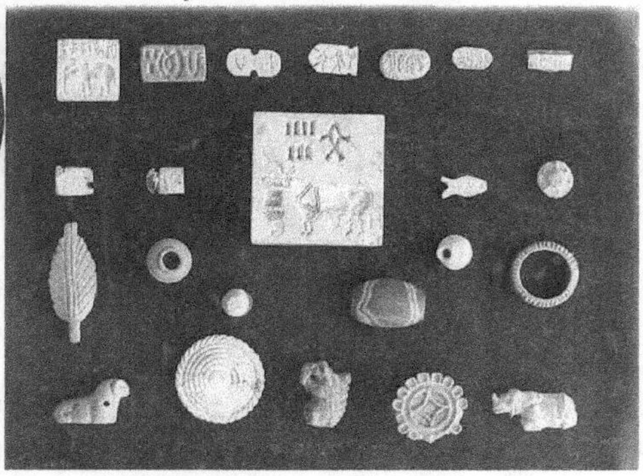

Harappa, seals, sealings and other miscellaneous objects of faience, stone, etc. selected for the Burdin Fine Arts Exhibition

http://www.photocentralasia.com/specialex/specialexphotos06.html

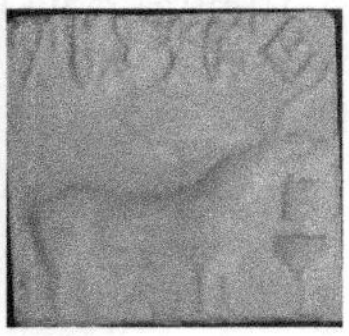

Seal impression. Royal Ontario Museum, Canada (No ROM number)

Unicorn seal ROM 996.74.5 Royal Ontario Museum, Canada

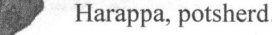

A group of six steatite seals, each with a depiction of an ox before an altar beneath a row of pictographic symbols; the reverse with a pierced boss.

http://www.asianartresource.co.uk/mall/asianartresourcecouk/products/product-823937.stm

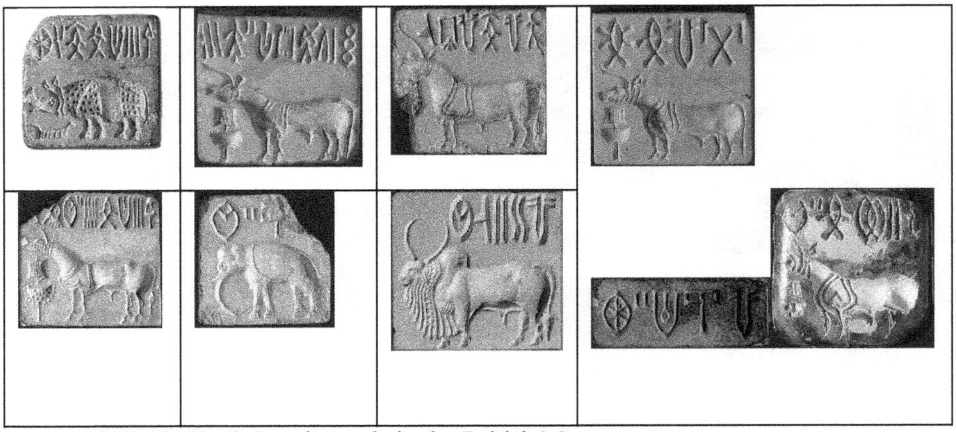

(British Museum1892-12-10, 1) Steatite seals in the British Museum

Impression of an Akkadian cylinder seal (ca. 2350-2100 BCE) variously interpreted as potting or cheese-making (after Boehmer 1965: no.693). Another interpretation could be that a man is offering a sword to the eagle-person. The three animals following this man could denote some metallurgical objects. The brazier is inscribing a vessel at the top-left.

Metal artifacts of the Bronze Age from southern Turkmenia. a,c.d Altin-depe; b Anau; e Ashkhabad; f Daina (After fig. 30 in: V.M. Masson and V.I. Sarianidi, 972, *Central Asia: Turkmenia before the Achaemen**ids*, New York, Praeger Publishers) Lead and arsenic was often added to

the bronze. Some objects from Namazga-depe contained as much as 8-0 lead and in one case the artifact was even made of brass (an alloy of copper and zinc). Twin moulds were used for casting; precious metals including gold and silver were also used. There are analogies of metal artifacts in the Harappan assemblages; for example, flag daggers without a midrib which were quite atypical for Hissar, were very widespread both in southern Turkmenia and in the Indus Valley.

Artifacts including golden head of bull. Southern Turkmenia, Margiana, Bactria: 4-7 golden head of bull and seals from Altyn depe (Developed Bronze Age); 8-21 seals and amulets of Bactria and Margiana (After Fig.4 in L.P'yankova, Central Asia in the Bronze Age: sedentary and nomadic cultures, in: *Antiquity* 68 (1994): 355-372).4.4 golden head of a bull with a turquoise sickle inlaid in the forehead; 4.5: steatite plate with an image of cross and half-moon.

Procession of animals

Bronze dish found by Layard at Nimrud: circular objects are decorated by consecutive chains of animals following each other round in a circle. A similar theme occurs on the famous silver vase of Entemena. In the innermost circle, a troop of gazelles (similar to the ones depicted on cylinder seals) march along in file; the middle register has a variety of animals, all marching in the same direction as the gazelles. A one-horned bull, a winged griffin, an ibex and a gazelle, are followed by two bulls who are being attacked by lions, and a griffin, a one-horned bull, and a gazelle, who are all respectively being attacked by leopards. In the outermost zone there is a stately procession of realistically conceived one-horned bulls marching in the opposite direction to the animals parading in the two inner circles. The dish has a handle. (Percy S.P.Handcock, 1912, *Mesopotamian Archaeology*, London, Macmillan and Co., p. 256). Cf. pasaramu, pasalamu = quadrupeds (Telugu); rebus: pasra = smithy ! (Santali) Smithy for varieties of minerals and metals, indeed.

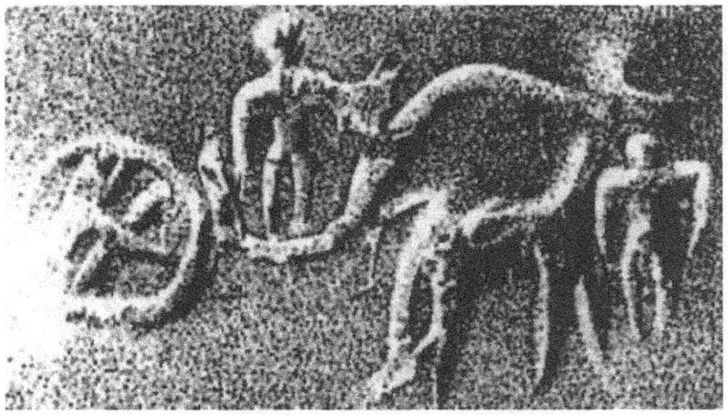

"Of lasting significance were attempts to lighten the disk wheels, as first seen on a third-millennium seal from Hissar IIIB (fig.2). On it, the central plank, through which the axle passes, is narrowed to a diametral bar; the flanking planks of the Hissar. Depiction of a wheel on a seal from Hissar IIIB. 3rd millennium BCE (After Figure 2, Littauer and Crouwel, 979). tripartite wheel are eliminated, and the former bonding slats are turned into sturdy transverse bars between the diametral bar and the felloe. This crossbar wheel is also clearly illustrated in the second millennium BCE, fixed on a revolving axle; it has remained in use with simple carts in various parts of the world.

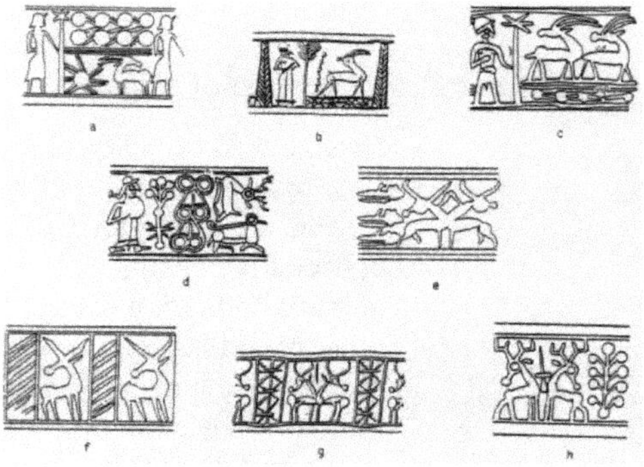

Cylinder seal impressions: (a) Nuzi (D. Stein); (b) Ugarit (Schaeffer-Forrer 1983); (c) Alalakh (Collon 1982); (d) Alalakh (Collon 1982); (e) Nuzi (D. Stein); (f) Nuzi (D.Stein); (g) Ugarit (Schaeffer-Forrer 1983); (h) Alalakh (Collon 1982).The styles are: juxtaposed antelope, humans and trees framed by geometric patters. The styles have prehistoric roots in Mesopotamia and glyphs such as an antelope with its head turned, jointed animal heads are also seen in Harappan inscription motifs.

Indus script hieroglyphs on Pandya coins. Madurai. kariba 'elephant trunk; ibha elephant' rebus: karba 'iron' ib iron' kuTi 'tree' rebus: kuThi 'smelter'aya 'fish' rebus: ayas, aya 'iron, metal' dATu 'cross' rebus: dhAtu 'element, ore'; dulo 'hole' rebus: dul 'cast metal'. *koṭhārī* f. 'crucible' rebus: treasurer; *khōṭa* 'alloy ingot'.

Dilmun seals with Indus Scrtipt

Dilmun seals (35) and decipherment through Indus Script Cipher

I am grateful to Luca Peyronel for selecting the following Dilmun seals from out of hundreds from Failaka, Bahrain and other Persian Gulf sites and categorizing them on iconographic frames (i.e. with the types of hieroglyphs signified on the seals). Peyronel gleans meanings of sacredness and ritual offerings from adorants explaining the iconograhic motifs.

The procedure for gleaning semantics (i.e. decipherment) of the hierolyphs is to treat them as Indus Script Cipher of rebus-metonymy-Meluhha speech renderings of metalwork proclamations.

I, therefore, suggest -- an alternative semantic framework -- that all the 35 Dilmun seals are Indus Script hieroglyph-multiplexes which are technical descriptions for documentation or proclamation as metalwork catalogues.

Proto-Prakritam or Meluhha hieroglyphs and rebus-metonymy readings of the hieroglyph-multiplexes on the 35 Dilmun seals:

Hieroglyph: *sā̃gaḍ* f. 'a body formed of two or more fruits or animals or men &c. linked together' (Marathi). *sā̃ghāṛɔ* (Gujarati) 'joined animal or animal parts, linked together'
Rebus: *sangara* 'proclamation'.

Hieroglyph: dula 'pair' Rebus: dul 'cast metal'

Hieroglyphs:

1. kolom 'three'

2. Hieroglyph: kolmo 'rice plant' Rebus: kolimi 'smithy, forge'.

Hieroglyph: 'human face': *mũhe* 'face' (Santali) Rebus: *mũh* opening or hole (in a stove for stoking (Bi.); ingot (Santali) *mũh* metal ingot (Santali) *mũhã̄* = the quantity of iron produced at one time in a native smelting furnace of the Kolhes; iron produced by the Kolhes and formed like a four-cornered piece a little pointed at each end; *mūhā mẽṛhẽt* = iron smelted by the Kolhes and formed into an equilateral lump a little pointed at each of four ends; *kolhe tehen mẽṛhẽt ko mūhā akata* = the Kolhes have to-day produced pig iron (Santali) *kaula mengro* 'blacksmith' (Gypsy) *mleccha-mukha* (Skt.) = *milakkhu* 'copper' (Pali) The Samskritam gloss *mleccha-mukha* should literally mean: copper-ingot absorbing the Santali gloss, *mũh*, as a suffix.

Hieroglyph: *करडूं or करडें [**karaḍū** or ṅkaraḍēṃ] n A* **kid**. *Rebus: karaḍa 'hard alloy of metal (Marathi) Allograph: करण्ड m.* a sort of duck L. కారండవము (p. 0274) [kāraṇḍavamu] *kāraṇḍavamu*. [Skt.] n. A sort of duck. (Telugu) karaṭa1 m. ' crow ' BhP., °*aka* -- m. lex. [Cf. *karaṭu* -- , *karkaṭu* -- m. ' Numidian crane ', *karēṭu* -- , °*ēṭavya* -- , °*ēḍuka* -- m. lex., *karaṇḍa*2 -- m. ' duck ' lex: see kāraṇḍava --]Pk. *karaḍa* --

m. ‘ crow ’, °*ḍā* -- f. ‘ a partic. kind of bird ’; S. *karaṛa* -- *ḍhī̃gu* m. ‘ a very large aquatic bird ’; L. *karṛā* m., °*ṛī* f. ‘ the common teal ’.(CDIAL 2787)

**koḍ `horn**' (Kuwi) Rebus: **koḍ** `artisan's workshop' (Gujarati).

kuṭhāru monkey (Samskritam) Rebus: armourer (Samskritam)

koṭhāri 'crucible' Rebus: *koṭhāri* 'treasurer' (If the hieroglyph on the leftmost is moon, a possible rebus reading: قمر ḳamar A قمر *ḳamar*, s.m. (9th) The **moon**. Sing. and Pl. See سپوږمي or سپوگمي (Pashto) Rebus: kamar 'blacksmith')

Hieroglyph: arka ‘sun’; agasāle ‘goldsmithy’ (Ka.) erka = ekke (Tbh. of arka) aka (Tbh. of arka) copper (metal); crystal (Ka.lex.) cf. eruvai = copper (Ta.lex.) eraka, er-aka = any metal infusion (Ka.Tu.); erako molten cast (Tulu) Rebus: eraka = copper (Ka.) eruvai = copper (Tamil); ere - a dark-red colour (Ka.)(DEDR 817). eraka, era, er-a = syn. erka, copper, weapons (Kannada)

Hierolyphs:

1. kuDi 'to drink'

2. kuTi 'tree' Rebus: **kuThi 'smelter'**

Hieroglyphs:

1. gaṇḍa 'four'

2. కాండము [kāṇḍamu] *kāṇḍamu*. [Skt.] n. Water. నీళ్లు (Telugu) kaṇṭhá -- : (b) ‘ water -- channel ’

3. khaṇḍ 'field,**division**' (Samskritam) Rebus 1: kaṇḍ 'fire-altar' (Santali) Rebus 2: khaṇḍa 'metal implements' *lokhãḍ, kāṇḍa* ‘flowing water’ ‘overflowing pot’ Rebus: *lokhãḍ, kāṇḍā* ‘metalware, tools, pots and pans’(Gujarati)

kole.l 'temple' Rebus: kole.l 'smithy' (Kota)

kāṅga 'comb' Rebus: *kanga* 'brazier, fireplace' (Kashmiri)
Hieroglyphs:

1. kula 'hooded snake'
2. kur.i 'woman'
3. kola ‘tiger’ (Telugu); kola ‘tiger, jackal’ (Kon.). Rebus: kol ‘working in iron’ (Tamil) kolhe 'smelter'
mẽḍh 'antelope, ram'; rebus: *mẽḍ* 'iron' (Mu.)
క్రమ్మర **krammara**. adv. క్రమ్మరిల్లు or క్రమరబడు Same as క్రమ్మరు 'look back' (Telugu). Rebus: krəm back’(Kho.)(CDIAL 3145) Rebus: kamar 'artisan, smith'

pattar 'trough' Rebus: **pattar** 'guild, goldsmith'.

ḍhangar 'bull' Rebus: *dhangar* 'blacksmith' (Maithili) *ḍangar* 'blacksmith' (Hindi)

balad m. 'ox ', gng. *bald*, (Ku.) *barad*, id. (Nepali. Tarai) Rebus: *bharat* (5 copper, 4 zinc and 1 tin)(Punjabi) *pattar* 'trough' Rebus*: pattar* 'guild, goldsmith'. Thus, copper-zinc-tin alloy (worker) guild. Rebus: bharata 'alloy of copper, pewter, tin' (Marathi) bhāraṇ = to bring out from a kiln (G.) bāraṇiyo = one whose profession it is to sift ashes or dust in a goldsmith's workshop (G.lex.) In the Punjab, the mixed alloys were generally called, bharat (5 copper, 4 zinc and 1 tin). In Bengal, an alloy called bharan or toul was created by adding some brass or zinc into pure bronze. bharata = casting metals in moulds; bharavum = to fill in; to put in; to pour into (G.lex.) Bengali. ভরন [bharana] n an inferior metal obtained from an alloy of coper, zinc and tin. *baran, bharat* 'mixed alloys' (5 copper, 4 zinc and 1 tin) (Punjabi)

Hieroglyph: 'hoof': Kumaon. khuṭo 'leg, foot', °ṭī 'goat's leg'; Nepalese. khuṭo 'leg, foot'(CDIAL 3894). S. khuṛī f. 'heel'; WPah. paṅ. khūṛ 'foot'. (CDIAL 3906). Rebus: khũṭ 'community, guild' (Santali)

Kur. kaṇḍō a stool. Malt. kanḍo stool, seat. (DEDR 1179) Rebus: kaṇḍ 'fire-altar, furnace' (Santali) kāṇḍa 'stone ore'. kāṇḍa 'tools, pots and pans

'scarf' hieroglyph: dhaṭu m. (also dhaṭhu) m. 'scarf' (Wpah.) (CDIAL 6707) Rebus: dhatu 'minerals' (Santali)

Seated person seated on a stool, with a tiara of a set of curved horns (sometimes with double crown as in al-Sindi 1994: no. 19; Kjærum 1983: no. 185 shown below). A pigtail hangs over the seated person's shoulders. Other hieroglyphs are: drinking through tubes from jar, bull -- sometimes paired, antelope (kid) -- sometimes paired, standard (portable brazier).

al-Sindi 1994: no. 17

al-Sindi 1994: no. 18

al-Sindi 1994: no. 19

Kjærum 1983: no. 185

Kjærum 1983: no. 186

al-Sindi 1994: no. 23

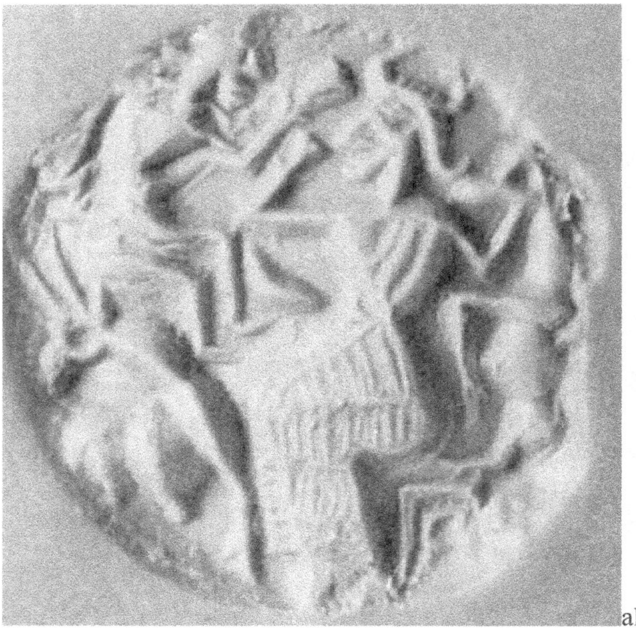

al-Sindi 1994: no. 24

al-Sindi 1994: no. 57

Kjærum 1983: no. 212

Kjærum 1983: no. 81

Kjærum 1983: no. 274

Kjærum 1983: no. 193

Dilmun seals with bullmen (human torso, bull's legs and tail, human face with bull's ears and horns)

.Peyronel 2000: no. 4.14 Bull-man holding a crescent standard

Kjærum 1983: no. 208

Kjærum 1983: no. 121

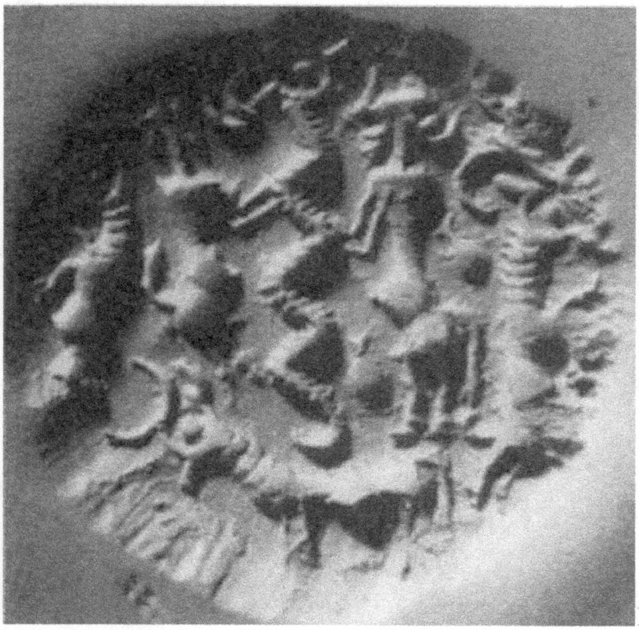

Kjærum 1983: no. 122

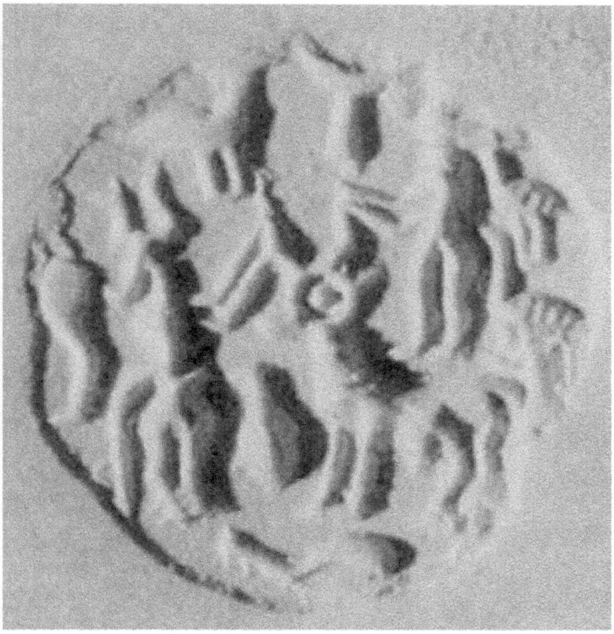

al-Sindi 1994: no. 254

Kjærum 1983: no. 274

[Peyronel, Luca, 2008, Some thoughts on iconographic relations between the Arabian Gulf and Syria-Mesopotamia during the Middle Bronze Age, in: Olijdam, E. & RH Spoor, eds., Intercultural relations between south and southwest Asia, studies in commemoration of ECL During Caspers (1934-1996), BAR International Series 1826 (2008): 236-252 "The relationship between bull-men and superimposed bulls or bull and gazelle (Kjaerum 1983: nos. 247-249) again suggests the complex pattern of ideological meanings which hides behind the animal repertoire in Dilmun stamp seals. Two crossed bull-men with raised hands stand across a net podium on a unique seal from Failaka (Kjaerum 1983: no. 261)…Another meaningful seal is engraved with a schematic shrine or door with symbols inside (hatched podium, sun-ring, hatched lentoid, net podium), flanked by a bull-man and a garbed man grasping the door-frame (Kjaerum 1983: no. 51). Rectangular structures appear on 9 seals (Kjaerum 1983: nos. 51-54, 126; al-Sindi 1994; nos. 202-203, 205, 263): they have symbols or human figures within and they can be considered schematic gates or chapels/shrines, without doubt linked with pecular ritual functions as revealed also by astral symbols, mythological figures (serpent monsters or bull-men) and worshippers on their sides." (p.242)

Dilmun seals with a pair of bull-men and other hieroglyphs (in addition to kids): rectangle with divisions, sun, crucible, bun ingot with infixed 3 numeral strokes, a rectangle with four infixed numeral strokes, temple gate (signifying temple).

Kjærum 1983: no. 93

Kjærum 1983: no. 70

Kjærum 1983: no. 248

Kjærum 1983: no. 249

Kjærum 1983: no. 261

Kjærum 1983: no. 51

Dilmun seals with a pair of bull-men and other hieroglyphs (crucible, sun, vase, pair of harrows, aquatic bird; pair of forked stakes)

al-Sindi 1994: no. 115

Pair of forked stakes, kids

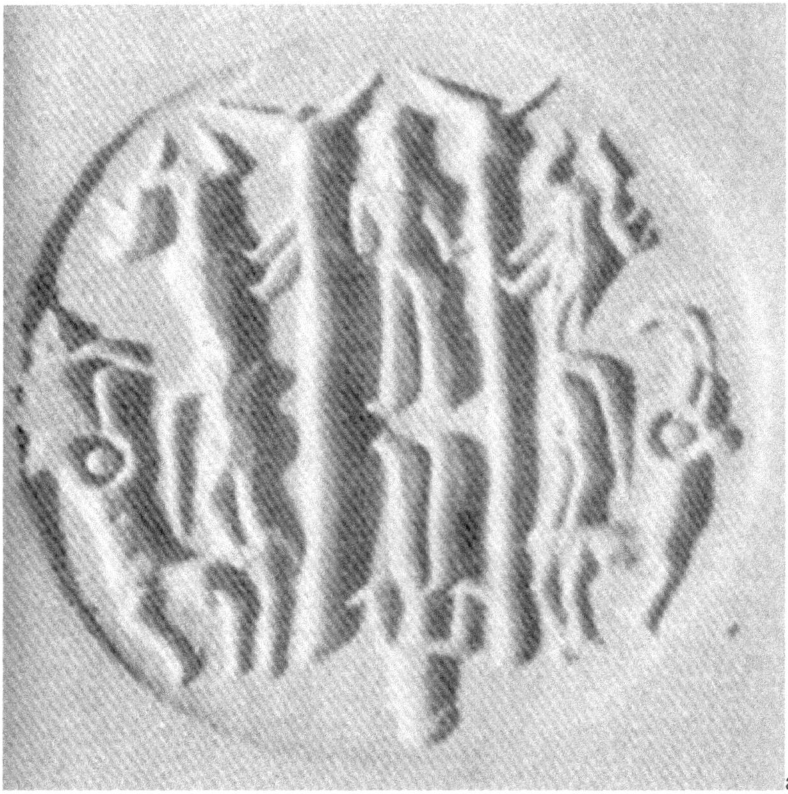

al-Sindi 1994: no. 116

Rectangle with divided squares, kids

al-Sindi 1994: no. 117

standard PLUS crucible PLUS sun PLUS rectangle with divided squares, antelopes, bull PLUS trouh

Kjærum 1983: no. 115

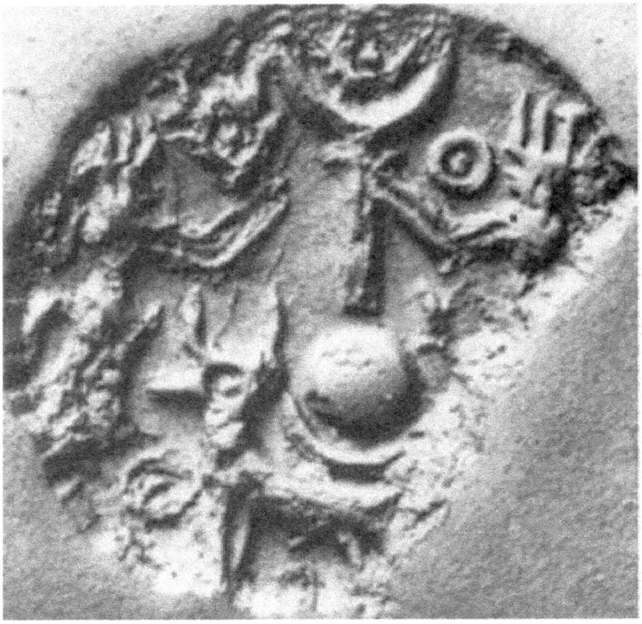
Kjærum 1983: no. 116

Kjærum 1983: no. 141 (Same as 115?)

"Bull-men are attested in Mesopotamian glyptic from the Early Dynastic II onwards. The iconographic elaboration probably happened at the end of the 4th or at the beginning of the 3rd millennium BCE in the Iranian milieu, where stamp and cylinder seals show hybrid creatures with mixed human and animal features since he prehistoric periods..."(opcit., pp.244-245) It has been noted in Indus Script Cipher that sangaDa ‘joined animals or animal parts’ is rebus sangara ‘proclamations’. The ‘hybrid creatures’ are thus metalwork proclamations detailing, for example, the metals as alloying components.

"Bull-men were represented during the Early Dynastic period only in contest scenes together with rampant animas, the naked hero and the human-headed bull. A lengthy discussion on these figures has involved Near Eastern scholars, some proposing to identify Enkidu and Gilgamesh with the bull-man and the hero with long hair with curls, other preferring to recognize in these figures different aspects of the god Dumuzi. More recently a simplistic correlation between Early Dynastic supernatural beings and those known from mythological tales was submitted to a strong criticism (Lambert 1987), despite the unequivocal connection with the religious sphere. It is now widely accepted that the ‘nude hero’ must be considered a protective and beneficent deity, in later periods associated with Enki (Akkadian period) or Marduk (from the 2nd millennium BCE), known by the name Lahmu…The corpus of seal impressions from Kultepe karum II (ca. 1920-1850 BCE) verifies the occurrence in the Anatolian, Syro-Cappadocian, Old Syrian, and Old Assyrian styles." (opcit. 244-245).

I would not venture critiquing these meanings and art expression evaluations based on faith. I would not also submit to the 'master of animals' metaphor. I would, instead, deploy an Occam's razor, suggest a simple, direct submission of Indus Script cipher based on Meluhha-rebus-metonymy yielding plain texts of metalwork catalogues involving multiple alloying metals and metalcastings to read the hieroglyph-multiplexes as cypher-texts, symbolic hyper-texts (as Dennys Frenez and Massimo Vidale would call them). See:

http://bharatkalyan97.blogspot.in/2015/10/art-historians-dilemma-and-occams-razor.html

Dilmun portable braziers with crucibles (offering tables with bull's hooves) and other hieroglyphs: aquatic bird, rice-plant, snake,

Kjærum 1983: no. 163

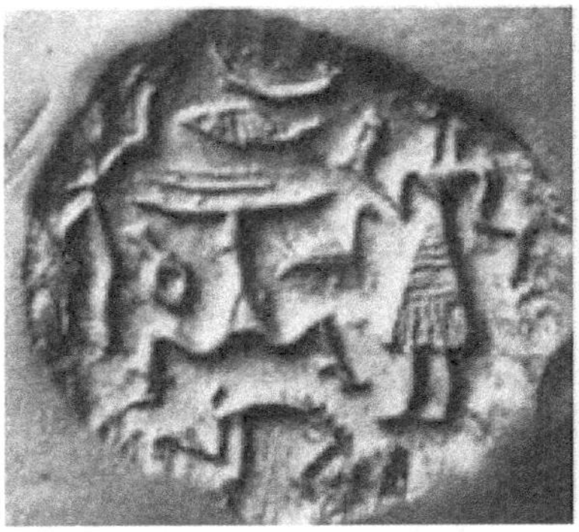
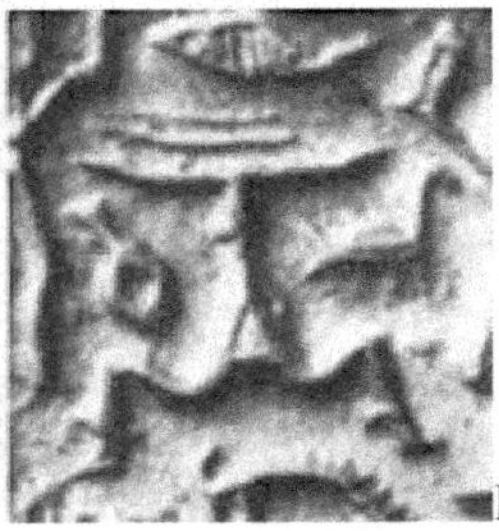
Kjærum 1983: no. 165

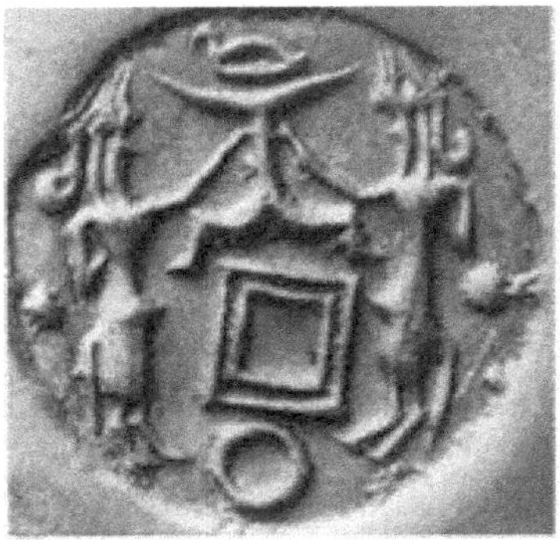

Kjærum 1983: no. 166

Kjærum 1983: no. 167

Kjærum 1983: no. 168

"Dilmunite seal designs with offering tables might testify not only to the iconographic knowledge but also to a circulation of that type of ceremonial furnishing between Western Syria and Arabian Gulf, i.e. as real imports. From an artistic point of view, Dilmun again shows the trend to assimilate themes and figurative motifs pertaining to the 'Amorite' Western and Northern Syrian milieu dating from the very beginning of the 2nd millennium till the end of the 17th century BCE...The wide web of intercultural contacts during the second half of the 3rd millennium BCE is well attested, for example, by the distribution of chlorite carved vessels and by imports or objects with Harappan influence in Mesopotamia (i.e. square or circular stamp seals, etched carnelian beads, weights, clay figurines, dice, kidney-shaped inlays. If it is very likely that the people from Meluhha had settled in the alluvium, but it is much more difficult to establish the presence of Mesopotamians in the Indus Valley on the basis of presumed Near Eastern 'cultural' traits in a handful of objects from Harappan cities."(opcit., p.246, 249, fn 9). It is possible that the assimilation of hieroglyphs onto Dilmun seals occurred because of Meluhhan presence and adoption of Meluhhan Indus Script cipher, with rebus-metonymy renderings of cyphertexts as hieroglyph-complexes.

See: http://archaeologydataservice.ac.uk/archiveDS/archiveDownload?t=arch-456-1/dissemination/pdf/Saar_Report_2.pdf Early Dilmun seals from Saar.

Concordance lists for epigraphs

An outstanding contribution to the study of the script problem is the publication of the Corpus of Indus Seals and Inscriptions (CISI) Three volumes have been published so far:

Corpus of Indus Seals and Inscriptions, 1. Collections in India, Helsinki, 1987 (eds. Jagat Pati Joshi and Asko Parpola)

Corpus of Indus Seals and Inscriptions, 2. Collections in Pakistan, Helsinki, 1991 (eds. Sayid Ghulam Mustafa Shah and Asko Parpola)

Corpus of Indus Seals and Inscriptions, 3. 1 Supplement to Mohenjo-daro and Harappa, 2010 (eds. Asko Parpola, B.M. Pande and Petteri Koskikallio) in collaboration with Richard H. Meadow and Jonathan Mark Kenoyer. (Annales Academiae Scientiarum Fennicae, B. 239-241.) Helsinki: Suomalainen Tiedeakatemia.

These volumes in which Asko Parpola is the co-author constitute the photographic corpus. The CISI contains all the seals including those without any inscriptions, for e.g. those with the geometrical motif called the 'svastika'. Parpola's initial corpus (1973) included a total number of 3204 texts. After compiling the pictorial corpus, Parpola notes that there are approximately 3700 legible inscriptions (including 1400 duplicate inscriptions, i.e. with repeated texts). Both the concordances of Parpola and Mahadevan complement each other because of the sort sequence adopted. Parpola's concordance was sorted according to the sign following the indexed sign. Mahadevan's concordance was sorted according to the sign preceding the indexed sign. The latter sort ordering helps in delineating signs which occur in final position. With the publication of CISI Vol. 3, Part 1, the total number of inscriptions from Mohenjo-daro totals 2134 and from Harappa totals 2589; thus, these two sites alone accounting for 4,723 bring the overall total number of inscriptions to over 6,000 from all sites (even after excluding comparable inscriptions on 'Persian Gulf type' circular seals from the total count).

Compendia of the efforts made since the discovery by Gen. Alexander Cunningham, in 1875, of the first known Indus seal (British Museum 1892-12-10, 1), to decipher the script appear in the following references:

A number of concordances and sign lists have been compiled, by many scholars, for the 'Indus' script:

Dani, A.H., *Indian Palaeography*, 1963, Pls. I-II

Gadd and Smith, *Mohenjodaro and the Indus Civilization*, London,1931,, vol. III, Pls. CXIX-CXXIX

Hunter, G.R., *JRAS*, 1932, pp. 491-503

Hunter, G.R., *Scripts of Harappa and Mohenjodaro*, 1934, pp. 203-10

Langdon, Mohenjodaro and the Indus Civilization*, London, 1931, vol. II, pp. 434-55*

Koskenniemi, Kimmo and Asko Parpola, *Corpus of texts in the Indus script,* Helsinki, 1979; *A concordance to the texts in the Indus script*, Helsinki, 1982

Mahadevan, I., *The Indus Script: Texts, concordance and tables*, Delhi, 1977, pp. 32-35

Parpola et al., *Materials for the study of the Indus script, I: A concordance to the Indus Inscriptions*, 1973, pp. xxii-xxvi

Vats, *Excavations at Harappa*, Calcutta, 1940, vol. II, Pls. CV-CXVI

http://www.scribd.com/doc/2232464/epigraphica (ebook)

DEDR Dravidian Etymological Dictionary

Munda:

- Comparative Munda (mostly North), rough draft ed. Stampe, based on Heinz-Jürgen Pinnow's *Versuch einer historischen Lautlehre der Kharia-Sprache* (Wiesbaden: Harrassowitz, 1959) and Ram Dayal Munda's *Proto-Kherwarian Phonology*, unpublished MA thesis, University of Chicago, 1968.
- Working files of South Munda lexical data by gloss assembled from collections of David Stampe, Patricia Donegan, H.-J. Pinnow, Sudhibhushan Bhattacharya, and Norman and Arlene Zide for a seminar by Stampe on Austroasiatic languages.

CDIAL Comparative Dictionary of Indo-Aryan Languages

Boas, Franz. 1917. Introduction. International Journal of American Linguistics. (Reprinted: Boas, Franz. 1940.

Race, language, and culture, 199-210. New York: The Free Press.)

1920. The classification of American languages. American Anthropologist 22.367-76. (Reprinted: Boas, Franz. 1940. Race, language, and culture, 211-8. New York: The Free Press.

1929. The classification of American Indian languages. Language 5.1-7

Campbell, 1997,.American Indian languages: the historical linguistics of Native America. Oxford: Oxford University Press, 62-6

Campbell, Lyle, 2006 Areal linguistics: a closer scrutiny. In: Linguistic Areas: Convergence in Historical and Typological Perspective, ed.by Yaron Matras April McMahon, and Nigel Vincent, 1-31.Houndmills, Basingstoke, Hampshire: Palgrave Macmillan

Campbell, Lyle, 2006, Areal linguistics. In: Keith Brown (ed.), 2006, Encylopaedia of Languages and Linguistics, 2nd edn., Oxford, Elsevier, pp. 454-460

Campbell, Lyle, and Marianne Mithun. 1979. North American Indian historical linguistics in current perspective. The Languages of Native America: an Historical and Comparative Assessment, ed. by L. Campbell and Marianne Mithun, 3-69. Austin: University of Texas Press

Dales, George F., Jr. 1967, South Asia's earliest writing – still undeciphered, Expedition 9 (2): 30-37

Darnell, Regna and Joel Sherzer. 1971. Areal linguistic studies in North America: a historical perspective.

International Journal of American Linguistics 37.20-8

Durante, Silvio, 1979,"Marine Shells from Balakot, Shahr-i Sokhta and Tepe Yahya: Their Significance for Trade Technology in Ancient Indo-Iran." In South Asian Archaeology 1977, Naples.

Emeneau, MB, 1956, India as a linguistic area, Language 32, 1956, 3-16.

Farmer, Steve, Richard Sproat, and Michael Witzel, 2004, The collapse of the Indusscript thesis: The myth of a literate Harappan Civilization. Electronic Journal of Vedic Studies 11 (2): 19–57

Gould, S.J., 2003, I have landed. Splashes and reflections in natural history, London.

Hunter, G.R., 1934, Script of Harappa and Mohenjodaro and its connection with other Scripts/G.R. Hunter.-London, p. 126

Jakobson, Roman, 1949 (1936), Sur la théorie des affinities phonologiques entre les langues. Actes du quatrieme congresinternational de linguists (tenu a Copenhague du 27 août 1 Septembre, 1936), 48-58. (Reprinted, 1949, as an appendix to: Principes de phonologie, by N. S. Troubetzkoy, 351-65. Paris: Klincksieck.)

1944. Franz Boas' approach to language. International Journal of American Linguistics 10.188-95

Kalyanaraman, S., 1988, *Indus Script: A bibliography*, Manila.

Kalyanaraman, S., 1992, Indian Lexicon, an etymological dictionary of south Asian languages. http://www.scribd.com/doc/2232617/lexicon (ebook)

Kalyanaraman, S., 2008, Sarasvati—Vedic river and Hindu civilization, Chennai, Sarasvati Research and Education Trust (ISBN 978-81-901126-1-1) http://www.scribd.com/doc/7734436/Sarasvati-Book (ebook)

Kalyanaraman, S., 2010, Indus Script Cipher – Hieroglyphs of Indian linguistic area (ISBN 978-0982897102)

Kenoyer, J. M. 1997 Trade and technology of the Indus Valley: new insights from Harappa, Pakistan. World Archaeology 29(2): 262-280.

Kenoyer, J. M. and R. H. Meadow 1999 Harappa: New Discoveries on its origins and growth. Lahore Museum Bulletin XII(1): 1-12.

Kharakwal, J.S., Y.S. Rawat and Toshiki Osada, 2007, Kanmer: A Harappan site in Kachchh, Gujarat, India. PP. 21-137 in: Toshiki Osada (Ed.), Linguistics, archaeology and the human past. (Occasional papers 2.) Kyoto: Indus Project. Research Institute for Humanity and Nature.

Koskenniemi, Seppo, Asko Parpola and Simo Parpola, 1973, Materials for the study of the Indus script, I. A concordance to the Indus inscriptions, Annales Academiae Scientiaram Fennicae, Ser. B, Tom. 185. xxviii, 528, 55 pp. + errata sheet. Helsinki: [Academia Scientiarum Fennica]

Koskenniemi and Parpola, 1982, A Concordance to the Texts in the Indus Script. Helsinki: [University of Helsinki]. 201pp. Department of Asian and African Studies, University of Helsinki. Research Reports, No. 3., pp. 10-11.

Kuiper, FBJ, 1948, Proto-Munda words in Sanskrit, Amsterdam, 1948

1967, The genesis of a linguistic area, IIJ 10, 1967, 81-102

Lal, B.B., 2002, The Sarasvati flows on: The continuity of Indian culture. New Delhi: Aryan Books International.

Mahadevan, Iravatham, 1966, "Towards a grammar of the Indus texts: 'intelligible to the eye, if not to the ears', Tamil Civilization, Vol. 4, Nos. 3 and 4, Tanjore, 1966.

Mahadevan, Iravatham, 1977, The Indus script: texts, concordance and tables. (Memoirs of the Archaeological Survey of India, 77) New Delhi: Archaeological Survey of India.

Mahadevan, Iravatham, 1978, "Recent advances in the study of the Indus script", *Puratattva*, Vol. 9.)

Mahadevan, I., *What do we know about the Indus Script? Neti neti ('Not this nor that'),* Presidential Address, section 5, Indian History Congress, 49th Session, Dharwar, 2-4 November 1988, Madras.

Marshall, J. 1931. Mohenjodaro and the Indus Civilization. Vol. I, II text, Vol. III plates. London: A. Probsthain

Masica, CP, 1971, Defining a Linguistic area. South Asia. Chicago: The University of Chicago Press.

Meadow, R. H., J. M. Kenoyer and R. P. Wright 1997 Harappa Archaeological Research Project: Harappa Excavations 1997, Report submitted to the Director General of Archaeology and Museums, Government of Pakistan, Karachi.

Meadow, Richard and Jonathan Mark Kenoyer, 1997, Excavations at Harappa 1994-1995: new perspectives on the Indus script, craft activities, and city organization, in: Raymond Allchin and Bridget Allchin, 1997, *South Asian Archaeology 1995*, Oxford and IBH Publishing, pp. 157-163.

Meadow, R. H., J. M. Kenoyer and R. P. Wright 1998 Harappa Archaeological Research Project: Harappa Excavations 1998, Report submitted to the Director General of Archaeology and Museums, Government of Pakistan, Karachi.

Meadow, R. H., J. M. Kenoyer and R. P. Wright 1999 Harappa Archaeological Research Project: Harappa Excavations 1999, Report submitted to the Director General of Archaeology and Museums, Government of Pakistan, Karachi.

Meadow, R. H., J. M. Kenoyer and R. P. Wright 2000 Harappa Archaeological Research Project: Harappa Excavations 2000, Report submitted to the Director General of Archaeology and Museums, Government of Pakistan, Karachi.

Meadow, R. H. and J. M. Kenoyer 2001 Harappa Excavations 1998-1999: New evidence for the development and manifestation of the Harappan phenomenon. In South Asian Archaeology 1999, edited by K. R. van Kooij and E. M. Raven, pp. in press. Leiden.

Mughal, M. R. 1990 Further Evidence of the Early Harappan Culture in the Greater Indus Valley: 1971-90. South Asian Studies 6: 175-200.

Mughal, M. R., F. Iqbal, M. A. K. Khan and M. Hassan 1996 Archaeological Sites and Monuments in Punjab: Preliminary report of Explorations: 1992-1996. Pakistan Archaeology 29: 1-474.

Parpola, Asko, 1994, Deciphering the Indus Script, Cambridge University Press, Cambridge, U.K. [Note: A comprehensive bibliography appears.]

Possehl, Gregory L., 1996, The Indus Age: The Writing System, Philadelphia: University of Pennsylvania Press.

Possehl, Gregory and Gullapalli, Praveena,1999, 'The Early Iron Age in South Asia'; in Vincent C. Piggott (ed.).The Archaeometallurgy of the Asian Old World; University Museum Monograph, MASCA Research Papers in Science and Archaeology, Volume 16; Pgs. 153-175; The University Museum, University of Pennsylvania; Philadelphia.

M. A. Probst, Alekseev, G. V., A. M. Kondratov, Y. V. Knorozov, I. K. Fedorova, and B. Y. Volchok, 1965, Preliminary report on the investigation of the Proto-Indian Texts. Academy of Sciences U.S.S.R., Soviet Institute of Scientific and Technical Information, Institute of Ethnography, Moscow

Przyludski, J., 1929, Further notes on non-aryan loans in Indo-Aryan in: Bagchi, P. C. (ed.), Pre-Aryan and Pre-Dravidian in Sanskrit. Calcutta : University of Calcutta: 145-149

Rajagopal, Sukumar, Priya Raju, and Sridhar Narayanan, 2009, Illiterate Indus?, Journal of Tamil Studies, December 2009 issue (#76), pp. 69-88, International Institute of Tamil Studies.

Southworth, F., 2005, Linguistic archaeology of South Asia, London, Routledge-Curzon.

Tewari, Rakesh, 2003, The origins of Iron-working in India: New evidence from the Central Ganga Plain and the Eastern Vindhyas, Antiquity, London http://www.antiquity.ac.uk/projgall/tewari298/tewari.pdf

Trubetzkoy 1939, Gedanken über das Indogermanenproblem Acta Linguistica 1.81-9

Vats, M.S., 1940, Excavations at Harappa, Being an Account of Archaeological Excavations at Harappa carried out between the Years 1920-1921 and 1933-34, Delhi, Archaeological Survey of India

Vidale, Massimo, 2007, The collapse melts down: A reply to Farmer, Sproat & Witzel. East and West 57 (1-4): 333-366. http://www.docstoc.com/docs

Agastya, 74
agate, 320
Akkadian, 69, 91, 133, 140, 291, 292, 303, 304, 314, 319, 334, 337, 338
alligator, 49, 299
allograph, 116, 121, 287
alloy, 44, 87, 116, 119, 120, 124, 128, 130, 133, 149, 151, 256, 257, 258, 260, 263, 269, 270, 272, 275, 277, 286, 289, 290, 292, 295, 302, 307, 338, 340
alloying, 98, 107, 149, 305
amśu, 121, 123, 124, 287
ancu, 123, 124
antelope, 49, 289, 292, 299, 317, 319, 320, 340
antimony, 133, 299
Anzu, 124
arch, 50
archer, 158, 266, 307, 337
arrow, 42, 116, 121, 123, 266, 287, 318
arsenic, 134, 149, 304, 338
artifact, 225, 294, 338
artifacts, 312
artisan, 125, 137, 138, 140, 145, 147, 170, 172, 255, 256, 258, 261, 262, 274, 285, 289, 302
ashur, 214
Austro-Asiatic, 52, 60, 71, 72
Avestan, 58, 79
awl, 50, 139
axe, 42, 50, 58, 295
ayas, 98, 116, 118, 120, 121, 123, 124, 125, 133, 140, 172, 235, 236, 261, 276, 285, 286, 287, 288, 293, 298, 299, 340
ayo, 116, 121, 288, 293, 298, 299
backbone, 128, 256, 272, 290
Bactria, 338
Bagchi, 366
Bahrain, 320
Baluchistan, 65
barley, 47
BB Lal, 320
bead, 50
beads, 140, 294, 313, 318, 320, 330
bed, 50
bha_s.a_, 70
Bharata, 70
bird, 48, 98, 100, 111, 116, 119, 124, 165, 286, 293, 305, 306, 317, 319, 335

Bisht, 139, 140
bison, 263, 264, 315, 324
blacksmith, 44, 87, 92, 93, 98, 112, 113, 114, 115, 123, 131, 132, 133, 137, 140, 147, 178, 256, 260, 261, 262, 263, 264, 275, 281, 282, 284, 292, 302, 304
boar, 39, 332, 333, 335, 337
Boas, 363, 364
boat, 50, 256, 274, 278
body, 35, 46, 49, 72, 86, 94, 99, 116, 118, 128, 143, 176, 178, 206, 228, 235, 255, 265, 266, 267, 268, 269, 270, 271, 272, 289, 292, 295, 315, 321, 323, 328, 335
bone, 45, 49
bos gaurus, 263
bos indicus, 97, 98
bovine, 98, 260
bow, 50, 77
Brahui, 55, 58
brass, 34, 35, 50, 130, 134, 140, 149, 254, 257, 258, 268, 271, 276, 280, 281, 282, 283, 293, 305, 338
brazier, 50, 65, 179, 257, 281, 290, 292, 293, 338
brick, 50, 65
bristle, 49
bronze, 50, 64, 102, 103, 115, 120, 124, 133, 134, 149, 179, 189, 202, 203, 204, 209, 210, 215, 216, 217, 218, 221, 222, 223, 257, 258, 268, 271, 276, 280, 281, 282, 284, 286, 294, 298, 301, 305, 310, 311, 338
Buddha, 71
buffalo, 49, 133, 165, 176, 178, 262, 263, 293, 316
bull, 42, 49, 56, 65, 69, 85, 90, 91, 99, 100, 108, 111, 133, 136, 256, 260, 262, 263, 274, 278, 280, 283, 284, 289, 290, 292, 293, 294, 303, 310, 315, 316, 317, 318, 319, 320, 321, 337, 338, 339
bush, 47
camel, 49
Campbell, 363
carnelian, 318, 320
carp, 67
carpenter, 34, 121, 257, 287
cart, 50
casting, 33, 64, 86, 130, 131, 165, 235, 236, 257, 269, 271, 276, 299, 302, 329, 338
Central Asia, 338
chalcedony, 174
Chatterjee, 366
chert, 320
chisel, 50
cipher, 1, 2, 3, 36, 81, 125, 141, 163, 235, 277, 294
citadel, 65, 137, 138, 139, 140
cities, 64, 65
city, 65, 68, 69
clay, 50, 65, 68
cloak, 50
cloth, 47, 68
comb, 50, 292
community, 77, 157, 260
composite animal, 260
conch, 42
conflict, 51
copper, 8, 9, 33, 34, 35, 59, 86, 94, 95, 98, 101, 112, 114, 115, 116, 118, 120, 124, 130, 133, 134, 137, 138, 140, 147, 149, 163, 166, 170, 226, 255, 256, 257, 258, 259, 260, 261, 262, 263, 268, 270, 271, 272, 275, 276, 277, 278, 279, 280, 281, 282, 283, 284, 287, 289, 290, 292, 294, 295, 296, 298, 299, 305, 306, 307, 310, 311, 318, 320, 321, 325, 329, 338
cotton, 47, 65
crab, 48, 137, 265, 266, 277, 278
crocodile, 69, 262, 264, 294
crucible, 50, 107, 133, 178, 307
cubical, 65, 320
cuneiform, 69
curve, 49, 271
curved, 93, 120, 172, 258, 261, 271, 277, 286, 293, 298
cylinder seal, 69, 338, 339
dagger, 178, 307
dance, 31, 49, 178, 179, 270
deciphering, 52, 54, 68
decoded, 371
deer, 49, 262, 336
deity, 51, 58
dhokra, 86, 90, 302
dice, 50
digger, 50
Dilmun, 138, 294, 313, 316
dog, 49, 320
domestic animals, 56
dotted circle, 44, 59, 294
Dravidian, 52, 55, 57, 59, 60, 61, 62, 63, 71, 72, 73, 74, 75, 79

drill, 50
drum, 50, 76, 96, 257, 273
duck, 48, 119, 120, 286
Durga, 73
eagle, 48, 86, 100, 123, 133, 213, 338
Egypt, 64, 71
electrum, 75, 123, 124
elephant, 49, 69, 73
Emeneau, 52, 62, 363, 364
eraka, 9, 86, 130, 133, 137, 138, 140, 147, 256, 258, 262, 268, 280, 289, 295, 310
Fabri, 366
Failaka, 316
ficus glomerata, 114, 115, 276, 277, 279, 280, 281, 284
ficus religiosa, 138, 259, 270, 280, 284
fin, 6, 8, 120, 121, 125, 140, 162, 163, 287
fish, 49, 116, 118, 119, 120, 121, 122, 123, 125, 133, 137, 139, 140, 145, 151, 157, 162, 167, 172, 235, 236, 274, 276, 277, 279, 282, 285, 286, 287, 288, 289, 290, 292, 293, 295, 298, 299, 302, 304, 305, 318, 319, 320, 321, 323, 328, 340
flag, 50, 271, 304, 307, 338
flow, 49
forge, 34, 50, 91, 111, 114, 147, 256, 263, 272, 275, 289, 290, 291, 293, 304, 307, 310
fox, 282
frog, 48, 319, 330
furnace, 34, 50, 98, 111, 112, 114, 116, 122, 133, 135, 137, 138, 178, 179, 236, 255, 256, 257, 258, 259, 260, 261, 263, 265, 266, 267, 268, 269, 270, 271, 272, 276, 277, 279, 281, 284, 289, 292, 293, 294, 299, 303, 304, 310
Gadd, 69, 135, 267, 317, 318, 321, 328, 362
gazelle, 339
gimlet, 310
gloss, 94, 96, 98, 107, 118, 124, 125, 135, 148, 172, 260, 261, 272, 275, 277, 285, 287, 294, 304, 306, 363
goat, 49, 91, 92, 93, 130, 165, 258, 270, 275, 281, 292, 298, 302, 317, 320
gold, 45, 50, 65, 75, 95, 96, 123, 124, 149, 165, 210, 221, 226, 258, 262, 273, 274, 282, 283, 290, 291, 294, 307, 318, 325, 326, 327, 328, 330, 335, 338
granary, 47
guild, 50, 116, 260, 283, 309, 310
Haifa, 136, 290, 303
hammer, 50
Harappa, 65
hare, 49
harrow, 236, 269, 292
hill, 50, 92, 281
Hindu, 72
hood, 87, 133, 167, 260, 263, 304, 307, 308
horn, 49, 65, 93, 98, 111, 258, 259, 274, 277, 278, 285, 289, 290, 293
horned, 320, 339
horse, 49, 73, 77
Hunter, 363, 364
ibex, 289, 290, 320, 334, 335, 339
implements, 39, 91, 114, 115, 116, 117, 118, 133, 265, 281, 283, 284
incised, 320
Indian Lexicon
  Indian Lexicon, 364
Indo-Aryan, 52, 55, 57, 59, 60, 61, 62, 74
ingot, 116, 121, 154, 155, 236, 256, 260, 261, 262, 264, 270, 272, 287, 293, 317, 340
inlaid, 338
inscription, 69, 78, 340
iron, 33, 35, 44, 86, 87, 93, 94, 96, 97, 98, 104, 107, 111, 112, 113, 114, 115, 116, 117, 118, 119, 120, 121, 122, 123, 128, 130, 132, 133, 135, 140, 147, 156, 162, 165, 172, 176, 178, 179, 199, 210, 235, 236, 255, 256, 257, 258, 259, 260, 261, 262, 263, 265,266, 267, 268, 269, 270, 271, 274, 275, 276, 277, 278, 279, 281, 282, 283, 284, 285, 286, 287, 288, 289, 290, 292, 293, 296, 298, 299, 302, 303, 304, 306, 307, 308, 340
iron ore, 107, 265, 268, 288
ivory, 49
jackal, 97, 256, 263
jar, 109, 111, 133, 174, 256, 258, 267, 290, 305, 318, 319, 320
Kalyanaraman, 36, 235, 363, 364
kamaḍha, 138, 256, 266, 284
Kannad.a, 54
Kashmiri, 55, 58
Kenoyer, 111, 264, 319, 328, 362, 364, 365, 366
kiln, 50
Kon
  kan.i, 54
Kuiper, 53, 364
ladder, 50, 71, 292

Lal, 320
language, 52, 53, 54, 55, 57, 59, 60, 61, 62, 63, 64, 65, 66, 67, 68, 69, 70, 71, 72, 73, 74, 75, 76, 77, 78
languages, 51, 52, 53, 54, 55, 56, 57, 58, 59, 60, 61, 62, 63, 66, 68, 70, 71, 72, 73, 74, 77, 79
lapidary, 47, 50, 312
lapis lazuli, 92, 320, 330
lathe, 50, 137, 138, 274, 278, 281, 283, 284, 303, 310
lattice, 50
lead, 51, 338
leafless tree, 262
Levi, 366
ligature, 236, 271, 272, 277, 278, 287, 298
lion, 49, 90, 140, 162, 323
lizard, 48
logo-semantic, 136
Lothal, 65
Mackay, 91, 125, 173, 267, 321
Magan, 138, 295
makara, 298, 299
Marshall, 313, 328, 365
Masica, 365
mason, 257, 284, 310
Meluhha, 1, 2, 36, 81, 86, 90, 94, 96, 103, 107, 132, 136, 139, 149, 151, 172, 178, 202, 209, 224, 235, 261, 275, 277, 283, 293, 294, 298, 301, 304, 306, 309, 310, 311, 315, 320
Meluhhan, 69
merchant, 69, 140, 260, 262, 270, 281, 291, 292, 298, 302, 337
merchants, 65
Mesopotamia, 65, 69, 340
metal, 312, 338
metals, 257, 338, 339
metalsmith, 91, 138, 284
mineral, 33, 34, 35, 44, 86, 95, 104, 107, 124, 140, 149, 151, 165, 236, 258, 260, 266, 273, 274, 277, 278, 289, 293, 310
mleccha, 3, 116, 130, 260, 261, 275, 281, 283, 292, 311
monkey, 49, 323
mortar, 64
mould, 50, 257
mountain, 42, 59, 92, 95, 124, 180, 181, 186, 199, 210, 271, 281, 292, 298, 314, 334
Munda, 43, 53, 54, 55, 57, 59, 60, 62, 75, 79, 87, 93, 94, 95, 107, 118, 120, 121, 122, 135, 259, 260, 267, 270, 271, 285, 286, 288, 298, 306, 363, 364
native metal, 96, 98, 107, 114, 117, 121, 122, 137, 256, 261, 263, 266, 269, 276, 287
neck, 49, 128, 208, 209, 260, 274, 284, 317, 323, 335
necklace, 50
numeral, 78, 95, 275, 328
one-horned, 339
ore, 9, 33, 44, 50, 75, 86, 94, 95, 96, 98, 104, 107, 114, 115, 117, 118, 121, 122, 123, 132, 137, 165, 176, 236, 255, 258, 260, 266, 270, 273, 276, 277, 278, 281, 282, 284, 287, 288, 289, 293, 294, 298, 310, 317, 340
organization, 62, 66
oval, 236, 317
Oxus, 320
Parpola, 320
penance, 256, 258, 260, 261, 264
perforated, 69
Persian Gulf, 65, 81, 125, 290, 313, 323, 362
pewter, 133, 149, 257, 262, 263, 275, 276, 290, 292, 302
pheasant, 48
pictographic, 65, 66
plant, 58, 64, 69, 75
plants, 63, 64, 66
platform, 69, 103, 151, 169, 281
pleiades, 50
Possehl, 103, 114, 317, 334, 365, 366
pottery, 59, 66, 320
Prakrit, 43, 54, 79, 128, 256, 290
present, 40, 56, 58, 62, 75, 78, 149, 204, 216, 221, 223, 292, 335, 336
Procession, 339
Proto-Dravidian, 52
Przyludski, 366
punch-marked, 141, 163, 169
Punjabi, 55, 58
R.gveda, 73, 74, 75
ram, 49, 56, 62, 93, 94, 96, 130, 131, 258, 261, 262, 289, 291, 292, 298, 299, 302
Ravi, 69
rebus, 57, 289, 312, 339
rhinoceros, 49, 69, 103
rice, 47, 65
Rigveda, 2, 66, 98, 123, 141, 261, 275, 311

rim of jar, 118, 236, 256, 259, 267, 290
rimless pot, 32, 34, 255, 270, 272, 278
road, 50, 69, 92
safflower, 212
Sanskrit, 53, 54, 55, 57, 58, 61, 62, 63, 67, 68, 70, 71, 72, 73, 74, 75, 76, 79
Santali, 52, 55, 58, 59, 62, 67, 68, 71, 72, 339
Sarasvati, 39, 44, 52, 54, 57, 64, 90, 101, 125, 141, 149, 169, 258, 283, 294, 311, 313, 322, 364
Sasson, 319
Saussure, 31, 32
saw, 50, 77
scarf, 33, 98, 136, 258, 260, 272, 310
scribe, 118, 133, 258, 259, 267
sealing, 68
sememe, 32, 56, 58, 62, 63, 67, 74
serpent, 90, 133, 260, 263, 304, 307, 308
shell, 50
ship, 56, 65
sign board, 140
silver, 50, 75, 95, 96, 117, 120, 123, 124, 128, 134, 148, 210, 226, 269, 274, 283, 286, 290, 307, 321, 335, 338, 339
Sindh, 52, 54, 57
Sindhi, 54, 55, 58, 65
smelter, 33, 44, 87, 112, 113, 118, 135, 137, 140, 153, 162, 165, 170, 172, 224, 225, 236, 255, 256, 262, 263, 264, 266, 267, 291, 292, 294, 304, 340
smithy, 91, 111, 112, 113, 114, 131, 137, 138, 147, 151, 152, 162, 179, 256, 258, 272, 275, 282, 283, 285, 289, 290, 291, 293, 304, 307, 309, 310, 339
snake, 48
soma, 50, 58, 64, 75
Southworth, 366
spinner, 50, 133, 331
spokes, 130, 140, 268
sprachbund, 9, 32, 33, 34, 36, 135, 136, 311
Sproat, 364, 366
spy, 50, 256, 258, 262
squirrel, 49
stalk, 281
steatite, 69, 320, 338
steel, 289
stool, 50, 209, 258, 259, 265
Sumer, 65, 94, 304, 306, 323, 335, 336, 337
Sumerian, 65, 69, 94, 212, 281, 306, 313, 317, 336, 337
summit, 271
Susa, 119, 285, 305, 306, 314, 315, 330, 331
svastika, 59, 148, 150, 167, 275, 276, 362
symbols, 63, 66, 68, 70
tablet, 45, 50, 169, 179, 254, 255, 256, 258, 263, 275, 310, 316, 332, 336
tablets, 59, 68
tail, 49, 163, 166, 225, 258, 260, 263, 289, 293, 318, 323
Tamil, 52, 54, 55, 58, 62, 66, 71, 73, 74
Telugu, 54, 339
temple, 42, 44, 45, 51, 70, 91, 99, 113, 135, 149, 151, 178, 187, 188, 199, 201, 214, 224, 225, 227, 258, 267, 294, 295, 303, 305
Tepe Yahya, 364
terracotta, 44, 111, 112, 176, 312, 319, 320
Tewari, 366
tiger, 49, 98, 111, 112, 113, 115, 140, 147, 162, 256, 260, 262, 275, 319
Tigris, 320
tin, 8, 50, 77, 95, 133, 137, 149, 209, 210, 255, 257, 258, 262, 263, 271, 272, 276, 289, 290, 291, 292, 293, 299, 302, 303, 304, 305, 307
Tocharian, 80, 123, 124
tools, 50
tortoise, 49
trader, 69, 281
traders, 65
tree, 42, 47, 91, 114, 115, 122, 140, 141, 153, 155, 158, 160, 161, 162, 206, 211, 213, 255, 256, 262, 278, 279, 280, 281, 284, 288, 291, 292, 314, 323, 340
turner, 117, 120, 138, 255, 258, 259, 262, 269, 278, 280, 281, 284, 286, 289, 290, 310
turquoise, 338
twig, 256, 258, 264
unsmelted metal, 236, 269
Ur, 69
Uruk, 131, 281, 332, 336
Vats, 101, 174, 363, 366
Vedic, 364
vessels, 65
Vidale, 366
war, 74
warehouse, 258, 274, 285
Warka, 305, 331
weapons, 50

weaving, 66, 67
weights, 65, 320
wheat, 47
wing, 9, 121, 125, 140, 164, 221, 287, 295
worship, 51
writing, 59, 64, 65, 69
zebu, 85, 87, 90, 91, 92, 93, 96, 97, 98, 108, 111, 114, 115, 116, 117, 118, 124, 260, 264, 290, 292, 319, 320, 321
zinc, 8, 134, 149, 255, 257, 258, 262, 272, 275, 276, 302, 305, 338
/8916249/Indus-script-decoded-language----Massimo-Vidale/

www.ingramcontent.com/pod-product-compliance
Lightning Source LLC
Chambersburg PA
CBHW050453110426
42743CB00017B/3340
* 9 7 8 0 9 9 1 1 0 4 8 6 4 *